CANADA
A National History

Margaret Conrad

UNIVERSITY OF NEW BRUNSWICK

Alvin Finkel

ATHABASCA UNIVERSITY

Longman

Toronto

For our students, past and present.
We hope that this is the kind of text that illuminates the present
and inspires further exploration into Canada's rich history.

National Library of Canada Cataloguing in Publication Data

Conrad, Margaret
    Canada: a national history / Margaret Conrad, Alvin Finkel.

Includes bibliographical references and index.
ISBN 0-201-73060-X

1. Canada—History. I. Finkel, Alvin, 1947– II. Title.

FC165.C65 2002   971   C2002-903442-6

ISBN 0-201-073060-X

Vice President, Editorial Director: Michael J. Young
Acquisitions Editor: Lori Will
Executive Marketing Manager: Christine Cozens
Developmental Editors: Susanne Marshall/Adrienne Shiffman
Production Editor: Tammy Scherer
Copy Editor: Karen Bennett
Proofreader: Nancy Carroll
Senior Production Coordinator: Peggy Brown
Page Layout: Carolyn E. Sebestyen
Art Director: Julia Hall
Cover and Interior Design: Michelle Bellemare
Front Cover Image: *Esquimaux Lady* by John Russell; courtesy of Institut für Ethnologie der Universität Göttigen/H. Hasse
Back Cover Image: Marshall McLuhan, 1966; Juster/*Montreal Star*/Public Archives of Canada/PA-133299

  2 3 4 5   07 06 05 04 03

Printed and bound in Canada.

Longman

CONTENTS

List of Maps

List of Figures and Tables

List of Boxes

VOICES FROM THE PAST

PREFACE

In 1993, the first edition of the two-volume text *History of the Canadian Peoples* was published. Our objective was to write a survey of Canadian history that incorporated new research in Canadian social history and included developments in the lives of all Canadians, not just the rich and powerful. While it was enthusiastically endorsed, our text also generated considerable controversy. Our focus on Aboriginal peoples, women, racial and ethnic minorities, the poor, and regions outside of the St Lawrence-Great Lakes heartland was deemed to have contributed to the demise of a cohesive narrative of the nation's history and even to the disintegration of the nation. Despite or perhaps because of these accusations, *History of the Canadian Peoples* is now in its third edition and is read by students all across the country and beyond.

Canada: A National History is a response to the demand from professors and students for a one-volume version of our text. Like the two-volume text, it attempts to introduce readers to the complexity of the past—the conflicts and failures, as well as the common goals and successes that make Canada what it is today. We also wanted to expose students to our view that history is socially constructed, using footnotes to document some of our sources and calling attention to conflicting interpretations of events. Although our detractors would suggest otherwise, we feel that we offer a balanced coverage of the economic, political, and social conditions that faced Canadians in the past. We, of course, recognize the limits of a national framework in assigning significance to events but we stand firm in our conviction that a critical examination of the past helps to develop a historical consciousness and sense of human agency that serves us well in our efforts to shape the future.

In constructing this text, we have kept the pedagogical features that characterize our two-volume text. "Historiographical Debates" alert readers to differing interpretation of past events while inserts offer "More to the Story," "Biography," and "Voices from the Past" to supplement our narrative. A timeline appears at the beginning of each chapter to place events in chronological perspective, and maps and illustrations give visual support to the written word. For those interested in researching topics in greater depth than we can provide here, we have included Selected Readings and Weblinks at the end of each chapter.

The text is divided into eight chronological sections that focus on major periods in Canada's past. In Part I, "Beginnings," we focus on the geography that helps to shape the experience of Canadians, as well as the early history of Aboriginal peoples, and their interaction with Europeans before 1663. Part II, "France in America, 1663–1763," explores the efforts of France to establish a North American Empire, while Part III, "British North America, 1763–1821," focuses on the establishment of British colonies across the territories of today's Canada. Part IV, "Maturing Colonial Societies, 1815–1867," takes the story of British North America beyond the pioneer stage to the point where commercial and social development led to Confederation, a nation-building project designed to unite the disparate British colonies from the Atlantic to the Pacific in a political union to serve as the framework for industrial growth and social reform. In Part V, "Inventing Canada, 1867–1914," we chart the nation-building process after Confederation and describe the economic and social trends that define the new industrial order. Part VI, "The Transitional Years, 1914–1945," chronicles the impact of two world wars, a major depression, and the onset of mass consumer culture on an increasingly diverse and complex Canadian society. In the wake of these momentous events, Canada embraced a new liberal consensus and closer relations with the United States, trends described in Part VII, "Reinventing Canada, 1945–1975." Part VIII, "Post-Modern Canada," explores Canada's responses to the new era of economic globalization and the neo-conservative agenda that called into question the values that many Canadians took for granted, including the very notion of a nation-state called Canada. Although Canadians entered the twenty-first century with their country's survival still in doubt, no one could deny that they had achieved much together and, whether united or divided, they were among the world's most fortunate peoples.

Our debts to others just keeps growing as we have passed from edition to edition of our two-volume *History of the Canadian Peoples*, and now with this inaugural edition of *Canada: A National History*. We thank Kathleen McGill, former senior acquisitions editor at Pearson Education Canada, who helped make publication of this text a reality. We owe a particular debt to our editors of the three editions of *History of the Canadian Peoples*: Curtis Fahey, Barbara Tessman, Dawn DuQuesnay, and Karen Bennett. For their contributions to this text, we extend thanks to our editors Lise Creurer, Susanne Marshall, Tammy Scherer, Karen Bennett, and Nancy Carroll.

We apologize to whose who have contributed but whom we have passed over here. We thank Douglas Baldwin, Marilyn Barber, Michael Behiels, John Belshaw, Rusty Bitterman, Ruth Brouwer, Sean Cadigan, Shawn Cafferky, Cynthia Comacchio, Cecilia Danysk, Catherine Desbarats, Graham Decarie, John Dickinson, Patricia Dirks, David Frank, Gerald Friesen, Thor Frohn-Nielsen, Roger Hall, Lorne Hammond, James Hiller, Norman Hillmer, Raymond Huel, Cornelius Jaenen, Linda Kerr, Jeff Keshen, Marcel Martel, Mark McGowan, Kathryn McPherson, Carmen Miller, Jim Miller, Wendy Mitchinson, Barry Moody, Suzanne Morton, Del Muise, Ken Munro, David Murray, Sharon Myers, Jan Noel, Peter Nunuda, Jim Pritchard, Adrian Shubert, Ron Stagg, John Steckley, Veronica Strong-Boag, Robert Sweeny, Georgina Taylor, Jeff Webb, Brian Young, and Suzanne Zeller.

Interpeting Canada's Past

In 1829, Shanawdithit, the last surviving Beothuk on the island of Newfoundland, died of tuberculosis. Thirty-eight years later, three British North American colonies united to form the Dominion of Canada. The second of these two events has always had a central place in Canadian history textbooks. The first, until recently, has been ignored. For students of history, it is important to understand why the focus of historical analysis changes and what factors influence historians in their approaches to their craft.

WHAT IS HISTORY?

Simply stated, history is the study of the past, but the past is a slippery concept. In non-literate societies, people passed oral traditions from one generation to the next, with each generation fashioning the story to meet the needs of the time. When writing was invented, history became fixed in texts. The story of the past was often revised, but earlier texts could be used to show how interpretations changed over time. Although ordinary people continued to tell their stories, they were considered less important than "official" written histories that reflected the interests of the most powerful members of society. Some of the official texts, such as the Bible and the Koran, were deemed to be divinely inspired and therefore less subject to revision than the accounts of mere mortals.

In the nineteenth century, history became an academic discipline in Europe and North America. Scholars in universities began to collect primary historical documents, compare texts, develop standards of accuracy, and train students to become professional historians. At first, professional historians focused on political and military events that chronicled the evolution of empires and nation-states. Gradually, they broadened their scope to include economic, social, and cultural developments.

THE CONTEXT OF THIS TEXT

The authors of this book are university-trained historians, schooled in the theories and methods of what was once called "the new social history." Since the new social history is now more than three decades old, it can no longer be considered new, but its findings have informed our decisions about what to include in this introductory textbook.

Social historians have made a concerted effort to broaden the scope of historical inquiry. To fill the gaps in written documents, they have taken an interdisciplinary approach, drawing upon other disciplines (including archaeology, anthropology, demography, and geography) to answer their questions. Such sources as oral traditions and the findings of archaeological excavations have enabled historians to explore the lives of the silent majority in past times. When personal computers became widely available in the 1970s, historians were able to process more efficiently large amounts of information found in such sources as censuses, immigration lists, and church registers. The science of demography, which analyzes population trends and draws upon vast quantities of data, has proven particularly useful in helping historians trace changes in family size, migration patterns, and life-cycle choices.

At the same time that new methodologies extended the scope of history, historians were being influenced by new theoretical approaches. Scholars who studied minorities, women, and the working class brought insights from multicultural studies, feminism, and Marxism to their analysis. Canadian history was also enriched by regional studies that integrated the perspectives of the West, North, and Atlantic Canada into the larger national story, hitherto dominated by Quebec and Ontario. By focusing on social structures such as class, culture, gender, race, and region, historians raised new questions about old topics and revolutionized the way the past is perceived.

Social history also has its critics. They argue that it focuses the energy of historians into narrow topics, that it yields interesting but ultimately insignificant findings, and that it destroys the unifying national focus that earlier political studies offered.[1] In response to such charges, we argue that the new social history offers a more comprehensive view of what happened in the past. We also maintain that there cannot be and never was an official version of Canada's history. The claim that there is only one way to view the past is, we believe, as damaging to the historical enterprise as are theories that dismiss history—and the belief that the present can be informed by an understanding of the past—as a figment of the modernist imagination.

CONSTRUCTING A TEXT

From the foregoing discussion, it is clear that history is a dynamic and evolving discipline. Debates rage, methods come and go, new sources are discovered, and different conclusions are drawn from the same body of evidence. We want students who use this text not only to learn about developments in Canada's past but also to gain some understanding of how history is written. At the beginning of and at various points throughout each chapter we cite from primary sources that historians use. We also discuss historiography—that is, reflections on historical interpretation—in sections entitled "Historiographical Debates." We conclude each chapter with a list of selected readings to acknowledge the sources that have informed our thinking and to offer direction for students who wish to explore topics in more depth.

Ultimately our goal is to integrate social and cultural history into the text so that readers can develop a clearer understanding of how economic and political developments influenced people's lives and vice versa. There is, we maintain, nothing inevitable about historical processes. At times in this text the limitations on an individual's behaviour set by age, class, culture, gender, race, or region may appear to suggest that many, perhaps most, of our ancestors were hopeless victims of forces beyond their control. A closer reading should reveal that people sought in various ways to transcend the limits placed on their lives. Social struggles of every sort changed, or at least sought to change, the course of history. As you read this book, we hope that you will gain a greater appreciation of how earlier generations of people in what is now called Canada responded to their environment and shaped their own history.

MORE TO THE STORY

What's in a Name?

Contemporary political movements that are changing the face of Canada are also forcing historians to think about the words they use. A half-century ago, most textbooks referred to people with black skin as "Negroes." In the 1960s, the term was replaced by "black," despite the fact that not all Africans are black, and more recently by "African Canadian." Similarly, the words used to describe Aboriginal peoples have changed in recent years. "Savages" was quickly dropped from textbooks in the 1960s. Although the misnomer "Indian" has particular applications that seem as yet unavoidable, the preferred terms are now "First Nations" or "Native peoples." "Amerindian" is a scholarly term used to encompass a wide range of Aboriginal cultures.

Women, too, have insisted on being described in more respectful terms. Feminists have objected strongly to the use of the word "girl" when adult women are being discussed, and dismiss "lady" as being condescending or elitist. Because "man" was adequate for the male of the species, "woman," they argued, was the most appropriate term, although some radical feminists prefer a different spelling, such as "wymyn." Only the most hidebound of scholars still insist that the word "man" can be used to describe the entire human species.

Many scholars complained loudly about being asked to abandon words long established in their vocabularies. A few even argued that "political correctness" restricted freedom of speech. We do not hold such views. Since English is a living language and changes over time, we see no reason why it should not continue to reflect the new consciousness of groups in Canadian society. In our view, the words "politically conscious" more accurately describe attempts by groups to name their own experience.

Language, of course, is not only about naming things; it is also about power. Attempts by oppressed groups to find new words to fit their experiences should be seen in the context of their struggles for empowerment. In this text, we attempt to keep up with the changing times while bearing in mind that people in the past used a different terminology. We are also aware that in the future we may revise the words we use, as groups continue to reinvent their identities. Even the word "Canada" has changed its meaning over the past 500 years, and it is our job as historians to shed light on the way this term came to be applied, for a time at least, to all the people living on the northern half of the North American continent.

NOTES

1 The now classic critique of social history in general and the first edition of our text in particular can be found in J.L. Granatstein, *Who Killed Canadian History?* (Toronto: HarperCollins, 1998). For a more nuanced critique see Michael Bliss, "Privatizing the Mind: The Sundering of Canadian History, the Sundering of Canada," *Journal of Canadian Studies* 26.4 (Winter 1991–92): 5-17. A.B. McKillop offers a thoughtful response in "Who Killed Canadian History? A View from the Trenches," *Canadian Historical Review* 80.2 (June 1999): 269–99. See also Jocelyn Létourneau, "L'Avenir du Canada: Par Rapport à Quelle Histoire?" *Canadian Historical Review* 81.2 (June 2000): 230–59, and Linda Kealey et al., "Teaching Canadian History in the 1990s: Whose 'National' History Are We Lamenting?" *Journal of Canadian Studies* 27.2 (Summer 1992): 129–31.

SELECTED READING

Students interested in the writing of Canadian history should start with the following: Carl Berger, *The Writing of Canadian History: Aspects of English-Canadian Historical Writing Since 1900*, 2nd ed., (Toronto: University of Toronto Press, 1986); Beverly Boutilier and Alison Prentice, eds., *Creating Historical Memory: English-Canadian Women and the Work of History* (Vancouver: University of British Columbia Press, 1997); Serge Gagnon, *Quebec and Its Historians: 1840–1920* (Montreal: Harvest House, 1982) and *Quebec and Its Historians: The Twentieth Century* (Montreal: Harvest House, 1985); Ronald Rudin, *Making History in Twentieth Century Quebec* (Toronto: University of Toronto, 1997); and M. Brook Taylor, *Promoters, Patriots, and Partisans: Historiography in Nineteenth-Century English Canada* (Toronto: University of Toronto Press, 1989).

More sources on various topics in pre-Confederation Canadian history can be found in M. Brook Taylor, ed., *Canadian History: A Reader's Guide*, vol. 1:, *Beginnings to Confederation* (Toronto: University of Toronto Press, 1994). Post-Confederation is covered in Doug Owram, ed., *Canadian History: Confederation to the Present* (Toronto: University of Toronto Press, 1994). Students of Canadian history should also become familiar with three important reference works: *The Dictionary of Canadian Biography* (14 volumes are currently in print, covering people who died up to 1920); *Historical Atlas of Canada*, 3 vols., published by the University of Toronto Press; and *The Canadian Encyclopedia*, 4 vols. (Edmonton: Hurtig, 1988).

WEBLINKS

NATIONAL LIBRARY OF CANADA
www.nlc-bnc.ca

The National Library's collections focus on works in all subjects written by or about, or of interest to, Canadians. A large number of electronic and research tools can be accessed at this site.

NATIONAL ARCHIVES OF CANADA
www.archives.ca

The mission of the National Archives is to preserve the collective memory of the nation and government of Canada. Virtual exhibits, portraits of featured people, places, and events, and a searchable research database and accompanying tools are available.

HISTORICA
www.histori.ca

The Historica Foundation's mandate is to provide Canadians with a deeper understanding of our history and its importance in shaping our future. This site features *Canadian Heritage Minutes* videos, lesson plans and resources for teachers, and games and project ideas for students.

THE CANADIAN ENCYCLOPEDIA
www.thecanadianencyclopedia.com

This site provides the full text of the Canadian Encyclopedia online, along with a variety of interactive activities and links.

CANADIAN HISTORY PORTAL
www.canadianhistory.ca

This multimedia site, maintained by the Canadian Historical Association, provides historiographical debates and links to primary sources, theme-based timelines, resources for students and teachers, and a searchable database.

VIRTUAL MUSEUM CANADA
www.virtualmuseum.ca

This rich website, produced by the Canadian Museum of Civilization, features an image gallery, interactive exhibits created by museums from around the country, a museum locator, and resources for teachers and students.

CANADIAN HERITAGE/PARKS CANADA NATIONAL HISTORIC SITES
parkscanada.pch.gc.ca/nhs/nhs_e.htm

Parks Canada provides information on existing national historic sites, with links to individual site websites. Determination and preservation policies and ongoing heritage initiatives are presented.

BEGINNINGS

By the seventeenth century, two peoples without a common history lived in what today is called Canada. The First Nations had been living for millennia in the northern regions of North America, while the Europeans were newcomers. Just like the Europeans, the First Nations had developed complex societies and belief systems. Neither group was very sympathetic to the other's culture or point of view. Part I of this text explores the culture of the two peoples and describes their early interaction to 1663.

Canada: A Bird's Eye View

timeline

80 000 BP	The last Ice Age begins
20 000 BP	Height of the last Ice Age
15 000 BP	Glaciers begin to melt
8 000 BP	End of the last Ice Age

For the Beaver people of northern Alberta, Earth's creation began when Muskrat retrieved a speck of dirt from the primordial sea. Muskrat drew a cross on the water's surface, and the cross provided the starting point for a set of paths carved in the land. Swan transformed creatures from beyond the sky into earthly forms, and each took up residence along particular pathways. For humans, dependent upon other species for their subsistence, knowledge of the trails that led to animals was essential to survival. This knowledge came from following the necessary rituals intended by the Great Spirit and the spirits of the animals.[1]

Views about the origins of the earth differ but, for everyone who has ever lived in Canada, the physical environment has been a crucial factor in shaping their life chances and choices. While geography alone does not determine human destiny, it places limits on the possibilities that individuals and groups enjoy. Most of this book focuses on ways people adapted to and transformed their environments and shaped complex societies. This chapter explores some of the features of the physical environment that provided challenges and opportunities to people in various regions as they went about the business of their daily lives.

THE PHYSICAL ENVIRONMENT

Canada is the second largest nation in the world, covering over 7 percent of the earth's surface. Only Russia is larger. Throughout much of its history, Canada was a cold and inhospitable place, buried under a vast sheet of glacial ice. The last Ice Age reached its maximum extent about 20 000 years ago (see Map 1.1). As the ice moved and melted, it created many of the geographical features we associate with present-day Canada.

Geographers have devised many ways of describing the natural environment. They define six major physiographic regions—areas with similar landforms—in Canada: east to west they are the Atlantic and Gulf region, the Great Lakes–St Lawrence Lowlands, the Canadian Shield, the Interior Plains, the Western Cordillera, and the North (see Map 1.2). The typology developed by Statistics Canada and Environment Canada in the 1980s suggests no fewer than 15 "ecozones"—regions distinguished by similar landforms, climate, and vegetation. There are also eight distinct forest regions, although the boreal (northern) forest region, dominated by white and black spruce, accounts for the greater part of Canada's wooded areas.

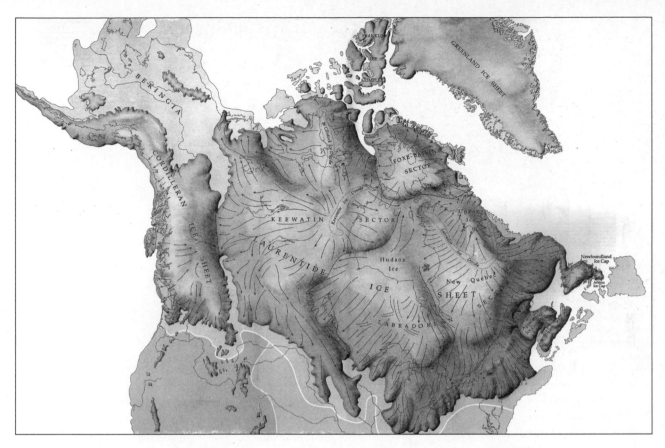

Map 1.1
The last Ice Age (Wisconsinan).

Adapted from *Historical Atlas of Canada*, vol. 1 (Toronto: University of Toronto Press, 1987) Plate 1

The Atlantic and Gulf region is the northern portion of a physiographic area usually referred to as Appalachia. The Appalachians straddle two national territories, as do most of Canada's other physiographic regions. Encompassing most of the Atlantic provinces of Canada (except for Labrador, which is part of the Canadian Shield), the Appalachians consist of ancient rounded hills and plateaus with a few large fertile areas, such as the Annapolis–Cornwallis Valley in Nova Scotia. Just east of this region, under water, is the continental shelf, home to what were once thought to be inexhaustible supplies of fish as well as oil and natural gas.

Climate and vegetation vary within the Atlantic and Gulf region. Near the coast, precipitation is heavy and temperatures are less extreme than in the drier inland areas. The island of Newfoundland forms part of the boreal forest, with few deciduous trees amid the conifers. Most of the Maritime provinces, by contrast, lie within the Acadian forest region, which includes both deciduous and evergreen trees. While 80 percent of the Maritimes is forested, only 35 percent of Newfoundland is covered with trees.

In the Atlantic region, population has concentrated in the coastal areas and along the St John River. The sea and the rivers yielded much of the food for the region's Native peoples, although hunting and plant gathering also provided important resources for survival. Systematic agriculture developed in the period of European settlement on the flat lowlands of Prince Edward Island and in the fertile valleys and plains of New Brunswick and Nova Scotia.

The Canadian Shield dominates 40 percent of Canada's land mass. Literally a great sheet of

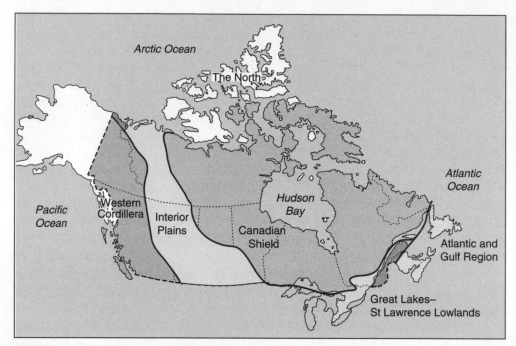

Map 1.2
Physiographic regions of Canada.

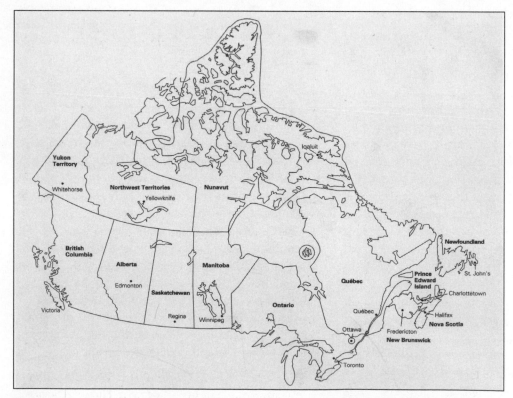

Map 1.3
Canada in the twenty-first century.

Precambrian rock, it represents one of the oldest land formations in the world. Although its hills are interspersed with areas where the land, soil, and drainage offer good farming possibilities, the cool summers and limited number of frost-free days restrict agricultural development. The abundant game within the region's forests supported dispersed Native populations, who faced little competition from European settlers before the nineteenth century. By then, minerals and forest resources in the region attracted commercial interest, as did the hydro-electric potential of the rivers in the twentieth century.

The Interior Plains were created over the course of several ice ages, as layers of sedimentary rock were imposed on Shield rock. Flat clay plains intersected by glacial meltwater produced valleys in a region characterized by plains and rolling hills. Although a large portion of the Interior Plains consists of good to excellent soil for farming, climatic conditions limit yields. Winters are harsh; the growing seasons are often short and uncertain. The lack of rain in southwestern Saskatchewan and southeastern Alberta further curtailed agriculture. In any event, the abundant game (especially buffalo) and vegetation in much of the region made a sedentary farming life unnecessary for Aboriginal people. By the nineteenth century, European farmers began to covet the Interior Plains region, which previously had been of interest only to Europeans involved in fur trading.

The Great Lakes–St Lawrence Lowlands, which includes southern Ontario and southern Quebec, is a region dominated by gentle rolling hills, the product of the last Ice Age, which ended about 10 000 years ago. As it receded, the ice ground down the sedimentary rock of the Canadian Shield, leaving an area with several major belts of fertile soil, particularly in southern Ontario. The lakes and rivers of the region provided accessible transportation routes for human inhabitants. Before extensive European settlement, deer, rabbit, beaver, bear, fowl, fish, and wild berries abounded, allowing Aboriginal populations to increase steadily. Population growth necessitated further food sources, encouraging some Native groups to begin planting crops in the fertile soil.

Like the Great Lakes–St Lawrence Lowlands, the Western Cordillera sustained a relatively large Aboriginal population. The region consists of a series of six mountain ranges extending through British Columbia and southwestern Alberta. Interspersed with plateaus, rivers, and valleys, the region in the pre-contact period was home to an abundance of freshwater fish, particularly salmon, as well as mountain sheep, bear, and deer. The mountain ranges offered a barrier to contact both among Aboriginal nations and, later, between European settlers and Native peoples. The temperate climate on the coast and in the southern interior of the Cordillera offers a marked contrast to the climate of the Interior Plains and attracted a large human population.

The North consists of a variety of subregions. Within the subarctic there are areas that might be seen as somewhat colder and less fertile extensions of the Cordillera and the Interior Plains. Further north is the Arctic, home to the Inuit. It is an area of no trees, little soil, and long, harsh winters. The underground permafrost—literally permanent frost—creates special problems for the construction of buildings. Only small concentrations of people dispersed throughout the region could be supported without depleting the caribou, moose, fish, waterfowl, and fur-bearing animals that people depended upon for survival. Europeans initially regarded the region as a barren wasteland inhospitable for settlement, and suitable only for exploitation of its furs. Over time, its metals and energy resources would lure Europeans into the North.

CONCLUSION

Six regions formed the environment that shaped the experiences of Canada's Aboriginal peoples and challenged early European explorers and settlers. Geography influenced the size of populations, the economic activities that were undertaken, and the extent to which mobility was required to sustain survival. As we shall see throughout this text, it also inspired the political systems and spiritual beliefs of the peoples who made the northern half of the North American continent their home.

NOTES

1 Robin Ridington, "Technology, World View and Adaptive Strategy in a Northern Hunting Society," *Canadian Review of Sociology and Anthropology* 19.4 (1982): 474–75.

SELECTED READING

Useful introductions to Canadian geography include J. Lewis Robinson, *Concepts and Themes in the Regional Geography of Canada* (Vancouver: Talon, 1989); Lawrence McCann, ed., *Heartland and Hinterland: Canadian Regions in Evolution* (Toronto: Prentice-Hall, 1987); D.F. Putman and R.G. Putnam, *Canada: A Regional Analysis* (Toronto: Dent, 1979); and Geoffrey J. Matthews and Robert Morrow Jr., *Canada and the World* (Scarborough, ON: Prentice-Hall, 1985). See also *Historical Atlas of Canada*, vol. 1, *Beginnings to 1800* (Toronto: University of Toronto Press, 1987).

 **WEBLINKS**

HISTORICAL ATLAS OF CANADA
www.mercator.geog.utoronto.ca/hacddp/page1.htm

The Atlas uses thematic mapping to describe events, issues or patterns in Canada's development. This site offers maps, graphs, and text based on print volumes, redesigned for online interactive viewing.

GEOGRAPHIC INFORMATION SYSTEMS
www.manifold.net

This site lets users view, convert, and edit map data using GIS technology.

GLACIER ICE
www.entrenet.com/~groedmed/glaciers.html

Diagrams, maps, terminology, and historical and geological information about glaciers and glacial activity are highlighted at this site.

GEOLOGICAL SURVEY OF CANADA
www.nrcan.gc.ca/gsc/index_e.html

The GSC is Canada's premier agency for geoscientific information and research, with world-class expertise focusing on geoscience surveys, sustainable development of Canada's resources, environmental protection, and technology innovation.

CHAPTER 2

The First Nations of Canada

30 000 BP	Native peoples begin to inhabit North America
10 000 BP	Native peoples use fluted points (sharpened points on a projectile) to kill giant mammals such as mastodons and mammoths; human remains are deposited near today's towns of Old Crow, Yukon; Taber, Alberta; and Debert, Nova Scotia
9 000 BP	Mastodons and mammoths become extinct
5 000 BP	Natives in Labrador build ritual burial mounds; Natives in Alberta use corrals to kill large mammals
4 000 BP	Southern Ontario Natives make use of fish nets, weirs, and grinding implements
1 000 BP	Chiefdoms begin to be established on Northwest Coast; southern Ontario Natives begin making pottery
900 BP	Algonkian-speaking groups enter the region north and west of the Great Lakes, previously the preserve of Siouan speakers
500 BP	Trade relations established between Natives in southern Ontario and Atlantic region
250 AD	Natives begin using the bow and arrow for hunting
500 AD	Farming is practised in southern Ontario
1 000 AD	Viking settlements in Newfoundland
1 300 AD	Iroquoian societies begin building palisaded villages
1 450 AD	Formation of Iroquois Confederacy

Annie Ned, a Yukon elder in her nineties, explained her understanding of oral history as practised by Native peoples to anthropologist Julie Cruickshank: "I'm going to put it down who we are. This is our Shagoon—our history. You don't put it down yourself, one story. You don't put it yourself and then tell a little more. You put what they tell you, older people. You've got to tell it right. Not you are telling it; it's the person who told you that's telling that story."[1]

Oral histories of the First Nations, once dismissed by non-Native scholars as unsubstantiated mythology, are now used in academic efforts to reconstruct the long history of human habitation in the Americas. Although scholars submit oral testimony to the same tests of accuracy as they do other sources—and therefore may question Annie Ned's claims to accuracy—they recognize its value in rounding out the story of Canada before and after the arrival of Europeans.

Because of the lack of written documents, the history of pre-contact Canada (roughly pre-1500) is pieced together from anthropological studies, archeological evidence, and relevant data provided by meteorologists, biologists, and other scientists, as well as oral testimony. The array of sources consulted by ethnohistorians often poses problems. The oral traditions of the Native peoples, accounts of early fur traders, priests, travellers, and other Europeans, and archeological evidence may each suggest different conclusions. In this chapter, we trace the broad outline of Canada's early human history as it is currently believed to have evolved, recognizing that new data from archeological studies, scientific findings, and oral testimony may alter the story.

FIRST NATIONS BEFORE 1500

Estimates of the Native population of the Americas at the time of continuous European contact around 1500 have varied greatly, from 30 million to over 100 million. Since most Aboriginal people lived in areas of the Americas with warm climates, the territory now called Canada was sparsely settled—scholars estimate a population of between half a million and two million people. The smaller figure is based on the observations of early European writers, and the larger on estimates (difficult to confirm) of the numbers of indigenous peoples who might have succumbed to European diseases before direct contact with the invaders. With the 500 000 figure in mind, the distribution of population is estimated to have been 150 000 to 200 000 on the Pacific Coast, 50 000 to 100 000 in the Western Interior, 100 000 to 150 000 in the Great Lakes–St Lawrence Lowlands region, and no more than 100 000 in the rest of the country.

Although the origins of the First Nations of the Americas are debated, most scholars argue that they are of Asiatic origin and arrived in the Americas in various waves of migration from 30 000 to 10 000 years ago. Many are believed to have crossed the land bridges that connected Siberia to Alaska during the ice ages. While accepting the migration theory, a few scholars speculate that some North American peoples sailed across the southern Pacific or perhaps along a North Atlantic route.

Native people themselves often reject the notion that they are descended from people who originated on other continents. Each Native group has a creation story that explains the origins of the world and its creatures, and these stories have in common the view that life began on the North American continent. As a Mi'kmaq legend claims, they have "lived here since the world began."[2]

At least 50 distinct cultures encompassing 11 language groupings have been identified among Canada's first peoples. The phrase "language grouping" refers

MORE TO THE STORY

Native Accounts of Creation

Each Aboriginal Nation has a narrative of how the world began. For the Five Nations Iroquois, the vast land area they lived on was an island on the back of a turtle. Long ago, according to one account, beings similar to humans lived in longhouses in the sky. In the centre of their principal village stood the celestial tree blossoming with lights, the symbols of peace and knowledge. One day a curious woman asked her husband to uproot this tree so she could discover the source of its power. As she bent forward to look into the hole where the tree had once been, she tumbled to a lower world. From the light that now shone through the hole into this lower world, the animals saw her plight. The Canada goose flew down to rescue her and then placed her on the back of the turtle. In this way Great Turtle Island, or North America, came into existence.

Yet another story of the origins of the planet and its creatures is the Cree-Ojibwa tale that suggests the earth had once been destroyed and was recreated by a culture hero named Weesakayjac. The story has some similarities with the biblical story of the flood and Noah's ark. It begins when Weesakayjac carries out a revenge killing of the leader of the powerful underwater cats:

> The remaining underwater cats were very angry when they saw this. They sunk the whole earth. The cats told Weesakayjac they would drown the whole earth and that Weesakayjac would drown too. After this warning, Weesakayjac built a big boat. Then he gathered all the animals. Then the rains came. It rained so much the earth was not visible any more. When the rains finally stopped, Weesakayjac called the water animals together. From the big boat, he wanted one of them to swim to the bottom, to reach the earth.

> First the otter, followed by the beaver and the muskrat make the effort. Finally, the explorations of the wolverine determine that it is safe for the animals to leave the boat. "That's how Weesakayjac made the earth again."[3]

to languages with a common origin, not necessarily mutually understandable languages. For example, the Iroquoian-speaking Huron of southern Ontario and the Five Nations Iroquois of New York spoke languages as different as the Romance languages of French and Portuguese are from one another.

In the sixteenth century, the First Nations lived in societies ranging from the scrupulously egalitarian model of the Athapaskan tribes of the subarctic to the slave-owning, highly stratified societies on the West Coast. Contact with the Europeans would bring dramatic and often unwanted changes to Aboriginal lifestyles, but change and adaptation had always been a feature of their lives.

Pre-contact change and adaptation was most dramatic in the lower St Lawrence-Great Lakes region.

When the last Ice Age receded about 10 000 years ago, the region's only inhabitants appear to have been a few Aboriginal groups hunting caribou. About 6000 years ago, the climate in the area had grown warmer, boreal forest had replaced tundra, and deer had supplanted caribou. People began catching fish in nets and weirs and using milling stones and mortars to grind nuts, berries, and roots. As the food supply became more varied and reliable, the population expanded significantly, and trade with other nations brought in copper from Lake Superior and marine shells from the Atlantic coast. Farming was introduced in the region about 1500 years ago and life became more sedentary than in earlier periods when the search for game forced frequent relocation. When the Europeans made contact with the Iroquoian-speaking peoples in

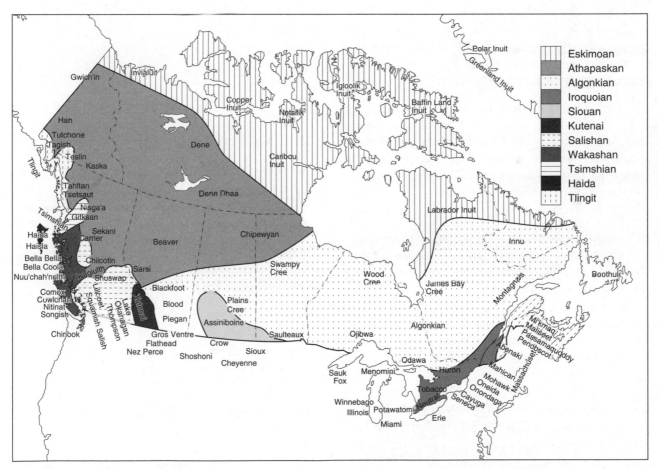

Map 2.1
Native tribes at the time of first contact.

Adapted from Olive Patricia Dickason, *Canada's First Nations: A History of Founding Peoples from Earliest Times*, Third Edition (Toronto: Oxford University Press Canada, 2002). Reprinted by permission of Oxford University Press Canada

the sixteenth century, they encountered palisaded settlements of 1500 to 2000 people. By that time, confederacies of various nations had been formed in an attempt to bring peace to a region that had been plagued with warfare. Well-crafted pottery suggests that the people had the wealth and leisure time to indulge in pursuits beyond mere survival.

Elsewhere hunting and gathering remained the primary means of obtaining food, but the process often changed dramatically with the development of new technologies. On the prairies, for example, the successive inventions of the spear thrower, the bow and arrow, and the buffalo pound increased the time available for spiritual and leisure activities, and attracted new migrants to the area. Three thousand years ago, only Siouan speakers lived on the plains of North America, but by the time of European contact the Blackfoot, who were Algonkian speakers, had come to dominate a portion of the region. The Sioux also disappeared from the thickly forested woodlands and the parklands north and west of the Great Lakes, replaced by Algonkian groups, including the Ojibwa and the Cree, who migrated in search of the caribou. By 1600, the Ojibwa and Cree were the chief inhabitants of northern Ontario, with the Sioux having been pushed southward and westward.

CULTURE AND SOCIETY

Change and diversity characterized Aboriginal life in the pre-contact period, but various groups shared a

Voices from the Past

Dreams and Cree Culture

A Plains Cree elder presented a testimony in the 1930s regarding the power of dreams for his people. His emphasis is on the experience of men, but women were equally guided in their lives by the interpretation of dreams.

> The spirit powers may come to you when you are sleeping in your own tipi when you are young. If you want to be still more powerful then you go and fast. The ordinary dreams you have while sleeping are called pawamuwin. They are not worth anything although sometimes you dream of things that are going to happen.

> You can tell a power dream in this way. You are invited into a painted tipi where there is only one man. The crier, who is the Raven Spirit, calls, and many come. I myself knew right away that they were spirit powers. I sat and thought to myself, "That is Horse, that is Buffalo spirit." The one that invited me said, "That's right."

> I was called many times and they always told me the same thing—that I must do more fasting. Each time they invite me to a different painted tipi. Often after I wake up I wonder why they didn't tell me anything. I had nothing to do with girls when I tried to dream.

> Finally, they told me that this would be the last time. They want me to go and fast for eight days. One of them said, "Try hard to finish these eight days, for that will be all." I gathered as many offerings as I could. It was during the moon just past [July] and there was plenty of food in camp so I knew the people wouldn't move for a while.

> I promised to stand and face the sun all day and to turn with the sun. Only after sunset would I sit down. I had heard that this was the hardest thing to do and that is why I resolved to do it out of my own mind. I thought that I could help myself a little that way. [By making himself suffer more, he would secure greater blessings]. The sun wasn't very high when I got tired. I suffered all day. I tried all kinds of ways to stand, but I was played out. I raised my hands and cried; I could hardly finish. The sun went down and I just fell over. That was the first day.

> The next morning I got very thirsty. I was not hungry but was thirsty all the time. On the fourth night my brother came with horses to get me. I told him I would stay. He came again on the sixth night but I said I would remain for two more nights. He said, "From the way you look, I may not find you alive."

> All kinds of different spirit powers came to see me every night. Each one who invited me gave me power and songs. Then one gave me the power to make the Sun dance. That is how I got power and how I know many songs. Pretty nearly every night now I sing some of those songs.[4]

number of features. In all societies, religion, as much as nature, regulated everyday life. Native religions are characterized by a belief in a divinity residing within all living creatures as well as within all natural objects. Because religion was all-encompassing, attempts to analyze pre-contact societies have been limited by an inability to comprehend the intricacies of spiritual practices. So, for example, among the Cree and Ojibwa, dreams and "vision fasts"—fasts undertaken to induce visions—played key roles in connecting individuals with their guardian spirits. Strict rules governed with whom a person could discuss either a dream or a vision, or with whom one could share a sacred object. When priests and traders in the post-contact period asked questions pertaining to various objects and ceremonies, they were often met with stony silence.

First Nations peoples did not see themselves as masters of their environment; rather, they believed that their communion with the spirits was the secret to any success they might have in staking out a living and achieving happiness. An outside observer might credit the Beaver people of today's northern Alberta with intricate knowledge of the whereabouts of animals and edible plants. The Beaver themselves believed that vision quests and dreams showed them the paths to these animals and plants, and that breaking faith with their traditional religious views and practices would result in the disappearance from their lands of their sources of food and other necessities.

A common feature of Native societies was their knowledge of the uses of a wide range of materials found in the natural world. After millennia of experience living in the Americas, they had unlocked an extensive botanical knowledge that was evident in the effective use of plants for medicinal purposes. Their familiarity with the properties of the various types of wood and other natural materials was displayed in the successful production of means of transportation (including canoes, snowshoes, and toboggans), homes of varying types, cooking utensils, and weapons. When the Europeans arrived, Native knowledge helped them exploit the resources of the Americas for profit. Historian Olive Dickason writes:

> Basque whalers availed themselves of Inuit harpooning technology to improve greatly the efficiency of their own techniques; Mi'kmaq...sea hunters put their expertise at the service of Europeans to pursue walrus for ivory, hides, and train oil [oil from the blubber of marine animals—Ed.], all much in demand by the latter; and later Amerindians did the same thing in the production of furs, so much sought after for the luxury trade, as status-conscious Europeans used furs (among other items) as symbols of rank. It has been estimated that by 1600 there may have been up to a thousand European ships a year engaged in commercial activities in Canada's northeastern coastal waters. Such activity would not have been possible without the co-operation and participation of the first nations of the land. When it came to penetrating the interior of the continent, Amerindians guided the way for the European "explorers," equipped them with the clothing and transportation facilities they needed, and provided them with food.[5]

Native willingness to participate in European trading ventures reflected continuity with earlier practices of trade among themselves. Before the arrival of the Europeans, Algonkian hunters of the eastern woodlands traded furs for corn and tobacco grown by Iroquoian-speaking peoples in the Great Lakes region and by the Mandans of the southern plains. Natives on the Prairies journeyed to the summer trade fairs on the Missouri where they could buy handicrafts and dried corn. On the Pacific coast Natives traded products of the sea with inland residents who could supply them with dried meat of caribou and mountain goats, moose hides, and goat-wool blankets. Extensive trade routes developed, and when the Europeans entered the Americas, Native people guided them along established water routes, forest paths, and prairie trails.

Trade was the peaceful side of relations among Native groups, but warfare between neighbours apparently also occurred in every region. While some battles had economic causes, Native rituals could also lead to warfare. Young men trained and prayed for opportunities to prove their battle-worthiness. The limited technology of warfare and the ritualistic motivations for battles meant that all-out warfare such as many European nations experienced was rare. As in Europe, torture or enslavement of captives was common, but sometimes captives were absorbed into the culture of their captors. Iroquoians, for example, occasionally launched "mourning wars," whose specific purpose was to capture members of other groups who could replace young people who had died prematurely. The captives were treated as if they were members of the victorious nation even though they might have no blood links with their captors.

SEX AND SEX ROLES

Aboriginal peoples also seemed to share a relatively relaxed attitude toward sexual and child-rearing practices. According to early European commentators, premarital sex was widely practised in Aboriginal society. While this was true in Europe as well, what was shocking to European observers was that Natives expressed their feelings about sex openly and apparently experienced no guilt. Monogamous marriages were the norm, although among the Pacific coastal peoples and the Blackfoot, leading males were often polygamous. To the dismay of the Europeans, divorce was not discouraged for couples who did not get along. The Europeans also criticized the tolerant attitude Natives displayed toward children. The young were subject to little of the discipline, physical punishment, and exploitation that were typically the lot of children in Europe.

Unlike Europeans, who ruthlessly proscribed erotic encounters between members of the same gender, First Nations people tolerated homosexual relations. Generally speaking, according to European observers, gays and lesbians cross-dressed and worked among members of the other gender, and sought same-sex partners in their sexual relationships.

The relative influence of men and women in social arrangements varied among Native societies, but women at the time of contact generally held relatively more power than European women could claim. As in Europe, each of the sexes had different roles: women usually produced and controlled the food resources of the tribe; men gained status through their prowess as hunters and protectors of their tribes. Among the Iroquoian First Nations, for example, village or tribal councils included only men, but important decisions required the approval of the women. Although the men might decide to go to war, there could be no war if the women, who controlled agriculture, refused to supply food for the warriors. Chiefs were men from certain family lines, but the women of the line could choose the chief and replace him if he failed to meet their expectations.

While rarely shamans (religious leaders), Ojibwa women benefited from a relatively equal sharing of goods and work among members of a band. Men were warriors and hunters of big game such as caribou and deer, as well as fishers and makers of snares, bows, and arrows. They also built the wigwams. Women hunted small game, gathered wild rice and berries, skinned the animals, prepared all the food, made the clothing, blankets, and cooking vessels, kept the wigwams in good repair, and took all responsibility for children.

Some First Nations restricted the role of women in religious activities. In particular, menstruating women were often forced to absent themselves from ceremonial events. Women may have welcomed this enforced seclusion. As explorer Samuel Hearne observed, among the Athapaskans, menstruation was used by women as justification for taking a holiday from sexual relations with their husbands. Established customs prevented husbands from protesting a woman leaving the tent for four or five days when she claimed to be menstruating, even if she made the argument several times a month.

Women had an important voice among Native groups, but the more valued position of men was reflected in the fact that during times of famine, female infanticide was practised in some tribes, while male infanticide remained rare. When European men arrived in North America, they tended to establish trading relations with First Nations men, thus often enhancing their status.

NATIVE ECONOMIES

While First Nations traded extensively, each Aboriginal group attempted as much as possible to achieve self-sufficiency. Geography determined what economic activities were possible in each region, and therefore the level of material comforts that were attainable. It also played the largest role in determining the size of a band—that is, the face-to-face group of people who worked together to guarantee subsistence—and the proximity of tribes, the collections of bands in given areas.

In the Atlantic and Gulf region, the various peoples, all speakers of Algonkian languages, had diverse resource bases. In Newfoundland, the harsh climate and rugged terrain limited the potential for population growth. The Beothuk, estimated to number only 1000 in the year 1500, depended heavily on the caribou for food and clothing, which they hunted during the herds' fall migrations. To accommodate their migratory lives, they travelled long distances in distinctive, light-weight birchbark canoes and lived in easily assembled wigwams covered with hides or birchbark.

The Mi'kmaq were relatively affluent, living in one of Canada's more favoured geographical areas. Population estimates vary widely, from 3500 to 35 000 before 1500. They occupied a territory stretching from the Gaspé Peninsula to Cape Breton, taking in present-day Nova Scotia, Prince Edward Island, and northern New Brunswick. Like the Beothuk, the Mi'kmaq were migratory, and their conical wigwams, dress, and diet were much the same at the time of European contact as archeology suggests they had been 1500 years earlier. Such continuity testifies to a culture extraordinarily well adjusted to its natural sur-

roundings, as well as a relatively stable environment capable of regenerating its resources.

The lives of the Mi'kmaq were governed by the seasons. Each year, when spring approached they set up camp near bays and river mouths and began setting up or repairing their fish weirs, or open-work fences, in anticipation of the runs of smelt, herring, salmon, and sturgeon. Spring also meant the return of migratory birds in great numbers, with birds and their eggs both providing additional sources of food. In summer, the Mi'kmaq hunted seals, walruses, dolphins, and small whales, and fished for cod, sea trout, and halibut. Autumn brought the hunt for large flocks of migratory birds and the eel catch, while winter meant a move inland in search of moose, caribou, otter, muskrat, and bear.

The Maliseet, who lived in the southern region of today's New Brunswick, had begun to cultivate corn and pumpkins just before the arrival of the Europeans. As a largely sedentary group, they built substantial year-round homes—"pit houses" framed with poles,

Maliseet wigwams depicted in William Robert Herries (1818–45), Indian Camp, New Brunswick, *n.d. water-colour on paper.*

Purchased with a Minister of Communications Cultural Property Grant and funds from the Marguerite and Murrray Vaughn Foundation and the Samuel Endowment. The Beaverbrook Art Gallery, Fredericton, NB, Canada

covered with bark and hides, and held in place by stones at the base. Like the Mi'kmaq, they were also blessed with abundant resources of fish.

Life was harder in the Canadian Shield, an area that includes 40 percent of Canada's land mass and consists of a great sheet of Precambrian rock. Abundant game in the region's forests supported dispersed Algonkian-speaking groups of between 20 and 400 people who survived by cooperative endeavour. In 1500 the nations of the Shield included the Innu (known as Montagnais and Naskapi to the Europeans), the Ojibwa, the Cree, the Nipissing and the Algonquin. Hunters and gatherers in an area that was hostile to agriculture, the size of their bands and the extent of the territory in which they travelled reflected the abundance of game within their territories.

The Ojibwa controlled the northern shores of Lake Huron and Lake Superior from Georgian Bay to the end of the prairies. With game aplenty in their homelands, the Ojibwa created large villages of dome-shaped, birchbark wigwams that served as their permanent homes. By contrast, the Cree, who lived north and west of the Ojibwa, were forced to be more nomadic and live in smaller groups than the Ojibwa to find the game they required to survive. Tipis made of caribou or moose hides, assembled and disassembled by the Cree women, provided them with shelter as they followed the caribou, moose, beaver, and bear. The Innu of northern Quebec and southern Labrador were similarly mobile.

In the Interior Plains, the buffalo hunt also dictated a semi-nomadic existence—semi-nomadic, rather than nomadic, because the Plains Natives, like many hunting and gathering peoples, had relatively fixed seasonal homes. Only Siouan-speaking groups lived in the area of present-day Prairie Canada 1000 years ago, but by the time of European contact in the eighteenth century, the Blackfoot, an Algonkian people, had achieved dominance on the northern plains of today's Saskatchewan and Alberta. Siouan groups remained in control of the plains of what is now Manitoba, with the Assiniboine (Nakota) constituting the largest Native grouping in that area. Writing about the Blackfoot, late-nineteenth-century missionary John McDougall summed up the role of the buffalo in pre-contact Interior Plain First Nations life:

> Without buffalo they would be helpless, and yet the whole nation did not own one. To look at them and to hear them, one would feel as if they were the most independent of all men; yet the fact was they were the most dependent among men. Moccasins, mittens, leggings, shirts and robes—all buffalo. With the sinews of the buffalo they stitched and sewed these. Their lariats, bridles, lines, stirrup-straps and saddles were manufactured out of buffalo hide. Women made scrapers out of the legbone for fleshing hides. The men fashioned knife handles out of the bones,

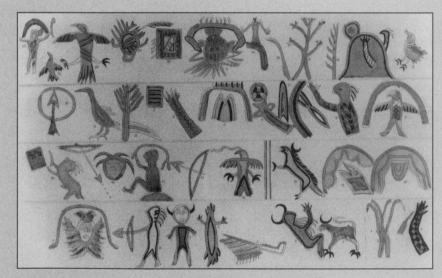

For the Aboriginal peoples of the Americas, art was interwoven with religion and with the activities of their daily struggles for survival. Artistic production varied from nation to nation, with sedentary nations like those of the Pacific Coast being most prolific. Even hunter-gatherer societies, like the Ojibwa, who moved their homes with the seasons, produced artistic representations of their daily lives and their religious beliefs. These Ojibwa pictographs depict scenes from everyday life as well as from the world of the spirits.

Newberry Library, Chicago

and the children made toboggans out of the same. The horns served for spoons and powder flasks. In short, they lived and had their physical being in the buffalo.[6]

Although most Aboriginal societies were organized around hunting, gathering, and fishing, the mainly Iroquoian-speaking tribes concentrated in southern Ontario and the St Lawrence River valley grew corn, beans, and squash. Taking advantage of moderate climate and good soils in the Great Lakes–St Lawrence Lowlands region, these nations were less dependent than other groups on an abundance of game or fish to guard against famine. The sedentary lifestyle encouraged population growth, with the result that the Iroquoian nations, including the St Lawrence Iroquoians, the Huron (in the Lake Simcoe-Georgian Bay area), and the Huron's neighbours, the Petun and the Neutral, together accounted for perhaps 50 000 people in 1500.

The Iroquoian groups lived in longhouses in large palisaded villages. Built of elm bark and attached to wooden frames, the longhouse was six metres wide and sometimes over 30 metres long, and within it about 40 members of an extended family lived and shared responsibilities. A village might contain 30 to 50 of these longhouses, each with a row of fires down the middle and bedrooms on both sides. Underground storage pits held part of the harvest to protect it from fire and mice.

If Iroquoian societies were generally well off materially, their economies were less wealthy than many of the coastal societies of British Columbia. The coastal societies included the Tsimshian on the northern mainland, the Coast Salish on the southern mainland and Vancouver Island, the Kwakwaka'wakw on the east coast of Vancouver Island, the Haida on the Queen Charlotte Islands, and the Nuu'chah'nulth on Vancouver Island's west coast—with a combined population of perhaps 200 000 people in the eighteenth century.

On the northwest coast of North America, a favourable geographical location and ingenious use of local resources created wealthy societies. Plants, almost exclusively gathered by women, and plentiful stocks of fish, particularly salmon and halibut, and shellfish provided the staples of the coastal diet. Like the Mi'kmaq and Maliseet on the Atlantic, Northwest coastal peoples built weirs to divert fish so they could be easily harpooned or netted. Abundant timber in the region provided the resources to build large homes for extended families. Among the Tsimshian, for example, homes made of massive timbers from red cedar measured 15 by 16.5 metres.

In contrast, the peoples of Canada's subarctic lived in easy-to-carry tipis so that they could travel quickly in search of local resources such as fish, small game, caribou, and berries. The Athapaskan-speaking peoples of the region lived in self-sufficient groups of about 20 or 30 related people, about the largest population that most areas could sustain.

By the sixteenth century, the Thule people, ancestors of today's Inuit, enjoyed undisputed control of the tundra region beyond the tree line from Labrador to the Yukon. The Thule, nomadic but originally concentrated in the western Arctic, had gradually followed the caribou to spread their domain as far as the Atlantic. With a language unrelated to other Native language groupings, they were alone among the First Nations of Canada in having claimed a home on two continents when the Europeans first arrived. Until political pressures in the nineteenth century forced them to choose to live either in Greenland or Canada, the Inuit moved freely between the Canadian Arctic and Greenland in search of whale, caribou, and seal.

SOCIAL ORGANIZATION

Despite cultural similarities, the diverse economies dictated by geography led to differences in social organization among Aboriginal peoples. Hunting and gathering peoples, living in relatively small groups and dependent on group solidarity for survival, tended to be the most egalitarian of all. In the western subarctic, Athapaskan societies were marked by cooperation in the tasks required for eking out a subsistence in a harsh terrain. A group that had a bad year could count on aid if it moved to an area where a local surplus existed. Although work was sex-segregated, there is little to suggest that women's work was less valued than men's. The men hunted big game, while women trapped smaller animals, prepared clothing from moose hides and rabbit skins, and carted the band's goods as groups moved from place to place in winter.

For the Innu, Cree, and Ojibwa, as well, there was an equal sharing of goods and involvement of everyone in decision-making. The Innu and Cree made decisions by the consensus of those affected by the decision, and men and women worked closely together to ensure survival. Neither the Cree nor the Ojibwa had a concept of land ownership. Rather, they believed that a particular group had the right to establish primacy in a particular area, giving it the first right to hunt and gather food there each season. It was also understood that if the area hunted by a band did not provide enough food in a given year, that band would have the right to hunt in the territory of a band that enjoyed a surplus. Large annual gatherings of Cree and Ojibwa tribes cemented the bonds that made sharing in times of famine possible.

Anthropologist Eleanor Leacock, describing the gendered division of labour among the Innu of southern Labrador, indicates the extent to which Algonkian nations appear to have established complementary relations among the sexes rather than relations of super-ordination and subordination:

> All adults participated in the procuring of food and manufacture of equipment necessary for life in the north. In general, women worked leather and bark, while men worked wood, with each making the tools they needed. For instance, women cut strips of leather and wove them into the snowshoe frames that were made by men, and women covered with birch bark the canoe frames the men made. Women skinned game animals and cured the hides for clothing, moccasins and lodge coverings. Everyone joined in putting up lodges; the women went into the forest to chop down lodge poles, while men cleared the snow from the ground where a lodge was to be erected.[7]

Perhaps due to their greater wealth and their focus on territorial expansion by military means, the Blackfoot developed somewhat less egalitarian customs than other Algonkian peoples. They created a relatively unified armed force under centralized control. Chiefs and male shamans had several spouses and larger tipis than other tribal members since the cere-

monial functions performed by these men were thought to require more space and people in the household. Because of male casualties in warfare and the adoption of female captives into the Blackfoot culture, women always outnumbered men. While there were some female shamans, they had no privileges. First or second wives had higher status than later wives. In the post-contact period, as some leaders acquired many wives, the number of low-status women increased dramatically.

The Mi'kmaq, the Iroquoians, and the Pacific Coastal Natives appear to have developed either

Cree woman fashioning pottery vessels from clay. Many of the items that women made in pre-contact times would be displaced by European manufactures in the era of the fur trade.

Courtesy of Manitoba Culture, Heritage and Tourism, Historic Resources Branch

more formal governmental structures or a more rigid social hierarchy than other nations. According to missionaries, the Mi'kmaq were peaceable, hospitable, and charitable, displaying little of the greed of European societies. They were relatively egalitarian and they exalted individual liberty. Close contacts among the various bands appear to have produced formal government structures that went beyond the level of bands or even tribes to include the entire Mi'kmaq people. Although the Mi'kmaq practice of choosing a grand chief to preside over all the tribes and seven district chiefs may have developed after European contact, it probably reflected pre-contact relations. The local chiefs were assisted by councils of male elders. Consent rather than coercion kept Mi'kmaq government in place without a state apparatus of courts or police.

Among the Iroquoians, confederacies had begun to form before European contact. The Five Nations Confederacy, which united Iroquoians in today's New York State, was the first and was followed by the Huron and Neutral confederacies, the latter two apparently not forming until the contact period. The Five Nations Confederacy—Mohawk, Onondaga, Oneida, Seneca, and Cayuga—was a response to a growing cycle of violence in Iroquoian societies resulting from blood feuds, and was formed sometime between the late fifteenth and sixteenth centuries.

biography

Dekanawidah and Hiawatha

The lives of Dekanawidah and his associate Hiawatha illustrate the dynamism of pre-contact First Nations life. But efforts to piece together their life stories also illustrate the difficulties in writing biographies of individuals in pre-literate societies. What we know of Dekanawidah and Hiawatha comes from the stories passed on from storytellers of their own time to later generations of Iroquois. The legends suggest they may have lived as early as the late fifteenth century or as late as a century afterwards.

Although Dekanawidah (which means the Peacemaker) was born a Huron in today's southeastern Ontario, he lived his adult life among the Seneca in today's New York State. Hiawatha, meanwhile, was born an Onondaga but lived with the Mohawk. We do not know the story of how either man ended up among a different Native group than the one of his birth. But we know they became leaders in their new homelands. These facts alone suggest societies that were in no way static.

Dekanawidah was disturbed by the extent of infighting that had developed among Iroquoian-speaking peoples, and concerned that their disunity might entice other First Nations to invade their territories. In his travels, he met Hiawatha, who shared his concerns. The two visited all the Iroquoian groups on the south shore of Lake Erie and Lake Ontario, and possibly along the St Lawrence. They organized a congress of all of these groups. Then, according to tradition, Dekanawidah proposed an elaborate constitution with 117 articles dealing with questions of relations among Iroquois peoples and between these peoples and other First Nations. Five groups—the Mohawk, Onondaga, Oneida, Seneca, and Cayuga—smoked the peace pipe to symbolize their acceptance of this constitution.

The constitution, like the legend of Dekanawidah, was preserved orally. It began: "I am Dekanawidah [the Peacemaker] and with the Five Nations' Confederate Lords I plant the tree of the Great Peace."[8] Its many clauses demonstrated an effort to create unity among the Five Nations but at the same time to ensure that representatives of the five nations in the Confederacy Council truly spoke for the women and men of these nations. The constitution not only codified elaborate rituals for decision making but also guaranteed each of the nations its religious rights, confirmed women's ownership of the land and soil, and ensured that traditional rights of clans would not be violated. Rules for adoption of individuals and nations into the Five Nations demonstrated that this was not a closed society.

The Iroquois constitution was detailed and sophisticated. It is believed to have had an influence on the men who drafted the American constitution, particularly Benjamin Franklin.

In the confederacies, men chosen by the women of the villages made decisions on war and peace and tried to settle disputes between villages or clans. They were not always effective. Unanimity was required before a decision could be approved, and even then a tribal council that disagreed with a confederacy-level decision could disavow it. The confederacy had no permanent officials, and its decisions required the consent of tribes to be put into effect. It was a system of government that seemed too loose to be effective to the recently arrived Europeans.

By contrast, the West Coast nations were chiefdoms characterized by social hierarchies that resembled the ordered patriarchal societies of Europe more than the relatively egalitarian Aboriginal societies of the rest of Canada. The chief, always a man, was regarded as a priest who owed his position of power and wealth to the gods. Generally holding his position by virtue of family descent and ruling between 100 and 500 people, the chief controlled the distribution of the resources of the community and took a larger proportion of the community's goods for his own use. Below the chief in the hierarchy were certain members of his family, members of several other wealthy leading families, free men (that is, non-slaves) and their families, and finally slaves.

The potlatch, a feast during which individuals distributed portions of their property in the form of gifts, reduced disparities somewhat and emphasized the connection between all free men and women of the tribe. It demonstrated that property belonged to the community even if custom dictated that its use was not equally shared. Status was indicated by a family's generosity at potlatch time. Ironically, the accumulation of goods for this ceremony encouraged aggressive competition between potlatches, and the elaborate rituals governing gift giving ensured that the social system reproduced itself. By redistributing wealth, potlatches legitimized the social structure and served diplomatic roles as well. Within a tribe, the potlatch provided all free people a certain share of the community's goods. Among tribes, potlatches between chiefs allowed one chief to demonstrate his control over an area by granting lavish wealth derived from it. Thus, potlatches served as a diplomatic way to stake out territory and fend off potential rivals.

Slaves, usually women and children captured in wartime (adult male captives were often killed), were almost universally excluded from the potlatches. Generally, a tribe would pay a ransom to free tribal members enslaved by an enemy, but slaves captured in forays far from the tribal home might never be freed; their slave status passed to their children. The treatment of slaves varied. In some villages there was little distinction between the slaves and free people except at potlatch and marriage time, while in other villages slaves were overworked and treated poorly.

Curing fish in a Nuu'chah'nulth dwelling. The large room, with its elaborate totem poles, would serve not only as a dining room and a living room, but also as a site for religious ceremonies and potlatches.

National Archives of Canada/C3676

CULTURAL PRODUCTION AND LEISURE

Because of the general success of First Nations in creating economies that provided their basic needs, they had a great deal of time to devote to artistic endeavours, games, and religious ceremonies, with the first two often related to the third. Ojibwa ball games, sometimes involving both sexes, were rough and noisy, often involving the entire community as participants and spectators and lasting entire days. Gambling was popular throughout First Nations societies. On the east coast, the Mi'kmaq played a game called *waltus*, in which discs like dice were tossed in a bowl and sticks were used to keep score.

On the West Coast the massive and intricately carved totem poles were closely linked with religious observances. Men were the woodworkers, producing not only totem poles but masks, house façades, feast dishes, canoes, storage boxes, helmets, cradles, and chamber pots. The free women wove intricate baskets from red and yellow cedar and the flexible roots of the spruce. They also made textiles from mountain-goat wool and the down of ducks and other birds. Both men and women participated in dramatic performances during the winter to appease the spirits and entertain the community, with the women producing the elaborate costumes necessary for these events.

Worshippers of sun and thunder, the Blackfoot attached special importance to Sun Dance bundles, which, along with medicine bundles, were kept in rawhide bags. They believed that each object in the bag played a role in ensuring good fortune. The transfer of a bundle from one person to another involved an elaborate ceremony lasting several weeks as the new owner was exposed slowly to the significance of each item in the bundle and to the visions and songs that justified the object's inclusion.

Voices from the Past

An Ojibwa Ball Game

In 1850, Kah-Ge-Gah-Bowh, an Ojibwa author, provided a graphic description of an Ojibwa ball game. His account is reproduced here with the typographical errors that are found in the original printed edition.

> Each man and each woman (women sometimes engage in the sport) is armed with a stick, one end of which bends somewhat like a small hoop, about four inches in circumference, to which is attached a net work of raw-hide, two inches deep, just large enough to admit the ball which is to be used on the occasion. Two poles are driven in the ground at a distance of four hundred paces from each other, which serves as goals for the two parties. It is the endeavour of each to take the ball to his hole. The party which carries the ball and strikes its pole wins the game.

> The warriors, very scantily attired, young and brave fantastically painted—and women, decorated with feathers, assemble around their commanders, who are generally men swift on the race. They are to take the ball either by running with it or throwing it in the air. As the ball falls in the crowd the excitement begins.—The clubs swing and roll from side to side, the players run and shout, fall upon and tread upon each other, and in the struggle some get rather rough treatment.

> When the ball is thrown some distance on each side, the party standing near instantly pick it up, and run at full speed with three or four after him.—The others send their shouts of encouragement to their own party. "Ha! ha! yah" "A-ne-gook!" and these shouts are heard even from the distant lodges, for children and all are deeply interested in the exciting scene. The spoils are not all on which their interest is fixed, but is directed to the falling and rolling of the crowds over and under each other. The loud and merry shouts of the spectators, who crowd the doors of the wigwams, go forth in one continued peal, and testify to their happy state.

> The players are clothed in fur. They receive blows whose marks are plainly visible after the scuffle. The hands and feet are unincumbered, and they exercise them to the extent of their power; and with such dexterity do they strike the ball, that it is sent out of sight. Another strikes it on its descent, and for ten minutes at a time the play is so adroitly managed that the ball does not touch the ground.

> No one is heard to complain, though he be bruised severely, or his nose come in close communion with a club. If the last-mentioned catastrophe befall him, he is up in a trice, and sends his laugh forth as loud as the rest, though it be floated at first on a tide of blood.[9]

The deceptively named Sun Dance was an elaborate set of religious ceremonies lasting several days and involving an entire nation. Presided over by a holy woman at a site chosen by a warrior society, it was organized by the extended family of a woman who had publicly promised the Sun Spirit to sponsor the event should the Spirit spare a male relative whose life was in danger.

In northern regions, Natives played a version of football, gambled, and developed songs and dances to celebrate their subsistence activities, beating drums made of caribou skins with sticks to accompany the dancers. Although they were less materially well off than most other Native groups in Canada, they made every effort to bring beauty into their lives. Author Keith J. Crowe notes:

> They tattooed their bodies and embroidered their clothing with beads of horn or soapstone, with the quills of goose and porcupine, with moosehair or strips of weasel skin. Some made toothmark patterns on birchbark containers. Some people painted their skin tents and shirts with paint from red ochre or black graphite. Any possession, a wooden bowl, a horn dipper, or a knife, might be decorated in some way. Painting, carving, embroidery, tassels, fringes, and beads, dyeing, and bleaching were all used.[10]

Inuit costume.

National Archives of Canada/PA533606

CONCLUSION

Throughout thousands of years, Aboriginal peoples in the area of present-day Canada not only adapted to various geographical environments but also carved out rich, dynamic lives and relationships. As part of this process, they defined their earthly existence by developing vibrant spiritual beliefs, which also changed over time. In the fifteenth century, when Europeans began to come regularly to the shores of the Americas, the resident nations entered relationships with people whose social values, religious beliefs, and cultural practices were at variance with their own.

NOTES

1 Julie Cruikshank, *Life Lived Like a Story* (Vancouver: UBC Press, 1992) 278.

2 Arthur J. Ray, *I Have Lived Here Since the World Began: An Illustrated History of Canada's Native People* (Toronto: Lester/Key Porter, 1996).

3 James R. Stevens and Chief Thomas Fiddler, *Legends from the Forest* (Toronto: Penumbra Press, 1991) 22.

4 David G. Mandelbaum, *The Plains Cree: An Ethnographic, Historical and Comparative Study* (Regina: Canadian Plains Research Centre, 1979) 160–61.

5 Olive Dickason, *Canada's First Nations: A History of Founding People from Earliest Times* (Toronto: McClelland and Stewart, 2002) xi.

6 John McDougall, *Saddle, Sled, and Snowshoe* (Toronto: William Biggs, 1896) 261-62.

7 Eleanor Leacock, "Women in Egalitarian Societies," in *Becoming Visible: Women in European History*, ed. Renate Bridenthal, Claudia Koonz, and Susan Stuard, 2nd ed. (Boston: Houghton Mifflin, 1987) 22–23.

8 Ronald Wright, Stolen Continents: The "New World" *Through Indian Eyes* (Toronto: Penguin, 1993) 120.

9 G. Copway or Kah-Ge-Gah-Bowh, Chief of the Ojibway Nation, *The Traditional History and Characteristic Sketches of the Ojibway Nation* (London, 1850; reprinted Toronto: Coles, 1972), 43–45.

10 Keith J. Crowe, *A History of the Original Peoples of Northern Canada* (Montreal: McGill-Queen's University Press, 1991) 22.

SELECTED READING

Sections of the following books grapple with general problems involved in studying the history of Native peoples: Arthur J. Ray, *I Have Lived Here Since the World Began: An Illustrated History of Canada's Native People* (Toronto: Lester/Key Porter, 1996); Olive P. Dickason, *Canada's First Nations: A History of Founding Peoples from Earliest Times* (Toronto: Oxford University Press, 2002); J.R. Miller, *Skyscrapers Hide the Heavens: A History of Indian-White Relations in Canada* (Toronto: University of Toronto Press, 1994); Bruce Trigger et al., *The Cambridge History of the Native Peoples of the Americas* (Cambridge: Cambridge University Press, 1996); Bruce G. Trigger, *Natives and Newcomers: Canada's "Heroic Age" Reconsidered* (Montreal: McGill-Queen's University Press, 1985); James Axtell, *The Invasion Within: The Contest of Cultures in Colonial North America* (New York: Oxford University Press, 1987); Cornelius Jaenen, *Friend and Foe: Aspects of French-Amerindian Cultural Contact in the Sixteenth and Seventeenth Centuries* (Toronto: McClelland and Stewart, 1976); and Barry Gough and Laird Christie, eds., *New Dimensions in Ethnohistory* (Ottawa: Canadian Museum of Civilization, 1991).

The historical geography of Native settlement is outlined in R. Cole Harris, ed., *Historical Atlas of Canada*, vol. 1, *Beginnings to 1800* (Toronto: University of Toronto Press, 1987).

Sources on Native societies in Atlantic Canada can be found in Bruce Trigger, *Handbook of North American Indians*, vol. 15, *The Northeast* (Washington: Smithsonian Institute, 1978); James A. Tuck, *Newfoundland and Labrador Prehistory* (Ottawa: National Museum, 1976) and *Maritime Provinces Prehistory* (Ottawa: National Museum, 1984); and Michael Deal and Susan Blair, eds., *Prehistoric Archeology in the Maritime Provinces: Past and Present Research* (Fredericton: The Council of Maritime Premiers, 1991).

Works on Aboriginals native to today's central Canada include Bruce Trigger, *The Children of Aataentsic: A History of the Huron People to 1600* (Montreal: McGill-Queen's University Press, 1987); Conrad Heidenreich, *Huronia: A History and Geography of the Huron Indians, 1600-1650* (Toronto: McClelland and Stewart, 1971); Peter S. Schmalz, *The Ojibwa of Southern Ontario* (Toronto: University of Toronto Press, 1991); and Eleanor Leacock, "The Montagnais-Naskapi of the Labrador Peninsula," in *Native Peoples: The Canadian Experience*, ed. R. Bruce Morrison and C. Roderick Wilson (Toronto: McClelland and Stewart, 1986).

On the early history of today's Prairie peoples, see David G. Mandelbaum, *The Plains Cree: An Ethnographic, Historical and Comparative Study* (Regina: Canadian Plains Research Centre, 1979); Jennifer Brown and Robert Brightman, eds., *The Orders of the Dreamed* (Winnipeg: Manitoba Studies in Native History, 1988); Treaty 7 Elders and Tribal Council et al., *The True Spirit and Original Intent of Treaty 7* (Montreal: McGill-Queen's University Press, 1996); and Oscar Lewis, *The Effects of White Contact Upon Blackfoot Culture with Special Reference to the Role of the Fur Trade* (Seattle: American Ethnological Society, 1942).

For the pre-contact history of Pacific Coast Natives, see Erna Guenther, *Indian Life on the Northwest Coast of North America as Seen by the Early Explorers and Fur Traders during the Last Decades of the Eighteenth Century* (Chicago: University of Chicago Press, 1972); and the early chapters of Mary-Ellen Kelm, *Colonizing Bodies: Aboriginal Health and Healing in British Columbia, 1900–1950* (Vancouver: UBC Press, 1998).

Excellent overviews of pre-contact Northern life are found in Keith J. Crowe, *A History of the Original Peoples of Northern Canada* (Montreal: McGill-Queen's

University Press, 1991); Kerry Abel, *Drum Songs: Glimpses of Dene History* (Montreal: McGill-Queen's University Press, 1993); and Robert McGhee, *Ancient People of the Arctic* (Vancouver: UBC Press, 1996). A vivid oral history is Julie Cruikshank's *Life Lived Like a Story* (Vancouver: UBC Press, 1992).

On Native sexuality, see Gary Kinsman, *The Regulation of Desire: Homo and Hetero Sexualities*, 2nd ed. (Montreal: Black Rose Books, 1996) and Evelyn Blackwood, "Sexuality and Gender in Certain Native American Tribes: The Case of Cross-Gender Females," *Signs* 10.1 (Autumn 1984): 27–42.

 **WEBLINKS**

ROYAL COMMISSION ON ABORIGINAL PEOPLES
www.ainc-inac.gc.ca/ch/rcap/index_e.html

This Government of Canada site allows access to the text of the RCAP.

VARIOUS ABORIGINAL SITES
Beothuk: www.mun.ca/rels/native/

Mi'kmaq: http://mrc.uccb.ns.ca/

Ojibwa: www.picriver.com/

Blackfoot: www.angelfire.com/ar/waakomimm

Haida: www.civilization.ca/aborig/haida/haindexe.html

These sites offer historical and cultural information.

CONSTITUTION OF THE IROQUOIS NATIONS
www.constitution.org/cons/iroquois.htm

This document outlines the official election processes, titles, duties, rights, use of symbols, and other legal matters concerning members of the Iroquois nations.

FIRST NATIONS OF NEW FRANCE
www.civilization.ca/vmnf/premieres_nations/en/index.html

Civilization.ca presents maps, images, historical descriptions, and resources concerning the First Nations of the New France era.

THE VIKINGS IN NEWFOUNDLAND
www.wordplay.com/tourism/viking.html

This site offers an informative historical account of Viking presence in Newfoundland, as well as documenting modern excavation of Viking settlements in Canada.

Natives and Newcomers, 1000–1663

When French explorer Jacques Cartier entered the Baie des Chaleurs in 1534, he met Natives, probably Mi'kmaq, who were clearly accustomed to trading with Europeans. According to Cartier:

> As soon as they saw us they began to run away, making signs to us that they had come to barter with us; and held up some furs of small value, with which they clothe themselves. We likewise made signs to them that we wished them no harm, and sent two men on shore, to offer them some knives and other iron goods, and a red cap to give to their chief. Seeing this, they sent on shore part of their people with some of their furs; and the two parties traded together.[1]

Fish attracted Europeans to the northern half of North America in the late fifteenth century. Soon, a fur trade developed between the Natives and newcomers. Initially, Europeans made only annual forays to fish and trade furs, but a variety of political and economic interests gave rise to efforts to settle in North America. In their competition for wealth, power, and glory, European kings and queens saw overseas colonies as a way to gain political advantage. Always short of money, they tried to build their empires on the cheap. They therefore granted monopolies over the increasingly lucrative fur trade to entrepreneurs who, in return, agreed to sponsor settlement and Christian missions in the "New World." While leery of the newcomers and their religious practices, the Natives saw advantages for themselves in the trade and military alliances that Europeans offered.

THE EUROPEAN CULTURAL HERITAGE

At the beginning of the sixteenth century, Europe was experiencing a period of rapid change. Feudal obligations, which for centuries had bound everyone—serfs, nobles, and monarchs—in hierarchical obligations, were breaking down. In towns, the guilds that had once made rules to ensure security for artisans increasingly gave way to capitalist enterprises that hired workers for a wage. Capitalists expanded the scope of trade and sponsored explorers who were pushing the boundaries of what was widely believed to be earth's geography. In both town and countryside, slaves served as domestic servants or concubines. Women, long subject to patriarchal authority in Europe, were increasingly being punished if they broke social norms, as the massive number of witchcraft trials attested.

Even the Christian church, which for centuries had united Europe across local cultures, fractured into Roman Catholic and Protestant variants. In 1517 Martin Luther, a priest in the German town of Wittenburg, led the challenge against the pope, who was head of the Roman Catholic Church. The "Reformation" of Christianity prompted the pope to launch a counter-Reformation, which encouraged the brutal suppression of Protestant dissenters. Wars between Catholics and Protestants swept across Europe and usually ended with only one variant of Christianity being allowed within a particular state.

These revolutionary developments were both the cause and the result of a new intellectual ferment that characterized European society at the dawn of the modern age. Just as trade was opening new vistas and challenging conventional notions about the world, scholars began questioning accepted verities. Starting in the Italian city-states, a Renaissance (or rebirth) of interest in the classical scholars of ancient Greece and Rome sparked debates about beliefs that the church held unassailable, including the assumption that God controlled everything that happened in the universe. Whether it was a Machiavelli expounding a secular political science or a da Vinci designing machines to make human flight possible, Renaissance intellectuals recognized few boundaries in the topics they explored.

Practical application of ideas was also part of the European genius that flourished during the Renaissance. Although the Chinese and Arabs had the technology to explore the world, it was the Europeans who led the way. Innovation in the techniques of ship construction, navigation, and armament production was a major factor in the successful overseas expansion of Europe. Other technological advances such as the printing press helped to spread new ideas and encourage individual initiative. In 1453 the European push to explore overseas was given new impetus when the Turks captured Constantinople, thereby blocking traders from travelling to the Far East, the source of many of the fabulous products that were much in demand in Europe.

By 1500, the nation-state headed by monarchs was emerging as the most powerful political institution in Europe. Overseas ventures, along with bloody wars at home, were sponsored by monarchs as part of their efforts to expand territory and national wealth. If successful, colonies would exploit Native labour, absorb the energies of their restive citizens, and enrich the mother country by shipping back valuable resources. They might also help spread the Christian faith, which, like capitalism and nationalism, fuelled the European drive for overseas expansion.

A BRIEF ENCOUNTER

Although the First Nations of the Americas may well have encountered peoples from abroad before the fifteenth century, there is little evidence to confirm it. The first contact leading to a settlement that has been documented by archeological evidence occurred at the end of the tenth century. By this time, the Norse, or Vikings, a seafaring people who had overrun much of Northern Europe, had established settlements in both Iceland and Greenland.

According to Norse sagas, Norwegian merchant-shipowner Bjarni Herjolfsson found himself lost along an unknown coastline while travelling to the new settlement of Greenland in 986. Leif Eiriksson later led an expedition to the coasts described by Herjolfsson, identifying three distinct areas of North America. The first, a land of rock and ice, he called *Helluland*; it was probably Baffin Island. The second, *Markland*, was flat and wooded, almost certainly part of southern Labrador. Leif then reached a country he called *Vinland*, which he described as having grassy meadows and well-stocked rivers.

The sagas indicate that Leif made several later expeditions and that Thorfinn Karscfni attempted to establish a settlement in Vinland. The settlement included women as well as men, and some children were born there. While the site of Vinland is still much disputed, the discovery of a Norse habitation at L'Anse-aux-Meadows in 1961 suggests a Newfoundland location. Evidence indicates that it was probably a base camp from which the Vikings travelled into the Gulf of St Lawrence and perhaps beyond.

The Viking settlements failed to take root in Vinland. While the area offered better agricultural prospects than either Iceland or Greenland, it was already settled. Hostilities quickly developed with the people living in the region, whom the Norse called *Skraelings*, a derogatory term meaning "wretches" or "savages." Lacking both the numbers and the military might to subdue the local residents, the Vikings retreated to Greenland. The Beothuk, Mi'kmaq, Innu, and Inuit peoples who may have came into contact with these ill-mannered European intruders were probably not significantly affected by this troublesome interlude.

EARLY EXPLORATIONS

Portugal and Spain led in the drive for overseas expansion. In 1440, Portuguese vessels had reached the Gulf of Guinea and began carrying back slaves, gold, and ivory from Africa. In 1487, Bartolomeu Diaz, a Portuguese navigator, sailed around the Cape of Good Hope. Ten years later his countryman, Vasco da Gama, sailed directly from Africa to India, returning in 1498 to Lisbon with jewels and spices.

Spain hoped to outstrip the wealth of its Iberian neighbour by finding a western passage to the riches of Asia. Its conquests began with Columbus's voyage of 1492, which prompted his subsequent efforts to establish colonies in the Caribbean. Between 1519 and 1521, Hernando Cortés conquered the Aztec Empire in Mexico. Cortés was soon followed by other conquistadores. Initially interested primarily in the precious metals of South and Central American empires, the conquistadors quickly found that there was

MORE TO THE STORY

Searching for Asia

While fish and furs were the attractions for most of Europe's early excursions to North America, the search for the Northwest Passage—which had alerted Europeans to these resources in the first place—continued to motivate expeditions to the Americas. Most of the European knowledge of the northern territories resulted from the continued search for a sea passage that would link the Atlantic to the Pacific and lead to the wealth of China and the East Indies. In 1576, 1577, and 1578, for example, explorer Martin Frobisher sailed west from Greenland in search of the elusive passage. He entered the bay that today bears his name and charted much of the eastern Arctic. Digging for ore on Baffin Island, Frobisher found little of value but managed to capture some Inuit, whom he offered to the king of England as evidence of his miraculous explorations.

Like Frobisher, Sir Humphrey Gilbert raised funds from English merchants who believed the passage existed and could guarantee their trading fortunes. In 1583, on his second voyage across the Atlantic, Gilbert took possession of Newfoundland in the name of England and made plans to establish a colony. Within two months, Gilbert had drowned at sea, and the only ship remaining of the original five that had sailed with him returned home. From 1585 to 1587, John Davis made three voyages along the Arctic coast to search for the passage and wrote sympathetically of the Inuit he encountered. Henry Hudson, working first for the Dutch and later the English, ascended the Hudson River in 1609 before braving the dangers of Hudson Strait the following year and sailing into Hudson Bay. Three centuries would elapse before the 1903–06 expedition of Norwegian Roald Amundsen finally traversed the Northwest Passage.

even more money to be earned by harnessing the agricultural labour of their new subjects. By 1600, Spanish rule extended over what is now the southwestern United States, Mexico, Central America, the Caribbean islands, and much of South America.

England, Scotland, France, and Holland soon joined the race for overseas riches. In 1497, fishing interests in the English port of Bristol commissioned Giovanni Caboto (John Cabot), an Italian navigator with an apparent knowledge of land beyond the "ocean sea," to carry out a voyage of exploration in uncharted territories. Cabot's "discovery" of "the new isle"—which became known as Newfoundland—and his description of the abundant cod off its shores, sparked widespread European interest. For Roman Catholics, who endured 153 meatless days a year, cod was an especially prized commodity. By 1580, over 400 Portuguese, Spanish, Basque, and French ships, with combined crews of about 10 000, were fishing cod in the waters off Newfoundland.

It was not long before a "dry fishery" developed, involving the cleaning and salting of fish on land. The dry fishery required a stay of two or three months on shore, and soon resulted in hired hands staying over winter on the island of Newfoundland and elsewhere in the Atlantic region to protect favoured fishing sites. Although France, Spain, and Portugal continued to use the "green-cure" method of preserving the fish aboard ship, England lacked the ready access to salt that those countries enjoyed. Its fishermen favoured the dry fishery, which required far less salt than green-curing did. They were therefore more likely to be found wintering in the "New World," especially on the shores of the Avalon Peninsula of Newfoundland.

FISH AND FUR

Conducted exclusively by Europeans for the European market, the cod fishery required little interaction with

Cod fishing and drying by the French in the eighteenth century.

Elizabeth Melau/National Archives of Canada/C05230

Aboriginal peoples. Nevertheless, trade with the First Nations soon became a sideline of Europeans in the fishing industry. Europeans traded iron pots, kettles, and glass beads, among other items, for the furs that the Native peoples were wearing. Trade goods made life easier for the Natives who acquired them and were held in high regard, as evidenced by their abundance in the burial sites. Mi'kmaq, Innu, and other First Nations in contact with Europeans also traded European goods with tribes further west. By 1530, European products had reached the upper St Lawrence, and before the end of the century they had penetrated Huron territory.

The fur trade picked up at the end of the sixteenth century when a rage for broad-brimmed beaver-felted hats took hold among the fashionable set on the European continent. As the Baltic sources of fur became exhausted, demand suddenly outstripped supply, leaving North America as the principal source. A race soon developed to secure Aboriginal trading partners.

While the cod fishery and the fur trade were the chief economic activities linking Europeans to North America, the hunting of whales was initially of equal significance. Whale oil lit most of Europe's lamps, and baleen, the large horny plates that took the place of teeth for whales, bolstered European dresses of the period. One of the earliest and most successful whaling operations in North America was conducted in the Strait of Belle Isle by the Basques. Their primary base was located at Red Bay on the southern coast of Labrador. At the height of the industry from the 1540s to the 1580s, some 30 Basque ships and 2500 men came annually to hunt and process right and bowhead whales. In the wake of the Basques came French, English, and Germanic whalers who hunted in the waters of the Gulf of St Lawrence before 1570.

ENGLISH COLONIZATION IN NEWFOUNDLAND

Between 1610 and 1630, the English made several attempts to establish settlements in Newfoundland. Most ended in failure. The generally impoverished people from England, Wales, and Ireland who were recruited to settle Newfoundland in this period

were among the earliest European immigrants to North America.

In 1610, the London and Bristol Company sponsored a settlement at Cupid's Cove, Conception Bay. It was designed to serve as a base for the Newfoundland fishery and trade in furs with the Beothuk. By 1612, about 50 men and women in the colony cleared land, planted gardens, and built homes, surrounding their small settlement with a palisade protected by mounted guns. The settlement quickly languished. It was harassed by pirates, agriculture proved difficult, and the Beothuk were not eager to trade in furs. Nor were the migratory fishermen enthusiastic about settlement on one of their prized fishing coves. These factors, added

Artifact from Ferryland excavations.
Colony of Avalon Foundation

to internal dissension, led to the plantation's breakup in the early 1620s.

The settlement in Ferryland was more enduring. Established in 1620 by Sir George Calvert, England's secretary of state for the colonies, it had substantial financial backing. Calvert recruited mostly Roman Catholic settlers, but he permitted both Protestant and Catholic clergy to minister in the colony. Religious bickering was the least of the problems that dogged the venture. French privateers and an outbreak of scurvy made the winter of 1628–29 unbearable, causing Calvert to withdraw his active interest in the colony and leave its operation to family agents. All the Catholic settlers in the total population of under 150 people departed either for England or English colonies further south, among them Calvert's colony in Maryland.

While a small number of Protestant settlers remained, they were soon caught in a crossfire between the Calvert family and the family of David Kirke. Having received royal recognition of his claims, Kirke forcibly seized Calvert's properties in 1639. Interested mainly in the fishery, Kirke also promoted agriculture and the production of salt. His widow Sarah Kirke was still in charge when a Dutch squadron virtually destroyed the colony in 1673. Despite its difficult beginnings, Ferryland survived to become one of the major English settlements in Newfoundland.

FRANCE IN AMERICA

French colonization in eastern North America was prompted by visions of emulating the success of Spain and Portugal in finding wealth in the New World. In 1524,

King Francis I hired Giovanni da Verrazzano to explore the North Atlantic coast for riches and a possible passage to Asia. Ten years later, he commissioned Jacques Cartier, a sea captain from St Malo, to discover and claim for France territory where gold and other precious metals might be found. Cartier undertook three voyages to North America between 1534 and 1541. The only gold he found was iron pyrite or "fool's gold," which he mistook for the real thing. Owing in large part to his duplicitous dealings with the Aboriginal peoples, his attempt at colonization was also a failure.

Cartier was a product of European society, which treated all pagan people with disdain. After leaving the

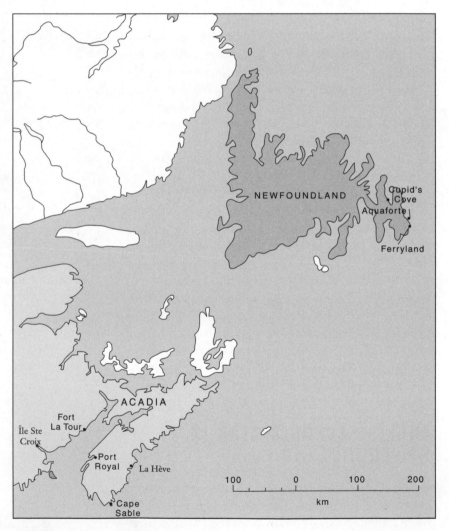

Map 3.1
European settlements in North America, 1632.

Baie des Chaleurs in 1534, Cartier sailed into Gaspé Bay and encountered a hunting party of Iroquoians from the village of Stadacona, located at the present site of Quebec City. Troubles began when he claimed the Stadaconans' territory for King Francis I and erected an imposing cross. Donnacona, the Stadaconan chief, objected to the presence of the cross. In response, Cartier took Donnacona captive and only freed him when he proved more amenable. The chastened chief gave reluctant consent to Cartier's plan to take two of the Native leader's sons to France for a year.

Returning in September 1535, Cartier again behaved arrogantly. The Stadaconans, perhaps trying to preserve their status as intermediaries between Natives further inland and the Europeans, expressed displeasure at Cartier's wish to travel up the St Lawrence. Cartier ignored their protests and sailed as far as Hochelaga, the site of present-day Montreal. The Hochelagans welcomed the French to their fortified villages and offered lavish gifts, but they had little interest in acquiring European goods.

Cartier returned to Stadacona, where he and his crew spent a difficult winter. Twenty-five of the European party of 110 died of scurvy before Native remedies prevented the rest from succumbing as well. The Stadaconans understood the curative powers of a broth and a poultice made from the bark and needles of the *anneda* (possibly white cedar), which is rich in the vitamin C needed to prevent scurvy. Cartier showed his gratitude by seizing Donnacona, two of his sons, and seven others to accompany his party back to France, where all but one soon died.

Cartier returned five years later as the leader of an advance party for Jean-François de La Rocque de Roberval, a nobleman from northern France who was commissioned to found a permanent settlement near Stadacona. By this time, the Stadaconans were not disposed to assist Cartier's colonists, who spent a rough winter and then headed home with a cargo of fool's gold. Deserted by his lieutenant, Roberval tried nonetheless to re-establish a settlement at the same site during the winter of 1542–43. The charms of his settlers, most of them ex-convicts, found little favour among the Stadaconans, and after a scurvy-ridden winter, they too departed.

For several decades thereafter, France give up on the idea of settlement so far north in the Americas. There was no rationale for a colony in the region as long as its only profitable economic activity was the cod fishery. Between 1562 and 1598, France was also wracked by religious wars which absorbed the attention and the wealth of monarchs. By 1600, the end of civil war in France and the dramatic increase in the demand for furs prompted a renewed interest in overseas ventures.

THE FOUNDING OF ACADIA

In 1603, Henri IV of France granted Pierre du Gua de Monts, a distinguished Protestant soldier and administrator, a 10-year monopoly of trade in the Atlantic region. In return, de Monts promised to settle 60 colonists a year and to promote Roman Catholicism among the Native peoples. In 1604, de Monts and 78 colonists wintered on an island at the mouth of the Ste Croix River on the present border between Maine and New Brunswick. Most of de Monts' colonists were gentlemen, artisans, and mariners. Among them was Samuel de Champlain, a Roman Catholic veteran of the recent religious wars, who would become a towering figure in Canadian history. The rigours of a Canadian winter defeated these men: 35 died of scurvy.

In the spring of 1605, de Monts moved across the Bay of Fundy to the shore of the Annapolis Basin. The new settlement, which was named Port Royal, quickly took root. The cooperation of the Mi'kmaq, who were prepared to welcome the intruders, was essential to the colony's success. The French planted wheat, built a grist mill, raised cattle, and grew fruit and vegetables. Delighting in the warmer winters at Port Royal, they developed innovative responses to the challenges of survival. Champlain founded l'Ordre de Bon Temps, its chief purpose to oblige each gentleman to take turns providing game and fish for the table.

De Monts lost his trade monopoly in 1607, but by then the small colony was, however precariously, on its feet. Jean de Poutrincourt et de Saint-Just, who became governor of the area, returned in 1610 with his son Charles de Biencourt and some 20 colonists,

MORE TO THE STORY

The Frontier and the Metropolis

Throughout this text, in order to better understand the dynamics of a given society, it is helpful to bear in mind two key questions. What is the locus of decision-making in the society? What are the influences that produce social change? Historians have developed the concepts of frontier and metropolis to help them analyze societies and formulate answers to these questions.

Within the context of the European exploration and settlement of what was to become Canada, the frontier includes the natural environment as well as the human inhabitants in the "New World." We could study the frontier in isolation, without reference to the impact of the power or the ideas of the metropolis, or "mother country." An emphasis on the frontier allows us to see how immigrants adapted their ideas and practices to a new environment, and how they were influenced by both geography and their encounters with the First Nations. Taken to its extreme, however, this perspective treats the colonists as if their lives began when they left their homelands. It ignores the continuing importance of imperial powers in shaping the ideas and institutions of the colonies. Moreover, it treats the Native peoples as if their lives and attitudes were unaffected by colonialism.

At the other end of the continuum, we could study metropolitan institutions as if they were puppet-masters controlling the lives of the colonists and the First Nations. Emphasis on the metropolis reminds us that imperial powers actively intervened in their colonies and that metropolitan ideas were important in shaping people's responses to a new society. If we focus on the roles of various institutions, both political and economic, we can also see that there is a chain of metropoles that can shape the lives of individuals. So, for example, the government in Paris might give orders to Montreal institutions, which, in turn, exerted power on the fur traders and First Nations in western Canada. Used exclusively, an emphasis on the power of the metropolis ignores the frontier influences that also moulded behaviour.

The relative impact of the metropolis and the frontier on colonial societies has occasioned much debate, but in recent years most historians concede that both had an influence on the peoples living in New France.

including a priest, Jessé Fléché. Membertou, an elderly Mi'kmaq chief, had maintained the habitation during the absence of the French. In short order, Fléché baptized Membertou and 20 members of his family and traders bartered for the much-desired furs. Armed with evidence of both financial and spiritual success, Biencourt returned to France and found a patron in the person of the Marquise de Guercheville. Her support was tied to the condition that the Jesuits, a Roman Catholic religious order that had become influential at the French Court, would control missionary work in Acadia and become partners in the trade.

In May 1611, Biencourt returned to Port Royal with 36 colonists and two Jesuit priests, the first mission by a French religious order in the Americas. When quarrels erupted between Biencourt and the Jesuits, the Marquise de Guercheville financed an expedition to move the Jesuits from Port Royal to Saint-Sauveur, a new colony established on a site opposite what is now known as Mount Desert Island on the Penobscot River in the state of Maine. Opposed to French colonization on his northern flank, the governor of the English colony of Virginia, established in 1607, sent an expedition under Samuel Argall to destroy Saint-Sauveur and Port Royal in the fall of 1613. The following year Poutrincourt took most of the colonists back to France. Only Biencourt, his cousin Charles de Saint-Étienne de La Tour, and a few others stayed on.

The Mi'kmaq and Maliseet, who had traded furs with Europeans for generations before French settlement took root, developed close ties with the French who lived among them. Not only did they gradually reconcile their spiritual beliefs with those of the persistent Roman Catholic missionaries in their midst, they also entered marriage relationships with the newcomers. Following the death of Biencourt in 1623, the direction of the colony was entrusted to Charles La Tour, who, with his father Claude, continued to make Acadia their home. Charles married a Mi'kmaq woman, probably the daughter of a local chief. Later blessed by a Récollet priest, the union produced three daughters, all of whom were baptized; one eventually entered a convent in Paris.

THE FOUNDING OF QUEBEC

Meanwhile, de Monts and Champlain had directed their attention toward the St Lawrence, where the fur trade had better prospects for success. By the time Quebec was founded in 1608, the area was known as Canada, derived from the St Lawrence Iroquoian word "kanata" meaning village or settlement. It soon became the term applied to the French colony based on the St Lawrence.

As de Monts' lieutenant, Samuel de Champlain chose the site of today's Quebec City as the new base of operation in Canada. It had several advantages. In addition to spectacular natural defences, it was also close to Tadoussac, where Europeans continued to trade with the Natives in violation of de Monts' fur-trading monopoly. Although Champlain soon became obsessed with making Quebec a settled, Christian community on a European model, his goal in 1608 was simply to monopolize the St Lawrence fur trade.

Quebec's beginnings were modest and inauspicious. Of 25 men who wintered there in 1608–9, only nine were alive the following spring after scurvy had taken its toll. The credit for the colony's survival belongs in large part to Champlain, who travelled to France to seek court and financial support for the struggling St Lawrence colony. A new commercial monopoly was established and Quebec was saved. Although Champlain never became the formal governor of Quebec, he had charge over its civil administration, enforcing the king's laws and overseeing relations with the Native peoples. He also invested a substantial sum in the colony, using the proceeds from a dowry he received when he married a 12-year-old French girl, Hélène Boullé, in 1610.

The survival of Quebec depended upon the goodwill of the Algonquin and Montagnais (Innu) who controlled the territory where Quebec was located. To cement his alliance with his prospective commercial partners, Champlain agreed in 1609 to support them in their ongoing war with the Five Nations Iroquois. The alliance also led to contact with the Algonquin's Huron allies and to direct involvement in battles against the Five Nations in 1609 and 1610. Within a short time, Native and European rivalries had intertwined. The Huron became partners with the Algonquin and the Innu in a military-commercial alliance with the French, while the Five Nations Iroquois became fur suppliers to the Dutch based at New Amsterdam and Albany in present-day New York.

Hoping to better the understanding between the French and their Native allies, as well as to create a supply of interpreters to carry on the fur trade, Champlain encouraged the men in his charge to live with Native allies and learn their languages. The first to volunteer was Étienne Brûlé. One of the survivors of the difficult winter of 1609, Brûlé was still in his teens when he became involved in the attempt to plant a French colony on the St Lawrence. Brûlé lived among the Huron, learning their language and customs. In turn, he was effectively adopted by the Huron, who complained nonetheless that he used the relative sexual freedom of Native society to practise uncontrolled lechery.

While serving as an interpreter of Native languages for French traders, Brûlé very likely became the first European to see Huronia, Lake Ontario, Lake Superior, and today's state of Pennsylvania. He was also branded a traitor for collaborating with the English after they seized Quebec in 1629. About 1633, for reasons unknown, the Huron turned against him, killing and eating him. This adventurous Frenchman became the prototype for the many young men who would live among the Native peoples later in the century, engaging in the fur trade and adopting Native culture.

CRISIS IN NEW FRANCE

In 1627, when the population of Quebec was only 107, Champlain's efforts to build a colony on the St. Lawrence received a boost from France. Cardinal

Richelieu, Louis XIII's chief minister, engineered a new trade monopoly, designed to encourage trade, settlement, and missionary activity. Known as the Compagnie de la Nouvelle France or Compagnie des Cents Associés, it was granted lands from Florida to the Arctic Circle and a monopoly of the fur trade and all other commerce except the fisheries for 15 years. In return, the monopoly holders would be required to settle at least 200 Catholic colonists a year for 15 years and fund missionary activities.

War broke out between England and France just as the Compagnie des Cents Associés was undertaking its first overseas initiatives. David Kirke and his four brothers, financed by London merchants and commissioned by King Charles I to displace the French from "Canida," seized Tadoussac and captured the company's ships, carrying 400 colonists, off Gaspé. Blockaded by the English, Quebec surrendered to David Kirke in July 1629. A few French colonists stayed, but most of the fur traders, led by Champlain, departed.

Meanwhile, French claims to Acadia were also being challenged. In 1621 King James of England granted the area encompassing Acadia to his fellow countryman, Sir William Alexander of Scotland. Alexander established a colony at Port Royal in 1628, but it survived only by making accommodations with both the Mi'kmaq and Claude de La Tour. Acadia, along with Canada, was restored to France by the Treaty of Saint-Germain-en-Laye in 1632, but the war had demonstrated just how tenuous French claims in New France actually were.

CIVIL WAR IN ACADIA

With the return of peace, the French government was determined to re-establish control over Acadia. Cardinal Richelieu appointed Isaac de Razilly as lieutenant-general in New France and provided a force of 3 ships and 300 men to take possession of Port Royal. From 1632 to 1635, Razilly, with his lieutenants Charles de Menou d'Aulnay and Nicholas Denys, laid the groundwork for a lasting colony. Razilly managed to maintain harmonious relations with Charles La Tour, who also claimed title to Acadia. Staying out of

Razilly's way, La Tour conducted trading operations from his bases at Cape Sable and on the St John River and dealt separately with the Compagnie des Cents Associés, which had authority over all of New France.

Following Razilly's death in 1635, his successor Charles de Menou d'Aulnay proved less accommodating to La Tour's claims. The battle between the d'Aulnays and the La Tours for control of early Acadia plunged the region into a bitter civil war. Charles La Tour's second wife, Marie, who arrived in the colony from France in 1640, died five years later after her unsuccessful attempt during her husband's absence to defend Fort La Tour on the St John River.

When the victorious d'Aulnay drowned in 1650, leaving an estate heavily in debt, his chief creditor, Emmanuel Le Borgne, seized Port Royal and attacked other nearby settlements in the region. D'Aulnay's widow, Jeanne Motin, battled creditors in the courts and even married Charles La Tour in a fruitless effort to secure her claims. The La Tours were joined in opposition to Le Borgne by Nicolas Denys, who by this time had substantial interests in the fishery and the fur trade between Canso and the Gaspé. In their desperation, they also sought financial support from colonists based in nearby Massachusetts, the largest colony in the area now known as New England.

In 1654, an expedition launched by the New Englanders plundered Port Royal and other settlements and took La Tour prisoner. La Tour was permitted to reoccupy his posts in Acadia on the condition that he swear allegiance to England and pay off his huge debts to English creditors, many of them based in Boston. To raise the money he needed to satisfy his captors, he sold most of his rights in Acadia to Thomas Temple (who became governor in 1662) and William Crowne. The English remained in control of Acadia until 1667 when, by the Treaty of Breda, the colony was returned to France.

Despite the difficulties, the European population in Acadia reached about 400 by the mid-seventeenth century. Both D'Aulnay and La Tour had recruited settlers, many of them indentured labourers and domestics. While many servants left once they had served their indenture, those who remained behind soon took root. The seizure of Port Royal by New Englanders in 1654 caused the French settlers in the

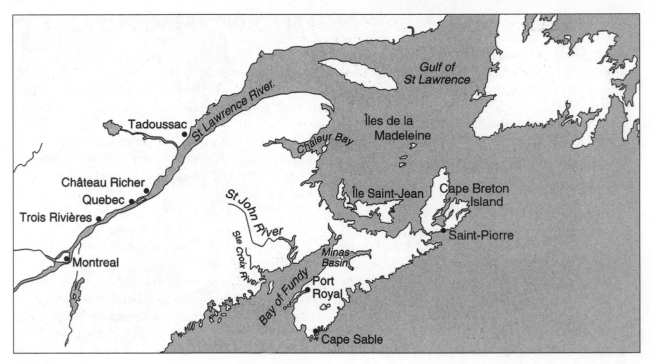

Map 3.2
New France in 1663.

area to move upriver. When French rule was restored, the "Acadians" had become accustomed to trading with New Englanders and resisting the demands of authorities, whether French or English.

CANADA, 1635–1663

Champlain had returned to Quebec in 1633 and the following year established a base at Trois–Rivières, further up the St Lawrence River. When he died in 1635, the colony remained primarily a fur trading outpost, not the settled agricultural community he had hoped to establish. Champlain had recruited a few farmers and his French patrons had contributed a few more, but the colony's total population in 1635 was only about 400. This number included some individuals who had taken up land, as well as officials and missionaries. The majority were indentured labourers who had been imported to build housing and work the land.

The Compagnie de la Nouvelle France made efforts to fulfil its charter pledges to bring colonists to

New France, but the fur trade, which was meant to provide the capital to sustain their efforts, let them down. When profits collapsed in the face of Iroquois attacks on the Huron fur flotillas in the 1640s, the company sublet the fur trade to the Communauté des Habitants, an organization composed of leading members of the colony. Although the Compagnie de la Nouvelle France retained administrative control of the colony, it lost interest in colonization.

After Champlain's death, the French court vested authority over civil administration in the colony in a governor, and in 1647 a council was named to direct trade and control justice in consultation with the governor. The governor enjoyed an effective veto over the council, and the conflict for political power lay between the governor and the Compagnie de la Nouvelle France. In 1659, the company obtained a ruling from France that gave it the greatest authority over the administration of justice in the colony, making power arrangements hopelessly confusing.

A shadowy presence in the emerging colony was the Compagnie du Saint-Sacrement, a secret organization of religious zealots who saw New France as a virgin territory that could be consecrated to God. Leading figures in this organization formed the Société de Notre-Dame, which founded Montreal in 1642. Initially named Ville Marie, Montreal was designed by its founders to be a settlement of strict piety. Only those who could demonstrate their complete devotion to the Catholic Church's teachings would be permitted to settle in the new community.

The influence of the zealots at court also secured the appointment in 1659 of the Jesuit-trained François de Laval-Montigny as New France's first bishop. Laval was a devoted servant of the sick and poor of the colony, but he was also a domineering individual who expected, as the emissary of both pope and king, to be obeyed by the civil authorities, the missionaries, and the colonists. With characteristic enthusiasm Laval set out to establish a seminary to train priests and to create parishes that would administer to the needs of the settlers in the colony.

PREACHING THE WORD

Religious enthusiasm also sustained Roman Catholic missions designed to convert the First Nations with whom New France traded. While French monarchs hoped to garner prestige for their efforts to Chritianize the "heathen," the Natives were not always eager to become Christians. Their usual response to the missionary efforts was: "such is not our custom; your world is different from ours; the God who created yours did not create ours."[2]

In the first half of the seventeenth century, Acadia was an open field for competing clerical orders. Récollet, Jesuit, and Capuchin priests conducted missions among the Mi'kmaq and Maliseet. The Capuchins were particularly active, sending at least 40 priests and 20 lay brothers to Acadia between 1632 and 1656. Most priests spent only a few years in Acadia, but they achieved their goal: a growing number of Mi'kmaq and Maliseet adopted Roman Catholic beliefs.

MORE TO THE STORY

Ste-Marie-Among-the-Hurons

The Jesuit ambition to spread the gospel is illustrated by the establishment of Ste-Marie-Among-the-Hurons, a fortified centre for the mission activity. Jérome Lalement, who arrived as the superior of the Jesuit mission in Huronia in 1638, conceived of such a centre as a means both of reducing missionary economic dependency on the Huron and of providing Christian Huron with a place of worship away from their pagan fellows.

Founded in 1639, Ste-Marie at its height in 1648 boasted 18 priests and 46 lay assistants. Among the assistants were four lay brothers, four boys, seven domestics, eight soldiers, and twenty-three *donnés*—that is, men who pledged their lives to the mission's work and received no wages but who took no priestly vows. The lay people included one or more surgeons, pharmacists, master builders, and shoemakers as well as many handymen. The farmers tended pigs and cows and grew crops.

By 1649, although some food was still obtained from the Huron, the diet of French men in Huronia had become similar to that of their counterparts in Quebec.

Alongside the enclosed compound, reserved for the missionaries, their lay helpers, and a few soldiers, was a Huron compound that included a chapel, a hospital, a cemetery for Christian Natives, and a longhouse for Huron visitors. While Huron converts were encouraged to relocate to Ste-Marie, few of them chose to abandon their villages and traditional customs, even though relations between the converts and traditionalists were becoming more strained. For the traditionalists, Ste-Marie was a symbol of the Jesuits' attitude of intolerant superiority toward Natives. Ste-Marie was burned to the ground by the Jesuits in 1649 to avoid its desecration by the Five Nations Iroquois.

The first group of missionaries in Canada were the Récollets, who began arriving in 1615. After failure among the migratory Algonquin, they focused their efforts on the sedentary agricultural Huron villages near Georgian Bay. Huronia was a significant location in both commercial and strategic terms: it was the point of exchange between the southern agricultural nations and the northern nomadic hunters. From these villages in the Great Lakes basin, travellers had access by waterways and relatively easy portages to the far western plains, the Mississippi River, and Hudson Bay.

The missionaries found aspects of Native society both to praise and criticize. While they denounced the relative power of women, the permissive upbringing of children, and the sexual freedom among youth, they acknowledged Native hospitality and generosity. Brother Gabriel Sagard, writing of the Huron in the 1620s, commented favourably on the skilled craftwork of the women and men, particularly their pottery, canoe making, and weaving. Sagard also found much to criticize about the Huron. While they were generous to a fault, they were also, in his opinion, unclean, ill-mannered, revenge seeking, incorrigible liars, and shameless belchers. The Huron made similar complaints about the French, whom they tended to regard as greedy and untruthful.

In 1625, Jesuits began arriving in Quebec, ostensibly to assist the Récollets with their missionary work, but soon to supplant them as the principal missionaries in the colony. French political intrigues decreed that the Jesuits, but not the Recollets, would be allowed to return to Canada in 1632. Like the Recollets, the Jesuits focused their missionary efforts on the Huron. In 1639, they built a headquarters called Sainte-Marie in Huronia to oversee their village missions. They also encouraged Christian Natives from several tribes to move to Sillery, a Jesuit-sponsored reserve outside of Quebec established in 1638. Here it was hoped that the new converts would farm under the guidance of the Jesuits and be free of contamination by "pagan" influences.

The Jesuits quickly realized that to succeed they needed to become more flexible in their approach to missionary work. They settled among the Natives, allowing themselves to be adopted by families, and accepted that, in some circumstances, hunting must be combined with, rather than replaced by, farming.

Teaching parishioners to say their catechism, using ideograms. Missionary Chrestien LeClercq prepared this illustration to celebrate the work of the Gaspé mission at Miscou. Established in 1633 to convert the local Natives, the mission was destroyed by English privateers from New York in 1690.

National Library of Canada NL22323

Many learned to speak the languages of the Aboriginal peoples fluently, and worked hard to understand in detail the cultures of those whom they wished to convert. Religious practices linking Native religious traditions with Christianity were tolerated. The Natives were impressed that the Jesuits, with their European technology, could foresee eclipses. Some were also fascinated by books and writing.

The extent of real conversions in the early years of Jesuit proselytizing is difficult to determine. Some converts were zealots who spurned their relatives and refused to participate in traditional religious ceremonies. Others may have accepted conversion to improve their trading position with the French. In Huronia, for example, only Christians converts received muskets in their trade with the French, who deemed converts to be the more reliable trading partners.

The persistence of the Jesuits and their desire for martyrdom impressed even those most resistant to their teachings. In the early years of their missions, several Jesuit priests were captured by the Iroquois and tortured to death, while others died less romantically of exposure, drowning, disease, or exhaustion. Jesuits were aware that the Natives, at least in the beginning, regarded them as strange and lacking in survival skills; and they knew that the "Savages" were determined to assert their superiority over Europeans. As Father Jean de Brébeuf, who would become one of the most celebrated martyrs, indicated in a letter to his superiors in France in 1637: "If you could go naked, and carry the load of a horse upon your back, as they do, then you would be wise according to their doctrine, and would be recognized as a great man, otherwise not."[3]

The Jesuits were convinced that formal education would socialize Native peoples to European ways. Paul Le Jeune, superior of the Canadian Jesuit missions, founded a Jesuit college at Quebec in 1635 to teach lessons in Christianity to Indian boys, among whom he hoped to find potential priests. Not surprisingly, Aboriginal families were not enthusiastic supporters of this endeavour.

FEMALE RELIGIOUS ORDERS

Following the European practice of gender segregation, the Jesuits accepted only boys in their schools. It was therefore necessary to call on female teachers to found schools for girls in the colony. The call was heeded by Marie de l'Incarnation, an Ursuline and the first of many energetic religious women to immigrate to New France. Requiring the Native girls to board at school so they could be shielded from non-Christian influences, the Ursulines taught them prayers and simple lessons. Some of the girls were fascinated by the devout women from France and sought to emulate them, but most tried to run away from their authoritarian European teachers.

In addition to their missionary activities among Native women, female religious orders played a major role in establishing schools and hospitals to serve the settler communities of New France. Marie de l'Incarnation and her Ursuline sisters devoted their lives to teaching in both Quebec and Trois-Rivières. In 1669, Marguerite Bourgeoys, who arrived in the colony in 1653, founded a teaching community in Montreal, the Soeurs de la Congrégation de Notre-Dame. Modelling her congregation on the non-cloistered Sisters of Charity in France, she concentrated on educating children from poorer families. She appears to have had some success, because illiteracy rates in early New France were lower than in France.

The first hospital in New France, the Hôtel-Dieu de Quebec, was founded in 1639 by the Soeurs Hospitalières under the leadership of Marie Guenet and Marie Forestier. Three years later a Hôtel-Dieu was established in Ville Marie by Jeanne Mance. Educated in France by the Ursulines, Jeanne Mance came to Canada in 1641. She participated in the founding of Ville Marie and devoted her life to the service of the colony. As a member of the Société de Notre-Dame, Mance was able to persuade a wealthy French woman to finance a plan to bring several Soeurs Hospitalières from La Flèche to Ville Marie in 1657. When Ville Marie needed money to hire soldiers for its battles with the Iroquois, Mance went to France to persuade her patron of the urgency, even though she had recently fallen on the ice and had to be carried about in France on a stretcher.

MISSIONS AND NATIVE CULTURE

While missionaries developed a significant presence in the colony, their attempts to convert Natives to European ways met with hostility, especially from women. Missionary proscriptions on premarital sex and divorce and the value placed on a family life cen-

biography

Marie de l'Incarnation

Marie de l'Incarnation was one of the most complex individuals to travel to New France in the early days of European settlement. Born Marie Guyart in Tours in 1599, she had a willingness to let her visions guide her life—much like the Natives whose religion she sought to displace. Visions led her as a young widow to put her 12-year-old son in a boarding school and join the cloistered Ursulines. Another vision persuaded her to heed the call of Paul Le Jeune for nuns to open a school for Native girls in Quebec.

Like many of her Ursuline and Jesuit counterparts, she was a religious zealot who lived a life of excruciating discipline. According to one biographer: "She wore a penitential shirt with knots and thorns, slept on a hair mattress that kept her always half awake, and sometimes rose at night to chastise herself, first with thongs, later with a whip of nettles.... She ate wormwood with her food, holding the bitterness in her mouth, and sometimes approached the fire to burn her skin."[4]

The founder of Canada's first school for Native girls was more than just an otherworldly self-flagellator. She had managed a large shipping company for her brother-in-law for a decade before devoting herself fully to Christ, and the administrative skills she had acquired proved invaluable in her religious endeavours. First she found a wealthy patron, Marie-Madeleine de La Peltrie, who funded and accompanied Marie and two other Ursulines to New France in 1639. Then she supervised the building of a school for Native and French girls and a convent for the nuns. When

Marie de l'Incarnation, as portrayed by C.W. Jeffreys.

National Archives of Canada

the convent burned down in 1650, she had a larger convent built to replace it. At the time of her retirement as superior in 1669, her convent housed between 50 and 55 people. Of these, 22, including four lay sisters and three novices, were members of the religious community.

tred around nuclear, male-headed households threatened women's considerable power within Native societies. Indeed, several Huron men who became Christians were barred from their longhouses by their angry mothers-in-law. The Huron women rejected, among other things, the European view that lineage must be determined patrilineally—that is, through the male line—and that non-marital sex must be forbidden so men could be certain about the paternity of offspring.

Some Native men, by contrast, appeared to relish the new powers that the Christians claimed they should take from the women. In 1640, a group of Innu women who summered along the St Lawrence River complained to the Jesuits of the audacity of three male captains, all Christian converts, who had ordered the women to appear before them. "They treated us so rudely that we were greatly astonished. 'It is you women,' they said to us, 'who keep the Demons among us; you do not urge to be baptized…When you pass before the cross you never salute it, you wish to be independent. Now know that you will obey your husbands and you young people know that you will obey your parents, and our captains, and if any fail to do so, we will give them nothing to eat.'"5

Before European contact, if a group of Innu men had demanded that the women accept subordinate status and that children be obedient, they would have been dismissed as madmen possessed by evil spirits. Their threat to withhold food would have been meaningless in a society that required its members to take collective responsibility for obtaining and preparing food.

Most Native women continued to assert their traditions, but a coterie of women zealots, imitating the nuns, gained notoriety. They whipped each other, wore hair shirts, mixed ashes in their food, stood naked in snowstorms, and one put glowing coals between her toes. Some worked to aid the poor and sick, and eventually some of these Native women were allowed to join the French women's religious orders. None, however, survived long enough to enjoy a fruitful religious career.

THE HURON–FIVE NATIONS WARS

Missionary activities, however destructive to Native culture, were overshadowed by the more serious impact of European germs and weapons. In the late 1630s, smallpox and measles wrought devastation among the French fur-trade allies, particularly the Huron and Innu. Huron numbers were reduced by between one-half to two-thirds, leaving only 10 000 Huron in the early 1640s. Death on this scale robbed the Huron of many of their leaders and played havoc with the delicate social arrangements of the four tribes of the loose Huron Confederacy.

These arrangements had already suffered the strains of quite different responses to the Jesuit teachings and presence. Two of the tribes were receptive to the Jesuits while the other two proved hostile. When

disease depleted their numbers, opponents of the "charcoal" men (alluding to their black robes) accused the missionaries of practising black magic to destroy them. Meanwhile, the converts increasingly refused to have their family members buried in non-Christian sites or to fight alongside non-Christian Huron in battles against enemies.

In 1649 those enemies destroyed Huronia. The Five Nations Iroquois had become dependent on the fur trade, but they had exhausted fur supplies within their own territory and began to seek new supplies on their northern frontier. In the 1640s, the Five Nations attempted to disrupt the annual flotilla of Huron canoes that made the long journey from Huronia to Quebec. When the attacks on fur convoys proved unsuccessful in forcing the Christianized Huron to bend to their demands for access to furs, the Five Nations launched direct attacks on Huronia itself.

An attack in 1648 was repulsed, but not without significant Huron casualties. In 1649, the Five Nations broke through Huron defences. Jesuit priests Jean de Brébeuf and Gabriel Lalement were brutally tortured, their tormentors baptizing them with boiling water before executing them. Terrorized by a hitherto unheard-of concentration of enemy warriors, and internally divided, the survivors burned their villages and dispersed. Some traditionalists simply surrendered to the Five Nations, who proved willing to adopt them into their tribes. Most residents of Huronia took the lead of the converts who followed the Jesuits to an island in Georgian Bay, subsequently known as Christian Island. Even there, they were dogged by disaster. A winter of starvation left 5000 people, more than half of the remaining Huron population, dead.

A majority of the Huron who survived the winter of devastation on Christian Island joined their ancient enemies, the Five Nations Iroquois. Others went to live among the Petun and Neutral, only to face another Five Nations raid and dispersal. A small but crucial group moved westwards to re-establish their villages among nations that had once supplied them with furs to sell to the French. They became known as the Wyandot and settled in today's Michigan, Kansas, and Oklahoma. About 600 Huron resettled near Quebec, where they were given aid by the religious orders.

View of the Huron village of Lorette, established near Quebec for Huron refugees from Iroquois warfare (by E. Walsh).

Clements Library, University of Michigan

For the struggling St Lawrence colony, the loss of Huronia had grave commercial, military, and even agricultural consequences. Before 1649, the French involved in the fur trade could receive furs in the colony without ever setting foot in the upper country where the furs originated. In addition, their allies had protected them against hostile Five Nations Iroquois; now those allies were gone. It would be several decades before their replacements would become a match for the Five Nations who had begun to torch crops and kill settlers in an effort to force fur traders to recognize them as the exclusive seller of furs to Europeans.

The vulnerability of the French was revealed in April 1660 when Adam Dollard des Ormeaux, a soldier and recent immigrant to New France, and 17 French men, with their Algonquin and Huron allies, attempted to ambush a party of Five Nations hunters along the Ottawa River. Surprised by their attackers at the foot of Long Sault rapids, all the French and an even larger group of their Native allies were killed.

NEW FRANCE IN QUESTION

Despite concerted efforts to lay the foundations of an overseas colony, the future of New France looked uncertain in 1660. Acadia, its development impeded by

Working a canoe up a rapid on the Ottawa River. The route followed by voyageurs in the 1600s remained in use until the nineteenth century, when this drawing was produced.

Newberry Library, Chicago

Both in Acadia and Canada, Native allies had a significant impact on the French immigrants, raising the question of whether France could successfully implant its institutions and values in North America. Natives were attracted to some European foodstuffs such as bread and, to their later chagrin, they believed that European alcohol helped bring them into closer contact with the spirit world. But Natives had an equally significant impact on the foods eaten by the early settlers, as well as on the transportation methods they employed, and even on their dress. Indian corn (maize), pumpkins, beaver flesh, tails, and feet, and the meat of moose, bears, dogs, and feathered game supplemented the colonists' more familiar food items. Tobacco, an indigenous crop that garnered great interest among Europeans, was also grown in New France. Without Native inventions such as the birchbark canoe, the toboggan, and snowshoes, the French would have had difficulty negotiating the unfamiliar terrain. Native medicine helped remedy scurvy and other ailments, although European haughtiness prevented the French from taking advantage of the full cornucopia of Native cures.

the battles of rival French claimants, was in English hands. Quebec was subject to raids by the Five Nations Confederacy, whose trade links with the Dutch and the English underscored the success of other European nations in developing overseas empires. England's American colonies, stretching along the Atlantic seaboard from New England to Virginia, were home to 70 000 colonists in 1660; Canada and Acadia together had less than 4000.

Despite the challenges it faced, Canada by 1660 was taking on the trappings of a settled European community. Two-thirds of the 3035 people living in the colony resided in the countryside and depended on farming for their livelihood. The urban population lived in the three towns of the colony: Quebec, founded 1608; Trois-Rivières, 1634; and Montreal, 1642. By 1660, Quebec, the most highly developed centre, could boast a church, seven chapels, a college, a convent school for girls, a hospital, nine mills, a brewery, and a bakery. The city was surrounded by five forts that protected area residents.

One group of colonists was particularly influenced by the free-spirited behaviour of the Native peoples. These were the young men who spent a good part of their lives trading in the bush. Most had liaisons with Native women while they lived in the upper country. Some remained in the Great Lakes basin and never returned to Quebec. Others abandoned their Native wives when they returned to the Laurentian settlements, but a few brought their wives back with them. Champlain and, for a time, the Jesuits, promoted interracial marriages as a means of encouraging assimilation. "Our sons shall marry your daughters and together we shall form one people," Champlain proclaimed.

CONCLUSION

After nearly a half-century of effort, France had staked its claim to the area that would become the eastern provinces of Canada, but it had fallen badly behind in the competition to establish North American colonies. Canada and Acadia were little more than fur trade outposts, vulnerable to internal dissension and external assault. They produced no great riches for the empire, nor were they high on the list of overseas destinations sought by French emigrants who would rather risk contracting malaria in the French West Indies than suffer a winter in New France. If the northern colonies were to thrive, they needed strong leadership and infusions of capital. On that, all elements in the colony—administrators, church leaders, fur traders, and settlers—agreed. As we will see in the next chapter, Louis XIV, the so-called "Sun King," would provide both—at least for a time.

A Historiographical Debate

The Destruction of Huronia

What caused the destruction of Huronia? At one level the answer is simple. The Five Nations Iroquois, with an estimated 500 guns in their possession, dispersed an enemy that could count on only 120 guns. French policy regarding provision of weapons to the Native peoples was inconsistent from region to region, but in Huronia only Christian converts received guns. In 1648, only about 15 percent of the Huron were nominal Christians, and a disproportionate number of those had the job of transporting furs to the French colony. Given the lack of guns, Huronia, including its Christians, became more vulnerable to Five Nations attack.

For historian Cornelius Jaenen, there is no conclusive evidence that Iroquois raiders made much use of guns in their attacks on the Huron. They may instead have resorted mainly to the traditional tomahawk and torch to terrorize their Huron and French enemies. Employing solid military tactics involving concentration of forces, surprise, and sustained attack, they moved quickly from one village to the next before the Huron could assemble and mount a counter-offensive. Since their opponents were already bitterly divided between Christians and traditionalists, their tactics were effective.[6]

Some scholars have maintained that arming the Huron would have been unnecessary if European trade rivalries had not promoted Huron-Iroquois hostility. Anthropologist George Hunt argued in 1940 that the Huron and the Five Nations Iroquois, sharing common origins, were unnatural enemies and that the fur trade created new and more intense rivalries between Native groups.[7] While Hunt's general point regarding the impact of the fur trade on the motivations for intertribal conflicts has merit, few researchers accept his claim that the Five Nations and Huron were on good terms in the immediate pre-contact period.

Geographer Conrad Heidenreich suggests that desperation of the Five Nations and guns alone do not explain their success in vanquishing the Huron. The cohesiveness of the Five Nations Confederacy, whose contact with Europeans was largely restricted to traders, was in contrast to the disunity of the Huron, whose society had been less integrated than the Five Nations to begin with and became even less so as a result of religious division and the removal of recognized leaders by diseases.[8] Anthropologist Bruce Trigger is still more emphatic in pinpointing Jesuit activities as the cause of the destruction of Huronia.[9] In contrast, Jesuit historian Lucien Campeau argues in the order's defence that the Iroquois destroyed both the Petun and the Neutral; and the Petun had only sporadic contacts with the Jesuits, while the Neutral had none at all. It was guns, Campeau says, not cultural and religious confusion, that destroyed the Huron, just as those guns also brought down the other two nations.[10]

A Huron writer suggests an interesting counter-thesis. Georges Sioui argues that the Iroquois understood the Europeans' threat to the Native way of life and so became engaged in a war of liberation against the French. Because they suffered a huge loss of life in this war, they could only survive as a people by absorbing new members into their nations, by force if necessary. For Sioui, the large-scale adoption by the Five Nations of the Huron, Petun, and Neutral was not the unintended consequence of the attack on Huronia, but indeed the objective of the attack. Sioui also maintains that historians of European origin have exaggerated the toll of the wars on Huron lives to disguise an essential fact: that European diseases, and not Native warfare, were responsible for the sharp decline of Native populations.[11]

American historian Daniel Richter supports Sioui's view that the chief aim of the Five Nations was to take captives, but his research questions Sioui's claims that such an aim was part of a Five Nations effort to build Native resistance against Europeans. "Mourning wars"—that is, wars meant to take captives to replace population losses among their own people—were part of ancient Iroquois tradition, Richter argues. The decimation caused by European diseases simply intensified such warfare. Moreover, the mourning wars did not promote unity among the Five Nations who fought among themselves for the right to various groups of captives.[12]

NOTES

1 *The Voyages of Jacques Cartier*, trans. and ed. H.P. Biggar (Ottawa: King's Printer, 1924) 52–53.

2 Quoted in James P. Ronda, "We Are Well as We Are: An Indian Critique of Seventeenth Century Missions," *William and Mary Quarterly*, 3rd ser. 34 (1977) 77.

3 *The Jesuit Relations and Allied Documents*, ed. S.R. Mealing (Toronto: McClelland and Stewart, 1963) 50.

4 Joyce Marshall, ed., *Word from New France: The Selected Letters of Marie de l'Incarnation* (Toronto: Oxford University Press, 1967) 5.

5 *The Jesuit Relations and Allied Documents*, ed. Reuben Gold Thwaites, vol. 18 (Cleveland: Burrows Brothers Co., 1896–1901) 105–07.

6 Cornelius Jaenen, The French *Relationship with the Native People of New France and Acadia* (Ottawa: Indian and Northern Affairs Canada, 1984).

7 George T. Hunt, *The Wars of the Iroquois* (Madison: University of Wisconsin Press, 1967).

8 Conrad Heidenreich, *Huronia: A History and Geography of the Huron Indians, 1600–1650* (Toronto: McClelland and Stewart, 1971).

9 Bruce G. Trigger, "The Jesuits and the Fur Trade" in *Sweet Promises: A Reader in Indian-White Relations in Canada*, ed. J.R. Miller (Toronto: University of Toronto Press, 1991) 15–16; Bruce G. Trigger, The Children of Aataentsic: A History of the Huron People to 1600 (Montreal: McGill-Queen's University Press, 1987).

10 Lucien Campeau, *La Mission des Jésuites chez les Hurons, 1634–1650* (Montreal: Éditions Bellarmin, 1987).

11 Georges Sioui, *For an American Autohistory: An Essay on the Foundations of a Social Ethic* (Montreal: McGill-Queen's University Press, 1992).

12 Daniel K. Richter, *The Ordeal of the Longhouse: The Peoples of the Iroquois League in the Era of European Colonization* (Chapel Hill: University of North Carolina Press, 1992).

SELECTED READING

On the Norse explorations, see P. H. Sawyer, ed., *The Oxford Illustrated History of the Vikings* (Oxford: Oxford University Press, 2000); and William W. Fitzhugh and Elisabeth I. Ward, eds., *The North Atlantic Saga* (Washington: Smithsonian Institution Press, 2000). A recent work on John Cabot is Peter Edward Pope, *The Many Landfalls of John Cabot* (Toronto: University of Toronto Press, 1997).

Cartier's account of his explorations is found in The *Voyages of Jacques Cartier*, ed. by Henry Percival Biggar and Ramsay Cook (Toronto: University of Toronto Press, 1993). Useful texts on Samuel de Champlain include Conrad Heidenreich, *Explorations and Mapping of Samuel de Champlain, 1603–1632* (Toronto: B.V. Gutsell, 1976), and Samuel de Champlain, *Algonquians, Hurons and Iroquois: Champlain Explores America, 1603–1616*, ed. Edward Gaylord Bourne and trans. Annie Nettleton Bourne (Dartmouth: Brook House Press, 2000).

The major surveys in English of the history of New France are W.J. Eccles, *The Canadian Frontier, 1534–1760* (New York: Holt, Rinehart and Winston, 1969); *The French in North America, 1500—1783*, rev. ed. (Markham, ON: Fitzhenry and Whiteside, 1998); and *France in America*, rev. ed. (East Lansing: Michigan State University Press, 1990). A detailed study of New France before 1663 is Marcel Trudel, *The Beginnings of New France, 1524–1663*, trans. Patricia Claxton (Toronto: McClelland and Stewart, 1973). Rich details on the social history of Montreal are found in Louise Dechêne, *Habitants and Merchants in Seventeenth Century Montreal* (Montreal: McGill-Queen's University Press, 1992).

The early history of Acadia is covered in John G. Reid, *Acadia, Maine and New Scotland: Marginal Colonies in the Seventeenth Century* (Toronto: University of Toronto Press, 1981); Naomi E.S. Griffiths, *The Contexts of Acadian History, 1686–1784* (Montreal: McGill-Queen's University Press, 1992) and *The Acadians: Creation of a People* (Toronto: McGraw-Hill Ryerson, 1973); Sally Ross and Alphonse Deveau, *The Acadians of Nova Scotia: Past and Present* (Halifax: Nimbus, 1992); Elizabeth Jones, *Gentlemen and Jesuits* (Toronto: University of Toronto Press, 1986); and Andrew Hill Clark, *Acadia: The Geography of Early Nova Scotia to 1760* (Madison: University of Wisconsin Press, 1968). Newfoundland in the seventeenth century is discussed in Gillian Cell, *English Enterprises in Newfoundland, 1557–1660* (Toronto: University of Toronto Press, 1969) and *Newfoundland Discovered* (London: Hakluyt Society, 1982); and H.A. Innis, *The Cod Fisheries: The History of an International Economy* (Toronto: University of Toronto Press, 1978). On whaling, see Daniel Francis, *A History of World Whaling* (Markham, ON: Penguin, 1990).

There is a growing literature on early European-Native relations in Canada. Some of these texts are referred to in Chapter 1. Additional sources include Denys Delâge, *Amerindians and Europeans in the American Northeast, 1600–1664* (Vancouver: UBC Press, 1993); L.C. Green and Olive P. Dickason, *The Law of Nations and the New World* (Edmonton: University of Alberta

Press, 1989); Cornelius Jaenen, *The French Relationship with the Native People of New France and Acadia* (Ottawa: Indian and Northern Affairs Canada, 1984); Bruce G. Trigger, *Natives and Newcomers: Canada's "Heroic Age" Reconsidered* (Montreal: McGill-Queen's University Press, 1986); and E.S. Rogers and Donald B. Smith, eds., *Aboriginal Ontario* (Toronto: Dundurn Press, 1994). On early missionaries to New France, see John Webster Grant, *Moon of Wintertime: Missionaries and the Indians of Canada in Encounter since 1534* (Toronto: University of Toronto Press, 1984).

On the fate of the Huron, see Daniel K. Richter, *The Ordeal of the Longhouse: The Peoples of the Iroquois League in the Era of European Colonization* (Chapel Hill: University of North Carolina Press, 1992), and Georges Sioui, *For an American Autohistory: An Essay on the Foundations of a Social Ethic* (Montreal: McGill-Queen's University Press, 1992). A Mi'kmaq's account of his people's post-contact history is Daniel N. Paul, *We Were Not the Savages: A Mi'kmaq Perspective on the Collision of European and Native American Civilization* (Halifax: Fernwood, 2000). The impact of contact on the lives of Aboriginal women is explored in Eleanor Leacock, "Montagnais Women and the Jesuit Program for Colonization," in *Rethinking Canada: The Promise of Women's History*, 3rd ed., ed. Veronica Strong-Boag and Anita Clair Fellman (Toronto: Oxford University Press, 1997). On the early history of residential schooling, see J.R. Miller, *Shingwauk's Vision: A History of Native Residential Schools* (Toronto: University of Toronto Press, 1996). Church perspectives both on Native-European relations and conditions in New France are found in S.R. Mealing, ed., *The Jesuit Relations and Allied Documents* (Ottawa: Carleton University Press, 1990); Joyce Marshall, ed., *Word from New France: The Selected Letters of Marie de l'Incarnation* (Toronto: Oxford University Press, 1967); and Father Gabriel Sagard, *The Long Journey to the Country of the Huron* (Toronto: Champlain Society, 1939). A work of synthesis is Cornelius Jaenen, *The Role of the Church in New France* (Toronto: McGraw-Hill Ryerson, 1976).

Apart from the general texts, works with information on the social history of early New France include R. Cole Harris, "The Extension of France into Rural Canada," in *European Settlement and Development in North America: Essays on Geographical Change in Honour and Memory of Andrew Hill Clark*, ed. James R. Gibson (Toronto: University of Toronto Press, 1978). On the society of origin of the first European colonists of Acadia and New France, a lively account is Pierre Goubert's, *The Ancien*

Régime: French Society, 1600–1750 (Paris: Colin, 1969).

On women in early New France, there is good general information in the Clio Collective, *Quebec Women: A History*, trans. Roger Gannon and Rosalind Gill (Toronto: Women's Press, 1987) as well as Isabel Foulché-Delbosc, "Women of Three Rivers: 1651–1663," in *The Neglected Majority: Essays in Women's History*, vol. 1, ed. Susan Mann Trofimenkoff and Alison Prentice (Toronto: McClelland and Stewart, 1977); Jan Noel, "New France: Les Femmes Favorisées," in *Rethinking Canada*, ed. Strong-Boag and Fellman, 28–50; and Raymond Brodeur, ed., *Mystique et missionaire: Marie Guyart de L'Incarnation* (Québec: Les Presses de l'Université Laval, 2001).

 WEBLINKS

CHRISTOPHER COLUMBUS
www1.minn.net/~keithp/index.htm

The Columbus Navigation Homepage provides information on navigation history, as well as general material on Columbus and his voyages. A timeline, maps of routes, and a select bibliography of further readings are available.

JACQUES CARTIER
www.win.tue.nl/~engels/discovery/cartier.html

This page, part of Discoverers Web, contains a biography of Cartier and links to related sites.

PORT ROYAL
http://parkscanada.pch.gc.ca/parks/nova_scotia/port_royal/Port_royal_e.htm

This Parks Canada site describes one of the earliest locations of European settlement in North America. It includes virtual tours and learning experiences for students.

MARIE DE L'INCARNATION
www.library.upenn.edu/special/gallery/kislak/religion/mincarnation.html

This site contains a portrait and a biography of Marie de L'Incarnation, and describes how missionaries and colonists aided in the preservation of native languages by attempting to convert indigenous peoples to Christianity. Other links are available.

JEAN DE BRÉBEUF
www.sfo.com/~denglish/wynaks/wn_stmar.htm

This site gives a brief description of mid-seventeenth century relations between Jesuit missionaries and the Huron people at Ste-Marie-Among-the-Hurons.

THE EUROPEAN ENLIGHTENMENT
www.newgenevacenter.org/west/enlightenment2.htm

The struggle between religious and secularist movements throughout European society and politics during the period of settlement in New France is outlined in this site.

PART I SUMMARY

FIRST NATIONS AND EUROPEANS HAD EACH ESTABLISHED complex, evolving societies over the millennia and each group judged the other through lenses shaped by its own history and social values. While cultural differences resulted in misunderstandings, they did not stand in the way of a partnership in the fur trade from which both sides seemed to benefit. The fur trade also increased competition among the First Nations and Europeans for advantage, sometimes with disastrous results. Neither the Huron, who were nearly wiped out by disease and warfare, nor the Europeans, who faced scurvy and attacks from European rivals, could have anticipated the horrors that the coming together of the two worlds precipitated. Nevertheless, by 1663 the fur trade, together with the North Atlantic fisheries, had inspired Europeans to stake a permanent claim in what to them was a "New World."

FRANCE IN AMERICA, 1663–1763

Between 1663 and 1763, the French built an empire in North America and then lost most of it to Great Britain. New France at its height included Newfoundland and Acadia, and extended along the St Lawrence and Great Lakes, into the Prairies, and down the Mississippi. Valued for the commerce (mostly in fish and furs), prestige, and military might it brought to the French monarchy, New France never attracted many settlers. Only close alliances with Native peoples enabled France to lay claim to such a vast domain. When wars erupted between Great Britain and France for dominance in Europe, they inevitably spilled into the colonies. France was defeated during the Seven Years' War but left a legacy of French settlement in North America that remains to this day.

CHAPTER 4

New France Takes Root, 1663–1689

It is pleasant to see now almost the entire extent of the shores of our River St Lawrence settled by new colonies, which continue to spread over more than eighty leagues of territory along the shores of this great River, where new hamlets are seen springing up here and there, which facilitate navigation—rendering it more agreeable by the sight of numerous houses, and more convenient by frequent resting places.... Fear of the enemy no longer prevents our labours from causing the forests to recede and from sowing their fields with all sorts of grain....The Savages our allies, no longer fearing that they will be surprised on the road, come in quest of us from all directions, from a distance of five or six hundred leagues —either to re-establish their trade interrupted by the wars; or to open new commercial dealings.[1]

This report from the Jesuits in 1668 suggests that the fortunes of Canada had changed dramatically in the five years since royal government had been proclaimed in 1663. With characteristic energy, Louis XIV had addressed the major problems facing the struggling colony— defence against the Iroquois, the lack of European population, and administrative instability. Royal intervention ensured that the colony would take root and survive.

THE AGE OF ABSOLUTISM

The transformation in the fortunes of New France came as a direct result of Louis XIV's decision in 1661 to assume personal charge of state affairs. This was a significant event, not only for France and its colonies but also for Europe as a whole. By creating a complex bureaucracy to administer state affairs and by making royal favour rather than hereditary privilege the chief source of power, Louis XIV emerged as Europe's most powerful monarch. The king insisted that the old aristocracy (*noblesse d'épée* or *de sang*) and the new elite created by royal favour (*noblesse de robe*) pay homage to him at his fabulous court at Versailles, where they could be kept under his watchful eye.

As absolute ruler, Louis XIV demanded that all power be embodied in the king. Aristocracy, merchants, artisans, and peasants—all were subordinate to him. Even the Roman Catholic Church in France collaborated in this consolidation of power, advancing the theory of the divine right of kings to justify the new political order. This theory proclaimed the monarch to be God's direct representative on earth. Few dared to defy the double-barrelled authority of state and church.

The king was his own first minister, but his policies were only as good as the advice he received from the ministers, secretaries, courtiers, clergy, family members, and mistresses who surrounded him. In the early years of the reign of Louis XIV, one of the most influential royal officials was Jean-Baptiste Colbert. He was controller-general of finances (1662–83) and, after 1669, minister of colonial and maritime affairs as well. To enhance the glory of the monarch, Colbert was determined to reform national finances, promote economic self-sufficiency, and build a colonial empire with a navy to defend it.

Louis XIV and His Heirs, by Nicolas de Largillière, 1710. So successful was Louis XIV in establishing his absolutist regime that other European monarchs tried to imitate his policies, but no one managed to outshine the "Sun King," and the period of his long reign (1661–1715) is often referred to as "the age of Louis XIV." Despite crippling losses on the battlefield towards the end of his rule, and a society periodically racked by famine and heavy taxation, the Sun King bequeathed one of the most powerful nations on earth to his successor, Louis XV (1715–74), who was the younger brother of the child in this portrait.

ABSOLUTISM IN NEW FRANCE

New France soon felt the impact of Louis XIV's absolute rule. In 1665, Alexandre de Prouville, Marquis de Tracy, and 1200 troops, most of them members of the Carignan-Salières regiment, arrived in the colony. Two expeditions were launched into Mohawk country in 1666. Although the European-trained army suffered more casualties than it inflicted, the show of force had the desired effect. The Five Nations sent delegates to Quebec and agreed to keep the peace. It lasted long enough to give French authorities the breathing space they needed to transform their colony on the St Lawrence.

Moving quickly to ensure sustained population growth, the royal government dispatched nearly 800 women, known as the *filles du roi*, to the colony. Most of the filles du roi were orphans, plucked from the state-sponsored institution in Paris that looked after the disadvantaged peoples of French society. Within a few months of their arrival, most of the women had found husbands in a colony where bachelors outnumbered marriageable European women six to one. Women were essential for bearing the next generation and for maintaining the household economy upon which basic survival in pre-industrial societies depended. As a result, they were eagerly sought as marriage partners.

In the decade following the declaration of royal government, the colony also became home to a significant number of French soldiers. The members of the Carignan-Salières regiment were encouraged to settle in the colony, and about 400 of them did so. Indentured servants (*engagés*), in contrast to their counterparts in earlier years, now more often chose to stay in New France once they had fulfilled their contractual obligations. Between 1663 and 1673, over 2000 immigrants arrived, nearly doubling the population of the colony and laying the foundations for stable community development.

The royal government, eager to increase the population base of New France, was not content to let nature take its course. For a short time it offered bonuses for families of 10 or more children and imposed penalties on people outside the church who clung to the single life.

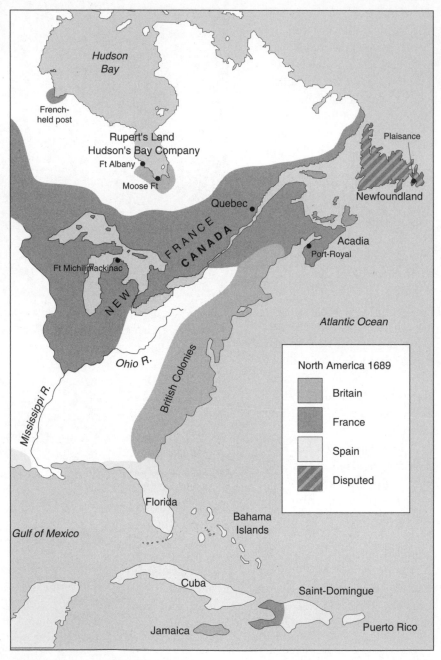

Map 4.1

North America, 1689.

Adapted from W.J. Eccles, *France in America* (East Lansing, MI: Michigan State University Press, 1990) 64

Evidence suggests that these "carrot and stick" policies had little impact on family formation. As in France, couples in New France did not practise birth control and, on the average, had a child every two years. Lower mortality rates, a higher standard of nutrition, less exposure to epidemic diseases, and a lower age of marriage for women than in France are the factors that seem to account for the rapid growth of the population to 15 000 by the end of the century and to 70 000 by 1763.

ACADIA

Acadia was theoretically subject to the same policies as Canada, but in practice it experienced royal authority quite differently. Held by the English between 1654 and 1667, the colony missed Louis XIV's brief burst of enthusiasm for colonial development. A governor, subordinate to the governor general based in Quebec, was finally appointed in 1670. With a motley garrison of 50 soldiers and 60 new settlers to augment the fewer than 500 people already living there, Governor Hector d'Andigne de Grandfontaine was expected to maintain the king's authority over an area that today roughly corresponds to the Maritime provinces of Canada and part of the state of Maine.

Not surprisingly, given its small population and dispersed settlement, Acadia lacked the institutional development that characterized the St Lawrence colony. Although 55 seigneuries were granted in the region, rents were rarely collected. The few priests in Acadia sometimes assumed legal duties in the absence of judicial officers. Without an effective military presence, the Acadians were reluctant to make enemies. They established amicable relations with the Abenaki, Mi'kmaq, and Maliseet who lived in the region and, in defiance of official injunctions, traded regularly with the New Englanders, who regarded Acadia as their northern outpost.

Dykeland agriculture emerged as a distinctive feature of Acadia. Instead of clearing the forests for planting, the settlers reclaimed the marshlands built up by the high tides of the Bay of Fundy. This difficult engineering feat produced rich soil that sustained cattle and crops in abundance. Because of the relative ease of making a living, the immigrant population married young, raised large families, and soon developed a reputation for displaying an independent attitude toward authorities, based at Port Royal.

NEWFOUNDLAND

Newfoundland's wealth was found in the vast quantities of cod found on the offshore "banks." Economically more important to France than beaver, cod supported a thriving bank fishery, based in the French ports of Le Havre, Honfleur, and Les Sables-d'Olonne. It supplied green fish to the huge market in and around Paris and along the Loire. Ships from the other major fishing ports produced dried cod for the southern European market. By the 1660s, the bank fishery accounted for about a third of the French fleet.

In 1662, Colbert had chosen the ice-free port of Plaisance, on the west coast of the Avalon Peninsula of Newfoundland, to serve as a base to protect the much valued French fishery. Served by a governor, and a few administrators, troops, and missionaries, it soon attracted settlers to its shore properties. By the end of the century, Plaisance consisted of 40 resident fishing families and served a France-based fishing fleet of over 400 vessels, employing an estimated 10 000 men. Like the men in the fisheries who could be forced to serve on naval vessels in time of war, Plaisance also had military potential, a fact that did not go unnoticed by the English based in St John's, the major centre on what was now called the "English shore" of the Avalon Peninsula.

COLONIAL ADMINISTRATION

Under royal government, New France was administered in much the same way as a province in France, with modifications adapted to the colonial reality. The chief officer in New France was the governor general based in Quebec. Always a military man, and usually a member of the old aristocracy (*noblesse d'épée*), the governor general controlled the military forces in the colony and was responsible for relations with the First Nations. Local governors in Montreal and Trois-Rivières reported to him, as did, in theory at least, governors located in Port Royal and Plaisance. With the arrival of the Troupes de la Marine in the 1680s, New France always had a substantial military force that the governor general could use to protect the colony from external attack and to quell any civilian unrest. The military establishment was also a significant source of revenue for the colony.

As in France, the intendant in New France was the chief provincial administrator, responsible for finance, economic development, justice, and civil administration. Intendants, usually members of the new aristocracy (*noblesse de robe*) beholden to the king for their newly acquired status, represented the efforts of the king to bring bureaucratic efficiency and centralized control to bear on distant provinces. By the eighteenth century, the intendant, like the governor general, was assisted by delegates in the main districts as well as a number of minor officials such as royal notaries, road surveyors, and customs officials.

Both the governor general and the intendant sat on the Sovereign Council, an appointed body modelled upon the provincial parlements in France. Its main functions were to serve as the court of appeal from the lower courts, to issue decrees for the governance of the colony in line with royal instructions, and to register the royal edicts that served as the constitutional framework for the colony. As the population grew, the number of councillors rose from the original five in 1663, to seven in 1675, and twelve in 1703. The Sovereign Council also included the bishop of the Roman Catholic Church and an attorney general who was trained in law. In 1703, at the behest of the king, the name was changed from Sovereign to Superior Council, reflecting the more modest role that the absolute ruler expected this colonial institution to play.

PATERNALISM IN NEW FRANCE

Power in the age of absolutism was exercised by the social elite. Any notion of authority emanating from the people was anathema to men such as Louis XIV and Colbert. Indeed, Colbert abolished the system whereby elected syndics from the major towns brought the concerns of the people to the Sovereign Council. Nor were people allowed to sign petitions. At the same time, the habitants were encouraged to take their problems to their superiors, both civilian and spiritual, and, on major issues, colonial authorities were instructed to convene consultative assemblies and report recommendations. While the advice thus rendered need not be acted upon, it was often in the best interest of absolute rulers to listen to the concerns of the people they governed.

Under the old regime, power may have been narrowly focused, but it was usually exercised with a sense

biography

Charles Le Moyne: A Self-Made Nobleman

The son of a French innkeeper, Charles Le Moyne arrived in New France in 1641, at the age of 15. He worked for the Jesuits for a time and then became a fur trader, interpreter, and soldier. In 1654, he married a commoner, Catherine Thierry, and together they had twelve sons and two daughters. Le Moyne, who became one of the most successful merchants in Montreal, distinguished himself in the wars against the Iroquois and received small seigneuries before being raised to noble status in 1668. Four years later, he was granted the seigneury of Longueuil. As members of a noble family, Le Moyne's sons easily found commissions in the military. His eldest son, Charles, was named Baron de Longueuil in 1700 and received the coveted Croix de St-Louis in 1703. Another son, Pierre Le Moyne d'Iberville, had a distinguished military career. Yet another, Jean-Baptiste, usually known by his noble title, Bienville, was a long-time governor of Louisiana.

of responsibility toward all classes of society. Such an approach, called paternalism, was particularly obvious in New France, where special circumstances—pioneer hardships, Iroquois hostility, and colonial rivalries—often elicited a sympathetic response from royal authority. As practised in New France, paternalism made it possible for the colony to be granted exceptions from the general rules prevailing in the mother country. For instance, the North American colonists were spared the crushing burden of taxation that was levied on the people of France on the grounds that frontier conditions made it difficult for them to pay their share.

Frontier conditions also produced institutional responses that were unique to North America. In 1669, Louis XIV ordered the governor general to enrol all male habitants between the ages of 16 and 60 into militia companies. The Iroquois threat and colonial rivalries made such an innovation necessary for the defence of the colony. With a company in every parish, everyone had easy access to a militia captain, a man chosen from the parish to lead the militia in times of war and to report local concerns to the intendant in times of peace. Ordinances from the civil authorities were also passed down this military hierarchy, in a society where the privileges of the elite were carefully assigned and jealously guarded.

View of Quebec, 1699, from the cartouche on a map by Franquelin.
National Archives of Canada/C15791

LAW AND ORDER

In 1664, Louis XIV decreed that the Custom of Paris—the legal code used in the Paris region of France—would be the basis for the civil law of the colony. The Sovereign Council served as supreme court in the colony, hearing appeals from royal courts established in major towns. On rare occasions, wealthy colonists appealed their cases to the Conseil des Parties in France. The intendant appointed all court officials, supervised the court system, and had wide legal authority, including judging cases under 100 livres if all parties agreed and intervening in cases where he felt justice was not being done. A few seigneurial and church courts existed in the colonies but, as in France, they were subordinate to royal policy.

It was in the royal interest to keep legal proceedings cheap and accessible. In France, the cost of going to court, driven high by efforts on the part of judges and lawyers to enrich themselves, deterred many people from seeking justice. Legal reforms introduced in New France included the barring of lawyers from the courts. According to one commentator, this policy had the desired effect: "I will in no wise say whether justice is more untainted or disinterested than in France, but at least if it is sold, it is much cheaper. We do not pass through the squeezing of the lawyers, the grasp of attorneys, nor the claws of the clerks; that vermin has not yet affected Canada. Each pleads his own cause, the decision is expeditious and it is not bristling with bribes, costs and expenses."[2]

While reforms made the courts more accessible in New France, justice was not free. Nor was it always equally rendered. There was a fixed schedule of court costs as well as fees for bailiffs and witnesses. Access to the system was always easier for the elite. Excepting some female servants who had been seduced by their employer or his son and had borne a child out of wedlock, domestic servants, apprentices, and slaves never brought charges against their masters. People in the countryside faced the added burden of travelling to one of the towns where the cases were heard. The peasantry, which made up about 80 percent of the population, comprised only 18 percent of the litigants who came before Quebec's royal court, which was known as the Prévôté.

Violence, bloodshed, and death were a fact of colonial life, and the criminal law in New France, as in all of Europe in the seventeenth century, was harsh. Under the French regime, criminal law recognized three categories of crimes: crimes against God, such as heresy, blasphemy, and sorcery; crimes against the Crown, such as treason, sedition, rebellion, desertion, duelling, and counterfeiting; and crimes against person or property, such as murder, suicide, rape, slander, libel, theft, and arson. The French inquisitorial system of justice was based on the interrogation of the accused, and the final decision as to guilt or innocence was rendered by the judge, not, as in the British system, by a jury of peers. Depending upon the seriousness of the charges, the accused might even be subjected to judicial torture, *la question extraordinaire*, to extract a confession.

Since harsh sentences were meant to act as a deterrent to potential criminals, they were conducted in public and with considerable fanfare. There were three categories of punishment—capital, infamous, and pecuniary—and within each a judge had some latitude. For capital crimes, death could be brought about by beheading, strangulation, burning at the stake, quartering, amputation of the limbs, mutilation,

or some combination of these methods. Members of the nobility condemned to death had the privilege of being beheaded rather than hanged. The total number of people executed in Canada during the French regime was eighty-five, six of them broken on the wheel. Infamous punishment included humiliation on a wooden horse, in the stocks, or at the pillory, and might also include exile or loss of civil rights. Pecuniary punishment consisted of fines or confiscation of property.

Although the law set forth brutal punishments for a wide range of offences, the judges in New France were often lenient on appeal. They also showed a marked reluctance to order that individuals have their tongue cut out for blasphemy, be drawn and quartered for passing counterfeit money, or have a fleur-de-lis branded on their cheek for a first offence of selling brandy to Natives. Had they pushed the law to the limit, many more people in New France would have been mutilated than actually was the case.

RELIGIOUS ESTABLISHMENT

Louis XIV kept a tight rein on the institutional church in his realm. Not only did he prosecute all non-Catholics, he also resisted any attempts on the part of the pope to interfere in the functioning of the church on French soil. The relationship of church and state reflected an ideology known as *gallicanism*. In the French context, gallicanism meant that the church was organized on a national scale, with all clergy answering to their superiors up the hierarchy through bishops and archbishops, who, in turn, were responsible to the king. The king, not the pope, nominated all church officials in France and controlled the rules and membership of all religious communities.

As ruler by divine right, Louis XIV claimed to be the supreme protector of the church, and any person or group opposing his claims was ruthlessly persecuted. Protestants, Jews, and Jansenists, the latter a puritanical group within the Catholic Church, bore the brunt of his zeal for spiritual uniformity. Following the revocation of the Edict of Nantes in 1685, which had granted Protestants limited toleration in France, one million Huguenots were faced with forced con-

---

MORE TO THE STORY

Witches and Warlocks in New France

Marie de l'Incarnation, writing to her son in 1668, described a case in which a young woman was "possessed by the devil," apparently when a young man, recently arrived from France, was refused permission to marry her. According to Marie de l'Incarnation, the young man "attempted to gain by spite what he could not obtain by fair means," using the offices of "certain magicians and sorcerers that had come from France." She continued:

> To be brief, the girl, who was continually pursued and agitated by demons, was put in a room in the hospital where sick persons are also kept, and, by the order of Monsigneur [Laval], Mother de Saint-Augustin was set to watch over her.... The good mother watched over the girl day and night. By day the demon did not appear, but he worked his ravages at night, agitating the girl greatly and from time to time giving her views of the magician, who appeared to her accompanied by many others. But all these hellish flies could never prevail over the girl, since they were always driven away by the one to whom the Church had committed her. Enraged because Mother de Saint-Augustin guarded the

girl's purity with such care, the demons appeared to her in hideous forms and beat her outrageously. The wounds and bruises that marked her body were enough to show that they were realities and not illusions.... Finally, the demons and magicians withdrew, through the intercession of this holy man [Father de Brébeuf], who had spilled his blood for the upholding of the Faith in this country.[3]

This incident points to the church's importance in fostering stability in a colony where the rigours of frontier life might easily have led to social unrest. In contrast, the Protestant community of Salem, Massachusetts, was racked in 1692 by a series of trials against people, most of them women, accused of being witches and warlocks. When the episode finally ended, 20 of the accused had been executed and 100 were awaiting trial. No such panic occurred in New France, primarily, it seems, because most people in the colony believed fervently in the ability of church authorities to exorcise demons. Nor would the church hierarchy in New France have allowed accusations to get out of hand, as they certainly did in Salem.

---

version to Catholicism. Many chose instead to leave France, taking their skills and their ambitions with them. New France suffered the same intolerance.

Officially sanctioned in its monopoly position, the Roman Catholic Church played an important role in the colony. It was charged with maintaining schools, hospitals, and charitable institutions, sustaining the social order by preaching obedience and submission, and cementing Native alliances through missionary endeavours. Upon his arrival in 1659, Bishop Laval began the process of carving out parishes to help the church minister to its expanding flock. In 1663, a seminary to train priests was established in Quebec and the tithe was introduced to support the church establishment. Institutions to take care of the poor, orphaned, and indigent—*bureaux des pauvres* and *hôpitals-généraux*—appeared in the colony before the end of the seventeenth century. Like the schools and

hospitals, they were entrusted to the administration of the church.

Despite the church's status in the colony, the bishop won few battles in confrontations with the secular authorities. Colbert was suspicious of clerical officials and even went to the length of sending the Récollets back to the colony in 1670 in an attempt to reduce the power of the Jesuits, who had been influential in the appointment of Laval. The Sulpicians, who became seigneurs of Montreal in 1663 and built their own seminary, also challenged the bishop's authority. Instructions from France deprived the bishop of his role in appointing and dismissing, jointly with the governor general, the members of the Sovereign Council, and authorized the intendant to discourage the bishop from attending council meetings. When Laval asked that the tithe be set at one-thirteenth of the produce of the land, parishioners objected and it

Governor Denonville Denounces Gangs, 1685

Both religious and civil authorities in New France were alarmed by the influence of the frontier on the culture of young men in the colony. In 1685 Governor Denonville expressed his concern to the Minister of Marine and Colonies:

> Monsieur de la Barre has suppressed a certain gang called the Chevaliers, but he has not taken away its manners or disorders. A way of dressing up like savages, stark naked, not only on carnival days but also on all days of feasting and de-

bauchery, has been treated as a clever action and a joke. These manners tend only to maintain the young people in the spirit of living like savages and to communicate with them and to be eternally profligate like them. I cannot express sufficiently to you, Monseigneur, the attraction that this savage life, of doing nothing, of being restrained by nothing, of following every whim and being beyond correction, has for the young men.[4]

was set at one-twenty-sixth and on grains alone, not the entire agricultural output. As a result, the church was dependent upon state subsidies for as much as one-third of its revenue.

It took some time for the church to get established in the countryside. When Laval's successor, Jean-Baptiste de la Croix de Saint-Vallier, arrived in Quebec in 1688, there were 21 priests resident in the parishes, of whom 12 lodged with parishioners because there was as yet no rectory. In only six localities was the tithe sufficient to assure a modest living. Until the eighteenth century, priests were often itinerant, visiting a parish for a few weeks each year rather than residing permanently there. Even at the end of the French regime, with 114 parishes to serve, there were only 169 priests, including the seminary, missionary, and chaplaincy personnel.

The church also struggled against the superstitions and questionable religious practices of their often uneducated flock. Bishop Saint-Vallier, sensing the lack of rigour in parish religious life, published a *Rituel*, or service book, for his priests and a catechism for the instruction of children and Native people. In the eighteenth century, the church faced an even greater challenge in the growing secular orientation of social life.

MERCANTILISM

Nowhere was the hand of the royal government more visible than in the economic development of New France. Under Louis XIV and Colbert the economic policy known as *mercantilism* reached its supreme expression. France's overseas colonies, according to this theory, were important only to the extent that they provided France with a market for French manufactures and the raw materials that the kingdom would otherwise have to import from foreign countries. By so doing, colonies would contribute to the imperial goal of increasing exports, reducing imports, and building up a substantial budgetary surplus. Trade with foreign nations and their colonies was strictly forbidden.

Colbert reasoned that the fur trade in New France had a detrimental influence on stable colonial development. He therefore set out to create a compact colony on the St Lawrence, a place with a diversified economy based on the exploitation of its primary resources of agricultural land, timber, fish, and minerals. The fur trade would be carried on by a company carefully controlled by the state. Once firmly rooted, the colony was expected to provide a range of raw materials to sustain the French economy.

The chief instrument for executing Colbert's goals for the colony was the intendant, one of the two most powerful royal officials in the colony. Jean Talon, the first intendant to arrive in New France, proved equal to the task defined by Colbert. During his terms of office (1665–68, 1670–72), he worked energetically to establish the colony on a firm economic base and explored the potential of the local resources. He promoted the development of agriculture, supervising the distribution of imported horses, cattle, sheep, and goats among the settlers, encouraged the cultivation of hemp and flax, and ordered the construction of a brewery. He laid the foundations for Canada's first shipyard at Quebec and envisioned the colony's vast timber resources being transformed into the casks, barrels, tar, potash, and soap required by the settlers. When he learned of deposits of iron near Trois-Rivières and coal on Île Royale (Cape Breton), he planned their development.

Talon also explored the possibility of "triangular" trade with France's West Indies possessions of Guadeloupe and Martinique. In 1667, wood, fish, seal oil, and dried peas were sent directly to the West Indies, and the vessel then loaded sugar bound for France, from which metropolitan goods would be shipped back to New France. This trading pattern failed to thrive to the extent that Colbert had hoped, in part because Canada was isolated in winter and proved to be a weak link in the system. Besides furs, it had no commodities that the other colonies could not get more easily elsewhere.

Canadians showed initiative in overcoming one of the ongoing difficulties of a colonial economy: the chronic shortage of *specie*, or hard money. Government expenditures were covered by money sent annually from France, but this source proved less than reliable. In 1685, Intendant Jacques de Meulles used playing cards as promissory notes to pay the troops and labourers when the ships failed to arrive from France until late in the season. This ingenious solution also enabled the authorities to carry on normal transactions when money was in short supply.

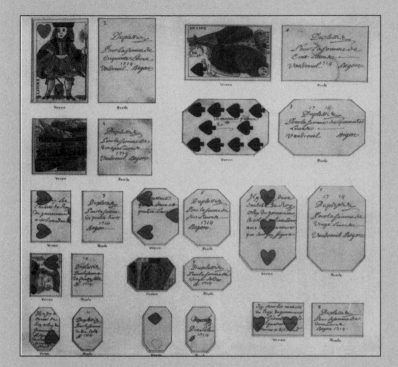

Beginning in 1685, intendants sometimes used playing cards, inscribed with a certain value, when they ran out of currency. The cards were refundable when the funds from the king arrived.

National Archives of Canada/C117059

SEIGNEURIALISM

Seigneurialism was the typical landholding system in France and the structure around which peasant agriculture took shape in Canada, though not in other areas of New France. According to seigneurial theory, all the land belonged to the Crown, which made grants of estates, or seigneuries, to the privileged orders—that is, the church and the nobility.

The seigneur was required to maintain a household on his estate and develop it with the help of peasant farmers, called *censitaires*. This term derived from the annual fees known as *cens et rentes* that the peasants paid for the privilege of working the land for themselves and their seigneur. Notaries in New France called such lots concessions, or habitations, and thus the people who lived on them became known as *habitants*. The seigneur could require his censitaires to work a certain number of days on his property, or *demesne*. He could also require that they grind their wheat in his mill for a price (*banalités*) and pay a fee (*lods et ventes*) if the concession changed hands. In these ways, the wealth of peasant labour was accumulated by the seigneur in the time-honoured manorial tradition.

As it developed in the colony, seigneurialism was intended to accomplish a number of objectives: to provide the colony with a basic land-survey system; to perpetuate a traditional class structure; to establish a

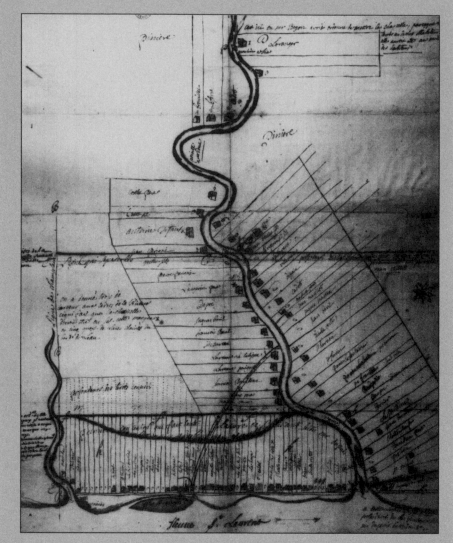

This survey of Batiscan, a seigneury belonging to the Jesuits, shows the names of the settlers and the buildings erected along rivers and roads.

Archives nationales, Paris: Section Outre-Mer (Colonies)

feit their grants. In 1711, royal decrees known as the Arrêts de Marly threatened to revoke undeveloped seigneurial grants and censitaire concessions. They also froze seigneurial dues at levels that remained in place until the British conquest.

The traditional survey system quickly adapted to the geography of the Laurentian lowlands. Instead of a three-field system encircling a village, as was typical in traditional feudal jurisdictions in Europe, the grants conformed to the river, becoming long, narrow trapezoids fronting along the St Lawrence River and other waterways. Seigneurial grants were on the average 10 times longer than they were wide, and tenant grants were similarly strip-like. When the first line of farms, or *côte*, was full, a second line, or *rang*, was opened along a road running behind the first settlements.

For a pioneer community, there were many advantages to this type of survey. In addition to being inexpensive to run, it permitted farmers to live near their own fields and to each other. It gave them access to fish and other marine life and to the best transportation route in the colony. By cutting across the ecological boundaries that tended to run parallel to the river, it gave each farmer—at least those with river frontage—access to a variety of soils and vegetation: marshlands for fodder near the river, rich heavy soils for cereals, upland meadows for grazing, woodlots for fuel, and timber at the upper reaches of the property. One disadvantage was that villages were slow to develop under such a system, and services, both com-

legal framework for relations between privileged landowners and dependent peasant families; and to develop a system for recruiting and settling immigrants. Not all of these objectives were achieved. Apart from the religious communities that ultimately accounted for about one-quarter of the 185 seigneuries granted, few seigneurs were successful immigration agents. To prevent land speculation, seigneurs and censitaires were obliged to bring the land into production or for-

mercial and religious, were often underdeveloped in the rural countryside.

Although the seigneurial system succeeded in reflecting the conservative class structure favoured in the age of absolutism, the foundations of the old nobility failed to develop in New France. Especially in the early years of settlement, some seigneurs were almost as poor as their censitaires and had difficulty providing such customary services as a grist mill and church. Once a seigneury had 30 or 40 well-established censitaires, it became profitable, and traditional seigneurial privileges—such as hunting and fishing rights, ownership of ferries and common pastures, and the reservation of building stone or wood supply—became carefully guarded. Nevertheless, seigneurs had no official military role, as they did under the feudal regimes of Europe. Indeed, in New France seigneurs were not always nobles and like the new nobility in France, owed their status to the kind offices of the king, not to time-honoured privileges.

In New France, the seigneur's income from rents was augmented by trade, military service, and government positions. So significant was commercial activity to the social structure of the colony that a special ordinance, issued in 1685, made it possible for the colonial nobility to engage in trade. In France, such involvement in pursuits "beneath one's station" had led to the loss of noble status. Thus, especially in the early years, the elite in New France was a fusion of noble and middle-class elements, and the *bourgeois-gentilhomme* was a typical member of the colonial upper class.

CONTROLLING THE FUR TRADE

When the Iroquois threat was reduced in 1666, furs again began moving through Montreal. Colbert hoped that Natives would bring the furs to the colony, but dreams of great wealth, coupled with stiff competition, drove young men to make the hazardous journey into the *pays d'en haut*, the area around the Great Lakes, to

As this drawing suggests, religious authorities in the colony were opposed to the sale of alcohol. Civil authorities, however, tolerated the traffic in spirits because it was a popular commodity in the fur trade.

Archives départementales de la Gironde, Bordeaux

cut out Native middlemen. By the end of the 1660s, Michilimackinac, at the northern tip of Lake Michigan, had become the focus for the fur trade in the interior, but it was only a short time before competition pushed French traders farther west. Missionaries and explorers in the interior also traded in furs to finance their costly activities.

In addition to the pressure to push ever westward, the fur trade created social problems that troubled authorities: the use of alcohol as a major trade item and the loss to the colony of so many young men who entered the trade, often in defiance of the law. Colbert introduced regulations to control both the sale of alcohol to Natives and to limit the role of the *coureurs de bois*, as the unlicensed fur traders were called, in the fur trade, but his efforts proved futile. In 1678, the intendant, at Colbert's request, convened a consultative assembly of leading laymen to advise on the alcohol trade. Not surprisingly, it recommended against major restrictions on the trade. A royal edict passed the following year forbade carrying brandy to Native dwellings but otherwise respected the wishes of the fur traders.

The problem of the coureurs de bois was equally difficult to solve. By 1680, over 600 coureurs de bois were trading in the interior in defiance of repeated ordinances. Admitting failure in the attempts to control the interior trade, Louis XIV issued two edicts on the matter in 1681: one granted amnesty to all coureurs de bois if they would return immediately to the colony; the other set up a system of trading permits, called *congés*, each of which initially permitted one canoe and three men to engage in the upcountry trade. The illicit traders paid little attention to the edicts, and the congés soon became little more than a source of revenue for the governor and intendant who sold them to the colonists.

THE HUDSON'S BAY COMPANY

The efforts of French officials to control the fur trade inadvertently gave the king of England an excuse to award a charter to the Hudson's Bay Company. In 1660, two St Lawrence-based traders, Pierre-Esprit Radisson and his brother-in-law Médard Chouart, Sieur des Groseilliers, returned from a trading expedition north of Lake Superior with a plan to ship furs to Europe through Hudson Bay. French officials refused to countenance such a proposal, and added insult to injury by accusing Radisson and Groseilliers of illegal trading. The pair took their idea to New England and eventually to England where a group of merchants agreed to finance an expedition to Hudson Bay. The *Nonsuch* and its intrepid crew spent the winter of 1668–69 at the mouth of the Rupert River on James Bay, and returned to England the following summer with a cargo of high-quality furs.

By 1670, English investors had created a company and applied for a charter from King Charles giving them a monopoly of all the territory drained by rivers flowing into Hudson Bay. The area, called Rupert's Land in honour of Prince Rupert, a cousin of the king and the company's first governor, included nearly one-third of the territory of present-day Canada. Largely ignorant of the size of their grant or the numbers of people already living there who could be deemed to have a prior claim, the Hudson's Bay Company would eventually make huge profits from North American holdings. As we indicate in the timeline, because the English took "New Amsterdam" (renamed New York) from the Dutch in 1664, they were well placed to restrict the French to a narrow band on the St Lawrence.

Throughout most of the seventeenth century, the English confined themselves to posts on the shores of Hudson Bay, while French traders based on the St Lawrence moved steadily westward in their search of furs. In 1682, Canadian entrepreneurs, assisted by an overland military expedition led by the Chevalier de Troyes, captured the English posts on Hudson Bay. Since France and England were technically at peace, Louis XIV was obliged to return the trading posts to the English, but the contest between the St Lawrence and Hudson Bay traders continued.

EXPLORATIONS WEST AND SOUTH

In 1671, Talon sent an expedition, which included the Jesuit Charles Albanel, into the Hudson Bay region and another under fur trader Daumont de Saint-Lusson into Lake Superior country in search of a route leading to the Pacific. Louis Jolliet, another experienced fur trader, was commissioned in 1672 to follow up on earlier efforts by Sulpician priests François Dollier de Casson and René de Bréhant de Galinée to find the rumoured river that flowed into the Gulf of Mexico. Jolliet was joined at Michilimackinac by Father Jacques Marquette, and together they explored the Mississippi as far as the mouth of the Arkansas River.

Talon returned to France in 1672, two years before Jolliet found his way back to the colony. By that time the initiative for territorial expansion had been seized by Louis de Buade, Comte de Frontenac, the new governor general of New France. A military man of great personal ambition, Frontenac defied Colbert's instructions. In 1673, he had a fortified trading post built at Cataraqui (present-day Kingston) and obtained rights for his friend René-Robert Chevalier de La Salle to build posts and to trade in the valley of the Mississippi River. La Salle finally reached the Gulf of Mexico in 1682, but he had disturbed Native and European fur traders with his irascible behaviour and aggressive trading activities.

The Iroquois, in particular, were alarmed by La Salle's alliances with their enemies, the Illinois. In 1684, the Seneca attacked La Salle's fort at St Louis. Governor La Barre, as deeply involved in the fur trade as Frontenac had been, sent an expedition to intimidate the Iroquois but was forced to accept a humiliating peace. La Barre was recalled for his failure, and his successor, the Marquis de Denonville, sent another expedition in 1687. This time the troops—832 regulars, 900 militiamen, and 400 Indian allies—had more success. English fur traders sent by Governor Thomas Dongan of New York were intercepted and the Seneca were subjected to a "scorched earth" policy. To guard French access to the Illinois country, a blockhouse with a garrison of 100 soldiers was built at the mouth of the Niagara.

Nevertheless, the Iroquois were still in control of the southern interior and posed a real threat to New France. In August 1689, 1500 Iroquois descended on Lachine, putting 56 homes to the torch and killing their captives. The tactics of the Iroquois were no better or worse than those of the French in this period of history. Before the 1687 expedition, Louis XIV had instructed Denonville to eliminate the Iroquois "barbarians" and ordered that captured warriors be sent to France, where they would become slaves for the Mediterranean fleet. Some 36 prisoners were seized for this purpose in 1687. In the same year, La Salle was murdered, apparently by his own men.

CONCLUSION

Between 1663 and 1689, French institutions took root in North America. French immigrants, though few in number, learned to adapt to their new environment and actually began to thrive. With church, state, military, and commercial institutions firmly in place—thanks to the will of Louis XIV—Canada was emerging as the heart of a genuine "Nouvelle France." Acadia and Newfoundland were outposts of Canada, prized for their strategic location and the rich fisheries off their coasts. Preoccupied by affairs at home, Louis XIV showed little inclination to expand his North American empire beyond these modest beginnings. The outbreak of war in Europe in 1689 changed everything.

A Historiographical Debate

Theocratic Tyranny or Benevolent Paternalism?

The noted American historian Francis Parkman, writing in the late nineteenth century, portrayed the inhabitants of New France as ignorant, superstitious, downtrodden colonials crushed under the heavy weight of stifling mercantilist restrictions, metropolitan intervention, an oppressive and despotic monarchy, and an even more powerful and fanatical church. He asserted that the "fault" of the absolutist monarchy and authoritarian church "was not that they exercised authority, but that they exercised too much of it, and, instead of weaning the child to go alone, kept him in perpetual leading strings, making him, if possible, more and more dependent, and less and less fit for freedom."[5]

Similar views of colonial rule were perpetuated until quite recently by both British imperial and English-Canadian historians. Among the French-Canadian historians, Canon Lionel Groulx, in formulating his views of the dominant role of the church in colonial life, came closest to the Parkman interpretation. However, Groulx celebrated rather than criticized

New France's authoritarianism. He described a "proper subordination" of the state to the church in the laying down of "the foundations of the social and political order" of his future Quebec.[6]

At the opposite pole of the debate came Guy Frégault's interpretation of French rule as benevolent paternalism. According to Frégault, colonial administration concerned itself with poor relief, hospitalization and medical care, building regulations, price controls, and the supervision of the church's charitable and educational institutions. Land was free, and there was no direct taxation. Although New France was not Utopia, it could stand favourable comparison with New England.[7]

It was William J. Eccles who documented and refined this interpretation, to the point that New France emerged as an embryonic welfare state in which the health, safety, security, and contentment of the population was a major concern of the governing class. As Eccles stated, "The basic premise, not merely of royal policy, but of all social institutions—indeed the basic premise upon which society in New France rested—was individual and collective responsibility for the needs of all."

This concern for the welfare of the community should not be confused with democracy: in France the Estates-General had not met since 1614, and there were no elected assemblies in the French colonies. Still, the people of New France were not completely powerless. Royal edicts contrary to the interests of the colonists were never implemented; the council at Quebec did not register and proclaim them, and delayed action by asking for further instructions and suggesting amendments in the time-consuming process of government through annual correspondence.

There were also avenues for the expression of popular will in the colony in the form of consultative assemblies, church boards and merchant associations. Moreover, several historians have noted that the colonists did not seem entirely submissive or as respectful of their social superiors as convention required. Eccles attributes this behaviour to the relative independence of the colonial farmer, to the influence of the Native peoples and fur traders, and also to the slow implantation of social distinctions.

Cornelius Jaenen concludes, in his study of the role of the church in Canada, as does Charles O'Neill for Louisiana,[9] that the clergy was frustrated in its attempts to dominate either socially or politically: "The colonists were far from docile, subservient, downtrodden, inarticulate, priest-ridden peasants. Contemporary documentation shows them to be remarkably independent, aggressive, self-assertive, freedom-loving and outspoken individuals."[10] Terence Crowley, in examining popular disturbances in the colony, found that people demonstrated against what they considered to be unfair impositions, or against government inaction to remedy perceived injustices such as hoarding or profiteering. They protested the abuse of power but did not rebel against constituted authority.[11]

New France, then, appears to have been neither a theocracy nor a tyranny. The clergy may have wielded great power in the period before 1663, but royal authority would soon assert itself in line with Gallican principles of the mother country. As for royal power, it was attenuated by a wide ocean, a cumbersome bureaucracy, and the relative unimportance of the colony. It was also more successful than private enterprise in populating and sustaining the colony in a difficult northern climate. The social legislation that Eccles underscores flowed not only from what Frégault and others called paternalism, but also from Catholic social teaching regarding the responsibilities of elites, just price, and charity. According to the prevailing views of the period, the common good should have priority over individual interest and advantage. The coming of British rule would introduce a different philosophy while providing an element of continuity.

NOTES

1 *The Jesuit Relations and Allied Documents*, ed. Reuben Gold Thwaites, 73 vols. (Cleveland: Burrows Brothers Co., 1896–1901), 51: 167–77.

2 Cited in André Vachon, "Le Notaire en Nouvelle-France," *Revue de l'Université Laval* 10.3 (1955–56) 235.

3 *Word from New France: The Selected Letters of Marie de l'Incarnation*, ed. and trans. Joyce Marshall (Toronto: Oxford University Press, 1967) 343–44.

4 Governor Denonville to Minister of Marine and Colonies, 13 November 1685, NAC MG 1, series C11A, Vol. VII, p. 46, cited in Cornelius Jaenen and

Cecilia Morgan, *Material Memory: Documents in Pre-Confederation History* (Don Mills, ON: Addison-Wesley, 1998) 35.

5 Francis Parkman, *The Old Régime in Canada*, vol. 1 (Toronto, 1899) 199.

6 Abbé Lionel Groulx, "Ce que nous devons au catholicisme," *Action française* (novembre 1923), cited in *Emerging Identities: Selected Problems and Interpretations in Canadian History*, ed. Paul W. Bennett and Cornelius Jaenen (Scarborough, ON: Prentice-Hall, 1986) 72.

7 Guy Frégault's views are summarized in *Canadian Society in the French Régime* (Ottawa: Canadian Historical Association, 1968).

8 W.J. Eccles, *Essays on New France* (Toronto: Oxford University Press, 1987) 39.

9 Charles O'Neill, *Church and State in French Colonial Louisiana: Policy and Politics to 1732* (New Haven, CT: Yale University Press, 1966).

10 Cornelius Jaenen, *The Role of the Church in New France* (Toronto: McGraw-Hill Ryerson, 1976) 155.

11 Terence Crowley, "'Thunder Gusts': Popular Disturbances in Early French Canada," *Canadian Historical Association Historical Papers* (1979): 11–32.

SELECTED READING

The age of Louis XIV is described in Pierre Goubert, *Louis XIV and Twenty Million Frenchmen* (New York: Random House, 1970) and Roger Mettam, *Power and Faction in Louis XIV's France* (Oxford: Basil Blackwell, 1988). The standard biography of the Sun King is J.B. Wolf, *Louis XIV* (New York: Norton, 1968).

On New France, see W.J. Eccles, *Canada Under Louis XIV, 1663–1701* (Toronto: McClelland and Stewart, 1964) as well as the three books by W.J. Eccles cited in Chapter 3. See also Leslie Chouquette, *Frenchmen into Peasants: Modernity and Tradition in the Peopling of French Canada* (Cambridge, MA: Harvard University Press, 1997); H. Charbonneau et al., *The First French Canadians: Pioneers in the St Lawrence Valley* (Newark: University of Delaware Press, 1993); Jacques Mathieu, *La Nouvelle-France: Les Français en Amérique du Nord XVIe–XVIIIe siècle* (Québec: Les Presses de l'Université Laval, 2001); Marcel Trudel, *An Introduction to New France* (Toronto: Holt, Reinhart and Winston, 1968); Dale Miquelon, *The First Canada to 1791* (Toronto: McGraw-Hill Ryerson, 1994) and Cornelius Jaenen, *The French Regime in the Upper Country of Canada in the Seventeenth Century* (Toronto: Champlain Society, 1996). On Acadia, see Naomi Griffiths, *The Contexts of Acadian History, 1686–1784* (Montreal: McGill-Queen's University Press, 1992); Jean Daigle, ed., *Acadia of the Maritimes: Thematic Studies from the Beginning to the Present* (Moncton: Chaire d'études acadiennes, Université de Moncton, 1995).

Aspects of social and institutional developments in New France are summarized in Peter N. Moogk, *La Nouvelle France: The Making of New France—A Cultural History* (East Lansing: Michigan State University Press, 2000); Alan Greer, *The People of New France* (Toronto: University of Toronto Press, 1997); R. Cole Harris and John Warkentin, *Canada Before Confederation* (Toronto: Oxford University Press, 1974); and John A. Dickinson and Brian Young, *A Short History of Quebec*, 2nd ed. (Toronto: Copp Clark Pitman, 1993). Volume 1 of R. Cole Harris and Geoffrey J. Matthews, *Historical Atlas of Canada* (Toronto: University of Toronto Press, 1988) provides a wealth of information on Native and European society under the French regime, as do volumes 1–4 of *Dictionary of Canadian Biography* (Toronto: University of Toronto Press, 1966–79).

Specialized studies include Marcel Trudel, *The Seigneurial Regime* (Ottawa: Canadian Historical Association, 1956); R. Cole Harris, *The Seigneurial System in Canada: A Geographical Study* (Madison: University of Wisconsin Press, 1966); Cornelius Jaenen, *The Role of the Church in New France* (Toronto: McGraw-Hill Ryerson, 1976); Roger Magnuson, *A Brief History of Quebec Education* (Montreal: Harvest House, 1980); Louise Dechêne, *Habitants and Merchants in Seventeenth-Century Montreal* (Montreal: McGill-Queen's University Press, 1992) and *Le Partage des subsistances au Canada sous le régime français* (Montreal: Boréal, 1994); Danielle Gauvreau, *Québec: Une ville et sa population au temps de la Nouvelle-France* (Montreal: Presses de l'Université du Québec, 1991); Louis Lavallée, *La Prairie en Nouvelle-France, 1647–1760: Étude d'histoire sociale* (Montreal: McGill-Queen's University Press, 1992); Lorraine Gadoury, *La noblesse de Nouvelle-France: Familles et alliances* (La Salle: Hurtubise HMH, 1992); Marie-Aimée Cliche, *Les Pratiques de dévotion en Nouvelle*-France (Sillery: Les Presses de l'Université du Québec, 1991); André Lachance, *Crimes et criminels en Nouvelle-France* (Montreal: Boréal Express, 1984) and *Les marginaux, les exclus et l'autre au Canada aux XVIIe et XVIIIe siècles* (Montreal: Fides, 1996); Jean-Charles Falardeau, "The Seventeenth Century Parish in French Canada" in *French Canadian Society*, ed. Marcel Rioux and Yves Martin (Toronto: McClelland and Stewart, 1964); and Jonathan Pearl, "Witchcraft in New France in the Seventeenth Century: The Social Aspect," *Historical Reflections* 4 (1977).

On women, see the Clio Collective, *Quebec Women: A History* (Toronto: Women's Press, 1987); Alison Prentice et al., *Canadian Women: A History*, 2nd ed. (Toronto: Harcourt Brace, 1996); Jan Noel, "New France: Les femmes favorisées," in *Rethinking Canada: The Promise of Women's History*, 3rd ed., ed. Veronica Strong-Boag and Anita Clair Fellman (Toronto: Oxford University Press, 1997), 33–56; Yves Landry, *Orphelines en France, pionnières au Canada: Les Filles de roi au XVIIe siècle* (Montreal: Leméac, 1992); an article summarizing his main findings, "Gender Imbalance, les Filles du Roi, and Choice of a Spouse in New France" in *Canadian Family History: Selected Readings*, ed. Bettina Bradbury (Toronto: Copp Clark Pitman, 1992), 14–32; and Marcel Trudel, *Les écolières des Ursulines de Québec, 1639–1686. Amérindiennes et canadiennes* (Montreal: HMH, 1999).

 **WEBLINKS**

LOUIS XIV
www.chateauversailles.fr/EN/220.asp

The official site of the palace of Versailles offers historical data on key figures of the period.

PLACENTIA
http://parkscanada.pch.gc.ca/parks/Newfoundland/ castle_hill/castle_hill_e.htm

This is the Parks Canada site for historic Castle Hill at Placentia.

PIERRE-ESPRIT RADISSON
www.nlc-bnc.ca/heroes/h6-235-e.html

The National Library of Canada offers a biography of Radisson, a bibliography, and additional links.

THE HUDSON'S BAY COMPANY MUSEUM COLLECTION
http://collections.ic.gc.ca/hbc/hbcen.htm

This extensive collection spans three centuries of the company's history and contains more than 10 000 artifacts that document the history of the fur trade in Canada.

CHAPTER 5

The Political Economy of a Strategic Outpost, 1689–1744

The Trade with the Natives is a necessary commerce; and even if the Colonists could get along without it, the State is, as it were, forced to maintain it, if it wishes to hold on to the country.... There is no middle course; one must have the native as either friend or foe; and whoever wants to have him as a friend must furnish him with his necessities at conditions which allow him to procure them.[1]

By 1717 when this statement appeared in an official memorandum from France, the fur trade, Native alliances, even social policy in New France were increasingly being dictated by strategic considerations. The challenge of the European rivals—in particular the Protestant English and Dutch—for power in Europe and overseas colonies had become the determining factor in French colonial policy. Although the fur trade might end up losing money, it was the key to maintaining Native alliances and ensuring the survival of the French empire in North America.

THE WAR OF THE LEAGUE OF AUGSBURG

While the Five Nations Iroquois were threatening the outlying settlements of Canada in 1689, Louis XIV become embroiled in a European war. Throughout the 1670s, he harassed the Dutch and then began asserting his right to occupy territories on the border of France and the United Provinces of the Netherlands. The so-called Glorious Revolution, which put the Protestant ruler of the United Provinces, William of Orange, and his wife Mary on the English throne in 1689, spelled disaster for Louis XIV's ambitions to expand French borders and to champion the cause of Roman Catholicism in Europe. When the Dutch ruler brought England into a defensive alliance known as the League of Augsburg, Louis XIV faced a formidable foe.

War in Europe made it easier for Governor Frontenac, who had returned to New France in 1689 for a second tour of duty, to launch raids against the English in New England and New York in an effort to convince them to abandon their alliance with the Five Nations Confederacy. Although the brutal border raids had the desired effect—the English trading base at Albany was temporarily rendered ineffective—they also brought a direct attack on Quebec.

The expedition against New France by land and sea was the idea of the feisty New Englanders who in the spring of 1690 attacked and looted Port Royal in Acadia and then attempted to take Quebec. While the force sent overland soon collapsed, Sir William Phips,

with his armada of 34 ships and 2000 men, appeared below the walls of Quebec in the middle of October 1690. But with winter approaching and smallpox ravaging his troops, Phips was forced to withdraw without achieving his objective. Frontenac is said to have responded to the demand to surrender with the words: "I have no reply to make to your general other than from the mouths of my cannon and muskets." So pleased was Louis XIV by the lifting of the siege that he struck a medal to commemorate the occasion. Its inscription read: "France in the New World Victorious, Quebec 1690."

biography

Madeleine de Verchères

In 1692 Madeleine de Verchères, a 14-year-old girl, became a hero when she helped to defend her community downriver from Montreal from an Iroquois attack. Her father, a seigneur and army officer, and her mother, who had repulsed a similar attack two years before, were absent at the time of the incident. According to the story, which became more exaggerated as time went on, she was pursued and quickly overtaken by the Iroquois, who seized her by the kerchief she was wearing around her neck. She loosened the scarf and ran into the stockade on her father's seigneury. "I went up on the bastion where the sentry was," she later explained. "I then transformed myself, putting the soldier's hat on my head, and with some small gestures tried to make it seem that there were many people, although there was only this soldier."[2] She fired a cannon shot to warn others in the settlement that they were under attack and to summon aid. The Iroquois retreated when armed troops arrived from Montreal the following day.

There seems to be little doubt that young Madeleine showed initiative under difficult circumstances and there were good reasons for her to do so. At the time of this attack, she had already lost two brothers and two brothers-in-law to the Iroquois. Later in life she told an embellished version of her story to secure a pension. It is the more dramatic version that often gets repeated in textbooks.

Madeleine de Verchères, *by C.W. Jeffreys.*

Jeffreys, Charles William/National Archives of Canada/C-010687. Reproduced with permission of C.W. Jeffreys Estate, Toronto

French bravado in the colonies continued to reap rewards. In 1694, the Canadian-born naval captain Pierre Le Moyne d'Iberville captured and burned St John's as well as a large number of English fishing bases along the coast of Newfoundland. He then proceeded to Hudson Bay where he captured Fort York from the Bay Company one week before peace was negotiated in Europe. In the colony itself, civilians, including women such as Madeleine de Verchères, distinguished themselves by showing exceptional initiative in the face of Iroqouis attacks. The War of the League of Augsburg ended in 1697 with the Treaty of Ryswick without any territorial losses to the French Empire in North America, but the truce did not last long.

Frontenac and his ambitious fur-trading friends had used the war to justify building more fortified posts in the interior. By 1695, French traders had made direct contact with the Sioux and the Assiniboine, traditional enemies of France's allies, the Ottawa. For a time it seemed as if the Iroquois would become allied with the aggrieved Ottawa, who together would force the French out of the interior and perhaps out of North America. Frontenac realized his strategic blunder soon enough to launch a blow to the heart of Iroquois territory. In 1696, an expedition destroyed the villages of the Onondaga and the Oneida.

The near-century of warfare between and among Natives and newcomers in North America prompted a general desire for peaceful relations. In September 1700, delegates from four Iroquois tribes (the Mohawk stayed away) made peace at Montreal with the Huron, Abenaki, and Ottawa who lived on reserves in the colony. In July of the following year, over 1300 Natives from 32 nations assembled near Montreal to negotiate peace among themselves and renew their alliances with the French. By the Treaty of Montreal, the French recognized the Iroquois as an independent nation and in return the Iroquois promised to remain neutral in any war between France and Britain.

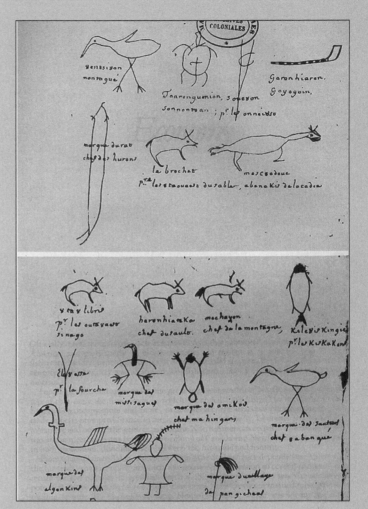

The peace treaty of 1701 that concluded the war between the Iroquois and the French was signed by the chiefs using the totemic animal representing each tribe.

Archives nationales, Paris, Fonds des Colonies, série C11A, vol. 19, fol. 43-43v

THE WAR OF THE SPANISH SUCCESSION

As people in North America were sorting out their relations, France became embroiled in another war. This time, Louis XIV hoped to establish his grandson on the throne of Spain, thus uniting two of Europe's great empires. As a pre-emptive move, Pierre Le Moyne d'Iberville was dispatched in 1698 to the mouth of the Mississippi to lay claim to the region for France.

Three years later, he was ordered to establish a colony there. Louisiana was to become the final link in a chain of posts reaching from the St Lawrence to the Spanish empire in Mexico. Antoine Laumet de Lamothe Cadillac, another prominent member of the "beaver aristocracy," also convinced the Minister of Marine and Colonies to move the western base from Michilimackinac to Detroit as part of the strategy to intimidate the Iroquois and contain the English.

These developments signalled a dramatic shift in colonial policy, one that was dictated by France's relations with foreign powers, both Native and European. From now on, economic aspects of the fur trade were superseded by military considerations. The fur trade would help cement Native alliances, while the *coureurs de bois*, with their skills in Native relations and guerrilla warfare, would become agents of the Crown rather than outlaws. This turn of events, driven by developments in Europe, put the final nail in the coffin of Colbert's earlier dream of a compact colony on the St Lawrence.

The War of the Spanish Succession broke out in 1702 with England and France ranged on opposing sides. Although unwilling to antagonize anew the recently subdued Iroquois, Governor Vaudreuil had no hesitation in attacking settlements on the New England frontier. Raiding expeditions conducted by the Canadian militia and their Native allies in 1703 and 1704 wrought havoc in outlying settlements and flooded New France with prisoners, many of them slaves of their Native captors. From the Deerfield raid alone, over 100 hostages were taken. In Newfoundland, English fishing communities were again the object of brutal raids. The greatest devastation occurred when a force of 450 Canadians and their Native allies under Daniel d'Auger de Subercase, Governor of Plaisance, spent the winter of 1705 burning, looting, and taking no fewer than 1200 prisoners on the "English shore."

The people who survived the Newfoundland raids could do little by way of retaliation, but the New Englanders, once again, struck back. In 1703, 1704, and 1707 they attacked the outlying settlements in Acadia, taking hostages of their own, but achieved no strategic objective. Finally, in 1710, a combined force of 1900 British and colonial troops led by General Francis Nicholson captured Port Royal, which was defended by its recently-appointed governor, Daniel d'Auger de Subercase, with a garrison of 258 soldiers. The English launched an ambitious attack led by Sir Hovenden Walker on Quebec in 1711, but they were forced to abandon their invasion following heavy losses of men and ships in the treacherous currents and shoals of the lower St Lawrence River.

With the exception of Port Royal, the French suffered few losses in North America and inflicted

Voices from the Past

Wartime Economic Crisis

After more than two decades of almost continuous warfare, New France in 1712 faced a serious financial crisis. Prices had skyrocketed, hard cash had evaporated, and colonial administrators were forced to pay the troops with playing cards that they hoped would be redeemed by the imperial treasury. As this communication from the Minister of Marine and Colonies in 1712 indicates, the colonies could expect little help from France:

> A number of people from Canada have told me this year that it will in future be absolutely impossible to find the means of supporting the troops and meeting ordinary expenses if the

treasurers general do not honour the bills of exchange when they fall due, and that the large quantity of cards issued in the country brings them into disrepute, which causes goods to quadruple in price, since [these cards] give the traders nothing but bills of exchange which go dishonoured, which ruins them in interest charges and brings suffering to the entire colony. I accept the truth of all these facts, but the unfortunate state of the kingdom in the past several years has prevented His Majesty from meeting both his expenses and those it was indispensable for him to make, on the other hand, to defend himself against the enemies of the state....The King is not in a position to provide for the colony.[3]

considerable damage on English settlements and posts in New England, Newfoundland, and the Hudson Bay area. But European considerations dictated the terms of the peace. To secure the Bourbon dynasty on the Spanish throne, Louis XIV was forced to make concessions in the Treaty of Utrecht, which ended the war. Colonial territory was thrown into the balance. France agreed to abandon Hudson Bay, Acadia, and Newfoundland to the British and to recognize British authority over the Iroquois Confederacy. France retained fishing rights on the north coast of Newfoundland (subsequently dubbed the Treaty Shore) as well as two islands protecting the entrance to the Gulf of St Lawrence: Île du Cap-Breton (soon to be rechristened Île Royale) and Île Saint-Jean (Prince Edward Island).

On the surface, the losses seemed inconsequential. France had invested little energy into developing these lost outposts of its emerging continental empire, and they had brought in little or no direct wealth. For New France, however, the signs were ominous: European interests alone seemed to determine the fate of colonies in the Americas. For the over 2000 Acadians in New France, it was the final conquest.

THE IMPERIAL FACTOR

The death of Louis XIV in 1715 brought a five-year-old child, Louis XV, to the throne of France. Between 1715 and 1723, Philip, Duc d'Orléans, acted as regent for the young king. As a

tool for an aristocracy determined to regain its power, the duke restored the authority of the *parlements* and replaced bureaucrats on the councils with eminent aristocrats who pursued their own supposedly enlightened policies. Even Protestants and Jews would be tolerated as long as they kept silent in public. On one

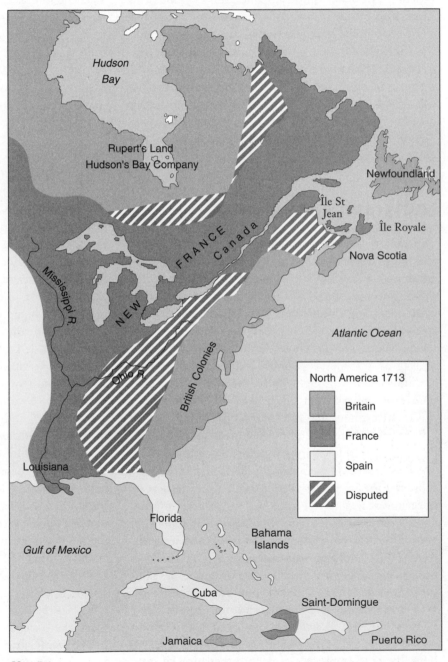

Map 5.1
North America, 1713.

Adapted from W.J. Eccles, *France in America* (East Lansing: Michigan State University Press, 1990) 122

issue, however, the duke carried on Louis XIV's tradition: colonies were valued only to the extent that they enhanced the wealth of France and restrained the growth of rivals to French imperial power.

The Regency ushered in three decades of peace. During this time, France moved to consolidate its North American empire. The forts along the Mississippi route between Louisiana and Canada were reoccupied and garrisoned, and the fur trade was subsidized to help sustain Native alliances. In the northwest, Canadians outflanked the Bay traders and set up trading networks with new nations in the far west. On Île Royale, the fortified town of Louisbourg rose to prominence. The British would have much to reckon with when they faced France again on the colonial battlefield.

LOUISIANA AND ILLINOIS

Officially a regional jurisdiction, subordinate to officials in Quebec, Louisiana was in practice directly administered from France, often with the help of Canadian-born officials. In the first two decades of its existence, a high death rate from disease and famine conditions gave the colony a bad name and caused surviving troops and settlers to desert to nearby Spanish or English colonies. Freehold land tenure, offered as an inducement, brought little response. The Duc d'Orléans embarked on a disastrous scheme to attract private investment, but the "Mississippi bubble" burst in 1720, as did the pocketbooks of many investors, undermining confidence in new colonial ventures.

Despite the odds, Louisiana survived, but only because the French state willed it so. In 1722, the seat of government was moved from Mobile to New Orleans, considered a healthier site. Between 1719 and 1729, 6000 African slaves were imported to do the hard work required to develop the economy. The colony's exports included pitch, tar, furs, hides, and eventually tobacco, silk, indigo, cotton, and rice. Troupes de la Marine were sent to defend the colony, and Ursuline, Jesuit, Carmelite, and Capuchin orders ministered to the spiritual and social needs of the settlers. By 1746, there was a white population of over 4000, one-fifth of them soldiers. The cost to the Crown of this ambitious colonization project was staggering: 20 million livres by 1731 and 800 000 livres a year thereafter to sustain the strategic outpost.

In 1717, the Illinois country was attached administratively to Louisiana. Sporadic military campaigns against the Fox nation slowed development, but by 1731 the Illinois country was home to 108 non-Native families, most of them originally from the Montreal area, as well as a few soldiers, missionaries, and traders. Twenty years later, the population had reached over 3000, including 1536 French and 890 African and Native slaves. By that time, large slave-worked estates were shipping wheat, flour, corn, cattle, and swine to Louisiana and the French West Indies.

THE PAYS D'EN HAUT

The French were determined to out-manoeuvre the Hudson's Bay Company on their northwestern frontier. By the middle of the eighteenth century, they had established trading alliances with the Natives in the Abitibi–Temiscaming region, along the north shore of Lake Superior, and into the Prairies. The man who played the biggest role in establishing the French presence on the Prairies was Pierre Gautier de Varennes et de La Vérendrye.

While serving as commander of a fur-trading post at the mouth of the Nipigon River, La Vérendrye heard from a variety of Aboriginal sources about a "muddy lake" and a "great river" to the west. In the spring of 1730, a chief of the Kenisteno, called La Martleblanche by the French, promised to guide La Vérendrye to these mysterious bodies of water, which he hoped would lead to the Pacific. La Vérendrye sought and secured from Louis XV a commission to find the Pacific Ocean and a monopoly of the trade in the territories claimed by the Hudson's Bay Company. In the summer of 1732, La Vérendrye, two of his sons, a priest, and at least 16 voyageurs joined an Aboriginal war party of 50 canoes on a journey into the interior.

Over the next 10 years, La Vérendrye and his sons established a chain of trading posts stretching from Lake Superior to the heart of the western plains: Fort St Pierre (Rainy Lake), Fort St Charles (Lake of the Woods), Fort Maurepas (on the Winnipeg River), Fort

Rouge (at the junction of the Red and Assiniboine rivers) Fort La Reine (Portage La Prairie), Fort Dauphin (on Lake Manitoba), Fort Bourbon (on Lake Winnipegosis), and Fort Pascoyac (on the Saskatchewan River). The success of the effort depended upon alliances with the Cree and the Assiniboine and their long-standing rivals, the Ojibwa and the Dakota. Eager to maintain good relations with the First Nations, La Vérendrye chose several young men from each post to live with the local tribes and permitted two of his sons to be adopted by the Cree. He also shipped Sioux slaves back to the colony and boasted that this trade in humans was one of the French regime's main benefits from his frontier activities.

Although La Vérendrye's party never found the Pacific, one of his sons reached the foothills of the Rockies. La Vérendrye himself lost his fur-trade monopoly and died a poor man in 1749. Nevertheless, he left a significant legacy. French trading posts in the interior were a more convenient source of supplies for Native peoples than the distant posts on Hudson Bay. Only the limited capacity of canoes, the principal vehicle of inland trade, restricted the ability of the French to totally undermine the commercial activities of the Bay traders.

Following La Vérendrye's death, Governor La Jonquière ordered Jacques Le Gardeur de Saint-Pierre

This watercolour by Mark Catesby in 1724 is one of the earliest European depictions of the buffalo that inhabited the western plains. A source of food, clothing, and housing for Native peoples of the plains, buffalo were so numerous that explorers and fur traders claimed that they were obliged to chase them away from their encampments.

Windsor Castle, Royal Library. Copyright © 1992 Her Majesty Queen Elizabeth II, RE 26090, detail

to take possession of La Vérendrye's posts, establish new ones, and continue the search for the elusive Western Sea. In 1754, Louis La Corne, who succeeded Le Gardeur, built Fort Saint-Louis, near the forks of the Saskatchewan River, which became the limit of western expansion under the French regime.

The English might well claim sovereignty over their posts on Hudson Bay, but they would have considerable difficulty controlling their inland supply routes. So aggressively did the French pursue their trading enterprises that the Bay men were forced to send their own traders into the interior. In 1754, Anthony

Henday embarked on a journey that took him to the site of what is today Edmonton, Alberta, in an effort to persuade the Natives to bring their pelts to the Hudson's Bay Company posts.

By the mid-eighteenth century, Canada's commercial hinterland consisted of most of the interior of the continent. Two main entrepôts, Detroit and Michilimackinac, served as headquarters for merchants, traders, and Jesuit missionaries as well as transshipment points. Detroit also had a garrison of troops and a summer population of over 400 people. Outside the fort, 500 settlers made a good living supplying the fur-trade network from their productive farms. The Jesuit mission at Detroit served a resident population of 2600, primarily Ottawa, Petun, and Potawatomi, the largest Aboriginal concentration in the Great Lakes basin.

Meanwhile, Russian and Spanish explorers had begun to explore the Pacific coast. In separate expeditions, the Russians Vitus Bering and Aleksei Chirikov explored the Alaska coast in 1741, their explorations leading to the sea otters' silky furs becoming available to an appreciative market in Russia and China. For the time being, the area that would become British Columbia and the Yukon were too remote for French influence to penetrate them. Aboriginal peoples in the area however, would soon feel the impact of European diseases and trade goods.

LOUISBOURG

Following the loss of Newfoundland, France decided to build a base on Île Royale. Named in honour of the king, Louisbourg was designed to protect the St Lawrence entrance to France's continental empire and provide a North American base for the lucrative fisheries. Like Louisiana, Louisbourg was an expensive venture, costing nearly 20 million livres to establish. Construction of the fortified town began in 1720. Although it fell both times it was attacked and was never very effective in protecting the St Lawrence, Louisbourg soon became a major fishing port and a thriving entrepôt for the North Atlantic trade.

Even before the ink was dry on the Treaty of Utrecht, Louisbourg had become home to evacuees from Plaisance. It proved more difficult to persuade the Acadians to leave their prosperous farms on the dyked marshlands of the Bay of Fundy for the rocky soil of Île Royale. The prospect of freehold land tenure—there would be no seigneuries on Île Royale—was no boon to the Acadians, who had enjoyed the benefits of, if not official title to, free land for nearly a century. Only 67 Acadian families immi-

This medal, one side of which shows the head of Louis XV, was struck to commemorate the founding of Louisbourg in 1720.

Parks Canada, Fortress of Louisbourg RAL-5437T, RAL-5438T. Photo by H.M. Moses, 1997

grated to Île Royale between 1713 and 1734. Most of them lived in areas outside the town where they could farm and fish for their subsistence.

For much of Louisbourg's short history under French rule, the majority of people who lived there came directly from France. Men involved in the fishery and navy often wintered in the town, some of them marrying local women and setting down roots. As in other French colonial possessions, the military were well represented, making up one-quarter to one-half of the population. The Récollets, Frères Hospitaliers, and Soeurs de la Congrégation de Notre-Dame located in the community.

Although most of the residents were French and Roman Catholic, Louisbourg attracted people from a variety of ethnic and religious backgrounds. A significant proportion of the fishing community was drawn from the Basque-speaking region of southern France, and between 1722 and 1745 about 20 percent of the garrison consisted of German and Swiss soldiers of the Karrer regiment. Louisbourg's inhabitants included black and Native "servants," a few Irish, Scottish, and Spanish sojourners, and at least one Jew. By the 1740s, there were over 2000 residents in the town, and the population of the island had grown to over 5000.

The first people on the spot, the primarily Newfoundland-born settlers from Placentia, took up the choice beach lots and the best land grants in and around Louisbourg. These fishing proprietors (*habitants-pêcheurs*) dominated the island's economy and helped to maintain a spirit of independence in the town. They also controlled the Superior Council until 1745, holding four of the five council positions. As in Canada, the leading officials in Louisbourg (a lieutenant-governor and commissaire-ordonnateur) were from France.

Open to sea traffic for much of the year—fogs permitting—Louisbourg was a busy commercial centre. An average of 154 ships a year called at the port, a number exceeded in North America only by Boston, New York, and Philadelphia. Although fish and fish oil were the only locally generated exports, the wharves in Louisbourg harbour were awash with manufactured goods, fishing supplies, and foodstuffs from France; molasses, sugar, and rum from the West Indies; foodstuffs and building supplies illegally shipped from

New England; and foodstuffs and forest products from Canada. There was a six-fold increase in French seaborne commerce in the years between 1710 and 1740, and Louisbourg was one of the major beneficiaries of this growth.

ÎLE SAINT-JEAN

French authorities also made efforts to entice the Acadians to move to Île Saint-Jean, but with no better results than they had on Île Royale. In 1719, the islands of Saint-Jean, Miscou, and Magdalen were granted to the Comte de Saint-Pierre with the stipulation that he settle the territory. The following year his Compagnie de l'Île Saint-Jean sent out over 250 colonists who established themselves at Port LaJoie (near present-day Charlottetown), Havre Saint-Pierre (St Peter's), and other coastal locations. Like most private ventures sponsored by France, this one failed within a few years and the settlers drifted away.

To confirm French sovereignty, the governor of Louisbourg was ordered to send an armed detachment —all of 30 men—to occupy Saint-Pierre's dilapidated buildings at Port La Joie. During the 1730s Jean-Pierre Roma, an energetic Parisian merchant, established fishing operations on the island. He built roads to connect his base at Trois-Rivières with Havre Saint Pierre and Port LaJoie, and attracted settlers to the island. According to a census taken in 1735, there were 432 colonists on Île Saint-Jean, about a third of them of Acadian origin. Roma hoped to establish a thriving fishing and trading centre. Had the War of the Austrian Succession not intervened, he may well have succeeded in his goal.

THE ST LAWRENCE ECONOMY

By the eighteenth century, most of Canada's population was colonial-born, but the economy of the St Lawrence colony was still largely shaped by the interests of the mother country. Canada's strategic importance to the French Empire in North America accounted for two of the three main sources of investment in the colony: the fur trade and the military. Agriculture, the third pillar of the St Lawrence economy, also benefited from the need to supply the troops stationed in the colony and at the interior posts.

THE FUR TRADE

Fur remained Canada's chief export and was the focus for French-Native relations. Although the supply of beaver continued to decline from overtrapping in the eighteenth century, other fur-bearing animals more than took up the slack. The slaughter in the wilderness netted over 250 000 pelts a year in 1728, rising to over 400 000 by the 1750s.

Montreal was the pivot of the trade, which reached far into the interior of the continent and back across the Atlantic to La Rochelle in France. Each year the convoys of canoes set out from Montreal for the *pays d'en haut* laden with items for the fur trade and supplies for the long journey and the interior posts. In the upper country, the trade developed on a three-tier system. Forts Frontenac and Niagara operated as king's posts in direct competition with British interlopers and their agents at Oswego. To ensure its success, the trade at these posts was heavily subsidized by the state. At Detroit, and Michilimackinac and other garrisoned posts, the trade was controlled through congés, or licences, but there were still unlicensed coureurs de bois operating in their own interests or on behalf of unnamed merchants and royal officials. At Green Bay and posts west of Sault Ste Marie—the *mer de l'ouest* region where the trade was now the most lucrative—monopolies were leased by the Crown to military officers and a few merchants, who used their privileges to enrich themselves.

Furs were also traded illegally. To avoid customs duties and export controls, furs shipped on the accounts of colonial officials were loaded onto fishing vessels at Kamouraska or the Gaspé or unloaded clandestinely in France before reaching La Rochelle. Other traders bypassed Quebec by shipping out of New Orleans, or even New York via Oswego and Albany. The trade through New York was officially condemned but unofficially winked at because of its many advantages. These included sizable profits, immediate payments, and access to English trade commodities, which were eagerly sought by Canadians and Natives alike.

Table 5.1
Fur Exports from Quebec

(number of pelts)

Year	Beaver	Other pelts	Total
1728	101 840	157 234	259 074
1732	106 929	176 078	283 007
1733	147 235	163 178	310 413
1735	118 353	187 035	305 388
1736	123 372	183 042	306 414
1737	82 524	273 609	356 133
1739	88 751	236 539	325 290
1754	88 301	320 327	408 628
1755	99 332	315 973	415 305

Source: H.A. Innis, *The Fur Trade in Canada: An Introduction to Canadian Economic History* (Toronto: University of Toronto Press, 1927) 153–54.

Table 5.2
Colonial Revenues and Expenditures

Year	Income	Expenditures
1713	442 348	445 455
1715	548 246	548 243
1720	381 499	381 499
1725	393 577	393 594
1730	496 253	494 217
1735	485 852	520 484
1740	417 968	503 766
1745	500 038	1 337 722
1750	904 722	1 774 715

Source: Cornelius Jaenen and Cecilia Morgan, *Material Memory: Documents in Pre-Confederation History* (Don Mills, ON: Addison Wesley Longman, 1998) 90. Reprinted with permission by Pearson Education Canada.

The necessity of satisfying their Native allies was an ongoing challenge. Far from being blindly exploited, taken in by inferior quality and short measure, the Native traders were discriminating in taste and value, and they commanded and received goods of acceptable standards. Manufacturers at Montpellier, Montauban, Carcassonne, and Rochefort in France made goods specifically for the fur trade and hoped to keep one step ahead of the British, whose manufactured goods were in high demand among Native clients.

An ancillary activity associated with the strategic role of the colony and the fur trade was the military establishment. Although it is impossible to separate the exact amounts that were spent maintaining troops and fortifications from the general Crown expenditures in New France, most years the military had the lion's share of the appropriations. When the colony was put on a wartime footing in 1744, the annual budget soared. The French government also spent large sums on arming and equipping the Canadian militia, which was of direct benefit to the colonists, and on presents to their Aboriginal allies. In wartime, the Crown provided subsistence for the families of the Native auxiliaries, who fought side by side with the colonial militia and the regular troops.

ECONOMIC INITIATIVES

Although the fur trade was the golden goose of the St Lawrence economy, the colonists briefly made fortunes on ginseng, a plant that grew wild in the region. The market boomed in the late 1740s when a regular trade was established through the Compagnie des Indes, which obtained the exclusive right to sell ginseng in

---

MORE TO THE STORY

The China Connection

The ginseng root was much prized in Asia for its reputed medicinal, restorative, and aphrodisiac properties. It came to the attention of the Jesuits through correspondence with their counterparts in Manchuria, where the root was harvested by the peasants. Father Joseph-François Lafitau at the Caughnawaga (Kahnawaké) reserve, near Montreal, identified the plant in the neighbouring woods. By 1721, Canadian ginseng shipped to France was being sold in Canton, China. The market boomed in the late 1740s when a regular trade was established through the Compagnie des Indes, which obtained the exclusive right to sell ginseng in Asia.

With the value of the ginseng trade at La Rochelle approaching 20 percent of the revenues from the fur trade, ginseng fever struck the colony. Even the religious communities sent their domestic servants and slaves to gather the precious root. When preparing his report on colonial agriculture, the engineer Louis Franquet remarked that the Canadian farmers were neglecting their harvests and could not find Natives willing to help them because everyone seemed bent on making quick money by gathering ginseng.

The bubble burst in 1752. Because of its inferior quality, the Chinese refused to purchase the Canadian product. Thereafter the Compagnie des Indes would buy only properly harvested and treated roots. A very modest trade continued until the conquest, by which time the plant had been hunted virtually to extinction. Abbé Raynal, who frequently commented on colonial affairs, noted that: "The colonists were severely punished for their excessive rapaciousness by the total loss of a branch of commerce, which if rightly managed, might have proved a source of opulence."[4]

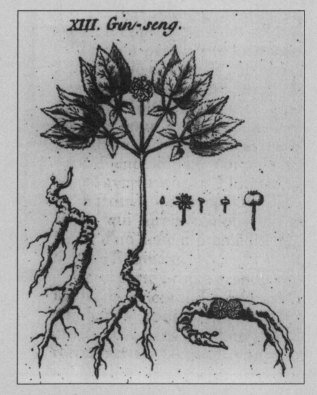

Etching of ginseng, 1744.

National Archives of Canada/C103993

Asia. As with so many colonial ventures, the ginseng boom was a short one, a victim of poor quality.

Other than furs and ginseng, few colonial resources proved successful as exports. Sawmills became a familiar site on the Canadian landscape—there were over 50 in operation by 1752—but they produced squared timber and lumber primarily for local use. Shipbuilding proved more successful. By the 1730s, colonists were building 150-ton and 200-ton vessels. A royal bounty of three livres per ton stimulated investment, and in most years Canadians completed eight to ten vessels that qualified for the subsidy. With the expansion of the West Indies trade, ships were built in the colony specifically to carry flour and wood products to the West Indies.

Military vessels were also built in the colony. In 1731, orders were placed for the construction of ships-of-the-line at the royal shipyards on the St Charles River near Quebec. Ten warships were built for the French navy in the 1740s and two more in the 1750s. Appropriately, the first warship launched was christened *Le Canada*, but the pride of the shipyards was *Le Caribou*, a 700-ton man-of-war. In the 1750s, four naval vessels were built to patrol Lake Ontario. While the colonials lacked the resources and skills to construct many of the huge ships required by the navy, they had no difficulty producing the thousands of fishing boats, coastal vessels, and bateaux that served their local needs.

In comparing New France's shipbuilding industry with that of nearby English colonies, contemporaries and later historians judge it a failure. Admittedly, there were problems. The imported skilled workers, sent to the colony under contract, complained that they had poor housing and unfair working conditions compared to the Canadians, who were sometimes better paid and given leave during inclement weather. In 1741, the disgruntled immigrant workers underlined their discontent by bringing construction activities to a halt. Intendant Gilles Hocquart responded by imprisoning the mutinous workers in irons, a measure that quickly brought an end to their protest. Constituted authority was prepared to deal harshly with insubordination from the

lower orders, and in pre-industrial society there was little working-class consciousness that might have induced the Canadian workers to cooperate with their metropolitan brothers to protect their collective economic interests.

The ships built in the colony also cost too much. In part, this was because of the corruption that characterized state activities in New France. Many expenses not associated with construction activities were charged to the company. An even bigger problem was the quality of the final product, which rotted quickly. Without proper facilities for drying and storing the lumber, it was exposed to the elements and soon deteriorated. Moreover, colonists rapidly depleted the supply of hard oak and pine in the St Lawrence lowlands and were forced to use less sturdy timbers, which led to an inferior product.

In the eighteenth century, mining got underway in Île Royale, where coal reserves near the ground surface were easily exploited. With the age of steam still a century away, coal was used primarily as a source for heat and could not as yet form the basis of a booming industry. Denys La Ronde spent 25 000 livres bringing equipment and two German experts to explore the possibilities of exploiting the copper deposits in the Lake Superior region, but little came of the venture.

Iron was a basic commodity for people in pre-industrial Europe, and Canada had an excellent source on the banks of the St Maurice River about 12 kilometres from Trois-Rivières. In 1730, a Montreal merchant, François Poulin de Francheville, opened a bog-iron plant to provide the colony with forged iron for stoves, cauldrons, pots, axeheads, and the small tools and implements required in the colony. After his death in 1735, the ironworks were taken over by François-Étienne Cugnet. With a royal subsidy of 100 000 livres, Cugnet began full-scale production, but within five years the company was bankrupt and the state assumed management of the forges.

Like the shipyards, the St Maurice ironworks were less than a complete success as an economic venture, and for some of the same reasons. Skilled workers had to be imported and mistakes were made in the construction and layout of the plant. One investigation also revealed that a number of people drew large salaries without having much to do with the ironworks. Clearly, capitalist notions of efficiency were not always uppermost in the minds of those pioneering such enterprises. In any case, industrial capitalism had yet to transform the way that people worked and planned their manufacturing ventures. What is significant is that the French state supported these new efforts in its colonies and that a new way of thinking about economic activities was beginning to take shape in the North Atlantic world.

CONCLUSION

Between 1663 and 1744, France had laid the foundation for a vast North American empire based on trade and Native alliances. The losses sustained by the Treaty of Utrecht were balanced by the construction of Louisbourg, a growing French presence on the St Lawrence and expansion into the Great Lakes and Mississippi regions. Life in a strategic outpost was always precarious but, as we shall see in the next chapter, it had its advantages, at least for those with ambition.

NOTES

1 National Archives of Canada, MG7, A–2, I, *Fonds français*, Ms. 12105, memorandum of le Maire [1717], 83.

2 André Vachon, "Jarret de Verchères, Marie-Madeleine," *Dictionary of Canadian Biography*, vol. 3, 308–13.

3 Cited in Guy Frégault, "La colonisation du Canada au XVIII siècle," *Cahiers de l'Academie canadienne-française* 2 (1957): 53-81.

4 Brian Evans, "Ginseng: Root of Chinese-Canadian Relations," *Canadian Historical Review* 61.1 (March 1985): 17.

SELECTED READING

In addition to the works by W.J. Eccles, Alan Greer, Jacques Mathieu, Dale Miquelon, Peter Moogk, and Marcel Trudel cited in the previous chapter, see Dale Miquelon, *New France, 1701–1744: "A Supplement to Europe"* (Toronto: McClelland and Stewart, 1987) and André Vachon et al., *Taking Root: Canada from 1700 to 1760* (Ottawa: Public Archives of Canada, 1985) for excellent surveys of developments in New France in the eighteenth century. French relations with Aboriginal peoples are covered in Gilles Havard, *The Great Peace of Montreal of 1701: French Native Diplomacy in the Seventeenth Century*, trans. Phyllis Aronoff and Howard Scott (Montreal: McGill-Queen's University Press, 2001). On the history of Louisbourg, see Christopher Moore, *Louisbourg Portraits: Life in an Eighteenth-Century Garrison Town* (Toronto: Macmillan, 1982) and A.J.B. Johnson, *Religion in Life at Louisbourg* (Montreal: McGill-Queen's University Press, 1984). See Georges Arsenault, *The Island Acadians, 1720–1980* (Charlottetown: Ragweed, 1989) for information on the early history of Île Saint-Jean. This period in Newfoundland history is

covered in the relevant chapters of Patrick O'Flaherty, *Old Newfoundland: A History to 1843* (St John's: Long Beach Press, 1999). On the "upper country," two studies deserve attention: Charles J. Balesi, *The Time of the French in the Heart of North America, 1673–1818* (Chicago: Alliance Française, 1992) and Joseph L. Peyser, *Letters from New France: The Upper Country, 1686–1783* (Urbana: University of Illinois Press, 1992). On the fur trade and other economic matters, see Harold Innis, *The Fur Trade in Canada: An Introduction to Canadian Economic History* (Toronto: University of Toronto Press, 1927); John F. Bosher, *The Canada Merchants* (Oxford: Oxford University Press, 1978); Cameron Nish, *Les bourgeois-gentilhommes de la Nouvelle-France, 1729–1748* (Montréal: Fides, 1975); Kathryn A. Young, *Kin, Commerce, Community: Merchants in the Port of Quebec, 1717–1745* (New York: Peter Lang, 1995); Jacques Mathieu, *La Construction navale royale à Québec, 1739–1759* (Quebec: Société historique de Québec, 1971); Réal Boissonnault, *Le forges du Saint-Maurice, 1729–1883* (Québec: Parcs Canada, 1983); Brian Evans, "Ginseng: Root of Chinese–Canadian Relations," *Canadian Historical Review* 61.1 (March 1985); James Pritchard, "The Pattern of

French Colonial Shipping to Canada before 1760," *Revue française d'histoire d'outre-mer* 63.231 (1976); Gratien Allaire, "Fur Trade Engagés, 1701–1745," in *Rendezvous: Selected Papers of the North American Fur Trade Conference 1981*, ed. Thomas C. Buckley (St Paul, MN: Minnesota Historical Society, 1984), and "Officiers et marchands: les sociétés de commerce des fourrures, 1715–1760," *Revue d'histoire de l'Amérique française* 40.3 (1987).

 **WEBLINKS**

TREATY OF UTRECHT
www.geocities.com/Yosemite/Rapids/3330/constitution/ utrecht.htm

A portion of the treaty text—in which France ceded its claim to Newfoundland, with the exception of fishing rights along the coast from Cape Bonavista to Pointe Riche—is available on this site.

LOUISBOURG
http://Collections.ic.gc.ca/louisbourg/enghome.html

This outstanding site provides a wealth of information on the fortress and the time period. There is an extensive subject index of site resources, and online access is available to parish records of births, marriages, and deaths from 1713 to 1758.

MCCORD MUSEUM
www.musee-mccord.qc.ca

The online library of the McCord Museum of Canadian History collection houses more than 950 000 objects, images, and documents documenting the history of Canada.

Society and Culture in New France

The common man in Canada is more civilized and clever than in any other place in the world that I have visited. On entering one of the peasant's houses, no matter where, and on beginning to talk with the men and women, one is quite amazed at the good breeding and courteous answers which are received, no matter what the question is.... Frenchmen who were born in Paris said themselves that one never finds in France among the country people the courtesy and good breeding which one observes everywhere in this land....[1]

When Peter Kalm, a Swedish scientist and university professor, visited the English and French colonies in 1749–50, he was especially impressed by New France. He found productive farms, happy peasants, and a sophisticated elite. Kalm also voiced an opinion held by many visitors to the colony: that a distinctive Canadian culture was emerging on the banks of the St Lawrence.

IMMIGRATION AND SOCIETY

Despite the opportunities it offered, few people settled in New France. Some 27 000 foreign-born individuals spent some time in Canada under the French regime, but nearly two-thirds of them went back home. In total, fewer than 10 000 Europeans immigrated to Canada. Another 500 settled in Acadia, most of them arriving before 1650. Over a quarter of the immigrants to Canada came in just two decades: 1660–1669 and 1750–1759.

People moving permanently to Canada tended to be concentrated into a few specific occupational groups. The most likely settlers were either soldiers released from military service or engagés committed to a specific term of service, usually three years. Over half of the 1500 women who migrated to Canada were filles du roi. Some 1000 petty criminals were sent to Canada, and at least 200 of them stayed. Other than some 500 clergy, most of them in the male religious orders, self-financing immigrants accounted for no more than 250 people. A few were *fils de famille*, a general term used to describe debauched sons sent abroad to save elite families further embarrassment. While a few errant sons stayed, most of them eventually returned home.

Four times as many men as women, and as many urban as rural people, chose Canada as their home. Nearly all immigrants were single; only one man in twenty and one woman in five were married or widowed. Most were relatively young. Although immigrants

MORE TO THE STORY

Demography

The science of demography analyzes population trends and is concerned with factors relating to births, marriages, deaths, and migrations of peoples. While present-day data-gathering techniques give demographers plenty of information upon which to base their conclusions, the sources for earlier periods are often elusive. Happily, the bureaucratic nature of the French regime had the unintended result of providing historians with a variety of sources—censuses, parish records, marriage contracts, confirmation lists, indenture agreements, death certificates, for example—that can be used to reconstitute the general trends in immigration, family formation, and life expectancy. From such sources, demographers have determined immigration patterns for Canada.

Historian Peter Moogk offers the following statistical summary:

Table 6.1

Immigration to Canada before 1760

Soldiers	3300
Acadians	1800
Women from France	1500
Indentured servants	1200
Slaves	900
British subjects	650
Other European foreigners	525
Male clergy	500
Self-financed immigrants	250
Transported prisoners	200
Total	10 825

Source: Peter Moogk, *La Nouvelle France: The Making of New France—A Cultural History* (East Lansing: Michigan State University Press, 2000) 113.

This summary of a census taken in Acadia in 1686 indicates that census takers were interested not only in the human population but also in the amount of cleared land, the number of farm animals, and the firearms held in the colony.

Archives nationales, Paris, Section Outre-Mer, Série G1, vol. 466, no. 10

came from all regions of France, Paris and the areas immediately surrounding ports such as La Rochelle, Rouen, St Malo, and Dieppe contributed a disproportionate number of settlers. Most immigrants were French citizens, but 525 Europeans from areas outside of France fetched up in the colony. So, too, against their will, did 900 slaves, both Native and African. In addition, 650 British subjects, over 500 of them captives of raids on English colonies or vessels, settled in

Canada, as did 1800 Acadians who escaped to the St Lawrence region following the initial deportation order in 1755.

By the end of the French regime, about 4000 Native people lived in Canada, most in reserves around Quebec and Montreal. The church played an important role in drawing Natives to the colony. In 1676, for example, the Jesuits established a mission at La Prairie for Aboriginal Christians, most of them

Iroquois. They moved several times before finally settling at Sault St-Louis, or Caughnawaga (Kahnawaké) in 1716. There they grew through natural increase and adoptions. Among the latter were Natives captured during wars, captives from British colonies, and French foundlings and children born out of wedlock. In the 1750s, 30 families from Kahnawaké, including a part-African Abenaki named Louis Cook, moved to St Regis-Akwesasné on Lake Francis to be nearer to the Iroquois in what is now the state of New York.

The intendant's palace at Quebec, 1761.

Richard Short/National Archives of Canada/C360

TOWN LIFE

About 20 percent of the people in New France lived in urban communities. Closely linked to France through church, state, and commercial institutions, the major colonial towns were quick to reflect the social and intellectual currents transforming European society. The French commander Montcalm, writing in 1757, judged Quebec to be the equal of most French towns. Visitors to Montreal and Louisbourg were often surprised by the vibrant urban life they encountered.

Located on one of the most imposing sites in North America, Quebec never failed to impress the first-time visitor. As the capital of New France and the chief port of Canada, Quebec had grown from a population of 500 in 1660 to 10 times the size a century later. Importers and artisans mixed in Lower Town, while administrative and religious institutions were concentrated in Upper Town. Dominating all was the Château Saint-Louis, the residence of the governor general. At the rear of the town stood the intendant's palace, which served as his official residence and the meeting place for the Superior Council, the Quebec Prévôté, and the Admiralty Court. Stone fortifications ran behind the town from the St Lawrence to the St Charles River. By 1750 many of the houses in the town

were also built of stone, a result of a ban on new wooden structures following a disastrous fire in 1726.

Quebec was a busy place, especially in the late spring and early summer when the ships began arriving from France. On weekly market days people from the countryside crowded the town's narrow streets. In backyards throughout Quebec, but especially in the expanding precincts of Upper Town, people grew gardens, kept live animals, and built their privies. Pigs and cattle commonly wandered the streets unattended. When citizens wanted to discard refuse, they simply spread it on the unpaved streets, thus adding new odours to those already wafting from the open sewers that carried the town's liquid sludge to the river's edge. Such practices were common to all colonial communities and in no way detracted from Quebec's pre-eminent position in New France. The town was home to the highest-ranking officials in church and state as well as over 350 artisans representing more than 30 different crafts. On religious holidays, Quebec could mount the most impressive processions, with all ranks of society accounted for.

By the middle of the eighteenth century, Quebec was a tenant's town, with over half of the town's population renting rather than owning their dwelling places. The mobility of the population and the com-

Street Scene, Quebec at Night, *by Clarence Gagnon. The painting depicts a large stone dwelling in the town of Quebec.*

National Gallery of Canada/1449

petitive economic climate made it difficult for labourers and artisans to earn enough money to purchase a home. While widows in Quebec had the highest rate of home ownership, they were also the most likely people to rent out rooms. The favourite time for moving to new lodgings, then as now, was in the first week in May, when spring encouraged new beginnings.

Montreal was Canada's second-largest town, with over 4000 inhabitants in the mid-eighteenth century. By that time, it had lost much of its earlier religious tone and taken on the trappings of a frontier garrison town, dominated by soldiers and men of the fur trade rather than by the Sulpicians. Flanked by Mount

Royal and protected by a stone wall, Montreal, like Quebec, made an impressive site. Its island location was surrounded by prosperous farms and Native communities. During the summer, Natives from the interior were frequent visitors. Rich and rowdy, especially when brigades were assembling for, or arriving from, the pays d'en haut, Montreal may have been less dignified than Quebec, but it was a more lively place.

By the 1740s, Louisbourg was a handsome town, reflecting the most advanced thinking in urban planning and defensive strategy. On top of the town's highest hill stood the major public buildings, all constructed in stone. The royal fleur-de-lis graced the elegant bell tower that capped the imposing citadel. A thick stone and mortar rampart, with outer rings of ditches and earthworks, encircled the town. Around the harbour, gun batteries were mounted with heavy cannon to ward off enemy attack. With a population of over 4000, and even more in the summer when the fishing fleets and merchant traders were in port, Louisbourg hummed with activity.

MUNICIPAL GOVERNMENT

Because there was no municipal government in New France, the royal courts also exercised administrative functions. A series of 42 by-laws issued by the Sovereign Council in 1676 constituted what today would be called a municipal code for Quebec. Included in this code were ordinances establishing a town market and setting the prices of essential commodities such as meat and bread. Building standards, fire protection, and town planning were also covered in the code. Because human and animal wastes constituted a major health hazard, by-laws were eventually passed to regulate their removal.

Poverty, begging, vagrancy, and prostitution were also subject to regulation. Vagrants, for example, were prohibited from remaining in the town without permission of the authorities, and the town's poor were not allowed to beg without a certificate of poverty signed by a priest or judge. The growing incidence of prostitution in the port town of Quebec resulted in a 1676 by-law forbidding all citizens to harbour women of dubious morals, as well as pimps and madams. By modern standards, the people of colonial towns were remarkably law-abiding. Tavern brawls and the occasional duel between officers were de rigueur, but the presence of the Troupes de la Marine made law and order a relatively easy matter for authorities.

As the size and complexity of town life increased, so too did the number of vagabonds and foundlings. In the 1730s, the state's cost of maintaining *enfants bâtards* in Canada became a cause for concern: nearly 5000 livres for Quebec and nearly 8000 livres in Montreal. The Crown responded by reducing the stipend for the care of the infants, but it was clear from their numbers and the proliferation of other proscribed activities— including maintaining mistresses, drinking, gambling,

and prostitution—that colonial society reflected the relaxed moral values that also characterized French society in this period.

In Montreal, the care of foundlings became one of the prime concerns of the Soeurs Grises, or Grey Nuns, a religious community that received official sanction from the king in 1753. Founded by Marie-Marguerite d'Youville, the Soeurs Grises devoted their energies to the care of the sick and poor. The problem of abandoned infants led them to take in about 20 babies a year. A death rate among the unfortunate foundlings of 80 percent—typical of such institutions in Europe—underscored the fragility of life in institutional settings in the pre-industrial world.

ARTS AND SCIENCES

The towns were the centres of the intellectual life in New France. In addition to the religious orders that had long provided the colonies with a high standard of education and social services, there developed a class of civilian intellectuals, both French and colonial-born, whose interests reflected the preoccupations of the enlightenment philosophers of France. Two eighteenth-century medical doctors, Michael Sarrazin and Jean-François Gauthier, for instance, sent reports on the natural history of Canada to the Academie Royale des Sciences in Paris. Governor Roland-Michel Barrin de La Galissonnière, who did much to encourage the intellectual life of the colony, impressed the visiting Peter Kalm in 1749 with his theories on the relationship between nature and politics.

Other than travel accounts and a few plays in verse for special occasions, Canadians produced little formal literature. Marie-Élisabeth Bégon, a resident of Montreal, excelled in the eighteenth-century art of letter writing, but few emulated her example. With France on the cutting edge of European intellectual life in the eighteenth century, the colonial elites relied heavily upon their mother country for the ideas that animated their dinner conversations. They neither produced their own newspaper nor bothered to import a printing press.

Painting, sculpture, and architecture were stimulated in New France by the demands of the growing

Jingdezhen china. Elites in New France lived in the manner of their counterparts in France. In Louisbourg tables were set with fine Jingdezhen porcelain, imported from China. Archeologists at the site have collected 69 000 fragments of this dinnerware.

Parks Canada, Fortress of Louisbourg National Historic Site of Canada (N.S.), Andrée Crépeau, RAL-6213t

second and sometimes even a third rang of seigneuries was being carved out behind original grants. Parish churches, a few seigneurial manors, and many small habitant houses dotted the landscape.

The process of creating a farm from the tree-covered banks of the St Lawrence was back-breaking and soul-destroying work. At best, a peasant family could clear two *arpents*—roughly one hectare—a year, and a farm of 30 to 40 arable arpents was the most that could be expected from a lifetime of labour. The children of the first generation had an easier task. Not only were they used to the hard work involved, but they could also live at home while starting their new farms. After three generations of settlement, families began developing strategies to avoid excessive subdivisions of their holdings. Such a prospect loomed large because the Custom of Paris required that all children in non-noble families share equally in inheritance—whereas in noble families a larger portion of the estate was bestowed upon one heir.

The habitants responded to overcrowding on the seigneuries in a variety of ways. One strategy involved an arrangement whereby one or two children acquired the family farm while the others took their inheritance in cash or kind and could then move to outlying regions individually or in groups. For some rural families, farm income was supplemented through winter employment on government construction projects or in the fur or timber trade. It was usually the more prosperous habitant families whose sons turned to wage labour. A few young men even managed to take up trades permanently and set up shop in the villages that had begun to develop in the rural countryside.

urban elite, as well as by church and state. While much of the fine furnishings that graced the elegant homes and public buildings of the towns came from France, local artisans also practised their skills in fine crafts. Surviving ex-votos, portraits of notable citizens, beautifully carved pine furniture, and locally crafted silver plate all testify to the rich level of material culture that was produced in eighteenth-century New France.

CANADIAN PEASANT SOCIETY

The preoccupations of the urban-based colonial elites had little impact on the habitants, some 80 per cent of the population, who lived in the rural countryside. Most of these habitants were Canadian-born and easily absorbed the common immigrants to the colony. By 1750, seigneurial farms had spread along both sides of the St Lawrence and down the Richelieu River. A

The most prosperous habitants bought farms from their poorer neighbours for their children, while the original owners moved to new settlements. Although undeveloped concessions were free, no one could enter farming without money to buy the tools, animals, seeds needed to get started, and enough provisions to last until the first crops were harvested.

The houses of the habitants were usually constructed of squared logs, whitewashed, and topped with a thatched or cedar roof. Their ground floors, averaging eight by six metres, were divided into two or three rooms. Manor houses tended to be more imposing and often built in stone, especially in the older more established regions. Besides the main house, a manor usually included a wooden barn with a central threshing floor and bays for storing hay and grain, stables for horses and cattle, a shed, and an outdoor oven.

In the eighteenth century, a typical peasant farm might consist of 100 arpents, about ten times the size of a peasant holding in France—although not all of this land was cleared or arable. The farm would produce heavy yields for the first decade and then drop well below the metropolitan level of production. Rapid soil depletion necessitated the clearing of more

forest land on the upper reaches of the river-front farm. Wheat was the chief cereal crop, but Canadians also grew flax, oats, barley, and peas. At the interior posts the colonists learned to grow corn, the staple crop of the Iroquois nations. Almost every farm in the St Lawrence valley had kitchen gardens planted with onions, cabbage, beans, carrots, lettuce, radishes, beets, parsnips, tobacco, and a variety of herbs. Around Montreal, which had more fertile soils and a longer growing season than Quebec, apple, pear, and plum trees, as well as melons and pumpkins, did particularly well. By the end of the French regime, horses, cattle, and sheep grazed on the marshes and uplands, and pigs and poultry roamed the farmyards. A 1709 ordinance stipulating that no person was to keep more than two horses and a foal seems to have been ignored. Canadians raised horses for farm work and transportation and even for racing.

Despite injunctions from intendants that crop rotation, fertilization, and selective breeding be practised, most peasants engaged in extensive, rather than intensive, agriculture. A majority of habitants produced mixed crops for their own subsistence and not for a specialized market. On the seigneuries around

MORE TO THE STORY

The Standard of Living of Peasants in New France

The similarity, in formal terms, between the position of the peasantry in France and New France has occasioned much debate. Some historians suggest that, despite feudal forms, the peasant in New France was virtually an independent farmer. Although habitants paid annual dues to the seigneur, tithes to the church, and taxes to the state, they experienced much lower levels of taxation than prevailed in France. Most of the peasants in New France, it is argued, were better housed than their European counterparts, and rarely encountered the prospect of famine, a fate common among the peasantry in many regions of France.

Other historians question this rosy picture of the habitant lifestyle, noting that many peasants in New France had great difficulty raising a crop that sustained their household needs. As a result, the exactions of seigneurs, clerics, and state bureaucrats, while not a large percentage of the crop, constituted

an oppressive burden. Most peasants in New France experienced a lower level of material culture than their French cousins, and were destined to remain near the bottom of the social hierarchy. They also had much lower literacy rates than their immigrant ancestors.

Whatever position is taken on this question, most historians agree that habitants in New France had more land, a greater likelihood of including meat and fish in their diets, and a better chance of being well fed than the chronically oppressed French peasantry. There is also general agreement that French peasants were more deferential to authority than their colonial counterparts, who were notorious for their lack of discipline. The widespread availability of land may help to account for this spirit of independence, which was typical of the lower classes generally in North America.

Quebec and Montreal, farmers made a systematic effort to respond to market demands and often had grain surpluses to export.

One of the biggest difficulties facing the peasant farmers was the fact that wheat was not ideally suited to the soil and climate of the St Lawrence lowland. Early frosts, smut, rust, drought, or infestations of grasshoppers and caterpillars reduced wheat yields. In years of poor harvest—17 times between 1700 and 1760—flour had to be imported. In 1749, hungry peasants congregated in the towns. Intendant François Bigot, reminded of the periodic bread riots in France, quickly opened the storehouses and enacted regulations to prohibit begging and vagrancy.

By the mid-eighteenth century, the habitants had become the solid base of the colony that Colbert had once hoped for. Soon the influence of France would be eliminated, the fur-trade frontier would be taken over by the Hudson's Bay Company traders, the military establishment would be staffed by foreigners, and the towns would be transformed by an influx of English-speaking administrators, soldiers, and merchants. But the farming communities along both sides of the St Lawrence would remain intact and largely French in culture—just as they are today.

THE FAMILY UNDER THE FRENCH REGIME

Among all the people of European origin in New France, the family was the fundamental social unit. It was in the family that most of the colony's production took place, where services were administered, and where pain and pleasure alike were experienced. Even on the frontier, families thrived. Commandants often took their wives and children with them to the interior posts or formed close relationships with Aboriginal women.

Canadian women married at a younger age than their European counterparts. In France, in the eighteenth century, the average age of marriage for women was 25; in New France, it was 22. There was little appreciable difference in the age of marriage for men in France and the colony, although in both cases husbands tended to be several years older than their wives.

In New France, men remarried within a year or two after losing a wife, women after three years of widowhood. Coureurs de bois often took Native companions and produced Métis children. No doubt owing to the influence of the church and the relatively young age of marriage, illegitimacy rates were low—only ten or twelve per thousand births.

Families in New France were large. Marrying younger and generally living longer, Canadian women had more children on the average than women in France. A woman who survived her childbearing years in the eighteenth century could expect to give birth to about seven or eight children. In Acadia, where the age of marriage was lower than on the St Lawrence, the average family was even larger. Families provided most of the social services that were taken up by the state in the twentieth century. Children were born at home with the assistance of an experienced midwife, and much of the education in practical and productive skills took place under the watchful eye of parents. When people were sick or injured, they were treated in their homes. Without a family, an individual was forced to rely on the church-operated public institutions.

Weddings were social events, surrounded by Christian and pagan customs. The rituals included the *charivari*, a noisy gathering of people in the community under the window of a recently married couple. If the marriage was socially questionable—a widow who had remarried too soon after the death of her husband, or a couple of too unequal age—the charivari could take a menacing tone. Occasionally couples married *à la gaumine* (without benefit of clergy), and common-law relationships were even more likely on the fur-trade frontier where marriage *à la façon du pays* reflected Native customs and the absence, or defiance, of priestly injunctions.

Death was a frequent visitor to families in pre-industrial society. Urban areas were particularly dangerous places to live, with their high vulnerability to the epidemics that periodically ravaged the colony. In 1702–3, an outbreak of smallpox in Quebec took the lives of 350 people—nearly 20 percent of the town's population. Accidental and violent deaths were also commonplace. Historian Allan Greer notes that of the 4587 accidental deaths recorded by priests in the sev-

Couple in Sunday clothes.

City of Montreal. Records Managment and Archives (BM7/42498.34-2-4-1)

enteenth century, 51 people were struck by lightning; 299 died in war; 71 were crushed by trees or other falling objects; 37 froze to death; 69 were killed by fire; and 1302 drowned.[2]

Because of the high death rate, marriage partners could expect their unions to last only 15 or 20 years or so before the grim reaper took one of them away. Women and children were the most vulnerable. On average, one in four children died in the first year of life, and childhood diseases prevented a good many of the rest from reaching the age of 15. It was a relatively common occurrence for women to die in childbirth, which meant the death rate for women between the ages of 15 and 49 was higher than the rate for men in the same age group.

THE FAMILY ECONOMY

In pre-industrial society, families were important economic units, with everyone working together to ensure collective survival. No peasant farm could thrive without the work of all members. Land was most commonly received through inheritance, or seigneurial grant, not through purchase. For elite families, patronage, or protection, went first to members of the family—as exemplified by the adeptness of the Colberts and Pontchartrains at finding positions for their relatives within the Ministry of Marine.

Marriage was a business partnership to which a woman brought a dowry in return for her husband's patronage. Dowries varied in amount according to class and, especially among the peasantry, might be largely in kind—household linen, items of furniture, clothes, or livestock. When her husband died, the law of dower entitled a widow to "the enjoyment" for life of one-half the husband's estate, but she was obliged to pay the outstanding debts and the dues on the land, and she was required to maintain the real property so it could pass intact to her husband's heirs. Most marriage contracts stated that a wife would receive a fixed dower no matter what outstanding debts were held against her deceased husband's estate.

Like society as a whole, families in New France were hierarchical, with the father at the head of the household. Unless a wife made a special contract, all of her possessions were controlled by her husband. Children belonged first to their fathers, and they could not marry without his consent until the age of 25 for daughters and 30 for sons. Because marriage was so critical to the family's economic well-being and social status, it was an event that could not be entrusted to the wishes of consenting partners alone.

The colony's approaches to childrearing and education were transplanted from France. Because so many children died in infancy, parents tried to avoid strong emotional attachments to their babies, and grieving parents found consolation in the popular belief that their deceased infants became angels who interceded on their behalf in heaven. Particularly in elite families, swaddling, wetnursing, and early toilet-training were part of the infant regime. To inculcate respect for authority, obedience, and discipline, corporal punishments were liberally administered.

Despite the seemingly harsh discipline, most families enjoyed a reasonable level of domestic harmony. The need for habitant families to function as a unit of production coupled with religious teachings encouraged co-operative behaviour. The cults of the infant Jesus and the Virgin Mary offered a less disciplinarian approach to those in subordinate positions within the family. Gradually, too, the examples of Native child-rearing practices may also have had an impact. French commentators often remarked on the fact that Aboriginal peoples treated their children with affection and kindness rather than strict discipline reinforced by violence.

Ex-votos (paintings commemorating miraculous events) also provide details of material life in the colony. This ex-voto shows people being saved from a shipwreck near Lévis.

Musée de sainte Anne, Sainte-Anne de Beaupré, QC

CHURCH AND SOCIETY

Although the institutional church lost some of its political power under Louis XIV, there is no question about the influence that the gallican brand of Roman Catholicism had on the social and cultural life of the colony. Virtually everyone belonged to the Roman Catholic Church, and those who did not were required by law to conform to its practices. Christian values and prejudices permeated the laws and customs of the colony and were imposed, when there was an opportunity to do so, upon the Aboriginal peoples. While Protestants were allowed to return to the colony in the eighteenth century, they posed no threat to the Roman Catholic Church, which remained the only institutional church in New France throughout the French regime.

Despite slow beginnings and seemingly endless obstacles, parish priests gradually became a significant presence in the countryside. They presided over the religious ceremonies that marked every stage of an individual's life. For many of the settlers, religious rituals offered much-needed comfort and reassurance in the face of the unfamiliar and often terrifying realities of colonial life. The priest also served as a key adviser to the *fabrique*, the board of trustees of the parish, which was one of the few local institutions in the colony.

In addition to their religious duties, priests kept parish registers, which today provide us with valuable vital statistics, and they even drew up legal documents. They also provided some of the basic education that country folk received. Ultimately the parish priest, recruited among the local population and trained in the seminary at Quebec, would identify with his parishioners much more than with the bishop, who, with the exception of Laval, spent more time in France than in his diocese.

Local boys were recruited for the seminary, but they were less welcome among the regular orders that drew their members mainly from France. Before the conquest, only three Canadians entered the Jesuit order and none became Sulpicians. No Canadian was appointed bishop or superior of a major religious order during the French regime. Although Canadian-born priests served the rural parishes in increasing numbers, there was always a shortage of clergy. At the end of the French regime, almost one-half of the clergy were still of French origin. In contrast, fully 20 percent of the girls in noble families in New France entered a convent, a reflection it seems, of parental strategies designed to pass as much of the family estate as possible to sons.

CLASS AND SOCIETY

There is little indication that New France in the eighteenth century had become more egalitarian than society in Europe. As the population grew and as communication across the Atlantic became more reliable, the values relating to class and status in Europe took firm root in the colony. The emphasis on class and rank under the ancien régime, and the privileges that went with such distinctions, eventually led to violent revolution in France in 1789. In New France, the conquest intervened before a revolution could occur, neatly removing the top echelons of the French ruling elite and substituting English conquerors.

Social structure in New France was not built on economic differences. Rather, social rank dictated economic behaviour. Social position, achieved by birth or influence, demanded a particular way of life, and people in New France, whether they could afford to or not, lived on a scale deemed appropriate to their rank. Those who did otherwise were widely scorned. Governor Jean de Lauson, for example, was criticized by his contemporaries because he lived without a personal servant and ate only pork and peas, like a common artisan or peasant. Peasants who used their horses for racing rather than farm work earned disapproving comments from authorities.

For many members of the colonial elite, maintaining the outward show of their status often kept

Table 6.2

Occupational Hierarchy of New France, Based on Conventional Dower

Ranking by average dower	Other occupations
1. The Elite (2000–8000 livres per annum)	
Commissioned military officers	Senior clergy and nuns
Senior judicial and administrative officers	
2. Honourable Employments (800–1500 livres)	
Architects	Minor clergy
Master builders in stone	Wholesale merchants
Silversmiths	Royal notaries
Non-commissioned officers	
3. Good Trades (600–750 livres)	
Hatmakers	Land surveyors
Surgeons	Hussiers
Shoemakers	
4. Modest Occupations (425–500 livres)	
Metalworkers	
Woodworkers	
Private soldiers	
5. Base Occupations (400 livres or less)	
Stonemasons	Food retailers
Tenant farmers	Carters
Tailors	Sailors
	Hired servants

Source: Peter Moogk, "Rank in New France: Restructuring a Society from Notarial Documents," *Histoire sociale/Social History* 7.15 (May 1975): 43.

them on the edge of bankruptcy. Those below them, in contrast, could live simply while accumulating wealth. One tanner in Quebec, for example, possessed only 82 livres of clothing and furniture when he died but held promissory notes to the amount of 4312 livres. Wealth, of course, usually went hand in hand with rank. Those higher up on the social ladder had access to more forms of wealth, including seigneurial grants, military appointments, and commercial opportunities.

While a great gulf existed between the nobility and the common folk, there was a precisely defined pecking order among the members of the middle classes. Fine craftsmen, for example, distinguished themselves from those who practised more common trades, and royal officers had more status than municipal officials. Rituals and ceremonies observed throughout the colony reinforced this hierarchy. In church, the benches were assigned so that the elite sat closest to the front, with the middle classes behind them. The lower orders sat or even stood at the back. People dressed, lived in homes, and behaved in public in ways that "befitted their station." Women usually derived their status from their husbands' position.

THE COLONIAL ELITE

At the top of the social hierarchy in New France was the noblesse, a class of military officers, administrators, and the highest-ranking church officials holding letters patent of nobility. Nobles in the colonies—unlike those in France—were allowed to engage in trade without being stripped of their titles. It was also possible, by combining seigneurial, military, commercial, and administrative functions in a way that would draw the attention of the king, for an ambitious young commoner to achieve noble status. As individuals rose up the social scale, they often managed to "marry up," especially in a second or third marriage—although upward mobility was easier in the seventeenth than in the eighteenth century. It was also easier in the early years of settlement for individuals to claim noble status that they did not have. In 1684, those who used the title *écuyer* (esquire) in legal documents were ordered to give proof of their pretensions. They were fined if they made false claims.

Because they had large families, the nobility was more than able to perpetuate itself, even though few colonials were ennobled in the eighteenth century. The restrictions on upward mobility did not, however, stop those in the upper echelons of the middle class from seeking the trappings of noble life. By 1760, nearly 50 percent of the seigneurs in the colony were members of the middle class. The middle class also sought places in the Troupes de la Marine for their sons, but these, too, dried up over the course of the eighteenth century. With only 112 positions in the officer corps and 56 cadetships, commissions in the Troupes were the objects of bitter competition among the leading families of the colony.

The church reflected the rigid class system that prevailed in Canada in the eighteenth century. While the Quebec seminary recruited most of its students from the colony, it was not an institution that advanced the careers of peasant boys. Most of the recruits came from wealthier middle-class families. Toward the end of the French regime, there was a marked increase in sons of artisans entering the priesthood, but only two of the 195 ordained colonial-born priests between 1611 and 1760 were sons of common farmers.

Its aristocratic ethos and military flavour made New France distinct from its English neighbours, where middle-class values prevailed. Puffed up by their knowledge that the French court was the centre of diplomatic life in Europe, colonials took their cue from their mother country. The strategic role defined for the colony, with its garrisoned towns and interior fur-trading posts, enhanced the arrogance of its ruling class. Even peasants aped the values of their social superiors. Unlike most Europeans in this period, they had access to land and were subject to military conscription. With the colony at war for much of its history, the military ethos penetrated deeply into the social fabric of New France.

MERCHANTS

All colonists had the right to engage in trade. In 1706, even foreign merchants were permitted to set up shop in the colony. Since the colony relied on France for a number of crucial commodities—cloth and clothing, wines and brandies, guns, powder and lead, utensils, salt, and a variety of luxury goods—a score of merchants did well in the import trade. Importers brought merchandise from France and sold it to the *négociants* —traders, outfitters, and shopkeepers— who proliferated in the colony.

Merchants in Quebec were active in organizing their own interests. In 1708, they established a *bourse*, an organization similar to a board of trade, and rented a house for its activities. A royal decree of 1717 authorized the merchants in Montreal and Quebec to meet every day in a suitable place to carry out their business and to make representations to the king on matters of policy that would benefit their trading activities.

As valued partners in family enterprises, women played a significant and direct role in the commercial life of New France. They worked with their husbands in commercial and artisan establishments and operated businesses as diverse as taverns and sawmills. Some women became active in trade when their husbands were away on business or died prematurely. Marie-Anne Barbel, for instance, took over her husband's business interests when he died in 1745, continuing his partnership in a fishing concession and his fur-trade operations. Just as any man would do in similar circumstances, she traded properties, established new businesses, and took her adversaries to court. She continued to make a comfortable living for herself and her unmarried children until her death at the age of 90.

By the 1740s, François Havy and Jean Lefebvre, representing the firm of Dugard in Rouen, were the most powerful merchants in Canada. They retailed goods in both Quebec and Montreal, invested in sealing expeditions along the Labrador coast, and exported wheat to Louisbourg. Smaller merchants in the towns and countryside stocked important items and made their living by retailing. So, too, did a few pedlars who travelled the seigneuries along the river.

In addition to the private trade, which occupied at least 15 vessels each year out of La Rochelle, the Crown shipped supplies to the colony to support its military establishment and related state activities. This was a highly profitable trade for the metropolitan merchants and their Canadian contacts. Supplies for colonial troops were bought at cheaper prices and the Crown bore the risks of the voyage—shipwreck, piracy, spoilage, and capture in wartime. Even if the ship were lost at sea or the cargo spoiled, the contractor would receive his commission. In some cases, contractors could also draw upon naval stores and sailors to outfit their ship.

La Rochelle and Rouen were the major ports in the trade with New France in the first half of the eighteenth century. During the 1750s, Bordeaux took on special significance. Intendant François Bigot organized a ring with Bordeaux merchants and Canadian collaborators to monopolize the lucrative supply trade. Members of this charmed circle amassed large personal fortunes by mismanaging military appropriations and defrauding the colonists. In all, 22 millionaires emerged from this operation. Bigot had developed his skills while stationed at Louisbourg, which was also a place where officials found easy opportunities for lining their pockets. In this busy entrepôt, clandestine trade was particularly lucrative. Port registers indicate that the greatest number of vessels clearing the harbour were from the English colonies and the West Indies. Even the vessels owned by Louisbourg residents were often of New England origin.

ARTISANS

Artisans produced most of the colony's goods and services and trained others in the skills of their trade. In urban areas of France, guilds controlled the progression from apprentice to journeyman and master craftsman and regulated the quality of their work, but the Crown restricted the operation of guilds in the colonies. When master roofers in Quebec asked for *la jurande*, or the right to control the standards of their trade, the Superior Council rejected their request on the grounds that there were no legally constituted master craftsmen in the colony with the exclusive rights to pursue a particular trade.

In the absence of guilds, the Crown regulated the bakers, butchers, surgeons, midwives, and notaries. The church was permitted to exercise regulatory authority over the activities of itinerant schoolmasters and private tutors. The Crown also encouraged the

biography

The Fate of François Bigot

François Bigot was born in 1703 in the Bordeaux region of France. The Bigot family had risen to prominence over three generations, and young François was probably attracted to the marine department because his cousin had briefly served as its chief minister. Known for his passion for gambling and pretty women as well as for his ambition, Bigot was appointed financial commissary to Louisbourg in 1739 and intendant to Canada in 1748. Bigot had no great desire to live in the colonies, but he saw service there as an opportunity to make his fortune. In taking advantage of his posting, he was no different than other colonial officials. He nevertheless differed from most of them because he was brought to trial for his corrupt administrative practices.

Following the surrender of Canada, Bigot and many of his former business associates were arrested. The state needed a scapegoat for the loss of the colony, and the activities of the *grande société* were so outrageous that they

had reached the ears of the highest authorities in France. By exposing Bigot, the king could also justify the decision to default on the colonial debts that had been accumulated during the war. Bigot spent nearly two years in the infamous Bastille before being brought to trial in 1763. A tribunal of 27 magistrates handed down a 78-page indictment, announcing Bigot's permanent banishment and the confiscation of all of his property. Several of Bigot's close associates were also heavily fined.

Shortly before the judgment was delivered, Bigot moved to Switzerland, where he lived under an assumed name. Although not destitute, he lived less elegantly than he had planned, and he suffered from poor health. He died on 12 January 1778 at Neuchatel. As requested in his will, he received a modest burial: "I desire that my body be buried in the cemetery at Cressier without any pomp, just as the poorest person in the parish would be."[3]

religious activities of these corporate groups. Within each trade, *confréries*, or fraternities, organized annual religious observances in honour of the craft's patron saint. While such organizations had the potential for collective political action, they remained essentially religious and social institutions.

The guild system was already breaking down in Europe by the time that colonists began moving to North America. Throughout the colonies, the ideal was to be free to work as needs determined. A few colonists in New France entered partnerships to learn a trade, and apprenticeship was still common, but these arrangements were often short-lived. Journeymen, those who had served their apprenticeship and were required to practise their trade as a wage earner for a period (usually six years) before becoming master craftsmen, virtually disappeared in New France. Most shops were small family affairs consisting of a master who worked with the help of his wife and older children, and perhaps one or two appren-

tices. They produced goods on order, not in large quantities, striving for honest subsistence and, if possible, an easy living, rather than ever-increasing wealth.

LABOUR

In pre-industrial society the problem of securing a reliable labour force had resulted in a variety of work-inducing institutions, including seigneurialism, indentured servitude, and slavery. All of these forms of labour took root in New France. Much of the work in New France conducted outside the family context was done within the structure of feudal obligations. Seigneurs could extract dues from their censitaires, who were also required to work a stipulated number of days on the seigneur's demesne. In addition, the Crown imposed the *corvée*, a requirement to work a certain number of days on public works. These obligations remained an important feature of the work world in New

France and, indeed, would be carried on for many years after the conquest.

Merchants or administrators requiring a fully committed workforce commonly used indentured labour, contracted for a specific period of time. The fur trade's *engagés*, or voyageurs, were usually recruited in the colony, as many as 400 a year. Perhaps because of the profits to be made and the adventure associated with the trade, it seems there was little difficulty finding enough young men willing to take the arduous trip into the interior. Because of the shortage of labourers, the Crown permitted soldiers in the colony to work for wages when they were not needed for military duties.

Acadians Repairing Dykes.

History Collection/Nova Scotia Museum NSM 871202

The shortage of labour led to the arrival of one of the largest groups of eighteenth-century immigrants: men who had been condemned as smugglers for attempting to circumvent the dreaded salt tax (*gabelle*). Between 1721 and 1749 over 700 salt smugglers and other petty criminals were shipped to New France to relieve the labour shortage. They do not seem to have been treated much differently from engagés. A dispatch from the Minister of Marine in 1739 announced that, of 81 salt smugglers sent to Canada, all had either been incorporated into the troops or distributed to individuals or communities offering good contracts. They were not hardened criminals and were regarded in the colony as individuals possessing a great deal of initiative, creativity, and independence of mind, all qualities admired and useful in a society itself in creation.

SLAVERY

Both Native and African peoples were employed as slaves in New France. While the numbers are difficult to determine, historians estimate that about 400 enslaved blacks came to Canada between 1690 and 1760 and at least 216 to Louisbourg. African slaves were more common in Louisiana, the Illinois country, and the French West Indies. Most of the African slaves who came to Canada and Île Royale were purchased from one of these colonies or picked up as "prizes" in raids on the English colonies. Native slaves formed a slight majority of the enslaved population in Canada. They began arriving in the colony in the late 1680s when French explorers and fur traders purchased a number of Pawnee in the Mississippi region. The French called all slaves of Native origin *panis* (Pawnee), but they took slaves from a number of First Nations.

Slave owners were uncertain of the status of their chattels, especially Native slaves, until 1709 when Intendant Jacques Raudot proclaimed slavery to be legal. Black slaves throughout the French Empire were governed by the Code Noir. Under its provisions, slaves could be bought and sold as property, but their owners were obliged to house, feed, and clothe them properly and care for the aged and infirm. Slaves were to be encouraged to marry, and all of them were to be instructed and baptized in the Roman Catholic religion. Although masters could whip their slaves, they could not imprison or execute them without recourse to the courts. Women were not to be sexually exploited, nor were children to be sold separately from their parents before reaching adolescence.

Slaves, whether black or Aboriginal, were expensive. The price of a black slave ranged between 200 and 2400 livres and averaged about 900 livres. Native slaves were worth less, about 400 livres, their lower life expectancy, abundant supply, and greater likelihood of escape all conspiring to suppress their value. Because of their cost, slaves were purchased only by the wealthier colonials. Governor Charles de Beauharnois owned 27 slaves. Bishop Laval owned slaves as did Marguerite d'Youville, founder of the Soeurs Grises. Institutions operated by the church often relied heavily on the labour of their unhappy chattels. Like all moveable property, slaves could be passed on by inheritance. Charles Le Moyne, the first Baron de Longueuil, left seven slaves when he died—a mother and father and their five children. He instructed that they be divided between his two sons.

Both black and Native slaves had an appallingly short life expectancy: 17.7 years for Natives and 25.2 for Africans, compared to nearly 50 for white colo-nials. Slaves could marry only with the permission of their owners, and their children became the master's property too. Baptismal records usually record only the master's name, not that of the mother. Nearly 60 percent of slave children were born out of wedlock, sometimes fathered by other slaves, more likely by the master or the master's son. As a result, Métis and mulatto children were relatively common in the elite families who owned slaves. Blacks and Natives were encouraged to marry each other, and 45 of these "mixed" marriages were recorded.

Few records have survived of slave resistance to their treatment. An exception is the case of Marie-Joseph Angélique who, when threatened with sale, set fire to her owner's house and ran away. She was caught and condemned to death for defying her master. A more positive case is recorded in 1753 in Louisbourg, where Jean-Baptiste Cupidon, a free black servant, purchased the freedom of his future bride Catherine from her owner for 500 livres, a sum equal to more than a year's wage for a common labourer or artisan.

CONCLUSION

By 1750, most of the people in New France had been born in North America and were beginning to call themselves "Canadians" and "Acadians." With little more than a century of colonial settlement behind them, they had succeeded in adapting to a new climate, in creating an uneasy alliance with their Aboriginal neighbours, and making North America their home. They may have been subjects of the French king, but they had also become citizens of their own new world.

Voices from the Past

Shipping a Slave to Louisbourg

Throughout the Americas, if slaves showed any sign of resisting their owners they were often sold to new owners. In 1753, the following letter was sent from a merchant in the French colony of Martinique in the West Indies to the Louisbourg firm of Beaubassin and Silvain. It reveals the degree to which slaves were treated as just another commodity to be bought and sold.

> I have put aboard the *Ste Rose* a Negro by the name of Toussaint, to ask that you get rid of him for me at any price. He belongs to one of my friends who wants to get [him] out of these islands because of the excessively strong habits he has here. Please do me the pleasure of rendering him the service of having him remain in Louisbourg, and of selling him to someone who will never bring him back here. He is a baker by trade. As for the price of the sale, you can use it for whatever you think best, whether cod or something else.[4]

The Status of Women in New France

Historians disagree about how to interpret the status of women in New France. Jan Noel has argued that the unusual conjunction of cultural heritage, demographic features, and economic conditions combined to make women in the colony "femmes favorisées."[5] She cites examples of 20 outstanding women in business, church, and politics who made their mark on the colony's history, and she comments on the level of education—usually better than that of men in the colony—and the range and freedom of action that colonial women enjoyed. Such examples, Noel maintains, suggest that women in New France had more opportunities than did their contemporaries in New England and Europe, and more even than women in the nineteenth century. More recently Terence Crowley echoes Noel's point that the role played by women in the church hierarchy "contrasted sharply with the situation in British possessions to the south," and "allowed them to make a vital contribution to colonial development."[6]

There is considerable evidence to back up Noel's position. In particular, the female religious orders produced women of outstanding intellectual achievements and administrative abilities. Marie de l'Incarnation, Jeanne Mance, and Marguerite Bourgeoys stand shoulder to shoulder with Champlain, Maisonneuve, and Laval for their pioneering activities in the New World. Moreover, women were often instrumental in raising the money needed for commercial and religious ventures in the colonies. For example, Hélène Boullé, who married Champlain at the age of 12, was a wealthy heiress whose dowry financed her husband's early expeditions. Another woman, Madame de Guercheville, never came to the New World but used her wealth to finance Jesuit activities in Acadia. When she became suspicious of the motives of the fur traders in charge of developing Port Royal, she purchased (with her husband's permission) de Monts' rights in New France. She held title to Acadia until she relinquished her claims to the Compagnie de la Nouvelle France in 1627.

Micheline Dumont, one of the authors of a collective history of Quebec women, takes issue with Noel's perspective. She maintains that women in the seventeenth century may have played a unique role because of the exceptional circumstances prevailing in the infant colony, but that by the eighteenth century their status had become more like that of their sisters in France.[7] And while it is true that women in New France were sometimes forced to do the tasks traditionally assigned to men, they saw their fate as an aberration, not a step toward some ideal of liberation. Madeleine de Verchères, for instance, who claimed to have organized the defence of her village against an Iroquois attack in 1692, argued for a pension on the grounds that she was an unusual woman with "feelings which lead me to glory, just like many men." Most women, she implied, would not aspire to such acts of heroism.

Dumont also cautions historians not to confuse privileges based on class with the experience of all women. As in France, elite women in New France had considerable scope for action under the laws of the ancien régime, especially when they acted on behalf of their husbands or in segregated religious orders. Marie La Tour fought to the death to defend her absent husband's fort in Acadia in 1645, but such leadership was expected of wives in this period. In New France, women may have stretched the boundaries of the limitations placed upon them, but at no time were those boundaries ever erased. Others have added that no woman ever served as a governor, a priest, an intendant, a military commander, a notary, a sovereign councillor, or a judge, and as far as we can tell no one ever argued that they should have done so.

Finally, by emphasizing exceptional women, Dumont argues, historians often overlook the significant contribution that women made to colonial society through their productive and reproductive work within the family. In pre-industrial European and colonial society, the family was the fundamental unit of economic life. The bearing and rearing of children, the growing and preparing of food, the making of cloth and warm clothing, and the nursing and nurturing of family and friends—all carried on almost exclusively within the domestic setting—were fundamental to the survival of the family, the community, and the colony.

Even if Dumont's cautions are correct, it remains the case that women in New France functioned in a different environment than the one that prevailed in France or even in nearby New England. The important institutional roles played by the church and state, the significance of the fur trade and the military establishment, the absence of deeply rooted traditions, the influence of First Nations, and perhaps even the particular cultural practices brought by the few thousand immigrants selected from French society to settle in North America: all these elements combined to produce, if not a totally new society, at least a considerably altered one.

Perhaps women in New France were not so much *favorisées* as challenged to adapt their traditional notions of gender roles to the colonial environment. The same could be said for men, whose roles were also reshaped by the colonizing experience. Together in New France, French women and men became Canadiennes and Canadiens, whose differences from their counterparts in old France became the cause for comment, and sometimes conflict, during the course of the eighteenth century.

NOTES

1 *Peter Kalm's Travels in North America*, vol. 2, ed. Aldolph B. Benson (New York: Dover Publications, 1966) 558.

2 Allan Greer, *The People of New France* (Toronto: University of Toronto Press, 1997) 24.

3 J.F. Bosher and J.-C. Dubé, "Bigot, François," in *Dictionary of Canadian Biography*, vol. 4, *1771 to 1800* (Toronto: University of Toronto Press, 1979) 59–70.

4 Kenneth Donovan, "Slaves in Ile Royale," *Acadiensis* 25.1 (Autumn 1995): 22.

5 Jan Noel, "New France: Les Femmes Favorisées," in *Rethinking Canada: The Promise of Women's History*, 3rd ed., ed. Veronica Strong-Boag and Anita Clair Fellman (Toronto: Oxford University Press, 1997) 33–56.

6 Terence Crowley, "Women, Religion and Freedom in New France," in *Women and Freedom in Early America*, ed. Larry Eldridge (New York: New York University Press, 1997) 110–11.

7 Micheline Dumont, "Les femmes de la Nouvelle-France: Étaient-elles favorisées?" *Atlantis* 8.1 (Fall 1982): 118–24; see also the Clio Collective, *Quebec Women: A History* (Toronto: Women's Press, 1987).

SELECTED READING

In addition to the works by Louise Dechêne, W.J. Eccles, Alan Greer, Jacques Mathieu, Dale Miquelon, Peter Moogk and Marcel Trudel cited in Chapter 4, see André Lachance, *La vie urbaine en Nouvelle-France* (Montreal: Boréal Express, 1987) and *Vivre, aimer et mourir en nouvelle France: La Vie quotidienne aux XVIIe et XVIIIe siècles* (Montreal: Libre Expression, 2000); Hubert Charbonneau, *Vie et mort de nos ancêtres* (Montreal: Les Presses de l'Université de Montréal, 1973) and *The First French Canadians* (Urbana: University of Illinois Press, 1993); and Lorraine Gadoury, *La famille dans son intime: Échanges epistolaires au sein de l'élite canadienne du XVIIIe siècle* (Montreal: Huburtise HMH, 1998).

Articles that explore specific topics include John F. Bosher, "The Family in New France," in *Readings in Canadian History: Pre-Confederation*, 3rd ed., ed. R. Douglas Francis and Donald B. Smith (Toronto: Holt, Rinehart and Winston, 1990); Allan Greer, "The Patterns of Literacy in Quebec, 1745–1899," *Histoire sociale/Social History* 11.22 (Nov. 1978); Terence Crowley, "'Thunder Gusts': Popular Disturbances in Early French Canada," *Historical Papers/ Communications historiques* (1979) and "Women, Religion and Freedom in New France," in *Women and Freedom in Early America*, ed. Larry Eldridge (New York: New York University Press, 1997); John Dickinson, "Reflexions sur la police en Nouvelle-France," *McGill Law Review* 32.2 (1987);

Kenneth Donovan, "Tattered Clothes and Powdered Wigs: Case Studies of the Poor and Well-to-Do in Eighteenth Century Louisbourg," in *Cape Breton at 200: Historical Essays in Honour of the Island's Bicentennial, 1785–1985*, ed. Kenneth Donovan (Sydney: University College of Cape Breton Press, 1985); Lilianne Plamondon, "A Businesswoman in New France: Marie-Anne Barbel, the Widow Fornel," in *Rethinking Canada: The Promise of Women's History*, ed. Veronica Strong-Boag and Anita Clair Fellman (Toronto:

Copp Clark Pitman, 1986); Louise Dechêne, "L'Évolution du régime seigneurial au Canada: le cas de Montréal aux XVIIe et XVIIIe siècles," *Recherches sociographiques* 12.2 (1971); and Yves Zoltvany, "Esquisse de la Coutume de Paris," *Revue d'histoire de l'Amérique française* 25.3 (1971). On slavery in New France, see Marcel Trudel, "Ties That Bind," *Horizon Canada* (1985) and Kenneth Donovan, "Slaves and Their Owners in Île Royale, 1713-1760," *Acadiensis* 25.1 (Autumn, 1995): 3–32.

WEBLINKS

SOUERS GRISES
www.newadvent.org/cathen/07031a.htm

An excerpt from the New Catholic Encyclopedia offers information on the origins of the Grey Nuns of Montreal.

CODE NOIR
www.ciral.ulaval.ca/alx/amlxmonde/amsudant/guyanefr1685.htm

This site offers the text of the Code Noir in French.

E-STAT
http://estat.statcan.ca

Census data on New France can be found at Statistics Canada's E-STAT, which offers reliable and timely statistics about Canada and its people.

UPPER TOWN
http://parkscanada.pch.gc.ca/unesco/QUEBEC/Quebec_e.htm

This site offers a brief description of the historic section of Quebec City, with links to other significant locations in and around the city.

LAVAL UNIVERSITY HISTORY DEPARTMENT
www.fl.ulaval.ca/hst/index.htm

Laval's site aims to give users links to resources on the study of history.

Empires in Conflict, 1715–1763

[This] part of my duty... is very disagreeable to my nature and temperament as I know [it] must be grievous to you who are of the same species...your lands and tenements, cattle of all kinds and livestock of all sorts are forfeited to the Crown with all other effects, except your money and household goods and you yourselves to be removed from this Province. [It is] his Majesty's orders that the whole French inhabitants of these districts be removed from this province....[1]

With these words, spoken on 5 September 1755, Colonel John Winslow informed the 418 Acadian men assembled at the church in Grand Pré that they and their families were to be expelled from Nova Scotia. The deportation of the Acadians was only one of a series of dramatic events that transformed North America in the mid-eighteenth century. Between 1744 and 1763 a state of almost continuous warfare scattered the Acadians to distant ports, sealed the fate of New France, and profoundly altered the relationships between Natives and newcomers. The War of the Austrian Succession (1744–48) set the ball rolling.

ENEMIES AND ALLIES

The long period of relatively peaceful relations between 1713 and 1744 had given Great Britain and France a chance to position themselves for another contest. On the surface, the British had the upper hand in North America. Their colonies had grown in population and wealth, while the French holdings remained sparsely settled and economically dependent upon their mother country. In theory, when the British colonies conscripted human resources for war, they could draw upon a population base of nearly one million people; French possessions, including Louisbourg and Louisiana, had less than one-tenth that number.

Balanced against this demographic reality was the Native population of North America. Although the Treaty of Utrecht gave Britain control over Iroquois territory and the Hudson Bay region, the new rulers were slow to establish control in these areas. France, in contrast, aggressively pursed Native alliances. By the 1740s, most of the interior of the continent and the Atlantic frontier were occupied by First Nations loosely allied with France.

The success of the French in developing alliances with the First Nations was a result, in part, of Louis XIV's decision to use the fur trade as a diplomatic tool. By supplying the Natives with manufactured items, including the weapons they needed for hunting and fighting, the French became valued trading partners.

The French had learned early in their colonization experience that Aboriginal peoples would accept neither European claims to land ownership and sovereignty nor French laws and taxes. If alliances were to succeed, the French were obliged to recognize the original inhabitants of North America as "free and independent people" with title to their ancestral lands. Alliances embodying such provisions were signed with much pomp and ceremony and were reinforced by the annual distribution of "King's presents." These agreements remained secure only as long as the French were willing to accept the fact that they were partners and protective patriarchs, not overlords.

Natives had their own reasons for entering into alliances with the foreigners in their midst. They enjoyed the increased material wealth that resulted from trade and used European alliances to enhance their power in relation to other First Nations. Moreover, after many years of contact, Aboriginal peoples in the eastern regions of North America had been drawn into family relationships with the French and converted to Roman Catholicism. Even had they wished to do so, they would have found it difficult to disentangle themselves from the Europeans who had made North America their home. Natives also recognized that wars among European nations were often waged on their ancestral lands, making it impossible for them to remain neutral. This reality was most obvious in the

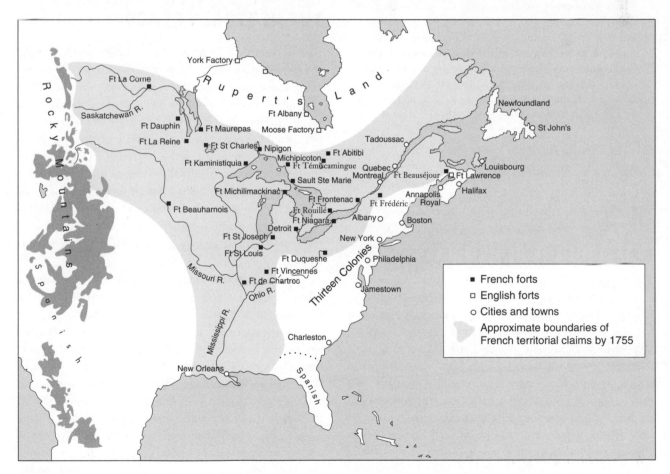

Map 7.1

France in America, 1755.

Adapted from J.L. Finlay, *Pre-Confederation Canada: The Structure of Canadian History*, 3rd. ed. (Scarborough, ON: Prentice-Hall, 1989) 68. Reprinted with permission by Pearson Education Canada.

Atlantic region and the Ohio territory, where the settlement frontier was fast encroaching on a "middle ground" of joint European–Native occupation.

Like the European nations, the First Nations differed in their approach to military alliances. The Iroquois initially tried to remain neutral and profit from European rivalries. Their strategic geographical location between the French and British colonies, and the hard lessons learned in earlier wars, made this the logical approach to take. In Acadia and the Ohio-Mississippi region, First Nations tended to form alliances with the French because of the threat that expanding Anglo-American settlement posed to their territorial claims. The Iroquois who sought sanctuary in the French missions understood this reality when they stated in 1754:

> Brethren, are you ignorant of the difference between our Father [the French] and the English? Go see the forts our Father has erected, and you will see that the land beneath his walls is still hunting ground, having fixed himself in those places we frequent, only to supply our wants; whilst the English, on the contrary, no sooner get possession of a country than the game is forced to leave it; the trees fall down before them, the earth becomes bare, and we find among them hardly wherewithal to shelter us when the night falls.[2]

For the Natives as much as for the French in North America, the rise of the British Empire and the birth of the United States of America in the second half of the eighteenth century would force major adjustments.

BRITISH RULE IN THE ATLANTIC REGION

Nowhere was the three-way struggle for power more intense than in the Atlantic region. By the Treaty of Utrecht, the French ceded "All Nova Scotia or Accadie, comprehending its ancient boundaries," to Great Britain. France tried to make the best out of a bad bargain by claiming that the "ancient boundaries" of Acadia included only the Nova Scotia peninsula. The British argued that the traditional French definition of Acadia included the area north of the Bay of Fundy. Because it was a critical territorial link in both colonial empires, Britain and France jockeyed for control over the borderland region.

The British were initially slow to establish a major presence in their Atlantic colonies. Following the 1710 capture of Port Royal, renamed Annapolis Royal in honour of Queen Anne, a garrison of fewer than 500 British and colonial soldiers was stationed in Nova Scotia. British fishing fleets returned to St John's, which had been sacked twice by the French during the war, but the official policy remained one of discouraging settlement in Newfoundland. With only a few British settlers and servants in Newfoundland—less than 3000 year-round residents in 1713—a population of about 2000 Roman Catholic Acadians in Nova Scotia, and hostile Beothuk, Mi'kmaq, and Maliseet throughout the region, there was little incentive to establish the full apparatus of colonial administration or to encourage immigration.

THE NEUTRAL FRENCH

By the Treaty of Utrecht, the Acadians were granted the liberty "to remove themselves within a year to any other place, as they shall think fit, together with their moveable effects." Those who decided to remain were to be "subject to the Kingdom of Great Britain" and permitted "to enjoy the free exercise of their religion, according to the usage of the church of Rome, as far as the laws of Great Britain allow the same." Most of the Acadians opted to remain on their farms in the Bay of Fundy region. Acadia had changed hands several times during the previous century, and it was possible that their homeland could once again be returned to France.

British officials tried to persuade the Acadians to take an oath of allegiance, but their new subjects made it clear that any oath of loyalty must include explicit guarantees that they not be required to take up arms against the French and Mi'kmaq. Such a provision was the only practical alternative to becoming the victims in the crossfire between the British and the French and their Native allies. In 1729 and 1730, Governor Richard Phillips verbally conceded this exemption when he administered an oath of allegiance to men over 15 years of age in many Acadian settlements. British authorities were thus forced to admit defeat in their efforts to secure an unqualified oath of allegiance from the people they sneeringly dubbed "neutral French."

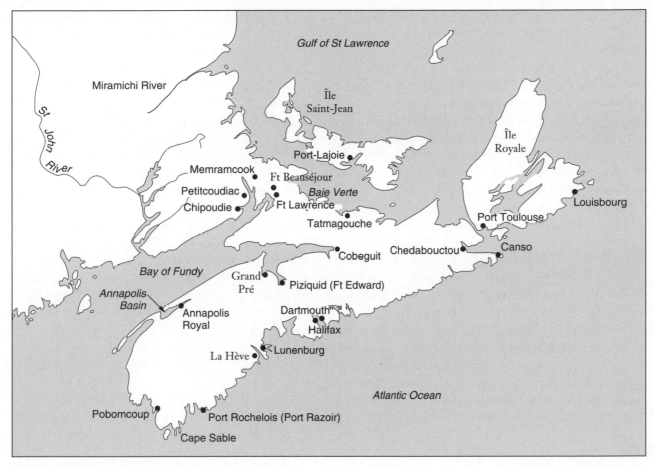

Map 7.2
Nova Scotia/Acadia in the eighteenth century.

The three decades following the conquest of 1713 must have seemed, in retrospect, a golden age to the Acadians. Family life flourished, population grew, economic opportunities beckoned, and the hand of authority was light. Settlement expanded up the Chipaudie, Petitcoudiac, and Memramcook estuaries, and along the eastern shore from Baie Verte to the Baie des Chaleurs. With the establishment of Louisbourg, the Acadians had an alternative to the Boston market for surplus products from their farms and fisheries. Hard work and a healthy climate gave them a better than average chance of reaching old age surrounded by an expanding network of kin. By 1750, there were over 9000 Acadians in "Nova Scotia or Accadie" and 3000 more scattered throughout the rest of the region.

MI'KMAQ AND MALISEET

Although the Treaty of Utrecht made no mention of any territorial rights of Natives in the Atlantic region, British authorities tried to insist that the Mi'kmaq and Maliseet, like the Acadians, swear an oath of allegiance to the British Crown. In return they were offered the same privileges that the Acadians enjoyed in religious matters and government-sponsored trading posts called "truck-houses." The Mi'kmaq and Maliseet were not impressed with the proposal. They had never sworn allegiance to the French, and they had no intention of doing so to the British. Nor did they have much need of trading posts; they usually obtained better prices from the

French or from the ships of various nations that arrived in their inshore waters every spring.

When French authorities learned that the British were attempting to exert control over the Natives in the Atlantic region, they sent Canadian-born missionary Antoine Gaulin to convince the Mi'kmaq to move to Île Royale. Like the Acadians, the Mi'kmaq were reluctant to do so, except on a seasonal basis to receive their "presents" from the French. Political priests were key to maintaining Native alliances. In addition to Gaulin, who served in the region from 1689 to 1731, Pierre-Antoine-Simon Maillard orchestrated French-Mi'kmaq relations from his base on Chapel Island, Île Royale from 1735 to 1758. Jean-Louis Le Loutre, whose missions on the mainland of Nova Scotia included the Acadians as well as Mi'kmaq from 1737 to 1755, was so effective in his political activities that the British finally put a price on his head.

The Mi'kmaq needed little encouragement from the French to challenge the British presence in Nova Scotia. In 1720, they drove the New England fishing fleet out of Canso, justifying their act as protecting the land that God had given them. During the summer of 1722, Mi'kmaq mariners were reported to have captured 36 vessels in the waters off Nova Scotia. The New Englanders and the British authorities in Nova Scotia were quick to retaliate. For the next three years, the New England–Nova Scotia frontier was embroiled in a bloody "Indian War." In the summer of 1724, the Mi'kmaq even attacked Annapolis Royal, burning part of the town and killing several British soldiers.

Peace treaties were concluded in Boston and Falmouth (in present-day Maine) in 1725 and ratified at Annapolis Royal the following year. These agreements included recognition of British sovereignty over "Nova Scotia or Accadie" as well as of the traditional hunting and fishing rights of the Mi'kmaq and Maliseet. It was the classic stand-off, with both sides interpreting the agreement in ways that the other failed, or refused, to understand.

WAR OF THE AUSTRIAN SUCCESSION, 1744–1748

The test of Acadian neutrality and Native alliances came in 1744, when the lack of a male heir in the Hapsburg line provoked a war in Europe over the succession to the Austrian throne. Britain and Holland supported the claims of the Archduchess Maria Theresa, while France and Prussia opposed her right to rule. Three weeks before the news reached Annapolis Royal and Boston, Governor Le Prévost Duquesnel at Louisbourg learned that war had been officially declared. Following his instructions from France, Duquesnel authorized privateers to attack New England shipping, dispatched a force to capture Canso, and made plans to attack Annapolis Royal.

Inevitably, the New Englanders were alarmed by these developments on their northeastern frontier. With the encouragement of Governor William Shirley of Massachusetts, a volunteer militia of 4300 men led by William Pepperell was organized to attack Louisbourg. A squadron from the West Indies under the command of Commodore Peter Warren provided naval support. In the spring of 1745, the New Englanders pounded the mighty fortress for seven weeks before forcing its surrender on 17 June. In 1746, the French sent a squadron of 54 ships carrying 7000 men, commanded by the Duc d'Anville, to recapture Louisbourg. The expedition was dogged with bad luck and retreated without even reaching its objective. With communications between France and its North American colonies at the mercy of the British fleet, the French colonials were left to pursue their own wartime strategies.

Authorities in Quebec took steps to secure their frontiers by launching raids against New York and Massachusetts, and increased the volume of trade and present-giving among their Native allies. On their eastern front, 300 militia men under Captain Louis Coulon de Villiers embarked on a classic guerrilla campaign against Annapolis Royal. They made their way through heavy winter snows to Grand Pré, where they encountered 500 New England troops quartered in Acadian homes. Alerted by several Acadians, de Villiers and his men surrounded the houses where the New Englanders were sleeping, killed 70 of them, including their leader Colonel Arthur Noble, and forced the rest to surrender.

The "Massacre of Grand Pré," as the English called it, put the Acadian strategy of neutrality in serious jeopardy. While it was clear that some of the Acadians had warned Noble about the French pres-

MORE TO THE STORY

Life in the Colonial Militia

The feats of bravery and endurance of Canadian militiamen have become the stuff of legend. In the eyes of their enemies, the Canadians possessed superhuman abilities. They were capable of travelling hundreds of kilometres in the dead of winter, their knowledge of the terrain equalled that of their Native allies, and they were crack shots with their flintlock muskets. As experts in *la petite guerre* (guerrilla warfare), they had few equals. They were also noted for their cunning and cruelty. In the early years of settlement, they commonly attacked their enemies at night, sometimes burned their captives in their homes, and spared neither women nor children. Although the cruelty of border raids abated considerably in the eighteenth century, the Canadian militia remained widely respected and feared.

The French authorities made every effort to keep their militia in top fighting condition. After 1669, every Canadian male between the ages of 16 and 60 who was capable of bearing arms was subject to conscription and monthly military training. In 1752, when Governor Ange de Menneville Duquesne discovered that the militia was not up to scratch, he ordered weekly exercises and required that each soldier have a rifle, a full powder horn, and at least 20 bullets. Militiamen wore civilian clothes and were thus spared the expense of buying a costly uniform. The young men who cut their teeth on the gruelling fur-trade expeditions into the pays d'en haut clearly had the advantage over their farm-based cousins in the militia, but most men in the colony were accustomed to hunting and knew the basics of frontier survival.

Few men, it seems, tried to shirk their military responsibilities, and many men aspired to the social and political rewards that went with the unpaid position of militia captain. The old feudal emphasis on military loyalties coupled with the desper-

A Canadian militiaman going into battle on showshoes.

National Archives of Canada/C1854

ate attempt to save the cherished homeland meant that almost all male colonists were willing to serve. Following the conquest of 1760, British commanders and British traditions dulled the Canadian enthusiasm for military exploits, but during the French regime the Canadian militia was, René Chartrand argues, the best fighting force on the continent.[3]

ence in the area, he had not believed them. After the event, when the English discussed Acadian policy, it would be the "treacherous informers" and "traitors," not those who had maintained a desperate neutrality, who would be remembered.

Further reprisals were temporarily averted when the two sides agreed to a negotiated peace. By the Treaty of

Aix-la-Chapelle in 1748, Britain and France restored their captured possessions. This policy meant that France gave up its conquests in the Netherlands and India in return for Louisbourg. The New Englanders were appalled by Britain's apparent lack of concern for their safety and well-being and insisted that their northeastern frontier be properly defended.

THE UNEASY PEACE IN ACADIA, 1749–1755

All sides—French, British, and Native—moved immediately to strengthen their positions for the war that was certain to come very soon. Again the activity was particularly intense in the Atlantic region. In 1749, the French reoccupied Louisbourg, and the British, aware of resentment in their colonies, decided to build a fortified base on the Nova Scotia peninsula. In the spring of 1749, Edward Cornwallis led an expedition of 2500 soldiers, settlers, and servants to found Halifax on the shores of Chebucto Bay.

As governor of Nova Scotia, Cornwallis was determined to bring both the Aboriginal peoples and the Acadians under his authority. Since the Treaty of Aix-la-Chapelle had failed to mention the Natives, the British claimed that it was necessary for the First Nations that had fought with the French to sign separate peace treaties. While the Maliseet and their allies the Passamaquoddy on the north shore of the Bay of Fundy were prepared to reconfirm the treaty of 1725–26 with Cornwallis and his emissaries, the Mi'kmaq were defiant. They resumed their attacks against the British on land and sea and harassed the British base at Halifax, which was located on one of the Mi'kmaq's favourite summer encampments. Cornwallis responded by offering a reward of 10 guineas for every "savage taken or his scalp." The Mi'kmaq in turn declared war on the British for having settled their lands without permission and for undertaking to exterminate them. A formal declaration of war was drawn up with the help of Abbé Maillard and Abbé Le Loutre.

The declaration of hostilites by the Mi'kmaq gave the French the opportunity they were looking for to extend their influence in the region. In 1750, they built Fort Beauséjour north of the Missaguash River on the Isthmus of Chignecto. Cornwallis reacted quickly, dispatching Lieutenant-Colonel Charles Lawrence and two regiments with orders to construct a fort within sight of Beauséjour. Meanwhile, the Mi'kmaq continued to attack the British. In 1751, they even conducted a successful raid on the new community of Dartmouth across the harbour from Halifax. Cornwallis's successor, Peregrine Hopson, managed to persuade a few Mi'kmaq to sign his treaty of peace and friendship in 1752, but it had little impact. With more than 1000 Acadian men within two days' march of Fort Beauséjour, and 400 Natives allies encamped at nearby Baie Verte, the French had proved once again that they were masters of war in time of peace.

THE SOUTHWESTERN FRONTIER IN QUESTION

In Canada, Governor La Galissonnière made impressive plans for defending French interests in North America. He sent a detachment to the mouth of the St John River, strengthened the forts in the Lake Champlain region, and dispatched a military expedition under Pierre-Joseph Céloron de Blainville into the Ohio Valley. Friendly Iroquois were gathered at La Présentation (Ogdensburg, New York) by Sulpician priest Abbé Picquet to serve as a buffer between New France and New York. To protect their communications from Fort Frontenac to Fort Niagara, the French put a small fleet on Lake Ontario. Fort Rouillé was built in 1750 at present-day Toronto, site of a strategic portage.

With British activity in the interior undermining Native alliances, it was imperative that the French act decisively. The scope of Anglo-American ambitions was revealed by the creation of the Ohio Company in 1748. Sustained by capital invested by London merchants and such powerful Virginia families as the Lees, Fairfaxes, and Washingtons, the Ohio Company planned to make vast profits by selling half a million acres to land-hungry settlers.

In 1752, a new governor, the Marquis de Duquesne, arrived at Quebec with orders to drive the British out of the Ohio. Duquesne sent 300 Troupes de la Marine, 1700 Canadian militia, and 200 allied Natives into the Lake Erie region to construct a road to the headwaters of the Ohio and establish forts at strategic locations. In 1753, Governor Robert Dinwiddie of Virginia sent George Washington to the region to officially protest French activities, but the delegation received a polite rebuff from French commander Jacques Saint-Pierre at Fort Le Boeuf (present-day Waterford, Pennsylvania). Fort

MORE TO THE STORY

Early Days in Halifax

Halifax, founded in 1749, represented Britain's first serious attempt to colonize the French possessions acquired by the Treaty of Utrecht of 1713. Named after the chief officer of the Board of Trade and Plantations, the garrison town attracted a curious mix of immigrants, including artisans from London, soldiers and sailors discharged from the recent war, and New Englanders eager to profit from the vast sums of money being invested in the frontier colony. With the arrival of 2500 German- and French-speaking "foreign Protestants" between 1750 and 1753, Halifax boasted a population of over 5000, making it one of the largest towns in North America.

The capital of Nova Scotia, Halifax represented the latest thinking in urban planning. The town was laid out according to a rigidly symmetrical model plan, with rectangular streets moving up the steep slope from the waterfront. In the centre was the Grand Parade, which served as the focus of community life. An Anglican and a Presbyterian church faced the parade grounds alongside storehouses for munitions. On the landward side, the town was protected by a palisade and five forts, while water approaches were secured by three batteries. A common burial ground was located just outside the palisade.

In year-round communication with the North Atlantic world, Haligonians were kept informed about the latest developments by their local newspaper, the *Halifax Gazette*, founded in 1752. Its four pages of cramped print was by no means the principal vehicle of communication in Halifax. Since most people could not read or write, news was conveyed by word of mouth, and major events were announced by the town crier. Gossip travelled quickly through Halifax's compact streets, helped along by an abundance of taverns—estimated at as many as 100 by 1760—where merchants, administrators, soldiers, and civilians mingled regularly.

In the first decade after its founding, Halifax was a divided and unhappy community. Old and New Englanders nurtured ancient grudges while merchants and government officials clashed over contracts and public policy. A Jersey-born merchant, Joshua Mauger, took advantage of the chaos to gain ascendancy over both the economy and political institutions of the colony. Using his vast wealth gained from the West Indies trade and smuggling with Louisbourg before its capture in 1758, he advanced credit to the merchants in Halifax and soon became their indispensable patron. His monopoly of the manufacture of rum, protected from imports by a high customs duty, ensured that his wealth and influence would both continue to increase. A major player in administrative circles, Mauger became so powerful in London that he could secure the dismissal of governors and other officials who challenged his authority.

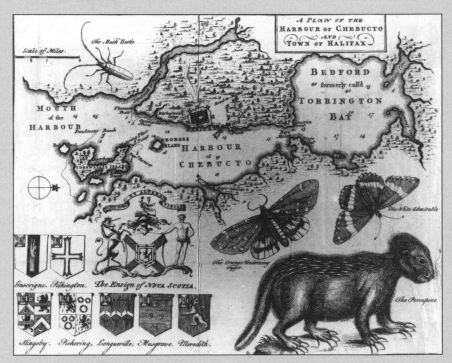

Map of Halifax with flora and fauna.
Nova Scotia Archives and Records Management PANS N-9893

Duquesne, built early in 1754 on the site of present-day Pittsburgh, stood as a symbol of French control over the region.

Washington returned in the spring of 1754 with a small detachment of militia to order the French out of the Ohio territory. When they encountered a French scouting party, led by Ensign Joseph de Jumonville, they attacked it, killing Jumonville and nine of his men. Such an attack at a time when the British and French were officially at peace brought a swift reaction. On 3 July, a force from Fort Duquesne, led by Jumonville's brother, Louis, caught up with Washington's party, which had taken refuge in a crude shelter aptly named Fort Necessity. After a bruising assault that lasted nine hours, Washington surrendered. He and his surviving men were allowed to retreat in safety, but by the terms of the capitulation agreement the Virginians promised to abandon all claims to the disputed Ohio territory.

THE BRITISH TAKE THE OFFENSIVE

The success of the French on the frontier forced the Anglo-American colonies into cooperation. In 1755, they launched a four-pronged attack against the outer defences of New France: Fort Beauséjour in Acadia, Fort Frédéric on Lake Champlain, Fort Niagara in the Great Lakes region, and Fort Duquesne. Major-General Edward Braddock and two regiments of regulars were sent by Britain to assist the colonial effort.

France in the meantime had sent out Jean-Armand, Baron de Dieskau, with 3000 Troupes de la Terre. Like the Troupes de la Marine, they were placed under the governor, who in 1755 was Pierre de Rigaud de Vaudreuil. The son of an earlier governor of the colony, he was the first Canadian-born appointee to the highest position in the colonial administration. Vaudreuil's strategy was to launch surprise attacks at various points along the American frontier. Guerrilla raids would keep the colonists terrorized, unnerve the British soldiers, put the enemy on the defensive, and take advantage of one of France's major assets: its Native alliances.

Major-General Braddock himself led the force that was organized to capture Fort Duquesne. Unused to frontier conditions, he failed miserably. A detachment of 108 colonial regulars, 146 Canadian militia, and 600 Indians defeated Braddock's army with little difficulty. Two-thirds of Braddock's 2200 men, and Braddock himself, were killed or wounded, while the French and their allies left the field with only 43 casualties. Braddock's papers, which revealed the plans for the other campaigns, were among the equipment abandoned by the British.

Governor Shirley of Massachusetts led the expedition against Fort Niagara, but his force of 2400 colonial militia was dissolved by disease and desertion before it reached its objective. The thrust toward Lake Champlain was blunted by a force led by Dieskau. Only on the Nova Scotia frontier were the British successful. A colonial militia of nearly 2500 men under the command of Lieutenant-Colonel Robert Monckton captured Fort Beauséjour on 12 June 1755 after a brief siege. With only 160 regular soldiers, and 300 Canadian militia and hastily conscripted Acadians, the French commander's position was hopeless.

THE ACADIAN DEPORTATION

Even before the fall of Beauséjour, British authorities had decided to expel the Acadians living north of the Missaguash River. The fate of the remaining Acadians was still to be decided, but when Fort Beauséjour surrendered, over 200 Acadians were discovered within its walls. With rumours circulating in the colony that the French were preparing to launch a counterattack, Lieutenant-Governor Charles Lawrence decided to act immediately to force the Acadians to do his bidding or face the consequences.

In July, delegates from the Acadian communities in peninsular Nova Scotia were summoned to Halifax and ordered to take an unqualified oath of allegiance. They refused to do so, promising only to remain neutral. Told that deportation would be the consequence of their refusal to take an unqualified oath, they stuck stubbornly to their position, even when given another chance to reconsider. Unfortunately for the Acadians, the strategies they had pursued in the past would no longer work. While these negotiations were taking place, word of Braddock's defeat reached Halifax. Panic spread throughout the town. The decision to deport the remaining Acadians was taken by Lawrence and his council on 28 July.

Lawrence moved quickly. Orders were sent to the military commanders at Chignecto, Piziquid, and Annapolis Royal instructing them to seize the men and boys so that the women and children would not try to escape. As soon as it could be arranged, transports from Boston would take them away. All Acadian land and livestock became the property of the Crown. The deportees could take only the goods they could carry with them. Their destination would be other British colonies in North America where they would be scattered like leaves before the wind.

Terror swept through the Acadian communities as the awful reality dawned. At Chignecto the men were summoned to Fort Cumberland (formerly Fort Beauséjour) to be told of their fate and held in captivity; 80 of them escaped by digging a tunnel and fleeing with their families into the nearby woods. The Acadians near Piziquid were imprisoned in Fort Edward. At Grand Pré, the parish church served as a makeshift prison until the transports arrived. Annapolis Royal was a different story. There the Acadians had prior warning, and many managed to escape before the authorities issued their fatal order. Whether free or captive, no Acadian was spared the horror of what followed. The British soldiers put

Acadian homes, barns, and churches to the torch and rounded up their cattle. In a few turbulent days in the late summer of 1755, the golden age of Acadian life came to a tragic end.

The horrors of the deportation did not end there. Authorities in the British colonies, with no idea that they were expected to receive hundreds of refugees, offered them little assistance. A few colonies even refused to accept their quota of "boat people" and sent them on their way. For many Acadians, their deportation from Nova Scotia marked the beginning of a lifetime of wandering that took some of them the length of North America and others to the West Indies, to Britain, or back to France. Nowhere did they feel at home. Even in France they felt like strangers and begged to be returned to the "New World" where they had been born.

Nor were the heart-rending events of 1755 the end of the deportations, which continued until 1762 and included the Acadians living in the captured colonies of Île Royale and Île Saint-Jean. In all, an estimated 11 000 Acadians had been removed from their native land. Many had died, including those drowned when their boats capsized during their endless wanderings. Nearly 1800 Acadians escaped to Canada, where they were among the most determined defenders of the colony during its siege in 1759–60. Acadians who were dumped in the southern colonies made their way to

Voices from the Past

Claude Bourgeois Pleads for Relief

Although there are no letters or diaries written by the deported Acadians, their desperate conditions while in exile prompted several petitions to authorities for relief. This petition, dated 24 May 1756, from Claude Bourgeois to the civil authorities in Massachusetts was signed with an X indicating that he found someone to help him write his plea for assistance.

> Claude Bourgeois, your Petitioner, one of the late French inhabitants of Nova Scotia, was sent with his family to Amesbury by order of the General Court [of Massachusetts], where he has resided constantly with his wife and six children; and begs leave to represent to your Honours, that about four weeks ago ten or twelve men came and took

away from him two of his daughters, one of the age of 25 years and the other 18, that his daughters were at that time employed in spinning for the Family, the poor remains of the Flax of wool which they had saved from Annapolis. Your Petitioner having fetched his Daughters home again, the Town have withheld their subsistence so that fourteen Days past he has received nothing at all to prevent them from starving, and the owner of the house where he lives threatens that he shall pay the rent of it by his children's labour. Your petitioner prays your Honours to relieve him under these circumstances, and your Petitioners shall ever pray, etc.[4]

Louisiana where their descendants, called *Cajuns*, still live. Those who remained in Nova Scotia survived by hiding out in the woods and living with the Mi'kmaq. A few were rounded up and used as prison labour in the colony during the war.

The departure of the Acadians made the Mi'kmaq more vulnerable to Lawrence's efforts to conquer them. In May 1756, he authorized both military forces and civilians to destroy the Aboriginal settlements and offered rewards for the capture of men, women, and children. The final battle for the control of the border colony had begun in earnest.

The Expulsion of the Acadians at Fort Amherst, *by Lewis Parker.*

Permission of the Artist, Lewis Parker, Courtesy of Parks Canada

THE SEVEN YEARS' WAR, 1756–1763

In 1756, warfare on the frontiers of New France finally merged into a larger contest, known as the Seven Years' War. It was essentially a continuation of the War of the Austrian Succession, this time with France and Austria pitted against Britain and Prussia. Fought both in Europe and its colonies, this war would profoundly alter the balance of power in North America and open the way for a dramatic confrontation between Britain and its American colonies.

When war was declared, the Canadians moved quickly to secure the approaches to their colony. In 1756, Dieskau's successor, Louis-Joseph, the Marquis de Montcalm, led a successful expedition against Oswego, thus blocking British entry to the Great Lakes. In the following year, another campaign down the Lake Champlain route resulted in the capture of Fort William Henry. After the surrender, Montcalm's Native allies fell on the retreating British forces, killing 29 and taking over 100 prisoners.

This incident added fuel to the fire of intense hatred that was building in the Thirteen Colonies against their adversaries. On the frontier, French and Native raiding parties had made life intolerable for the English colonists. Governor Vaudreuil informed his superiors in 1756 that one of his commanders had been "occupied more than eight days merely in receiving scalps; that there is not an English party but loses some men, and that it was out of his power to render me an exact report of all the attacks our Indians made."[5]

Oswego and Fort William Henry were important victories for Montcalm, but they brought criticism from Vaudreuil, who felt that the European style of warfare was too formal for frontier conditions. As commander of the Troupes de la Marine, the militia, and Native forces, Vaudreuil championed the flexible guerrilla tactics of his army and was afraid that the conventional European fighting techniques used by Montcalm and his Troupes de la Terre would lead to disaster.

In 1757 William Pitt's accession as prime minister brought new energy to the British cause. Pitt focused military strategy on the colonies, directing British troops in large numbers—at least 23 000—and naval resources to the conquest of New France. While the Canadians were experts in frontier wars, they were more vulnerable to the formal campaigns envisioned by Pitt. If the British blockaded the northern coastline, the colonials would be required to provision their military and civilian population without help from France. Withstanding a prolonged siege would be virtually impossible.

As the British converged on the colony in 1758, the conflict between Montcalm and Vaudreuil intensified. Montcalm, with a force of 3600 men, won another major victory at Carillon (Ticonderoga) against a massive British army of 15 000 men, but he remained convinced that the best strategy was to abandon outlying defences and concentrate all available manpower on the St Lawrence heartland. Vaudreuil continued to insist that the outlying forts be defended and that guerrilla tactics were the best way of keeping the British troops divided and defeated. Montcalm was so discouraged by the situation in North America that he asked to be recalled. Instead, he was promoted to lieutenant-general, a rank that made him supreme commander of all French forces in North America. Vaudreuil was now required to submit to the dictates of his superior officer and watch his Canadian forces become secondary to the Troupes de la Terre from France.

While Vaudreuil and Montcalm were quarrelling over strategy, Louisbourg had been captured for the second time by the British. Jeffrey Amherst led a force of over 13 000 men who took the fortress, defended by 4000 soldiers, on 26 July 1758 after a seven-week siege. With the British navy under Admiral Edward Boscawen preventing the French from receiving provisions or reinforcements, there was little that people in Louisbourg could do other than keep the British engaged long enough to prevent a campaign against Quebec that summer.

THE SIEGE OF QUEBEC

It was clear that the British were circling ever closer on their prey. Following the capture of Louisbourg, the British occupied Île Saint-Jean (now anglicized as St John's Island) and squelched any remaining Mi'kmaq and Acadian resistance in the Atlantic region. In August, Colonel Bradstreet took Fort Frontenac, effectively cutting the French supply line to the Ohio region. The French were forced to blow up Fort Duquesne to prevent it from falling into British hands. In June 1759, the Royal Navy, under the command of Vice-Admiral Charles Saunders, appeared on the St Lawrence. As well as 18 000 sailors, the expedition carried over 8600 seasoned troops under the command of General James Wolfe. The siege of Quebec had begun.

The arrival of the British on the St Lawrence made it impossible for the French to hold the interior.

A view of Louisbourg as seen from the lighthouse during the siege of 1758.

P. Ince/National Archives of Canada/C5907

On 25 July, Fort Niagara surrendered after a siege of three weeks and Fort Rouillé was destroyed to prevent its capture by the British. Similarly, Fort Carillon and Fort Frédéric were blown up by the French as they retreated before an advancing army led by Jeffrey Amherst, who had become chief of the British forces in North America. The French commander Bourlamaque entrenched his troops at Île-aux-Noix on the Richelieu River, his last line of defence against the capture of Montreal.

Conditions in Quebec had become desperate even before British ships appeared on the St Lawrence. While Montcalm, Bigot, and their friends indulged themselves in the good times of the casino, ballroom, and banquet hall, the ordinary people faced rationing and even starvation. The presence of nearly 16 000 regular, militia, and Native soldiers added pressure to the limited supplies of food available in the colony. Prices had risen dramatically for any commodities that were still available, and even horses were being slaughtered to feed hungry mouths. Crop failure and an outbreak of typhus added to the misery. Only the arrival of 22 supply ships from France in May 1759 made it possible to feed the soldiers and civilians in the town until the fall harvest.

The British reasoned that the capture of Quebec would ensure the eventual surrender of the entire colony, but success would not come easily. Although the British succeeded in taking Pointe Lévis across the river from Quebec and laid waste to much of the surrounding countryside, they failed to land on the left flank of the town. Nor could they cut communications to the main supply base at Batiscan, 80 kilometres upstream from Quebec. Wolfe's forces launched an artillery bombardment from their base on Pointe Lévis, but the walled town remained invincible. Repeated landing attempts were driven back by a combined force of 4000 regular French troops, up to 10 000 Canadian militiamen, and 1000 Native warriors. In each encounter the British suffered heavy casualties.

Good luck rather than good management determined victory. On the night of 12 September, Wolfe managed to land nearly 4500 men at Anse-au-Foulon, a cove about three kilometres above Quebec. They scrambled up a steep cliff to the Plains of Abraham, where they stood in battle array on the morning of 13 September.

From a tactical point of view, the Battle of the Plains of Abraham was a blundering fiasco for both the French and the British. Wolfe ordered his men to form two lines below a crest of higher ground to await the French army, which arrived breathless from Beauport. With few rations, no reserves, and only one field gun, his position was tenuous. Montcalm could have waited for the British to charge uphill against his winded troops, or he could have remained within the stout walls of the town until reinforcements under Bougainville arrived from Batiscan to attack the British from the rear. He did neither. Instead, he lined up his troops outside the town walls and ordered them to charge in three columns. This strategy severely limited the number of men who could fire at any one time and resulted in the breaking of the charge under a withering British volley. As the French retreated in disarray to the protection of the town, Montcalm was mortally wounded and Wolfe lay dead on the battlefield.

Casualties were heavy on both sides—658 for the British and 644 for the French. Despite the retreat of the French, the British still held only the Plains of Abraham. Nevertheless, the war-weary inhabitants of the town, as well as the jaded Troupes de la Terre, were eager to surrender. On 19 September, the French troops left the fortress of Quebec, their flags unfurled, torches lit, drums beating, and fifes playing. The British navy returned home, and a garrison under Brigadier James Murray was left behind in the shambles of the old capital. They faced a cold winter, short rations, and a devastating outbreak of scurvy. Whenever they ventured outside the walls of the town for food or firewood, the British were attacked by Canadian militiamen and their Native allies, who also harassed anyone caught collaborating with the conqueror.

In the spring, a contingent of 7000 men under the Chevalier de Lévis, who had succeeded Montcalm, attempted to retake Quebec. Murray then made the same tactical blunder as Montcalm. Instead of waiting for an assault on the walled fortress, he ordered his troops to meet the French at Sainte-Foy. The British charged without success, were routed by a bayonet charge, and fled in disarray to Quebec. The arrival of the British navy with reinforcements prevented Lévis from following up his victory. Sainte-Foy was the last major engagement of the war. Although the French won that battle, they lost the war and the colony.

SURRENDER AND NEGOTIATION

Governor Vaudreuil surrendered New France to General Amherst on 8 September 1760. Although Amherst refused to grant the honours of war to the French troops, he responded in a practical way to Vaudreuil's pleas for leniency in dealing with the conquered Canadians. Under the Articles of Capitulation, everyone who wished to do so could leave the colony and take their possessions with them. Those who remained were granted security of property and person. Canadians were granted freedom to practise their Roman Catholic faith, but the status of enforced tithing remained in doubt. Amherst refused Vaudreuil's request to permit the king of France to name the Roman Catholic bishop of the colony, and he reserved decision on the rights of the Jesuits, Récollets, and Sulpicians to continue their ministries. In contrast, the female religious orders were granted their customary privileges.

The Acadians who had sought refuge in Canada were given permission to go to France, but they were specifically excluded from the guarantees against deportation that were given to the French and Canadians. Afraid that the British would deprive the conquered people of their valuable human property, Vaudreuil secured guarantees for the continuance of black and Aboriginal slavery and the right of owners to bring up their slaves "in the Roman Religion." Vaudreuil

also attempted to protect his Native allies from the wrath of the conqueror. Article XL provided that "Indian allies" of the French were to be "maintained in the lands they inhabit" and were not to be "molested" for having fought against the British.

Until the peace treaty was signed in Paris on 10 February 1763, New France was ruled by martial law. The British gave some thought to exchanging their conquered territory for Guadaloupe, but the Treaty of Paris confirmed British possession of all of New France, except for Saint-Pierre and Miquelon. The French were also granted permission to fish on the Treaty Shore of Newfoundland. Louisiana, which had not been a theatre of war, was divided along the Mississippi, with Britain receiving the eastern section and navigational rights to the mighty river. In a separate treaty, France ceded the area west of the Mississippi to its ally Spain.

During the negotiations, France showed surprisingly little interest in regaining Canada, which philosopher Voltaire dismissed as "a few acres of snow." As well, the French took some pleasure in

This engraving is one of 12 views of Quebec City based on drawings by Richard Short, a naval officer with the British fleet in 1759. It offers evidence of the effects on the city of months of British bombardment, during which one-third of the buildings were destroyed and many more so badly damaged that they had to be pulled down.

National Archives of Canada/C350

biography

Montcalm and Wolfe
The Marquis de Montcalm

Born in 1712 to a distinguished family in France, young Louis-Joseph de Montcalm was commissioned as an ensign in the Hainault Regiment at the age of nine. He began his active military career in 1732 after being educated at home. His tutor found him stubborn and opinionated, a view shared by his colonial nemesis Governor Vaudreuil. Married in 1736 to Angelique-Louise Talon de Boulay, the daughter of another aristocratic family, Montcalm rose easily through the military ranks and was knighted in 1743. He saw plenty of military action in Europe during the War of the Austrian Succession. Claiming long service (31 years, 11 campaigns, and 5 wounds), he applied for and in 1753 received a substantial pension. Montcalm might have ended his days enjoying the tranquil life of a gentleman at his chateau at Candiac. Instead, he responded to the call to serve in New France following Dieskau's capture in 1755. Montcalm arrived in Quebec in May 1756 and never returned to his native land. He died in the early morning hours of 14 September following his defeat on the Plains of Abraham and was buried in a shell crater under the floor of the chapel of the Ursuline nuns.

The Marquis de Montcalm had the dubious distinction of suffering one of the most disastrous military defeats of the eighteenth century. While some historians argue that he was the author of his own defeat, others see him as the victim of the French military system that was long overdue for major reform.

The Marquis de Montcalm.

National Archives of Canada/C27665

James Wolfe

Born in 1727, James Wolfe was educated in Westerham and Greenwich, England. He received his first military appointment in the 1st Regiment of Marines in which his father was a colonel. Like Montcalm, Wolfe saw action on the European continent during the War of the Austrian Succession. He also participated in the Battle of Culloden against the Scots in 1746 and was stationed in Scotland after the war. It was perhaps during the Scottish campaign that Wolfe developed the tough military policies for which he became infamous in New France. Following the capture of Louisbourg, in which he showed himself to be a gifted officer, Wolfe urged "an offensive and destructive" war in the region to prevent the Canadian "hell-hounds" from securing an advantage. He personally helped to lay waste to the settlements and fisheries in what is now northern New Brunswick and the Gaspé region as a prelude to the campaign against Quebec.

Despite his poor health, he was chosen by Sir William Pitt to command the expedition against the heart of New France. Like Montcalm, Wolfe died in the conflict, but, unlike his beaten adversary, Wolfe's reputation grew after the Battle of the Plains of Abraham. Many portraits and statues of Wolfe were produced to commemorate the hero of the hour, none more widely circulated than that by Benjamin West depicting, in a highly idealized style, Wolfe's death.

The Death of General Wolfe, *by Benjamin West.*

National Gallery of Canada/8007

the prospect of a full-scale confrontation erupting between Britain and its Thirteen Colonies, now that the French threat on the continent had been eliminated. In all of these negotiations the Natives were not represented, and their homelands were parcelled out to European powers as if North America were an empty frontier ripe for exploitation.

CONCLUSION

Britain emerged from the Seven Years' War as the dominant imperial power in North America. As we will see in the next chapter, its efforts to administer the colonial possessions met with failure on all sides. Not only did the British find themselves fighting a war with the First Nations on the frontier, but they also faced a rebellion in their colonies. The attempt to impose British political and legal institutions in Quebec also failed. As the British responded to these troublesome colonial realities, their policies increasingly resembled those of their French predecessors. Like the French, the British found themselves fighting the Thirteen Colonies, forging Native alliances, and resorting to aristocratic paternalism in a desperate attempt to maintain their North American empire.

NOTES

1 John Winslow's *Journal, Report of the Public Archives of Canada for 1905*, vol. II (Ottawa: King's Printer, 1906-1909), cited in Cornelius Jaenen, *Material Memory: Documents in Pre-Confederation History* (Don Mills: Addison Wesley, 1998) 69.

2 W.J. Eccles, *The Canadian Frontier, 1534–1760* (New York: Holt, Rinehart and Winston, 1969) 158.

3 See René Chartrand, "Death Walks on Snowshoes," *Horizon Canada* (1987) 1: 260–64.

4 Sally Ross and Alphonse Deveau, *The Acadians of Nova Scotia: Past and Present* (Halifax: Nimbus, 1992) 66.

5 G.F.G. Stanley, *New France: The Last Phase, 1744–1760* (Toronto: McClelland and Stewart, 1968) 147.

SELECTED READING

On Native-European relations in the eighteenth century, see texts by Olive Dickason, J.R. Miller, and Arthur Ray cited in Chapter 2. See also, L.S.F. Upton, *Micmacs and Colonists: Indian–White Relations in the Maritimes, 1713–1867* (Vancouver: UBC Press, 1979); Richard White, *The Middle Ground: Indians, Empires, and Republics in the Great Lakes Region, 1650–1815* (Cambridge: Cambridge University Press, 1991); Cornelius J. Jaenen, "French Sovereignty and Native Nationhood during the French Regime," *Native Studies Review* 2.1 (1986); Olive Dickason, "Amerindians between French and English in Nova Scotia, 1713–1763," *American Indian Culture and Research Journal* 10.4 (1986): 31–56, and "Louisbourg and the Indians: A Study in Imperial Race Relations," *History and Archaeology* 6 (1976): 1–206; Jennifer Reid, *Myth, Symbol, and Colonial Encounter: British and Mi'kmaq in Acadia* (Ottawa: University of Ottawa Press, 1996), and Stephen E. Patterson, "Indian–White Relations in Nova Scotia, 1749–1761: A Study in Political Interaction," *Acadiensis* 23.1 (Autumn 1993): 23–59.

On the Acadians, see Naomi Griffiths, *The Acadians: Creation of a People* (Toronto: McGraw-Hill Ryerson, 1973) and *The Contexts of Acadian History, 1686–1784* (Montreal: McGill-Queen's University Press, 1992); and Andrew Hill Clark, *Acadia: The Geography of Early Nova Scotia to 1760* (Madison: University of Wisconsin Press, 1968); Sally Ross and Alphonse Deveau, *The Acadians of Nova Scotia: Past and Present* (Halifax: Nimbus, 1992). Earle Lockerby offers details on the appalling death rate of the Acadians deported from Île Saint-Jean in "The Deportation of the Acadians from Île St-Jean, 1758," *Acadiensis* 27.2 (Spring 1998): 45-94. Jean Daigle, ed., *Acadia of the Maritimes: Thematic Studies* (Moncton: Chaire d'études acadiennes, Université de Moncton, 1995) brings the Acadian odyssey up to the twentieth century. J.B. Brebner, *New England's Outpost: Acadia before the Conquest of Canada* (New York: Columbia University Press, 1927), and George A. Rawlyk, *Nova Scotia's Massachusetts: A Study of Massachusetts-Nova Scotia Relations, 1630–1784* (Montreal: McGill-Queen's

University Press, 1973) offer valuable insights on geopolitical developments in the Atlantic region in the early eighteenth century. See also the relevant chapters in Phillip A. Buckner and John G. Reid, eds., *The Atlantic Region to Confederation: A History* (Toronto: University of Toronto Press, 1994).

On the military history of the eighteenth century, see I.K. Steele, *Guerrillas and Grenadiers: The Struggle for Canada, 1689–1760* (Toronto: Ryerson Press, 1969); George F.G. Stanley, *New France: The Last Phase,* *1744–1760* (Toronto: McClelland and Stewart, 1968); James Pritchard, *The Anatomy of a Naval Disaster: The 1746 French Expedition to North America* (Montreal: McGill-Queen's University Press, 1995); C.P. Stacey, *Quebec, 1759: The Siege and the Battle* (New York: St Martin's Press, 1959); and Guy Frégault, *Canada: The War of the Conquest*, trans. Margaret M. Cameron (Toronto: Oxford University Press, 1969). The careers of Montcalm and Wolfe are judiciously assessed by W.J. Eccles in *Dictionary of Canadian Biography*, vol 3. (1974) 115–43.

 ## WEBLINKS

EDWARD CORNWALLIS
www.schoolnet.ca/aboriginal/treaties/maritim5-e.html

This site provides portions of the text of the maritime treaties signed between Edward Cornwallis and representatives of the Chinecto and St John's tribes.

FORT ROUILLÉ
www.interlog.com/~jarvisci/toronto/rouille.htm

This site describes the French settlement of 1750 at Fort Rouillé, in what is now Toronto.

MI'KMAQ RESOURCE CENTRE
http://mrc.uccb.ns.ca/

A history of the Mi'kmaq people, transcriptions of oral histories, related essays, treaties, further readings, and other resources highlight this extensive site.

WAR OF THE AUSTRIAN SUCCESSION
www.usahistory.com/wars/austsucc.htm

This online encyclopedia entry refers to the attack on Port Royal by French forces and the capture of Louisbourg by New Englanders as the conflict spilled over into North America.

PART II SUMMARY

IN THE CENTURY FROM 1660 TO 1760, FRANCE established several distinct communities in North America. Acadia, largely ignored by France in the seventeenth century, and, after 1713, a British colony called Nova Scotia, sustained, through dykeland farming and fishing, a small but relatively prosperous population. Canada, the headquarters of France's North American fur trade, received more attention from the mother country, particularly from 1663 to 1672, and became home to an even larger farm population. While the demands of the fur trade could have been met by a compact colony with strategic alliances with several Native groups, France's imperial policies after 1698 dictated a strategy of vigorous colonial expansion. From a full-blown colony in Louisiana and a fortress in Louisbourg to an expanding set of thinly-populated trading posts across much of the western three-quarters of the continent, France was on the move in North America until the 1750s. The Seven Years' War brought an end to the French regime in North America and marked the high point of British power in North America.

PART III

BRITISH NORTH AMERICA, 1763–1821

Great Britain emerged from the Seven Years' War as the dominant imperial power in North America, but its power was soon challenged. In 1776, most of the British colonies along the Atlantic seaboard declared independence and fought a successful war to establish their claim. Britain and the world were forced to recognize a new nation—the United States of America—in 1783. Within a decade Great Britain was again at war with France and, for a brief time (1812–1814), with the United States. The French Revolution and Napoleonic Wars dragged on from 1793 to1815. Meanwhile, the "old regime" that had characterized European nations and their colonies was being rapidly swept away. The American and French Revolutions signaled the birth of the "modern" era characterized by liberal democratic political systems, industrial capitalism, and new social values. Despite its embarrassing losses in North America, Great Britain emerged as the dominant power in this new world order. The remaining British North American colonies, for better or worse, would be defined in the crucible of this revolutionary age.

CHAPTER 8

Making Adjustments, 1763–1783

Why do you suffer the white men to dwell among you?...Why do you not clothe yourselves in skins, as your ancestors did, and use the bows and arrows, and the stone-pointed lances, which they used?...You have bought guns, knives, kettles, and blankets, from the white men, until you can no longer do without them; and what is worse, you have drunk the poison firewater, which turns you into fools. Fling all these things away...and as for these English...you must lift the hatchet against them.[1]

These insights, voiced by Pontiac, the Ottawa chief who led an uprising against the British in 1763, came too late to save his people or himself. Although the First Nations living along the Anglo-American frontier scored spectacular successes against the British, they no longer had access to European supplies of guns and ammunition and were soon forced to surrender the posts they had captured. Pontiac himself became a victim of the confusion and desperation of his people, whose world had been turned upside down by the British conquest of New France. In 1769, he was assassinated by the nephew of a Peoria chief in Cahokia, who resented Pontiac for having finally agreed to peaceful relations with the British and for monopolizing the attention of the white authorities.

THE CONQUEST AND NATIVE POLICY

The transfer of New France to British control was as traumatic for the First Nations of North America as it was for the Canadians. With the rivalry of the British and French removed, the Natives could no longer play one side against the other to their advantage. The price of furs plummeted, the quality and quantity of European trade goods declined, and the custom of giving annual presents to secure military alliances was abandoned. In many areas of the continent, Aboriginal peoples were now at the mercy of land-hungry settlers.

The fate of Native peoples in Nova Scotia reflected a pattern that was subsequently repeated across the continent. After the fall of Louisbourg and Quebec, the Mi'kmaq, Maliseet, and Passamaquoddy were hounded by bloodthirsty militia and finally made peace with their conquerors in a series of treaties signed in 1760 and 1761. Without a supply of guns and ammunition, they had little alternative but to surrender. Lieutenant-Governor Jonathan Belcher was instructed by British authorities to draw up a proclamation forbidding encroachment on Native lands, which he obediently did, but he refused to publicize it. As he told his superiors: "If the proclamation had been issued at large, the Indians might have been incited...to have extravagant and unwarranted demands, to the disquiet and perplexity of the New Settlements in the province."[2]

Natives in Nova Scotia faced a dismal prospect as settlers poured into the colony at the end of the Seven Years' War. Expected to petition the British Crown for land in the same way as immigrants, they were forced to forfeit any uncultivated holdings. Land was periodically reserved for the region's First Nations, but it remained unprotected from the encroachment of immigrants and never formed the basis of a significant reserve system. The Mi'kmaq and Maliseet were also handicapped by their linguistic and religious differences: they spoke very little English and were Roman Catholics. When British authorities refused to continue the French practice of annual gift-giving and using the services of a Roman Catholic priest, a few Mi'kmaq made their way to Newfoundland to contact the French based at Saint-Pierre. They inevitably incurred the hostility of the Beothuk, who were fighting a losing battle for existence.

On the western frontier, the British faced a Native uprising in the spring of 1763. Encouraged by French traders still resident in the interior and Pontiac's stirring rhetoric, the First Nations prepared to wipe the "dogs dressed in red" from "the face of the earth." The Natives captured most of the posts in the upper Mississippi and Ohio River basins and killed over 2000 settlers. Warned of the attack, the commander at Detroit managed to hold out. It took the British nearly two years to regain control of the frontier. In desperation Amherst even considered resorting to biological warfare. He suggested to his commanders that they use blankets infected with smallpox "to extirpate this execrable race," and at least one officer, Captain Ecuyer at Fort Pitt, acted on this suggestion.[3]

THE ROYAL PROCLAMATION OF 1763

The Royal Proclamation of October 1763 reflected the efforts of the British Crown to control the Native uprising on the frontier and to protect Natives from the greed of immigrants. A decree of the Crown, not a law of Parliament, the proclamation set out the policy for governing the newly acquired territories and for relations with Native people in North America. Canada was reduced in size (see Map 8.1) and renamed Quebec. Labrador was attached to Newfoundland, while the interior region west of the Allegheny Mountains was declared to be Indian territory.

According to the Proclamation, any lands that had "not been ceded to or purchased" by Britain in the colonies were reserved for "the said Indians." The British "strictly" forbade any individual "on Pain of our Displeasure," to purchase Native land. If Natives wished to sell their land, they could do so only through the British Crown "at some public Meeting or assembly of the said Indians, to be held for the Purpose by the Governor or Commander in Chief of our Colony." And only those who held a licence from the governor could participate in the Native trade.

Pontiac's revolt placed pressure on the British to resume the fur trade out of Montreal as a means of maintaining Native goodwill. Through the mediation of William Johnson, the superintendent of Indian affairs in the Mohawk valley, efforts were made to define a boundary for Indian territory. More than 3000 Natives, mostly Iroquois and their allies, met with Johnson at Fort Stanwix in 1768 to establish a permanent boundary between white settlements and Native hunting grounds. Since neither the Iroquois nor the British could control the people they claimed to bargain for, the new boundary line was widely ignored. As independent traders and settlers clashed with Native communities, the Anglo-American frontier dissolved into chaos. William Johnson's nephew, Guy Johnson, was instrumental in convincing the British to exert

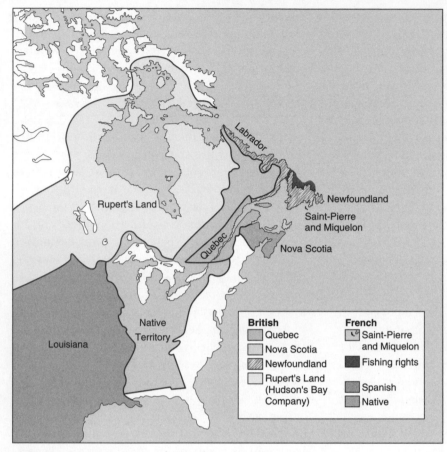

Map 8.1
North America, 1763.

Adapted from *Historical Atlas of Canada*, vol. 1 (Toronto: University of Toronto Press, 1987) plate 42.

more control over the region by placing the Ohio territory under the jurisdiction of Quebec in 1774.

THE CONQUEST AND QUEBEC

The people living in the new British colony of Quebec also made a difficult adjustment. In the aftermath of the conquest, between 2000 and 3000 people —primarily administrators, merchants, and military leaders—moved to France. Most of the 70 000 people living in Quebec had been born in the colony and had little choice but to accept the fact that they were now British subjects by conquest. Required to take an oath of allegiance to the British king, they did so with lit-

tle resistance. Their conquerors had taken the precaution of disarming them, and the fate of the Acadians was still fresh in their minds.

Until 1764, the colony remained under military rule and military occupation. The commander of the occupying forces, James Murray, was a fiery Scot who maintained a strict discipline among his troops and pursed a lenient policy toward the conquered people. He introduced a form of military rule that resembled the political system under the French regime, governing with an appointed council and subordinates in the three jurisdictions of Quebec, Trois-Rivières, and Montreal. Since the chief military officers all spoke French and French laws were respected, the transition to British authority was eased considerably. Murray granted new commissions to former militia captains, and most of them adequately performed the required duties.

If they had wished to do so, the British could have crippled the Roman Catholic Church by refusing to appoint a successor to Bishop Pontbriand, who had died in 1760. Without an official head of the church, no priests could be consecrated, and in short order the whole structure of the institutional church would crumble. Murray, however, recognized the critical role played by the church in the social and spiritual life of the colony and paved the way to having Abbé Jean-Olivier Briand consecrated by French bishops in 1766. For the time being at least, the institutional structure of the church remained intact.

Less tolerance was granted to the male religious orders, particularly the Jesuits who were notorious around the world for their political intrigues. The capitulation agreement reflected this distrust by stipulating that only the female religious orders could continue their activities. Since the male religious communities were forbidden to recruit new members, they would gradually die out.

Murray's biggest problem was addressing the economic crisis induced by a generation of warfare and profiteering. During the Seven Years' War, paper money had flooded the market and prices had skyrocketed. The British introduced hard currency, imposed price controls, and regulated the supply of necessities. Paper money was registered and, although heavily discounted, gradually disappeared from circulation. When there was a shortage of essential supplies in the colony, the British made military stores available to civilians, an act of generosity that surprised the demoralized Canadians.

CIVILIAN RULE

Once the Treaty of Paris had been signed, British officials began to make plans to incorporate New France into the British colonial empire. James Murray was appointed governor of the new British colony of Quebec and his commission, dated 10 August 1764, together with the Royal Proclamation of 1763, served as the foundation of civilian government.

Under these regulations, British authorities made little attempt to accommodate the cultural differences of their new subjects. Quebec was to become a colony like most of the others in North America, ruled by a governor advised by an appointed council and an elected assembly. British law would be introduced and justices of the peace appointed at the local level. Roman Catholics were denied political rights under British law, so only the few hundred Protestants in the colony would be eligible to vote and hold public office.

Both Murray and his successor, Sir Guy Carleton, quickly realized that British institutions were not suited to the newly conquered colony. The Canadians complained about the cost and complexity of the British legal system as well as the harsh penalties it imposed for minor offences. Because only Protestants could serve as lawyers, jurors, justices of the peace, and judges, cultural antagonism soon coloured the judicial process. Murray eased the tension by permitting Roman Catholics to practise law and serve on juries, but it was clear that the conquered people longed for a return to the French civil code.

As British institutions began to take root, the whole social structure of Canadian society was put in jeopardy. The seigneurs no longer derived income and status from their military and political offices, which had previously supplemented their seigneurial dues. Although they retained ownership of their estates, their seigneurial privileges remained in question under British law.

Canadian merchants also faced predictable difficulties in their attempts to adjust to the British mercantile system. In the wake of Wolfe's army, British and New England merchants arrived in the colony and quickly gained the upper hand. There were not many of them—the immigrant British population remained under 1000 in the decade following the conquest—but they had the connections, the capital, and the competitive edge over their French rivals in the British mercantile system. The Canadians even lost control of the fur trade, becoming guides, interpreters, and labour rather than commanders of the posts and policy makers.

The ordinary inhabitants faced no such challenges. In the years immediately following the conquest, agricultural production increased and the population grew at a rapid rate. Although a few seigneurs tried to shore up their declining fortunes by increasing rents which were no longer subject to the controls applied during the French regime, this practice only became widespread after seigneurial dues were sanctioned in law in 1774.

To prevent the British minority from using its power to exploit the Canadians, Murray postponed calling an assembly. The English merchants were outraged. They were also annoyed both by the restrictions on the fur trade that Murray enforced and by his attempts to conciliate the conquered Canadians. Ignoring the protests of the anglophones in the colony, Murray tried to bolster the old aristocratic ideal as reflected in seigneuries, which stood in sharp contrast to the grasping commercialism, typical of the small knot of British and New England merchants in the urban centres. In 1764, Murray had informed the Board of Trade in London:

Portrait of novelist Frances Brooke, painted in 1771 by her friend Catherine Read. Between 1763 and 1768, Frances Brooke, one of Britain's leading literary figures, lived in Quebec and produced the first novel written in what would become Canada. The History of Emily Montague, *published in London in 1769, described the rich social life that prevailed in administrative and military circles in Quebec. As the wife of the Reverend John Brooke, who served as garrison chaplain, Frances Brooke was in a good position to observe the behaviour of her social set. The rapid rise in literacy in the English-speaking world in the second half of the eighteenth century meant that there was a larger audience for written material designed to entertain as well as educate.*

Catherine Read/National Archives of Canada/C117373

Little, very little, will content the New subjects; but nothing will satisfy the licentious fanatics trading here but the expulsion of the Canadians, who are perhaps the bravest and the best race upon the face of the globe, a race, who could they be indulged with a few privileges which the laws of England deny to Roman Catholics at home, would soon get

the better of every national antipathy to their conquerors, and become the most faithful and most useful set of men in this American empire.[4]

Murray's bias toward the Canadiens led to his recall in 1765. His successor, Sir Guy Carleton, arrived in Quebec in 1766 prepared to address the concerns of the small British community in the colony, but he soon adopted the views of his predecessor. Both men were influenced by the larger political forces emerging on the North American continent. With France no longer a threat to their development, the Anglo-American colonists were beginning to question imperial policies. Murray and Carleton were military men charged with protecting their colony in the event of war. The conquered Canadians, they reasoned, still subscribed to conservative political ideals that would shore up the British Empire better than the republican notions that inspired the rebellious Anglo-American colonists.

THE QUEBEC ACT, 1774

Carleton's views were reflected in the Quebec Act, passed by the British Parliament in 1774. Designed to strengthen the traditional elites in the colony, the act was based on the mistaken belief that seigneurs and church leaders would ensure the loyalty of the masses in time of war. To that end, the tithes of the church were guaranteed, the seigneurial system was legally recognized, and French civil law was reintroduced in the colony. English criminal law would remain in force.

The status of the Canadien elite was also enhanced by the decision to permit Roman Catholics to participate in colonial government. Under the Quebec Act, the colony was to be ruled with the advice of an appointed council rather than an elected assembly. Canadians could be appointed to the council, but all councillors would serve at the pleasure of the governor. No rabble-rousing assembly like the ones that existed in the colonies of Massachusetts and Virginia would stir up problems for imperial authorities in Quebec.

The Quebec Act also dramatically increased the size of the colony. Quebec's boundaries were extended southwest into the Ohio territory, eastward to include Labrador, and north to the borders of Rupert's Land. Here, too, strategic interests seem to have dominated the thinking of British authorities. By attaching the Ohio region to the fur-trade interests of Montreal, it would be easier to forestall land-hungry Anglo-American settlers and restore order in what had been defined as Native territory.

There is little doubt that the seigneurs and clerical leaders were pleased by the restoration of their traditional privileges, but other segments of Quebec society were less enthusiastic. Although delighted with the extension of the boundaries of their fur-trade empire, the Protestant merchants resented the loss of their democratic right to an elected assembly they could dominate, assuming that Catholics were barred from voting as they were in England. The habitants also had mixed feelings about an act that left them more beholden than ever before to the seigneurs and clergy. Would not an elected assembly work for the ordinary people of Quebec as it was claimed to do in other British colonies?

ANGLICIZING NOVA SCOTIA

British authorities were more open to developing elected institutions in Nova Scotia. Following the capture of Louisbourg in 1758, they forced a reluctant Governor Lawrence to call an elected assembly and issue a proclamation inviting prospective immigrants to the frontier colony. A second proclamation in 1759 outlined the rights guaranteed in the new Nova Scotia: two elected assembly members for each settled town-

This cartoon, which appeared in London Magazine *in July 1774, is a satirical comment on the religious implications of the Quebec Act. With the devil looking on, British politicians and Anglican priests support a bill that lifts some of the restrictions on Roman Catholics in Britain's North American colony.*

National Archives of Canada/C38989

ship, a judicial system like the one in New England, and freedom of religion for Protestant dissenters.

With these matters seemingly settled, over 8 000 New Englanders responded to Lawrence's call. Known as "Planters," the old English term for settlers, they created a new New England in the western portions of the old colony of Nova Scotia. Fishing families from Massachusetts moved into the sheltered bays and harbours of Nova Scotia's south shore; farming families from Connecticut, Rhode Island, and Massachusetts filled up the townships located in the Annapolis Valley and around the Isthmus of Chignecto. James Simonds, James White, and William Hazen, New England merchants associated with Joshua Mauger, established trading operations near the mouth of the St John River in what is now New Brunswick. A group of farmers from Essex County, Massachusetts, squatted further up the river on land that was occupied by Acadians and Maliseet. Helped by Joshua Mauger's intervention, the New Englanders received title to the land and promptly named their settlement Maugerville in honour of their champion.

Mi'kmaq craft and hunting skills are highlighted in this early nineteenth century drawing.

National Gallery of Canada/6663

giance. This decision served as a signal for those in hiding to lay claim to land and for those in exile to return to their beloved "Acadie."

By 1775, Nova Scotia had been transformed into a colony of pioneer settlements. In addition to New Englanders and Acadians, its rich cultural mosaic included: German- and French-speaking Protestants from continental Europe, many of them based in Lunenburg; fish merchants and their employees from the Channel Islands located in areas of the Gaspé and Cape Breton; Yorkshire English who took up land in the Chignecto region; Irish, both Protestant and Roman Catholic, who settled in several locations throughout the colony; and, with the arrival of the *Hector* in Pictou harbour in 1773, the first of successive waves of Scottish immigration.

By the end of the 1760s, the New England migration had slowed to a trickle. Land speculation contributed to the decline: in one 17-day period in 1765, some 1.2 million hectares of land had been granted, leaving little arable land for potential settlers. The opening of the western territories in 1768 also pulled New England settlement in a westerly rather than a northerly direction. By that time, well over half the 14 000 people in Nova Scotia could trace their origins to New England. With their dissenting religious views, penchant for trading, and fierce individualism, the Planters brought a distinctly "Yankee" culture to the shores of Nova Scotia.

The New Englanders were only the largest of several immigrant groups to locate in Nova Scotia in the two decades following the expulsion of the Acadians. Indeed, the Acadians themselves became one of the largest groups of "planters" in their former homeland—though not in the areas that they had previously inhabited. In 1764, the British agreed to permit the Acadians to stay in Nova Scotia on condition that they take an oath of alle-

ST JOHN'S ISLAND

Scots made up a significant portion of the British pioneers on St John's Island. Of great interest to land speculators once it was confirmed as a British possession in 1763, the island was surveyed into 67 townships by Captain Samuel Holland in 1764. Three years later, in one of the most spectacular "lotteries" in Canadian history, the British government gave 64 of the lots to favourites of the king and court in London. According to the conditions of the grants, the proprietors were required to bring out Protestant settlers, improve their properties, and sustain early colonial administration through the payment of land taxes, known as quitrent.

As in New France, there was a twofold purpose in resorting to this method of planting colonies. One was

MORE TO THE STORY

Elizabeth and Edmund Doane

Elizabeth and Edmund Doane were enterprising New England Planters who settled in Barrington, Nova Scotia. According to family tradition, the Doanes dismantled their two-storey house in the Cape Cod community of Eastham and loaded it, together with their seven children, livestock, and provisions, on a boat for the journey to Nova Scotia. Bad weather and shipwreck dogged their journey northward in the fall of 1761, but they finally reached Barrington the following spring.

In addition to running their own farm, they kept a shop that held accounts for 50 of the community's families. Elizabeth Doane also served as doctor and midwife for her neighbours. When the Doanes began to talk of returning to New England because of hard times in the pioneer community, their neighbours encouraged them to stay by suggesting that Elizabeth Doane submit a petition for a land grant in her own name. Her petition, dated 13 May 1770, stated: "Elizabeth Done Being Destitute of Accomodation of Land to Set a House upon But am Nevertheless free and willing to Exert my facilities and Skil [in physic and surgery and midwifery] and having a Love for the People...Request the favour of...a Small tract of Land." Thirty-eight proprietors of the Township of Barrington—all men—signed her petition, and her grant was approved. Elizabeth Doane continued to provide medical care for her Barrington neighbours for many years, and when she became too old to make house calls by foot, two men carried her in a basket suspended by a pole across their shoulders. She died in 1798 at the age of 82.[5]

to maintain a conservative social structure that placed power and wealth in the hands of a colonial elite. The other consideration was to have private initiative bear the cost of colonial settlement. Theoretically there was little risk involved in delegating authority in this way. If the proprietors failed to fulfil the conditions of their grants, their titles could be escheated, or cancelled, and the ownership of the land would revert to the Crown.

Unfortunately for St John's Island, the escheat process never worked well in practice. The proprietors used their influence to have a separate administration for the island proclaimed in 1769. In 1770, Governor Walter Patterson arrived in the colonial capital, named Charlottetown in honour of the queen, and by 1773 the first assembly was elected. Thereafter, any policy for land reform had to be approved by the colonial legislature as well as by British authorities. Since proprietorial interests had strong supporters both on the island and in Britain, movements to improve the land system were easily frustrated. The lottery of 1767 thus marked the beginning of the great "land question" that would bedevil Island society until the proprietorial system was abolished in the 1870s.

In their initial flush of enthusiasm, several proprietors made serious efforts to fulfil their settlement obligations. Many of the proprietors were Scots, who recognized that conditions in the Highlands—a disintegrating clan structure, overcrowding on meager tenant properties, and rising rents—made emigration an attractive option. The first Scottish settlers, recruited by Captain Robert Stewart for Lot 18, arrived on the *Annabella* in 1770. Tenants from Ulster were tempted by what seemed like reasonable terms for leasing land, and a colony of London Quakers established a base at Elizabethtown. In the early years of settlement, lack of provisions, social conflict, and crop failures—plagues of mice were a recurring menace—threatened survival. Many who could afford to do so left their farms for better opportunities elsewhere. Nevertheless, St John's Island had nearly 1500 residents by 1775 and, in the words of historian J.M. Bumsted, "appeared to be teetering on the brink of success."[6]

NEWFOUNDLAND AND LABRADOR

Notwithstanding official policy discouraging settlement, Newfoundland in the eighteenth century drew a

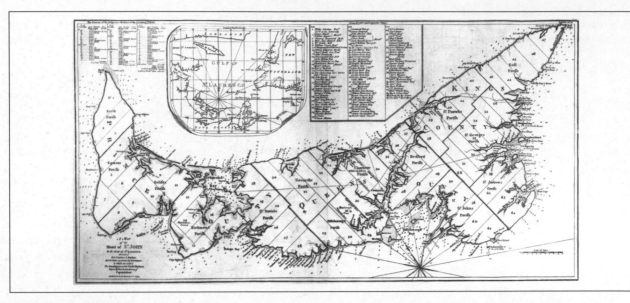

Map 8.2
Holland's map of PEI.

Public Archives and Records Office of Prince Edward Island, Acc. 0. 247

steady stream of immigrants from the home ports of the British fleet and the south coast of Ireland where crews were recruited for the fishing season. The advantages of wintering in Newfoundland were obvious to the fishermen. They could get a head start on the fishery in the spring, protect their shore bases from interlopers, and live without tax or trouble on a sheltered patch of the coastline. By 1775, over 12 000 people called themselves "Newfoundlanders," a term apparently used as early as the 1760s.

In the eighteenth century, the shore-based fishery grew steadily, while the catch of the migratory fleet declined. Recognizing the obvious, British merchants sent an increasing number of "sack ships"—the large ocean carriers of the eighteenth century—to purchase the product of the resident fisheries for their European markets. By the 1750s, New Englanders were competing with British merchants in supplying Newfoundlanders with manufactured goods, provisions, and rum in return for fish, which they sold in the West Indies. This activity contravened the British navigation acts that restricted colonial trade to British vessels, but as long as the acts were not enforced in Newfoundland waters, New England and foreign vessels could trade with impunity.

Following the Seven Years' War, Britain took steps to establish tighter control over the Newfoundland fishery. In 1764, laws were passed giving British authorities more power to arrest smugglers. A customs house was built at St John's to collect duties on imports, followed by a Court of Vice-Admiralty to handle disputes relating to trade. Between 1762 and 1770, Captain James Cook and his successor Michael Lane carried out a survey of Newfoundland, providing the British with a more accurate picture of the colony over which they officially had control.

The imperial thrust was epitomized in the person of Captain Hugh Palliser, who became governor of Newfoundland in 1764. He expelled as many as 5000 fugitives during his four-year tenure, challenged the rights of "owners" of shoreline property, and, in his well-meaning efforts to protect Native people, seized the bases of the Labrador seal fishermen. In the so-called Palliser's Act of 1775, the British government reaffirmed its commitment to discourage settlement in Newfoundland and increase the competitive edge of the British-based fishing fleet. Like many of Britain's imperial policies in this period, Palliser's Act flew in the face of colonial reality and only consolidated the growing resentment within the older British North American possessions.

Labrador, dominated by a population of Inuit and Innu, also opened to outside influences following the Seven Years' War. In 1770 George Cartwright built a fur-trading and fishing base at Cape Charles and later moved to Sandwich Bay. He was followed by other British-based companies, but it was not until 1834 that the Hudson's Bay Company built its first trading post at Rigolet. Until that time, Moravian missionaries of the United Brethren, a highly disciplined Protestant sect, were the major European presence in Labrador. The first of several Moravian missions in Labrador was founded at Nain in 1770–71. The Moravians established schools, taught practical skills, provided medical services, and kept close control over the trade of the region.

FUR-TRADE RIVALRIES IN THE NORTHWEST

The British conquest of New France resulted in an intensification rather than the elimination of the rivalry between the fur traders based on the St Lawrence and Hudson Bay. Even before the Treaty of Paris was signed, British traders moved to Montreal and began to occupy French posts in the interior. At first, the area south and west of the Great Lakes was the favoured area for fur-trade operations, but most traders recognized that their success in the long term lay in developing the great Northwest.

As the Montreal traders moved into the Northwest they were welcomed by Natives, who had become increasingly reliant on European trade goods. The Blackfoot, Cree, and Assiniboine, who had acquired horses through trade with First Nations to the south, were particularly eager to purchase firearms to enhance their roles as hunters and warriors. In competition with each other for dominance in the fur trade, they also encouraged the competition among fur trade companies. Not only did they get better prices this way but also better service as posts prolifer-

Esquimaux Lady, *by John Russell. In the mid-1700s, Mikak, an Inuit woman, and her son were kidnapped and taken to England by British marines intent on rounding up a group of Natives suspected of plundering a whaling station. After she returned home, Mikak served as a guide to the first Moravian missionaries when they arrived at Nain in 1770.*

Institut und Sammlung für Völkerkunde der Universität Göttingen

ated throughout the interior to cater to the demands of the fur-trading First Nations.

The Hudson's Bay Company opened its first interior post in 1774, at Cumberland House some 800 kilometres from Hudson Bay. By that time, Bay men were crisscrossing the West in their efforts to outdistance their rivals based in Montreal. Samuel Hearne reached the Arctic Ocean by way of the Coppermine River in 1772, putting an end to speculation about a water passage from Hudson Bay to the Pacific. The Montreal traders were slow to organize into a single company to compete more effectively, but the American Revolution would serve as a catalyst for such a development.

Voices from the Past

The Impact of the Fur Trade on Natives: A Trader's View

In 1774, Samuel Hearne, a former officer in the Royal Navy, was placed in charge of Cumberland House, a post set up by the Hudson's Bay Company to compete with the Montreal traders for customers among the First Nations. He had proved his mettle by surviving in the Canadian interior and dealing on a friendly basis with the Aboriginal people during a 1900-kilometre journey in 1771–72 that led him as far as the Arctic Ocean. His description of the Chipewyan in the early 1770s reflects the views of a trader who admired the Natives and had few illusions about the impact of the fur trade on their culture:

> The real wants of these people are few, and easily supplied; a hatchet, an ice-chisel, a file, and a knife, are all that is required to enable them, with a little industry, to procure a comfortable livelihood, and those who endeavour to possess more, are always the most unhappy, and may, in fact, be said to be only slaves and carriers to the rest, whose ambition never leads them to anything beyond the means of procuring food and clothing. It is true, the carriers pride themselves much on the respect which is shown to them at the Factory; to obtain which they frequently run great risques of being starved to death in their way thither and back; and all they can possibly get for the furrs they procure after a year's toil, seldom amounts to more than is sufficient to yield a bare subsistence, and a few furrs for the ensuing year's market; while those whom they call indolent and mean-spirited live generally in a state of plenty, without trouble or risque; and consequently must be the most happy, and, in truth, the most independent also. It must be allowed that they are by far the greatest philosophers, as they never give themselves the trouble to acquire what they can do well enough without. The deer they kill, furnishes them with food, and a variety of warm and comfortable clothing, either with or without the hair, according as the seasons require; and it must be very hard indeed, if they cannot get furs enough in the course of two or three years, to purchase a hatchet, and such other edge-tools as are necessary for their purpose. Indeed, those who take no concern at all about procuring furrs, have generally an opportunity of providing themselves with all their real wants from their more industrious countrymen, in exchange for provisions, and ready-dressed skins for clothing.

> It is undoubtedly the duty of every one of the company's servants [employees] to encourage a spirit of industry among the natives, and to use every means in their power to induce them to procure furrs and other commodities for trade, by assuring them of a ready purchase and good payment for every thing they bring to the Factory; and I can truly say that this has ever been the grand object of my intention. But I must at the same time confess, that such conduct is by no means for the real benefit of the poor Indians; it being well known that those who have the least intercourse with the Factories [posts], are by far the happiest. As their whole aim is to procure a comfortable subsistence, they take the most prudent methods to accomplish it, and by always following the lead of the deer, are seldom exposed to the gripping hand of famine, so frequently felt by those who are called the annual traders.[7]

THE AMERICAN REVOLUTION

There is no easy answer as to why Quebec, Newfoundland, Nova Scotia, and St John's Island failed to become part of the new United States of America. A series of developments—the failure of an American invasion of Quebec in 1775–76 and the attack on Fort Cumberland in Nova Scotia in 1776, the presence of British troops, and the caution of the population—seems to have combined to keep the northern colonies within the British sphere of influence.

British policy as expressed in the Quebec Act and Palliser's Act was included among the grievances cited by the Americans against their mother country. By annexing the Ohio country to Quebec, granting privileges to Roman Catholics, and restricting access to the Newfoundland fisheries, British authorities had simply gone too far. Such policies seemed to be of a piece with other "intolerable" acts passed by the British Parliament. Determined to make the colonies cover the enormous costs of their defence and administration, King George III and his chief ministers had introduced a series of unpopular measures, including taxes on paper, sugar, and tea, without the approval of the elected colonial legislatures. When colonists in Massachusetts erupted in riotous indignation over mercantile restrictions on their trade and the quartering of soldiers in private homes, British authorities closed the port of Boston, suspended the Massachusetts assembly, and sent in more troops.

In September 1774, delegates from 12 colonies—all except for Newfoundland, St John's Island, Nova Scotia, Quebec, and Georgia—met in Philadelphia to co-ordinate a response to Britain's arbitrary colonial policy. The First Continental Congress demanded the repeal of the coercive acts. When Britain refused to back down, colonial militia were placed on alert. Clashes between the two sides occurred at Lexington and Concord in Massachusetts in the spring of 1775. A second Continental Congress voted to raise an army under George Washington to defend "American liberty." After driving the British out of Boston, they planned to march on Quebec.

QUEBEC IN QUESTION

This decision to invade Quebec was based on a number of assumptions. There was every reason to expect that the Canadians would be eager to throw off the yoke of their recent conquerors, and a few of the English-speaking merchants were sympathetic to the republican cause. If there were spontaneous uprisings in support of the invading armies, all to the good. Nova Scotia was also home to a sympathetic population, fully half of New England origin, but the colony was impossible to attack without supporting seapower. The British forces in Quebec, however, might succumb during a winter siege.

In September 1775, an army of 2000 men led by Richard Montgomery moved down the Lake Champlain–Richelieu River route toward Montreal. The plan was to take Montreal and proceed to Quebec, where they would meet another army under Benedict Arnold, which was marching overland along the Kennebec and Chaudière rivers. Because Carleton had sent half of his garrison to assist General Gage in Boston, he was left with only 600 regulars for the defence of his colony. The fate of Quebec hung on the reaction of the colonists to the invading forces.

To Carleton's dismay, Montgomery's troops met considerable support. The citizens of Montreal capitulated without a fight, and Carleton himself narrowly escaped capture as he fled to Quebec. In Quebec, Carleton found the people more disposed to repel the invading forces, whose popularity had quickly dwindled when they commandeered supplies without compensation and desecrated Roman Catholic shrines and churches. By the time winter had set in, few Canadiens saw the Anglo-Americans as their liberators.

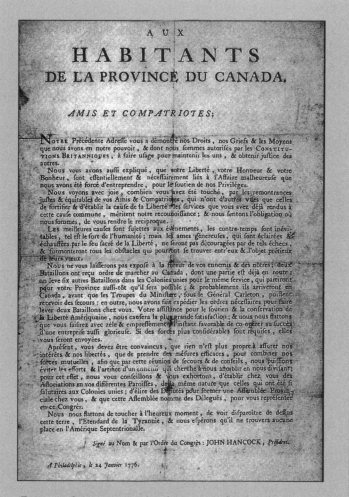

Prior to the invasion, the Americans flooded Quebec with propaganda to persuade Canadians to join their democratic cause. It is difficult to assess what impact their call to arms had on the common people. What was clear is that one of the issues fuelling the war was democratic idealism, which contrasted sharply with the monarchical traditions of European nations.

National Archives of Canada/C111468

Like Wolfe before him, Montgomery had difficulty breaching the natural defences that surrounded Quebec. A desperate attack launched on the evening of 31 December failed. Montgomery was killed during the encounter and Arnold was wounded. In May 1776, the Americans beat a hasty retreat when British ships arrived bearing 10 000 troops. The large military force also guaranteed the good behaviour of the civilian population. Carleton's successor, Sir Frederick Haldimand, handed out stiff sentences to those who resisted the hated military corvée and kept a close watch on anyone suspected of disloyalty.

During the nine-month occupation by the Americans, Carleton found little to criticize about the behaviour of the seigneurs and clerical officials. They had enthusiastically supported his efforts to raise a colonial militia to save the colony from republicanism. In contrast, the habitants, who were experiencing the second war on their native soil in two decades, were reluctant to fight. Both sides in the conflict were led by English-speaking Protestants whose goals seemed to have little relevance to the lives of ordinary people. While a few habitants voluntarily participated in the fighting on both sides, most of them waited out the conflict, selling supplies to those who offered hard cash, and preserving their neutrality as long as possible.

The British element in the colony was no more reliable than the habitants. Some of the merchants acted as informers for Montgomery. As the war dragged on, fur traders such as Peter Pond found it a convenient time to make a trip into the interior to discover new customers and communication routes. Pond established a post on Lake Athabasca in 1778 at the behest of the Chipewyan, who were particularly aggressive in courting trading partners. The Montreal traders were soon tapping the furs along the Peace and Mackenzie rivers as well.

While the Natives in the Northwest were spared involvement in the war, others were not so fortunate. Like the Canadians, the Iroquois had armies marching across their territories and, again like the Canadians, they were divided about what to do. Joseph Brant and his Mohawk followers and some Seneca, as well as the Iroquois of the Kahnawaké and St Regis reserves, fought with the British. The Oneida and Tuscarora, perhaps influenced by their ties with Congregational ministers, leaned toward the Americans. The Onondaga and Cayuga remained neutral until 1779, when American troops invaded their territory. This provoked them into retaliatory raids on American settlements. With their homelands at stake, the Natives proved to be among Britain's most effective combatants, although they were fighting for themselves, not for any European power.

Carleton's failure to pursue the retreating militiamen meant that the Americans lived to fight another day. On 4 July 1776, the Thirteen Colonies declared independence from Britain. When Britain's forces were defeated in the battle of Saratoga in 1777, its European enemies could not resist the chance to strike a mortal blow. France joined the fray in 1778, followed by Spain the next year. With France as an ally of the Americans, another invasion of Quebec was planned, but because neither side could agree on who should rule the colony if it were captured, Quebec was spared a second invasion.

THE WAR IN THE ATLANTIC REGION

Like Quebeckers, people in the Atlantic region were forced to choose sides. Newfoundland's situation was perhaps the most clear-cut. Its fisheries were part of the great triangular trade dominated by Great Britain. It would have been economic suicide to cut the ties that bound that trade together. Even if Newfoundlanders had chosen to take the side of the Thirteen Colonies, they would have had difficulty doing so in any formal way. There were no local institutions on the island that could respond to an invitation from the Continental Congress to join in the crusade for liberty.

Halifax was similarly a creation of the imperial system, and the people there considered British soldiers an economic boon rather than a social irritant. In the outlying regions of the colony, there was much sympathy for the rebel position but little enthusiasm for battle. A religious revival led by Henry Alline in the townships settled by New England Planters attracted as much attention as, if not more than, the secular battles raging around them. On St John's Island, the inhabitants were too busy putting down roots to participate in a war for independence.

biography

Joseph and Molly Brant

Mary Brant—generally known as Molly—and her brother Joseph were members of a powerful Mohawk family who allied themselves with the British during the Seven Years' War. In 1758, as a young man of 15, Joseph Brant took part in Abercrombie's campaign to invade Canada. He subsequently joined Indian superintendent Sir William Johnson in the capture of Niagara in 1759 and participated in the siege of Montreal the following year. It was around this time that Molly Brant established a relationship with Johnson. Their first child was born in 1759, and before Johnson's death in 1774 they had seven more children who survived infancy. Molly Brant presided over Johnson's household in the Mohawk valley and proved a valuable partner in his fur-trade and diplomatic activities. In his will Johnson left his estate to his white son, John, and gave Molly Brant a good portion of land, a black female slave, and £200. With her legacy she opened a store which sold rum and other trade items to her people.

When the American Revolutionary War broke out, Joseph and Molly Brant allied themselves with the British. Joseph Brant led a force of Native and white soldiers in frontier battles that included campaigns against the Oneida and Tuscarora, who had sided with the United States. Like white Americans, the Six Nations experienced the American Revolution as a civil war. Meanwhile, Molly Brant helped to provision the Loyalist forces and kept them informed about rebel activities. In 1777, the victorious Oneida took revenge on the Mohawk. Brant's home was looted and she took refuge at Onondaga (near Syracuse, New York) and later at Niagara.

As head of the Six Nations matrons, Molly exercised her considerable influence to prevent the Mohawk from wavering in their support of the British. During the darkest days of the war, she went to Carleton Island, New York, to convince her discouraged people there to continue the fight. When the war ended, Molly Brant moved to Kingston, where Governor Haldimand had a house built for her use. She was also awarded an annual pension of

Portrait of Joseph Brant, *by George Romney, painted during Brant's visit to Britain in* 1776.

National Gallery of Canada/8005

£100, the highest paid to an Aboriginal ally. Joseph Brant, embittered by Britain's decision to relinquish sovereignty over all the territory west of the Mississippi to the Americans, tried in vain to forge a confederacy that would, by war or diplomacy, produce a better deal for his people.[8]

Still, for most people in the Atlantic region, the issues fuelling the conflict were sharply drawn. To take up with the wrong side could result in the loss of property, position, and even life itself. Seizure of rebel property by British soldiers or attacks by New England privateers could wipe out a generation of hard-earned subsistence. Few of the pioneer colonists could risk such a fate, and as a result behaved cautiously.

Raids by New England privateers were a feature of the war for most people living in the seabound Atlantic colonies. In November 1775, privateers landed in Charlottetown, plundering homes, seizing provisions, and carrying away the colony's leading officials, including the acting governor, Phillips Callbeck. Most raids were similarly selective, leaving all but targeted victims unmolested, but such activities did little to endear pioneer settlers to the revolutionary cause. Virtually every outport settlement from Yarmouth Township to Labrador was visited by privateers, an indication that republican forces perceived the northern colonies as an extension of the British frontier of influence in North America rather than as allies in the cause.

The presence of a British fleet in the North Atlantic during much of the war discouraged George Washington from any serious thought of invading the region. There was a brief flurry of rebel activity in the fall of 1776 when Jonathan Eddy, a member of the Nova Scotia assembly for Cumberland, and John Allan, a Scottish–born resident in the area, led a force of nearly 180 men against the British garrison at Fort Cumberland (formerly Fort Beauséjour). Eddy's ranks included 19 Natives from the St John River area and about 40 Acadians prepared to use the occasion to strike at their British conquerors. The rest were mostly New England-born settlers. While the attack was easily repulsed by soldiers sent from Halifax, the tension among settlers in the area around Fort Cumberland resulted in bloodshed, looting, and litigation that continued for over a decade.

After the defeat of British forces at Saratoga in 1777, the scene of fighting moved to the middle and southern American colonies. Thereafter, the North Atlantic colonies became even more British in orientation. The increased military presence in colonial capitals, the profit to be gained by supplying British troops, and the influx of Loyalists fleeing from rebel-held strongholds sealed the fate of Nova Scotia and St John's Island. In 1781, the British army under Edward Cornwallis suffered a crushing defeat at Yorktown, Virginia.

Two years later in another treaty negotiated in Paris, the British agreed to recognize the independence of the United States, a decision that would have profound implications for what was left of "British" North America. Although the victorious Americans suggested that the British might want to withdraw completely from North America, they never seriously considered such a policy. The boundary was set at the St Croix River in the east, vague highlands along the Quebec border to the 45th parallel, and then a line running along the St Lawrence and through the middle of the Great Lakes. Because the maps used during the negotiations were faulty, it would take more than half a century of negotiation to determine the exact border between the two emerging nations.

CONCLUSION

Between 1763 and 1775, the British tried to impose order on their North American colonies but their efforts ended in failure. They lost 13 of their most valued colonies and were left with only the possessions that they had acquired from France by treaties signed in 1713 and 1763. As we will see in the next chapter, the impact of the American Revolutionary War was as great on the North American colonies that remained in the British Empire as on those that joined the new United States of America. A flood of immigrants, a reorganized colonial administration, and a new boundary line followed in the wake of the war. In one crucial decade, the British Empire in North America was reduced to a shadow of its former self, and the foundations of a second transcontinental nation on the North American continent were tentatively laid.

Culture and Conquest

Historians have little difficulty agreeing upon the immediate impact of the conquest on the Canadians. As stated most bluntly by Susan Mann Trofimenkoff, "Conquest is like rape."[9] Scholars are less likely to agree upon the long-term impact of such a traumatic event. As with most historical debates, events in the present very often shape the way historians view this critical moment in Quebec's history. There were other conquests in Canadian history—for instance, that of Acadia in 1710–13 and the centuries-long subordination of the First Nations—but the conquest of Quebec has generated the most comment because many historians see it as a causal factor in the problems facing the Québécois in the nineteenth and twentieth centuries.[10]

Early French-Canadian historians were inclined to see the conquest as a tragedy that blunted the colony's cultural and institutional development. Conservative in their political philosophy, they argued that New France was devastated when the leading citizens departed for France following the conquest and French political structures were replaced by "barbaric" British institutions. In the words of one of French Canada's first historians, François-Xavier Garneau, "The evils they had previously endured seemed light to them compared to the sufferings and humiliations which were in preparation, they feared, for them and their posterity."[11]

A contrasting view, popular among nineteenth-century clerics, saw the hand of God in a conquest that spared Quebec the evils—in particular the liberalism and atheism—of the French Revolution. Only a few liberal French-Canadian historians, such as Benjamin Sulte, saw virtue in the conquest because Britain replaced absolute rule with constitutional government. This view had been typically argued by anglophone historians, most notably Francis Parkman, who maintained, "A happier calamity never befell a people than the conquest of Canada by British arms."[12] For Parkman, the most important theme in history was the broadening of liberty as represented in the Protestant Reformation, representative institutions, and laissez-faire economic policies. New France, with its Roman Catholic hierarchy, authoritarian political institutions, and mercantile economy, clearly had, in his view, little to offer to the progress of Western civilization.

As the Industrial Revolution began drawing more and more Canadiens into the ranks of the urban working class, conservative historians in Quebec gradually made the habitant farmer the hero of New France. It was in the countryside that the seeds of French-Canadian nationalism were well and truly planted, they argued, and where Christian virtues remained uncorrupted. Abbé Lionel Groulx, writing in the interwar years, even claimed that the French Canadians were a superior race, purified by the fires of the conquest and guided throughout by the steady influence of the Roman Catholic Church. In Groulx's estimation, the Québécois were "perhaps the purest race on the whole continent," a characteristic not easy to verify by demographic evidence, but one that clearly meant much to him.[13]

As Quebec entered a period of rapid social and economic transformation following the Second World War, *la survivance* in the countryside was no longer enough, and the interpretations of the conservative school were squarely challenged. Maurice Séguin, an influential historian at the Université de Montréal, called upon Canadiens to lift themselves from the paralyzing hold of the "agrarian retreat." For Séguin, Canada under the ancien régime was "colonization in the full sense of the term," while the conquest was a "catastrophe" forcing the Canadiens back on an ever-declining agricultural economy. His call to action inspired many of the students who attended his classes: "Let us take the land, but also the forest, the mines, the watercourses, the fisheries; in a word; all the resources of our country, their processing and their trade, if we want to save our nationality by ensuring its unrestricted economic life."[14]

Two of Séguin's colleagues at the Université de Montréal, Guy Frégault and Michel Brunet, were the most articulate advocates of what became known as the "Montreal School." Frégault concluded that New France was, like all colonies, dependent upon imperial investment, but its evolution was "normal" within the context of North American colonial development. The Canadian community in 1763, however, was "conquered, impoverished, socially decapitated, and politically in bonds," while "French colonization, more vital than ever, was conclusively halted."[15]

Michel Brunet went even further. Drawing directly upon Marxist theory, which held that the bourgeoisie was the dynamic class in capitalist society, he explored the impact of the conquest on the Canadian middle class in the 30 years following the conquest. He concluded that French-Canadian business people were unable to hold their own against their English competitors. For Brunet, the excessive emphasis on agriculture, the domination of social and intellectual life by the Roman Catholic Church, and the distrust of democracy all stemmed from the "decapitation" of the Canadian society in 1763.[16]

The Montreal School's position reflected contemporary concerns over the English domination of the Quebec economy. By the 1960s, they were politically linked with the nationalistes who were seeking independence for Quebec. Historians at Université Laval in Quebec City, who were branded as "federalists" for their historical interpretations, challenged the views put forward by the Montrealers. Jean Hamelin led the way, calling into question the notion that there was a dynamic middle class in pre-conquest New France. "The essential fact on this subject that emerges from the intendants' correspondence," he maintained in 1960, "is the poverty of merchants and traders as a group throughout the period of French rule." For Hamelin, "The absence in 1800 of a vigorous French-Canadian bourgeoisie ...emerges not as a result of the Conquest but as the culmination of the French regime."[17]

Hamelin's views were echoed by Fernand Ouellet, who accepted the finding that there was a weak middle class in the pre-conquest period. Unlike Hamelin, however, Ouellet concluded that this fact was irrelevant to the economic condition of French Canadians in the post-conquest period. For Ouellet, the profound changes wrought by the Industrial Revolution were reasons enough for the economic underdevelopment that characterized Quebec in the nineteenth and twentieth centuries. In recent years, most historians have followed Ouellet's lead in moving away from overly deterministic interpretations of the conquest.

NOTES

1 W.J. Eccles, *The Ordeal of New France* (Montreal: Canadian Broadcasting Service, 1966) 142.

2 G.P. Gould and A.J. Semple, eds., *Our Land: The Maritimes* (Fredericton: Sainte Annes Point Press, 1980) 177.

3 Cited in W.J. Eccles, *The Ordeal of New France*.

4 Governor James Murray to the Lords of Trade, 29 October 1764, cited in *Documents Relating to the Constitutional History of Canada, 1759–1791*, ed. A. Shortt and A.G. Doughty (Ottawa, 1918), Part 1, 231.

5 Phyllis Blakeley, "And Having a Love for the People," *Nova Scotia Historical Quarterly* 5,2 (June 1975): 172-73.

6 J.M. Bumsted, *Land, Settlement, and Politics on Eighteenth-Century Prince Edward Island* (Montreal: McGill-Queen's University Press, 1987) 64.

7 Samuel Hearne, *A Journey from Prince of Wales's Fort in Hudson's Bay, to the Northern Ocean* (London, 1795) 51–52.

8 See Barbara Graymont, "Koñwatsiʔtsiaienni" in *Dictionary of Canadian Biography*, vol. 4, 1771 to 1800 (Toronto: University of Toronto Press, 1979) 416–18; and Barbara Graymont, "Thayendanegea" in *Dictionary of Canadian Biography*, vol. 5, 1801 to 1820 (Toronto: University of Toronto Press, 1983) 803–12.

9 Susan Mann Trofimenkoff, *The Dream of Nation: A Social and Intellectual History of Quebec* (Toronto: Gage, 1982) 31.

10 For a summary of the debate, see Dale Miquelon, ed., *Society and Conquest: The Debate on the Bourgeoisie and Social Change in French Canada, 1700–1850* (Toronto: Copp Clark Pitman, 1977); "The Conquest of 1760: Were Its Consequences Traumatic?" in *Emerging Identities: Selected Problems and Interpretations in Canadian History*, ed. Paul Bennett and Cornelius Jaenen (Scarborough, ON: Prentice-Hall, 1986) 76–105; and Serge Gagnon, *Quebec and Its Historians: The Twentieth Century* (Montreal: Harvest House, 1985) 53–89.

11 François-Xavier Garneau, *History of Canada, from the Time of Its Discovery till the Union Year* (1840–1841), vol. 2, trans. Andrew Bell (Montreal: n.p., 1860) 84–86.

12 Francis Parkman, *The Old Regime in Canada*, vol. 2 (Toronto, 1899) 205.

[13] Lionel Groulx, *Lendemains de conquête* (Montreal, 1920), 234–35, cited in *Emerging Identities*, ed. Bennett and Jaenen, 90.

[14] Maurice Séguin, "La Conquête et la vie économique des Canadiens," *Action nationale* 28 (1947), cited in Miquelon, *Society and Conquest*, 78.

[15] Guy Frégault, "La colonisation du Canada au XVIIe siècle," *Cahiers de l'Académie canadienne-française* 2 (1957): 53–81.

[16] Michel Brunet, *La présence anglaise et les canadiens* (Montreal: Beauchemin, 1958).

[17] Jean Hamelin, *Économie et société en Nouvelle-France* (Quebec, 1960), cited in Miquelon, *Society and Conquest*, 105, 114.

SELECTED READING

On Quebec following the conquest, see A.L. Burt, *The Old Province of Quebec* (Ottawa: Carleton University Press, 1933; reprinted 1968); Hilda Neatby, *Quebec: The Revolutionary Age, 1760–1791* (Toronto: McClelland and Stewart, 1966); Fernand Ouellet, *Social and Economic History of Quebec*, trans. Robert Mandron (Toronto: Gage, 1980); Allan Greer, *Peasant, Lord and Merchant: Rural Society in Three Quebec Parishes, 1740–1840* (Toronto: University of Toronto Press, 1985); and José Iguartua, "A Change in Climate: The Conquest and the Marchands of Montreal," *Canadian Historical Association Historical Papers* (1974): 115–43. Debates surrounding the conquest are usefully summarized and discussed in Cameron Nish, ed., *The French Canadians, 1759–1766: Conquered? Half Conquered? Liberated?* (Toronto: Copp Clark Pitman, 1966) and Dale Miquelon, ed., *Society and Conquest: The Debate on the Bourgeoisie and Social Change in French Canada, 1700–1850* (Toronto: Copp Clark Pitman, 1977).

In addition to the sources on Native issues cited in Chapter 7, see Howard H. Peckham, *Pontiac and the Indian Uprising* (Chicago: Russell, 1971); Jack Stagg, *Anglo-Indian Relations in North America to 1763 and an Analysis of the Royal Proclamation of 7 October 1763* (Ottawa: Department of Indian Affairs and Northern Development, Research Branch, 1981); Robert J. Surtees, "Canadian Indian Treaties," in Wilcomb Washburn, ed., *Handbook of North American Indians 4: History of Indian-White Relations* (Washington DC: Smithsonian Institution, 1988); and William C. Wicken, "The Mi'kmaq and Wuastukwiuk Treaties," *University of New Brunswick Law Journal* 43 (1994): 241-53. See also John Reid et al., "History, Native Issues and the Courts: A Forum," in *Acadiensis* 28.1 (Autumn, 1998): 3-26.

Developments in the Atlantic region are covered in relevant chapters of Phillip A. Buckner and John G. Reid, eds., *The Atlantic Region to Confederation: A History* (Toronto: University of Toronto Press, 1994), W.S. MacNutt, *The Atlantic Provinces: The Emergence of Colonial Society, 1713–1857* (Toronto: McClelland and Stewart, 1965), and Margaret R. Conrad and James K. Hiller, *Atlantic Canada: A Region in the Making* (Toronto: Oxford University Press, 2001). Specialized studies include Andrew Hill Clark, *Three Centuries and the Island: A Historical Geography of Settlement and Agriculture in Prince Edward Island* (Toronto: University of Toronto Press, 1959); J.M. Bumsted, *Land, Settlement and Politics on Eighteenth-Century Prince Edward Island* (Montreal: McGill-Queen's University Press, 1987); and Frederick W. Rowe, *History of Newfoundland and Labrador* (Toronto: McGraw-Hill Ryerson, 1980). The post-expulsion Acadian odyssey is described by Naomi Griffiths, *Acadians: Creation of a People* (Toronto: McGraw-Hill Ryerson, 1973) and Jean Daigle, ed., *Acadia of the Maritimes: Thematic Studies* (Moncton: Chaire d'études acadiennes, Université de Moncton, 1995).

New England's influence on the Maritime region is explored by *The Neutral Yankees of Nova Scotia* (New Haven, CT: Yale University Press, 1937) and George A. Rawlyk, *Nova Scotia's Massachusetts: A Study of Massachusetts-Nova Scotia Relations, 1630–1784* (Montreal: McGill-Queen's University Press, 1973). Articles in *They Planted Well: New England Planters in Maritime Canada* (Fredericton: Acadiensis Press, 1988), *Making Adjustments: Change and Continuity in Planter Nova Scotia, 1759–1800* (Fredericton: Acadiensis Press, 1991), and *Intimate Relations: Family and Community in Planter Nova Scotia, 1759–1800* (Fredericton: Acadensis Press, 1995), all edited by Margaret Conrad, offer wide-ranging perspectives on this early wave of anglophone immigrants. The Yorkshire settlers are the subject of James D. Snowdon, *Footprints in the Marsh Mud: Politics and Land Settlement in the Township of Sackville, 1760–1800* (Sackville: Tantramar Heritage Trust and R.P. Bell Library Maritime Literature Reprint Series, 2000). The Scots in the region are covered in Donald MacKay, *The People of the Hector* (Toronto: McGraw-Hill Ryerson, 1980), and J.M. Bumsted, *The People's Clearance: Highland Emigration to British North America, 1770–1815* (Winnipeg: University of Manitoba Press, 1982). The German and French Protestants who were transported to Nova Scotia between 1750 and 1753 have received detailed treatment in Winthrop Bell, *The "Foreign Protestants" and the Settlement of Nova Scotia* (Toronto: University of Toronto Press, 1961), republished in 1991 by Acadiensis Press.

The American invasion of Canada is discussed in George F.G. Stanley, *Canada Invaded, 1775–1776* (Toronto: Hakkert, 1973) and Robert McConnell Hatch, *Thrust for Canada: The American Attempt on Quebec in 1775–1776* (Boston: Houghton Mifflin, 1979). See also

Barbara Graymont, *The Iroquois in the American Revolution* (Syracuse, NY: Syracuse University Press, 1972); Isabel Thompson Kelsay, *Joseph Brant, 1743–1807: Man of Two Worlds* (Syracuse, NY: Syracuse University Press, 1984); and Richard White, *The Middle Ground: Indians, Empires, and Republics in the Great Lakes Region, 1650–1815* (Cambridge: Cambridge University Press, 1991). The Maritimes during the American Revolution are the focus of George A. Rawlyk and Gordon Stewart, *A People Highly Favoured of God: The Nova Scotia Yankees and the American Revolution* (Hamdon, CT: Archon Books, 1972) and J.M. Bumsted, *Henry Alline* (Toronto: University of Toronto Press, 1971). The Eddy rebellion of 1776 is well chronicled in Ernest Clarke, *The Siege of Fort Cumberland: An Episode in the American Revolution* (Montreal: McGill-Queen's University Press, 1995).

 WEBLINKS

TREATY OF PARIS (1763)
http://odur.let.rug.nl/~usa/D/1751-1775/7yearswar/ paris.htm

This site offers an English translation of the Treaty text.

THE QUEBEC ACT (1774)
http://insight.mcmaster.ca/org/efc/pages/law/cons/ Constitutions/Canada/English/PreConfederation/ qa_1774.html

This site provides the English text for Articles 1–18 of the Quebec Act.

PROCLAMATION OF 1763
www.solon.org/Constitutions/Canada/English/ PreConfederation/rp_1763.html

The royal proclamation on North America, as delivered on 7 October 1763 by George III, is presented at this site.

"PLANTERS"
http://ace.acadiau.ca/history/plstcntr.htm

Sponsored by the Planters Studies Centre at Acadia University, this site provides information on the history of the New England residents who migrated to Nova Scotia between 1759 and 1774. Internal links lead to brief articles on Planter architecture and artifacts.

LES REVUES D'UN AUTRE SIÈCLE
www.bnquebec.ca/illustrations/accueil.htm

The National Library of Quebec Collection site contains nearly 7000 illustrations relating to Quebec.

LE BILAN DU SIÈCLE
www.bilan.usherb.ca

The University of Sherbrooke presents a history of Quebec, featuring information, pictures, and biographies.

CHAPTER 9

Redefining British North America, 1783–1815

I have received your two Letters and the Trunk, and I feel the good effects of the Clothes you sent me and my Children, and I value them to be worth more than I could have valued a thousand Pounds sterling in the year 1774. Alas, my Brother, that Providence should permit so many Evils to fall on me and my Fatherless Children.... Since I wrote you, I have been twice burnt out, and left destitute of Food and Raiment; and in this dreary Country I know not where to find Relief—for Poverty has expelled Friendship and Charity from the human heart and planted in its stead the Law of self-preservation—which scarcely can preserve alive the rustic Hero in this frozen Climate and barren Wilderness.[1]

Polly Diblee, writing in 1787 to her brother William Jarvis, then living in London, England, was not exaggerating her hard luck. In 1783, she and her husband Filer, a lawyer from Connecticut, and their five children, arrived on the shores of what would soon become the British colony of New Brunswick. They were part of the movement of Loyalist refugees from the new United States of America. Arriving destitute, the Diblee family spent their first rough winter in a log cabin. Unable to bear the prospect of imprisonment for debt, Filer committed suicide in March 1784. Not all Loyalists experienced such despair at being cast adrift by the exigencies of war, but for many refugees, especially those accustomed to an urban lifestyle, the frontier experience was overwhelming.

THE LOYALIST INFLUX

When the American Revolutionary War ended, the losers were forced to flee. Branded as "Tories" or "Royalists" by the triumphant American patriots, 70 000 self-styled "Loyalists" left the United States to start their lives over again. Nearly half of them went to Nova Scotia and another 12 000 to Quebec. Although their suffering during the first years was genuine, they were luckier than many refugee peoples. They were given land, provisions, and temporary shelter; a few eventually received financial compensation from the British government for their losses.

While historians often discuss the Loyalists as if they were a homogeneous group, they were as socially and culturally diverse as the society they came from. Many of the Loyalist grantees were soldiers disbanded from volunteer and regular regiments. Others were refugees who had burned their bridges behind them when they sided with the British; still others were opportunists attracted by the British promise of free land and provisions for three years in what was left of British North America. Over half of the Loyalists were women and children whose fortunes were dictated by family decisions to support the British cause. A number of widows whose husbands had served in the war were included in the land grants. Like most pioneer women, Loyalist women were forced to adjust to the circumstances thrust upon them and raise their families in conditions not of their choosing.

A disproportionate number of the Nova Scotia Loyalists came from urban centres such as Boston, New York, and Charleston, where British armies had been stationed at various times during the war. Unsuited to the hardships of pioneer life, they were tempted to sell their land and ship out. Port Roseway, renamed Shelburne, in Nova Scotia, was perhaps the most extreme example of Loyalist mobility. Its population of nearly 10 000 in 1783 had dwindled to less than 1000 a decade later. In contrast, many of the refugees who flooded into Quebec were farmers from upstate New York and the back country of Pennsylvania and New England, who were better prepared for the challenges that confronted them on the frontier.

The greatest number of Loyalists were drawn from the lower and middle classes of labourers, farmers, artisans, and merchants. Although a few highly placed colonial officials and Harvard-trained professionals moved to Nova Scotia and Quebec, most of the wealthy Loyalist elite went to Britain or the West Indies. Nor were the pretensions of a few Loyalists well received by the mass of refugees. When 55 prominent New Brunswick Loyalists petitioned for estates of 5000 acres rather than the basic allowance of 100 acres for each head of household and 50 for each family member, there was such an outcry that British officials were forced to bow to the wishes of the majority.

Culture as well as class divided the Loyalists. While most of the migrants were colonial-born, 10 percent were recent immigrants from Britain and elsewhere. People of Dutch and Huguenot ancestry swelled the Loyalist ranks, as did religious minorities. During the war, pacifist groups such as the Quakers were particularly vulnerable to patriot demands that people take sides, with the result that they became Loyalists by default.

Slave-holding Loyalists brought their "property" with them, and over 3000 free black Loyalists chose to settle in Nova Scotia. During the war, the British had encouraged slaves to leave their rebel masters by promising them their freedom if they fought in British regiments. Black Loyalists were offered land, but were given smaller grants in less desirable areas and became the objects of hostility and violence during the tension-ridden early years of settlement. In 1792, nearly 1200 black Loyalists chose to leave the Maritimes when offered passage to the new colony of Sierra Leone in Africa.

SETTLING THE LOYALISTS

Getting the Loyalists established in their new homes posed a huge administrative challenge. In Nova Scotia, Governor John Parr in Halifax

This painting by William Booth shows a black woodcutter in Shelburne, Nova Scotia, in 1788.

National Archives of Canada/C40162

MORE TO THE STORY

Black Loyalist Preachers in Nova Scotia and Sierra Leone

Shelburne, Nova Scotia, was the initial destination of nearly half of the free black Loyalists. Pushed to the opposite shore of the harbour, they founded a community they called Birchtown in honour of the British commander in New York who had signed their embarkation certificates. Religious leaders played an important role in the African-American community. Many of the Birchtown settlers were under the pastoral care of Methodist minister Moses Wilkinson, a former slave. Blind from birth, he was a fiery and persuasive preacher who inspired Boston King, another black Loyalist, to take up the ministry. King was appointed to the Methodist society in Preston, near Halifax, in 1791. Another member of Wilkinson's congregation, John Ball, became an itinerant Methodist preacher in the colony.

After the arrival of the Loyalists, one-quarter of the Methodists in Nova Scotia were African Americans, a fact that did not go unnoticed by the denomination's founder, John Wesley. In a letter to the white Methodist Loyalist James Barry in July 1784, Wesley noted: "The work of God among the blacks in your neighbourhood is a wonderful instance of the power of God; and the little town they have built is, I suppose, the only town of negroes that has been built in America—nay perhaps in any part of the world, except only in Africa."[2] Wesley vowed to keep his black followers supplied with religious books and encouraged white Methodists to "give them all the assistance you can in every possible way."

Not all the citizens of Birchtown were Methodists. The Reverend John Murrant attracted about 40 families to the evangelical Anglican sect known as the Huntingdonians named after Countess Huntingdon who funded their missions. When Murrant left Nova Scotia in 1791, his successor as chief pastor to the black Huntingdonians was Birchtown resident Cato Perkins. David George, by far the most controversial and successful of the black Loyalist preachers in the Shelburne area, was Baptist.

Converted to the Baptist faith while still a slave in Georgia, George was a founding member, in 1773, of North America's first African-American church, Silver Bluff Baptist, in South Carolina, and the first slave to serve as its pastor. When the Revolutionary War broke out, he escaped to the British lines and came to Shelburne in 1784. His meetings were attended by both black and white settlers, but rioting soldiers tore down his house and drove him out of the town. Birchtown residents, it seems, also found his message too radical and forced him to return to Shelburne.

In addition to their emphasis on salvation through faith rather than good works, Baptists also insisted on adult rather than infant baptism and baptism by immersion rather than by sprinkling. By adopting these beliefs and practices, Baptists defied the teachings of established churches and were widely perceived as encouraging opposition to law and order. As George's following grew and his fame spread, he incurred the hostility of people who liked neither his message nor the colour of his skin. In New Brunswick, the lieutenant-governor insisted that he preach only to black people. Riots broke out when he baptized a white couple in Shelburne.

The dream of a "promised land," where they could escape prejudice, own property, and live independently, had inspired black Loyalists to move to Nova Scotia. This dream also led nearly 1200 of them to emigrate to Sierra Leone in 1792. Assisted by philanthropists in Britain who believed that blacks would have a better life in their African homeland, they were also encouraged by their religious leaders to make this last pilgrimage. Over one-third of the blacks in Shelburne, including virtually all of David George's congregation as well as most of Moses Wilkinson's Methodists and Cato Perkins's Huntingdonians, accepted the challenge. The members of Boston King's Methodist chapel in Preston also joined the exodus.

Despite their short sojourn in Nova Scotia, the black Loyalist ministers and their followers had a significant impact on the colony. They left a legacy of literacy, religious conviction, and self-help in both of their adopted homelands, and to this day in Sierra Leone the descendants of the black Loyalists are identified by their Nova Scotia heritage.

moved quickly to escheat unoccupied land that had been granted in the colony and carve out townships for the refugees. Cities sprang up at Port Roseway (Shelburne) and Parrtown (Saint John), and dozens of villages—Aylesford, Digby, Gagetown, Guysborough, Rawden, Ship Harbour, Sussex Vale—emerged from the forest-covered wilderness. When Loyalists on the St John River complained that Halifax was too remote from their concerns, the British government responded by reorganizing colonial administration. In 1784, the old province of Nova Scotia was reduced in size and two new colonies were created: New Brunswick and Cape Breton, with capitals at Fredericton and Sydney respectively.

Governor Walter Patterson of St John's Island tried to lure Loyalists to his estates there, but few wanted to begin their new lives as tenant farmers. Since there was no effort to escheat unsettled land on the island, most of the refugees looked elsewhere for a place to live. Over half of the 500 Loyalists on the island were disbanded soldiers who had been stationed there during the hostilities.

In Quebec, Governor Frederick Haldimand diverted many of the Loyalist immigrants to the north shore of Lake Ontario. Here, he believed, they would be safer from American attack than in the Eastern Townships, where they had originally hoped to settle. Another war might come at any time, and it would be difficult for British forces to protect such an exposed frontier. However, before he could establish settlements in what would become the province of Ontario, Haldimand was obliged under the terms of the Proclamation of 1763 to secure the agreement of Natives living in the region.

First Nations had been neither consulted nor involved in the negotiations ending the war. Under the terms of the peace treaty, the British ceded all territorial claims south of the Great Lakes to the Americans. This left the Natives living there at the mercy of land-hungry American settlers, who were no longer restrained by the provisions of the Proclamation of 1763. Pressured by their desperate Native allies and the merchant community of Montreal who had lost a lucrative fur trade frontier, the British continued to occupy the western posts south of the Great Lakes until Aboriginal policy in the region could be determined.

Fearing another frontier war like the one that had erupted in 1763, Governor Frederick Haldimand made arrangements for a tract of land along the Grand River, which the Mississauga Ojibwa had recently relinquished, to be provided for the Mohawk and other members of the Six Nations and their allies who wanted to move to British-held territory. A census taken in 1785 indicates that over 1800 Aboriginal Loyalists moved to the colony of Quebec, including 400 Mohawk, several hundred Cayuga and Onondaga, and smaller groups of Seneca, Tuscarora, Delaware, Nanticoke, Tutelo, Creek, and Cherokee.

Until the 1780s, the present-day southern Ontario peninsula was the homeland of the Ojibwa, Ottawa, and Algonquin, collectively called the Anishinabeg, a word meaning "true human beings." These nations had a history of nearly two centuries of contact with Europeans. When approached by Haldimand, they relinquished control over some of the best agricultural land in British North America, often for seemingly little in return. The Mississauga, for instance, exchanged a strip of land near Fort Niagara for "three hundred suits of clothing" in 1781. By 1788, most of the rest of the land north of Lake Ontario had been ceded in return for guns, ammunition, clothing, and other material items. While the British believed they were engaging in real-estate deals, the First Nations expected to share the land with the Loyalist refugees. They could scarcely imagine that in less than a century millions of white settlers would claim the land as their own.

In 1784, surveyors began laying out townships in the St Lawrence–Bay of Quinte area. Five of the townships went to John Johnson's Royal Yorkers, who arranged themselves in cultural groupings: Catholic Highlanders, Scottish Presbyterians, German Calvinists, German Lutherans, and Anglicans. Other townships in the region were allotted to Major Edward Jessup's corps, Robert Rogers's corps, and refugees from New York organized under Captain Michael Grass and Major Peter Van Alstine. Loyalists arriving from the frontier districts of New York and Pennsylvania settled around Fort Niagara. Others located at Sandwich (present-day Windsor) and across the river at Amherstburg, where they mingled with French settlers already long established near Fort

Detroit. Loyalists also settled in Saint-Jean, Chambly, Yamachiche, Pointe-Claire, Sorel, Gaspé, St Armand, Foucault, and Montreal.

When the British finally agreed to evacuate the posts in the southwest by Jay's Treaty in 1794, settlers moved from Detroit to British-controlled territory. These were the last "real" Loyalists. By that time, the colony had also become the destination of "late Loyalists," residents of the United States who had second thoughts about staying in the new republic, and relatives of Loyalists living in Upper Canada. The generous terms for land grants in Upper Canada also attracted a continuing flow of American immigrants to the frontier colony of Upper Canada.

Although they were only about 10 percent of the population of Quebec, the Loyalists brought powerful pressures to bear on authorities to address their needs. They demanded an elected assembly, common law, freehold tenure, and all the other "rights of Englishmen." The French middle class of merchants and professionals in Quebec also supported the establishment of an elected assembly in the colony—as long as Roman Catholics retained political rights. Since the conquest, the number of French-Canadians had more than doubled, reaching over 160 000 by 1790. They could easily dominate any elected institution.

THE CONSTITUTIONAL ACT, 1791

In 1791, the British Parliament passed the Constitutional Act, the third attempt to establish institutions for Quebec in as many decades. By this act, Quebec became two colonies: Upper and Lower Canada. In Upper Canada, where the English-speaking Loyalists made up the majority of the population, British laws, including freehold land tenure, prevailed. Lower Canada, with its overwhelmingly French-speaking population, retained the seigneurial system and French civil law. As a compensation to the English settlers in Lower Canada, provision was made for freehold tenure outside of seigneurial tracts, and the Eastern Townships were opened for settlement.

Each colony was granted a bicameral legislature, with an appointed legislative council and an elected assembly. Anyone with a 40-shilling freehold in rural areas or who paid rent at the rate of 10 pounds per annum was qualified to vote. Because of the availability of land in North America, a larger proportion of the men in the colonies could vote than in Great Britain. Women rarely held property in their own name, and even if they did, they seldom exercised the franchise, which was considered a male prerogative. A special oath of allegiance was devised to permit Roman Catholics to vote and hold public office.

The Constitutional Act represented an attempt on the part of British authorities to stem the tide of democratic sentiment sweeping the North Atlantic world. To do so they hoped to blunt the power of the elected assembly by strengthening the institutions embodying monarchical and aristocratic ideals. The monarchy was represented by a governor in Lower Canada and a lieutenant-governor in Upper Canada, while the aristocracy was represented in appointed legislative and executive councils. The governor (or lieutenant-governor), acting on behalf of the Crown, appointed individuals to the legislative council, which could introduce its own bills and veto all bills originating in the assembly. Because the members of the legislative council held office for life, were granted huge tracts of land, and were even eligible for titles, they were clearly meant to become the nucleus of a colonial aristocracy. The governor was also authorized to appoint an executive council to advise him on colonial matters. As was the case with the legislative councils, the men chosen to serve on the executive councils tended to hold office for life and were in a strong position to pursue their self-seeking policies.

The powers of the governor added more control over the activities of the assemblies. A governor could withhold consent from a bill passed by the colonial legislature, or he could reserve it for consideration by British authorities, who could disallow the bill within two years of its passage. He could also dismiss an assembly whose policies he found not to his liking. Reserves of Crown land and funds from Britain ensured that there would be sources of independent revenue to sustain the governor's independence from monies granted by the assembly.

Under the act, one-seventh of the land granted in every township was reserved for "the Support and Maintenance of a Protestant Clergy." The wording was vague and would soon be subject to much debate, but the intent was clear. In Upper Canada there would be an established church, presumably the Church of England, to add strength to the monarchical principle. The separation of church and state, a policy favoured by democrats everywhere by the end of the eighteenth century, was still too radical a concept for British colonial policy-makers.

Colonial officials hoped that the granting of an elected assembly would encourage the colonists to tax themselves to pay the cost of local improvements and ensure their loyalty in the event of another war. The test would come all too soon. In the aftermath of the American Revolution, support for democratic ideals had grown quickly in Europe. A popular revolution broke out in France in 1789 and three years later the triumphant republicans set out to export their revolutionary ideals. Britain and other European monarchies went to war to stop them. When Napoleon seized control of his war-ravaged country in 1799, he, too, took on his European rivals. The French and Napoleonic Wars finally ended in 1815 but not before they had induced a nasty little sideshow in North America known as the War of 1812.

UPPER CANADA, 1791–1812

Nowhere was loyalty more of an issue than in Upper Canada. In the years from 1791 to 1812, the population of the frontier colony increased ninefold, with most of the new residents coming from the United States. Immigration from the former Thirteen Colonies had been encouraged by Upper Canada's first lieutenant-governor, John Graves Simcoe (1792–98). In Simcoe's estimation, the Americans who came to Upper Canada to farm would again become loyal subjects of the king if administrators took care to cultivate British institutions in the colony.

Simcoe had commanded a Loyalist unit, the Queen's Rangers, during the American Revolution and was eager to recreate British institutions in the backwoods of British North America. He appointed officials with views similar to his own and, in return for their services, granted them vast tracts of land that they held for speculative purposes. Along with the

Clergy and Crown reserves, these grants constituted a major grievance for early immigrants. New settlements, instead of being compact, were generally widely dispersed, making the provision of local services such as roads and schools costly, and separating neighbours by inconvenient distances. In 1839, when Lord Durham reviewed the state of surveyed land in Upper Canada, he found that over half of it had been either granted to "classes of grantees whose station would preclude them from settling in the wilderness" or set aside as Clergy reserves.[3]

The badges of elite membership were a land grant along with a government post and membership in the Law Society of Upper Canada, which controlled entry into the legal profession in the colony. Living in large, comfortable homes, they hired servants and educated their children in private schools. Their male children generally also joined the elite. William Jarvis, for example, owed his appointment by Simcoe as provincial secretary and registrar to his rank as an officer in the Queen's Rangers. A generation later his son Samuel was deputy provincial secretary and chief superintendent of Indian affairs, while his other son, William, became sheriff of Gore District.

Women in elite families lived more restricted lives. Following the injunctions of an emerging cult of domesticity among the British middle class, women of means in Upper Canada were expected to marry sons of other elite families and make motherhood, household work, and charity their major preoccupations.

In the early years of Upper Canada, the land-rich political elite was concentrated in York (renamed Toronto in 1834), a site selected as the capital in 1793 because it was less vulnerable to American attack than Niagara, where the capital had originally been located. Kingston, the largest town, boasted only 50 houses. The majority of people lived in the countryside. Compared to most colonies, rural residents were well served by roads. The British government paid the cost of building a network of military roads—Yonge Street, for example—that became commercial routes as well.

Simcoe established a system of local government along British lines that provided a framework for legal and social services. Upper Canada was divided into districts, which were in turn divided into townships. The township became the unit of local administration, and its

York, *by Elizabeth Francis Hale, 1804.*

property owners elected the men who assessed property values for tax purposes, collected these taxes, and oversaw the highways. As in the Maritime colonies, these unpaid local officials were less important than the justices of the peace, appointed by the lieutenant-governor. The justices of the peace levied local taxes, appointed district treasurers, and superintended the building of jails and highways and the sale of liquor licences.

In the early years of settlement, the British government provided most of the funds that sustained the colonial economy. Government jobs and contracts, dispensed at the discretion of the lieutenant-governor and officials appointed by him, helped to create local oligarchies loyal to the government throughout Upper Canada. Not surprisingly, opposition to this privileged elite soon found a voice in the elected assembly. Simcoe left the colony in 1798 but his successors were confronted by a population increasingly democratic in sympathy and distrustful of their rulers.

In the Upper Canadian Assembly, challenges to the government's authority before 1812 were usually identified closely with three Irish-born men: William Weekes, Robert Thorpe, and Joseph Willcocks. While misgivings about Britain's brutal suppression of an Irish uprising in 1798 and the subsequent Act of Union (1801) between Great Britain and Ireland had initially kindled these men's criticism of colonial governance, their focus was on the denial of democracy in Upper Canada. Their supporters were united by a sense of grievance rather than by ethnicity.

LOWER CANADA, 1791–1812

In Lower Canada, governors used patronage to sustain the power of an English-speaking elite, despite the overwhelming preponderance of French-speaking people in the colony. Some members of the English elite were merchants who had made their fortunes in the fur trade. After 1800, this wealth was supplemented by investments in local industries such as brewing and distilling as well as the burgeoning timber trade.

Equivalent in importance to oil in the twentieth century, timber was essential to the successful prosecution of overseas trade and global wars. Until the 1790s, the British navy relied primarily on Baltic suppliers for timber. This source was seriously restricted when Napoleon entered into alliances with Russia, Prussia, Sweden, and Denmark in 1807. Britain moved quickly to raise duties on foreign timber, thereby offering some guarantee of long-term protection for capitalists prepared to invest in colonial production. By 1810, 74 percent of exports from Lower Canada were forest products. Furs, which accounted for 76 percent of exports in 1770, made up less than 10 percent of export receipts in 1810. British demands for squared timber also encouraged other ventures, such as John Molson's steamboat service on the St Lawrence and the beginnings of a Quebec shipbuilding industry.

With commercial connections in Great Britain, English-speaking merchants and capitalists had a major advantage over their French counterparts. Anglophones who had made money in the fur trade bought seigneuries both to gain access to timberlands and to earn income from habitants' dues. By 1812, an estimated two-thirds of the seigneuries were in the hands of English-speaking merchants. The predominantly English-speaking merchant group of Montreal also accumulated about 2.5 million hectares of land outside the seigneurial belt, granted by the Crown under the "leader and associate" system. A leader received 2500 hectares for every farmer he settled on a 500-hectare farm; the leader's grant supposedly repaid his costs of both recruiting and transporting settlers and provisioning them until they could grow their first crop. In practice the leaders, many of them wealthy merchants, provided the government with inflated lists of alleged settlers and generally provided few services to the real settlers.

Most of the new settlers moved north from the New England states. By 1812, about 20 000 of them had been enticed by promises of free land in the Eastern Townships south and east of Montreal. Because they received their lands in freehold tenure, the settlers did not have to contend with the seigneurial system, but they did have to cope with rocky soil, poor transportation, and huge areas of wilderness held aside for Clergy reserves, Crown reserves, and speculative purposes. The modest lives of these immigrants underscore the fact that only a small proportion of the English-speaking residents of Lower Canada, who in 1812 numbered 50 000 or about 15 percent of the population, were wealthy.

The French-speaking majority included only a small number of wealthy merchants and seigneurs. With commercial avenues blocked, there was a dramatic growth in the number of French-speaking

A View of the Château-Richer, Cape Torment, and the Lower End of the Isle of Orleans near Quebec, 1787, *by Thomas Davies.*

National Gallery of Canada/6275

professionals in the early nineteenth century. The leaders of the Roman Catholic Church welcomed priests fleeing the excesses of the French Revolution, who staffed a number of the new classical colleges in the colony. Although the colleges were designed to train a native-born priesthood, about 50 percent of the classical-college graduates sought employment in secular occupations, using their academic talents to become notaries, lawyers, journalists, and clerks. The socially ambitious continued to look to the purchase of a seigneury as a badge of their success. For instance, Louis-Joseph Papineau, who became the leader of the opponents of the government after 1815, was the son of a notary who purchased a seigneury called Petite Nation on the Ottawa River in 1801.

Frustrated by their failure to penetrate the government bureaucracy, the French-speaking middle class became increasingly nationalistic. Its members saw themselves as the natural leaders of French Canada. Through the Parti canadien, established in 1805, they focused upon the elected House of Assembly as a forum for demanding greater popular control over government. Supportive of the seigneurial system, and initially favourable to church control over education and social services, most members of the Parti canadien saw democracy as a tool for cultural survival. It could be used to protect French Canada's laws and language, limit the power of the merchants, and ensure that economic development was not controlled from abroad.

In 1806, the nationalists had their own newspaper, *Le Canadien*, edited by Pierre Bédard and François Blanchet. It was used to denounce the administration of Governor James Craig and assert the right of the assembly to shape policy for the colony. Craig retaliated in 1810 by imprisoning the editors and dissolving the assembly for a second straight year, which forced new elections. Since war with the United States seemed imminent, British authorities moved in 1811 to replace Craig with a more conciliatory governor, but this

biography

Ezekiel Hart

Ezekiel Hart was born in Trois-Rivières in 1770, the son of a Jewish merchant. There were fewer than 100 Jews in the Canadas before 1800, but their number included enterprising and prosperous individuals. Hart and his two brothers had run a successful brewery and potashery before Ezekiel established his own import-export business and a general store and began to purchase a great deal of land. In 1807, Hart won a by-election in Trois-Rivières, but the Parti canadien, regarding him as a supporter of the government, declared him ineligible to serve. The following year, Hart was re-elected and took the Christian oath of office required of members, but the assembly majority argued that his adhesion to the Jewish faith invalidated his oath.

Although Governor Craig supported Hart's right to take his seat in the assembly, the colonial secretary confirmed that Jews were unable to serve in British legislatures. Catholics in Britain suffered from the same legal restrictions as Jews, so it was ironic that the mainly

Catholic assemblymen of Lower Canada embraced the British ban on Jews in government. In 1832, with religious toleration established in British law, Ezekiel Hart's son Samuel won a seat in the Lower Canadian Assembly and became the first Jew to hold a seat in a British legislature.

The Parti canadien's rejection of Ezekiel Hart may suggest that the Canadiens were anti-Semitic. Anti-Semitism was indeed widespread in Christian societies in the nineteenth century, as it had been earlier. But Hart had been elected on both occasions by an electorate that was predominantly French-speaking. The Parti canadien, in turn, was most likely using Hart's Jewishness as a pretext to exclude a rich merchant suspected of being a supporter of the governor. The judge rejected by the same assembly was, after all, a Canadien. Nevertheless, the Parti canadien's willingness to use a man's religion as an excuse to ban him from its midst demonstrates that the party was not prepared to defend individual freedom of conscience.

only postponed what became the norm in all British North American colonies: confrontation between elected and appointed officials.

AGRICULTURAL CRISIS ON THE SEIGNEURIES

Secret instructions to the governor accompanying the Constitutional Act forbade the expansion of the seigneurial system beyond the boundaries established in 1791. As the population on the seigneuries grew, land in some areas became subdivided to the point where farm units were unproductive. Most habitants lacked the funds necessary to buy land and were therefore forced to seek alternative ways of making a living. In many farm families, fathers and sons pursued seasonal work in the fur trade, the lumber camps, on canal construction, or in shipbuilding, while women took responsibility for farm management. Agriculture under these circumstances remained largely for family subsistence rather than for commercial profit.

While men who could not be supported on the farms might find employment in the timber trade, fisheries, or fur trade, women had fewer options. Many women became domestic workers in the cities; others became prostitutes. In the city of Quebec, with a population of only about 14 000 in 1810, 400 to 600 prostitutes, native-born and immigrant, tried to earn a living off their bodies, relying particularly on the members of a local British garrison that averaged close to 2500 men from 1810 to 1816.

The agricultural crisis was most evident in areas where it was difficult to engage in farming for export. In Sorel, along the Richelieu River, at least one-third of the adult male population in the 1790s contracted with the North West Company (NWC) to work in the western fur trade. Some two-thirds of these men went west during the growing season. Wheat, the exportable crop, had a modest yield in the Sorel area. When the NWC merged with the Hudson's Bay Company in 1821 and implemented large layoffs, Sorel was thrust into poverty.

Similarly, in the Gaspé where farming was often marginal, over 5000 individuals in 1800 depended for most of their income on the Robins and other Channel Island families who bought their fish for re-

sale in Britain. Unable to subsist on agriculture, Gaspésiens depended for their survival on merchants who paid them not in cash but in credits, which could be redeemed only at the merchants' stores. Above all, in Lower Canada after 1806, it was seasonal work for lumberjacks, teamsters, drivers, and raftsmen in the timber trade that added cash to hard-pressed subsistence-agriculture households.

Overpopulation and outdated agricultural practices were not the only problems facing the habitants. While the impact of seigneurial dues on the habitants is much debated for the post-conquest period, evidence in some areas suggests that they had a crippling effect. In the Richelieu region, for example, over half of the habitants' agricultural surpluses were remitted to the seigneurs. This situation left little possibility of saving for the poor crop years that, because of wheat-fly infestations, became more frequent in Lower Canada after 1800. It also made it difficult for habitants to invest in new farming practices revolutionizing agriculture in other areas of North America and Europe.

The British officials tended to dismiss poverty in Quebec as the fault of its allegedly unprogressive victims. This was a distortion of reality. Both before and after the conquest, the Canadiens demonstrated an ability to take advantage of market opportunities. Furthermore, whatever the anti-materialist ideology of their church, the Canadiens were far from otherworldly. Rather, their problems were rooted in the failure of the British either to fix seigneurial dues, which had been done before 1760, to prevent gouging, or to grant free lands to capital-short farmers. British policies—or the lack thereof—on these fronts stymied the Canadiens economically and stimulated their desire for political reforms.

THE WAR OF 1812

In 1812, demands for political reform were temporarily halted when war was declared between Great Britain and the United States. Although the issues that ultimately led to war—Native policy on the frontier and the rights of neutral shipping on the high seas—directly affected the British North American colonies, they were handled by authorities in London. So, too, was the military side of the war. British troops assisted by their Native allies living in American territory did most of the fighting. Even the resolution of the conflict was negotiated between Britain and the United States without taking British North American interests into consideration. Nevertheless, the war created powerful mythologies, especially in the two Canadas, reinforcing anti-democratic ideology among the elite in Upper Canada and nationalism among the French-speaking middle class in Lower Canada.

THE CANADAS

The main goal of the United States in the war was to seize Britain's thinly populated North American colonies. Since the Canadas seemed the easiest target—the Maritimes could be protected by the British navy—they became the object of attack. The fact that so many Upper Canadians had immigrated from the United States convinced some American authorities that the capture of Upper Canada would be a "mere matter of marching." On the eve of leading his army into Upper Canada, American General William Hull issued a declaration indicating that he came to liberate the people of Upper Canada from the yoke of British oppression, not to conquer them.

Most Upper Canadians appear to have opposed the idea of breaking links with Great Britain, but a significant minority supported the American cause. During the course of the war, several hundred American immigrants in Upper Canada moved back to the United States to avoid being called upon to fight their former homeland. Many who remained in the colony pointedly took no role in the fighting until it became clear that Great Britain was prepared to make a major commitment to defence. In the final analysis, about 11 000 colonists were active in the militia, poorly trained as it was, while members of the elite received officer commissions.

Despite the enlistments, the military commander, Major-General Isaac Brock, regarded the population as defeatist. He informed his superiors in 1812:

> My situation is most critical, not from any thing the enemy can do, but from the disposition of the people—The population [of Upper Canada], believe me, is essentially bad—A full belief possesses them that this Province must inevitably succumb. This prepossession is fatal to every exertion—

> Legislators, Magistrates, Militia, Officers, all, have imbibed the idea, and are so sluggish and indifferent in all their respective offices that the artful and active scoundrel is allowed to parade the Country without interruption, and commit all imaginable mischief... Most of the people have lost all confidence—I however speak loud and look big."[4]

To demonstrate that Britain could win a war with the Americans, Brock authorized a victorious assault on Michilimackinac soon after war was declared. This aggressive posture won the British the support of the Native peoples of the Ohio valley, who united under the Shawnee chief Tecumseh after receiving promises that Britain would seek to win the return of this vast area to Native control. With Native help, Brock went on to seize Detroit, but then his luck ran out.

At a battle in October 1812, on the heights above the village of Queenston, in the Niagara region, Brock and 28 of his men were slain. His army, which included 1000 British regulars, 500 Iroquois, and 600 Upper Canadian militia, nevertheless carried the day. Over 900 Americans were taken prisoner when they were trapped by reinforcements from Fort George led by Major-General Roger Hale Sheaffe. The victory, following the earlier capture of Detroit, helped to raise the morale of the Upper Canadians and stiffen their resolve to resist the invaders.

In September 1813, the Americans under Commodore Oliver Perry defeated the British fleet on Lake Erie at the Battle of Put-in-Bay. This victory forced the British to abandon Detroit. Soon thereafter, the American army defeated British forces under Lieutenant Brock's successor Colonel Henry Proctor at Moraviantown. Tecumseh died in the battle, which undermined the effect of the Native alliance. Meanwhile, the American army ranged freely in the western peninsula, burning Newark (Niagara-on-the-Lake) to the ground before departing in December 1813. On the eastern frontier, American forces had been unable to capture Kingston and thereby gain control of Lake Ontario. As a consolation prize, they occupied York for a few days in the spring of 1813, and torched its parliament buildings. The British in turn razed sections of Buffalo in the state of New York as well as the city of Washington, DC.

In 1814, battles in the Niagara peninsula exhausted both sides. The bloodiest occurred in pitch darkness at Lundy's Lane, not far from Queenston

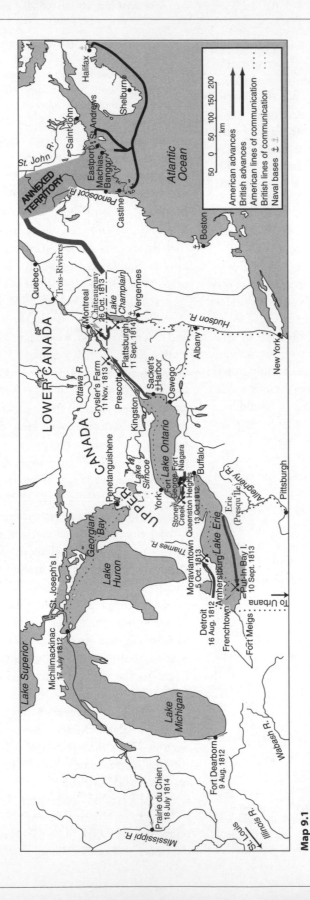

Map 9.1
The War of 1812.

Adapted from D.G.G. Kerr, *Historical Atlas of Canada*, 3rd ed. (Scarborough: Nelson, 1975) 38.

Voices from the Past

The Legend of Brock and the Loyal Militia

Following the Battle of Queenston Heights, Upper and Lower Canadians began singing the praises of brave General Brock and the loyal militia who supposedly saved British North America from the invading Americans. This effusive outburst appeared in the Montreal *Gazette* on 26 October 1812.

> The intelligence received last week from [Upper Canada] is such as cannot but call forth the astonishment, the gratitude, and the applause of all classes of His Majesty's Subjects in British America when we consider the number of assailants, compared to that of the little band of heroes who so nobly defended this devoted portion of the British Empire and the brilliant results of their exertions at Queenston on the 13th.... The Historian in handing down to posterity the details of this historic achievement will dwell with rapture on the undaunted courage displayed and the unshaken loyalty evinced by a little army not exceeding 800 British subjects against an enemy at least three times their numbers,

> and while he bedews with merited regret the memory of the illustrious Chief and his heroic companions who so nobly fell on this glorious day, he will inscribe the name of BROCK on the imperishable list of British Heroes and class the victory that resulted among the most brilliant events which adorn the page of British History. —Our fellow subjects in the United Kingdom will, no doubt, duly appreciate the splendid exertions of their Canadian brethren, and will freely confess that they are worthy of the King whom they serve and the Constitution which they enjoy, and that the men who have come forward so cheerfully in defence of the cause of their country and who have conspicuously distinguished themselves in sharing with British Troops in the capture of Michilimackinac and Detroit, and in this latter glorious defeat of the enemy at Queenston, are well entitled to the friendship and protection of their mother-country.— May the union between Britain and such heroic descendants be eternal....

Heights, on 25 July 1814. British regulars, assisted by the militia, confronted American troops, who could barely be seen in the dark. By morning the casualties on both sides were enormous. While the Upper Canadian authorities touted Lundy's Lane as a glorious victory, it actually confirmed the pattern of rough equivalence between the two sides and deepened war-weariness in both Washington and London.

In Lower Canada, the squabbles between the Parti canadien and the governor were set aside as both factions united to defend the colony. The Lower Canadian Assembly authorized the new governor, Sir George Prevost, to conscript manpower and to keep as many as 6000 men in the field for a full year. The Roman Catholic Church, under Bishop Joseph-Octave Plessis, supported the British cause. In October 1813, a force of about 1300 men, consisting of the French Canadian Voltigeurs under Lieutenant-Colonel Charles de Salaberry and 150 Iroquois, fended off 4200 undisciplined, poorly trained American recruits who crossed the river Châteauguay en route to Montreal.

THE MARITIME COLONIES

Unlike Upper and Lower Canada, the Maritime colonies were spared invading armies during the War of 1812. They were nevertheless greatly influenced by the wartime economy that prevailed for more than two decades. As alternative sources of supply were cut off, Atlantic colonies found a ready market for their timber, fish, and foodstuffs. The timber trade reached boom proportions, and shipbuilding and the carrying trade made promising beginnings. In St John's Island (renamed Prince Edward Island in 1799) and other fertile areas of the Maritimes, farmers were spurred to greater production. There were even signs that the Maritimes could become a major player in the lucrative West Indies trade.

New Brunswick's economy was transformed following Napoleon's blockade of the Baltic supply. Between 1805 and 1812, the fir and pine timber reaching Britain from New Brunswick increased more than 20-fold. Businessmen, many of them based in the Scottish port city of Greenock, brought their capital, labour, and technology to the shores of the Miramichi and St John rivers. By 1815, forest products accounted for nearly two-thirds of the colony's exports. Control over Crown lands and the revenue of the timber trade became issues that would dominate New Brunswick's social and political life long after the wars that prompted the timber boom had come to an end.

The War of 1812 also expanded the potential for privateering, which had been carried on against French shipping, with more or less success, throughout the Napoleonic Wars. Thirty-seven vessels from the Atlantic colonies engaged in privateering activities during the conflict, recording 207 captures. The *Liverpool Packet* was the champion of the privateering fleet, taking 50 "prizes," most of them from Massachusetts. These captures helped to line the pockets of ambitious Halifax merchants who bought the vessels at prize courts and sold them at a profit. The war also inspired moments of great excitement. In June 1813, for example, Haligonians were treated to the spectacle of the HMS *Shannon* arriving with the USS *Chesapeake* in tow following a brief engagement off Boston harbour. The following year, a British army under Sir John Sherbrooke occupied part of the coast of present-day Maine, providing more opportunities for commercial profit.

View of Saint John, New Brunswick, 1814, *by Joseph Brown Comingo (1784–1821)*.

New Brunswick Museum, Saint John, NB

The wars with France and the United States encouraged more black immigration to the Maritimes. In 1796, some 550 Maroons from Jamaica, freedom fighters who had lost their most recent battle in their 140-year war against the British, worked on the town's fortifications. They, like many Black Loyalists before them, decided to relocate in Sierra Leone. Following the War of 1812, over 2000 African Americans who fought for the British in the War of 1812 were brought to the Maritimes. After spending a difficult winter in Halifax, they were finally settled in communities outside the city. Preston and Hammonds Plains absorbed most of the immigrants; 500 settled at Loch Lomond in New Brunswick. After the abolition of the slave trade in 1807, slavery was not upheld in the courts and gradually died out in the Maritimes.

NEWFOUNDLAND

Newfoundland was transformed by two decades of war. With the decline in the number of West Country vessels sent to the banks and inshore fishery, Newfoundlanders increasingly dominated the salt-fish trade. Their dominance was further augmented by the exclusion of the French and Americans from the Newfoundland fishery. During the wars, St Pierre and Miquelon were occupied by British troops and the French Treaty Shore was patrolled, bringing the French fishery to a standstill. The wars also encouraged economic diversity, including a lucrative seal fishery and a local shipbuilding industry.

With opportunities beckoning to those willing to work, Newfoundland attracted immigrants. Among them were merchants and fishing crews determined to avoid wartime restrictions and impressment. By 1815, the population of the colony had reached 20 000, and St John's had emerged as the commercial capital of the North Atlantic fisheries. As historian Shannon Ryan put it, Newfoundland "had always been a fishery based around an island." Now, with the French and Napoleonic Wars serving as a catalyst, it "would finally become a colony based on the fishery."[5]

A colony in all but name and status, Newfoundland had also expanded its territorial jurisdiction. In 1809, Labrador, which had been part of Quebec/Lower Canada since 1774, was re-annexed to Newfoundland. This was a result, in part, of imperial policy developed for the protection of Labrador, but it was also a reflection of the growing presence of Newfoundlanders in the Labrador inshore and seal fisheries. Since Europeans were confined largely to the coast, the inland boundary between Lower Canada and Labrador remained undefined and the matter remained unsettled until the twentieth century.

THE WAR OF 1812: MYTH AND REALITY

While the war of 1812 receives little attention in British and American textbooks, it features prominently in most accounts of Canadian history. Especially in Upper and Lower Canada where most of the battles were fought, the failure of the United States to capture the less powerful British colonies became a source of pride and the inspiration for a remarkable number of commemorative heritage sites. Historical memory also dimmed with the passage of time. In many Canadian accounts of the war, the fact that British regulars did much of the fighting became less significant than the role played by the brave colonial militia in such battles as Queenston Heights and Châteauguay. The war was even seen in retrospect as the seed bed of Canadian nationalism, with English and French Canadians co-operating to push back the aggressive Americans.

The War of 1812 also deeply affected political values in the colonies. Along with the American Revolution, it served as a rationale in Conservative thought for maintaining a hierarchical, class-stratified society rather than an egalitarian one. The alternative to British rule and British class structures, it was argued, was a slide into atheist republicanism and even annexation to the United States. Conservatives used

the war to justify appointing to public office only an elite loyal to British values, suppressing dissent of any kind, and discouraging further American immigration.

No colony was more influenced by the War of 1812 than Upper Canada. In the aftermath of the war, the colony increasingly became dominated by a small clique of officials often described as a "Family Compact." Claims to service during the War of 1812 played a significant role for those seeking patronage. It was rather more difficult for a woman to take advantage of her contributions to the military effort to receive favours from the state, as Laura Secord would learn. In 1813, she had walked through enemy lines from Queenston to Beaver Dams to warn British troops of an impending American assault. Efforts both by her husband and herself to elicit government patronage on the basis of this service yielded little, although later generations, for their own reasons, would come to venerate Secord.

THE DEFENDED BORDER

The War of 1812 was the last official war between Britain and the United States. By the Treaty of Ghent, signed 24 December 1814, both parties agreed to return any enemy territory that they had occupied. Two agreements reached after the war helped to establish peaceful relations between the United States and Britain in North America. The Rush-Bagot agreement of 1817 limited the number of armed vessels on the Great Lakes and Lake Champlain to those required to control smuggling. In the same year, agreement was reached over the disputed islands in Passamaquoddy Bay. Boundaries were further clarified by the Anglo-American Convention of 1818, in which the 49th parallel was recognized as the boundary between the Lake of the Woods and the Rockies, and the disputed territory on the Pacific coast was to be subject to joint occupation until an agreement could be reached. American rights to the inshore fisheries of the Atlantic region were also restricted.

Although the United States and Britain never again declared war on each other, both sides continued to see the other as a potential enemy. Military bases were constructed and strengthened on both sides of the border over the next century. Between 1826 and 1832, the British built the Rideau Canal linking Kingston and Ottawa as an alternative water route to the vulnerable international section of the St Lawrence River between Montreal and Kingston. The route of the Intercolonial Railway was also chosen with military considerations in mind. This was yet another legacy for British North America of the War of 1812.

CULTURE IN COLONIAL SOCIETY

While war and rumours of war dominated colonial society between 1783 and 1815, it was also a period in which high culture took root. The arrival of the Loyalists and the prosperity associated with the French and Napoleonic Wars encouraged the refinement, literary output, and scholarly debate. These were features of a new intellectual awakening known as the Enlightenment that was increasingly animating the North Atlantic world.

Many of the Loyalists had enjoyed the amenities of urban life and were impatient to establish churches, schools, and newspapers in their new homeland. While only a minority of them belonged to the Church of England, the structure of the established church of Britain was strengthened by the Loyalist presence. In 1787, Charles Inglis, the Loyalist rector of Trinity Church in New York, was consecrated the first Church of England bishop of Nova Scotia, with jurisdiction over all the British North American colonies. The first overseas bishop in the British Empire, Inglis was eager to enhance the status of Anglicanism in the colonies. He supported the founding in 1789 of King's College in Windsor, Nova Scotia, as an exclusive institution for sons of the Anglican elite and backed various missionary efforts—most of them futile—to draw the mass of the population from their dissenting religious views. In New Brunswick, the Loyalists were instrumental in founding the Provincial Academy of Arts and Sciences, which received its charter as the College of New Brunswick in 1800.

As a "consolation to their distress," many educated Loyalists turned to literature. They produced poems, essays, and sermons, and were avid readers of British fiction and advice books. In 1789, John Howe, a Loyalist from Massachusetts, and William Cochran, an Anglican clergyman and classical scholar, attempted to provide a forum for colonial writers. Although their *Nova Scotia Magazine*, published in Halifax, lasted less than two years, it ranks as the first literary journal in the British North American colonies. By the late 1780s, there were two bilingual newspapers in Quebec: the *Quebec Gazette* and the *Montreal Gazette*. The latter was the more radical of the two, advocating greater social equality, public education, and restrictions on the powers of the church.

With the Loyalists came the full range of eighteenth-century political ideologies, which raised the level of political debate. The Loyalist elite was unable to curtail the democratic tendencies taking root in the era of the American and French Revolutions, but they added weight to the conservative side of the political spectrum. In rare cases they also proved far-sighted. William Smith, a Loyalist from New York who became chief justice of Quebec, proposed a federated British North America under a "governor-general" to serve as a "showcase of the continent." His "grand design" for the British colonies in North America was a little premature, but it had merits that would soon be recognized by colonial politicians.

In the years during and following the American Revolutionary War, voluntary organizations emerged in colonial towns. Service organizations, such as the Charitable Irish Society, and private clubs, such as the Masonic Lodge, were established and informal literary salons, popular in Britain, became a feature of polite society. In the summer of 1791, a debating club christened the Robin Hood Society—its name was later changed to the Montreal Society—was formed. Among the topics of debate were the "duty of electors" and the relative merits of marriage and celibacy.

As one of the major military bases in the British Empire and an emerging commercial centre, Halifax reflected many of the cultural trends of the times. Several of the town's finest public buildings were also constructed in this period. New Hampshire-born Loyalist Sir John Wentworth, who served as

MORE TO THE STORY

Artists in a New World

Native artists in British North America produced intricate carving, beading, baskets, and painted skins. By the eighteenth century, Europeans were systematically collecting Native artwork, some of which found its way into galleries and museums.

The first European artists in the colony were soldiers, draftsmen, and natural scientists who had received some training in drawing. Because drawing was the only method of creating a visual record before the introduction of photography in the mid-nineteenth century, it was a valuable skill taught in many professions.

Eighteenth-century European-born artists were trained to impose a rigid order on their subject matter, omitting any details that might offend European sensibilities. The idealized North American environment can be seen in the work of Richard Short, a purser with James Wolfe's expedition.

Joseph Frederick Wallet DesBarres was a Swiss-born army officer who, together with Samuel Holland and James Cook, surveyed most of the Atlantic region in the period following the Seven Years' War. DesBarres included landscape views in his much-praised *Atlantic Neptune*, a four-volume guide to navigation in the region. In their detail and colour, the paintings of Thomas Davies represent a departure from the topographic watercolours done by students of the military academy. Davies was posted in the British colonies from 1755

A painted robe, Sioux type.

Canadian Museum of Civilization, CMC 74-7928

View of the River La Puce Near Quebec in Canada, 1792, *by Thomas Davies.*

National Gallery of Canada/6274

Miniature of Jane Harbel Drake, *by Joseph Brown Comingo.*

New Brunswick Museum, Saint John, NB/989.13.1

The Woolsey Family, 1809, *by William Berczy.*

National Gallery of Canada/5875

to 1790, and his work, such as *View of the River La Puce*, offers an exceptional visual record of the eighteenth-century landscape.

By the eighteenth century, it had become fashionable among the middle class in Europe and North America to have their portraits painted. The first colonial-born portrait artist in the Atlantic region was Joseph Brown Comingo, from Lunenburg, Nova Scotia. Although little is known about his artistic training, he worked extensively throughout Nova Scotia and New Brunswick, painting both portraits and landscapes. His miniatures, such as the one of Jane Harbel Drake, were particularly popular in the eighteenth and early nineteenth centuries.

One of British North America's most accomplished artists was William Berczy. Born in Wallerstein (Germany) in 1744, Berczy arrived in 1794 in Upper Canada, where he was involved in various colonization schemes. During his sojourn in the colony, he supplemented his income by painting miniatures and portraits. His portrait of Joseph Brant is considered an accurate portrayal of the Mohawk chief, and art historian Dennis Reid argues that Berczy's *The Woolsey Family* is "one of the few exceptional Canadian paintings" of the early nineteenth century.

In the private schools that flourished following the arrival of the Loyalists, young ladies received training in the "polite" accomplishments of drawing and watercolour painting. Women were also occasionally taught to draw by their formally trained fathers and brothers. Because they had few practical outlets for their work, women rarely earned a living from their artistic endeavours, and very few signed pieces of their work have survived the ravages of time and neglect.

Prince's Lodge Rotunda, Halifax.

Nova Scotia Archives and Records Management PANS N-6384

lieutenant-governor of Nova Scotia from 1792 to 1808, and his wife Frances, oversaw the construction of Government House, an elegant Georgian mansion that still serves as the official residence of the lieutenant-governor of the province.

Between 1794 and 1799 Halifax was also the home of Prince Edward, who commanded the garrison. He, along with his mistress, who was publicly addressed as Madame St Laurent, brought glamour and excitement to Halifax social life. Struck by "the miserable state of all the works and public buildings," the prince devoted his considerable energy to overhauling Halifax's defences and was instrumental in the construction of three exquisite round structures: St George's Anglican Church, the Old Town Clock, and the Prince's Lodge Rotunda. Created Duke of Kent in 1799, Prince Edward later became the father of Queen Victoria (1837–1901).

CONCLUSION

Between 1783 and 1815 the social, economic, and political ties linking Upper and Lower Canada and the Maritimes to Great Britain became stronger. The immigration of Loyalists and settlers from Great Britain helped to anglicize the colonies, while the French and Napoleonic Wars drew them more fully into the British mercantile system of production and trade. In the Canadas, the War of 1812 encouraged commitment to the British parliamentary system rather than its republican counterparts in the United States and France. With a thriving fishery and growing population, Newfoundland and Labrador began to take on the trappings of the other colonies of settlement. The rest of British North America—the great Northwest and the Arctic—as we shall see in the next chapter, were also increasingly subject to the world's greatest empire.

NOTES

1 Wallace Brown, The Good Americans: *The Loyalists in the American Revolution* (New York: William Morrow, 1969) 206.

2 James W. St. G. Walker, *The Black Loyalists: The Search for a Promised Land in Nova Scotia and Sierra Leone, 1783–1870* (New York: Longman, 1976) 73.

3 *Lord Durham's Report: An Abridgement of Report on the Affairs of British North America by Lord Durham*, ed. Gerald M. Craig (Toronto: McClelland and Stewart, 1963) 119.

4 Gerald M. Craig, *Upper Canada: The Formative Years, 1784-1841* (Toronto: McClelland and Stewart, 1963) 70-71.

5 Shannon Ryan, "Fishery to Colony: A Newfoundland Watershed, 1793–1815," *Acadiensis* 12.2 (Spring 1983): 52.

SELECTED READING

There is an extensive literature on the Loyalists. In *The United Empire Loyalists: Men and Myths* (Toronto: Copp Clark Pitman, 1967), L.F.S. Upton discusses the historiographical issues that haunt the topic. Specialized studies that avoid most of the historiographical traps include Norman Knowles, *Inventing the Loyalists: The Ontario Loyalist Tradition and the Creation of a Usable Past* (Toronto: University of Toronto Press, 1997); Esther Clark Wright's *The Loyalists of New Brunswick* (Wolfville, NS: Wright, 1955); Neil MacKinnon, *This Unfriendly Soil: The Loyalist Experience in Nova Scotia, 1783–1791* (Montreal: McGill-Queen's University Press, 1989); Marion Robertson, *King's Bounty: A History of Early Shelburne* (Halifax: Nova Scotia Museum, 1983); David Bell, *Early Loyalist Saint John: The Origins of New Brunswick Politics* (Fredericton: New Ireland Press, 1983); and Ann Gorman Condon, *The Envy of the American States: The Loyalists of New Brunswick* (Fredericton: New Ireland Press, 1984). The black Loyalist experience is described in James Walker, *The Black Loyalists: The Search for a Promised Land in Nova Scotia and Sierra Leone, 1783–1870* (1976, reprinted Toronto: University of Toronto Press, 1992) and William Spray, *The Blacks in New Brunswick* (Fredericton: Brunswick Press, 1972). Literary issues are discussed in Dennis Duffy, *Gardens, Covenants, Exiles: Loyalism in the Literature of Upper Canada/Ontario* (Toronto: University of Toronto Press, 1982), and Gwen Davies, "Consolation to Distress: Loyalist Literary Activity in the Maritimes," in *Studies in Maritime Literary History* (Fredericton: Acadiensis Press, 1991): 30–47. On Loyalist women, see Mary Beth Norton's pioneering article, "Eighteenth-Century American Women in Peace and War: The Case of the Loyalists," *William and Mary*

Quarterly 3.33 (1976): 386–409, and Janice Potter-MacKinnon, *While Women Only Wept: Loyalist Refugee Women* (Montreal: McGill-Queen's University Press, 1993). Overviews are provided by Christopher Moore in *The Loyalists: Revolution, Exile and Settlement* (Toronto: Macmillan, 1984), and Wallace Brown and Hereward Senior, *Victorious in Defeat: The Loyalists in Canada* (Toronto: Methuen, 1984).

Quebec in the aftermath of the American Revolution is covered in A. L. Burt, Allen Greer, Fernand Ouellet, and Hilda Neatby, cited earlier, as well as Philip Lawson, *The Imperial Challenge: Quebec and Britain in the Age of the American Revolution* (Montreal, McGill-Queen's University Press, 1989) and F. Murray Greenwood, *Legacies of Fear: Law and Politics in Quebec in the Era of the French Revolution* (Toronto: University of Toronto Press, 1993).

The social history of early Ontario is examined in a variety of excellent essays in J.K. Johnson and B. Wilson, eds., *Historical Essays on Upper Canada: New Perspectives* (Ottawa: Carleton University Press, 1989) and an earlier volume, *Historical Essays on Upper Canada* (Ottawa: Carleton University Press, 1975). On elite formation in the colony, see Johnson's *Becoming Prominent: Regional Leadership in Upper Canada, 1791–1841* (Montreal: McGill-Queen's University Press, 1989), and Bruce Wilson, *The Enterprises of Robert Hamilton: A Study of Wealth and Influence in Early Upper Canada* (Ottawa: Carleton University Press, 1983). The colony's economic history is surveyed in Douglas McCalla, *Planting the Province: The Economic History of Upper Canada* (Toronto: University of Toronto Press, 1993). The gendered public discourse of Upper Canada is explored in Cecilia Morgan, *Public Men and Virtuous Women: The Gendered Language of Religion and Politics in Upper Canada, 1791–1850* (Toronto: University of Toronto Press, 1996). On women in Upper Canada, see Elizabeth Jane Errington, *Wives and Mothers, School Mistresses and Scullery Maids: Working Women in Upper Canada, 1790–1840* (Montreal: McGill-Queen's University Press, 1995) and Katherine M.J. McKenna, *Anne Murray Powell and Her Family, 1755–1849* (Montreal: McGill-Queen's University Press, 1994). On Upper Canadian politics, see Gerald Craig's *Upper Canada: The Formative Years* (Toronto: McClelland and Stewart, 1963); David Mills, *The Idea of Loyalty in Upper Canada, 1784–1850* (Montreal: McGill-Queen's University Press, 1988); and Jane Errington, *The Lion, the Eagle, and Upper Canada: A Developing Colonial Ideology* (Montreal: McGill-Queen's University Press, 1987).

For Lower Canada, Fernand Ouellet, *Lower Canada, 1791–1840: Social Change and Nationalism* (Toronto: McClelland and Stewart, 1980) and his *Economic and Social History of Quebec* (Toronto: Macmillan, 1981) provide abundant information as well as suggestive interpretations of the economic, social, and political history of Quebec during this period. Jean-Pierre Wallot, *Un Québec qui bougeait: trame socio-politique au tournant du XIXe siècle* (Trois-Rivières: Boréal Express, 1973) offers a view of Lower Canada's economy and society before 1815 at variance with Ouellet's. Closer to Ouellet's views but far more sympathetic to the British merchants is Donald Creighton, *The Empire of the St Lawrence* (Toronto: Macmillan, 1956). Case studies of rural life are found in Allan Greer, *Peasant, Lord, and Merchant: Rural Society in Three Quebec Parishes, 1740–1840* (Toronto: University of Toronto Press, 1985). On the English-speaking minority, see Ronald Rudin, *The Forgotten Quebecers: A History of English-Speaking Quebec, 1759–1980* (Quebec:

Institut québécois de recherche sur la culture, 1985).

The causes of the War of 1812 are assessed in Harry L. Coles, *The War of 1812* (Chicago: University of Chicago Press, 1965). Military aspects of the war are dealt with both in Coles and G.F.G. Stanley, *The War of 1812: Land Operations* (Toronto: Macmillan, 1983). On the social impact of war, see George Sheppard, *Plunder, Profit, and Paroles: A Social History of the War of 1812 in Upper Canada* (Montreal: McGill-Queen's University Press, 1994). A two-volume popular history of the war is Pierre Berton, *The Invasion of Canada, 1812–1813* and *Flames Across the Border, 1813–1814* (Toronto: McClelland and Stewart, 1980; 1984).

Developments in Atlantic Canada in this period are covered in Buckner and Reid, Conrad and Hiller, McNutt and Bumsted, cited earlier. See also Shannon Ryan, "Fishery to Colony; a Newfoundland Watershed, 1793–1815," *Acadiensis* 12.2 (Spring 1983): 34–52; Keith Matthews, *Lectures on the History of Newfoundland, 1500–1830* (St John's: Breakwater Books, 1988); Sean T. Cadigan, *Hope and Deception in Conception Bay: Merchant-Settler Relations in Newfoundland, 1785–1855* (Toronto: University of Toronto Press, 1995) and Julian Gwyn, *Excessive Expectations: Maritime Commerce and the Economic Development of Nova Scotia, 1740–1870* (Montreal and Kingston: McGill-Queen's University Press, 1998). The significance of privateering for the Maritimes in this period is summarized in Daniel Conlin, "They Plundered Well: Planters as Privateers, 1793–1805," in Margaret Conrad and Barry Moody, eds., *Planter Links: Community and Culture in Colonial Nova Scotia* (Fredericton: Acadiensis Press, 2001): 20–35. The Maroon and Black Refugee migration in this period is covered in the two volumes of Bridglal Pachai's *Beneath the Clouds of the Promised Land: The Survival of Nova Scotia Blacks* (Halifax: Black Educator's Association of Nova Scotia, 1987/1990).

 **WEBLINKS**

CONTSITUTION ACT OF 1791
www.solon.org/Constitutions/Canada/English/PreConfed
eration/ca_1791.html

This site offers a complete account of the 1791 Constitutional Act.

TREATY OF 1783
http://earlyamerica.com/earlyamerica/milestones/paris/

In addition to the complete text of the Paris Peace Treaty of 1783, this site offers contextual background regarding the creation of this document.

NEWFOUNDLAND AND LABRADOR HERITAGE
www.heritage.nf.ca/

This Heritage site explores the history, society, culture, and natural environment of Newfoundland and Labrador.

NAPOLEON
www.wtj.com/archives/napoleon/

This War Times Journal site offers transcripts of Napoleon's correspondence regarding his campaigns, as well as archives and articles relating to the Napoleonic Wars.

PRIVATEERING
www.chebucto.ns.ca/~jacktar/privateering.html

The Canadian Privateering Homepage offers definitions, documents, answers to frequently asked questions, and internal links to related topics.

THE WAR OF 1812
www.militaryheritage.com/1812.htm

This site offers articles, uniform charts, book reviews, extensive links, and the largest collection of War of 1812 images available on the Internet.

LOUISA'S WORLD
www3.ns.sympatico.ca/dmcclare/home.htm

"Louisa's World" explores the 1815 diary of a Nova Scotia farm girl who lived in Dartmouth, NS. In addition to mentioning the defeat of Napoleon, she describes farming rhythms and courtship practices in spare but fascinating detail. Dale McClare, who created the site, has done a good job of explaining the context, finding illustrations, and tracking down diary references. This is an excellent site for students of social history.

Natives and the Fur Trade in the West, 1775–1821

Mulks, a Squamish elder who spoke only his Coast Salish mother tongue, was about 100 years old in 1896 when he recounted the Squamish people's tale of a smallpox epidemic that had ravaged the peoples of the Strait of Georgia in the period before they had seen any Europeans. The master of an Anglican college in Vancouver, who transcribed the account that the Squamish translators provided, wrote:

> A dreadful skin disease, loathsome to look upon, broke out upon all alike. None were spared. Men, women and children sickened, took the disease and died in agony by hundreds, so that when the spring arrived and fresh food was procurable, there was scarcely a person left of all their numbers to get it. Camp after camp, village after village, was left desolate. The remains of which, said the old man...are found today in the old camp sites or midden-heaps over which the forest has been growing for so many generations. Little by little the remnant left by the disease grew into a nation once more, and when the first white men sailed up the Squamish in their big boats, the tribe was strong and numerous again.[1]

The epidemic was the Pacific coastal leg of a smallpox pandemic among Natives of the Americas that broke out in central Mexico in 1779. Spreading rapidly north and south, smallpox killed half the people of the Assiniboine, Ojibwa, Cree, and Blackfoot nations. By 1782 it had reached the northern plains, leaving its deadly mark on the Chipewyan, and had crossed the Rockies to devastate First Nations in southern British Columbia, few of whom had yet encountered Europeans. Captain George Vancouver, exploring the territory around Puget Sound and the Strait of Georgia in the early 1790s, was astonished by the number of deserted villages with hundreds of human skeletons lying on the beaches.

An expanding fur trade across the plains helps to account for the speed with which the epidemic moved. Trade opened up a pathway for pathogens such as smallpox and diphtheria, bringing to the plains the tragedies that had already befallen the Natives east of the Great Lakes. While smallpox's course was slower in British Columbia, where many of the coastal nations remained relatively isolated from other Native groups, the fur trade would eventually introduce all of the Western First Nations to a variety of diseases that would take a heavy toll in human lives.

The Aboriginal peoples of the Western Cordillera, the Interior Plains, and the North survived European diseases. In the period from 1775 to 1815 Natives continued to vastly outnumber the Europeans throughout these regions, and they became willing, often enthusiastic, participants in the fur trade. The rivalry between the Montreal traders and the Hudson's Bay Company would ensure that, at least in the short term, the Natives would be well served.

FUR-TRADE RIVALRIES IN THE NORTHWEST

With the outbreak of the American Revolution, the Montreal-based fur traders were forced to reconsider their strategy. Their trade in the southwest was devastated by war and the posts ultimately abandoned to the United States. To secure their advantage against the Hudson's Bay Company, the leading traders in the western territories—the "wintering partners"—pooled their resources with the Montreal merchants who marketed their furs abroad. Together they formed the North West Company (NWC) in 1783. The main Montreal partners were Benjamin and Joseph Frobisher and Simon McTavish. In the years that followed, the western fur trade would make fortunes for these and other Montreal businessmen—fortunes invested in land, the timber trade, and other ventures in Lower Canada.

Competition between the river and the bay led to the proliferation of trading posts. In 1774, there were only seventeen posts in the Northwest, seven belonging to the Hudson's Bay Company and ten to the St Lawrence traders. By 1804, there were 430 posts. Scarcely a Native living in the Northwest was more than 200 kilometres from a trading post. The Montreal traders were also aggressive explorers. In 1789, Alexander Mackenzie, exploring on behalf of the North West Company of Montreal, reached the Arctic Ocean along the river that bears his name, and in 1793 reached the Pacific by an overland route.

The new company's main advantages over the Hudson's Bay Company were its experienced French-Canadian voyageurs, its Native-style birch-bark canoes, and its wintering partners. In a short time, however, the HBC put into operation large numbers of York boats, flat-bottomed vessels made of spruce and rowed by eight men with long oars. The experienced boatmen hired for the purpose were

Fort Prince of Wales (Churchill, Manitoba), c. 1777.

Hearne, Samuel/National Archives of Canada/C-41292

found mainly in the Orkney Isles north of the Scottish coast. To match the wintering partners of the "Nor'Westers," the HBC placed its posts in the hands of inland masters. Although these traders, unlike the wintering Nor'Westers, did not initially share in profits, they were permanently stationed in the interior.

NATIVE PEOPLES AND THE TRADE

For Native peoples, it mattered little whether their furs went to London or Montreal merchants. Their goal remained the receipt of as many high-quality goods as possible for their furs at a conveniently located post. During the period of HBC-NWC competition, this goal was often met. Aggressive attempts by the companies to enlist new groups of Natives to their posts drew an ever-expanding number of nations into the trade. A new "middle ground" of Native-European culture soon developed. The companies depended upon the Natives as trappers and providers of local food. Living in proximity to them, company employees often married Native women.

In Northern regions competition among the companies was often more a curse than a blessing. Fur-trader "marriages" to Native women sometimes appeared to the Dene as forced confinement of the women rather than willing partnerships. A trader would simply use force or intimidation to acquire a woman whom he wanted to live with, rather than seek her consent or the consent of her family. Taking advantage of the smaller concentrations of people and relative lack of firearms in the North, traders imposed a harsher regime than they dared among the more populous and better-armed First Nations further south.

The North West Company was particularly notorious in this regard. After the Hudson's Bay Company began to establish posts in the Athabasca District in 1790, the Nor'Westers had little hesitation in employing violence against both their competitor and their Native suppliers to try to maintain as much of their former monopoly in the region as possible. The violence reached new levels between 1798 and 1804, when the XY Company, a loose grouping of traders who had broken from the NWC, attempted to gain a foothold in the region. Although the XY group had returned to the NWC fold by 1804, the violence in the North continued.

Some Dene groups responded to trader violence by withdrawing from the trade. From the early days of contact, many tribes had refused to become part of the fur trade, and appeared to live happily enough without the white man's goods. While withdrawal from the trade was the usual response to a pattern of fur-trader violence, retaliation was common. In the Fort Chipewyan area at the turn of the nineteenth century, there were several incidents of Dene murders of traders deemed to have treated the Natives abusively.

If such abuse was less common further south, the First Nations that lived there also got more than they bargained for. The Ojibwa of what is now northwestern Ontario experienced a cycle that would be repeated for many tribes on the parklands and plains of the West. In the late eighteenth century, the Ojibwa were indispensable to the traders north and west of Lake Superior not only as trappers, but also as guides to the many superficially similar rivers of the area, as providers of venison, and as labourers on the supply boats. They were able to command good prices for their furs and to influence the location of trading posts. Continuing as ever to hunt big game and to provide themselves with most of the necessities of life, the Ojibwa valued the trade in beaver pelts for the firearms and metal utensils that made their lives easier.

The easy partnership would not last. From 1804 onwards, there were reports that beaver were becoming scarce in the region trapped by the Ojibwa. Soon it became clear that big game in the area was also disappearing. Reports of death from starvation and rumours of cannibalism underlined the gravity of the situation. With few furs to sell and food supplies low, the Ojibwa had to work harder and to travel further in search of game. This was an ironic outcome of the fur trade, given that European goods had once been attractive because they reduced the amount of work necessary for survival. Overtrapping and overhunting had jeopardized Ojibwa independence.

The experience of the Blackfoot was different from that of the Ojibwa. By about 1730, the Blackfoot had come into indirect contact with the European presence when they received their first horses from the Shoshoni, another plains nation, and firearms and iron from the Cree and Assiniboine. At the time, the Blackfoot lived on the northern plains of Saskatchewan, but their new weapons and an outbreak of smallpox among the Shoshoni allowed them to expand south and west and eventually to dominate southern Alberta as well as Montana. As the Peigan, followed by the Blood and Blackfoot, pushed west to the foothills of the Rockies, the Shoshoni and Kutenai were forced across the mountains.

During his travels to the West in 1754, Anthony Henday encountered the Blood, one of the groups that made up the Blackfoot Confederacy. They made clear their lack of interest in journeying from their territory to trade in furs. Their livelihood, they noted, was the buffalo hunt, and their territorial expansion was focused on areas where buffalo were plentiful. In 1787, David Thompson was sent by the HBC to persuade the Blackfoot to bring furs to company posts on the South Saskatchewan River, but he met with the same response.

By the 1790s, the Blackfoot apparently had a change of heart. As the HBC and NWC built posts on the northern fringe of Blackfoot country, this once aloof nation began to bring wolf and fox skins to trading posts, although they still refused to trap beaver. The major item that the Blackfoot traded with the Europeans quickly became pemmican, a mixture of dried buffalo and berries that became the mainstay of officers and employees at fur-trade posts as other game became less plentiful.

The Blackfoot, unlike the Ojibwa, did not become dependent on the Europeans during the fur-trading period because the large number of buffalo in their territory continued to provide them with self-sufficiency in food, clothing, and much else besides. They were not interested in either the Europeans' food or, for a long period, clothing—the women in particular refused to respond to the traders' blandishments to purchase their woollens—so the Blackfoot traded for guns, powder, awls, iron, beads, tobacco, and liquor.

A Buffalo Rift, *by Alfred Jacob Miller.*

National Archives of Canada/C-403

To some extent, the trade was profitable for the Blackfoot. It allowed them to expand their territory, increase the size of their tipis and buffalo corrals, and generally to prosper. At the same time, their self-sufficient economy was slowly transformed into an increasingly commercial one, and tendencies toward inequality dating from the pre-contact period were reinforced. The traders from the two companies, wooing the Blackfoot tipi by tipi, encouraged a degree of individualism that eroded the unity of the tribes.

As a result of these developments, the scale of warfare increased dramatically. Young men were the chief victims of an increasingly violent society. The balance in numbers of men and women evident at the time of David Thompson's 1787 visit gave way in two generations to a three-to-one preponderance of women over men. While the men who survived were often able to marry four or even eight wives and live in huge tipis, the women were not as fortunate. A sorority of wives had characterized polygamy in an earlier period when most men had one or two wives. With larger numbers of wives, that tendency broke down. Beyond a third or fourth marriage, new wives were regarded almost as slaves, were excluded from the sun dance, and were otherwise discriminated against.

Still, the Blackfoot remained in control of their destiny and regarded the fur trade as beneficial. Other tribes of the parklands and plains felt the same way. Apart from the Blackfoot, the major groups in the area that now forms the southern half of the Prairie provinces were Cree, Ojibwa, and Assiniboine, many

Blackfoot woman pounding dried meat.

Glenbow Archives, Calgary, NA-667-72

of them immigrants during the fur-trade period. All had experienced a degree of cultural change after moving onto the plains, mainly through the adoption of a number of the beliefs and rituals of the original plains nations. The sun dance, for example, was adopted by all the new residents of the northern plains.

THE BIRTH OF THE MÉTIS NATION

The term Métis theoretically refers to "mixed-blood" people—that is, people whose known ancestral heritage is a mixture of European and Native Indian. In practice, only a fraction of mixed-blood individuals ever identified themselves as Métis. During the French regime, intermarriage between white men involved in the fur trade and Indian women was so common that one demographer suggests that as many as 40 percent of French-Canadians in Quebec today have at least one Native ancestor. Children of part-Native descent who integrated into Quebec society did not develop a sense of being members of a separate nation, nor did the offspring of Native-white liaisons who rejoined the tribes of their mothers.

The term Métis, then, is probably most usefully applied to persons who were members of mixed-blood communities and whose sense of identity was with other mixed-bloods rather than with a particular Native or European group. Before the end of the French regime, sizeable Métis communities had sprung up in the territory of the upper Great Lakes, and more such communities developed in the area of the modern-day Prairie provinces during the years that followed.

Forbidden by the HBC, liaisons between fur traders and Native women were frowned upon by the Roman Catholic Church. The church had little impact upon young men who lived much of their lives in the interior, but the HBC was somewhat more successful in restraining its employees—at least until competition from the North West Company forced it to relax its regulation that only officers of posts could have sexual relations with Native women. Native society approved of marriages between its women and European traders. Such unions were consistent with pre-contact practices in which intertribal marriages cemented trade and military relationships between groups.

Both in the French regime and afterwards, the traders often proved fickle marriage partners. When it came time to retire, they would often abandon long-term relationships that had produced many children. In the French period, most of the abandoned Native wives and their children were reintegrated into their former communities. Later, as it became common both for the traders and First Nations to move frequently, Native women could no longer easily return home. Many abandoned wives and their children became dependent upon the fur-trade posts for their survival and were preferred over full-blooded Native women as marriage partners for white fur traders.

Métis men played a special role in the plans of the two fur-trade companies. For the most part, the sons of British employees, whether officers or clerks, were hired as labourers at the posts. The French-speaking Métis, who had started their own settlements, were valued as providers of pemmican, as boatmen, and as guides. Significantly, all the jobs reserved for Métis were low in status and pay. Even the Métis sons of officers or partners were blocked from advancement.

The Métis communities developed cultural patterns that set them apart from both Native and Euro-Canadian culture. The offspring of the French developed their own language, Michif, which combined French and the plains Cree language in almost equal quantities. English-speaking Métis also developed their own language, Bungi, a combination of Cree with the Scots dialect of the Orkneys. The dances of the Métis combined the intricate footwork of Natives with Scottish and French forms, including reels and jigs. In the Red River area, Métis travelled in carts with "dished"—saucer-shaped—wheels to avoid getting stuck in the Prairie mud. The carts were made entirely of wood, the parts bound together by wet rawhide that shrank after drying and proved particularly sturdy. The Métis women, maintaining the leather-work skills of their Aboriginal ancestors, used beads rather than porcupine quills to decorate the coats, belts, and moccasins they produced. Later the women of the plains nations also adopted this practice.

THE FOUNDING OF THE RED RIVER SETTLEMENT

Although the Métis played a crucial role in the life of the two rival fur-trade companies, they were not consulted by the HBC when it established the Red River settlement near present-day Winnipeg. The settlement's origins reflected a convenient mix of philanthropic and commercial objectives. Lord Selkirk, a Scottish landowner and peer in the British House of Lords, regarded with concern the fate of Scots Highlanders deprived of their land by his fellow landowners who wanted land for sheep enclosures. Selkirk began to promote colonization as a commercial venture that would not only enrich its promoters but also rid Great Britain of a surplus population for which the new industrial order offered no employment.

In 1808 and 1809, Selkirk and a group of associates purchased a third of the HBC's shares and used their voting power within the company to promote an agricultural settlement in the Red River valley. Selkirk's partner, Andrew Colvile, argued that the settlement could help provision the western fur trade, reducing the costs associated with importing supplies from Britain.

The settlement began modestly in 1812 with 35 people, whose numbers were reduced by scurvy the first winter. Although most of the settlers were able to survive with the help of local Saulteaux (Ojibwa), their early attempts at farming were disastrous. They did not begin to sow viable crops until the late 1820s.

While the experienced HBC fur traders viewed Selkirk's settlement derisively, the Nor'Westers suspected that it was a ploy to create a strategic outpost that could disrupt their company's river links between Montreal and the interior. The Métis, with several large settlements in the area, also believed that the Red River colony threatened their future, and NWC traders encouraged them in this view. As it turned out, the actions of the colony's governor, Miles Macdonnell, suggested that their suspicions were justified.

With poor crops and more settlers arriving annually, the fledgling colony was dependent on pemmican supplies for its survival. In January 1814, Macdonnell issued a proclamation against the export of pemmican from the vast region—known as Assiniboia—that had been placed under his control as a potential area of settlement. This proclamation threatened the NWC's supplies and confirmed fears about the real purposes of the colony. It was also a blow to the Métis, who were the main producers and exporters of pemmican.

The Métis had another reason to dislike Macdonnell. Emulating the plains nations, the Métis hunted the buffalo by running them on horseback, a practice that was gradually driving the animals away from the lower Red River. Hoping to avoid a situation in which the colony would depend on Natives and Métis for provisions, Macdonnell issued a proclamation in July 1814 forbidding the running of buffalo. The NWC encouraged the Métis to respond belligerently to this outrage. Nor'Wester Duncan Cameron named three prominent Métis "captains" and in 1816 made one of them, Cuthbert Grant, "Captain-General of the Métis." The militia led by these captains solidified the sense of identity among the Métis of the Prairies.

In 1815, the NWC's intrigues forced Macdonnell to leave the settlement, which was being besieged by Métis attackers. His interim replacement, Peter Fidler, a long-time fur trader and father to a large Métis family, capitulated to Métis demands to disband the colony, but the colonists had only been gone a few months before they returned under new leadership and with reinforcements. Governor Robert Semple, like his predecessor, was insensitive to Métis interests and antagonistic toward the NWC. He reinstated the pemmican ban and, to make it last, ordered the seizure of Fort Gibraltar, the NWC's post in the Red River area, in March 1816.

In retaliation, the Métis under Grant seized pemmican from HBC posts on the Qu'Appelle River to provision the Nor'Westers on Lake Winnipeg. On their way to the Nor'Westers, Grant's Métis militia was surprised by Semple and a group of armed colonists at a place called Seven Oaks. Semple, misjudging the numbers under Grant's direction, demanded that the Métis disarm. In the ensuing confrontation, Semple and twenty of his men were killed; on Grant's side, there were only two casualties.

Lord Selkirk, determined to punish the Métis as well as the Nor'Westers, whom he blamed for the Métis aggressiveness, hired Swiss mercenaries to improve the colony's defences. He also had Grant and other Métis leaders charged with murder and forced to appear before Canadian courts, but no one was convicted. Selkirk's actions against several NWC officials were similarly unsuccessful. The court rulings confirmed the finding of a British-appointed commission that no premeditated Métis massacre of Selkirk settlers had occurred at Seven Oaks. In his report William Bachelor Coltman, the principal commissioner, concluded that the Selkirk party had fired the first shot. Coltman believed that the Métis had subsequently killed wounded men rather than taking prisoners, and he suggested that the heavy casualties of the HBC men were the result of their "standing together in a crowd, unaccustomed to the use, of fire-arms, or any of the practices of irregular warfare" while they

MORE TO THE STORY

Native Agriculture in the Northwest

While archeological research suggests that in the pre-contact period, agriculture was practised in the Northwest as far north as today's Lockport, Manitoba, it had ceased during the early fur-trading period, probably because corn, tobacco, and other cultivated products had become available through trade. Trade goods received from the Europeans in exchange for furs were, in turn, traded with agricultural nations further south. As the availability of both fur-bearing animals and game declined in areas under Ojibwa control, many Native peoples tried to adapt to the new circumstances by taking up agriculture.

The Ottawa living in the Red River village of Netley Creek reintroduced agriculture to the Northwest in 1805 after receiving seed from trader Alexander Henry. They planted corn, potatoes, and other crops. In turn, the Ottawa taught the Ojibwa, migrants from parklands areas with no farming tradition, how to plant corn. Initially the HBC and the NWC discouraged Natives from planting crops, fearing it would diminish their participation in the fur trade. Later, as game became more scarce in the region, it was accepted that Native farmers could contribute to the traders' food requirements. Agriculture spread among the Ojibwa despite the early lack of enthusiasm on the part of fur traders. South of Lake Manitoba corn was the major crop; north of the lake it was potatoes. While no group

gave up the hunt and became completely sedentary, agricultural sites often became the centre of ceremonial gatherings for the Ojibwa. A description by HBC trader William Brown in 1819 indicates the impact of agriculture on Ojibwa life, including the division of labour by gender:

> A considerable number of the Indians particularly those of Fort Dauphin, and the Manitoba, have ground under cultivation, and raise a great many Potatoes, but that is their only crop.... Those of the Manitoba...[cultivate] on an Island towards the North end of the Lake, they have erected there what they call a Big Tent, where they all assemble in spring, hold Councils and go thro' their Religious Ceremonies—The soil here is excellent and each family has a portion of it under cultivation, which the women and old men remain, and take care of during the summer—while the young men go a hunting—In the fall of the year when they are going to abandon the place, they secure that part of the produce, under ground till spring, which they cannot carry along with them—During favourable years, they generally make a considerable quantity of maple sugar, part of which they also put in Cache—The Big Tent is constructed in the form of an arch, and consists of a slight frame of wood covered on the outside with the bark of the pine tree, and lined in the inside with bulrush mats. It is 60 ft. long—15 ft. wide—and 10 ft. high.[2]

faced "excellent marksmen, advantageously posted in superior numbers around their opponents."[3]

The competition between the HBC and NWC nearly ruined both companies financially and placed a severe strain on fur-bearing animals and game in the Northwest. Political pressures in Britain, as well as these economic pressures, forced the two companies to merge in 1821. The new company took the Hudson's Bay Company's name and was required by the British Parliament to end the use of liquor as a trade item in the fur trade. Fast on the heels of the merger came massive layoffs as rival posts were consolidated.

The Selkirk settlement, where poor crops, floods, and locusts were driving away many settlers, received a

much-needed boost from the arrival of many of these discharged employees. Henceforth, large numbers of retired HBC men, usually the fathers of Métis families, would choose to spend their declining years with their families as farmers in the Red River settlement. The strengthening of the settlement was only one of the far-reaching consequences for Western Canada of the amalgamation of the two rival fur-trading companies.

TRADE ON THE WEST COAST

West of the Rockies, European contact came later and under different conditions. The continuous European history in British Columbia began in 1778 when

Captain James Cook surveyed the northwest coast in his search for the elusive Northwest Passage from Hudson Bay to the Pacific. Before that time, Russian and Spanish explorers had opened the region to a vigorous sea otter trade. A growing Russian presence on the Pacific coast led the Spanish to send expeditions from San Blas, their naval base in Mexico, to search for interlopers and establish a Spanish claim to the region. In 1774, Juan Perez sighted what would become known as the Queen Charlotte Islands and traded with the Haida, who sailed out to meet his ship. The following year, Juan Francisco de la Bodega y Quadra officially claimed the North Pacific coast for King Carlos III of Spain.

Nuu'chah'nulth village, drawn by John Webber during Captain Cook's 1778 voyage.

National Archives of Canada/C-6641

In 1789, the Spanish sent Captain Esteban Jose Martinez to establish a fortified base at Nootka Sound, where Cook had landed 11 years earlier. War over the North Pacific coast was avoided in 1790 with the Nootka Sound Convention, which permitted joint occupation of the Pacific coast north of San Francisco. Five years later, the Spanish abandoned their fortified base on Nootka Sound. By that time, Europeans and Aboriginal peoples had taken stock of each other and found a common ground of interest in the exchange of material goods. During his four-week stay with the Nuu'chah'nulth (Nootka) in 1778, Cook and his crew traded a variety of goods for sea-otter pelts, food, and artifacts. Cook reported that the Native demand for European products was insatiable:

> Hardly a bit of it [brass] was left in the ships except what belonged to our necessary instruments. Whole suits of clothes were stripped of every button; bureaus of their furniture; and copper kettles, tin cannisters, candlesticks and the like, all went to wreck; so that our American friends got a greater medley and variety of things from us, than any other nations whom we had visited.[4]

The profits that Cook gained from the sale of sea-otter skins in China opened a thriving trade for the Nuu'chah'nulth from the 1780s to the 1820s. British, French, Spanish, and American traders participated in the exchange of goods—usually iron tools—for pelts collected by the Nuu'chah'nulth and other coastal peoples, including the Haida of the Queen Charlotte Islands area. The trade was dominated by the Americans (the "Boston men") and the British ("King George men").

The Natives were hard bargainers who were not dependent on European goods and refused to trade except on their own terms. As in other areas of North America, the coastal Natives initially held the upper hand in the transactions with Europeans. The maritime trade and the new trade goods it brought into their territories gave the Aboriginal peoples more time and scope to develop their much-cherished crafts, such as totem poles and masks. The end result was an enhancement of the existing culture rather than an adaptation to the culture of the traders. Indeed, the shipbound traders made no attempt to impose cultural change on the Native peoples—their only interest was in acquiring pelts.

biography

A Tale of Two Maquinnas

Maquinna was the chief of the Mowachaht people, a Nuu'chah'nulth group that numbered about 1500, when the Europeans first ventured into Nuu'chah'nulth territory. His first encounter with Europeans came in 1774, when the Spanish, after meeting the Haida, encountered storms and, forced southwards, sought shelter in Nootka Sound. Four years later Captain Cook's ships ventured past the Mowachaht summer home at Yuquot, on the southeast of Nootka Island, a large island off the west coast of Vancouver Island, in 1778. Maquinna sent some of his people to greet the strangers on their boats, and then presided over the beginnings of trade with the British, giving Cook his royal robe of sea-otter skins as a gift.

Maquinna presided over the Mowachaht trade with the Europeans until his death in 1795. While he allowed the Spanish to establish a fortified base on Nootka Sound in the late 1780s, he was eager both to preserve good relations with all the white groups interested in trading with his people and to compel them to recognize Nuu'chah'nulth control over a homeland that Natives had occupied for 4300 years. In 1792, he hosted a meeting of Captain Vancouver for the English and Captain Quadra for the Spanish that settled the two countries' dispute regarding trading rights in the area. Maquinna insisted that Europeans must pay each time they fished in Mowachaht waters or cut trees on their land.

Despite his best efforts, Maquinna could not prevent some traders from treating his people without respect. In 1785, as the trade began in earnest, a ship's captain, in retaliation for a stolen chisel, unleashed a cannon attack on the Nootka Sound people that left 20 dead. That same year Maquinna's successor, who would take the same name at the time of his succession, was scarred permanently by gunpowder placed under him by a ship crew that had invited him aboard. Meanwhile, the smallpox epidemic a few years earlier, which many Natives correctly associated with the newcomers, had killed about half the Nuu'chah'nulth population.

Outrages occurred periodically, often the result of crews taking a swift and terrible revenge on an entire group because of petty thievery or assault by a few of its members. In turn, the Nuu'chah'nulth were prepared to take a collective revenge on the whites whom they regarded as having collectively abused Natives even if it was a relatively small number of traders who engaged in murderous behaviour. In 1803, under the second Maquinna's orders, the Mowachaht warriors planned the murder of the crew members of the American ship *Boston*. American ships did not allow armed Natives aboard, but Maquinna's followers, after being strip-searched, overpowered the ship's crew using paddles and equipment as weapons. They then used weapons aboard to murder all but two of the twenty-seven crew members.

The two men, when they were freed, produced a classic captivity book in which they described in excruciating detail the daily horrors they allegedly faced at the hands of their captors. The book, like others of its sort, was used by American officials and landgrabbers to make Natives appear less than human and therefore unfit to have sovereignty over their traditional lands. Of course, the provocations of the whites and the many cold-blooded murders of Natives were conveniently ignored in such accounts.

Callicum and Maquinna, Nuu'chah'nulth leaders, 1789.

National Archives of Canada/C-27699

Meanwhile, Alexander Mackenzie's arrival on the west coast via an overland route in 1793 marked the beginning of contact between traders and the Natives in the interior of British Columbia. As beaver on the plains became scarce, the Nor'Westers began to seriously pursue the idea of trading in the British Columbia interior. The first steps were made with the explorations of David Thompson and Simon Fraser, who, aided by the Natives of the region, provided the NWC with critical knowledge of the area's river systems. Fraser established posts across the Rockies in Carrier and Sekani territories during a journey from 1806 to 1808, and Thompson descended the Columbia to its mouth in 1811, discovering that it offered a satisfactory connection to the coast.

In the central interior of British Columbia, posts such as Fort Fraser, Fort St James, and Fort George became year-round homes to some Nor'Westers. Like their counterparts further east, most of these men formed liaisons with Native women. Although some of them abandoned their Native families when they left the posts, many remained, retiring with their families to Red River or, after its founding in 1843, Fort Victoria.

CONCLUSION

While the West continued to provide homelands for a variety of First Nations in 1821, much of the region had also become an area of European trade in beaver and sea-otter pelts. The Natives were partners in the fur trade. As long as competition among the Europeans and good markets for furs prevailed, First Nations significantly influenced the terms of trade. They also retained control over their own territories and maintained traditional religious and cultural practices. After 1821, however, the fur-trade monopoly, declining supplies of furs, and increasing European interest in the West as an area of settlement would all threaten the Natives' dominance in their homelands.

NOTES

1 Cole Harris, "Voices of Disaster: Smallpox Around the Strait of Georgia in 1782," *Ethnohistory* 41.4 (Fall 1994) 595.

2 D. Wayne Moody and Barry Kaye, "Indian Agriculture in the Fur-trade Northwest," *Prairie Forum* 11.2 (Fall 1986) 176.

3 Lyle Dick, "The Seven Oaks Incident and the Construction of a Historical Tradition, 1816 to 1970," *Journal of the Canadian Historical Association* (n.s.) 2 (1992) 97.

4 John Douglas, ed., *A Voyage to the Pacific Ocean in the Years 1776, 1777, 1778, 1779, and 1780...vol. 2, by Captain J. Cook*, cited in J.C. H. King, "The Nootka of Vancouver Island," in *Cook's Voyages and Peoples of the Pacific*, ed. Hugh Cobbe (London: British Museum Publications, 1979) 102.

SELECTED READING

For the Prairies and northern Ontario, the period covered in this chapter is surveyed in the early chapters of Gerald Friesen, *The Canadian Prairies: A History* (Toronto: University of Toronto Press, 1987). Also see the opening chapters of the major provincial histories: Howard Palmer with Tamara Palmer, *Alberta: A New History* (Edmonton: Hurtig, 1990); John Archer, *Saskatchewan: A History* (Saskatoon: Western Producer Prairie Books, 1980); and W.L. Morton, *Manitoba: A History* (Toronto: University of Toronto Press, 1957).

The early history of British Columbia is the subject of the opening chapters of Margaret Ormsby, *British Columbia: A History* (Toronto: Macmillan, 1976) and Jean Barman, *The West Beyond the West: A History of British Columbia* (Toronto: University of Toronto Press, 1996).

For Native peoples, a good place to start is Chapters 11 and 12 of Arthur J. Ray, *I Have Lived Here Since the World Began: An Illustrated History of Canada's Native People* (Toronto: Lester, 1996) or with the parallel chapters in the textbooks by Olive Patricia Dickason and J. R.

Miller mentioned in Chapter 2. Several essay collections focus on Prairie and Northern Canadian Native peoples, particularly R. Bruce Morrison and C. Roderick Wilson, eds., *Native Peoples: The Canadian Experience* (Toronto: McClelland and Stewart, 1986). Philip Drucker, *Cultures of the North Pacific Coast* (San Francisco: Chander Publishing, 1965) outlines the pre-contact history of Pacific Coast Natives. Mike Robinson, *Sea Otter Chiefs* (Calgary: Bayeux Arts, 1996) provides background on the coastal Native leaders in the early years of contact.

Among excellent studies of the religious and cultural life of Native peoples are Jennifer Brown, Robert Brightman, and George Nelson, *The Orders of the Dreamed: George Nelson on Cree and Northern Ojibwa Religion and Myth* (Winnipeg: University of Manitoba Press, 1988) and David G. Mandelbaum, *The Plains Cree: An Ethnographic, Historical and Comparative Study* (Regina: Canadian Plains Research Centre, 1979).

Studies of the impact of the fur trade on major Native societies include Robin Fisher, *Contact and Conflict: Indian–European Relations in British Columbia, 1774–1890* (Vancouver: UBC Press, 1979); Arthur J. Ray, *Indians in the Fur Trade: Their Role as Trappers, Hunters, and Middlemen in the Lands Southwest of Hudson Bay, 1660–1870* (Toronto: University of Toronto Press, 1974); Laura Peers, *The Ojibwa of Western Canada, 1780–1870* (St Paul: Minnesota Historical Society Press, 1994); Charles A. Bishop, *The Northern Ojibwa and the Fur Trade: An Historical and Ecological Study* (Toronto: Holt, Rinehart and Winston, 1974); Oscar Lewis, *The Effects of White Contact upon Blackfoot Culture with Special Reference to the Role of the Fur Trade* (Seattle: American Ethnological Society, 1942); John S. Milloy, *The Plains Cree: Trade, Diplomacy and War* (Winnipeg: University of Manitoba Press, 1990); and Paul C. Thistle, *Indian-European Trade Relations in the Lower Saskatchewan River Region to 1840* (Winnipeg: University of Manitoba Press, 1986).

A good short introduction to the fur trade is Frits Pannekoek, *The Fur Trade and Western Canadian Society, 1670–1870* (Ottawa: Canadian Historical Association, 1987). A lengthier but highly readable account is Daniel Francis, *Battle for the West: Fur Traders and the Birth of Western Canada* (Edmonton: Hurtig, 1982). On the west coast trade, see James Gibson, *Otter Skins, Boston Ships and China Goods: The Maritime Fur Trade of the Northwest Coast, 1785–1841* (Montreal: McGill-Queen's University Press, 1992); Richard Mackie, *Trading beyond the Mountains: The British Fur Trade on the Pacific, 1793–1843* (Vancouver: UBC Press, 1996); and Elizabeth Vibert, *Traders' Tales: Narratives of Cultural Encounters in the Columbian Plateau, 1807–1846* (Norman: University of Oklahoma, 1997). On the northern trade, see Kerry Abel, *Drum Songs: Glimpses of Dene History* (Montreal: McGill-Queen's University Press, 1993). The Hudson's Bay Company's history to 1870 is surveyed in Glyndwr Williams, "Highlights of the First 200 Years of the Hudson's Bay Company," *The Beaver*, special issue (Autumn 1970). A detailed account of the company's history is E.E. Rich, *The Hudson's Bay Company*, 3 vols. (Toronto: Hudson's Bay Records Society, 1960).

On key explorers, see Barry M. Gough, *First Across the Continent: Sir Alexander Mackenzie* (Norman: University of Oklahoma Press, 1997); Samuel Hearne, *Journals of Samuel Hearne and Philip Turner Between the Years 1792 and 1794*, ed. J.B. Tyrell (Toronto: Greenwood, 1934); and J.B. Tyrrell, ed., *David Thompson's Narrative of His Explorations in Western America, 1784–1812* (New York: Greenwood Press, 1968). Two excellent accounts of women in the fur trade are Sylvia Van Kirk, *"Many Tender Ties": Women in Fur Trade Society in Western Canada, 1670–1870* (Winnipeg: Watson and Dwyer, 1980) and Jennifer S.H. Brown, *Strangers in Blood: Fur Trade Company Families in the Indian Country* (Vancouver: UBC Press, 1980).

Barry Kaye, "The Red River Settlement: Lord Selkirk's Isolated Colony in the Wilderness," *Prairie Forum* 11.1 (Spring 1986): 1–20 outlines how a decision was made to establish a colony at the forks of the Red and Assiniboine rivers. The confrontation between the settlement and the Métis is detailed in Margaret Macleod and W.L. Morton, *Cuthbert Grant of Grantown: Warden of the Plains of Red River* (Toronto: McClelland and Stewart, 1974). A critique of their account and the historical tradition within which it was written is in Lyle Dick, "The Seven Oaks Incident and the Construction of a Historical Tradition, 1816 to 1870," *Journal of the Canadian Historical Association* (n.s.) 2 (1992): 91–113.

 **WEBLINKS**

HUDSON'S BAY COMPANY CHARTER
www.solon.org/Constitutions/Canada/English/PreConfed
eration/hbc_charter_1670.html

This site contains the complete text of the HBC charter.

YORK BOATS
www.nelson.com/nelson/school/discovery/cantext/west-
ern/1871york.htm

A firsthand description of York boats, details of crew organization, and how such boats were used are contained on this site.

RED RIVER
www.televar.com/~gmorin/27rrs.htm

This site offers the text of the Red River Settlement Census for 1827. For an index of related sites, including searchable archives, see www.televar.com/~gmorin/places.htm.

DAVID THOMPSON
www.archives.ca/02/020123_e.html

The National Archives of Canada's ArchiviaNet allows users to follow search routes to find holdings on David Thompson. A brief biography is available, along with listings of his papers and journals.

PART III SUMMARY

BY 1821, THE SUCCESS OF BRITISH SETTLEMENT AND enterprise in North America was evident. The British presence in the region until the late 1740s had been limited to a small military and civilian establishment in Acadia, small fishing communities in Newfoundland, and a few posts on Hudson Bay. Eighty years later, the demography of the new colonies of New Brunswick, Newfoundland, Nova Scotia, Prince Edward Island, and Upper Canada reflected the attraction of British North America to both British and Anglo-American emigrants. While Lower Canada was still largely inhabited by the Canadiens and the West was mainly home to its First Nations, the imperial government dominated the former while English-speaking fur traders exercised growing control over the latter. Peace with the Americans after 1814 removed fears of external threats to Britain's remaining North American possessions, but efforts of colonial administrators to impose imperial economic control and the British social order on the monarch's curious mix of North American subjects would meet many challenges.

Maturing Colonial Societies, 1815–1867

Between 1815 and 1867 the British North American colonies and territories went their separate ways but were drawing closer in culture and values. The Atlantic colonies and the Canadas grew in population and political maturity, their leaders increasingly determined that British North Americans manage their own affairs under a system of "responsible government." On the west coast, the colonies of Vancouver Island (1849) and British Columbia (1858) were carved out of the vast territory under the jurisdiction of the Hudson's Bay Company, which was beginning to feel the impact of outside influences and the growing power of the Métis.

When Great Britain dismantled the mercantile system and began reshaping the apparatus of colonial governance in the 1840s, British North Americans faced a common crisis: how to adjust to a world where old colonial empires were crumbling and new industrial empires were emerging. Leading businessmen, professionals, and politicians in the Canadas and the Maritimes began to dream of a nation from sea to sea, bound together by railways and political institutions adapted from their British heritage. Despite the very real obstacles in their path, the promoters of "confederation" were successful. A new nation called Canada came into being on 1 July 1867, and within less than a decade had expanded its boundaries to the Pacific Coast.

CHAPTER 11

Developing Colonies, 1815–1867

timeline

1818	Roman Catholic missions arrive in Red River
1820	Cape Breton annexed to Nova Scotia
1829	Death of Shanawdithit, the last Beothuk
1829	Catholic Emancipation throughout the British Empire
1830	Grand Orange Lodge of British North America established
1832	Cholera epidemic in the Canadas
1833	British Parliament passes an act to abolish slavery throughout the British Empire
1837–1901	Reign of Queen Victoria
1835–38	Smallpox epidemic sweeps across the West
1840	Act of Union unites Upper and Lower Canada
1842	Webster-Ashburton Treaty
1845	John Franklin's expedition lost in an effort to find a Northwest Passage
1846	Great Britain adopts free trade; Oregon Treaty
1849	Vancouver Island becomes Crown colony
1850	Fugitive Slave Law passed in the United States
1854–66	Reciprocity Treaty
1858	Gold Rush on Fraser and Thompson rivers; British Columbia becomes Crown colony
1866	Vancouver Island and British Columbia united
1867	Confederation

We in Canada have this glorious privilege that the ground where on we tread is our own and our children's after us.... No dangers of the leases expiring and the laird saying pay me so much more rent, or bundle and go, for here we are laird ourselves. I may thank my stars that I am out of such a place.[1]

This is how George Forbes, son of a Scottish tenant farmer, described his situation in a letter to his brothers in 1856. One of the more than a million British immigrants to arrive in the British North American colonies between 1815 and 1860, Forbes had improved his social status by moving to a new home across the sea, but others were not so fortunate. Discontent reached such a pitch that rebellions broke out in both Upper and Lower Canada in 1837–38.

Within a decade of the rebellions the British government had abandoned the old mercantile system that bound colonies to the mother country and had conceded more power to the colonial assemblies. There was little support for complete independence because many colonials still valued the British connection and basked in the imperial glory that characterized the long reign of Queen Victoria (1837–1901). In this chapter, we will trace the economic and social conditions in the colonies that served as the context for political developments that will be discussed in the following chapter.

DRAWING BOUNDARIES AND CREATING COLONIES

Colonial jurisdictions and boundaries were periodically redrawn in this period. Following the uprisings in Upper and Lower Canada, British authorities passed the Act of Union in 1840, creating an uneasy political entity: the United Canadas. Canada West (formerly

Upper Canada) and Canada East (formerly Lower Canada) retained their own distinct identities and never worked well together in harness.

After functioning as a separate colonial jurisdiction for 35 years, Cape Breton was re-annexed with Nova Scotia in 1820. The Colonial Office justified this administrative decision on the grounds that the officials at Sydney had failed to call an assembly. Given the prejudices of the time, it was difficult to do so in a colony settled primarily by Scots, Irish, and Acadians, most of whom were Roman Catholic and who spoke either French or Gaelic.

New Brunswick's border with the United States, in contention since the American Revolution, proved difficult to establish. Despite continuing efforts, the identity of the Ste Croix River, part of the boundary defined by the peace treaty, was only determined in 1798 when the site of Champlain's settlement of 1604 was located. The Webster-Ashburton Treaty, named after the principal American and British negotiators, finally put an end to wrangling over territory in the Aroostook-Madawaska region on the upper St John River in 1842. The division of the disputed territory, which left a hump of land between New Brunswick and the Eastern Townships, came as a disappointment to British North Americans.

Boundaries on the West Coast were also in contention. In 1825, the British government ceded the territory on the Pacific coast north of 54° 40° to Russia. The growing influence of the United States in the region and the claims of presidential candidate James Polk in 1844 that the Americans would extend their border to "Fifty-four Forty or Fight" eventually led to a diplomatic solution. Under the provisions of the Oregon Treaty signed in 1846, the 49th parallel was set as the boundary between American and British territory from the Rockies to the Pacific.

In an effort to assert its authority on the West Coast, Great Britain made Vancouver Island a Crown colony in 1849. The discovery of gold on the shores of the Fraser and Thompson rivers prompted the creation of the Crown colony of British Columbia in 1858. Neither colony was initially granted an elected assembly and both were ruled by former governors of the Hudson's Bay Company, which continued to dominate the region. In 1862, British Columbia was expanded to 60 degrees North and the Queen Charlotte Islands were added to its jurisdiction. As a cost-saving measure, British Columbia and Vancouver Island were united into one colony in 1866. New Westminster was declared to be the capital of the new colony but, after lobbying from aggrieved islanders, it was moved to Victoria in 1868.

Meanwhile, the far north still lured European explorers eager to find an elusive "Northwest Passage." The most famous was Englishman John Franklin. In 1819 and 1825, Franklin's attempts to penetrate the northern waters ended in disappointment. Franklin set out again in 1845, but failed to return. Between 1848 and 1859, some 30 rescue missions attempted to find the missing Franklin expedition. One group, headed by the resourceful Captain Robert McClure, actually traversed the Northwest Passage by foot and sled in a desperate attempt to escape the Arctic ice.

POSTWAR IMMIGRATION

Between 1815 and 1860, the British North American colonies witnessed an unprecedented level of immigration. Most new settlers came from Great Britain, where poverty and unemployment followed in the wake of the Napoleonic Wars and the economic adjustments associated with the Industrial Revolution. At the end of the war, military officers, soldiers, and sailors found little demand for their services, while the new social order dominated by industrial entrepreneurs weighed heavily against tenant farmers, artisans, and the rural gentry. For those being squeezed by these circumstances, the colonies offered hope for a new beginning.

The most dramatic social collapse took place in Ireland, whose people had become reluctant British subjects by the Act of Union in 1801. The combination of a growing population, periodic famines due to potato crop failures, and political oppression was a powerful stimulus to emigration. Between 1825 and 1845, at least 450 000 Irish emigrants landed in British North American ports, about one-third of them moving on to the United States. These emigrants were the lucky ones. As a result of a disastrous famine that began in 1845, some 800 000 Irish died and another two million emigrated to other parts of Great Britain

Main street of Barkerville during the gold rush in the 1860s.

National Archives of Canada/PA-61940

and overseas. Of the latter, more than 300 000 came to British North America.

Even people who had good prospects in Britain were often pulled by the opportunities that North America seemed to offer. Merchants eager to expand their operations, farmers with visions of becoming gentlemen, artisans with skills in demand in the colonies, and any number of adventurers turned their sights on British North America. Some immigrants brought traditional values with them, spurred by the desire for economic and spiritual independence as much as by a thirst for wealth. Others were converts to the values of industrial capitalism, more anxious to "get ahead" than to re-establish a way of life rapidly disappearing in Britain.

Following the War of 1812, the British North American colonies were no longer the preferred desti-

nation of immigrants from the United States. An exception to this generalization were African Americans. Upper Canada, where Simcoe had introduced an act to gradually eliminate slavery in 1793, became a popular destination of free blacks and refugee slaves. Most black immigrants settled in white communities, but there were also attempts to organize group settlements. For example, in 1829, near London, Ontario, African-American immigrants founded the community of Wilberforce, named after a prominent British abolitionist.

The discovery of gold on the Pacific coast in 1858 brought an influx of immigrants from all over the world. Virtually overnight, Victoria, the capital of the colony of Vancouver Island, became an overcrowded town of 6000 people and instant communities such as Boston Bar, Lytton, and Barkerville appeared near the gold fields in British Columbia. While most of the immigrants drifted away after the gold rush ran its course, the multicultural community that remained included African Americans, Chinese, and Hawaiians, as well as Americans, British, and British North Americans.

As the number of immigrants increased, British North America's Native population declined. No longer a military threat, they were at best objects of charity, at worst targets of exploitation by rapacious immigrants. Disease and poverty inevitably took their toll. By 1850, it is estimated that fewer than 25 000 Native peoples lived in the Atlantic colonies and the Canadas, most of them relegated to reserves on the outskirts of immigrant communities. The approximately 100 000 Natives in the West fared better, remaining the workforce of a still vital fur trade dominated by the Husdon's Bay Company. Yet, they, too, were experiencing the impact of immigration, especially in British Columbia where the Natives were often dispossessed of their lands in the wake of the gold rush.

By the 1860s the tide of immigration had receded, but the "British" character of the colonial population was set. The Irish made up 25 percent of a British North American population approaching 2.5 million, while those who identified themselves as English and Welsh accounted for about 20 percent, and the Scottish nearly 16 percent. At 45 and 33 percent, respectively, Prince Edward Island and Nova Scotia had the highest proportion of people claiming Scottish ancestry, and Scots fur traders were the overwhelming majority of the Europeans in the West.

The Irish represented about 30 percent of the population of Canada West. Unlike the Maritime colonies, where Irish Protestants and Catholics were represented in nearly equal numbers, Ontario attracted a majority of Irish Protestant immigrants. In Newfoundland, Catholics were the dominant element among the nearly half of the population who claimed Irish origins. About 50 000 British immigrants settled in Lower Canada, where francophones, who made up nearly 70 per cent of the colony's population, predominated. By the mid-nineteenth century over half the population of Montreal and one-third of Quebec City were anglophones.

THE IMMIGRANT EXPERIENCE

While it was widely claimed in Great Britain that any industrious male emigrant could acquire land in the colonies, many would never do so. They were forced to eke out a living in an urban centre, become a tenant on someone else's land, or find work in the fisheries, the timber trade, or some public construction project such as road or canal building. In both town and countryside, a disproportionate number of the poor were Irish Catholics who—even though they were not of the poorest class at home—often arrived penniless after they had paid the costs of passage to Canada.

The emigration experience was sometimes tragic. In 1832, a large group of military pensioners were persuaded to exchange their pensions for a lump sum of money and land in the Canadian bush. Anna Brownell Jameson, the wife of Upper Canada's attorney general, was shocked in 1836 to find a hamlet at Penetanguishene peopled with old, sick veterans,

Emigrants.

National Archives of Canada/C4986

many unable to raise enough food to feed themselves. Since the area had no roads, those who had farm surpluses had difficulty taking their produce to market. Jameson was appalled that "men who fought our battles in Egypt, Spain, and France" were living in shacks, often reduced to begging in order to survive.[2]

Clearing the land was a daunting task for most pioneer settlers. They assaulted the forests as if trees were an enemy to be conquered. Despite the lessons learned in Britain, where most of the forests were gone and hunting had become a sport reserved for the aristocracy, immigrants showed little interest in conservation. In their haste to establish themselves, they cut down giant hardwood stands and burned the stumps, a process often leading to runaway fires that destroyed both the forests and those who inhabited them. Walter Johnstone, a Scottish visitor to Prince Edward Island, remarked in 1820, "Burnt woods are to be seen in the neighbourhood of almost every settlement, some of them of considerable magnitude."[3]

Inevitably, the arrival of immigrants created social tensions. The newcomers were rivals for land and jobs, and often brought cultural values that offended local residents. In the Ottawa Valley, Irish labourers were notorious for using violence to force employers to hire them. Wealthy timber merchant Peter Aylen, seeking personal control of the valley, led the Irish in open warfare against francophone lumbermen in the late 1830s and early 1840s. The so-called Shiners' War continued until Aylen unleashed his troops on the respectable middle-class citizens of Bytown (renamed Ottawa in 1855), who then invoked state authority to stop the armed confrontations.

Quebec City was the most common port of entry for post-1815 immigrants. As a result, Lower Canadians were most vulnerable to the diseases that the immigrants sometimes brought with them. A cholera epidemic swept through Britain in 1831 and arrived in British North America with infected immigrants the following year. Health officials reported 5820 deaths from cholera in Lower Canada in 1832, most of them recent immigrants and Canadiens in Quebec and Montreal. An immigrant station was established at Grosse Île, an island in the St Lawrence near Quebec City, but it did little to prevent the spread of disease. In 1834, another outbreak claimed 2358 victims in Lower Canada, compared to 555 in Upper Canada and 320 in Nova Scotia.

While disease and economic rivalries fuelled tension between immigrants and the settled population, old-country hatreds afflicted the immigrants themselves. This was particularly the case among the Irish, who brought their religious rivalries with them. In the 1830s the Orange Order, devoted to maintaining Protestant ascendancy over Roman Catholics, took root in the colonies. By 1860, the Orange Order claimed 100 000 members in British North America. Members of the Orange Order favoured Protestants over Catholics for jobs and political office, and violent clashes between the Orange and the Green punctuated elections and annual celebrations designed to keep religious hatred alive.

THE COMMERCIAL ECONOMY

Despite social tensions and economic uncertainty in the first half of the nineteenth century, colonial economies grew impressively. Immigrants invested capital in their new homeland and colonial staples—fish, fur, minerals, timber, and wheat—found ready markets in Great Britain, where they were accorded preference under the mercantile system. Britain's decision to adopt a policy of free trade in 1846 caused anxiety among colonial producers but they managed to weather the crisis. Taking advantage of an expanding global economy, British North Americans sold their staples wherever they could find markets. Under a system of free trade with the United States that prevailed form 1854 to 1866, primary products from the eastern colonies found expanding markets south of the border.

The cod fishery, which first attracted Europeans to the northern half of North America, continued to be a mainstay of the British North American economy. Although the fishery was important to all sea-bound colonies, Newfoundland was defined by its saltfish trade. No other British North American colony was so dependent upon imported food or a single staple product. Unlike the other British North American colonies, which traded primarily with Great Britain and the United States, Newfoundland's export trade was largely to southern Europe, Brazil, and the British West Indies. From 1815 to 1914 Newfoundlanders exported on the average 1 million hundredweights of salt fish a year, a testimony to the continuing demand for the product and the amazing fertility of the lowly cod.

Economic diversification in Newfoundland came primarily in the form of another sea-based industry: the seal fishery. North Atlantic harp seals visit coastal Newfoundland and Labrador in the late winter and early spring to feed and give birth to their calves on the ice floes before moving into the Arctic. In addition to their skins, seals yield a fatty blubber which was rendered into oil for lighting and lubricants. The seal fishery was a brutal and dangerous enterprise, but it offered both adventure and profit. At its height

in the 1850s, it employed 14 000 "ice hunters" and accounted for nearly a quarter of the colony's exports by value.

Local demand for construction materials and Great Britain's insatiable market for squared timber sustained a vigorous forest industry in eastern British North America. Each spring, lumberjacks drove the winter's harvest of logs down rivers such as the Ottawa, Saguenay, Miramichi, and St John that led to colonial ports and overseas markets. The forest industry created seasonal employment, albeit at low wages, for many men. Work could also be found in the sawmills that dotted the forest frontier in British North America. In Lower Canada alone there were 727 sawmills in 1831, and the number continued to

St John's fleet departing for the seal fishery, c. 1860. As this image indicates, the sealers were obliged to cut channels in the harbour ice so that the vessels could be towed to open water.

Courtesy of Centre for Newfoundland Studies Archives, Queen Elizabeth II Library, Memorial University of Newfoundland

grow. Farmers throughout the colonies supplemented their income by producing staves, hoops, and barrel ends for local and export markets.

Shipbuilding, financed by British and colonial capitalists, emerged as the most important sideline of the forest industry. Although Saint John was the largest shipbuilding centre in the Maritimes, shipyards were scattered throughout the region. Quebec City, where seven shipyards employed 1338 people in 1851, was the major shipbuilding port in the Canadas. In addition to building and selling vessels, British North Americans became involved in the carrying trade. Initially, most of their vessels carried local staples such as timber or fish. When shipping capacity outstripped the resources, merchants found cargoes elsewhere. By mid-century, ships from the colonies were plying the seven seas, full participants in the rapid expansion of the carrying trade.

The sailing ship was queen of the seas in the first half of the nineteenth century, but colonial entrepreneurs were quick to recognize the importance of steam transportation. In 1809, John Molson, an ambitious Montreal brewer, in partnership with two Englishmen, launched the steamship *Accommodation*. Although the vessel was a commercial failure, its successors did a roaring trade on the Great Lakes and St Lawrence, and competition for traffic among the "river barons" was keen. In 1833, the *Royal William*, launched from Quebec yards in 1831, became the first ship to cross the Atlantic using steam, taking 25 days to make the trip from Pictou, Nova Scotia, to Gravesend, England. Maritime capitalist Samuel Cunard inaugurated the first regular steam-powered trans-Atlantic service from Great Britain to North America in 1840.

Although over half the population in the eastern colonies farmed for a living, most agricultural produce was consumed locally. Potatoes, wheat, and coarse grains were the staples of colonial diets and surpluses of the season's crops were regularly exported. In the Maritimes, potatoes, along with dried fish, filled the holds of ships bound for the West Indies. Farmers in Prince Edward Island and the Annapolis and St John River valleys produced food for local markets, including the workforce employed in the region's forestry and fishing industries, but wheat had to be imported.

Lacking agricultural potential, Newfoundlanders were dependent on imported food.

By 1840, Upper Canada was emerging as the wheat basket of British North America. Wheat exports from the colony increased dramatically between 1830 and 1850, enabling many farm families to rise above subsistence. Nevertheless, about half of the cash income on the farms in Upper Canada came not from exported wheat but from other products sold locally. Farmers on Lake Ontario raised pigs to satisfy local markets for pork; western Upper Canada farmers produced rye, tobacco, and barley.

While hard-working farmers in Upper Canada were experiencing an increase in their standard of living, their counterparts in Lower Canada were facing an agricultural crisis. Soil exhaustion and the reduced size of seigneurial holdings forced farmers in Lower Canada to switch from wheat to mixed crops and livestock. In 1800, wheat had accounted for over 60 percent of agricultural production in Lower Canada, but only 21 percent in 1831. The average farm in Canada West in 1851 could boast a net value of production twice that of a Canada East farm and sold about four times as much in the market. In rural areas of Canada East, there were almost as many agricultural labourers (63 365) as farmers (78 437) in 1851, testimony to the fact that the seigneurial system could no longer sustain the growing farming population.

After 1821, the Hudson's Bay Company had a virtual monopoly of the fur trade in British North America. Company officials streamlined operations in the old Northwest, while expanding their trading activities on the Pacific coast and in Labrador to tap new resources. By the 1850s, it was becoming clear that the fur trade frontier would soon recede as settlers took up farming on the plains. Before that happened, a growing American market for buffalo hides, used to make sturdy leather belts for power transmission in factory machinery, precipitated the mass slaughter of one of the main food sources for the Natives of the plains. Aboriginal peoples participated in the massacre, but their refusal to do so would have made little difference—white buffalo hunters would simply have stepped in to maintain the supply.

British North America's mineral wealth began to be exploited in this period. In 1826, the London-based

General Mining Association was created to develop Nova Scotia's mineral resources, over which it had a virtual monopoly. The company brought skilled British miners to the coal fields of Cape Breton and Pictou County and introduced modern technology, including steam-driven machinery and vessels. Even before the gold rush swept all before it on the Pacific coast in 1858, the Hudson's Bay Company had begun exploiting coal resources in 1852, using both Scottish and Native labourers in its Nanaimo mines.

The founding of banking institutions testifies to the attempts of British North America's mercantile elite to organize their wealth for systematic investment. In the wake of the War of 1812, the Bank of Montreal (1817) the Bank of New Brunswick (1820), the Bank of Upper Canada (1821), and the Halifax Banking Company (1825) began operations. These institutions were usually dominated by a small number of men whose lending policies soon drew criticism. By the 1830s more banks were being established in major centres and smaller communities began mobilizing their capital, sometimes in branches of already established banks, but more often in locally incorporated operations.

THE DOMESTIC ECONOMY

Although the world of staples trade and colonial shipping touched the lives of people in the colonies both directly and indirectly, the seasonal rhythms of household production determined most people's general well-being. Pre-industrial rural families produced most of their own food, clothing and shelter, selling any surpluses of their labour to secure imported commodities such as tea, spices, and metal products. What

Clearing the town plot, Stanley, New Brunswick, 1834, *by W.P. Kay.*

National Archives of Canada/C17

was most important was that everyone work together to support the family which was the basic unit of economic production.

On the agricultural frontier, men's labour, which involved the clearing of land and producing marketable crops, was essential to the achievement of an improved standard of living. It took years for a pioneer farm family to clear enough land to have surpluses. In areas where the soil was poor or the climate uncertain, farming could never sustain a family, and other sources of income were necessary. Survival in such cases depended on a careful combination of rudimentary farming, fishing, and forestry work, and wage labour wherever it could be found.

In pre-industrial society, women's work was largely confined to the domestic realm, where most of the food and clothing was produced. Women's paid labour usually took the form of domestic service in the homes of other women where they learned and practised housewifery skills. Women produced the goods for household consumption that allowed the family to meet its basic needs and sold surpluses from the dairy, garden, and loom. In fishing communities women were often involved in the shore-based processing of fish.

Women also produced the next generation. Before mid-century, the average colonial woman bore on average seven or eight children, roughly one child every 26–28 months. Infant mortality was high, with one in five children dying in the first year of life; one in 20 births resulted in the death of the mother. As a result of these realities and the likelihood of death from infections, diseases, malnutrition, and accidents, men and women in colonial British North America had an average life expectancy of less than 50 years. Those who managed to survive to the age of 20 could still, on the average, expect to live only to 60 years of age.

The unpaid labour of older children was an essential element in a household economy that left little room for hiring farm labourers or house servants. By the age of 15, sometimes even earlier, most children were expected to do the work of an adult. Children in poor families were often sent out to work at the age of seven or eight to gain additional family income. It was common for children to be "adopted out" through a formal contract that outlined the duties of the child, the proscriptions on the child's behaviour, and the responsibilities of the family to whom the child was indentured.

While there is no question that families were the basic economic and social unit, they often varied widely from the ideal. A significant proportion of British North Americans at any given time (more than 25 percent in most regions) inhabited households extended by the presence of another family, a relative, or boarders. At least 7 percent of British North Americans never married, while a growing proportion of families were headed by women who had been widowed or abandoned by their husbands. Step-parents were common in many family units. Despite clerical and legal injunctions to the contrary, marriage between cousins was considered a positive match in families attempting to retain control of property or other forms of wealth. Throughout British North America, most marriages were endogamous—that is, within the same cultural group.

At mid-century, the average family size was beginning to decrease. For the rich, too many children brought complicated claims on their estates; for the poor they brought additional stress on the family economy. Although late marriage was the most acceptable form of family limitation, artificial methods of birth control were practised. Douches, condoms, and diaphragms were available by mid-century but not widely used. The rhythm method was inadequately understood, and patent medicines to "regulate" menstruation were highly unreliable and sometimes dangerous to a woman's health. Most married women who wanted to limit the size of their families either abstained from sexual intercourse or practised extended breast-feeding to reduce their fertility.

COLONIAL CITIES

In the first half of the nineteenth century, fewer than one in five British North Americans lived in communities of 1000 people or more. The largest cities in the Canadas in 1851 were Montreal (57 000), Quebec City (42 000), and Toronto (30 000). With a population of nearly 30 000, Saint John was the largest city in the Atlantic region. Montreal, Toronto, and Saint John owed much of their recent growth to the expansion of manufacturing. Benefiting from a ready supply of power from the Lachine Canal and cheap labour from nearby rural areas, Montreal boasted the highest concentration of manufacturing and processing operations.

Despite such developments, most cities remained little more than overgrown villages. Even Montreal was still a "walking" city in 1850, its commercial section crowded near the port. Markets, where farm families hawked their produce, were the centres of urban life. In the nearby streets merchants and artisans sold specialized goods and services that were unavailable in the rural areas. At mid-century, cities in British North America were building imposing new structures to house their markets and other activities of urban civic life. Bonsecours market in Montreal was, not surprisingly, the biggest of them all.

Unlike their twenty-first century counterparts, colonial cities were not planned around business and residential activities. Merchants, artisans, and apprentices usually lived and worked in the same building, and the "seedy" side of town was often only a block away from elite business and residential areas. While colonial elites were inclined to build their "estates" on the edge of the city, working people were clustered in the centre of town and were often grouped according to ethnicity and occupation. Census records indicate that widows and single women gravitated to urban areas, where they found more opportunities for making a living than in the countryside.

Notwithstanding the opportunities cities offered, they were not always pleasant places to live. Decaying garbage and the excrement of thousands of horses, cows, and pigs filled the streets. Market squares were awash with animal carcasses, fish heads, and rotting vegetables. In the lower regions of the town, noxious cesspools accumulated to become a breeding place of foul odours, enormous rats, and dreaded disease. Outdoor toilets still graced the backyards of many urban homes along with pigs, chickens, and even cattle. Fires frequently created havoc. In 1845, two huge fires left 20 000 people, or half the population, in

Bonsecours market, Montreal.

National Archives of Canada/C6730

As this picture shows, pigs roamed freely along Sparks Street in Ottawa in the 1860s.

Ottawa City Archives/CA-0219

Quebec City homeless. A major fire in Montreal in 1852 razed 11 000 homes, leaving one-sixth of the population without shelter.

By 1850, city councils were beginning to install rudimentary water and sewer systems and street lighting, but even in the most progressive cities, only a few wealthy wards had access to such services. For those unable to afford the cost of indoor plumbing, public wells and private carters provided water. The condition of the urban water supply helped to account for a higher death rate in cities than in rural areas.

Major British North American cities boasted a military presence to protect citizens against invasion from without and civil strife from within. Over 10 000 British soldiers were scattered from St John's to Victoria, with Halifax, Montreal, and Kingston serving as the major garrison towns. As well as infusing money into the colonial economy, the military made a substantial contribution to urban social life. Amateur theatre, sports events, and libraries were sponsored by the military, while grog shops, taverns, and prostitution flourished in the vicinity of the barracks.

Town and country in British North America were bound together by commercial exchange, which extended to the frontiers of settlement. In the Canadas, Montreal and Toronto were emerging as the focus for

road, water, and eventually rail transportation networks to their economic hinterlands, but no city had assumed metropolitan dominance over the whole colony. In the Atlantic region, year-round ocean communication enabled Boston, New York, Liverpool, and London to compete directly with Halifax, Saint John, Charlottetown, and St John's for economic control over the regional economy. Victoria's closest links were with San Francisco, which grew rapidly following the California gold rush of 1849. As the American frontier moved steadily westward, inhabitants of Red River also felt the inexorable pull of their southern neighbour.

WEBS OF DEPENDENCY

In colonial society, all of its members—men and women, rich and poor, immigrant and native-born—were bound together by the mercantile and domestic economies, which functioned on barter and mutual dependence as much as on hard currency. Women's work was performed within the context of the family, where, by law, the male head of the household controlled the wealth of his wife and children. Both the fisheries and timber trade nurtured the "truck system" in which merchants provided their labourers with the equipment and provisions they needed for the season's work in return for the product of their labour. Many workers never saw their wages and were perpetually bound to their merchant-supplier by a web of debt.

The same system often prevailed in farming communities, where merchants held mortgages on indebted farms. In Lower Canada and Prince Edward Island, rents to seigneurs and proprietors were notoriously in arrears, and tenants could be—though they rarely were—forcibly ejected from their lands. An increasing proportion of the Aboriginal population, having incorporated European society into traditional seasonal rhythms of the fur trade and artisan production, was now part of the network of dependency.

What is most obvious about these economic relationships is a fundamental inequality. Patriarchy, the belief that men should have power over women and children, and paternalism, the practice by which people in authority rule benevolently but intrusively over those below them on the social scale, encouraged duty

King Street East, Toronto, 1853.

Metropolitan Toronto Reference Library/J. Ross Robertson Collection/T10248

and deference in colonial society. Women and children were socialized to obey the male head of the household, and members of the labouring class deferred to their social superiors. Both patriarchy and social inequality came under strong attack in the nineteenth century, but the majority of people remained locked in unequal relationships. For people whose skin was not white, rationales for racial prejudice, which guaranteed perpetual subordination, were being more firmly entrenched.

CLASS AND CULTURE

Class in colonial society was based on kinship, wealth, and relationship to production. Although hereditary privileges were largely absent in North America, ac-

cess to sources of wealth and power was narrowly restricted. Tight little cliques of merchants, professionals, and politicians dominated all aspects of life in the settled colonies. In the early years of settlement, this class consisted almost exclusively of immigrants from Britain and the United States, but native-born elites soon asserted themselves. Individual members of the colonial elite might experience failure, but as a group they were growing more powerful. Michael Katz's studies show that at mid-century less than 10 percent of the adult men in Hamilton, Canada West, held "virtually all of the resources necessary to the health, well-being, and prosperity" of the rest of the community. "The rulers, the owners, and the rich," he concluded, "were by and large the same people."[4]

A middle class of farmers and artisans constituted the "bone and sinew" of colonial society. A term first used in England in 1811, "middle class" was beginning to take on a new, more complex meaning in the nineteenth century as some colonial producers expanded their operations beyond the family farm and the artisan's shop to emerge as successful entrepreneurs. Respectable artisans in British North America joined fraternal organizations and were elected to city councils. On the lower end of the middle-class spectrum, farming, fishing, and artisan families struggled to survive, their fate never far removed from the uncertainty of wage dependency.

In both town and country, a class of propertyless labour survived by doing manual work, often on a seasonal basis. Skilled labourers, such as printers and ship pilots, earned a living wage, while unskilled labourers were subject to cycles of boom and bust, the rhythms of the seasons, and payment in kind rather than cash. For some British North Americans, wage labour was only a stage in their life cycle, a chance to earn a little money before returning to the family farm or setting up in business. But for most labourers, these possibilities were receding in a society where class lines hardened over the course of the early nineteenth century.

GENDER AND SOCIETY

The old adage "women to the hearth and men to the plough" was firmly rooted in the pre-industrial division of labour. No distinction in colonial society was more fundamental than that between the sexes. Men and women performed distinct tasks in the colonial economy and were treated differently under the law. Ultimately separate gender roles, believed to be complementary, were brought together in the family, the basic unit of production in colonial society.

Under British common law which prevailed outside of Lower Canada, men were recognized as household heads with wives and children as their property. Despite her crucial economic role, a woman was legally subordinate to the husband, father, or even brother for whom she performed labour. The husband's right to dispose of the family property was limited only by a widow's legal claim to one-third of it, and most men willed their farm homes to a son, grandson, or son-in-law. In Lower Canada where the

Custom of Paris governed civil law, a couple married under a system of community of property. After marriage, all wealth acquired became their joint property, but was administered by the husband alone. The surviving widow had a dower right to half the estate, while the other half was divided equally among the children.

Widowhood was a difficult period in the lives of many colonial women. In Peel County, Canada West, for example, only one-quarter of widows in the mid-nineteenth century received a separate inheritance from their husbands. The others became boarders in the homes of a male heir. Wills generally indicated what provisions the heir was to make for the widow, and over 20 percent of the documents explicitly forbade the widow to remarry, on pain of being forced to surrender the property her labour had helped to create.

In this patriarchal system, women's sexuality and reproductive powers were carefully controlled. Girls and women were supervised within families, while church, state, and collective community pressure encouraged strict conformity to acceptable sexual behaviour. Women considered to be of easy sexual virtue were publicly ridiculed and socially ostracized, while men who failed to provide for their families or were dominated by their wives were subject to criticism.

There was often great sympathy expressed for single mothers, but their lot was not an easy one. In a curious twist of legal logic, a woman could not sue a man for the support of their child, but her own father could sue the man for the loss of his daughter's services, as well as his personal distress and dishonour. Denied any recourse under the law, children without legal fathers were called "illegitimate" and carried that stigma for life. Fewer than 5 percent of all colonial births were deemed illegitimate, although a considerably higher percentage of first children were born less than nine months after the wedding day.

For young women who found themselves pregnant outside marriage, the alternatives could be grim. Infanticide was the desperate resort of many unwed mothers in the mid-nineteenth century. The mothers who were caught were usually destitute, unmarried, working-class women with no family to share the burden of their shame or help them raise a child. Unwanted children were often placed in charitable in-

Susannah Moodie Describes an Upper Canadian Charivari

In the 1830s, quoting a neighbour's report, author Susannah Moodie provided a detailed description of a charivari, a community effort to assert social control, in her book *Roughing It in the Bush*:

> When an old man marries a young wife, or an old woman a young husband, or two old people, who ought to be thinking of their graves, enter for the second or third time into the holy estate of wedlock, as the priest calls it, all the idle young fellows in the neighbourhood meet together to charivari them. For this purpose they disguise themselves, blackening their faces, putting their clothes on hind part before, and wearing horrible masks, with grotesque caps on their heads, adorned with cocks' feathers and bells. They then form in a regular body, and proceed to the bridegroom's house, to the sound of tin kettles, horns and drums, cracked fiddles, and all the discordant instruments they can collect together. Thus equipped, they surround the house where the wedding is held, just at the hour when the happy couple are supposed to be about to retire to rest—beating upon the door with clubs and staves, and demanding of the bridegroom admittance to drink the bride's health, or in lieu thereof to receive a certain sum of money to treat the band at the nearest tavern.

> If the bridegroom refuses to appear and grant their request, they commence the horrible din you heard, firing guns charged with peas against the doors and windows, rattling old pots and kettles, and abusing him for his stinginess in no measured terms. Sometimes they break open the doors, and seize upon the bridegroom.... I have known many fatal accidents arise out of an imprudent refusal to satisfy the demands of the assailants.[5]

Moodie's neighbour observed that mob justice sometimes had an ugly side. In one instance a mob, seeking to penalize a black barber for marrying a local Irishwoman, dragged him nearly naked from his wedding bed and rode him upon a rail. The ordeal resulted in the death of the victim, but no one was brought to trial.

stitutions, where many of them died. Although anyone convicted of infanticide, abortion, or rape was subject to the death penalty, lighter sentences for these crimes were usually imposed.

Throughout British North America, divorces were difficult to obtain, frowned upon by the church and state as a threat to social stability. Before mid-century, a woman who left her husband received no property settlement, and custody of the children invariably went to the father. A divorce could be granted by a special act of the legislature in cases where the husband was proved to be guilty of incest, sodomy, bestiality, bigamy, or rape of a woman other than his wife (under the law it was impossible for a husband to rape his own wife). Except in Nova Scotia, cruelty was not a legal justification for divorce in British North America: as the head of the family, a man was considered to have the right to inflict physical "discipline" on his wife and children, provided he did not use "excessive force." In the Maritime colonies, the divorce laws were less rigid than in Canada West, where only five divorces were granted before Confederation. The Custom of Paris was even more stringent and did not recognize divorce at all.

The state also played a role in attempting to force individuals to conform to community moral standards. Although homosexuality was a capital crime under British law, the records of court cases in the colonies suggest that gay males in the army, the elite, and the middle class had secret networks. Those caught faced the loss of their careers and long jail sentences. In Canada West in 1842, Samuel Moore, lance corporal, and Patrick Kelly, private, of the 89th regiment of Foot, were discovered making love and were tried and sentenced to hang for "sodomy." They did not hang, but they both spent long terms in Kingston Penitentiary.

RACE AND RACISM

People whose skin was not white suffered most from the smug, small worlds of class and culture in British

North America. Treated with a mixture of disdain and paternalism, Aboriginal peoples and immigrants from Africa and Asia faced major obstacles in their efforts to get ahead.

ABORIGINAL PEOPLES

The lives of Aboriginal peoples in British North America varied considerably. By 1850, the fur-trade frontier was little more than a memory in most areas of the Atlantic colonies. Each summer the Mi'kmaq and Maliseet emerged from their winter retreats to peddle their wares in markets and from door to door in white communities. Sought by collectors throughout the world, Native crafts were prominent among colonial exhibits appearing at the Industrial Exhibition in London in 1851. Gifted Native artists such as Nova Scotia's Mary Christianne Paul Morris could earn a reasonable living from their labours. Most, however, lived a precarious existence. Newfoundland's Beothuk disappeared entirely when their last surviving member, Shanawdithit, died in 1829.

In the Canadas, Aboriginal peoples living within the confines of white settlement found the world around them changing rapidly in the mid-nineteenth century. They were not only increasingly isolated on reserves but also had to contend with constant interference by white bureaucracies. For example, in the Grand River area of Canada West, the superintendent of Indian affairs invested $38 000 of the Six Nations band's money in the failing Grand River Navigation Company (of which the superintendent was a director) without consulting the band.

Aboriginal peoples in the Canadas still dependent upon the hunt moved north and west with the receding fur-trade frontier, but the white bureaucracies followed them there as well. By the late 1840s armed skirmishes between Ojibwa and the Quebec Mining Company on Manitoulin Island in Lake Huron resulted in a new series of treaties covering the areas on the boundary separating Canada from the HBC territory. The treaties arranged by W.B. Robinson with the Ojibwa in the upper Great Lakes region in 1850 included several new provisions, reflecting the changing circumstances. Among them were the rights to royalties on any

Mary Christianne Paul Morris made a living from her sale of traditional Mi'kmaq crafts.

Nova Scotia Archives and Record Management Album No 5; No 76; N-6454

biography

Shanawdithit

Unlike many other Native groups, the Beothuk of Newfoundland shunned trade with Europeans and developed hostile relations with settlers living in coastal communities. They retreated to the interior where their living conditions deteriorated. Diseases, carried by the goods they scavenged and occasional contact with Europeans, easily ravaged a people whose diets no longer sustained good health. By the late eighteenth century stories of piteous deaths from hunger and disease, as well as outright murder by fur traders and fishers, drew the attention of authorities. Humanitarian efforts proved futile. Shanawdithit, the last surviving Beothuk on the island of Newfoundland died in 1829.

Little is known about Shanawdithit. Born around 1801, she was captured along with her mother and sister in 1823. The women were brought to St John's, where they attracted much attention. The Reverend William Wilson recorded his impressions: "The ladies had dressed them in English garb," he observed, "but over their dresses they all had on their, to them indispensable, deer-skin shawl." The youngest, Shanawdithit, renamed Nancy or Nancy April by her captors, was fascinated by her new surroundings. She decorated her forehead and arms with tinsel and coloured paper, chased onlookers, and was curious about the townfolk's material possessions. When she was given pencil and paper, Wilson reported, "she was in raptures. She made a few marks on the paper, apparently to try the pencil, then in one flourish she drew a deer perfectly."[6]

Following a brief sojourn in the interior and the death of her mother and sister, Shanawdithit was taken into the household of John Peyton Jr, a merchant who lived on the Bay of Exploits. There she worked as a servant for her keep and developed a close relationship with Peyton's three young children but reportedly refused to be pushed around. Occasionally, she would go into the woods where she claimed to have talked to her mother and sister. While she tolerated her captors, she was afraid of Mi'kmaq, who increasingly dominated the interior of the island, reporting that one, "bad Noel boss," had shot her while she was washing venison, wounding her in the back and legs.

In the last year of her life, Shanawdithit was taken to St John's where she lived with William Eppes Cormack, president of the recently established Beothuk Institution. This organization was too late to save the Beothuk from extinction, but it was largely because of Cormack's efforts that Shanawdithit's knowledge of her people was preserved. She helped Cormack develop a Beothuk vocabulary and drew sketches depicting the culture of her people as she knew it. Even in death, she continued to satisfy the curiosity of the people who had inadvertently brought the Beothuk to such a sad end. Before her body was interred in a St John's military cemetery in 1829, her skull and scalp were removed by Dr Carson, who performed the autopsy, to be sent to the Royal Society of Physicians in London.

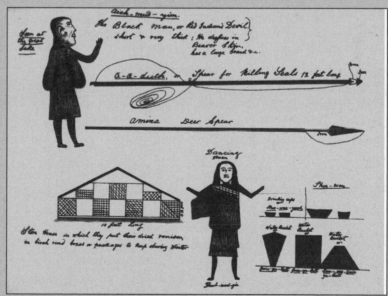

Shanawdithit's pictures of spears for killing whales and deer, smokehouses for curing meat, storehouses for winter supplies, a dancing woman, and a devil clad in beaver skin reflect the cultural practices and beliefs of her people.

National Archives of Canada/C87698

minerals found on their reserves and an "escalator" clause providing for an increase in the annuity payments should the value of the surrendered land increase dramatically.

On the West Coast, Native treaties with the Hudson's Bay Company recognized Native rights to land only if it had been settled and cultivated. Natives thus deprived of their traditional hunting and fishing territories often responded by attacking HBC property and personnel. In 1844, Cowichan, Songhee, and Clallum destroyed livestock belonging to the Hudson's Bay Company and attacked Fort Victoria. The Company met violence with violence. In 1850, for example, two warships were sent to destroy a Newitty village when its inhabitants refused to surrender the culprits believed to have killed three HBC men on Vancouver island. The gold rush heightened racial tensions. In the Fraser canyon, gold seekers created their own de facto government and resisted efforts by officials to maintain law and order. Miners grabbed the land they wanted and sometimes burned Native villages to force the terrified people to move out of their way.

By mid-century, responsibility for Native policy in the eastern colonies was gradually being transferred from British to colonial governments. The colonies were even more reluctant than Britain to spend public money on Aboriginal people. In Nova Scotia, Joseph Howe was appointed first Indian commissioner under new colonial legislation in 1842, but the position carried no salary. Not surprisingly his enthusiasm soon flagged. In 1857, the colony ceased special relief payments to the Mi'kmaq and insisted that they be included under the general municipal poor laws.

Church and philanthropic agencies frequently filled the vacuum left by sluggish colonial administrations. In 1845, Methodist minister Peter Jones, son of a white surveyor father and a Mississauga mother, established the Mount Elgin Industrial Institution at Munceytown Reserve, Canada West. The objective of the institution was to inculcate Christian values and the work ethic. While boys learned trades such as shoemaking and carpentry, girls were taught sewing, knitting, spinning, and the general skills of housewifery. In the Maritimes, Silas Rand tried to convert the Mi'kmaq, who had practised Roman Catholicism

since the time of the French regime, to the Baptist faith. Rand's evangelical efforts had less impact than his work in collecting Mi'kmaq legends and compiling a Mi'kmaq dictionary.

Beginning in 1818, Catholic missionaries arrived in Red River, led by Bishop Joseph-Norbert Provencher, and Protestant ministers, particularly Anglicans, soon followed. The Oblates, a Roman Catholic congregation of French origin with Canadian headquarters in Montreal, set up their first mission at Red River in 1845. They dispersed quickly through the West, reaching the Columbia River in 1847 and Vancouver Island in 1858.

In the West a few missionaries followed a path dating back at least to the Jesuits' establishment of Sillery: they founded Native-only Christian communities. The Anglican missionary William Duncan in 1862 gathered a group of about 50 Tsimshians in a settlement called Metlakatla at a site across from today's Prince Rupert. Modelled on a Victorian village, Metlakatla was governed in an authoritarian manner. Duncan established a volunteer police force whose duties included surveillance of sexual relations, church attendance, and work habits. As elsewhere, the paternalistic approach ended in failure.

While Natives in the eastern colonies had gradually developed immunities to many European diseases, epidemics still ravaged the West. Smallpox cut a swath on the West coast in 1835–36 and wiped out an estimated two-thirds of the 9000 Blackfoot peoples in 1837–38. Some plains Cree were spared a similar fate because the company made use of a new vaccine against smallpox to immunize the Native suppliers at Fort Pelley. Some Native populations appear to have recovered quickly, but others were not so resilient. From a population of 6000 in 1835, the Haida, whose culture flourished in the early years of contact, shrank to only 800 people in 1885.

As in eastern British North America, many Natives in the West became demoralized as their intricate societies collapsed around them. Others integrated themselves into the resource-based economy established by the European settlers. From the 1850s onward, many Natives on the West coast worked at commercial fishing, canning, sailing, coal mining, farming, and lumbering. Working in a white man's world did not mean that Natives fully abandoned their culture. For example, Natives often used their wages to acquire goods for distribution at potlatches rather than as a way to assimilate into European material and religious traditions.

THE MÉTIS

The history of the Métis community in this period is intertwined with the history of the Red River colony, which had developed slowly following the debacle of Seven Oaks. Encouraged by the missionaries in their midst, English and French Métis took up farming, planting their crops on lots along the river. They also continued their hunting activities. Without the meat provided by the Métis hunters, the colonists would often have faced starvation. By 1850, the colony's population was estimated at 5000. A majority were Métis; most non-Métis were retired company servants.

Relations among the various groups in the colony were strained by religious, linguistic, and racial divisions. The French-speaking Métis developed a strong sense of being a distinctive community. Their language and religion separated them from the Natives, while their Native heritage separated them from the French. Although their economic activities parallelled those of the English-speaking Métis, many of the anglophones desperately sought respectability in European eyes; the French-speaking Métis largely sought autonomy. English-speaking white settlers tended to be the most prosperous group in the colony and were more likely to be included by the HBC in political decision-making.

Marriage practices reflected the growing racism that infected Red River society. Initially the fur traders, dependent on Native knowledge and skills, gladly married Native women, who knew the country and participated in the trade alongside their husbands. For the white fur trader, a liaison with a Native woman had the additional advantage of cementing an alliance with a Native community, on which the fur traders depended for a steady supply of furs and provisions. As time passed, a new generation of fur traders married Métis women—the offspring of these European-Native relationships—or, if at all possible, white women.

George Simpson, governor-in-chief of the Hudson's Bay Company between 1826 and 1860, set the tone for changing racial values in Red River. Like other fur traders, he had initially found it expedient to develop relationships with mixed-blood women. In 1829, he had married his cousin Frances Ramsey Simpson while on leave in England. As the couple settled into domestic life back in Red River, it became clear that the Simpson household, a centre of activity in the pioneer community, no longer welcomed the non-white wives of fur traders. The Simpsons began treating these women with disdain, signaling the view that "mixed" marriages were inappropriate.

Underlying this transition in marriage partners was a new attitude toward Aboriginal people. As the Hudson's Bay Company traders became more confident of their ability to dictate the terms of the fur trade, their positive views of Natives and Métis gradually gave way to increasingly racist attitudes. After 1850, the arrival in today's Western Canada of a growing number of white settlers, who were not involved in the fur trade and who saw Native peoples as competitors for resources, hardened that racism.

BLACKS

Discrimination against blacks in British North America was less formal but equally crippling in its impact. Compared with the United States, where slavery was still practised, British North America appeared to be a mecca, and refugees from the United States arrived in substantial numbers throughout the first half of the nineteenth century. They soon separated themselves both from white settlement and from the descendants of the black Loyalists. Blacks had their cultural differences, but in the eyes of whites these were often blurred by the overriding factor of colour.

Notwithstanding strong anti-slavery sentiment in the colonies, the treatment of blacks was characterized by little Christian charity. Two decades after the arrival of the black refugees following the War of 1812, land title in Nova Scotia and New Brunswick was still uncertain. When their complaints were eventually addressed, blacks were given small allocations. The grants to their white neighbours were both larger and more efficiently registered. Following the abolition of slavery in the British Empire in 1833, the Nova Scotia Assembly passed "An Act to prevent the Clandestine Landing of Liberated Slaves...from Vessels arriving in the Province."

In every area of public life, blacks faced discrimination. Although black men who owned land could vote in British North America, they complained in Nova Scotia that they could not do so without being questioned and browbeaten. They were also denied equal access to public schooling. Only through the initiative of religious and philanthropic societies such as the Society for the Propagation of the Gospel, Dr Bray's Associates, and the Society for Promoting Christian Knowledge were schools provided for blacks in the Maritimes.

By the 1830s, Canada West had become the preferred destination for free blacks and refugee slaves who crossed the border to settle near Windsor and Niagara Falls. One of the most publicized efforts to plant a black colony in Canada was initiated in 1842 under the auspices of the British–American Institute. Josiah Henson, a slave who escaped to Upper Canada in 1830, was the moving spirit behind the settlement, located near Chatham. Christened Dawn, the community attracted over 500 settlers, who raised tobacco, wheat, and coarse grains and engaged in lumbering activities. The publication of Harriet Beecher Stowe's novel *Uncle Tom's Cabin* in 1851 brought immediate fame to Dawn, because Henson was reputedly the prototype for the character of Uncle Tom.

Following the passage of the Fugitive Slave Law in the United States in 1850, which permitted slave owners to pursue their property into non-slave states, Canada West became the main terminal for the "underground railroad." This was the name given to an informal network of anti-slavery activists who helped slaves escape to

In the middle of the nineteenth century, many slaves made their way to British North America, and freedom, by an informal network of sympathizers in the United States, known collectively as the "underground railroad," who provided shelter, food, and transportation in defiance of the Fugitive Slave Law.

National Archives of Canada/PA-123708

British North America. While estimates of the number of fugitive slaves living in Canada West in 1861 usually range into the tens of thousands, a recent study suggests that the number was much smaller, perhaps 20 percent of a total black population of about 23 000. More than 40 percent of the blacks living in the colony in 1861 were colonial born, and most of the black immigrants were free settlers, not runaway slaves.[7]

Whether immigrant or colonial born, fugitive or free, blacks in Canada West could not escape the cold shoulder of racial prejudice. In London, for example, whites insisted that blacks be taught in separate schools because of "the inbred feeling of repugnance in the breast of almost every white person at hybridism, which must to some extent be the result of a commingling of the races." Segregated schools were officially sanctioned in Canada West in 1850, and communities near black settlements petitioned against further black immigrants.

Mary Ann Shadd Cary, who in the 1850s edited a newspaper for her people called the Provincial Freeman, argued against the separatist tendencies of both whites and blacks, but to little avail. When John Anderson, a fugitive slave accused of killing his master, was tried in Toronto in 1860, two of the three judges argued that by killing a man Anderson had made himself liable to extradition to the United States to stand trial for his crime. Following massive protests from the international abolitionist community and a threat of intervention by Britain, the case was dismissed on a technicality. Meanwhile, Anderson was taken to Britain by his abolitionist friends and he eventually settled in the West African state of Liberia.

RELIGION AND CULTURE

Perhaps no single source of identity in colonial society was more important than organized religion. In the nineteenth century, Christian churches were sprouting like mushrooms across the colonial landscape. Churches competed with each other for adherents and played an increasingly important role in shaping aspects of the intellectual, social, and political life of British North Americans.

The political emancipation of Roman Catholics was one of the most important developments in this period. While the laws preventing Roman Catholics from voting, acquiring land, and worshiping in public had been abolished in Nova Scotia in 1789 and New Brunswick in 1810, outside of Upper and Lower Canada, they still could not hold public office. This ban was first lifted in 1823 for Lawrence Kavanagh, a Cape Breton merchant elected to the Nova Scotia Assembly. In 1829, Great Britain removed restrictions on the civil rights of Roman Catholics at home and throughout the empire.

Nowhere was the new power of the Roman Catholic Church more obvious than in Canada East. Following the conquest, the Roman Catholic church struggled to maintain its central role in the lives of francophones. Church attendance dropped off and it was often difficult to staff clerical positions. Inspired by the return of the Jesuits to Canada East in the 1840s and a quickening of religious devotion throughout colonial society at mid-century, the Roman Catholic Church made a comeback. More French Canadians opted to become priests and nuns and church attendance increased dramatically. Led by energetic bishops such as Jean-Jacques Lartigue and his successor, Ignace Bourget, the church established newspapers and associations to reassert its influence and counter liberalizing tendencies.

Another significant development in this period was the rise of evangelicalism, a movement that swept Europe and North America in the eighteenth and early nineteenth centuries. Those who embraced evangelicalism emphasized individual piety, personal "conversion," and direct communication with God. Such views defied the notions of hierarchy and social order advocated by the "established" Anglican, Presbyterian, and Roman Catholic churches and paralleled the secular demand for greater personal freedom and democratic consent that was gaining ground in the nineteenth century. The Methodist and Baptist churches grew more rapidly than other evangelical denominations in the colonies, but Quakers, Lutherans, Congregationalists, Mennonites, and Tunkers all had their followings, along with several smaller sects.

By the mid-nineteenth century, four out of ten British North Americans were Roman Catholics, but only in Assiniboia and Canada East were Roman Catholics in the majority. Over 40 percent of the population of Newfoundland and Prince Edward Island, a third of New Brunswickers, and one-quarter of Nova Scotians also subscribed to the Roman Catholic faith. Canada West, where Roman Catholics accounted for only 20 percent of the population, was the most Protestant region in British North America. Methodists, Presbyterians, and Anglicans were the largest Protestant denominations. In the western portions of Nova Scotia and New Brunswick, Baptist churches attracted a significant following.

While religious affiliation was closely tied to ethnic origin, it also had a bearing on class. The Methodists and Baptists, for instance, were particularly adept at winning converts among farmers and artisans. Although Methodists and Baptists could be found among those who had already acquired wealth and status, members of the Church of England and the Church of Scotland were overrepresented among colonial elites. Outside Canada East, Roman Catholics were excluded from the corridors of wealth and power, and throughout British North America they were heavily concentrated in the labouring class. The correlation between class and religion was not always a perfect fit. In Leeds and Lansdowne townships in Canada West, Irish Roman Catholics were among the most successful farmers and no more likely to be found among the ranks of the labouring class than their Canadian-born neighbours.

By the 1840s, most denominations sponsored their own newspapers, which debated global and local political events as well as religious questions. Churches also emerged as important dispensers of charity in a society characterized by rampant poverty and disaster. In urban centres, orphanages, hospitals, and shelters were usually church-sponsored institutions. Evangelical churches were also among the first to develop home and overseas missions. In 1845 Maritime Baptists sent Richard Burpee to India and, in the following year, the Presbyterian Church of Nova Scotia agreed to send John Geddes to the Hebrides.

In addition to educational, charitable, and mission activities, the church served as the focus for various reform movements in colonial society. The most successful by far was the temperance movement, which, from its beginnings in the late 1820s, soon engulfed all of British North America. Even the Anglican and Roman Catholic churches encouraged temperance among their followers, although they were much less likely than their evangelical counterparts to countenance total prohibition of alcoholic beverages as a solution to society's ills. According to temperance advocates excessive drinking undermined family life and was both a waste of money and a detriment to hard work.

CONCLUSION

By the 1850s, the hierarchical class system, unequal distribution of wealth and status, and carefully prescribed roles of men and women that prevailed in much of British North America were increasingly being called into question. New political values stressed greater equality of opportunity and encouraged people to question the status quo which allowed a privileged few to exercise power over the majority. As we will see in the next chapter, the new liberal values were hotly contested and they had their limits, especially when it came to racial minorities, but they nevertheless began to dominate the political discourses in the maturing British North American colonies.

A Historiographical Debate

Native Women and the Fur Trade

Before 1980, historians studied the fur trade as a virtually all-male affair. That year saw the publication of two books highlighting the role of Native women in the trade. The books, by Sylvia Van Kirk and Jennifer Brown, not only filled in an important gap but also reshaped historical perspectives on the fur trade itself.

Discussion of relations between European men and Native women in earlier histories often reflected traditional

European race and gender biases. E.E. Rich's authoritative three-volume history of the Hudson's Bay Company, which appeared from 1958 to 1960, devoted scarcely two out of over 1500 pages of text to the subject. Repeating misunderstandings common since the writings of the Jesuits in the seventeenth century, Rich asserted that Native women were promiscuous and Native men were willing to prostitute their wives and daughters for a bottle of brandy. Despite the HBC's prohibitions against sexual intercourse with Native women, Rich said, "Such behaviour was almost inevitable when active men were quartered for long periods among those with the concepts and habits of the Indians."[8]

While Rich appeared to believe that sexual availability was the only attraction of Native women, he also recognized that "domestic ties to some extent explained the willingness with which men spent year after year at the posts, willingly renewed their engagements, and volunteered to settle there if the Company's Charter were overthrown."[9] For Rich, like other early historians of the fur trade, this incidental observation merited little further exploration. The real focus of his and similar studies of the fur trade was the leading European male figures in the trade: HBC officials in Canada, partners in the North West Company, explorers, and the like. Family life received scant concern in accounts centred on the public sphere of company life.

Brown and Van Kirk, in contrast, focused on the domestic realm and thereby demonstrated the danger of separating family life from the overall operation of the fur trade. Native women provided their fur-trading husbands with far more than sex, companionship, and babies, although all of these were important. Their unpaid labour was crucial to the fur trade—the women made moccasins and snowshoes, prepared pemmican, fished, collected food supplies such as wild rice and berries, snared small game, tended crops at company posts, and assisted in making and powering canoes. Their knowledge of local language and geography also made them invaluable as interpreters, guides, and diplomats.

Van Kirk, relying on fur traders' accounts, concludes that many Native women actively sought alliances with the traders. Many of these women believed that the Europeans offered an easier life with more material goods. Furthermore, their new husbands quickly learned that Native women, more so than European women, enjoyed autonomy within their domestic sphere and brooked no interference from men. Even the trading of furs, often viewed as a male-only activity, tended to be a shared husband-and-wife venture. The Native women, knowing the people who were supplying the furs

and often having excellent business acumen, became indispensable to many traders. Madame Lamallice, the wife of the brigade guide at an HBC fort on Lake Athabasca, was the only interpreter in the area and could demand extra rations for her family. She also carried on "her own private trade in pounded meat, beaver tails and moose skins, with a hoarded stock of trade goods, including cloth and ribbons."[10] She threatened that if the HBC tried to stop her trade, she would turn the Indians against the company.

Van Kirk emphasizes that while many Native women were abandoned by fur traders whom they had married *à la façon du pays*, fur-trade society on the whole was characterized by stable interracial marriages. Yet over time, the female progeny of these marriages, rather than Native women, became the favoured marriage partners of fur traders: "The replacement of the Native wife by the mixed-blood wife resulted in a widespread and complex pattern of intermarriage among fur-trade families. It produced a close-knit society in which family life was highly valued. James Douglas echoed the sentiments of many of his colleagues when he declared that without 'the many tender ties' of family, the monotonous life of a fur trader would be unbearable."[11]

Although Native wives tried to pass on their practical skills to their children, daughters were often encouraged by their fathers to emulate European examples of what was considered to be ladylike behaviour. Compounding the resultant crisis of identity was the fact that, after the 1820s, the gradual arrival of European women in fur-trade society provoked an unfavourable re-evaluation of Métis wives. Officers began to marry European women, and these new wives snubbed the Métis wives of traders as racially inferior and unladylike, making the Métis women victims of racist and sexist stereotypes. By then, the fur trade itself was in decline and the white wife in the Red River settlement, like the missionary, "symbolized the coming of a settled agrarian order" where "native women would have little role to play."[12]

These insights had a negligible effect on Peter C. Newman, who in the 1980s wrote a lively popular history of the Hudson's Bay Company. In the first volume of his work, Newman gave scant attention to the role of women in the trade and presented a traditional image of larger-than-life male adventurers rather than the family men portrayed by Van Kirk and Brown. The fur traders, he claimed, saw the women as "bits of brown," and he added: "Love-making on the frontier did not carry much emotional baggage, being routinely offered and casually accepted."[13] Academic historians, unlike journalists, largely rejected Newman's approach and conclusions, and the second volume of his study gave more credence to the Van Kirk-Brown thesis.

There is little doubt that including women in the story of the fur trade does far more than sharpen the focus of an existing picture. It changes our image of the trade and the male traders completely. They were not lone adventurers passing through a wilderness for excitement and profit. Rather they were part of a complex interaction between Europeans and Natives, and they led lives that gave them emotional and economic ties to both groups.

NOTES

1 Peter A. Russell, "Forest into Farmland: Upper Canadian Clearing Rates, 1822–1839," in *Historical Essays on Upper Canada: New Perspectives*, ed. J.K. Johnson and Bruce G. Wilson (Ottawa: Carleton University Press, 1989) 132.

2 Anna Brownell Jameson, *Winter Studies and Summer Rambles in Canada: Selections* (Toronto: McClelland and Stewart, 1965) 167.

3 D.C. Harvey, ed., *Journeys to the Island of St. John or Prince Edward Island, 1775–1832* (Toronto: Macmillan, 1955) 104.

4 Michael B. Katz, *The People of Hamilton, Canada West: Family and Class in a Mid-Nineteenth-Century City* (Cambridge: Harvard University Press, 1975) 43.

5 Susannah Moodie, *Roughing it in the Bush; or Life in Canada*, ed. Elizabeth Thompson (Ottawa: Tecumseh Press, 1997) 152.

6 L.F. S. Upton, "The Extermination of the Beothuk of Newfoundland," *Canadian Historical Review* 58.2 (1977): 133-53.

7 Michael Wayne, "The Black Population of Canada West on the Eve of the American Civil War: A Reassessment Based on the Manuscript Census of 1861," *Histoire sociale/Social History* 28.56 (Nov. 1995): 465–81.

8 E.E. Rich, *The History of the Hudson's Bay Company, 1670–1870, vol. 1, 1670–1763* (London: Hudson's Bay Records Society, 1958) 605.

9 Ibid.

10 Sylvia Van Kirk, *"Many Tender Ties": Women in Fur Trade Society in Western Canada, 1670–1870* (Winnipeg: Watson and Dwyer, 1980) 84–85.

11 Ibid.

12 Ibid.

13 Peter C. Newman, *Company of Adventurers* (Markham, ON: Viking, 1985) 1: 205.

SELECTED READING

R.C. Harris and J. Warkentin, *Canada before Confederation* (Toronto: Oxford University Press, 1974) and *The Historical Atlas of Canada*, vol. 2 are the most comprehensive sources for the history of British North America in the nineteenth century. Raw data on the population and production from pre-Confederation censuses are contained in the *Census of Canada*, 1871, vol. 4, and analyzed in M.C. Urquhart and K.A.H. Buckley, eds., *Historical Statistics of Canada* (Cambridge: Cambridge University Press, 1965); F.H. Lacey, ed., *Historical Statistics of Canada*, 2nd ed. (Ottawa: Statistics Canada, 1983); and Jacques Henripin, *Tendances et facteurs de fécondité au Canada* (Ottawa: Ministry of Supply and Services, 1968).

There is a vast literature on immigration and settlement in this period. Irish immigration to Upper Canada/Canada West is thoughtfully analyzed in Donald Harmon Akenson, *The Irish in Ontario: A Study in Rural History* (Montreal: McGill-Queen's University Press, 1984) and Bruce S. Elliott, *Irish Migrants in the Canadas: A New Approach* (Montreal: McGill-Queen's University

Press, 1988). Two recent studies focusing on the Upper Canadian immigrant experience are Wendy Cameron and Mary McDougall Maude, *Assisting Emigration to Upper Canada: The Petworth Project, 1832–1837* (Montreal: McGill-Queen's University Press, 2000) and Wendy Cameron, ed., *English Immigrant Voices: Labourers' Letters from Upper Canada in the 1830s* (Montreal: McGill-Queen's University Press, 2000). Two good community studies with information regarding landholding patterns in Canada West are David Gagan, *Hopeful Travellers: Families, Land, and Social Change in Mid-Victorian Peel County, Canada West* (Toronto: University of Toronto Press, 1981) and Leo A. Johnson, "Land Policy, Population Growth, and Social Structure in the Home District, 1793–1851," *Ontario History* 69 (1977): 151–68. Michael Katz offers a detailed urban study in *The People of Hamilton, Canada West: Family and Class in a Mid-Nineteenth-Century City* (Cambridge: Harvard University Press, 1976). See also Gordon Darroch and Lee Saltow, *Property and Inequality in Victorian Ontario: Structural Patterns and Cultural Communities in the 1871 Census* (Toronto: University of Toronto Press, 1994); Peter A. Russell, *Attitudes to Social Structure and Mobility in Upper Canada, 1815–1840: "Here We Are Laird Ourselves"* (Lewiston, NY: Edwin Mellen Press, 1990), and the books by McCalla and Johnston cited in Chapter 9.

Suggestive interpretations on the economic, social, and political conditions in Lower Canada/Canada East in this period can be found in the works by Creighton, Ouellet, Greer, and Rudin cited in Chapter 9. See also Normand Séguin, *La Conquête du sol au 19è siècle* (Montreal: Boréal Express, 1977). Lower Canada/Canada East is well served by a number of fine case studies including Peter Gossage, *Families in Transition: Industry and Population in Saint-Hyacinthe* (Montreal: McGill-Queen's University Press, 1999); Gérard Bouchard, *Quelque arpents d'Amérique: population, économie, famille au Saguenay, 1838–1971* (Monrtéal: Boréal, 1996); Claude Baribeau, *La seigneurie de la Petite Nation, 1801–1854: le rôle économique et social du seigneur* (Hull, PQ: Éditions Asticou, 1983); René Hardy, *La sidérurgie dans le monde rural: les hauts fourneaux du Québec au XIXe siècle* (Saint-Foy: Les Presses de l'Université Laval, 1995); and three books by John I. Little, *Crofters and Habitants: Settler Society and Culture in a Quebec Township, 1848–1881* (Montreal: McGill-Queen's University Press, 1992), *Nationalism, Capitalism, and Colonization in Nineteenth-Century Quebec: The Upper St Francis District* (Montreal: McGill-Queen's University

Press, 1989), and *The Child Letters: Public and Private Life in a Canadian Merchant-Politician's Family, 1841–1845* (Montreal: McGill-Queen's University Press, 1995).

In addition to general studies of the Atlantic colonies cited in earlier chapters, see W.S. MacNutt, *New Brunswick: A History, 1784–1867* (Toronto: Macmillan, 1984); Graeme Wynn, *Timber Colony: A Historical Geography of Early-Nineteenth-Century New Brunswick* (Toronto: University of Toronto Press, 1981); Andrew Hill Clark, *Three Centuries and the Island* (Toronto: University of Toronto Press, 1959); Stephen Hornsby, *Nineteenth-Century Cape Breton: A Historical Geography* (Montreal: McGill-Queen's University Press, 1992); Donald Macgillivray and Brian Tennyson, eds., *Cape Breton Historical Essays* (Sydney, NS: University College of Cape Breton Press, 1980); and the early essays in two books edited by Kenneth Donovan: *Cape Breton at 200: Historical Essays in Honour of the Island's Bicentennial, 1785–1985* (Sydney, NS: University College of Cape Breton Press, 1985) and *The Island: New Perspectives on Cape Breton's History, 1713–1975* (Fredericton: Acadiensis Press, 1990). Douglas Baldwin and Thomas Spira explore aspects of society in Prince Edward Island in *Gaslights, Epidemics and Vagabond Cows: Charlottetown in the Victorian Era* (Charlottetown: Ragweed Press, 1988). The political implications of the land question in Prince Edward Island are analyzed in Ian Ross Robertson *The Tenant League of Prince Edward Island, 1864–1867: Leasehold Tenure in the New World* (Toronto: University of Toronto Press, 1996). Scott W. See explores religious violence in *Riots in New Brunswick: Orange Nativism and Social Violence in the 1840s* (Toronto: University of Toronto Press, 1993). Urban developments are discussed in T.W. Acheson, *Saint John: The Making of a Colonial Urban Community* (Toronto: University of Toronto Press, 1985) and Judith Fingard, Janet Guildford, and David Sutherland, *Halifax: The First 2500 Years* (Halifax: Formac, 1999).

Specific studies on immigration and settlement in Newfoundland include W. Gordon Handcock, *"Soe longe as there comes noe women": Origins of English Settlement in Newfoundland* (St John's: Breakwater Press, 1989) and John J. Mannion ed., *The Peopling of Newfoundland: Essays in Historical Geography* (St John's: Institute for Social and Economic Research, 1977). The early nineteenth century is analyzed in the works by Cadigan, Matthews, and O'Flaherty cited earlier. For the history of St John's see Patrick O'Neill, *The Story of St. John's, Newfoundland* (Erin, ON: Boston Mills Press, 1975). On the salt-fish trade and sealing in this period see two books by Shannon Ryan, *Fish Out of Water: The Newfoundland Saltfish Trade,*

1814–1914 (St. John's: Breakwater, 1986) and *The Ice Hunters: A History of Newfoundland Sealing to 1914* (St. John's: Breakwater, 1984).

For British Columbia, the Prairies, and northern Ontario, the period covered in this chapter is the subject of the early chapters of regional and provincial surveys cited in Chapter 10. On colonization generally, see Sarah Carter, *Aboriginal People and Colonizers of Western Canada to 1900* (Toronto: University of Toronto Press, 1999). The early history of Métis communities is explored in Jennifer Brown and Jacqueline Petersen, eds., *The New Peoples: Being and Becoming Métis in North America* (Winnipeg: University of Manitoba Press, 1985). On Red River, see Gerhard Ens, *Homeland to Hinterland: Changing Worlds of the Red River Métis in the Nineteenth Century* (Toronto: University of Toronto Press, 1996) and Frits Pannekoek, *A Snug Little Flock: The Social Origins of the Riel Resistance of 1869–1870* (Winnipeg: Watson and Dwyer, 1991). See also the excellent accounts of women in the fur trade by Brown and Van Kirk cited in Chapter 10.

On European-Native relations in the early period of settlement in British Columbia, see works by Robin Fisher and Cole Harris cited in earlier chapters. See also Barry M. Gough, *Gunboat Frontier: British Maritime Authority and Northwest Coast Indians, 1846–1890* (Vancouver: UBC Press, 1983); Paul Tennant, *Aboriginal Peoples and Politics: The Indian Land Question in British Columbia, 1849–1989* (Vancouver: UBC Press, 1990); Tina Loo, *Making Law, Order, and Authority in British Columbia, 1821–1871* (Toronto: University of Toronto Press, 1994); and Hamar Foster, "Letting Go the Bone: The Idea of Indian Title in British Columbia, 1849–1927," in *Essays in the History of Canadian Law*, vol. 6, *British Columbia and the Yukon*, ed. Hamar Foster and John McLaren (Toronto: Osgoode Society for Canadian Legal History, 1995). The impact of epidemics is discussed in Cole Harris, *The Resettlement of British Columbia*, Chapter 1; and Robert Galois, "Measles, 1847-1850: The First Modern Epidemic in British Columbia," *BC Studies* 109 (Spring 1996): 31-46. On early settlement more generally, see also Richard S. Mackie, *The Wilderness Profound: Victorian Life on the Gulf of Georgia* (Victoria: Sono Nis Press, 1995); and *Vancouver and Its Region*, ed. Graeme Wynn and Timothy Oke (Vancouver: UBC Press, 1992). The beginnings of the lumber industry in British Columbia are detailed in Gordon Hak, *Turning Trees into Dollars: the Columbia Coastal Lumber Industry, 1858–1913* (Toronto: University of Toronto Press, 2000).

Economic developments in this period are covered in Michael Bliss, *Northern Enterprise: Five Centuries of Canadian Business* (Toronto: McClelland and Stewart, 1987); Kenneth Norrie and Douglas Owram, *A History of the Canadian Economy* (Toronto: Harcourt Brace Jovanovich, 1991); G.N. Tucker, *The Canadian Commercial Revolution, 1845–1851* (Ottawa: Carleton University Press, 1964); A.R.M. Lower, *Great Britain's Woodyard: British America and the Timber Trade, 1763–1867* (Montreal: McGill-Queen's University Press, 1973); G.P. de T. Glazebrook, *A History of Transportation in Canada*, vol. 1 (Ottawa: Carleton University Press, 1964); John McCallum, *Unequal Beginnings: Agriculture and Economic Development in Quebec and Ontario until 1870* (Toronto: University of Toronto Press, 1980); Marjorie Griffen Cohen, *Women's Work, Markets, and Economic Development in Nineteenth-Century Ontario* (Toronto: University of Toronto Press, 1988); S.A. Saunders, *The Economic History of the Maritime Provinces* (1939; reprinted Fredericton: Acadiensis Press, 1984); and Jacob Spelt, *Urban Development in South Central Ontario* (Ottawa: Carleton University Press, 1972).

The impact of sea-based industries on the Atlantic region has been extensively explored by the Maritime History Group, based at Memorial University in St John's. In addition to five books of published proceedings, several monographs have appeared, including two by Eric Sager: *Seafaring Labour: The Merchant Marine in Atlantic Canada* (Montreal: McGill-Queen's University Press, 1989) and *Maritime Capital: The Shipping Industry in Atlantic Canada, 1820–1914* (Montreal: McGill-Queen's University Press, 1990), and two books by Rosemary Ommer: *Merchant Credit and Labour Strategies in Historical Perspective* (Fredericton: Acadiensis Press, 1990) and *From Outpost to Outport: A Structural Analysis of the Jersey–Gaspé Cod Fishery, 1767–1886* (Montreal: McGill-Queen's University Press, 1991). The fisheries generally are the subject of James E. Candow and Carol Corbin, eds., *How Deep is the Ocean? Historical Essays on Canada's Atlantic Fishery* (Sydney: University College of Cape Breton Press, 1997). On economic development in Nova Scotia in this period, see Julian Gwyn, *Excessive Expectations: Maritime Commerce and the Economic Development of Nova Scotia, 1740–1870* (Montreal: McGill-Queen's University Press, 1998).

In addition to the sources on the fur trade cited in Chapter 10, see *Fur Trade and Empire: George Simpson's Journal*, ed. Frederick Merk (Cambridge: Harvard University Press, 1968); and Lorne Hammond, "Marketing Wildlife: The Hudson's Bay Company and the Pacific Northwest, 1821–49," *Forest and Conservation History* 37 (Jan. 1993): 14-25. Local documentary studies include Morag McLachlan, *The Fort Langley Journals, 1827–30* (Vancouver: University of British Columbia Press, 1998), and Neil J. Sterritt et al., *Tribal Boundaries in the Nass Watershed* (Vancouver: University of British Columbia Press, 1998).

Transportation and urban amenities in this period are described in Norman R. Ball, ed., *Building Canada: A History of Public Works* (Toronto: University of Toronto Press, 1988). The role of the military is the subject of Elinor Kyte Senior, *British Regulars in Montreal: An Imperial Garrison, 1832–1854* (Montreal: McGill-Queen's University Press, 1981) and the early chapters of Desmond Morton, *Canada and War: A Military and Political History* (Toronto: Butterworths, 1981). The cholera threat is discussed in Geoffrey Bilson, *A Darkened House: Cholera in Nineteenth-Century Canada* (Toronto: University of Toronto Press, 1980). On medical care, see Wendy Mitchinson, *The Nature of Their Bodies: Women and Their Doctors in Victorian Canada* (Toronto: University of Toronto Press, 1991), and Charles G. Roland, ed., *Health, Disease and Medicine: Essays in Canadian History* (Toronto: Irwin, 1984)

Women's experience is summarized in Alison Prentice, et al., *Canadian Women: A History*, 2nd ed. (Toronto: Harcourt Brace, 1996) and the Clio Collective, *Quebec Women: A History* (Toronto: Women's Press, 1986). See also Peggy Bristow, et al., *"We're Rooted Here and They Can't Pull Us Up": Essays in African-Canadian Women's History* (Toronto: University of Toronto Press, 1994); Cecilia Morgan, *Public Men and Virtuous Women: The Gendered Language of Religion and Politics in Upper Canada, 1791–1850* (Toronto: University of Toronto Press, 1996); Elizabeth Jane Errington, *Wives and Mothers, School Mistresses and Scullery Maids: Working Women in Upper Canada, 1790–1840* (Montreal: McGill-Queen's University Press, 1995); Katherine M.J. McKenna, *Anne Murray Powell and Her Family, 1755–1849* (Montreal: McGill-Queen's University Press, 1994); Janet Guildford and Suzanne Morton, eds., *Separate Spheres: Women's Worlds in the Nineteenth-Century Maritimes* (Fredericton: Acadiensis Press, 1994); Linda Kealey, ed., *Pursuing Equality: Historical Perspectives on Women in Newfoundland and Labrador* (St John's: Institute for Social and Economic Research, 1993); Marilyn Porter, *Place and Persistence in the Lives of Newfoundland Women* (Aldershot: Avebury, 1993); and Peter Ward, *Courtship, Love, and Marriage in Nineteenth-Century English Canada* (Montreal: McGill-Queen's University Press, 1990). Studies of visible minor-

ity women in early British Columbia include Tamara Adilman, "A Preliminary Sketch of Chinese Women and Work in British Columbia, 1858–1920," in *Not Just Pin Money: Selected Essays on the History of Women's Work in British Columbia*, eds. Barbara K. Latham and Roberta J. Pazdro (Victoria: Camosum College, 1984), and Sherry Edmunds-Flett, "19th-Century African-Canadian Women on Vancouver Island," in *Telling Tales: Essays in Western Women's History*, eds. Catherine A. Cavanaugh and Randi R. Warne (Vancouver: University of British Columbia Press, 2000).

The working class in the nineteenth century has received considerable attention, most notably in Bryan D. Palmer's *The Working-Class Experience: Rethinking the History of Canadian Labour, 1800–1991*, 2nd ed. (Toronto: McClelland and Stewart, 1992); M.S. Cross, ed., *The Workingman in the Nineteenth Century* (Toronto: Oxford University Press, 1975); and Steven Langdon, *The Emergence of the Working-Class Movement, 1845–1875* (Toronto: New Hogtown, 1975). Class and culture are the subjects of J.I. Cooper, "The Social Structure in Montreal in the 1850s," *Canadian Historical Association, Report* (1956); and Fernand Ouellet, "Libéré ou exploité: le paysan québécois d'avant 1850," *Histoire sociale/Social History* 13.26 (Nov. 1980): 339–68. On the nineteenth-century marine labour force, see Judith Fingard, *Jack in Port: Sailortowns of Eastern Canada* (Toronto: University of Toronto Press, 1982).

The experience of Aboriginal peoples in this period is covered in the surveys by Olive Dickason, J.R. Miller, Arthur J. Ray, and L.F.S. Upton cited earlier. See also Ian A.L. Getty and Antoine S. Lussier, eds., *As Long as the Sun Shines and the Rivers Flow: A Reader in Canadian Native Studies* (Vancouver: UBC Press, 1983); Robin Fisher and Kenneth Coates, eds., *Out of the Background: Readings in Canadian Native History*, 2nd ed. (Toronto: Copp Clark, 1996); and Donald Smith, *The Reverend Peter Jones (Kahkewaquonaby) and the Mississauga Indians* (Toronto: University of Toronto Press, 1987). Two articles by Judith Fingard describe aspects of Protestant missionary activity directed toward Native peoples in this period: "English Humanitarianism and the Colonial Mind: Walter Bromley in Nova Scotia, 1813–1825," *Canadian Historical Review* 54.2 (June 1973): 123–51 and "The New England Company and the New Brunswick Indians, 1786–1826: A Comment on the Colonial Perversion of British Benevolence," *Acadiensis* 1.2 (Spring 1972): 29–42. For the Beothuk, see Ingeborg Marshall, *The History and Ethnography of the Beothuk* (Montreal: McGill-Queen's University Press, 1996), and Ralph

Pastore, *Shanawdithit's People* (St John's: Atlantic Archaeology, 1992) and "The Collapse of the Beothuk World," *Acadiensis* 19.1 (Autumn 1989): 52–71. The Aboriginal peoples of Labrador are discussed in Robert McGhee, *The Native Peoples of Atlantic Canada* (Toronto: McClelland and Stewart, 1974) and *Ancient Peoples of the Arctic* (Vancouver: University of British Columbia Press, 1996); Helge Kleivan, *The Eskimos of Northeast Labrador: A History of Eskimo-White Relations, 1771–1955* (Oslo: Norsk Polarinstitutt, 1966); and José Mailhot, *The People of Sheshatshit: In the Land of the Innu* (St John's: Institute for Social and Economic Research, 1997).

Studies of the impact of the fur trade on Northwest Native societies are itemized in Chapter 10. On the North, see Kerry Abel, *Drum Songs: Glimpses of Dene History* (Montreal: McGill-Queen's University Press, 1993); Ken S. Coates, *Best Left as Indians: Native-White Relations in the Yukon Territory, 1840–1973* (Montreal: McGill-Queen's University Press, 1991); and his *Canada's Colonies: A History of the Yukon and Northwest Territories* (Toronto: Lorimer, 1985). See also Kenneth Coates and William R. Morrison, eds., *Interpreting Canada's North* (Toronto: Copp Clark Pitman, 1989). On the work of missionaries among the Native peoples, see John Webster Grant, *Moon of Wintertime: Missionaries and the Indians of Canada in Encounter since 1534* (Toronto: University of Toronto Press, 1984); Martha McCarthy, *From the Great River: Oblate Missions in the Dine, 1847–1921* (Edmonton: University of Alberta Press, 1995); and Robert Choquette, *The Oblate Assault on Canada's Northwest* (Ottawa: University of Ottawa Press, 1995).

The history of Blacks in this period is covered in Robin W. Winks, *The Blacks in Canada: A History*, 2nd. ed. (Montreal: McGill-Queen's University Press, 1997); Bridglal Pachai, *Beneath the Clouds of the Promised Land: The Survival of Nova Scotia Blacks*, vol II, *1800–1989* (Halifax: The Black Educators Association of Nova Scotia, 1990); W.A. Spray, *The Blacks in New Brunswick* (Fredericton: Brunswick Press, 1972); Jim Hornsby, *Black Islanders: Prince Edward Island's Historical Black Community* (Charlottetown: Institute of Island Studies, 1991); and Daniel Hill, *The Blacks in Early Canada: The Freedom-Seekers* (Agincourt, ON: Book Society, 1981).

Religion in the early nineteenth century is the focus of work by Michael Gauvreau, *The Evangelical Century: College and Creed in English Canada from the Great Revival to the Great Depression* (Montreal: McGill-Queen's University Press, 1991); William Westfall, *Two Worlds: The Protestant Culture of Nineteenth-Century Ontario* (Montreal: McGill-Queen's University Press, 1989); John Webster Grant, *A Profusion of Spires: Religion in Nineteenth-Century Ontario* (Toronto: University of Toronto Press, 1988); Jacques Monet, *The Last Cannon Shot: A Study of French-Canadian Nationalism* (Toronto: University of Toronto Press, 1969); Nire Voisine and Jean Hamelin, eds., *Les Ultramontanes Canadiens-français* (Montreal: Boréal Express, 1985); Goldwin French, *Parsons and Politics: The Role of the Wesleyan Methodists in Upper Canada and the Maritimes, 1780–1855* (Toronto: Ryerson Press, 1962); and George Rawlyk, *Ravished by the Spirit: Religious Revivals, Baptists, and Henry Alline* (Montreal: McGill-Queen's University Press, 1984) and *Canadian Baptists and Christian Higher Education* (Montreal: McGill-Queen's University Press, 1988). For a discussion of perspectives on the evangelical tradition, see Michael Gauvreau, "Beyond the Half-Way House: Evangelicalism and the Shaping of English-Canadian Culture," *Acadiensis* 20.2 (Spring 1991): 158–77. Religious restrictions on the franchise are discussed in John Garner, *The Franchise and Politics in British North Ameria, 1755–1867* (Toronto: University of Toronto Press, 1969). Jan Noel, in *Canada Dry: Temperance Crusades before Confederation* (Toronto: University of Toronto Press, 1995) examines the early history of the temperance movement.

 **WEBLINKS**

WEBSTER-ASHBURTON TREATY
www.yale.edu/lawweb/avalon/diplomacy/br1842m.htm

The Avalon Project at the Yale Law School offers the text of the treaty and related documents.

1858 GOLD RUSH
www.bcarchives.gov.bc.ca/exhibits/timemach/galler04/frames/index.htm

The British Columbia Archives present an exploration of the Cariboo gold rush, detailing the people, conditions, terrain, equipment and methodology, and commerce of the gold rush regions.

PARTRIDGE ISLAND
www.saintjohn.nbcc.nb.ca/~Heritage/PartridgeIsland

This site offers documentary material on the history of Partridge Island.

MARITIME HISTORY
www.mun.ca/mha/holdings.html

The Maritime History Archive at Memorial University in Newfoundland includes parish and mercantile records, photographs, and maps.

SALT FISHERIES
http://collections.ic.gc.ca/fisheries/main.asp?frame=on

The Newfoundland Salt Fisheries digital exhibit provides essays on various aspects of the fisheries, thematic slide shows, photo galleries, a selection of audio and video clips, maps, primary documents, and illustrations.

SIR JOHN FRANKLIN
www.ric.edu/rpotter/sjfranklin.html

The Franklin expedition is documented at this site, which includes multimedia documents, images of the Arctic in popular culture, links to further reading, and details of the search for evidence of his travels.

GROSSE ÎLE
www.parkscanada.gc.ca/parks/quebec/grosseile/en/stopover_e.html

This site provides a brief history of Grosse Île in the wake of the Napoloenic Wars.

THE UNDERGROUND RAILROAD
http://education.ucdavis.edu/new/STC/lesson/socstud/railroad/Map.htm

This site, prepared by two education students at the University of California—Davis, offers two maps showing the routes used in the Underground Railroad. Also available are internal links to online resources and a short bibliography.

CHAPTER 12

Rebellions, Reform, and Responsible Government

In September 1837, opponents of British rule in Lower Canada, known as Patriotes, held a noisy charivari outside the home of Rosalie Cherrier in St Denis, a village in the District of Montreal. Cherrier was an outspoken "Constitutionalist," the name adopted by supporters of British rule in the colony. The evening before the charivari, she had harangued a Patriote demonstration, denouncing the revolutionaries who were calling for Lower Canada's political independence from Great Britain. During the commotion, shots rang out from her house, seriously wounding two men. Although it was unclear who had fired the weapon, Cherrier, whose home was destroyed during the charivari, was charged with attempted murder. She was later acquitted of the crime.[1]

Cherrier's experience demonstrates the deep political divisions in Lower Canada that ultimately led to rebellion against British rule in 1837. In the same year, tensions in Upper Canada also led to armed uprisings. The political unrest in the Canadas may have been exceptional in the degree of violence it inspired, but the concerns raised by leaders of the rebellions were echoed in every British North American colony between 1815 and 1867. Although the rebellions were defeated, they forced Great Britain to reassess its relationship with its colonies. By 1848 British authorities had conceded the principle of "responsible government," which gave more power to the elected members of the colonial Assembly.

EMERGING POLITICAL CULTURES

Political values in British North America evolved within the larger framework of western political thought. In Europe and the Americas, the concentration of power in the hands of monarchs and a small hereditary landed elite, bolstered by a state-supported church and a standing army, were being challenged by leaders of the rising middle class. Their demand that power be shared among all men with a stake in society, usually defined as those possessing property or wealth, was a popular rallying cry in both the American and French Revolutions. By the nineteenth century, wider concepts of democracy were being advanced. Why not give every man—and even every woman—an equal political voice? Indeed, why not create a society in which equality of condition, not just equality of opportunity, prevailed? In the British North American colonies, as in much of the North Atlantic world, political discussions were informed by these three perspectives: conservatism, liberalism, and socialism.

When calling for political reforms, colonial politicians could draw upon the practical experience of an evolving parliamentary democracy in Great Britain and a full-fledged republican system in the United States. On the European continent, popular unrest flared in 1830 and 1848, threatening monarchs and inspiring revolutionary tracts such as the *Communist Manifesto*, written by Karl Marx in 1848. Those denied access to formal political processes in British North America wondered if they, too, should resort to violence to advance their cause. Among Irish Catholics in the colonies, the movement for repeal of the legislation uniting Great Britain and Ireland in 1801 became a model for mobilizing mass support for a political cause. The British labour movement, still in its infancy, offered yet other ways by which ordinary people could exert influence.

For colonial elites who lamented the erosion of traditional institutions, European conservatism served as a source of inspiration. Conservatism was still a force to be reckoned with in Great Britain, and the papacy, emerging from a century of retreat, sounded the clarion call to all Roman Catholics to resist the "sins" of liberalism and socialism. In British North America, conservative political values and loyalty to the British Empire had been given a new lease on life following the War of 1812.

It is within this context that the eastern colonies of British North America moved along the continuum from imperial dependency to responsible government, an essentially liberal response to the issue of political power. "Responsible government" refers to a system in which the executive council (cabinet) is drawn from the majority party in the elected assembly and requires a majority of votes in the assembly to pass their legislation. As this definition implies, it is the political system that, with some modification, exists in Canada today. The road to responsible government was not always an easy one. Nor was it necessarily the democratic triumph that is often portrayed. Only a relatively small number of men emerged as the power brokers under responsible government, and their values were revealed in the laws they imposed on the society they governed.

REBELLION IN THE CANADAS

LOWER CANADA

The agricultural crisis, coupled with the frustration of a Canadien middle class excluded from the Executive and Legislative Councils, provided a backdrop to the rebellions in Lower Canada in 1837 and 1838. Following the War of 1812, the Parti canadien, dominated by the new middle class of French-speaking lawyers, doctors, and journalists, began to agitate for political reform that would reduce the power of appointed officials in the colony. As in other colonies, a small group of government officials and wealthy merchants favoured by the governor appeared to monopolize political appointments, Crown land grants, and government contracts. In Lower Canada, they were labelled the Château Clique because they could often be found at the Château St-Louis, the governor's residence in Quebec City.

The Parti canadien handily won all elections for the House of Assembly. By defending Canadien culture, in particular the Roman Catholic Church, the seigneurial system, and the French language, the Parti canadien gained the support of the majority of francophones in the colony. The Parti canadien proved especially popular with the habitants because it campaigned for the opening of new seigneuries. Even English-speaking settlers in the Eastern Townships, while hesitant about supporting political organizations dominated by French-Canadians, opposed the government's policies, complaining about administrative incompetence and corruption. Scots, Irish, and English immigrants, many of them sympathetic to democratic principles, also demanded political reform.

The stature of the Parti canadien had been raised significantly in 1822 when it joined with the clergy to fend off a proposal by the British government to unite Lower Canada and Upper Canada into one colony. This proposal was a direct attempt by the Montreal merchants and their imperial allies to reduce the influence of the Canadien representatives in the Assembly who balked at proposals for state-funded canal construction on the St Lawrence and demanded grants of new seigneuries before they would approve road-building expenditures for the Eastern Townships. With the completion of the Erie Canal in 1825, a development that gave New York State an advantage over Montreal in shipping, the clamour of the Montreal merchants for canal expenditures grew louder, and their resolve to oppose Assembly demands for more power in colonial politics stiffened.

In the late 1820s, the program of the Parti canadien, which changed its name to Parti patriote in 1826, became more radical. The refusal of governors to respond to the Assembly's demands and the close relationship between the Roman Catholic hierarchy and the governing clique helped to fuel the discontent of the Parti patriote. The party's leaders were also influenced by developments in Europe and the United States which were advancing the cause of liberalism. While Papineau remained a defender of the seigneurial system, he and other leaders were increasingly drawn to republicanism and state control of education, policies that were fiercely opposed by the leaders of the Roman Catholic Church.

In 1834, Papineau put forward in the Assembly a list of 92 resolutions designed to make the authority of an electoral majority supreme. The resolutions demanded an Executive Council chosen by the Assembly, an elected Legislative Council, and the Assembly's approval of government appointments and salaries. The resolutions made thinly veiled threats that if Britain did not accept their proposals, the Canadiens would demand independence from the British Empire.

The party's growing radicalism prompted the defection of some of its earlier supporters, both English and French. Seventeen members of the Parti patriote voted against the 92 resolutions, finding them too extreme. Similarly, John Neilson, editor of the *Quebec Gazette* and a long-time supporter of Papineau, turned away from a party that rejected the monarchical system. In the 1834 election, the Parti patriote expelled most of the moderates from its ranks. At the same time, anglophone radicals such as Dr Edmund O'Callaghan and Dr Wolfred Nelson won election in French-Canadian ridings under the Patriote banner.

By 1834 the lines had been firmly drawn between the Parti patriote and the governing clique. Governor Lord Matthew Whitworth-Aylmer responded to the Assembly's refusal to pass money bills by selling over 2.1 million hectares of land to the British American Land Company as a means of providing the Executive with the revenue it needed to meet administrative costs. His action appalled Patriote supporters and crystallized the popular view that the government was determined to deny ordinary people both land and democracy.

Tired of continued obstructionism by the Lower Canadian Assembly, Colonial Secretary Lord John Russell decided to act. In March 1837, he issued 10 resolutions approved by the British Parliament, which permitted the new governor, Lord Gosford, to appropriate provincial revenue without the authority of the elected Assembly. Russell also rejected calls for an elected Legislative Council and confirmed the title of the British American Land Company to the lands it was selling at prohibitive prices. For many Patriote leaders, this marked the end of the constitutional avenue to reform. They resolved to overthrow British rule by a campaign of civil disobedience if possible, by violence if necessary.

By the summer of 1837, tensions were running high. In Montreal English-speaking defenders of the government formed a paramilitary loyalist association, known as the Doric Club, to break up Patriote meetings. The Patriotes responded with the creation of a paramilitary organization of their own, the Fils de la liberté. Meanwhile, Lord Gosford, following Russell's orders, dismissed the Assembly for refusing to vote support for long-term funding for salaries of government appointees. The Patriote central committee responded with a call for a constitutional convention for Lower Canada in December 1837, to be preceded by an economic boycott, large rallies, and petitions.

The boycott movement was led by Patriote women who produced homespun to replace imported cloth and bought manufactured goods only from merchants known to be Patriote supporters. Nonetheless the Patriotes were not supporters of women's rights. Indeed, they had joined the government members of the Assembly in 1834 to place a legislative ban on women's right to vote. In Lower Canada and elsewhere in the colonies there were limits to the liberalism of those purporting to be reformers.

When it became clear that the boycott was having no effect on the government's resolve to resist the demands of the Assembly majority, the Patriotes stepped up their pressures with a campaign against minor officials. They called on all government appointees, including justices of the peace, militia captains, and battalion lieutenants, to resign their posts or face harassment. On 6 November a street battle in Montreal between the Doric Club and the Fils de la liberté became Gosford's pretext for ordering the arrest of Patriote leaders and calling in troops from the other British American colonies to suppress the protest movement. When Papineau fled to the United States, many of his supporters began to lose their patriotic zeal. Other Patriote leaders, convinced that peaceful protest was futile, resorted to armed rebellion.

On 23 November, a mainly habitant Patriote army under Wolfred Nelson defeated British troops at St Denis on the Richelieu River, but they could not follow up their victory. Two days later, the British defeated the Patriotes who had mobilized at St Charles farther south on the Richelieu. They destroyed St Denis on 1 December and two weeks later sacked the Patriote stronghold of St Eustache, leaving 58 Patriotes dead and 60 homes burned. Two days later, British forces burned and looted the village of St Benoît, another Patriote stronghold, and the first rebellion was over. Martial law was declared, and more Patriote leaders fled to the United States.

In the United States, a core of exiles regrouped under the name Frères Chasseurs and proposed a more militant program to gather popular support for another uprising. The new program included a proposal to end all seigneurial dues, with lands to be freely granted to the habitants. The rebels entered Lower Canada in November 1838 and gathered about 4000 insurgents. No match for the British troops, they were easily defeated. The Iroquois of Kahnawaké joined the attack on the Patriotes. Although they had their own grievances with the government, the Iroquois decided to make common cause against the rebels after the latter invaded Kahnawaké on their march to Montreal.

St Denis insurgents.
Henri Julien/National Archives of Canada/C18294

Determined to prevent future attempts at rebellion, the British forces went on a rampage of looting and burning of farms and houses in Patriote centres of resistance in the Montreal area and on the Richelieu. The government also arrested 850 Patriotes for their roles in the rebellions: 12 of them were hanged, 58 deported to Australian penal colonies, and 2 banished. The Australian deportees described the pain of their exile in the haunting folksong, "Un canadien errant," that would inspire generations of Quebec nationalists.

UPPER CANADA

Upper Canadians also experienced social unrest leading to rebellion in the 1830s. In the wake of the War of 1812, conservative values became strongly entrenched in Upper Canada. Government leaders equated political reform with American republicanism and used the threat of American expansion to suppress dissent. For a time, American immigration to Upper Canada was actively discouraged and the political and property rights of American-born residents in the colony were called into question. Anyone who advocated political reform was accused of sowing disunity, which could weaken Upper Canada's ability to resist future American attacks.

The experience of Robert Gourlay, a Scot who emigrated to Upper Canada in 1817, demonstrated the limits of tolerance. Soon after his arrival, Gourlay organized township meetings to record settlers' complaints about the system of land grants in the colony. When he published the proceedings of a settlers' meeting in Niagara, that had been drawn up as a petition to the Prince Regent, members of the elite charged him with seditious libel. Twice charged and twice acquitted by juries that accepted his claim that he was upholding citizens' rights to petition their monarch, he was banished by the government anyway in 1819.

Opponents of the government accused it of having created an oligarchy, which the reformers called the Family Compact. The term implied somewhat misleadingly that the members of the oligarchy were interrelated and located in one geographical area. In practice, there were small cliques throughout the province and their members were not, at least initially, related by blood. But there was indeed a colonial oligarchy whose members were favoured by most of the lieutenant-governors. Its members saw themselves as the gentlemen of the colony, a class akin to the British aristocracy. To their opponents, they were pretentious and corrupt beneficiaries of undeserved patronage.

The Family Compact resisted growing opposition demands for land reforms, secularization of clergy reserves (or at least their distribution among all religious denominations), and greater power for the elected Assembly. In Assembly elections, the oligarchy could count on significant support from British immigrants against the allegedly pro-American Reformers. Leaders of the Roman Catholic Church, who feared the consequences for a religious minority of majoritarian rule espoused by the Reformers, also supported the status quo. By the 1830s, an uneasy electoral alliance existed between the Family Compact and the fiercely Protestant Orange Order, the Roman Catholic hierarchy, and some moderate Reformers.

In the Assembly, Reform members had difficulty uniting as a cohesive party, although they shared some common objectives. The land issue in Upper Canada provoked widespread resentment that could be focused on the political elite. While new settlers were increasingly forced to buy land or move to remote areas of the colony, speculators were able to purchase choice lands relatively cheaply. The Upper Canadian government was particularly generous to the Canada Land Company, headed by John Galt, which received grants of millions of hectares of Crown land. To the Reformers, already insensed by the grants of land to Family Compact members and their supporters, the sale of land to a new group of speculators added insult to injury.

Reformers also united around the defence of the civil rights of Upper Canada's American-born population. Following the War of 1812, the Anglican bishop, John Strachan, and his supporters called into question the property rights of "aliens" and, by inference, the voting rights for American immigrants. Only British intervention in 1828 settled this issue in the immigrants' favour. The clergy reserves issue also briefly united Reformers, who resented Strachan's claims that the Church of England remain the exclusive beneficiary of the monies earned from the sale of the reserves.

biography

Papineau and Mackenzie: Rebels with a Cause
Louis-Joseph Papineau

Louis-Joseph Papineau was born in 1786, the son of a notary who served in the Assembly and purchased a seigneury in 1801. He studied law before following his father into politics. Elected to the Assembly in June 1808, Papineau quickly rose to leadership positions within the Parti canadien, and was chosen by the Assembly majority as speaker in 1815, a position he held until 1837. Papineau served as a militia captain in the War of 1812, and until the late 1820s supported British parliamentary institutions, arguing that rule by an Assembly majority would be consistent with British political traditions. In 1822, Papineau and John Neilson lead a delegation to London to oppose British plans to unite the two Canadas. Papineau soured on British institutions and became more enamoured of American democracy as he tired of the contempt with which the British-appointed lieutenant- governors treated resolutions passed by the people's representatives in the Assembly.

Louis-Joseph Papineau, his wife, Julie Bruneau, and their daughter, Eliza.

National Archives of Canada/C21005; Antoine Plamandon, National Gallery of Canada/17920

In many ways, Papineau's views seemed a bundle of contradictions. By 1837, he was a republican, a democrat, and an anticlerical nationalist who denounced Britain's political and economic oppression of Lower Canadians. Yet he was also a vigorous supporter of the seigneurial system. After purchasing his father's seigneury in 1817, he had become lord of the manor to about 300 people, a number that swelled as a result of both migration and births to over 3000 in 1852. He was not an ideal master. In an analysis of Petite Nation, Papineu's seigneury on the north shore of the Ottawa River, Claude Baribeau concludes: "On the one hand, he took part in a feudal type of exploitation that he condemned elsewhere; on the other, he gave to anglophone capitalists the responsibility of exploiting the forestry resources of his seigneury, commercializing agriculture and to an extent proletarianizing his people, activities that he reproached elsewhere as an agrarian, anti-capitalist nationalist."[2] The contradictions in his personal life aside, there is little doubt that he spoke for a Lower Canadian majority in rejecting the notion of land as simply capitalist real estate to be bought and sold for whatever price speculators believed it could fetch.

Reluctant to turn to armed force in 1837, Papineau played little role in the military side of the rebellion. He fled to the United States and attempted both there and in France to encourage official efforts to dislodge Britain from Canada. His efforts met with little success. Amnestied in 1844, Papineau returned to Quebec in 1845. He was re-elected to the Assembly in 1847 and remained there until 1854, serving as an inspiration for the opposition group that became the Parti Rouge. At the same time he supervised the construction of a manor house inspired by castles on the Loire River, to which he retired from politics in 1854, the year the seigneurial system was abolished. He died at his manor house at Montebello in 1871.

William Lyon Mackenzie

Born in 1795 in Dundee, Scotland, Mackenzie had a peasant background. He received a modest business education and in 1820 set sail for Upper Canada, seeking advancement beyond the modest clerical jobs he had found at home. Four years of shopkeeping later, he started the *Colonial Advocate* in Queenston, moving his family (which eventually included seven children) and the paper to York later that year. The *Advocate* became the leading voice of the radicals in the colony, particularly after several younger members of the elite destroyed Mackenzie's printing press in 1826. Elected to the Assembly in 1828, he was expelled five times by the Tory majority for allegedly libelling them, but he was always re-elected in the subsequent by-election. Mackenzie regarded the Compact as a collection of corrupt, pompous individuals whose public high-mindedness concealed an attachment to the public trough.

Against Tory assertions of the need for a hierarchical society where each person knew his or her place, Mackenzie extolled a society of small farmers and small businessmen of relatively equal wealth and equal opportunities for education. Influenced like Papineau by romanticized notions of what the United States represented, Mackenzie railed against land speculators, special privileges for the Church of England, corporate entities such as the Compact-controlled Bank of Upper Canada, and a myriad of policies that he blamed for the creation of a system of social classes in Upper Canada.

Elected the first mayor of Toronto in 1834, Mackenzie's Assembly influence peaked in 1835 when the reformers won an electoral majority. He published his *Seventh Report of the Committee on Grievances*, demanding that elected politicians rather than British appointees have power in the colony. When the reformers lost their majority and Mackenzie his seat in the 1836 election orchestrated by Governor Head, Mackenzie abandoned any hope of peaceful change. He made preparations for armed resistance, coordinating his efforts to a degree with Papineau with whom he corresponded frequently.

After the rebellion failed, Mackenzie fled to the United States, and attempted to organize exiles on Navy Island in Niagara River for an invasion of Upper Canada. This earned him 11 months in prison in Rochester, New York, and disillusioned him regarding the Americans' concern for spreading democracy. Allowed to return to Canada in 1849, Mackenzie was re-elected to the Assembly in 1851 and continued to press for radical reforms until illness forced his retirement in 1858. He died in 1861.

William Lyon Mackenzie.
National Archives of Canada/C1993, detail

By refusing to budge on this issue, the Upper Canadian administration prompted conservative reformers such as Egerton Ryerson, a leader of one of the Methodist churches, to make common cause for a time with radical politicians.

By the 1830s, two poles of reform were to be found in the Assembly. One, associated with Dr W.W. Baldwin and his son Robert, called for a continued role for Britain in colonial government and even accepted an appointed Executive Council as long as the members had the support of a majority in the elected Assembly. Radical Reformers supported the notion of an Executive Council drawn from the majority group in the legislature but went further in their reform demands. Led by William Lyon Mackenzie, the radicals wanted the Executive Council, like the Assembly, to be an elected body with the lieutenant-governor reduced to a figurehead. They also demanded that other government positions in the colony be elected rather than appointed.

As in Lower Canada, when the Reformers controlled the Upper Canadian Assembly, they were reluctant to pass money bills, most notably the civil list which authorized the salaries of the lieutenant-governor's appointees. Given its support from a large percentage of new British immigrants, the governing clique had no need to fear, as it did in Lower Canada, the constant dominance of the Assembly by Reform members. The squabbling Reformers lost their majority in 1830, regained it in 1834, and lost it again in 1836.

Sir Francis Bond Head, a gentleman-adventurer who became lieutenant-governor in late 1835, was less willing than some of his predecessors to attempt to reconcile the competing claims of Compact and Reformers. Faced with a truculent Assembly in 1836, he dissolved it and called new elections. Making a mockery of the electoral process, Head condoned intimidation by Orangemen at the polls and used government-appointed returning officers to manipulate voting procedures. He also made extravagant claims throughout the election that a vote for the Reformers was a vote for annexation to the United States. After the election, only 17 Reformers held their seats in the 63-member Assembly. Moderate Reformers such as Robert Baldwin, while appalled by Head, believed that they would eventually achieve political change in Upper Canada if they bided their time and continued to apply pressure in London. The radicals were less sanguine.

By the fall of 1837, Mackenzie was convinced that an armed uprising would be necessary to bring his vision of a frontier agrarian democracy into being. His blueprint for the state of Upper Canada was modelled on the American constitution. Convinced by his oratory that the government was planning to confiscate their land, many Reformers joined Mackenzie's cause out of sheer desperation. The departure of Upper Canadian troops to quell the rebellion in Lower Canada gave Mackenzie and his confederates the chance they were waiting for. With Toronto now largely unprotected, military success seemed within their grasp.

Unfortunately for Mackenzie and his supporters, the planning for a rebellion, undertaken mainly in the taverns that dotted the Home District around Toronto, was amateurish and confused. Mackenzie's original plan was to seize a large cache of government arms in Toronto on Thursday, 7 December. Due to developments in Lower Canada, his lieutenants, in his absence, decided to push the date ahead to the 4th, gathering men at Montgomery's Tavern north of Toronto for the assault on the capital. Since news of the change of date did not reach all the rebels, confusion about the timing of the uprising limited the number of men available for the attack on Toronto.

Meanwhile, the gathering on the 4th tipped off loyalists in the area, who warned Governor Head of the insurgency. He quickly assembled 1500 volunteers. Reports of the size of this force caused many of the rebels to think twice about taking up arms. On the fateful Thursday, Mackenzie's rag-tag army, numbering only about 400 men, was quickly dispersed.

Word of rebellion in the Home District quickly spread throughout the colony. In the London District Dr Charles Duncombe hurriedly organized local Reformers to make a stand. As in the Toronto area, American-born settlers proved to be the most willing to take up arms. The pro-government volunteers, better armed than their opponents, carried the day in the London District as they did in other areas of the colony where the Reformers took up arms.

The Upper Canadian rebellion of 1837 resulted in 885 arrests: 422 of them in the Home District, 163 in the London District, 90 in Gore (which included the present-day cities of Hamilton, Guelph, Kitchener, and Brantford), and 75 in Midland (which included Kingston). Most of those arrested were established farmers or tradesmen, men neither wealthy nor poor. For their part in the rebellion, two men were hanged: Samuel Lount, a blacksmith, and Peter Matthews, a farmer. While Lount hailed from Pennsylvania, Matthews was a veteran of the War of 1812 on the British side.

Mackenzie and other rebel leaders fled to the United States. With the help of sympathetic Americans, the exiles, along with their Lower Canadian counterparts, formed "Hunters' Lodges" and conducted raids across the border in hopes of rallying opposition within the colony. A combination of British troops, lack of popular enthusiasm, and the unwillingness of the United States to alienate Great Britain by supporting the rebels doomed their efforts. On 14 January 1838,

Mackenzie was forced to withdraw from Navy Island on the Canadian side of the Niagara River, where he had proclaimed the republic of Upper Canada, and where subsequent raids, including substantial incursions at Pelée Island, Prescott, and Windsor, were crushed. The authorities moved quickly to punish those responsible for perpetrating turmoil in border communities: 156 people were jailed, 99 deported, and 18 hanged.

REFORM MOVEMENTS IN THE MARITIMES

Despite sharing many of the political problems identified in the Canadas, none of the Maritime colonies erupted in full-scale rebellion. Nevertheless, each colony spawned reform movements that were organized around ideas of liberal democracy and specific grievances relating to the structure and processes of colonial governance.

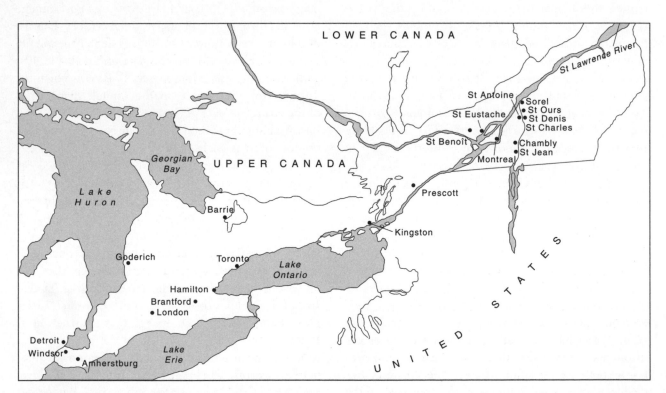

Map 12.1
Sites of the 1837–38 rebellions.

PRINCE EDWARD ISLAND

The land question was the animating force of political life on Prince Edward Island. In 1767, most of the land in the colony had been granted to proprietors, many of whom resided in Great Britain. Few of the proprietors fulfilled the terms of their grants which required that they recruit settlers, build roads, and pay taxes. As a result there were vast tracts of vacant land, little revenue to support the cost of colonial administration, and a growing number of angry tenant farmers who resented paying fees to absentee proprietors.

In the early nineteenth century, more of the proprietors were wealthy islanders who had acquired tracts of land from the original grantees. They rented land to immigrants but were even more likely than their absentee counterparts to insist that tenants pay their dues. Inevitably, tensions erupted when agents for the proprietors attempted to collect rents or to evict tenants who had fallen behind in their payments. Because of the power of the proprietors, both on the island and in Great Britain, demands for reform of the land system were resisted. By the early 1830s, landlords still controlled about 90 percent of the colony's farmland, and 65 per cent of the island's 33 000 inhabitants were either tenants or squatters.

In 1831, William Cooper, a former land agent for absentee proprietor Lord James Townsend, won a hard-fought election for a seat in the island legislature on a platform of "our country's freedom and farmers' rights." He soon emerged as leader of the Escheat Movement, which won an overwhelming victory in the 1838 election. When Cooper travelled to London to plead his case for a general escheat, or cancellation, of the proprietary grants, he was refused even a hearing from Colonial Secretary Lord John Russell.

EXECUTION OF LOUNT AND MATTHEWS.

Upper Canadian rebels Samuel Lount and Peter Matthews were hanged in 1838. After the execution, Lount's widow, Elizabeth, wrote a public letter accusing Chief Justice John Beverley Robinson of callousness and treachery in her husband's death. Her letter, which raged against "the series of hardships brought upon me and my orphan children by you, and others of the tory party of Canada," was one of the few pieces of writing by a woman that was to appear in the Reform press.

National Archives of Canada/C1242

Thereafter, reform on the island focused on responsible government as the only means of achieving a satisfactory conclusion to the interminable land question.

NEW BRUNSWICK

In New Brunswick, the timber trade dominated the political process. The revenues from the sale, leasing, and licensing of Crown lands, spent at the lieutenant-governor's prerogative, became the object of the Assembly's reform efforts and were a prize worth fighting for. The issue became more contentious with the appointment of Thomas Baillie as commissioner of Crown lands in 1824. Charged with bringing bureaucratic efficiency to the administration of Crown lands, Baillie alienated virtually everyone in the colony while chalking up vast surpluses in the colonial treasury.

Political power in the colony was concentrated in an appointed Council that exercised both legislative and executive functions. As elsewhere, this self-seeking group often opposed the wishes of the elected Assembly and dispensed patronage to themselves and their friends. Reform opposition coalesced in the Assembly in 1833 when the Colonial Office decided to divide the Council into legislative and executive branches of government. At the top of the list of appointments to the new Executive Council was none other than the hated Thomas Baillie.

Charles Simonds, a powerful member of New Brunswick's timber aristocracy and president of the Bank of New Brunswick, led the Assembly's efforts to reform what was increasingly viewed as a heavy-handed and corrupt political structure. In 1833 and again in 1836, the Assembly sent a delegation to London to negotiate a solution to the mounting political unrest in the colony. The Colonial Office, recognizing that the Reformers were gaining strength and had the support of some of the most powerful men in New Brunswick, agreed to a compromise. In return for a "civil list" guaranteeing the salaries of government appointees, including the hated Thomas Baillie, the revenues from Crown lands would be turned over to the Assembly's disposal. When Lieutenant-Governor Archibald Campbell, a staunch upholder of the old regime, refused to accept the new order, the Colonial Secretary, Lord Glenelg, dismissed him.

Campbell's successor, Sir John Harvey, had no such qualms. Moreover, he acquiesced to the Colonial Secretary's injunction to choose councillors who had the confidence of the Assembly, thus relieving the new Executive Council of the dead weight of lifetime appointments. With Simonds the chief adviser to the lieutenant-governor, New Brunswick had achieved one of the most important conditions for the operation of responsible government: executive responsibility to the majority in the Assembly. What was still missing was a full-fledged party system to exercise power and a governor who withdrew from the governing executive.

NOVA SCOTIA

Resentment against appointed colonial officials, who held their positions virtually for life, was also a cause of complaint in Nova Scotia. As in New Brunswick, Nova Scotia had a single appointed council—the hated Council of Twelve—which focused democratic opposition. Reformers tended to find considerable support in the countryside where resentment against a clique concentrated in Halifax was steadily mounting. Between 1828 and 1831, Joseph Howe, the son of a Loyalist, began touring the province to promote his Halifax-based newspaper, the *Nova Scotian*. Howe's "rambles" helped to convince him that the economic and social well-being of the colony depended on wresting power from the hands of a powerful and increasingly autocratic political clique.

In 1835, Joseph Howe successfully defended himself against a charge of libel when he published a letter criticizing the colony's appointed magistrates. Riding on his popular acclaim, he won a seat in the Assembly where he continued his battle for political reform. Early in 1837 Howe introduced resolutions in the Assembly that criticized the composition of the Council of Twelve which, he charged, consisted of eight members of the Church of England including the bishop; a chief justice who for all intents and purposes was the leader of the Conservative Party; five members with close family connections; and five who were partners in the same bank. Howe's resolutions carried in the Assembly by 26 to 20 votes.

Having made concessions in New Brunswick, Lord Glenelg quickly responded to the demands of the Nova Scotia Reformers as well. In 1838, Lieutenant-Governor Sir Colin Campbell was instructed to surrender the casual revenues to the disposal of the Assembly and divide the Council of Twelve into legislative and executive branches. In addition, the governor was ordered to put four assemblymen, including one reformer, Herbert Huntington, on the Executive Council, while at the same time to avoid the appearance of favouritism toward the

Church of England, exclude all judges, and appoint no more than one member of the commercial elite. The concessions were welcome but they still fell short of full responsible government.

More than any other colonial politician, Joseph Howe knew what he wanted: the same constitutional rights for British subjects in the colonies as they enjoyed at home. Howe pressed his case in London and expounded his position in a series of public letters to the colonial secretary in 1839. "Every poor boy in Nova Scotia…knows that he has the same rights to the honours and emoluments of office as he would have if he lived in Britain or the United States," Howe concluded. "And he feels, that while the great honours of the empire are almost beyond his reach, he ought to

have a chance of dispensing the patronage and guiding the administration of his native country without any sacrifice of principle or diminution of self-respect."[3]

THE COLONIAL CONDITION IN NEWFOUNDLAND

In the early nineteenth century, Newfoundland differed from the other settled colonies in being denied the apparatus of colonial government. Governors were notable by their absence, preferring to leave the island when autumn arrived. Fishing admirals continued to enforce English laws during the summer months, but their handling of cases was often harsh and open to

The Town and Harbour of St John's from Signal Hill, 1831, *by William Edgar. By the time this image was painted, St John's had emerged as a great commercial entrepôt, a major naval base, and the political capital of the colony. It was also the refuge of discharged servants, known as "dieters," who wrought havoc in the community when the fisheries failed and unemployment escalated.*

Pyall, Henry/National Archives of Canada/C-041605

corruption. During the winter, people were left to their own devices and justices of the peace coped as best they could with problems as they arose.

By the beginning of the nineteenth century, any complacency about the lack of representative government was being swept away. Uncertainty about land tenure, the lack of schools, and assistance for the poor became the substance of a petition to the Prince Regent in 1811. One of the authors of this document was Dr. William Carson, a recent immigrant from Scotland, who was convinced that representative government, security of land tenure, and the full range of English civil rights were long overdue on the island.

A lingering post-war depression, compounded by several years of poor fish catches and a disastrous fire in St John's in 1816, resulted in bankruptcies and human misery. With immigrants arriving in larger numbers than ever, most of them from Ireland, social tensions intensified. Sporadic looting of merchant property and hungry mobs demanding provisions in communities such as St John's, Carbonnear, and Harbour Grace made officials uneasy. Although the British Parliament granted relief, it refused to consider political concessions.

In 1820, two separate court cases brought matters to a head. Two indebted Irish fishermen, James Landrigan and Philip Butler, were convicted of contempt of court in refusing to respond to the magistrates' summons to appear in court. Their property was promptly seized and both men were sentenced to receive 36 lashes with a cat-o'-nine-tails. Many people were outraged by what they saw as an unjustified overreaction on the part of officialdom. Backed by the reformers, Landrigan and Butler sued the magistrates for assault and false imprisonment. They were unsuccessful, but the scandal served as a catalyst for change.

The reform movement in the colony was led by Carson and Irish-born merchant Patrick Morris, and promoted by two reform newspapers, the *Newfoundland Sentinel* and the *Public Ledger*. While an elected legislature was not immediately forthcoming, other reforms were implemented. In 1824–25 circuit courts were instituted and Newfoundland was declared a Crown colony. Sir Thomas Cochrane became the first civil governor in 1825. Cochrane ruled with an appointed council and lived in grand style, building an elegant Government House in St John's. He also set about building roads to connect St John's to nearby districts and providing relief to the destitute.

When Great Britain itself began to broaden its electoral base though Catholic Emancipation in 1829 and the Reform Bill of 1832, it became even more difficult to deny similar rights to colonies settled by British populations. Newfoundland was granted representative government in 1832 with a broad male franchise. Every man who owned or occupied a house for at least one year was eligible to vote and after two years could run for elected office. As in most of British North America, political parties in Newfoundland took the names of their British counterparts. The Reformers or Liberals drew support primarily from Irish Roman Catholic voters, while the Tories or Conservatives represented English Protestant interests.

During the early years of representative government, the Reformers dominated the elected Assembly, which inevitably came in conflict with the appointed council dominated by Conservatives. The Colonial Office tried to mute divisions in 1842 by creating an amalgamated legislature, in which a portion of the members were appointed rather than elected. But the time for treating Newfoundland as an exception among the British North American colonies was fast disappearing. Full representative government was restored in 1848.

THE STRUGGLE FOR RESPONSIBLE GOVERNMENT

By that time, other British North American colonies were moving along the road to responsible government. In 1838, John George Lambton, Earl of Durham, was named governor general of British North America and charged with the responsibility of preparing a report on the causes of the Canadian rebellions. Heir to coal mines in Newcastle, England, he was, like many capitalists, suspicious of aristocratic landowners and conservative political values. After spending only a few months in the colonies, he produced a report early in 1839. Two of its main recommendations were union of Lower

Canada and Upper Canada, and the granting of responsible government.

Durham was impressed with the moderate Reformers of Upper Canada, who shared his liberal vision. He blamed the Family Compact for the colony's slow development, accepting the Reformers' view that undeveloped land held for speculative purposes stood in the way of progress. Responsible government, Durham felt, would weaken the power of the landholding oligarchy and open the way to capitalist development. To ensure that an elected government in the Canadas would not harm British interests, he recommended that Britain retain control over foreign relations, trade, and the distribution of public lands.

While Durham was prepared to accept the perspective of the moderate Upper Canadian reformers, he showed no such tendency in Lower Canada. After spending a mere eight days in Lower Canada, Durham concluded that the rebellion there had been largely an ethnic issue. He claimed to have found "two nations warring in the bosom of a single state."[4] Ignoring the conservatism of colonial policy and the extent to which the Patriotes had embraced liberal political ideology, Durham blamed Lower Canada's economic problems on the reactionary prejudices of the Canadiens. To ensure harmony and progress, he recommended assimilating the French Canadians whom he called "a people with no literature and no history." From his point of view, an amalgamation of the two Canadas and the granting of official status to only the English language would be a step along the road to material advancement for the Canadiens.

In 1840, the British Parliament passed the Act of Union which created the United Province of Canada. Durham's call for responsible government was, however, rejected. The governor would continue to appoint members to the Executive and Legislative Councils according to his own perception of which individuals could best be counted upon to reflect British colonial interests. The elected Assembly would remain a relatively powerless body. The institutional structure that prevailed before the rebellions was thus restored, except that where there had been two governors, two Executive Councils, two Legislative Councils, and two Assemblies, there would now be only one of each.

The union was unpopular in both Canadas. Although the 84 Assembly seats were divided equally between Canada East and Canada West, Upper Canadians generally feared French and Catholic domination. Lower Canadians, for their part, were convinced that union was a plot to achieve their assimilation and were determined to dissolve it.

With the radicals routed by the defeat of the rebellions, only moderate reformers in the two Canadas were left to mount an opposition to conservative forces. The Reformers in Canada West were led by Robert Baldwin, a Toronto lawyer, and railway promoter Francis Hincks. In Canada East, Louis-Hippolyte LaFontaine, a lawyer and former Patriote who had not taken part in the rebellions, emerged as leader of the Reformers. He took the courageous step of forming an alliance with the Upper Canadian Reformers.

LaFontaine's political position was carefully calculated. He argued that by winning responsible government and ensuring the formation of a progressive administration requiring Canadien cooperation, the French culture of Lower Canada could be preserved despite Durham's wishes. Initially regarded as a traitor by francophone Reformers for proposing these views, LaFontaine failed to win a Lower Canadian riding in the Assembly elections of 1841 and eventually sat in the Assembly for the riding of York in Canada West. Once it became clear that Britain would not allow Lower Canada to exist as a separate province, LaFontaine's option began to appear realistic, if not entirely palatable, to his compatriots.

The reform alliance demonstrated considerable strength in Assembly elections through the 1840s, but successive governors proved unwilling to grant the degree of colonial autonomy implied in the phrase "responsible government." Lord Sydenham (1840–41), Sir Charles Bagot (1841–43), and Sir Charles Metcalfe (1843–46) attempted, in varying degrees, to retain the former powers of the lieutenant-governors, although Bagot, in particular, was prepared to go a long way to meet the Reformers' demands for some degree of power-sharing.

Metcalfe's successor, Lord Elgin, arrived at a time when British trade and colonial policy were in the process of a significant transformation. Following the adoption of free trade in 1846, imperial authorities softened their attitude toward political reform. Elgin became the agent of this new British attitude in the Canadas. After elections held in 1848 returned a large reform majority in the two sections of the United Canadas, Elgin called upon LaFontaine and Robert Baldwin to form a ministry. The power of patronage, once in the hands of the governor, was handed over to an Executive Council (cabinet) that enjoyed a majority in the elected Assembly.

By this time Nova Scotia had already made history. In 1847, Nova Scotia's recently-appointed lieutenant-governor, Sir John Harvey, was instructed by Colonial Secretary Lord Grey to choose his advisers from the party that commanded a majority in the Assembly. The Reformers were victorious in an election held later that year and they stood firm in their resolve to take exclusive control of the reins of power. In February 1848, a Liberal government under the leadership of James Boyle Uniacke became the first "responsible" administration in the British Empire.

The remaining Atlantic colonies were not far behind Nova Scotia and the Canadas. In 1851, responsible government came into effect in Prince Edward Island. In New Brunswick, where the principle of responsible government had arrived piecemeal in 1837 and 1848, it was fully implemented in 1854. Once it was clear that responsible government had not led to chaos elsewhere, it was granted in Newfoundland as well in 1855.

This did not mean that the colonies were politically independent. The Colonial Office still kept a watchful administrative eye over colonial politics; the British Parliament continued to legislate on matters relating to defence, foreign policy, and constitutional amendment; and the Privy Council in Britain remained the final court of appeal for the colonies. Another century would pass before these ties of empire would be fully dissolved in "British" North America.

Responsible government represented the official transfer of power from the British to the colonial middle class. In some ways, it was a clever tactical move binding the colonies ever closer to Britain, which was steadily extending the boundaries of its informal empire based on trade and naval power. The significance of responsible government lay in its potential. After it was granted, colonial politicians had a much wider scope for using the powers of the state for achieving their own ends.

RESPONSIBLE GOVERNMENT IN ACTION

Most of the colonies used their newly-won powers to symbolically lay to rest deeply entrenched claims to privilege. In Nova Scotia the legislature repealed the law banning trade unions, revoked the special status of the Church of England, put an end to the General Mining Association's monopoly over the colony's mineral resources, and experimented with universal manhood suffrage. The New Brunswick Assembly transformed King's College, an Anglican institution, into the secular University of New Brunswick, introduced the secret ballot at election time, and adopted the prohibition of alcohol. In Prince Edward Island, Reform leaders George Coles and Edward Whelan failed to solve the land question—there was not enough money to buy out the landlords—but they managed to introduce a Free Schools Act and to extend voting privileges to a larger segment of the tenant population.

In Newfoundland, religious strife made it difficult to establish stable administrations. The Roman Catholic bishop, John Mullock, intervened directly in political matters and priests often managed elections in the outports. During the 1861 election, rival factions in St John's came to blows and troops fired on the crowd, killing three people and wounding 20 more. This tragedy finally brought compromise. Mullock and other religious leaders in the colony voluntarily withdrew from political activity and the Conservatives, who won the election, offered cabinet positions to a number of Roman Catholic politicians. Premier Hugh Hoyles tried to move beyond religious divisions by pursing policies that would lead to economic and social development in the colony and by dispensing patronage with an even hand.

In the Canadas, the ministry headed by LaFontaine and Baldwin enthusiastically embraced the idea of economic progress, the separation of church and state, and legal reform. They passed a bill making the University of Toronto a non-denominational institution, created a Court of Chancery, and implemented the Guarantee Act pledging the government's credit for the construction of railways. They also supported a controversial bill designed to compensate people in Canada East, including rebels, for losses suffered during the rebellions of 1837–38. Since an earlier bill gave similar compensation to Upper Canadians, the Rebellion Losses Bill offered a necessary proof to Lower Canadians of ethnic equality that they demanded in the new regime.

The Tories, believing that they had been abandoned by Britain, were outraged. First the trade laws that gave protected markets to Canadian products had been abandoned. Then the political power of the oligarchy had been swept away. The Rebellion Losses Bill proved to be the last straw. A Tory mob in Montreal attacked the governor's carriage and burned the Parliament building to the ground. Thereafter, the capital of the United Canadas alternated between Toronto and Quebec City because legislators could not agree on where a permanent capital should be located in the sprawling colony.

Baldwin and LaFontaine retired from the political scene in the early 1850s and the old divisions between Tories and Reformers gave way to new Conservative and Liberal alliances. In 1854 Conservatives in Canada East, known as the *Bleus*, agreed to join a coalition with the Conservatives in Canada West led by the "laird of Hamilton,"Allan MacNab. A charter member of the old Family Compact, MacNab had extensive land, railroad, and other business interests. He is alleged to have stated that "Railways are my politics," when asked how he could join forces with his old political enemies. Two policies of the new conservative regime, acts abolishing seigneurial tenure in Canada East and clergy reserves in Canada West in 1854, testify to the change in conservative values in the 1850s.

HUDSON'S BAY COMPANY RULE IN THE NORTHWEST

Europeans living in the Northwest and on the Pacific coast in this period had little hope of experiencing re-sponsible government. After its amalgamation with the North West Company in 1821, the Hudson's Bay Company was the undisputed authority in the Northwest. Its power was embodied in the person of George Simpson, who was in charge of the Northern Department of Rupert's Land from 1821 to 1826 and thereafter governor-in-chief of all HBC territory in North America until his death in 1860. Although an annual council meeting of all chief factors and traders assisted him in his work and his authority could be countermanded by the governor and board of the company in London, in practice he made company policy in the field. With company profits never below 10 percent of invested capital each year from 1826 to 1860, neither the London officers nor his subordinates had much interest in challenging Simpson's autocratic rule. Determined to trim staff costs, Simpson reduced the HBC's full-time staff from 1983 in 1821 to 827 in 1825 and cut the wages of those workers who remained in the company's employ.

Chief factors and traders were at the top of a status-and-pay hierarchy. Clerks ranked just below field officers in the hierarchy, although many of them were in charge of posts and expeditions. Apprentice clerks kept the posts' accounts and earned half the salary of full clerks. A variety of engagés were next to the bottom of the hierarchy and held jobs that included postmaster, interpreter, voyageur, and labourer. At the very bottom were apprentice labourers. Métis held an increasing number of company jobs, but none was ever named chief factor or trader and few were even given the position of clerk. Native men served the HBC as crew members of canoe brigades, provision hunters, and unskilled labourers at posts, while Native women produced footwear and canoe sails, planted vegetables, trapped small animals, dressed furs, and preserved fish.

From the time of its founding in 1670, the directors of the Hudson's Bay Company attempted to control all aspects of the lives of its servants. Employees of the company were expected to attend church, deal with the Natives in a prescribed manner, avoid drunkenness and adultery, and submit their letters to responsible officials for censorship before sending them. Not surprisingly, company employees often flouted their employer's all-encompassing regulations.

Fort Edmonton, *by Paul Kane, 1846.*

Royal Ontario Museum, 912.1.38

Occasionally, company servants beat up or even murdered a superior. Such acts of rebellion never seriously threatened company profits or control over its workforce. A series of fur-trading posts, mostly sparsely staffed, spread over thousands of miles, provided little opportunity for collective protest. Rebellion against a cruel officer or arbitrary rules at one post would be put down before it could spread to others.

After 1821, the company also implemented conservation measures. Outposts with low volumes of trade were abandoned; steel traps, which made trapping easier, were proscribed; and quotas on pelts were imposed. At the same time, the amount of goods exchanged with the First Nations for beaver pelts was reduced. In pursing these policies, Simpson recognized that his success was proportional to the degree of dependence of specific Native groups on the company. Natives who could make a good living by hunting, fishing, and gathering simply ignored company injunctions, as did Natives of the plains who increasingly took advantage of the growing American market for buffalo hides and tongues. With game in the region north of the Great Lakes already scarce, the Ojibwa found their dependence on the company heightened at the same time that the company appeared to want their services less and at a cheaper rate. Many Ojibwa, like many Cree and Assiniboine from the northern parklands, simply moved to the plains where the company felt obliged to remain more generous in its trading policies to maintain Native allegiance.

The Métis living within and near the Red River settlement also expanded their involvement in the lucrative buffalo hunt. By 1860, over 2500 Métis reportedly took part in the hunt, more than a five-fold increase from 40 years earlier. Most French-speaking Métis remained more aloof from the HBC than their English-speaking counterparts. As company orders for pemmican and furs fell along with the prices for these products, many Métis, particularly French-speaking ones, began to do business with American traders in direct violation of the HBC rule that only the company could act as a buyer of furs or pemmican within its claimed territories.

In 1849, the company charged a Métis trader named Pierre-Guillaume Sayer with infringing the company's

Voices from the Past

Views of the Métis

Alexander Ross, patriarch of a large English-speaking Métis family, accompanied the Métis on the buffalo hunt of 1840. He found much to admire, but objected to their hostility to the HBC and white rule.

I must say, I found less selfishness and more liberality among these ordinary men than I had been accustomed to find in higher circles. Their conversation was free, practical and interesting; and the time passed more agreeably than could be expected among such people, till we touched on politics. Like the American peasantry these people are all politicians, but of a peculiar creed, favouring a barbarous state of society and self-will; for they cordially detest all the laws and restraints of civilized life, believing all men were born to be free. In their own estimation, they are all great men, and wonderfully wise; and so long as they wander about on these wild and lawless expeditions, they will never become a thoroughly civilized people, nor orderly subjects in a civilized community. Feeling their own strength, from being constantly armed, and free from control, they despise all others; but above all, they are marvellously tenacious of their own original habits. They cherish freedom as they cherish life.[5]

Red River cart.

National Archives of Canada/C61689

---

trade monopoly by selling furs to American traders. Some 200 armed and angry Métis milled menacingly outside the courthouse as Sayer's trial proceeded. Aware of what was going on outside, the jury found Sayer guilty but recommended mercy on the grounds that he truly believed he had the right to sell furs freely. The HBC then avoided a possible confrontation by dropping the charges. Although the company monopoly had been broken, it would prove a pyrrhic victory, because both the fur-bearing animals and the buffalo declined drastically over the next three decades.

By this time, the Hudson's Bay Company's monopoly was being challenged in other ways as well. The silk hat had begun to overtake felt hats among the fashion-minded, while American muskrat hats could

be sold for less than those made of beaver pelts. In 1847, with inventory piling up, the company sold off its surplus at rates only 10 percent of the price that beaver furs had fetched in 1821. Nor was the HBC as influential in imperial policy circles as it had once been. The rapid rate of settlement in the American West in the 1840s and 1850s raised concerns that the thinly populated fur-trade empire of the HBC would eventually be seized by the Americans. British settlement would be necessary to secure title to the region.

Furthermore, a vocal minority in Canada West was promoting the idea of westward expansion. For these expansionists, the HBC and its fur trade were an anachronism and a barrier to progress. Under such conditions, British authorities began to question both the fur trade and the company that had become synonymous with that industry in British North America.

THE PACIFIC COAST

The new thinking in the Colonial Office was first reflected in policy relating to the Pacific coast. In January 1848, shipping magnate Samuel Cunard alerted the Admiralty that action must be taken to protect Vancouver Island coal from the Americans. The British government was receptive to this argument, and it soon came to the view that an agriculturally-based colony must be established on the island to shore up British control in the area. While HBC field governor George Simpson argued that colonization and the fur trade made a bad mix, he was overruled by the London governor of the HBC.

In an effort to assert its authority on the West Coast, Great Britain made Vancouver Island a Crown colony in 1849. The HBC was given a ten-year lease of Vancouver Island, but the British government named a governor for the colony and required the HBC to recruit permanent settlers of British descent within five years or forfeit its lease. Land sales were to be used to finance roads, churches, schools, and other necessary services. The first governor, Richard Blanshard, a British lawyer, quit after nine months in the position, charging obstruction by the HBC hierarchy.

James Douglas was named the second governor in 1851. Although he established schools, roads, and a courthouse, Douglas opposed democratic institutions, believing that only a small number of men in any society were fit to rule. Instructed by Britain in 1856 to have an assembly elected, Douglas subverted this request by setting a stiff property qualification for voting and holding office, a move that restricted political participation to a fraction of the population.

When gold was discovered on the mainland in 1858, Douglas moved quickly to impose order. He is-

Victoria in its early days.
Glenbow Archives NA-674-20

sued decrees forbidding the entry of foreign vessels on the Fraser River, but the miners questioned the right of an HBC officer to make this kind of regulation. Britain, recognizing the need for imperial rather than company control over both the mainland and the island, cancelled the company's lease on Vancouver Island and made the mainland a formal Crown colony. After agreeing to resign his HBC posts, Douglas was named governor of British Columbia (which then referred only to the mainland) in November 1858, while retaining his position as governor of Vancouver Island. New Westminster, now a suburb of Vancouver, was named the capital of the mainland colony.

Douglas made use of mining licences and judges to control the behaviour of the miners. His main aim was to keep the territory under British control and to fend off any efforts on the part of American immigrants to reverse the boundary treaty of 1846. Part of the plan included construction of some 600 kilometres of highway connecting settlements and gold-mining territories with New Westminster. Throughout these changes, the First Nations people remained the major-

ity of residents of British Columbia. The Census of Canada, which almost certainly underestimated Native numbers, suggested that in 1870, over 70 percent of British Columbia's population of 36 247 was Native while 25 percent was white and 4 percent was Asian.

CONCLUSION

By the mid-nineteenth century, parliamentary democracy had been established in the eastern British North American colonies and the Hudson's Bay Company's authority over the Northwest had been successfully challenged. Those who supported a more conservative political order may have regretted new political arrangements but they were forced to adjust or be left behind in a world that was rapidly changing to accommodate the goals and values of the new industrial age. As we shall see in the following chapter, no corner of colonial society could escape the winds of change that swept the colonial landscape in the mid-nineteenth century.

A Historiographical Debate

Causes of the Rebellion in Lower Canada

What were the causes of the rebellion of 1837–38 in Lower Canada? Historians, often using many of the same documents, have provided dramatically different accounts of the events leading to the rebellion, the key demands of the rebels, and ultimately the character of the society that was in rebellion against the British conquerors. Two poles of the debate are represented by Fernand Ouellet and Allan Greer.

Fernand Ouellet stresses two elements in explaining the outbreak of the rebellion and its large degree of habitant support, in the rural region of the District of Montreal. First, he emphasizes the determination of the Patriote leadership, mainly French-Canadian petit-bourgeois men, to assert not only the political independence of the French-Canadian nation, but also their right, as the better educated or more affluent members of that nation, to hold political power.

Second, he asserts that the habitants supported the Patriote program because they were suffering from acute poverty as a result of a series of agricultural crises. The habitants blamed these recurring crises on government policy that allowed large numbers of anglophone agricultural immigrants into the colony but did little to help habitants open new lands for a burgeoning population.

In Ouellet's opinion, the Patriotes were elitists and reactionaries who hoped to reinforce the feudal structures that pre-dated the conquest. Their goal was to usurp power from the English and the minority of French Canadians who supported the British program for a capitalist land-holding system and commercial society. Ouellet argues that the Patriotes opportunistically used the language of democracy to further their cause: in reality, they opposed the extension of the franchise to the landless—a growing group in the colony—and turned back efforts by habitants to have feudal dues abolished. When the British government refused to respond to their demands, the Patriotes, according to Ouellet, used intimidation and violence to break Britain's control over local power structures. They then called local "democratic" assemblies to support the Patriote program, cynically manipulating these meetings by providing predetermined resolutions and brooking no debate. While Ouellet in no way minimizes the poverty of the habitants, he tends to attribute their plight to their own unwillingness to change outdated agricultural practices, not to specific policies pursued by the colonial government.[6]

Allan Greer presents the Patriotes primarily as democrats rather than nationalists. He believes they should be viewed, like the Upper Canadian rebels, as supporters of representative democracy in opposition to authoritarian rule. Patriote views reflected the republican and democratic spirit that had taken hold of much of Europe and the Americas since the American and French Revolutions. Greer argues that the habitants had imbibed something of that spirit, and it was Britain's efforts to limit or destroy Lower Canada's evolution toward democracy that mobilized habitant opposition to British rule. Greer sees poverty as a secondary cause and notes that most of the fighting occurred in the Montreal region, which was more prosperous than the rest of the colony. Greer maintains that "to understand the habitants in the Rebellion, we must look at the habitants."[7] As they demonstrated in the popular assemblies, the habitants were interested in popular control of government—or, at least male popular control. They were neither pro-capitalism nor pro-feudalism; like the settlers of Upper Canada, their goal was to achieve self-sufficiency. They fought feudal exactions that they regarded as excessive, but they had every reason as tenants to oppose the campaign of seigneurs, many of whom were English, for the right of landlords to do whatever they wished with their land.

Greer regards the Patriotes as the intellectual leaders of the revolt but insists that the habitants had long played an independent political role in Quebec and continued to do so during the rebellion. The habitants, he argues, exercised a degree of control over government-appointed militia officers through popular ceremonies approving investitures. Moreover, they circumvented the authority of both the curés and justices of the peace by imposing their own notions of justice on individuals through charivaris and ostracism. They spontaneously made use of such measures of popular control to enforce their campaign for non-compliance with British rule in the months leading to the rebellion.

Greer suggests that the Patriote leaders provided intellectual direction for the habitants but did not control the events that produced the military conflict between Britain and the rebels. He argues that the Patriotes were democrats first and nationalists second, and that they attempted to rally anglophones as well as francophones in their campaign for a more democratic system of government. Such attempts were unsuccessful because anglophones, especially recent immigrants, largely viewed the Patriotes as French Canadians opposing British rule. With their support thus restricted to francophone districts, the Patriotes often combined appeals to democracy with appeals to nationhood.

Clearly, historical sources regarding Lower Canada during the rebellion and the period leading up to it lend themselves to several interpretations. For example, Greer makes use of the resolutions passed by the various assemblies to posit the view that a relatively homogeneous habitant population had developed a particular view of the problems facing their colony and the best ways of resolving them. Ouellet, by contrast, suggests that such a uniformity of views must have been stage-managed by the Parti patriote leadership. Greer challenges such a view, arguing that the habitants would not go along with, much less take up arms to defend, a revolution whose course they had little chance to influence. Ouellet maintains that habitant participation resulted from their frustration with government policies that they blamed for poverty that left many on the brink of starvation. The details of the Patriote program were less important to them than the fact that the Patriotes were fellow French Canadians who promised them some relief from their economic hardships if the *maudits anglais* were defeated.

NOTES

1   Allan Greer, *The Patriots and the People: The Rebellion of 1837 in Rural Lower Canada* (Toronto: University of Toronto Press, 1993) 79.

2   Translated from Claude Baribeau, *La seigneurie de la Petite-Nation 1801–1859: Le rôle économique et social du seigneur* (Hull, PQ: Éditions Asticou, 1983) 112.

3   Howe's Fourth Letter to Lord John Russell, 1839, cited in *The Speeches and Letters of Joseph Howe*, ed. J.A. Chisholm (Halifax: n.p., 1909) 266.

4   Gerald M. Craig, ed., *Lord Durham's Report: An Abridgement of Report on the Affairs of British North America* (Toronto: McClelland and Stewart, 1963) 23.

5   George Woodcock, *Gabriel Dumont* (Edmonton: Hurtig, 1975) 35-36.

6   Fernand Ouellet's views are developed in *Lower Canada 1791–1840: Social Change and Nationalism* (Toronto: McClelland and Stewart, 1980) and *Economic and Social History of Quebec* (Toronto: Macmillan, 1981). His response to Greer's interpretation of Lower Canadian social, political, and economic developments is found in a review essay in Histoire sociale/Social History 28.56 (Nov. 1996): 541-54.

7   Greer, *The Patriots and the People*, xi.

SELECTED READING

See also Selected Reading for Chapter 11.

The imperial context of political developments in this period is comprehensively discussed in P.A. Buckner, *The Transition to Responsible Government: British Policy in British North America, 1815–1850* (Westport, CT: Greenwood, 1985). See also Stanley Ryerson, *Unequal Union: Confederation and the Roots of Conflict in the Canadas, 1815–1873*, 2nd ed. (Toronto: Progress Books, 1983) for a Marxist's perspective on the period.

For Lower Canada, the causes of the 1837–38 rebellions are explored in Jean-Paul Bernard, *Les rébellions de 1837–1838* (Montreal: Boréal Express, 1983) and in the works by Ouellet and Creighton cited in Chapter 11. More favourable treatment of the unsuccessful revolutionaries is found in Allan Greer, *The Patriots and the People: The Rebellion of 1837 in Rural Lower Canada* (Toronto: University of Toronto Press, 1993), and Ouellet's *Louis-Joseph Papineau: A Divided Soul* (Ottawa: Canadian Historical Association, 1964) provides a brief biography of the key Patriote. Events of the rebellions are outlined in Elinor Kyte Senior, *Redcoats and Patriotes: The Rebellions in Lower Canada* (Montreal: McGill-Queen's University Press, 1981). On the treatment of the defeated rebels see Beverley Boissery, *A Deep Sense of Wrong: The Treason Trials of Lower Canadian Rebels After the 1838 Rebellion* (Toronto: Dundurn, 1995).

On Upper Canadian politics, see Gerald Craig's *Upper Canada: The Formative Years* (Toronto: McClelland and Stewart, 1963). An attempt to gauge popular thinking regarding public issues of this period is Jeffrey L. McNairn, *Public Opinion and Deliberative Democracy* (Toronto: University of Toronto Press, 2000). The ideological battles of the period are discussed in David Mills, *The Idea of Loyalty in Upper Canada, 1784–1850* (Montreal: McGill-Queen's University Press, 1988) and Jane Errington, *The Lion, the Eagle, and Upper Canada: A Developing Colonial Ideology* (Montreal: McGill-Queen's University Press, 1987). Events leading to the rebellions of 1837 and 1838 and the conduct of the rebellions are outlined in Colin Read and Ronald J. Stagg, eds., *The Rebellion of 1837 in Upper Canada: A Collection of Documents* (Toronto: Champlain Society, 1985) and Colin Read, *The Rising in Western Upper Canada, 1837–1838* (Toronto: University of Toronto Press, 1982).

The politics of the 1840s and 1850s are discussed in J.M.S. Careless, *The Union of the Canadas: The Growth of Canadian Institutions 1841–1857* (Toronto: McClelland and Stewart, 1967) and Jacques Monet, *The Last Cannon Shot: A Study of French-Canadian Nationalism, 1837–1850* (Toronto: University of Toronto Press, 1969). Monet's positive assessment of the post-rebellion political elite contrasts with Brian Young's critical evaluation of a key member in *George-Étienne Cartier: Montreal Bourgeois* (Montreal: McGill-Queen's University Press, 1981). A continuing rebel tradition is discussed in Jean-Paul Bernard, *Les Rouges: libéralisme, nationalisme et anticlericalisme au milieu du XIXe siècle* (Montreal: Les Presses de l'Université du Québec, 1971) and Allan Greer, "The Birth of the Police in Canada," in *Colonial Leviathan: State Formation in Mid-Nineteenth-Century Canada*, ed. Allan Greer and Ian Radforth (Toronto: University of Toronto Press, 1992) 17–49. On Lord Durham, see Janet

Ajzenstat, *The Political Thought of Lord Durham* (Montreal: McGill-Queen's University Press, 1988).

The politics of pre-Confederation Nova Scotia have been described in J. Murray Beck, *Politics of Nova Scotia*, vol. 1, *1710–1896* (Tantallon, NS: Four East Publications, 1985). Beck's earlier work, *The Government of Nova Scotia* (Toronto: University of Toronto Press, 1957) offers detailed information on the structures of colonial government, and his two-volume biography, *Joseph Howe* (Montreal: McGill-Queen's University Press, 1982, 1984), is by far the most thorough study undertaken of a Maritime politician in this period. The political implications of the land question in Prince Edward Island are summarized in Ian Ross Robertson's introduction to *The Prince Edward Island Land Commission of 1860* (Fredericton: Acadiensis Press, 1988) and his book *The Tenant League of Prince Edward Island, 1864–1867: Leasehold Tenure in the New World* (Toronto: University of Toronto Press, 1996). Newfoundland politics in the mid-nineteenth century is the subject of Gertrude Gunn, *The Political History of Newfoundland,* *1832–1864* (Toronto: University of Toronto Press, 1966) as well as the books by Cadigan, Matthews, and O'Flaherty cited earlier.

On Hudson's Bay Company organization and officials in this period, see Frederick Merk, ed., *Fur Trade and Empire: George Simpson's Journal* (Cambridge: Harvard University Press, 1968); J.S. Galbraith, *The Little Emperor: Governor Simpson of the Hudson's Bay Company* (Toronto: Macmillan, 1976); and J.G. McGregor, *John Rowand: Czar of the Prairies* (Saskatoon: Western Producer Prairie Books, 1979). Resistance by company employees to HBC authoritarianism is detailed in Edith I. Burley, *Servants of the Honourable Company: Work, Discipline and Conflict in the Hudson's Bay Company, 1770–1879* (Toronto: Oxford University Press, 1997).

Political developments in British Columbia are discussed in relevant chapters of surveys by Barman, Ormsman, and other titles mentioned in Chapter 10 and Chapter 11. See also the early essays of *A History of British Columbia: Selected Readings,* ed. Patricia Roy (Toronto: Copp Clark Pitman, 1989).

 **WEBLINKS**

1837 REBELLIONS
www.edunetconnect.com/cat/rebellions/index.html

This site offers a chronology of events, biographical information on rebel leaders, issues which provoked conflict, consequences, and suggestions for further reading.

LORD DURHAM
www.canadiana.org/citm/biographies/durham.html

This site provides a biography of John George Lambton, as well as several useful links and suggested reading.

THE UNION ACT OF 1840
http://home.cc.umanitoba.ca/~sprague/union40.htm

The full text of the Union Act is available on this University of Manitoba site.

British North America's Revolutionary Age

On 21 July 1836, a 23-kilometre railway line between La Prairie on the south shore of the St Lawrence and St Jean on the Richelieu was inaugurated with much fanfare. The onlookers were in awe of the Dorchester, the new wood-burning locomotive imported from Newcastle-upon-Tyne in England to run the train. Despite the technical difficulties keeping it working properly, British North Americans were optimistic about the potential of the iron horse. "Too much praise cannot be bestowed," wrote Thomas Storrow Brown reporting on the new line in Montreal's radical newspaper *The Vindicator*. "We in Canada are so accustomed to see things done ill, that a work well done is a miracle."[1]

In the mid-nineteenth century, British North Americans were conscious of living in an era of rapid change and miraculous events. New ideas, new methods of transportation, and new ways of producing goods and services were quickening the pace of everyday life. The Industrial Revolution was the catalyst for this change. Along with the new economic arrangements, it laid the groundwork for deep social transformation and intellectual departures that challenged virtually everything people had hitherto believed about the earth and its inhabitants.

THE INDUSTRIAL REVOLUTION

The Industrial Revolution takes its name from fundamental changes in technology and the organization of production that gradually transformed how people lived. The world's first industrial nation was Great Britain. It pioneered in the application of steam power to machines and machines to production in key sectors of the economy: agriculture, manufacturing, and transportation.

Beginning in the eighteenth century, machines were developed to perform a wide range of tasks, multiplying output far beyond anything that could be

The Dorchester, the locomotive that pulled British North America's first train along the Champlain-St Lawrence line, is illustrated in this commemorative stamp issued by Canada Post.

Canada Post Corporation

As they grew in numbers and wealth, capitalists had little difficulty incorporating people and resources into their exchange processes. They were also adept at convincing governments to pass legislation to protect their new interests. Under the pressure from this new entrepreneurial class, the communal management of land in the countryside, the guild control of industry in the towns, and the privilege of monopoly were all eventually pushed aside to facilitate the new industrial order.

Industrial capitalism transformed Britain and eventually the whole world. It introduced a new materialism that challenged traditional spiritual values, encouraged the growth of cities at the expense of the countryside, and created a new class structure based on relationship to production rather than heredity. It redistributed wealth geographically as well as socially and drove a wedge between the public world of work and the private realm of the family. It altered the relationship among men, women, and children and the relationship of human beings to their natural environment.

British North Americans were no strangers to this revolutionary process. They read about the new machines in their newspapers, purchased the products of Britain's factories with their hard-earned cash, and sent an increasing volume of their own raw resources to sustain Britain's expanding industrial economy. As the output of British factories began to dominate world markets, even colonial policy was transformed to accommodate new industrial interests. Colonies, it was argued, were an expensive luxury. Let the invisible hand of supply and demand be allowed to operate freely and Britain would soon conquer the whole world economically rather than militarily. For the colonies the triumph of this perspective led to free trade and responsible government.

done by human hands. Mechanization encouraged the division of labour into repetitive tasks, the centralization of work at factories where the machines were located, and control of the factory system in the hands of a few capitalists who could finance such extensive operations. Under the factory system, labourers lost control over their work, and factory owners, if they were competitive and shrewd, became wealthy from their entrepreneurial activities.

There was nothing particularly inevitable about this process, except that commercial societies in Britain and North America had a well-developed exchange system that adapted easily to industrialism. Since the fifteenth century, successful merchants, artisans, and farmers in the North Atlantic world had gradually adopted a capitalist perspective. They worked for profit instead of subsistence; they translated all transactions into monetary value; they established structures such as joint-stock companies and banks to accumulate capital; and they developed laws to protect their property and the market system from fraud, piracy, and theft.

FREE TRADE, RECIPROCITY, AND PROTECTION

The mercantile community in the colonies were thrown into a tailspin by the commercial revolution of the 1840s, which ushered in free trade throughout the British Empire. Fortunately, it was a good time to experience economic and political crises. The British economy was entering a boom period that would last for over two decades and the United States, also an early convert to industrialization, was gobbling up resources at an amazing rate. The discovery of gold in California, Australia, British Columbia, and New Zealand fuelled the global economy. The Crimean War (1854–56) in Europe and the Civil War in the United States (1861–65) further increased the demand for colonial products. If circumstances had thrust the colonies back on their own devices, the context was favourable for developing strategies to adjust to the new world order.

A few merchants, especially those closely tied to the timber and wheat trade, saw annexation to the United States as the solution to their temporarily failing fortunes. Others advocated a protectionist strategy to develop internal markets. The British–American League, which was formed in 1849 to respond to the perceived economic crisis, included tariff protection as a plank in its platform and called for a union of all British North America as a means of "creating large home markets for the consumption of agricultural products and domestic manufactures."[2] Still others, eyeing the nearest booming industrial economy, sug-

Voices from the Past

The Annexation Manifesto

In October 1849, a number of leading Montreal merchants issued a manifesto calling for annexation to the United States. The first paragraph read, in part: "Of all the remedies that have been suggested for the acknowledged and insufferable ills with which our country is afflicted, there remains but one to be considered....this remedy consists in a friendly and peaceful separation from the British connection and a union upon equitable terms with the great North American confederacy of sovereign states." The manifesto also outlined the advantages that the merchants felt would come from such a union:

> The proposed union would render Canada a field for American capital, into which it would enter as freely for the prosecution of public works and private enterprise as into any of the present States. It would equalise the value of real estate upon both sides of the boundary, thereby probably doubling at once the entire present value of property in Canada, whilst, by giving stability to our institutions, and introducing prosperity, it would raise our public corporate and private credit. It would increase our commerce, both with the United States and foreign countries, and would not necessarily diminish to any great extent our intercourse with Great Britain, into which our products would for the most part enter on the same terms as present. It would render our rivers and canals the highway for the immigration to and exports from, the West, to the incalculable benefit of our country. It would also introduce manufacturers into Canada as rapidly as they have been introduced into the northern states; and to Lower Canada especially, where water privileges and labour are abundant and cheap, it would attract manufacturing capital, enhancing the value of property and agricultural produce and giving remunerative employment to what is at present a comparatively non-producing population. Nor would the United States merely furnish the capital for our manufacturers. They would also supply them the most extensive market in the world, without the intervention of a custom house officer. Railways would forthwith be constructed by American capital as feeders for all the great lines now approaching the frontiers; and railway enterprise in general would doubtless be as active and prosperous among us as among our neighbours. The value of our agricultural produce would be raised at once to a par with that of the United States, whilst agricultural implements and many of the necessities of life, such as tea, coffee and sugar, would be greatly reduced in price.[3]

Among those who signed the manifesto were John Abbott, who would one day be a Canadian prime minister, and Alexander Galt, who would serve as finance minister for the United Canadas in the 1850s.

gested free trade with the United States as the best policy for sustaining British North America's primary industries.

Annexation was quickly abandoned by all but the most principled republicans, and a union of British North America still seemed highly impractical. Tariff protection was perceived as an inadequate measure by a business community dominated by mercantile interests. Free trade, perhaps, was an idea whose time had come. In 1851, the eastern British North American colonies agreed to free trade among themselves in natural products. Three years later, Britain negotiated a reciprocity treaty that provided for the free exchange of natural products between the British North American colonies and the United States. Under the Reciprocity Treaty, which remained in effect until 1866, colonial staples such as foodstuffs, wheat, timber, fish, and coal found American markets, while Americans enjoyed access to the inshore fisheries of the Atlantic region and access to the Great Lakes–St Lawrence canal system. In the 1850s and 1860s, British North Americans adopted decimal currency, which was both easier to calculate than British pounds and shillings and increasingly popular in the age of reciprocity with the United States.

Despite the widespread support for free trade, protectionists managed to win small victories. Businessmen in Saint John established a Provincial Association in 1844 to lobby the government for a protective tariff policy. Following the introduction of free trade, the New Brunswick legislature raised the tariffs on imported manufactures. In Canada, the tariff was set at 12.5 percent of the value of imports in 1849 and raised even higher in 1858 and 1859.

Although the goal was still to raise revenue, or so Finance Minister Alexander Galt argued in 1859, it clearly served to protect local producers from cheaper imports.

TRANSPORTATION AND COMMUNICATION

In addition to revolutionizing production techniques, mechanization also inspired new methods of transportation. Steam applied to sea and land transport offered a stronger and more reliable source of power than wind, water, and animals. Steamboats became commercially viable in the first decade of the nineteenth century, railways in the 1820s and 1830s. In Great Britain, industrialization was under way before the transportation revolution wrought by steam, but in British North America the steamboat as well as the telegraph and the railway accompanied and accelerated the industrialization process.

In the early 1860s, Father George-Antoine Belcourt helped his fellow Prince Edward Island Acadians to establish a banking co-operative, the Farmer's Bank of Rustico.

Public Archives and Records Office of PEI

By 1850, telegraph and railway communication promised an end to colonial isolation, but the cost of building intercolonial links was prohibitive for a population of less than three million. A telegraph line linking Canada to the American system was completed in 1847, and in the following year New Brunswick was linked with Calais, Maine. Thus, in a roundabout way, Maritimers could communicate telegraphically with Canadians. Underwater cable connected Prince Edward Island to the mainland in 1851 and Newfoundland in 1856.

In the years between 1852 and 1867, the British North American colonies built over 3200 kilometres of railway track and sank over $100 million into railways. Much of the capital came from Great Britain, as did the expertise required to build the new transportation systems. Colonial governments, whatever their political stripe, were obliging in their efforts to support railway development.

Joseph Howe was a great railway booster, and the Liberal government in which he served sponsored lines from Halifax to Windsor and Pictou. His Conservative nemesis, Charles Tupper, was equally enthusiastic about the potential of railways in his native province, especially a railroad that would make his Cumberland County constituency the link between Nova Scotia and the rest of the continent. Meanwhile, New Brunswickers sank money into a railway, grandly labelled the European and North American, between Shediac on the Northumberland Strait and Saint John on the Bay of Fundy. A line connecting St Andrews with Quebec was abandoned in the backwoods of New Brunswick when its promoters ran out of money in 1863. In the United Canadas, politicians of all political parties supported railways and, in the 1850s, brought the colony to the brink of bankruptcy with their decision to build the Grand Trunk Railway. When it was completed in 1859, it was the longest railway in the world, stretching from Quebec City to Sarnia and on American lines to Chicago.

In the initial flush of railway enthusiasm, British North American politicians made plans for an intercolonial railway that would link Canadians to an ice-free Atlantic port. Failure to agree on a route or to secure imperial backing caused the expensive project to be abandoned. In the meantime, a Montreal–Portland line, completed in 1853, gave the colony of Canada its much-desired winter port. By the end of the decade, railways crisscrossed the colony, reaching northward to the timber stands of the Ottawa Valley and Lake Huron and linking the market towns of the Ontario peninsula.

Despite the enthusiasm of their promoters, government-sponsored railways proved a burden to colonial taxpayers. The decision to raise tariffs in both New Brunswick and the Canadas in the 1850s had as much to do with the need to raise revenue to finance the growing railway debt as it did with the protection of colonial producers. In a curious feat of convoluted logic, colonial politicians and promoters argued that the solution to failing railways was more railways—to link the colonies with each other and

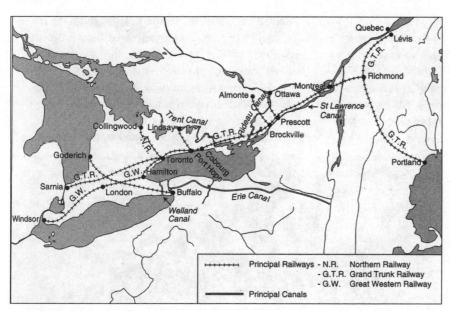

Map 13.1

Canals and railways in the United Canadas before Confederation.

Adapted from P.G. Cornell, et al., *Canada: Unity in Diversity* (Toronto: Holt, Rinehart, and Winston, 1967) 239.

with American lines, and even with the Pacific Ocean. Only by expanding could railways tap new frontiers and secure the traffic that would make them pay.

The close link between railway promoters and politicians in the United Canadas inevitably led to scandals. Politicians bought shares in railway companies and sat on their boards. Although the line between public and private interests was not then as carefully drawn as it would be later on, the revelation in 1854 that government leader Francis Hincks made £10 000 on the Great Northern Railway contract raised more than a few eyebrows. Hincks was forced to resign over the "Ten Thousand Pound Job" but he did not go to jail, nor was he made to give back the money.

If railways were sometimes a failing and scandalous proposition, they nevertheless fulfilled many of the expectations outlined by their promoters. Areas where the railway ran invariably experienced a quickening of economic pace. In the cities where railway-repair shops were located, heavy industry was given a tremendous boost. Railway companies were Canada's first large-scale integrated corporations and were among the largest employers in the colonies. Through their practices relating to management, division of labour, accounting, quality control, and even waste recycling, they introduced advanced capitalist practices into British North American society. In Montreal, the Grand Trunk, which eventually employed nearly 2000 people and included a wide range of metal-producing shops, was a monument to the industrial era.

British North America's Industrial Revolution came of age with the railway, but its origins can be found in earlier transportation developments. In the 1840s, industries located along the Lachine Canal were near transportation routes and potential hydraulic power. Between 1847 and 1854, $500 000 was invested in 30 industries in Lachine by entrepreneurs from Canada, Britain, and the United States. Mills and factories producing flour, beer, iron, furniture, sewing machines, steam engines, heating and ventilating equipment, paints, rubber, footwear, clothes, and drugs employed nearly 2000 people who crowded into the nearby suburbs of St Ann, Point St Charles, and Verdun. By 1856, Montrealers boasted that their city was "the best site for a manufacturing city in Canada, perhaps on the Continent."

LABOUR AND INDUSTRY

Without a supply of cheap and willing labour to work in the new factories, the Industrial Revolution would have been stillborn. Two developments, one demographic and the other economic, interacted with each other to guarantee the labour supply needed both in Britain and North America.

Over the course of the eighteenth century, the population of Europe in general and Britain in particular grew dramatically. From a population of five million in 1700, Britain grew to nine million a century later. Higher birth rates, lower death rates, better living standards, more efficient exchange networks, and even improved psychological conditions seem to account for some of the growth. At the same time, overcrowding in the countryside and the commercialization of agriculture pushed people off the land and into the cities to find work. Factory towns, like the colonies, became magnets for the rural dispossessed. In 1700, 80 percent of people in Britain made their living in agriculture; by 1800 only 40 percent did so.

Those fleeing the economic dislocation of the Industrial Revolution in Great Britain also found the land frontier disappearing in British North America. Even in Canada West immigrants were confronting the rugged Canadian Shield, which proved an inhospitable barrier to the farmer's plough. With the free land virtually gone and the cost of labour in British North America relatively high, the capital requirements of farming were steadily mounting. A prosperous farm was beyond the reach of many people, who found themselves forced into other occupations. Irish famine immigration in the late 1840s further added to the pool of available labour.

Many immigrants brought with them traditions of resistance against unfair labour practices. Craftsmen, whose skills were often rendered obsolete by the new machines, and work crews, whose livelihood was jeopardized by attempts to lower wages, protested efforts by employers to exploit them. At first, workers tried to destroy the new machines that threatened their traditional practices, as was the case among shoemakers in Montreal when the sewing machine was introduced in 1852. Gradually, workers began organizing to press

Most of the canals in British North America were built by man- and horse-power. In the 1840s, as many as 10 000 men, many of them poor Irish immigrants, worked from dawn to dusk digging, hauling, and quarrying for about 50 cents a day. The workers moved from job to job with their families, who lived in shantytowns that were established near construction sites. Given the poor working and living conditions, it is little wonder that strikes were a frequent occurrence.

National Archives of Canada/C61471

for better working conditions and a fairer distribution of the profits of mechanized production.

Only skilled labourers could risk joining unions, which were considered seditious conspiracies by factory owners. Unskilled workers, who could easily be replaced, were fired if they were caught trying to organize the shop floor. Only a tiny minority of workers belonged to unions, but whether unionized or not, wage earners were determined not to become slaves to their capitalist masters. On 10 June 1867, just three weeks before the first Dominion Day, over 10 000 workers in Montreal, parading behind the patriote flag of the Lower Canadian rebels of 1837, took to the street in a show of worker solidarity.

The state assisted the interests of capital by creating conditions conducive to managerial control over labour. Various master and servant acts passed in the colonies included provisions for punishing craftsmen, labourers, and servants who left their jobs. Couched in the language of pre-industrial labour relations, these acts were designed primarily to control servants, timber workers, and ship crews. Nevertheless, they reveal the bias in favour of employers that would continue to prevail in industrial settings and would make labour's lot a difficult one.

LAW AND INDUSTRY

The law was a vital instrument in capitalist accumulation during the Industrial Revolution. In the colonies, however, legal principles and practices were quickly outdated by the pace of economic change. Based on a belief in eternal principles and natural law, colonial legal systems lacked the extensive laws and trained personnel required to deal with the complexities of commercial transactions. In most colonies, executive councillors sat in judicial capacities, and their lack of specialized legal knowledge coupled with their busy schedules was a growing cause for complaint.

Legal reform followed hard on the heels of responsible government. In most colonial jurisdictions, new laws relating to contracts, partnerships, patents, and property were introduced, while the courts were reorganized to separate executive and judicial functions, to increase efficiency, and to incorporate change into legal decisions. Reform extended beyond commercial law and court procedures to the fundamental basis of law itself. No longer paternalistic and protective in its thrust, the law became an instrument for individual accumulation and economic development.

Nowhere in British North America was legal reform more at issue than in the Canadas. In 1849, William Hume Blake, solicitor general in the Baldwin-LaFontaine administration, introduced legislation to establish a Court of Common Pleas and a Court of Error and Appeals as well as to reform the Court of Queen's Bench and Court of Chancery. The latter was designed to administer jurisprudence to supplement and remedy the limitations and inflexibility of the common law. As chancellor from 1849 to 1862, Blake attempted to inject the principles of freedom and progress into his legal decisions.

Legal reform was not confined solely to English jurisdictions. In 1857, George-Étienne Cartier, lawyer and leader of the Bleus in Canada East, introduced bills to make the legal system more centralized and uniform. He also chaired the committee that produced a new Civil Code to replace the antiquated Custom of Paris. The code brought major revisions to contract and labour law. It also introduced changes in the property provisions of family law, abolishing dower rights except in cases where they were formally registered. In practice, this freed husbands from any claims held by their wives and children on family property.

THE STRUCTURE OF INDUSTRIAL CAPITALISM

The Industrial Revolution proceeded unevenly, its impact varying from sector to sector and from one region to another. Only a few colonial industries, following the precedents set in Britain and the United States, initially lent themselves to large-scale production: metal trades, locomotives, textiles, footwear, furniture, agricultural implements, tobacco, beer and ale, biscuits and bread, candies, carriages, and sails and rope.

Young women sorting ore at the Huntington Copper Mining Company Works, Quebec, 1867.

McCord Museum of Canadian History/Notman Photographic Archives, 28, 901-MISC-I

While most factories adopted techniques for division of labour (as in the shoe industry) or included a number of skills under one roof (as in carriage-making), not all industries relied on steam-powered machinery. Cheap hand labour remained central to the Industrial Revolution and in certain sectors, such as textiles and cigar-making, guaranteed success against foreign competitors.

Manufacturing in British North America, as elsewhere, tended to be geographically concentrated. Montreal, Toronto and Saint John led the way in the industrial process. With its large domestic market, low-wage structure, and pivotal location in the St Lawrence trading system, Montreal was British North America's leading industrial city before Confederation. Toronto was transformed from a city of artisans to one where over 70 percent of the labour force worked in units of over 30 people between 1851 and 1871. In Atlantic Canada, Saint John, a city that thrived on the timber trade and shipbuilding, emerged as the major manufacturing centre. By the 1860s, the foundry, footwear, and clothing industries in Saint John each exceeded shipbuilding in the value of their output.

Entrepreneurs came from every class and culture. A few, such as John Molson of Montreal, had a long tradition of capitalist investment in everything from beer to railroads. Many "captains of industry" emerged from the ranks of the merchant class that had accumulated capital in its commercial ventures to invest in new frontiers of opportunity. Successful primary producers and artisans were also in a good position to expand their operations in such areas as milling, tanning, or carriage-making. Most of British North America's entrepreneurs were anglophones, but one French-Canadian exception was Augustin Cantin, Montreal's major steamboat builder and the first person to integrate ship construction and marine engineering.

British North America's industrial workforce was overwhelmingly male. The milling, woodworking, and metal industries hired men almost exclusively and supervisory positions were reserved for them throughout the industrial structure. Women and children, some as young as eight or nine years of age, were employed in the clothing and tobacco industries and made up a sig-

nificant proportion of the people hired in printing, footwear, and confectionery work. Women and children also formed the bulk of workers employed in the "sweated trades," the term used to describe industrial tasks performed at home at appallingly low rates.

As the Industrial Revolution gathered steam in the 1850s, British North Americans experienced an economic revolution. Artisans in industries where the new processes prevailed were either thrown out of work or found their jobs radically altered. While it had once taken days to travel from Toronto to Quebec City, it now took hours. By 1859, even Red River had a steamboat. On the West Coast, fur-trade society was rapidly receding in the wake of the gold rush of 1858. There was nowhere to hide from the transforming processes of the new industrial order.

INTELLECTUAL REVOLUTIONS

The Industrial Revolution was a child of the Age of Enlightenment, a term applied to the dramatic shift in the tenor of European intellectual life in the eighteenth century. Building on developments in science and philosophy that had been gaining momentum since the Renaissance, intellectuals in the eighteenth century called into question the claims of revealed religion and a divinely-ordained social order. They argued that societies could be studied rationally and scientifically, and that social conditions could be improved by human planning and purposeful action. Once held by a tiny minority, these ideas gradually gained wide acceptance, especially among members of the rising middle class. Scientific innovation was the source of much of their newfound wealth, and their desire to change antiquated laws and institutions that restricted their advancement gave impetus to the reforming spirit of the age.

Nothing excited British North Americans as much as the promise and practice of science. By the mid-nineteenth century, natural history, a comprehensive term applied to the general study of science, was popular in educated circles. Natural scientists combed the colonies classifying the flora and fauna and studying geological formations. Organizations devoted to the study of science were founded in most colonial cities, and large audiences turned out to hear lectures on scientific topics and participate in field trips. Any university worthy of the name hired a professor of science. Required to be an accomplished generalist, the science professor taught subjects that today would include everything from chemistry and physics to biology and geology.

British North Americans not only gobbled up scientific knowledge; they also helped to advance it. Andrew Downs, creator of a zoological garden in Halifax in 1847, supplied specimens to museums in Europe and the United States. William Logan, director of the Geological Survey of the Province of Canada, was knighted in 1856 for his pioneer work on the geology of Canada. In the 1860s, Hudson's Bay Company fur traders, at the behest of scientists from the Smithsonian Institution in Washington, DC, began collecting information on everything from birds' eggs to the weather. Scientists such as James Robb at the University of New Brunswick, William Dawson at McGill, and George Lawson at Queen's developed close contacts with the larger scientific community for whom they published their findings.

biography

J. William Dawson

In 1855, in his book *Acadian Geology*, J. William Dawson (1820–1899) announced that the Maritime region was formed millions of years ago and that giant reptiles once roamed the land. For British North Americans raised on the Christian Bible such claims seemed not only far-fetched but perhaps even blasphemous.

One of the leading scientists of his generation, Dawson was born in Pictou, Nova Scotia, and educated at Pictou Academy and the University of Edinburgh. He was a pioneer in the field of geology, which was challenging everything people believed about the earth and its inhabitants. Dawson's discovery of ancient fossils in the cliffs along the Bay of Fundy helped to establish new theories about the earth's origins. A committed Presbyterian, Dawson went to great lengths to make geological time agree with Biblical creation accounts and he refused to accept the evolutionary theories that were expounded by his great contemporary Charles Darwin.

Dawson also had a brilliant administrative career. He was appointed Superintendent of Education in Nova Scotia in 1850 and Principal of McGill in 1855, a position he held for 38 years. In addition to making McGill one of the world's leading universities, he taught classes, published 20 books, became the only individual to preside over both the American and British Associations for the Advancement of Science, and helped to establish the

Royal Society of Canada in 1882. He was knighted for his public services in 1884.

J. William Dawson.

Reproduced with the permission of the Minister of Public Works and Government Services Canada, 2002. Courtesy of Natural Resources Canada, Geological Survey of Canada

British North American inventors also had a wide impact. Abraham Gesner, a medical doctor, geologist, and museum curator in the Maritimes, developed a process for making kerosene oil in 1847 and promptly established a factory on Long Island, New York, to market his product. Ironically, Gesner's process was eclipsed by drilled oil, with the first well dug by James Williams in Enniskillen Township in the late 1850s. In turn, Canada West's boom town, Petrolia, was superseded by oil fields in Ohio and Pennsylvania. Practical inventions, such as the timber crib or the steam fog-whistle, were the stock and trade of British North Americans who, like their southern neighbours, were obsessed with finding better ways of doing things.

By the mid-nineteenth century, most British North Americans had adjusted to the "age of progress," accepting the new science as part of the larger movement toward a better society. Scientific pronouncements concerning the age of the earth or aggressive tendencies in the animal kingdom seemed consistent with God's purpose for human beings. But this complacency was undermined when Charles Darwin published *The Origin of Species* in 1859. His view that all living things had evolved from a single, primitive form of life and had developed by a process of natural selection and survival of the fittest flew in the face of Christianity's human-centred view of creation and the notion of a benevolent God.

As the long debate over "Darwinism" dragged its weary way through the second half of the nineteenth century, most Christians simply accepted the discrepancy between Darwin's findings and divine revelation as a mystery that would be explained in God's good time. Others became more sceptical about religion, and a few deserted the church for the cold comfort of atheism. Still others attempted to refute Darwin's theories on a scientific basis. Geologist William Dawson of McGill, renowned for his study of fossilized plants and animals in the rock formations along the Bay of Fundy, became one of the world's foremost apologists for the creationist view. Although millions of years old, these fossils showed no evidence of evolutionary development, he argued, a view which, both then and now, offered comfort to the creationists.

THE RAGE FOR REFORM

Given the changes taking place in their society in the mid-nineteenth century, it is not surprising that British North Americans experienced a sense of crisis. Nor is it surprising that they began advocating sweeping changes to the institutions that governed their lives. Reforms were sometimes spearheaded by governments but more often originated with voluntary groups, many of them associated with colonial churches. Although the separation of church and state became an accepted policy in all colonial jurisdictions, it did little to halt the power of organized religion in British North American society. Determined to maintain their intellectual and social influence, church leaders by mid-century were advocating a variety of reforms and taking institutional initiatives to achieve their goals.

Evangelical churches were the first to take up the cause of social reform. Using Christ's sermon on the Mount as their inspiration, evangelicals formed missionary societies, fought slavery, encouraged education, founded hospitals for the sick and asylums for the insane, and urged temperance and civic reform. The evangelical impulse was strongest among Methodists, Presbyterians, and Baptists, but it touched all Protestant denominations. By mid-century the Anglican and Roman Catholic churches had climbed on the reform bandwagon.

Colonial churches played a particularly prominent role in the temperance movement. Arguably the first mass movement in Canadian history, temperance in the use of alcohol was encouraged by evangelicals as a means of self-help, but it also supposedly offered a solution to what seemed to be the effects of intemperance: crime, insanity, poverty, violence, and the abuse of women and children. People of evangelical leanings in the Maritimes began forming the first temperance societies in the late 1820s. By 1850 temperance had gained a following among all classes, religions, and cultures from St John's to Red River. The temperance crusade was so successful that it seemed possible to go one step further—state prohibition of the manufacture and sale of intoxicating beverages.

In New Brunswick, the Liberals, fresh from their success in achieving responsible government, passed a prohibition bill in 1855. The problems created by prohibition were quickly revealed. Not only were the regulations difficult to enforce in the face of opposition from brewers, distillers, sellers, and drinkers of alcoholic beverages, they also precipitated a drastic drop in customs revenues. The lieutenant-governor stepped in, prompting the government to resign. In the ensuing election the Liberals were defeated and the offensive legislation was repealed. Other colonies avoided the New Brunswick experience by letting individuals and municipal corporations make the difficult decision on the thorny temperance question.

REINVENTING EDUCATION

It was not so easy to delegate responsibility for education to individuals and local communities. Acts by colonial legislatures encouraging local initiative in education had led to a hodge-podge of schools in British North America. Some schools were privately sponsored, many church-affiliated, and the whole system lacked the efficiency and uniformity so dear to the hearts of educational reformers. Like temperance, education was expected to accomplish many purposes. Egerton Ryerson, the Methodist superintendent of education for Canada West from 1844 to 1876, defined education in 1846 as "not the mere acquisition of certain arts, or of certain branches of knowledge, but that instruction and discipline which qualify and dispose the subjects of it for their appropriate duties and employments of life, as Christians, as persons of business, and also as members of the civil community in which they live."[4]

Systems of non-denominational state-supported schools in Prussia, Ireland, and the United States offered models for British North American reformers to follow. Only three obstacles stood in the way of success: class, religion, and race. Like prohibition, the notion of state-supported schools open to all classes and cultures was one that sparked controversy. The supporters of the idea, again a loose alliance of Protestant middle-class reformers, hoped to establish social harmony through a universal curriculum and a "common" school experience. In contrast, working-class families feared that schools would take children away from productive labour at home and in the workforce and impose taxes they were ill-equipped to pay, while the colonial elite opposed the "levelling" impact of common schools and the low standards that would surely prevail in such a system.

The question that concerned many British North Americans was the role of religion in a common-school system. While education reformers left little doubt that Christian morality would have a high priority in their classrooms, opponents of the system charged that morality could not be divorced from religious instruction. Roman Catholics were particularly wary of state-supported schools, which, with their daily Bible readings and prayers, seemed little more than Protestant schools in disguise. Between 1856 and 1860, Prince Edward Islanders were caught up in controversy over the question of Bible reading in its publicly funded school system, a practice demanded by a "Protestant Combination" and staunchly opposed by Roman Catholics. Although a compromise was effected—Bible reading in the common schools would be mandatory by law, but children who found it offensive could be excused from attendance—the controversy altered the political alignment in the colony.

Common-school legislation was so controversial that most colonial administrations championed its cause only at their peril. Nevertheless, Egerton Ryerson managed to achieve most of his objectives during his long tenure in office. Under Ryerson's careful guidance, Canada West adopted general tax assessment to finance public schools, uniform textbooks, a system of graded subjects, the bureaucratization of administration, and the centralization of power at the expense of local school boards. He also pointed teachers on the path to professionalization through his encouragement of normal-school training, teachers' institutes and associations, and the publication of the *Journal of Education for Upper Canada*. In Nova Scotia, Theodore Harding Rand followed Ryerson's lead.

Despite their opposition to separate schools, both Ryerson and Rand were forced to accept compromises with the politically powerful Roman Catholics, who insisted that confessional schools be eligible for state support. In contrast, Canada East and Newfoundland, where the Roman Catholic Church and Church of England were strong, made denominational schools the basis for public education. Racial and linguistic differences were also reflected in the public school systems. Both Nova Scotia and Canada West had "Negro Separate Schools." Canada West also administered separate schools after 1860 for Algonkian children. In addition, there were bilingual schools where instruction was given in French, German, or Gaelic.

In their quest for improvement, Canadians had laid the foundations for 17 universities by the time of Confederation. Most institutions of higher learning were sponsored by churches, and those claiming to be non-denominational, including Dalhousie, the University of New Brunswick, McGill, and the University of Toronto, often had close ties to one of the major churches. Opened only to men, universities catered primarily to a small elite. Only about 1500 male students attended Canadian universities in 1867. While law and medicine were taught in a few of the larger universities, the liberal arts, dominated by courses in Greek, Latin, and philosophy, was the most popular program of study.

The education revolution that occurred during the middle decades of the nineteenth century had a profound effect on the course of childhood in British North America. Since that time, most children have left home for a significant portion of the day during the school year to receive moral and academic training at the hands of a professional teacher, rather than from their parents. Increasingly, that teacher was drawn from the ranks of young women between the ages of 16 and 25—women prepared to work long hours for low wages. In this way, people avoided paying higher taxes for their new educational institutions. The overall effect of this schooling experience on children was to prepare them for the vastly different ways in which they would make their living in a rapidly industrializing British North America.

THE DISCOVERY OF THE ASYLUM

By 1850, the notion that poverty, criminal behaviour, and mental illness should be cured rather than endured was beginning to gain currency. Emphasis was therefore placed on providing the needy with skills and values necessary for them to become self-support-ing citizens. By helping unfortunate people to help themselves, it was argued, society in general and the taxpayer in particular would benefit. Reformers also argued that specialized institutions designed to focus on specific problems would be more effective than the family in achieving the desired results. With appropriate treatment, there was even hope for the rehabilitation of the criminal and the insane, two groups hitherto considered beyond redemption.

Social policy relating to the poor in mid-nineteenth-century British North America was a haphazard mixture of public and private initiatives. Although colonial cities maintained jails, alms-houses, and orphanages where the poor could take refuge, rural areas required the poor to work for assistance—perhaps breaking rocks for roads—or be auctioned off to the bidder who would agree to provide room and board at the lowest price. Only the disabled, the old, and the very young were considered "deserving" of charity. The "able-bodied" poor—victims of seasonal-employment patterns, the absence of kinship networks, crude exploitation, or their own human weaknesses—were given little public assistance and even less sympathy.

Following the lead of Great Britain, which had instituted a new Poor Law in 1834, urban British North Americans erected Houses of Industry where the poor would not only find shelter but also be taught habits of industry and self-discipline. Private subscriptions led to the construction of a House of Industry in Toronto in 1836. While such institutions were sometimes open to all poor people, they were often targeted at women and children. As early as 1832, a group of reform-minded women in St John's set up a factory to teach carding, spinning, and net-making to the children of the poor. Saint John established a House of Female Industry in 1834. In the wake of the Irish famine migration of the 1840s, orphanages were established in colonial cities to care for homeless children.

Houses of Industry were designed to reduce the cost of relief and avoid the practice of committing the poor to common jails. At the same time, they would offer an ideal setting for moral uplift. Reformers promoted "reformatories" as alternatives to prisons for juveniles in trouble with the law. It was argued that by separating impressionable youths from hard-bitten criminals and by teaching them appropriate behaviour, they might be "saved" from a life of crime. Since social services were the responsibility of local authorities and continued to remain so after the achievement of responsible government, the reach of reform was limited. Only affluent municipalities, which in practice meant cities, could sustain such asylums for their poor.

Asylums were also built for the treatment of the insane. In 1836, the citizens of Saint John established British North America's first "lunatic asylum," but it housed both the poor and the insane until 1848. The spate of new asylums in colonial cities at mid-century was inspired by the view motivating the commissioners of the Beauport Asylum near Quebec. They argued that their new institution was a place where the insane could "exchange their chains, gloom and filth for liberty, cheerfulness and cleanliness, where they are subject to the remedial powers and moral influences, and to the mode of treatment in accordance with the most improved principles of the present day." Institutional treatment of the insane was so significant on the reform agenda in Canada West that when the Lunatic Asylum opened its doors in Toronto in 1850 it was the largest building in the colony.

Under the reform impulse, prisons, too, became institutions of reform rather than punishment. The Kingston Penitentiary, which had opened in 1835, was designed "to correct" deviant behaviour by imposing rigid discipline in a closely controlled environment. Like many of the new asylums, Kingston Penitentiary soon came under severe criticism for the harsh treatment of its inmates. Prisoners, who included men, women, and children, were flogged for minor infractions, confined for days to a dark cell, and fed on diets of bread and water. In 1848–49, George Brown, a rising star in the Reform Party of Upper Canada, chaired a commission of inquiry into conditions at the Kingston Penitentiary that laid bare the cruel and corrupt regime of warden Henry Smith. Brown's charges earned him the undying enmity of Conservative Assemblyman John A. Macdonald, in whose constituency the penitentiary was located. They also resulted in the appointment of a paid inspector to investigate prison operations.

By the 1850s, social reform and the institutions it encouraged had run aground on the shoals of denominational rivalry. The high incidence of Roman Catholics among those committed to institutional care prompted Protestants to complain about the costs of treating Roman Catholics and to conclude that social problems were associated with religious belief. In an effort to avoid the proselytizing tendencies of custodians in public institutions, a reinvigorated Roman Catholic Church expanded its social services to assist its own people. Protestants, not to be outdone, established separate institutions for themselves. Most British North American cities in mid-century spawned church-sponsored asylums, hospitals, and hostels, thus creating a patchwork of state, church, and privately supported efforts, vastly uneven in quality and accessible to only a fraction of the potential clients.

Provincial Lunatic Asylum in Toronto, designed by John G. Howard.

City of Toronto Art Collection

The rage for reform among the colonial middle classes in the mid-nineteenth century was motivated by altruism and by the example of their counterparts in Britain and the United States. It also served to disguise the growing disparity between rich and poor that increasingly characterized colonial society. Operating on the democratic belief that self-discipline and education would enable everyone to benefit from the new economic and political order, middle-class reformers made life even more difficult for those excluded from the race for success. Once merely perceived as the world's unfortunates, the poor were increasingly attacked for their lack of character and moral fibre. By placing the blame on individuals rather than on the system that created and tolerated inequality, reformers avoided any wholesale critique of the social order that sustained their own affluence.

PUBLIC AND PRIVATE WORLDS

New social values and attitudes toward work also had a profound influence on the family. Home in the pre-industrial world was the centre of work and play, business and politics, religion and education. By the mid-nineteenth century British North Americans were increasingly making a distinction between their public and private lives. The public world of business, paid labour, and politics, it was argued, should be separate from the domestic realm of the family, which should serve as a refuge from the outside world of exploitation and competition.

The impact of these changes was felt first in urban middle-class families where marriages were based on sentimental as well as economic considerations and where fewer children were being raised. In these families, the work performed by women in the home changed with the introduction of manufactured goods such as textiles, the increasing number of servants, and the tendency to send children to public schools. As the productive and reproductive roles of women decreased, more emphasis was placed on motherhood, household management, and charity. The careful delineation of separate spheres for men and women that had prevailed in the pre-industrial world was thus maintained: men dominated the public sphere with all its attendant opportunities while women were relegated to the private sphere of domesticity and good works.

Life-cycle choices were also being gradually altered to accommodate the new social reality. Both men and women married later, and they spent more time in the paid labour force before they married. Although the work of unmarried women was largely confined to domestic service, new professions such as school teaching gave educated women experience in the public sphere and the possibility of economic independence outside the institution of marriage. With the delaying of marriage, adolescence—a word coined only in the late nineteenth century—was emerging as a stage in the life cycle of British North Americans. Childhood was also becoming distinct from infancy and adulthood, and children were perceived as innocent and angelic rather than primitive creatures to be socialized to adult behaviour as quickly as possible.

Working-class family life was far removed from concerns for privacy and sentimentality that preoccupied the middle class. In the working-class district of St Jacques in Montreal, for example, families dependent on wage labour for survival lived a precarious existence. Faced with unemployment, illness, death, and unplanned pregnancy, families were often forced to commit their younger children to Saint-Alexis Orphanage, run by the Sisters of Providence. The majority of children at Saint-Alexis in the mid-nineteenth century were not technically orphans but had lived in families that were too poor to care for them at home.

Despite objections of middle-class moralists to "working wives," a working-class family could often survive only if more than one of its members engaged in paid labour. Middle-class families might live very well on the income of the male head of household and hire servants to attend to household chores, but the work of wives and children was crucial to the survival of working-class families. Although a wife's work in the home was not calculated in monetary terms, the family could not survive without her labour at home and, when necessary, in the paid work force. By the same token, children who were not old enough to work threatened the delicately balanced economy of the working-class family.

WOMEN'S RIGHTS

Efforts to exclude women from the public sphere soon drew a spirited response. In the United States, women involved in the anti-slavery movement recognized their own lack of civil rights and began organizing to remove the legal and attitudinal barriers that made women subordinate to men. American abolitionist women, led by Elizabeth Cady Stanton and Lucretia Mott, held a convention at Seneca Falls, New York, where a Declaration of Sentiments and Resolutions was adopted in 1848. Using the language of the earlier Declaration of Independence, the advocates of women's rights charged that "the history of mankind is a history of repeated injuries and usurpations on the part of man toward woman, having its direct object the establishment of an absolute tyranny over her."5 Such views were certain to draw the fire of men whose power was directly challenged by women's rights advocates.

Although they were slow to take up the campaign for female suffrage, British North American women were close observers of the women's movement taking shape south of the border. They often travelled to the United States to take advantage of educational opportunities denied them at home, and they lobbied against practices that discriminated against them. Between 1852 and 1857, three groups of women petitioned the legislature in Canada West for reform of laws relating to control of married women's property. In 1852, a landmark statute passed by the Prince Edward Island legislature permitted cases of seduction to be brought in the name of the woman seduced rather than in the name of the father. In Canada West, an 1855 law gave the court discretion to permit mothers to have access to or custody of infant children in cases where judges "saw fit." Subsequent decisions rendered by the courts recognized the enhanced status of motherhood in British North American society.

THE CREATIVE ARTS

The forces animating colonial society at mid-century, most notably the rise of literacy, had an impact on the creative arts. Not only were British North Americans

enthusiastic consumers of literature produced abroad, they also began to generate some of their own. Colonial newspapers carried British and North American authors in serial form, making Walter Scott, Anthony Trollope, and Charles Dickens as well as local authors easily accessible to colonials. Libraries and bookstores could be found in most urban centres. Although cheap pirated reprints of popular fiction flourished briefly in the early 1840s, they were quickly suppressed by copyright laws.

In 1824, Julia Catherine Beckwith of Fredericton became the first native-born British North American novelist with the publication of *St Ursula's Convent*, written when she was 17 years old. By 1850, Thomas Chandler Haliburton and Susannah Moodie had gained an international reputation for their work, which consisted primarily of humorous sketches of colonial life. Moodie's sister, Catharine Parr Traill, was one of several British writers who wrote guides for fellow immigrants. Traill's *Backwoods of Canada* (1836) and *The Canadian Settler's Guide* (1855) presented a mixture of sound advice, pious homilies, and natural history that reflected the literary taste of the time. New England poet Henry Wadsworth Longfellow—who never visited the Maritimes—immortalized the deportation of the Acadians with his poem "Evangeline," published in 1847. Although this had not been his goal, the poem helped to spark a new sense of collective identity among Acadians both in the Maritimes and elsewhere.

An intellectual awakening in French Canada was one of the major cultural developments of the mid-nineteenth century. Following Durham's cruel comment that the French Canadians were a people with no literature and no history, histories and creative writing appeared to prove the British lord wrong. François-Xavier Garneau's *Histoire du Canada*, which appeared in several volumes between 1845 and 1852, was an inspired piece of scholarship. In the Maritimes, Peter Fisher and Haliburton had also turned their hands to writing history, and in Canada West, John Richardson published *The War of 1812* in 1842. Robert Christie's *History of the Late Province of Lower Canada*, published in six ponderous volumes, began appearing in 1848.

Magazines published in British North America had a difficult time competing with American publications and colonial newspapers that contained popular works of British and American writers. *The Literary Garland*, based in Montreal, expired in 1851 after a valiant effort to provide a forum for colonial writers. In the same year, Halifax-born poet Mary Eliza Herbert began publishing *The Mayflower*. Devoted to literature for those who wished "to roam a while in the flowery field of romance,—to hold communion with the Muses," it survived for only nine issues and most of the contributions came from Herbert herself.

Despite the paucity of colonial contributors, the reading audience was growing and the pace of intellectual life quickening noticeably. Mechanics' Institutes, founded in Scotland to promote scientific education among the artisan class, took root in many colonial communities in the 1830s. Its focus in British North America was broadened to include literary, dramatic, and artistic as well as scientific pursuits and it appealed to a wide range of working and middle-class colonials sold on the idea of self-improvement. In Canada East, branches of the Institut Canadien were hotbeds for intellectual exchange, their offices serving as libraries, newsrooms, and conference halls all rolled into one.

Colonial theatres hosted a variety of functions, including live plays, music concerts, and dramatic readings. Toronto's much-praised St Lawrence Hall was opened in 1851 to accommodate, among other things, the increasing variety of local and international artists. In 1846, Haligonians converted a hay barn into the Theatre Royal, which in the following decade became the Sothern Lyceum, named after E.A. Sothern whose troupe was located briefly in the city. No British North American writer made a living from producing plays, but a few actors did well on the theatre circuit. Although art was still confined primarily to polite drawing-room sketches—nudes were the source of much head-shaking—a few art teachers survived in the colonies, and art shows were no longer a rare event.

In the mid-nineteenth century, music appealed to a wider audience than most artistic forms. Regimental bands, operas, operettas, symphonies, and choral recitals were well attended. Even in the backwoods, itinerant teachers inspired the formation of singing schools—all the rage in the 1850s—in which the basics of hymn and psalm singing were taught. Any parlour worthy of the name was incomplete without a pump organ, the perfect accompaniment to hymns and popular tunes. With its elite Grenadier and Coldstream Guards, Quebec City boasted the best band concerts in the colonies.

Those British North Americans too poor or in regions too remote to attend gala performances made their own music, using their own voices and whatever musical instrument happened to be at hand. Combs, spoons, saws, and stepping feet would serve as reasonable accompaniment if nothing else was available. Many families treasured a violin or harpsichord brought from their homelands, and the very talented could often fashion instruments from local resources.

French Canadians had a rich musical heritage, which was enhanced by European immigrants such as Charles-Wugk Sabatier, who arrived from Paris in 1848. A student of the famous Conservatoire de Paris, Sabatier taught Calixa Lavallée, the future composer of "O Canada." By 1850, Joseph Casavant, who had installed his first church organ in 1840, was already well on his way to establishing a worldwide reputation as an organ manufacturer. British North Americans were also beginning to develop careers that took them outside of their homeland. Emma (Lajeunesse) Albani, the child prodigy destined to become an international singing star, made her debut at the Mechanics' Hall in Montreal in 1856.

SPORTS AND LEISURE

Most British North Americans had little time for what in the twenty-first century is called leisure activity. Yet weekly and seasonal rhythms incorporated social activity as a break from the monotony of daily toil. The "Sabbath" was rigorously observed among those of evangelical persuasion, and church services were important community occasions for all Christians. In rural areas, "bees" brought people together for quilting, building, planting, and harvest activities. Priests and parsons often complained of the drunkenness and immorality that prevailed at rural "frolics" that were popular throughout the colonies.

During winter months, enforced relaxation provided a good opportunity for sleighing parties, weddings, and extended visits with friends and relatives. Winter travel over well-packed snow or ice was often a welcome alternative to muddy and uncomfortably rough roads in other seasons of the year. Diaries and letters of the colonial middle class often tell of family members reading and writing letters around a flickering candle or oil lamp on a chilly winter's evening.

In 1850, religious holidays had yet to take on the crass materialism that developed later in the century, but most cultural groups formally marked Christmas and Easter as well as the passing of the old year and the arrival of spring. For Aboriginal peoples in the Maritime colonies, the feast of Saint Anne on 26 July was a time to meet at Shubenacadie, Chapel Island, Lennox Island, and Burnt Church to reaffirm their culture. Days devoted to St George, St Patrick, and St Andrew were celebrated by the English, Irish, and Scots respectively. Irish Protestants, and increasingly Protestants generally, remembered the anniversary of the Battle of the Boyne. Many of these cultural events preserved limited identities and made a sense of a larger community identity difficult to establish.

Games, sports, and competitions were part of the festive and communal occasions of all pre-industrial cultures. Unorganized, unsophisticated, and accompanied by drinking and brawling, they were often scenes of cracked heads and hard feelings. In rural areas of British North America, cock fighting, bearbaiting, horse races, wrestling, and fisticuffs were popular. The colonial elite increasingly criticized such activities. They participated in organized sports, copied, for the most part, from events held among the British aristocracy. Clubs devoted to racing, yachting, rowing, and curling could be found from St John's to Toronto by the mid-nineteenth century and would soon take root in Victoria. Sports developed by Aboriginal peoples, most notably lacrosse and snowshoeing, were also popular in elite circles.

As the largest British North American city, and one with a significant military presence, Montreal emerged as the centre of organized sports. It boasted the first organized club—the Montreal Curling Club—in 1807, the first cricket, lacrosse, hunt, and snowshoeing clubs, and the first specialized sports facilities. Cricket was the game of champions in mid-nineteenth century British North America and

Toronto was the cricket capital of British North America, in part because of the influence of the first headmaster of Upper Canada College, which was founded in 1829. Considered a vehicle for teaching elite values, cricket was initially the sport of British immigrants and others who aped British sporting ideology. On 13 July 1836, the editor of the *Toronto Patriot* even claimed that a "cricketer as a matter of course, detests democracy and is staunch in his allegiance to his King." By the 1850s, cricket enjoyed a wide popularity and cricket clubs had mushroomed all over British North America. International matches with American teams began in 1844 and became annual events after 1853.

In June 1859, Blondin, the famous French funambulist, walked a tightrope over the even more famous Niagara Falls. By this time this dramatic natural attraction had emerged as a popular destination for the travelling public not only from within the colony, but also from the United States and Europe. Promoters of the Falls created an image of a sublime, wild, and romantic locale for European travellers. As early as the 1820s, the Falls had lost much of its natural beauty, surrounded as it was by efforts to make money from the growing number of tourists. Entrepreneurs set up hotels, museums, sea gardens, souvenir shops, steamboat services, and coach services, and guidebooks directed tourists through the area. Native women fashioned crafts that they and their children sold to visitors happy to purchase mementoes of such exotic people. Old soldiers served as guides to battle sites of the War of 1812. With the growth of train travel, the Falls became a site for newly-married couples who indulged in a new fad called "the honeymoon."

CONCLUSION

The industrial and intellectual revolutions of the mid-nineteenth century offered British North Americans both challenges and opportunities. For those who clung to the older notions of class privilege, patriarchal authority, religious certainty, and family self-sufficiency the challenges would be daunting. Even those who embraced new ideas were often disappointed in their practical results. Yet the opportunities continued to beckon. The new industrial order prompted a few British North Americans to dream big. Why not create a transcontinental nation? The ingredients were there: a shared British heritage, the potential of the railway to bring unity across vast distances, the promise of national greatness, and the lure of private profit. All that was needed was a little push and the pieces of the British North American puzzle would fall in place. As we will see in the next chapter, that push would come from a variety of sources in the heady atmosphere of the 1860s.

NOTES

1 John Thompson, "The First Last Spike," *Horizon Canada* 4 (1987) 1032.

2 Cited in Gregory S. Kealey, *Toronto Workers Respond to Industrial Capitalism, 1867–1892* (Toronto: University of Toronto Press, 1980) 6.

3 Cited in Michael Cross, ed., *Free Trade, Annexation and Reciprocity, 1846–1854* (Toronto: Holt, Rinehart, and Winston, 1971) 53-54.

4 Cited in Susan Houston, "Politics, Schools, and Change in Upper Canada," *Canadian Historical Review* 53.3 (Sept. 1972) 265.

5 Aileen S. Kraditor, ed., *Up from the Pedestal: Selected Writings in the History of American Feminism* (New York: Quadrangle, 1968) 184.

SELECTED READING

The classic discussion of the impact of industrialism is Karl Polanyi, *The Great Transformation: The Political and Economic Origins of Our Time* (Boston: Beacon Press, 1957). Canadian studies include Donald Creighton, *The Commercial Empire of the Saint Lawrence, 1760–1850* (Toronto: Macmillan, 1937); Stanley Ryerson, *Unequal Union: Confederation and the Roots of Conflict in the Canadas, 1815–1873* (Toronto: Progress Books, 1968); Gerald Tulchinsky, *The River Barons: Montreal Businessmen and the Growth of Industry and Transportation, 1837–1853* (Toronto: University of Toronto Press, 1977); Douglas McCalla, *The Upper Canada Trade, 1834–1872: A Study of Buchanan's Business* (Toronto: University of Toronto Press, 1979); and T.W. Acheson, *Saint John: The Making of a Colonial Urban Community* (Toronto: University of Toronto Press, 1985). Michael Bliss usefully summarizes the general trends in *Northern Enterprise: Five Centuries of Canadian Business* (Toronto: McClelland and Stewart, 1987). Other general studies include Kenneth Norrie and Douglas Owram, *A History of the Canadian Economy* (Toronto: Harcourt Brace Jovanovich, 1991); W.L. Marr and D.G. Paterson, *Canada: An Economic History* (Toronto: Macmillan, 1980); and W.T. Easterbrook and H.G.J. Aitken, *Canadian Economic History* (Toronto: Macmillan, 1963). A valuable perspective on the industrializing process is offered in the introductory chapters to R.T. Naylor, *The History of Canadian Business*, vol. 1, *1867–1914* (Toronto: Lorimer, 1975); Bryan Palmer, *A Culture in Conflict: Skilled Workers and Industrial Capitalism in Hamilton, Ontario, 1860–1914* (Montreal: McGill-Queen's University Press, 1979); and Gregory S. Kealey, *Toronto Responds to Industrial Capitalism, 1867–1892* (Toronto: University of Toronto Press, 1980). See also Ian McKay, "Capital and Labour in the Halifax Baking and Confectionary Industry during the Last Half of the Nineteenth Century," in *Essays in Canadian Business History*, ed. Tom Traves (Toronto: McClelland and Stewart, 1984) 47–81, and Paul Craven and Tom Traves, "Canadian Railways as Manufacturers, 1850–1880," *Canadian Historical Association Historical Papers* (1983), 254–81.

On legal reform see three volumes of *Essays in the History of Canadian Law* (Toronto: University of Toronto Press, 1981, 1983, and 1990); Peter Waite et al., *Law in a Colonial Society: The Nova Scotia Experience* (Toronto: Carswell, 1984); W. Wesley Pue and Barry Wright, *Canadian Perspectives on Law and Society: Issues in Legal History* (Ottawa: Carleton University Press, 1988); R.C.

Macleod, ed., *Lawful Authority: Readings on the History of Criminal Justice in Canada* (Toronto: Copp Clark Pitman, 1988); Constance Backhouse, *Petticoats and Prejudice: Women and Law in Nineteenth-Century Canada* (Toronto: Women's Press, 1991), and "Married Women's Property Law in Nineteenth-Century Canada," in *Canadian Family History: Selected Readings*, ed. Bettina Bradbury (Toronto: Copp Clark Pitman, 1992) 320–59; and R.C.B. Risk, "The Law and the Economy in Mid-Nineteenth-Century Ontario: A Perspective," in *Essays in the History of Canadian Law*, vol. 1, ed. David H. Flaherty (Toronto: University of Toronto Press, 1981) 88–131.

Other studies on nineteenth-century economic development include T.C. Keefer, *Philosophy of Railroads* (1850; reprinted Toronto: University of Toronto Press, 1972); S.A. Saunders, *The Economic History of the Maritime Provinces* (1939; reprinted Fredericton: Acadiensis Press, 1984); G.N. Tucker, *The Canadian Commercial Revolution, 1845–1851* (Ottawa: Carleton University Press, 1964); D.C. Masters, *The Reciprocity Treaty of 1854* (Toronto: McClelland and Stewart, 1963); John McCallum, *Unequal Beginnings: Agriculture and Economic Development in Quebec and Ontario until 1870* (Toronto: University of Toronto Press, 1980); A.R.M. Lower, *Great Britain's Woodyard: British America and the Timber Trade, 1763–1867* (Montreal: McGill-Queen's University Press, 1973); G.P. de T. Glazebrook, *A History of Transportation in Canada*, vol. 1 (Ottawa: Carleton University Press, 1964); Brian Young, *Promoters and Politicians: The North-Shore Railways in the History of Quebec* (Toronto: University of Toronto Press, 1978); and Jacob Spelt, *Urban Development in South Central Ontario* (Ottawa: Carleton University Press, 1972).

Gerald Friesen offers a valuable assessment of the relation between technology and society in this and other periods of Canadian history in *Citizens and Nation: An Essay on History, Communication, and Canada* (Toronto: University of Toronto Press, 2000). Sources on nineteenth-century intellectual history include Carl Berger, *Science, God, and Nature in Victorian Canada* (Toronto: University of Toronto Press, 1983); Susan Sheets-Pyenson, *John William Dawson: Faith, Hope, and Science* (Montreal: McGill-Queen's University Press, 1996); and A.B. McKillop: *A Disciplined Intelligence: Critical Inquiry and Canadian Thought in the Victorian Era* (Montreal: McGill-Queen's University Press, 1979) and *Contours of Canadian Thought* (Toronto: University of Toronto Press, 1987).

The plight of poor and easily exploited groups in Victorian society is a major theme in Judith Fingard's *The Dark Side of Life in Victorian Halifax* (Porters Lake, NS: Pottersfield, 1989), *Jack in Port: Sailortowns of Eastern Canada* (Toronto: University of Toronto Press, 1982), and in her much-quoted article, "The Winter's Tale: The Seasonal Contours of Pre-Industrial Poverty in British North America, 1815–1860," *Canadian Historical Association Historical Papers* (1974): 65–94. See also Richard B. Splane, *Social Welfare in Ontario, 1791–1893: A Study of Public Welfare Administration* (Toronto: University of Toronto Press, 1965).

General surveys on educational development covering this period include Charles E. Phillips, *The Development of Public Education in Canada* (Toronto: Gage, 1957); J. Donald Wilson, Robert M. Stamp, and Louis-Philippe Audet, *Canadian Education: A History* (Toronto: Prentice-Hall, 1970); Roger Magnuson, *A Brief History of Quebec Education* (Montreal: Harvest House, 1980); and Paul Axelrod, *The Promise of Schooling, 1800–1914* (Toronto: University of Toronto Press, 1997). The causes and character of educational changes are treated somewhat differently in Susan Houston and Alison Prentice, *Schooling and Scholars in Nineteenth-Century Ontario* (Toronto: University of Toronto Press, 1988) and Bruce Curtis, *Building the Educational State: Canada West, 1836–1871* (London, ON: Althouse, 1988). See also Alison Prentice, *The School Promoters: Education and Social Class in Mid-Nineteenth-Century Upper Canada* (Toronto: McClelland and Stewart, 1977). Rural responses to taxation levied to support public schools and municipal government in Canada East are explored in Chad Gaffield, *Language, Schooling, and Cultural Conflict: The Origins of the French-Language Controversy* (Montreal: McGill-Queen's University Press, 1987) and Wendie Nelson, "'Rage Against the Dying of the Light': Interpreting the Guerre des Éteignoirs," *Canadian Historical Review* 81.4 (Dec. 2000): 551–81. Educational reform in Prince Edward Island is discussed in Ian Robertson, "The Bible Question in Prince Edward Island from 1856 to 1860," *Acadiensis* 5.2 (Spring 1976): 3–25. On Nova Scotia's movement to create public schools see Margaret Conrad, "'An abiding conviction of the paramount importance of Christian Education,': Theodore Harding Rand as Educator, 1860–1900," in Robert S. Wilson, ed., *An Abiding Conviction: Maritime Baptists and Their World* (Saint John: Acadia Divinity College and the Baptist Historical Committee, 1988) 155–95.

Literature is discussed in Carl Klinck, *Literary History of Canada* (Toronto: University of Toronto Press, 1976). Historiographical developments are the subject of M. Brook Taylor, *Promoters, Patriots, and Partisans:*

Historiography in Nineteenth-Century English Canada (Toronto: University of Toronto Press, 1989) and Serge Gagnon, *Quebec and Its Historians* (Montreal: Harvest House, 1982). The architecture of the period is examined in Harold Kalman, *A History of Canadian Architecture*, vol. 1 (Toronto: University of Toronto Press, 1994) and Peter Ennals and Deryck W. Holdsworth, *Homeplace: The Making of the Canadian Dwelling over Three Centuries* (Toronto: University of Toronto Press, 1998). J. Russell Harper has written extensively on nineteenth-century art and artists. A good place to start is his *Painting in Canada: A History* (Toronto: University of Toronto Press, 1977). See also Sandra Paikowsky, "Landscape Painting in Canada," in

Profiles of Canada, ed. Kenneth G. Pryke and Walter R. Soderlund (Toronto: Copp Clark Pitman, 1992) 336–45.

Sports in the nineteenth century are the focus of Alan Metcalfe, *Canada Learns to Play: The Emergence of Organized Sport, 1807–1914* (Toronto: McClelland and Stewart, 1987); Morris Mott, ed., *Sports in Canada: Historical Readings* (Toronto: Copp Clark Pitman, 1989); and Don Morrow et al., *A Concise History of Sports in Canada* (Toronto: Oxford University Press, 1989). Aspects of tourism and leisure are discussed in Patricia Jasen, *Wild Things: Nature, Culture and Tourism in Ontario, 1790–1914* (Toronto: University of Toronto Press, 1995).

 **WEBLINKS**

GEOLOGICAL SURVEY OF CANADA
www.nrcan.gc.ca/gsc/history_e.html

Maintaine by Natural Resources Canada, this site offers a comprehensive historical overview of the Geological Survey of Canada.

CRIMEAN WAR
www.hillsdale.edu/academics/history/Documents/War/19Crim.htm

This site provides primary documents relating to the Crimean War, detailing general accounts and offering commentary on specific battles.

INDUSTRIAL REVOLUTION
http://encarta.msn.com/index/conciseindex/67/0678a000.htm

This Encarta.com entry describes the effects of the Revolution on Great Britain, the United States, and around the world, and recommends additional readings.

RECIPROCITY TREATY OF 1854
www.ola.bc.ca/online/cf/documents/1854ReciprocityTreaty.html

Read the full text of the Reciprocity Treaty online.

EARLY CANADIANA ONLINE
www.canadiana.org

This site consists of several collections, each with a particular scope and focus in Canadian history.

The Road to Confederation

The House was in an unmistakeably seedy condition, having, as it was positively declared, eaten the saloon keeper clean out, drunk him entirely dry, and got all the fitful naps of sleep that the benches along the passages could be made to yield. For who cared at one, two, three, and four in the morning, to sit in the House, to hear the stale talk of Mr. Ferguson, of South Simcoe, or to listen even to the polished and pointed sentences of Mr. Huntingdon? Men with the strongest constitutions for Parliamentary twaddle were sick of the debate, and the great bulk of the members were scattered about the building, with an up-all-night, get-tight-in-the-morning air, impatient for the sound of the division bell. It rang at last, at quarter past four, and the jaded representatives of the people swarmed in to the discharge of the most important duty of all their lives.[1]

At a conference in Quebec City in October 1864, delegates from several British North American colonies hammered out a proposal for political union and agreed to submit the "confederation" proposal to their respective legislatures. The debate on confederation in the Assembly of the United Province of Canada stretched from 2 February 1865 to 11 March 1865 and featured long, often raucous sittings. As the *Stratford Beacon's* account of the last hours of the debate suggests, there was considerable scepticism about the proposal. In Nova Scotia, Joseph Howe lamented the attempts by the United Province to lure the Atlantic colonies into confederation and ridiculed the notion that "a new nationality" would result from the project. The French and English of the United Province, were, in his view, incompatible. "A more unpromising nucleus of a new nation could hardly be found on the face of the earth," he concluded.[2]

NATIONALISM AND COLONIAL IDENTITY

Howe had not always been so negative in his musings on British North American unity. Like other political leaders in the colonies he had been inspired by national sentiments that were sweeping the Western world. Periodic nationalist uprisings, most notably in

1830 and 1848, rocked European empires. In the name of nationalism, Irish patriots demanded an end to the hated union between Britain and Ireland. National rhetoric fuelled movements to unify the Italian and German states and inspired the "rebels of '37," especially among French Canadians, whose common language, religion, and history provided the basis for a cohesive national identity. British immigrants to the colonies had brought their cultural identities with them, a confusing mixture of the ethnic, democratic, national, and imperial sentiment that prevailed in Great Britain itself.

By the mid-nineteenth century, there were voices calling for a larger British North American nationalism to mute class and cultural cleavages. The concept of a united British North America was not new. In the late eighteenth century, Loyalists had voiced such sentiments and Lord Durham had been a proponent of the idea. In 1851 Joseph Howe, trying to garner support for an intercolonial railroad, asked his constituents to "stand by me now in this last effort to improve our country, elevate these noble Provinces, and form them into a Nation."

One of British North America's most passionate nationalists was Thomas D'Arcy McGee. An Irish patriot who had participated in the Irish rebellion of 1848, McGee fled to the United States and in 1857 moved to Montreal. As a newspaperman and later a member of the legislature in the Canadas, McGee became a supporter of a "new Northern nationality" within the larger British imperial context. For McGee, nationalism offered a solution to the ethnic and sectional conflicts that he felt impeded the progress of British North America just as they had poisoned the potential of his native Ireland.

As in Ireland, nationalist sentiment posed problems for British North Americans because one patriot's nationalism often proved to be another patriot's bigotry. Safer ground for the new nationalism was the economic potential of the northern half of the continent, which stirred the hearts and imagination of both the romantic idealist and the practical businessman. Such an alternative vision of national destiny came not from across the Atlantic but from south of the border. By mid-century, the Americans were advancing across the continent, dazzling the world with the speed and scope of their economic achievement.

Like their southern neighbours, British North Americans began to argue that it was their manifest destiny to develop their own transcontinental nation. Eyeing the Northwest as their next resource frontier, empire builders in Montreal and Toronto dreamed of railways that would link them to their economic hinterland. In 1857, the government of the United Canadas sponsored Henry Youle Hind, a University of Toronto professor of chemistry and geology, to head a fact-finding expedition through HBC territories east of the Rockies and sent delegates to the commission of inquiry into the Hudson's Bay Company monopoly, where they laid claim to Rupert's Land by virtue of French exploration. In the same year, John Palliser, a scion of wealthy Irish landowners, convinced the Royal Geographical Society to sponsor an expedition that covered much of the same ground as Hind. Both men concluded that the Northwest, particularly the Red River and North Saskatchewan River valleys, was suitable for agricultural settlement.

The Hind and Palliser reports confirmed the view of Canada West expansionists that areas of Rupert's Land could become an agricultural paradise. Toronto's merchant community, concerned about its future as the city's western hinterland filled up, regarded the far-flung territories further west as an extension of that hinterland. In this goal, they were led by the most powerful Reformer in Canada West, George Brown, the editor of the *Globe* and a businessman with a variety of speculative investments whose future returns were tied to Toronto's prosperity. The expansionists found sympathetic ears in the British government and financial circles. They also gradually won over the colony's farmers, who were looking for a new agricultural frontier for their children.

With dramatic suddenness, the notion of a formidable and inaccessible western territory gave way to glowing reports of agricultural potential and unlimited opportunity. The Fraser valley gold rush of 1858 only added to the enthusiasm. Alexander Morris, who published *The Hudson's Bay and Pacific Territories* in 1859, expressed the optimism of many British North Americans when he described the possibilities offered by westward expansion:

With two powerful colonies on the Pacific, with another or more in the region between Canada and the Rocky Mountains, with a railway and a telegraph linking the Atlantic and the Pacific and absorbing the newly-opened and fast-developing trade with China and Japan...who can doubt of the reality and accuracy of the vision which rises distinctly and clearly before us, as the Great Britannic Empire of the North stands out in all its grandeur.[3]

All that stood in the way of pursuing such a grand vision was the political impasse in the Canadas.

THE CANADAS: ECONOMIC SUCCESS AND POLITICAL IMPASSE

During its brief existence as a political entity, the United Province of Canada experienced steady economic growth, but political stability proved elusive. Part of the problem lay in the unequal population growth of the two Canadas. At the time of the union in 1841, Lower Canada had a population of 650 000, compared to 450 000 in Upper Canada. Immigration over the next two decades raised the population of Canada West well over that of Canada East (see Table 14.1), prompting many Upper Canadian politicians to demand representation by population in the legislature to replace the equal division of seats provided for in the Act of Union.

Support for "rep by pop" among Canada West Reformers was matched by French-Canadian resistance to the idea. The claim that democracy demanded representation proportional to population was met by the charge that the undemocratic union of 1840 had provided no protection of French Catholic rights other than representation in the Assembly. Capitalizing on sectional tensions, George Brown shaped a Reform Party organization in Canada West that resembled in embryo a modern political party. Apart from the goal of representation by population, the glue bonding Reformers together was support for annexation of the Northwest to Canada and opposition to public moneys for separate schools and for subsidies to the Grand Trunk Railway.

John A. Macdonald emerged as the leader of an equally organized bloc of Conservative politicians who resisted the Reformers' demands. Relying on the skillful use of patronage, sentimental ties to Great Britain, and the importance of the economic link to the St Lawrence River, Macdonald persuaded many voters in Canada West to reject reforms that would alienate the French-speaking majority of Canada East. Increasingly, however, the majority in Canada West preferred the Reformers' message. In the 1863 election, the Conservatives won just 20 of Canada West's 65 seats. Only the success of the Conservatives in Canada East, known as the Bleus, prevented the opposition from achieving a majority.

Macdonald's counterpart in Canada East was George Étienne Cartier. A former Patriote turned wealthy lawyer, Cartier's corporate links typified the dramatic change in the preoccupations of many leading French-Canadian politicians. His clients included the Grand Trunk Railway, the Seminary of Montreal, the French government, and various insurance, mining, and railway companies. By aligning their capitalist interests with the hierarchy of the Roman Catholic Church, the

Table 14.1

Population of British North America, 1851–1871

	1851	1861	1871
Ontario	952 004	1 396 091	1 620 851
Quebec	890 261	1 111 566	1 191 516
Nova Scotia	276 854	330 857	387 800
New Brunswick	193 800	252 047	285 594
Prince Edward Island	62 678*	80 857	94 021
Newfoundland†	–	122 638	158 958
British Columbia	55 000	51 524	36 247**
Manitoba	–	–	25 228
Northwest Territories	–	–	48 000

* Figure is from 1848
† Figures are from 1857 and 1874
** This figure probably understates the Native population of the province by about 15 000

Source: "Series A 2-14. Population of Canada by province, census dates, 1851 to 1976," in *Historical Statistics of Canada*, 2nd ed., ed. F.H. Leacy (Ottawa: Minister of Supply and Services, 1983) and James Hiller, "Confederation Defeated: The Newfoundland Election of 1869," in *Newfoundland in the Nineteenth and Twentieth Centuries: Essays in Interpretation*, ed. James Hiller and Peter Neary (Toronto: University of Toronto Press, 1980).

Bleus under Cartier clinched their dominance of Canada East politics. The Bleus consistently defended the role of the Church in education in the United Province of Canada and generally could be counted upon to champion the Church's involvement in social services and the family life of Roman Catholics in Canada East. In return, the clergy thundered against the liberal opponents of the Bleus who supported separation of church and state.

Reformers in Canada East never won more than 25 of the 65 seats. Divided between the Rouges and independents, the reformist element in Canada East formed neither a coherent party nor an easy ally of the Canada West Reformers. A Reform ministry created in 1862 under the leadership of John Sandfield Macdonald survived just a year and a half and only by abandoning principles of "rep by pop" and opposition to public support of denominational schools. By 1864, the chances of forming a government acceptable to both halves of the United Province seemed remote. A "double majority"—majority support in each of the two sections of the province—was not constitutionally necessary, but most politicians accepted it as a practical necessity for commanding legitimacy.

The schools issue demonstrated the difficulties facing supporters of a "double majority." In 1841, the Common School Act for Canada West had established the right of religious minorities to share in the provincial grant for schools. In 1853, the Liberal Hincks-Morin ministry, relying mainly on the vote of Canada East politicians, strengthened the government's commitment to separate schools in Canada West by explicitly exempting separate-school ratepayers from property taxes for the support of common schools. A majority in Canada West opposed the bill and railed against Canada East politicians who thought they could impose legislation upon Canada West. Ten years later, a bill to allow Canada West's separate schools to license their own teachers passed because once again francophones in Canada East provided a massive vote in favour of a bill that the majority of elected members from Canada West opposed.

There were additional problems facing the administration of the Canadas. Under the Guarantee Act of 1849, several railways had received bond guarantees from an Assembly filled with railway investors. The most costly railway by far was the Grand Trunk, whose investors included major British banking concerns and the usual crew of Canadian politicians. In 1853, the Grand Trunk, which initially sought only to build lines from Montreal to Hamilton, recognized the need for an Atlantic link and bought the assets of the St Lawrence and Atlantic Railway, in which leading Conservative politician and railway promoter Alexander Galt was a leading figure. By 1859, the Grand Trunk was a nest of corruption and an enormous drain on the public purse. Increasingly, Canada's British creditors balked at making loans to a colony that could not live within its own means and had no apparent plans to expand its revenue base.

THE CANADIANS MAKE THEIR MOVE

By 1864, the political and economic impasse caused a coterie of leading Canadian politicians to look to a confederation of the British North American colonies as a solution. At George Brown's instigation, the assembly appointed a constitutional committee to examine options for the Canadas. In June 1864, the committee issued a report calling for consideration of a federal union of the British North American colonies.

This was not the first time that Brown had made such a proposal. In 1860, he had introduced a motion into the Assembly for the adoption of a federal union of the two Canadas: a central government with specific responsibilities for legislation would continue to exist, but provincial governments with their own responsibilities would also be created. Brown hoped that by making the provincial governments powerful enough—for example, by giving them complete control over education—Canada East's ability to impose legislation on Canada West would be greatly reduced. At the time, no member from Canada East was willing to support such a proposal, but the continuing impasse in the legislature gave Brown another chance to achieve his goals.

After the release of the Assembly committee's report in June 1864, Brown approached George-Étienne Cartier and John A. Macdonald, who were

biography

John A. Macdonald: The Changing Face of Toryism in Canada West

John A. Macdonald was born in Glasgow, Scotland, in 1815 and immigrated to Upper Canada with his parents five years later. The family moved to Kingston, and his father's merchant activities were sufficiently successful for young John A. to attend private and grammar schools. At age 15, he began to article in a Kingston law office, and he was called to the bar in 1836. An active Presbyterian and Kingston clubman, Macdonald became the solicitor for several major financial concerns by the early 1840s. His entry into politics in 1843 began with a successful run for the Kingston town council, followed by election to the Assembly in 1844.

When Macdonald was first elected as a Conservative in 1844, he opposed responsible government, the secularization of clergy reserves, and the broadening of the franchise. He argued that the democratic changes favoured by Reformers would weaken both the British connection and property rights. Although his support of the British connection and of the propertied classes never waned, he adapted quickly to the introduction of responsible government in 1848. He recognized that pragmatism, patronage, and party organization could keep conservatism alive in an age of democratic competition.

Appointed to the cabinet in 1847, he was Canada West's first minister, chief Conservative strategist, fundraiser, and campaign organizer by 1856. No candidate could be elected by a Conservative riding in Canada West without Macdonald's approval. He developed a centralized system of government patronage that guaranteed the personal loyalty of many state employees and recipients of government contracts. Attempting to create a mass base for conservatism, he appealed for support to leaders of disparate groups such as the Orange Order and the Catholic and Methodist churches. He not only dropped his opposition to secularization of clergy reserves but also, as attorney general, steered the government's legislation on the subject through the Assembly in 1854. Such a pragmatic change of heart would be repeated 10 years later when, in the interests of retaining office, he agreed to lead the fight for a Confederation agreement—a project he had

John A. Macdonald.

National Archives of Canada/PA-12848

denounced just days before becoming one of the leaders of a coalition government formed for the sole end of achieving confederation of the British North American colonies.

As Canada's first prime minister, Macdonald proved himself to be a quick-witted and practical politician, but he was overly fond of alcohol. His drinking frequently caused embarrassment for his government and may well have contributed to the mismanagement of the railway negotiations that resulted in the Pacific Scandal and the defeat of his government in 1873. Nevertheless, Macdonald remained leader of the Conservative Party and led it to victory in 1878. Championing a national policy of industrialization, railway building, and western settlement, he remained in office until his death in May 1891.

having great difficulty establishing a functioning majority in the Assembly, with the idea of a "Great Coalition" whose goal would be the achievement of British North American Confederation. The coalition would include the supporters of Cartier, Macdonald, and Brown and would thus command a strong majority in both sections of Canada. Only the recalcitrant Rouges would be excluded. Macdonald would remain the government leader for Canada West.

Macdonald favoured a legislative union over the federal union proposed by Brown. He was also initially lukewarm to the proposal for annexing the Hudson's Bay Company territories to Canada. But he wanted a political system that worked and he wanted to remain in office. He and Cartier quickly came to terms with Brown, and a new ministry dedicated to achieving a confederation of the British American colonies was sworn in.

Macdonald was a consummate political organizer whose persuasive skills could only be an asset in promoting his newfound project. Like most leading Canadian politicians of the period, Macdonald was a businessman-politician. Both a workaholic and an alcoholic, he was a lawyer with directorships in banks, insurance, railway, and utility companies in his home constituency of Kingston. Like Brown, he came to view the Northwest as a vast territory awaiting Upper Canadian settlement and the Maritimes as another potential market for Upper Canadian manufactures. As it happened, the premiers of the Maritime colonies were also considering new political arrangements.

GREAT EXPECTATIONS IN THE MARITIMES

In the Atlantic region, Nova Scotia and New Brunswick were the most receptive to the idea of British North American union. The healthy state of the coastal trade, shipbuilding, and the fisheries as well as increased demand for Nova Scotia coal and New Brunswick lumber fattened the treasuries of these two colonies but, like their Canadian counterparts, elected governments in the two colonies chose to spend much of this money on the building of railways and soon found themselves with revenue shortfalls.

Joseph Howe was the towering figure in the Reform ministries that prevailed in Nova Scotia before the Conservatives won a clear legislative majority in 1863. By that time, Howe's railway projects had contributed heavily to a provincial debt of $4.5 million. His favourite venture was a line linking Halifax to the St Lawrence, generally referred to as the Intercolonial Railway. Howe believed the Intercolonial would provide a military highway for Britain in time of war as well as stimulate British North American trade, but the project failed to attract the necessary investment from British financiers.

By 1864 Charles Tupper, a medical doctor who had represented Cumberland County since 1855, had emerged as Conservative Party leader and premier of Nova Scotia. The Conservatives continued the Reformers' commitment to railway development and also passed legislation to implement a public school system, thereby pushing up the public debt. With substantial investments in the county's coal mines, Tupper was deeply concerned when the Americans decided to abrogate the Reciprocity Treaty. An intercolonial railway might provide new markets for Nova Scotia's coal, but the colony was in no position financially to proceed. Ambitious for his province, Tupper inadvertently started the confederation ball rolling by promoting the idea of Maritime Union. Early in 1864, the issue was debated in the Nova Scotia Assembly, which agreed to send delegates to a conference on the subject.

New Brunswick politicians were receptive to the idea of Maritime Union and, like Nova Scotia, were eager to pursue railway development. In the 1850s, the province had followed a pied piper from Maine named John Alfred Poor, who was promoting a railway to link Maine with the Maritimes. When Poor declared bankruptcy in 1855, the colony managed to complete a line linking Shediac to Saint John but the extension into the United States was put on hold. Samuel Leonard Tilley, temperance leader and former apothecary, became premier in 1861. Like Tupper, he wanted to press forward with the Intercolonial, but with a $5-million railway debt and annual revenues of only $600 000, the legislature voted in 1862 against any new railway construction.

Prince Edward Island built no railways until 1871 and for a time its Assembly had increasing revenues at

Joseph Howe (left) and George Brown (right).

its disposal, chiefly because reciprocity increased demand for the island's potatoes and fish. Indeed, in the years 1855 to 1865, exports to the United States as a proportion of all island exports grew from 22 percent to 42 percent. In 1866, the figure fell to 9 percent. The land question still nagged at successive island administrations. In the 1850s, Liberal premier George Coles used provincial revenues to enable some tenants to become landowners, but this policy only heightened the sense of grievance of those still living as tenants.

In 1864, when the Conservative Protestant-dominated government on the island proved slow in pressing for more land reform, a Tenant League was formed. The league crossed denominational barriers, and its members, who supported a tenant takeover of rented land with rates of compensation to landlords to be set by townships, vowed to pay no further rents. Their collective action to resist the rent collectors resulted in the government using soldiers to serve writs on tenants in arrears and to repress the league. With the land issue on the minds of most islanders, the Maritime Union proposal fell on stony ground.

Party loyalties in Newfoundland, as in Prince Edward Island, had a strong denominational flavour, with the Liberals mainly Catholic and the Conservatives exclusively Protestant. In an effort to reduce sectarian tensions, politicians on both sides of the Assembly agreed in the 1860s to provide public support to both Protestant and Catholic schools and to split civil-service positions in proportion to the numbers of Catholics and Protestants. Newfoundland's flagging economy caused Premier Hugh Hoyles to take an interest in the idea of a union of the Atlantic colonies— Newfoundland, however, was not invited to the conference on Maritime union planned for Charlottetown in 1864.

EXTERNAL PRESSURES

The Colonial Office watched developments in the British North American colonies with great interest. By the 1860s, British governments, whether Liberal or Conservative, were eager to reduce the costs of colonial administration and military protection. Political union of the colonies seemed to be a step in the right direction. At the very least, it would enable the Colonial Office to deal with one government rather than many.

Edward Cardwell, who became colonial secretary in March 1864, enthusiastically supported the Canadian initiative for union of the British North American colonies. Regarding Britain's white-settler colonies as unnecessary financial burdens on the British treasury, he was particularly eager to see the colonies shoulder a greater share of their own defence costs. The defence issue was driven home to British North Americans by the American Civil War (1861–65), which pitted the slave-holding South against the industrial North. As the war dragged on, a number of incidents on the high seas and along the border helped to increase tensions between Britain and the North and exposed the vulnerability of the British North American colonies.

MORE TO THE STORY

Canadians and the American Civil War

An estimated 40 000 to 50 000 British North American men took part in the American Civil War, many of them having emigrated to the United States before the war started. While they served on both sides of the conflict, more enlisted in the Northern forces, both because they lived in closer proximity to that region, and because they tended to favour the anti-slavery cause. Among them was Calixa Lavallée, later the composer of "O Canada." Born at Verchères, Quebec, in 1842, Lavallée had lived in the United States since 1857 and enlisted in the Union army in 1861.

A few British North American women also served in the war. A most unusual combatant was Sarah Emma Emmonds. An anti-slavery advocate from New Brunswick, Emmonds posed as a man and enlisted in the Union army in 1861. Apart from her role in combat, Emmonds served the Northern cause as a "male" nurse, a spy, and a general's aide. Her former comrades-in-arms did not discover her true identity until a regimental reunion in 1884. By that time, Emmonds had married and settled in the United States.

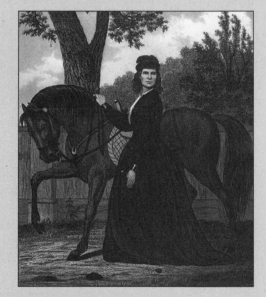

Sarah Emmonds, nurse and spy in the Union army.

Metropolitan Toronto Reference Library

In November 1861, a Northern naval ship seized the *Trent*, a British steamer en route from Cuba to Britain, and arrested two Confederate agents aboard. The North eventually yielded to Britain's protests and released the two agents, but tensions remained high. Since war with the United States was a distinct possibility, Great Britain felt obliged to send 15 000 troops to British North America to supplement the 3000 soldiers already stationed there. The Colonial Office nevertheless served notice to the colonies in 1864 that troops would soon be withdrawn and that the colonists were responsible for their own defence.

Meanwhile, British-built destroyers purchased by the Confederacy, including the *Alabama*, the *Florida*, and the *Shenandoah*, sank over 100 vessels. The North in turn pursued Confederate ships into British waters. Border raids conducted by southern agents from within British North America also strained relations. The US government was livid in 1864 when a Montreal magistrate set free Confederate agents who had robbed three banks in St Albans, Vermont, and then crossed back into Canada.

While military goals dominated Colonial Office policy in the period when the colonies debated Confederation, there were also economic interests pressing for British North American union. The British financiers who bought the Hudson's Bay Company in 1863 hoped to make a fortune when the expansion-minded Canadians incorporated the Northwest into their union. Only the political impasse in the United Province of Canada and the railway debt impeded efforts to develop the West for agricultural settlement. A new union with a strong central government might be more efficient.

American pressure also influenced the Confederation debate. In 1863, the United States warned that it would not renew the Reciprocity agreement after it expired in 1866. The treaty had encouraged the colonies to integrate their economies with that of the United States, and its termination struck fear in the hearts of colonial producers. While most colonial politicians supported free trade with the United States, many of them began to see a united British North America as an economic alternative to the American embrace.

The military threat posed by a triumphant United States also preyed on colonial minds. Confederation, it was argued, would make it easier for the colonials to defend themselves against any attempt by the Americans to annex Canada by force. Fears of such expansionism were not unfounded. The United States had, in recent memory, conquered large sections of Mexican territory, and several American statesmen were calling for the annexation of the Hudson's Bay Company's empire in the West. In the minds of some expansionists, it was the "manifest destiny" of the United States to dominate the entire North American continent. It was in this context of crisis and change that colonial politicians came together to discuss colonial union in 1864.

PLANNING CONFEDERATION

When the Canadians asked to attend the conference on Maritime union, lieutenant-governors in Nova Scotia and New Brunswick used their influence to ensure that the event went ahead. In an effort to get the support of Prince Edward Islanders, as well as to make it easier for the Canadians who would come down the St Lawrence by ship, Charlottetown was chosen as the site of the proposed meeting on 1 September 1864.

The Charlottetown Conference in September 1864 quickly shelved discussion of Maritime union to focus on Canada's proposal for a British North American federation. The delegates agreed to reassemble in Quebec City in October to produce a detailed proposal that could be presented to their respective legislatures. Representatives from Newfoundland joined the Quebec Conference, where the basis of union was hammered out.

The major issue was how much power to delegate to the central government. Macdonald favoured a legislative union of the colonies, a constitutional arrangement that would have eliminated provincial legislatures and avoided the strife between state and federal authorities that seemed to plague the United States. Outside of Canada West, this approach met universal hostility. Each colony had interests that they wished to maintain within their own jurisdiction.

With a legislative union out of the question, Macdonald sought to ensure the primacy of the cen-

Prelude to Confederation: William Henry Pope welcomes delegates to the Charlottetown conference.

Courtesy of Rogers Communications Inc.

Under the Quebec agreement, power was to be divided between a federal government and provincial governments. The federal government had control over "peace, order and good government" in the new nation, and it was given authority over international and interprovincial trade; foreign policy and defence; criminal law; Indian affairs; currency and banking; and interprovincial transportation. The provinces could legislate on matters concerning "civil rights and property," which included control over commerce within their borders, natural resources and public lands, civil law, municipal administration, education, and social services. Federal and provincial governments would split authority in the areas of agriculture and immigration.

tral government in a federal union. All important economic and diplomatic matters, he argued, ought to be in federal hands, leaving matters of purely local concern, such as education and care of the indigent, to the provinces. Cartier and Brown supported Macdonald's position. The leaders of the Atlantic colonies were generally suspicious of the motives of the Canadians and their centralizing policies, but the views of the Canadians prevailed.

The agreement reached at Quebec City made provisions for the creation of two provinces, Quebec and Ontario, out of the United Province of Canada. Representation in the elected federal assembly (House of Commons) would be proportional to population. To appease complaints from the Maritimes that the smaller provinces would be powerless in the Commons, the plan also called for an appointed Senate that gave Quebec, Ontario, and the Maritimes equal representation.

Both levels of government would have taxing powers; however, only the federal government's powers in this area were unrestricted. Tariffs and excise duties, at the time the source of most income for colonies, could be collected only by the federal government. Loss of such revenues would be compensated by a federal per capita grant to the provinces.

A limit on provincial powers regarding education enshrined, in perpetuity, educational rights acquired by law or custom before Confederation. This protected the tax-supported separate schools of Canada West and the Protestant schools of Canada East. Attempts by Catholic minorities in the Maritimes to achieve guarantees for equality between secular and confessional schools failed, but groups that believed their rights had been violated by a province could ask the federal government for "remedial" legislation. French and English were made official languages in the House of Commons and federal courts, and

Quebec was to be recognized as bilingual, but the status of French outside Quebec was ignored, even by Quebec's francophone politicians.

SELLING CONFEDERATION

While most of the delegates who attended the Quebec Conference were sold on Confederation, it took three years to sell the idea to the voters back home and even then not everyone bought it. Two premiers would prove unable to bring their colonies into the union in 1867; a third lost an election over the Confederation issue in 1865; and one only managed to advance the idea by refusing to submit the Confederation proposals to a vote in the Assembly.

Given the growing emphasis on "responsible" government and democratic principles in the mid-nineteenth century, the premiers required, at a minimum, a majority vote from their legislatures. In Prince Edward Island, Premier John Hamilton Gray faced stiff opposition to the Quebec proposals, even within his own party. The Canadians, who had dominated the discussions in Quebec City, had made Gray's task impossible by rejecting Prince Edward Island's request for an extra seat in the House of Commons. According to the formula developed for Commons representation, the island received only five seats, an awkward number to divide among its three counties. The Quebec City delegates were also unwilling to find a solution to the island's land question. Following a debate in the Assembly, the Confederation proposal was defeated and Gray had little choice but to shelve the idea.

Premier Hoyles of Newfoundland was also unable to muster the votes needed in his province's legislature, and the issue was resolved in 1869 when the electorate decisively rejected a surrender of independence. Newfoundland supporters of union argued that it would provide new markets for local products as well as grants that would allow them to build roads and other public works. The importance of federal subsidies, however, had to be balanced against the likely costs to Newfoundlanders of paying taxes to build mainland railroads and support elaborate defence measures.

For merchants and shippers in Nova Scotia and New Brunswick, the agreement to transfer the right to impose tariffs to the federal government was a major cause for concern. They feared that their international trading interests would be jeopardized by the protectionist tendencies of the Canadians. Many Maritimers, including those who did not reject the notion of a confederation of the colonies out of hand, were appalled that the Quebec Resolutions granted all monetary and most fiscal powers to the federal government, which would be dominated by Quebec and Ontario. The argument that the colonies together could muster the military forces to fend off American invaders struck opponents as spurious: in their view it was the bellicose Canadians who had courted American hostility. Now, using their crushing majority in the House of Commons, the Canadians were about to drag Maritimers into their disputes.

Anti-Confederates in the Maritimes noted, with some justification, that Confederation was a scheme of Canadian politicians and business interests who regarded the proposed new nation as an extension of the boundaries of the United Canadas. By virtue of the concentration of over three-quarters of the colonial population within its territory, it would dominate the new federation. Moreover, anti-Confederates argued, the financial proposals in the Quebec Resolutions gave the provinces inadequate income to pay for the responsibilities assigned to them, such as schools, roads, and social services. The small population base in the Maritimes would mean that their provincial governments would have little money to work with. Although Maritimers desperately wanted to be connected to the other colonies by a railway, they saw little benefit coming their way from a line to the Pacific, or indeed from an agricultural frontier on the distant Prairies. Many Acadians and Irish Catholics in the region were suspicious, on principle, of any union that reflected British models in Ireland, Scotland, and Wales.

Premier Tilley, leader of a divided party, agreed to face the New Brunswick electorate in March 1865. The anti-Confederates, led by Albert J. Smith, won three-quarters of the legislative seats, but their victory was short-lived. In spring 1865, the American government gave notice of the abrogation of the Reciprocity Treaty. In December, the American wing of the Fenian

Brotherhood, a group dedicated to Irish independence, made a raid on New Brunswick from Maine. Fenian raids and rumours of impending raids sowed fear among all British North Americans and emphasized their dependence on British protection—protection that the British were loudly indicating could not continue indefinitely. In New Brunswick, Protestant pro-confederates, all the while seeking the support of the Catholic hierarchy for their cause, sowed suspicion among their co-religionists that Irish Catholics in the colony and American Fenians were in league.

British backing for Confederation played the major role in unravelling popular opposition to the project in New Brunswick. Lieutenant-Governor Arthur Gordon succeeded in winning support for the union from the Catholic bishops of the province as well as from the timber merchants. He also forced an election in May 1866 and left little doubt in the electorate's mind about what the mother country expected from loyal voters. This time Tilley's pro-confederates carried the day.

Like his counterparts in the other Maritime provinces, Premier Tupper of Nova Scotia soon found that he lacked the legislative majority to bring Nova Scotia into Confederation on the terms arrived at in Quebec City. While Tupper had powerful supporters, including the colony's religious leaders, he faced almost universal opposition from the merchants. This group soon aligned itself with former premier Joseph Howe. Tupper retreated from Confederation to the less-radical ground of Maritime union.

The new lieutenant-governor, Sir William Fenwick Williams, a Nova Scotia native, helped to get Confederation back on track. By twisting the arms of enough politicians, he convinced the cautious Tupper to risk a legislative showdown on the issue in April 1866. His task had been aided by John A. Macdonald's assurance that the building of the Intercolonial Railway would be guaranteed in the act of union of the colonies. The Confederation resolution introduced into the Nova Scotia legislature in April 1866 tactfully made no reference to the Quebec City plan. Authorizing only continued negotiation on the issue of British North American union, Tupper's resolution won majority support and a call for a referendum was rejected.

In the Canadas, there was neither a referendum nor an election on the Quebec proposals. Macdonald, Cartier, and Brown collectively controlled enough votes to win easy passage of a motion supporting Confederation both in the Legislative Assembly and in the Legislative Council. The anti-confederate opposition in the United Province was led by

Fenian raid, Fort Erie, Canada West, 1866. Although only a tiny minority of Irish Americans joined the Fenians, British North Americans in undefended border towns considered these armed bands of marauding soldiers to be a real threat to their lives and property.

National Archives of Canada/C18737

A.A. Dorion, the Rouge leader, and John Sandfield Macdonald, the leader of moderate reformers in Canada West. They had different reasons for rejecting the Quebec City resolutions. John Sandfield Macdonald had established a political fiefdom among the Scottish Highlanders of Stormont and Glengarry counties. For him, the proposed confederation detached the Ottawa Valley from the upper St Lawrence by dividing the United Province of Canada into two provinces. The region would exchange the political hegemony of Montreal for that of Toronto, to Macdonald's chagrin.

A.A. Dorion, by contrast, supported the division of the United Province of Canada into two provinces. Like many Canadiens he regretted the loss of a separate Lower Canada in 1840. Recognizing that Britain was still unlikely to grant Lower Canada independent status, he hoped that something approaching sovereignty might be achieved if a loose federal union between the two sections of the United Province replaced the union. Now, not only was a federal union with a strong central government being proposed, but the union was to include the largely English-speaking Atlantic colonies.

Fears that Canada East would be drowned in an English sea aroused Quebec nationalism and allowed the Rouges to get signatures for monster petitions against Confederation. In a speech to the assembly during the debate on the confederation motion in February 1865, Dorion made a last-ditch attempt to have the political impasse in the Canadas resolved by way of a loose federal union. Among other things, Dorion invoked a popular theme of anti-confederate spokesmen: the allegedly overweening influence of the Grand Trunk in the project. A large number of cabinet members were involved in the Grand Trunk, including Cartier, the railway's chief solicitor.

Economic arguments certainly were as important as political issues such as "rep by pop" in influencing the Canadian supporters of Confederation. In the assembly, the confederates argued forcefully that the Canadas would be the major economic beneficiaries of Confederation. Galt prophesied that the acquisition and settlement of the western territories would stimulate both manufacturing and mercantile activity in Quebec and Ontario. The Maritimes, too, would provide new markets for what would, after 1867, be Central Canada. Ontario farmers were particularly receptive to the economic arguments for Confederation because their eyes were fixed westwards: Assiniboia would provide agricultural opportunities for farmers' sons who faced hard times in Ontario after the most fertile lands were occupied.

In Canada East, outside of the business circles of the Grand Trunk and the Bank of Montreal, both of which saw Montreal as the metropolitan centre serving a developing West, there was little interest in the Northwest. Not only was it far away, but the Catholic missionaries had insisted for some time that its soil was inimical to agriculture. Confederation was sold in Canada East on political grounds as much as on its economic potential. To the Rouge claim that Confederation meant centralization, Cartier and the Bleus countered by focusing on the re-establishment of a separate province of Quebec. That province, because of the powers granted provincial governments, would be able to assure its continued French and Catholic character. The confederate cause was also supported by the Catholic Church, persuaded by guarantees in the Quebec City resolutions for continued public support of the separate school system in Ontario.

In the end, a majority of the elected members from each of the two sections of the Province of Canada voted in favour of Confederation. Even among the French-Canadian members, a small majority supported it, but popular enthusiasm for Confederation was largely confined to Canada West. In Canada East, as in New Brunswick, the acceptance of Confederation seemed to amount more to resignation than to a wholehearted embrace of the concept.

The Canadians, having first sponsored the idea of a confederation of the colonies, were determined to control its shape. At a third and final conference on Confederation held in London in the fall of 1866, the Canadian delegates resisted any substantive changes to the Quebec resolutions. The only major concessions to the Nova Scotia and New Brunswick delegates were a clause guaranteeing the construction of the Intercolonial "by the Government of Canada" and the addition of a few areas of jurisdiction, among them the fisheries, to the list of federal responsibilities.

biography

A.A. Dorion: The Changing Face of Quebec Liberalism

While Antoine-Aimé Dorion led the anti-Confederation forces in Canada East in the 1860s, he was no radical nationalist in the mould of the Patriotes of 1837. Rather, he was a moderate liberal who recognized the political realities of the post-rebellion period. He distanced himself from the anticlericalism of the early Rouge leadership and ignored campaigns for the complete dissolution of the union of the Canadas. He won considerable support from Montreal's English-speaking electors because he fought for development of the port of Montreal and improved trade with the United States. He had worked with the annexationists of 1849 and, over time, his close association with English speakers showed itself in a loss of facility in his first language.

As the son and grandson of Patriote assemblymen, Dorion had received an education in the classics at the Séminaire de Nicolet in the 1830s before articling in a law firm. Called to the bar in 1844, he became well-known in liberal circles in Montreal and in 1849 helped found the Club National Démocratique, an organization committed to universal male suffrage and state support for education. Elected as a Rouge in 1854, Dorion, a practising Catholic, attempted to alleviate church concerns about his party's goals. Nevertheless, church authorities were alarmed by his attempts to cooperate with the Reformers of Canada West, led by George Brown, who was hated by the Catholic hierarchy for his attacks on public subsidies for Catholic schools.

Dorion served in the short-lived pre-Confederation Liberal ministries. In October 1862, he resigned from the Liberal cabinet, accusing its members of being too uncritical of proposals for an intercolonial railway. From the late 1850s onwards, Dorion had advanced schemes for a federal union of the two sections of the United Province, in all

Antoine-Aimé Dorion.

National Archives of Canada/C23599

cases granting jurisdiction in most domestic areas to the provinces. For Dorion, the confederation agreement of 1864 represented a repudiation of his notions of a loose federation and less government funding to privately owned railway companies.

The Quebec resolutions thus modified became the basis for the British North America Act, which was passed by the British House of Commons, with little debate, in March 1867. On 1 July 1867, the "Dominion of Canada" officially came into being. "Dominion" was chosen as an alternative to the

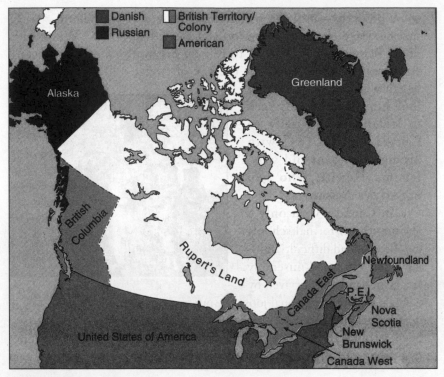

Map 14.1
British North America, 1866.

stronger term "kingdom," which might have offended the sensibilities of the United States. It was suggested by Tilley, who was inspired by his reading of Psalm 72: "And he shall also have dominion from sea to sea, and from the river unto the ends of the earth." Ottawa became the capital of the new political entity and the existing civil service of the United Province of Canada staffed the federal offices on Parliament Hill. Even the name of the new nation underscored the power relations upon which Confederation was built.

THE MEANING OF CONFEDERATION

"With the first dawn of this gladsome midsummer morn," trumpeted the Toronto *Globe*, "we hail this birthday of a new nationality. A united British America...takes its place among the nations of the world."[4] What was the character of this new nationality? Could its centre hold against the forces that seemed determined to tear it apart?

Focusing on railways that would link the former colonies, the supporters of Confederation evoked the progressive spirit of the age. Theirs was a vision of ever-expanding factories, whose goods would move by rail to every corner of the new dominion along with the products of farm, forest, sea, and mines, linking once-separate peoples with bonds of prosperity. Continuing ties with Britain would cement these bonds and discourage the expansionist tendencies of their aggressive southern neighbour.

Opponents of the proposals approved at Quebec City in 1864 usually embraced similar nineteenth-century capitalist notions of progress, and many of them were not averse to a federation on different terms. For them, the vision embodied in the British North America Act was a centralizing force, ignoring regional and linguistic communities. Confederation's supporters retorted that thinly populated colonies hugging the northern boundaries of the United States had no future as semi-independent entities in an era of capitalist expansionism.

Confederation was essentially a top-down exercise. The failure to hold referenda or elections (except in New Brunswick and Newfoundland) on the issue suggested a continuity with British North America's tradition of limited democracy. In the era of responsible government, the old oligarchies were forced to accept a degree of openness both in government and in the economy, but government remained in the hands of a small group of wealthy white men. Women played no role in the deliberations regarding the new constitution, and the document was silent on issues related to gender; patriarchy was an assumed part of the "new nationality." First Nations peoples were similarly excluded from participation. The BNA Act recognized their existence only to the extent of giving the federal authorities responsibility for their welfare.

CONCLUSION

From the beginnings of human occupation of what is now Canada, the peoples living there had shaped a multitude of societies, sometimes in harmony with nature, sometimes in blind disregard of nature's limits. Collectively they would also shape the "new nationality"—in reality a gathering of nationalities within a single nation-state. The sun that shone brilliantly in clear blue skies over most of the new country on 1 July 1867 seemed to announce new beginnings, but the people of the new nation were not marked out for a particular destiny. Rather they would continue to shape their own destinies, both in concert and in conflict with others. Confederation on 1 July 1867 was simply a document and a territorial map; in the days and years following, the peoples of the new nation-state would define, through their struggles, the real shape of the new nation.

A Historiographical Debate

Economic Elites and Confederation

The emergence of Canada as a modern state is inevitably a part of the spread of industrialism and capitalism. Confederation became an effective credit institution with the demands for long-term securities which accompanied the spread of industrialism especially as shown in transportation. The rise of Canada was in a sense the result of the demand for adequate imperial cost accounting which arose with Gladstonian Liberalism.[5]

This unlovely account of the Canadian Confederation movement was provided in 1933 by Harold Innis, the dean of Canada's economic historians. According to Innis, British financial interests required the creation of the Canadian state to ensure protection for railway investments in British North America. Most scholars agree that economic elites and economic arguments provided the real impetus for the Confederation movement. They differ, however, on whether British or Canadian capitalists had the greatest impact on that movement.

The economic historian Vernon Fowke, while acknowledging the role of Canadian and Maritime economic interests in pursuing a confederation agreement, also stresses the role of British capitalists in promoting the project. According to Fowke, the British politician-businessman Edward W. Watkin exemplified imperial attitudes to the economic potential of Confederation. Watkin "accepted the task of salvaging the finances of the newly constructed Grand Trunk Railway for its British owners," but only after "exacting the pledge that the Imperial government would give consideration to a scheme for the union of the British American colonies to be followed eventually by a railway from coast to coast."[6] Fowke says that Watkin's influence was evident in the Quebec City round of negotiations, which devised the terms of the new constitution. Watkin also led the groups that bought controlling interest in the Hudson's Bay Company in 1863, removing that firm as a possible obstacle to a takeover of the territories north and west of the United Province of Canada.

For Watkin, a railway across Canada would be simply a means of linking British trade with China, Japan, India, and California and a stimulus to natural development (mainly resource extraction). Above all, he foresaw the Grand Trunk Railway surviving because of the international commerce that this company would come to handle. Railway investors within Canada and the Maritimes, generally men with important political connections, also saw economic merit in the notion of a British North American federation. In Canada, the impending end of reciprocity and the prospect of having to rely on the tiny population base of British North America caused many businessmen to look to Confederation to produce a viable alternative to existing economic arrangements. But what alternative did they seek?

Economic historian R.T. Naylor argues that the Canadian promoters of Confederation, like their British counterparts, envisioned profitable exploitation of resources rather than the development of manufacturing as the aim of the new nation:

> Far from being the response of a rising industrial capitalism striving to break down intercolonial tariff walls, Confederation and the national policy were the work of the descendants of the mercantile class which had aligned itself with the Colonial Office in 1837 to crush the indigenous petite bourgeoisie and nascent industrialists.... The direct line of descent runs from merchant capital, not to industrial capital but to banking and finance, railways, utilities, land speculation, and so on.[7]

This characterization of the Canadian business interests supporting Confederation has been contested. The railway companies were vertically integrated operations involved not only in moving goods but also in many manufacturing activities. The Grand Trunk and the Great Western built rail cars and locomotives as well as the machinery required in railway construction.

Apart from the railway executives, whose interests appear to have been both industrial and commercial, there were many businessmen prominent in the Confederation movement whose interests seemed to straddle mercantile and manufacturing activity. George Brown and Charles Tupper, as businessmen, were certainly in this category.

As for those whose main field of activity was manufacturing, key elements favoured the project for British North American unity. In Saint John, for example, most of the principal manufacturers as well as the master tradesmen signed a pro-Confederation address that a local newspaper reproduced before the Confederation election in the colony in 1865. The signatories believed that the railway construction promised in the Quebec resolutions would "enable our rising manufacturers to take a firm stand, and instead of the periodical stagnation of trade caused by the fluctuations of our only articles of export—Lumber and Ships—we shall have manufactures that will be a continual source of prosperity, not affected by the changes in the European Market, and giving our working people employment all the year round."[8] By contrast, small manufacturers in Prince Edward Island and parts of Nova Scotia resisted plans for a common British North American market as a threat to local tariffs and therefore local and international markets.

It is difficult to draw a clear dividing line between business supporters and opponents of Confederation. Attitudes to publicly subsidized railway projects, however, based on the perceived usefulness of such projects to a particular business, were often pivotal in the positions taken on Confederation: those who believed that railway extension would enhance their economic futures usually supported Confederation, while advocates of laissez-faire railway development usually opposed the Quebec City resolutions.

NOTES

1 P.B. Waite, *The Life and Times of Confederation 1864–1867: Politics, Newspapers, and the Union of British North America* (Toronto: University of Toronto Press, 1962) 156.

2 Quoted in James L. Sturgis, "The Opposition to Confederation in Nova Scotia, 1864–1868," in *The Causes of Canadian Confederation*, ed. Ged Martin (Fredericton: Acadiensis Press, 1990) 125.

3 Alexander Morris, *The Hudson's Bay and Pacific Territories* (Montreal: John Lovell, 1959).

4 Waite, *The Life and Times of Confederation*, 322.

5 Quoted in Tom Traves, "Business-Government Relations in Canadian History," in *Government and Enterprise in Canada*, ed. K.J. Rea and Nelson Wiseman (Toronto: Methuen, 1985) 13–14.

6 Vernon C. Fowke, *The National Policy and the Wheat Economy* (Toronto: University of Toronto Press, 1973) 31.

7 R.T. Naylor, "The Rise and Fall of the Third Commercial Empire of the St Lawrence," in *Capitalism and the National Question in Canada*, ed. Gary Teeple (Toronto: University of Toronto Press, 1972) 16.

8 Quoted in Rosemarie Langhout, "About Face," *Horizons Canada* 53 (1986): 1252.

SELECTED READING

The political and economic history of the Confederation years is surveyed in W.L. Morton, *The Critical Years: The Union of British North America, 1857–1873* (Toronto: McClelland and Stewart, 1964). Stanley Ryerson's *Unequal Union: Roots of Crisis in the Canadas* (Toronto: Progress Books, 1968) provides a Marxist perspective on the period. Insights into the state of the public accounts in the United Province of Canada and its influence on political developments are found in Michael Piva, *The Borrowing Process: Public Finance in the Province of Canada, 1840–1867* (Ottawa: University of Ottawa Press, 1992). The years immediately preceding Confederation are examined closely in P.B. Waite, *The Life and Times of Confederation, 1864–1867: Politics, Newspapers, and the Union of British North America* (Toronto: University of Toronto Press, 1962) and Donald Creighton, *The Road to Confederation: The Emergence of Canada 1863–1867* (Toronto: Macmillan, 1964). Several important essays on Confederation appear in Ramsay Cook, ed., *Confederation* (Toronto: University of Toronto Press, 1967) and Ged Martin, ed., *The Causes of Canadian Confederation* (Fredericton: Acadiensis Press, 1990). See also Phillip A. Buckner, "The 1860s: An End and a Beginning," in *The Atlantic Region to Confederation: A History*, ed. Phillip A. Buckner and John G. Reid (Toronto: University of Toronto Press, 1994).

On Canadians' attitudes toward slavery and the American Civil War, see Tom Brooks and Robert Trueman, *Anxious for a Little War: The Involvement of Canadians in the Civil War in the United States* (Toronto: WWEC, 1993); Allen P. Stouffer, *The Light of Nature and the Law of God: Antislavery in Ontario, 1833–1877* (Montreal: McGill-Queen's University Press, 1992); and Greg Marquis, *In Armageddon's Shadow: the Civil War and Canada's Maritime Provinces* (Halifax: Gorsebrook Institute for Atlantic Canadian Studies, St. Mary's University; Montreal: McGill-Queen's University Press: 1998).

Quebec attitudes to Confederation are discussed in A.I. Silver, *The French-Canadian Idea of Confederation, 1864–1900* (Toronto: University of Toronto Press, 1982). Quebec society at the time of Confederation is analyzed in Paul-André Linteau, René Durocher, and Jean-Claude Robert, *Quebec: A History, 1867–1929* (Toronto: Lorimer, 1983). The key Quebec pro-confederate politicians are the subjects of critical biographies: Brian Young, *George-Étienne Cartier: Montreal Bourgeois* (Montreal: McGill-Queen's University Press, 1981) and A.A. den Otter, *Civilizing the West: The Galts and the Development of Western Canada* (Edmonton: University of Alberta Press, 1982). Ontario's key Confederation politicians are also the subjects of biographies. The major biography of John A. Macdonald is D.G. Creighton's laudatory two-volume *John A. Macdonald* (Toronto: Macmillan, 1965). George Brown's political and journalistic career is traced in a two-part biography, *Brown of the Globe* (Toronto: Macmillan, 1959), by J.M.S. Careless.

Two books edited by George Rawlyk, *The Atlantic Provinces and the Problem of Confederation* (St John's: Breakwater, 1980) and *Historical Essays on the Atlantic Provinces* (Ottawa: Carleton University Press, 1967), contain articles on the Confederation period. Economic conditions in the region are treated in S.A. Saunders, *The Economic History of the Maritime Provinces* (Fredericton: Acadiensis Press, 1984). *Nova Scotia and Confederation, 1864–74*, by Kenneth G. Pryke (Toronto: University of Toronto Press, 1979) provides detail on Nova Scotia politics in the 1860s and 1870s. The leading anti-confederate is portrayed in J. Murray Beck, *Joseph Howe*, vol. 2, *The Briton Becomes Canadian, 1848–1873* (Montreal: McGill-Queen's University Press, 1983). New Brunswick politics during this period are discussed in W.S. MacNutt, *New Brunswick: A History, 1784–1867* (Toronto: Macmillan, 1984); William M. Baker, "Squelching the Disloyal, Fenian-Sympathizing Brood: T.W. Anglin and Confederation in New Brunswick, 1865–1866," *Canadian Historical Review* 55.2 (June 1974): 141–58; William M. Baker, *Timothy Warren Anglin, 1822–1896: Irish Catholic Canadian* (Toronto: University of Toronto Press, 1977); and Alfred G. Bailey, "The Basis and Persistence of Opposition to Confederation in New Brunswick," *Canadian Historical Review* 23.4 (Dec. 1942): 374–97. Prince Edward Island politics are discussed in Ian Ross Robertson, "Prince Edward Island Politics in the 1860s," *Acadiensis* 15.1 (Autumn 1985): 35–58; David Weale and Harry Baglole, *The Island and Confederation: The End of an Era* (Summerside, PEI: Williams and Crue, 1973); and F.W.P. Bolger, *Prince Edward Island and Confederation* (Charlottetown: St Dunstan's University Press, 1964). On Newfoundland's rejection of Confederation, see James Hiller, "Confederation Defeated: The Newfoundland Election of 1869," in *Newfoundland in the Nineteenth and Twentieth Centuries: Essays in Interpretation*, ed. James Hiller and Peter Neary (Toronto: University of Toronto Press, 1980) 67–94. Newfoundland politics in the period are discussed in S.J. Noel, *Politics of Newfoundland* (Toronto: University of Toronto Press, 1971).

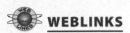
WEBLINKS

CONFEDERATION
www.nlc-bnc.ca/2/18/index-e.html

This site describes the path to Canadian Confederation, noting the influence of the American Civil War. It contains links to relevant historical documents, key terms, notable public figures, a bibliography, and maps outlining the changing shape of Canada from the seventeenth century to the present.

AMERICAN CIVIL WAR
www.cwc.lsu.edu/cwc/civlink.htm

The site of the United States Civil War Center contains a list of over 7000 thematic links to Civil War resources on the Internet.

GEORGE-ÉTIENNE CARTIER
http://collections.ic.gc.ca/charlottetown/fathers/cartier.html

This site on the Charlottetown Conference of 1864 offers a profile of Cartier. Numerous internal links are available.

GEORGE BROWN
http://collections.ic.gc.ca/charlottetown/fathers/brown.html

This site provides an overview of George Brown's career, the Charlottetown Conference, and several useful links.

SAMUEL LEONARD TILLEY
http://collections.ic.gc.ca/charlottetown/fathers/tilley.html

This site offers a brief profile of Tilley and his political career.

PART IV SUMMARY

THE YEARS PRECEDING CONFEDERATION WERE MARKED by an increasing emphasis on individualism and the virtues of the marketplace as well as by a growing reliance on the state to promote economic development and social compliance with the ways of the new economic order. In their private lives, British North Americans struggled to reconcile traditional religious beliefs and social values with new concepts represented by Darwinism, consumerism, and class conflict. As the financial costs of going it alone became clear, support grew for a union of the colonies to produce a new nation with a federal government capable of undertaking projects, such as the development of the West, for the economic benefit of everyone. Time would tell whether a Confederation of four eastern colonies could carry out such an ambitious project and just who would benefit.

PART V

INVENTING CANADA, 1867–1914

Between 1867 and 1914 Canada was transformed from a string of isolated British colonies into a nation that was ready to make its mark on the world's stage during the First World War (1914–18). In this period, immigration, western settlement, the growth of cities, and new social values signalled the onset of what historians call the "modern age." Two trends are particularly noteworthy: first, the emergence of the state—federal, provincial, and municipal—as a major force in nation-building; and second, the role of industrial capitalism in defining Canada's economic and social realities. Together, the interventionist state and vigorous industrial growth changed the lives of all Canadians and "invented" a nation that was vastly different from the one that had come together so inauspiciously in 1867.

Nation-Building, 1867–1896

On 1 July 1867, Canadians celebrated Confederation Day. The *Globe* described festivities in the city of Toronto:

On the roofs of houses and elsewhere, in all directions, flagpoles were being hoisted into the air to do their part in the celebration of Confederation Day. A programme of celebration arranged by the Government included a grand review of Her Majesty's Troops, regulars and volunteers, on the Bathurst Street Commons at ten a.m. At three o'clock there was a grand Balloon Ascension from Queen's Park. In the evening there were concerts given by the Bands of the Tenth Royal Regiment and the Grand Trunk Brigade in the form of a grand promenade at Queen's Park accompanied by the most magnificent display of fireworks ever exhibited in Canada.

The *Globe* also recorded that "an immense ox" was roasted and the meat "distributed among the poor of the city."

Some communities in the new Dominion marked Confederation differently. In Nova Scotia and New Brunswick, several editors printed black banners on the front pages of their newspapers, and die-hard anti-Confederates hoisted black flags. Francophones in Quebec were also restrained in their enthusiasm.

Quebec City at the time of Confederation.

National Library of Canada/C-117822

CONSOLIDATING THE UNION

The task of choosing the nation's first prime minister fell to the governor general, Lord Monck. He selected John A. Macdonald. If anyone could bring the scattered elements of the new nation together, it would be John A., whose ability to charm his opponents and sustain the faithful with well-placed patronage was legendary.

Macdonald had hoped to maintain the coalition that had championed Confederation, but there were defections. In 1865, George Brown resigned over disagreements regarding the handling of negotiations to renew the reciprocity treaty with the United States. Macdonald persuaded the remaining Reform ministers in the coalition to support his leadership, and he also maintained his partnership with the Bleus led by George-Étienne Cartier. Samuel Leonard Tilley, the Liberal premier of New Brunswick, and Charles Tupper, Conservative premier of Nova Scotia, also agreed to bring their pro-Confederation forces into Macdonald's Liberal-Conservative party.

The regional, religious, and cultural issues that plagued the colonies before Confederation lingered. When Macdonald created his first cabinet, he was obliged to accommodate various interests—Protestant and Catholic, French and English, province and nation. He did well enough that the new ministry carried 108 of the 180 seats in the first election. Almost half of the popular vote, however, went to candidates opposed to the Liberal-Conservatives. The opposition included George Brown's Reformers, A. A. Dorion's Rouges, and the Maritime anti-Confederates. In time, they would form a coalition that would become the basis of the Liberal Party.

Voting in the New Dominion

In 1867, elections were quite different from today's elections. Voters openly announced the candidate of their choice, under the watchful eyes of relatives, employers, and party workers. Violence between supporters of opposing sides was not uncommon. For example, no member was elected for the riding of Kamouraska in 1867 because of riots that made polling impossible.

The lack of a national franchise policy also caused difficulties. From 1867 to 1884, provincial election lists determined who could vote. Except in Nova Scotia, where voting occurred simultaneously in all constituencies, elections were conducted at different times across the Dominion. Thus, voting took place from late July to September in the 180 constituencies electing members to the first Canadian House of Commons. As government leader, Macdonald could ensure that elections were held in the easy ridings first so that momentum could be used to sway votes in the constituencies where government support was uncertain.

The number of people eligible to cast ballots was relatively small. All provinces limited the vote to men over 21 who owned or rented property of a certain value. Status Indians, regarded as wards of the state, had no vote, and property qualifications disenfranchised most unskilled workers and farm labourers. As a result of gender, property, and age restrictions, only 15 percent of the Quebec population, for example, could vote in the provincial or federal elections in 1867, and only about 20 percent had this right by 1900. Today, by contrast, under universal suffrage for people over 18, almost 70 percent of the population can vote, with most of the disenfranchised being either children or immigrants who have not yet fulfilled the requirements for citizenship.

NOVA SCOTIA'S SECESSIONIST MOVEMENT

The election results highlighted regional divisions. Although the Liberal-Conservatives won handily in Ontario and Quebec, pro-Confederation candidates won barely half the seats in New Brunswick, while Tupper was the only government candidate elected in Nova Scotia. Tupper's Conservative government was also mauled in the elections to the provincial assembly. A Repeal League quickly formed, and Joseph Howe was dispatched to London to get permission for Nova Scotia to leave Confederation.

Responding to the threat of secession was difficult for Macdonald, whose vision of Confederation included incorporation of the Maritime colonies and the Northwest into a union dominated by the United Province of Canada. Nova Scotia's alienation only increased when Parliament opened on 8 November 1867. A majority of members endorsed a rise in the tariff rate from 10 to 15 percent, which pleased Montreal industrialists but angered Maritime commercial interests dependent on international trade.

In Great Britain, Howe's request for repeal fell on deaf ears. Accepting defeat, Howe began negotiating with the Canadians for better terms for Nova Scotia. Neither a populist nor a republican, Howe was repulsed by talk of popular revolt or annexation to the United States, which many Repealers saw as their only alternatives to the hated union. It was wiser, Howe reasoned, to make the best of a bad bargain than to risk the possibility of severing ties with the mother country.

Eventually, the federal government agreed to pay an additional $1 million of pre-Confederation Nova Scotia debt and to increase the province's annual grant by $82 698 per year for 10 years. Howe and Hugh MacDonald, another anti-Confederate from Nova Scotia, were given cabinet posts. Repeal sentiment remained strong, strengthening Howe, along with Tupper, as they urged their colleagues to move quickly on the construction of the Intercolonial Railway and to press for a new reciprocity treaty with the United States.

Macdonald hoped that negotiations between the United States and Great Britain to resolve difficulties resulting from the American Civil War would provide an opportunity to pressure the Americans to accept free trade. In 1871, he represented Canada in a British delegation that met with their American counterparts in Washington, but headway on tariffs was difficult in the face of a protectionist Republican Congress. The Treaty of Washington offered some relief to Canadians involved in the fisheries. Their catch was granted free entry into the United States, and financial compensation, to be decided by arbitration, would be forthcoming in return for American access to Canada's inshore waters.

There were cries of "sell-out" in Nova Scotia, and many Canadians felt that British negotiators had put imperial interests in securing good relations with the United States ahead of Canada's well-being. Still, much of the energy had gone out of Nova Scotia's fight, at least for the time being. In the 1872 election, two-thirds of Nova Scotia's Members of Parliament supported Macdonald.

ANNEXING THE NORTHWEST: THE RED RIVER REBELLION

The Macdonald government moved swiftly to transfer the Northwest to the new country. By 1869, an agreement had been reached with the Hudson's Bay Company to sell its claim to the land for £300 000 (about $1.5 million) and a grant to the company of one-twentieth of the land most suitable for farming. This agreement proved lucrative to the financiers who had bought control of the company in 1863 for about $7.5 million. They retained their fur-trading operations, and eventually netted $120 million from land sales.

The Métis and Aboriginal peoples were treated less generously. Eager to open the Northwest to immigrants, the federal government sent land surveyors to the Red River colony in August 1869. Consulted by neither the company nor the Canadians, the Métis feared the loss of the land they farmed.

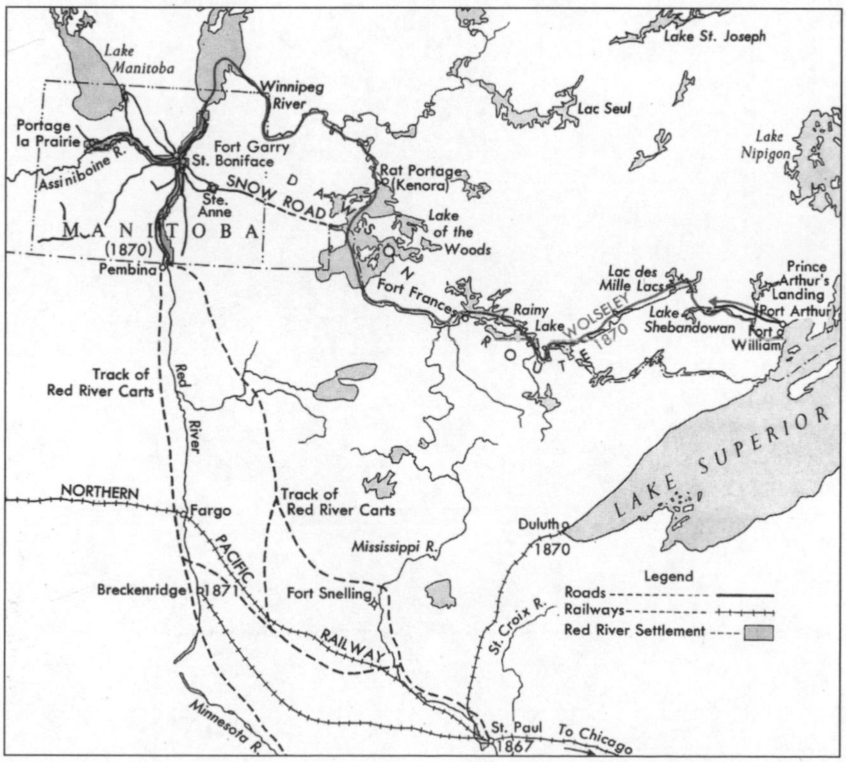

The behaviour of the Canadians already living in the Red River area reinforced Métis anxieties. The "Canadian Party" regarded Natives as uncivilized people whose presence in the region deterred European settlement. Although a minority in the community—that, according to the 1871 census, included 5757 French-speaking Métis, 4083 English-speaking Métis, 1500 whites, and 558 Natives—the "Canadians" had the ear of Ottawa. Many were land speculators who hoped to make their fortunes when Canada acquired the Northwest.

On 11 October 1869, a group of unarmed Métis stopped a road-building party from its work. Five days later, a Métis National Committee was formed to block Canada's takeover of Red River until guarantees for Métis land rights had been granted. As secretary to the committee, the Métis

Map 15.1
Red River colony and environs.

chose Louis Riel. The 25-year-old Riel had spent nearly 10 years in Catholic educational institutions in Quebec. Literate and articulate, he was seen as someone who could negotiate with the Canadians on their own terms.

Meanwhile, William McDougall, the Minister of Public Works in Macdonald's cabinet, was appointed the first lieutenant-governor of what became known as the Northwest Territories. Armed Métis thwarted McDougall's attempt to enter Hudson's Bay territory on 2 November. Early in December, the Métis established a provisional government under John Bruce and Louis Riel to coordinate resistance to Canadian imperialism.

The Canadian Party attempted to overthrow the provisional government, but they were no match for the well-organized Métis. One prisoner captured in an attempted insurrection in February 1870 was Thomas Scott, an Ontario Orangeman. Scott exhorted his fellow prisoners to overpower their guards and escape. Pressured by angry Métis guards, as well as by the challenge to his government's legitimacy, Riel ordered Scott executed in March 1870.

The situation was further complicated by the presence of American agents in Red River. Afraid that the United States would use the political crisis to seize control of the region, Macdonald reluctantly agreed to negotiate with representatives of the provisional government. They were led by Abbé N.J. Ritchot, who had Riel's confidence.

By May 1870, negotiations between the Canadian and provisional Red River governments concluded with an agreement that met most Métis demands. The Red River colony and its environs would become the

Louis Riel (second row, centre) with his provisional government.

National Archives of Canada/C6692

province of Manitoba, a tiny jurisdiction that initially encompassed only the area around Red River. Both English and French were officially recognized in legislative and court proceedings; denominational schools, Protestant and Catholic, would be maintained. Unlike other provinces, Manitoba would, until the federal government decided otherwise, have its land and other resources controlled by Ottawa. For the Métis, the major victory was the guarantee in the Manitoba Act that they would receive title for lands they currently farmed as well as for 1.4 million acres of farmland to be distributed to their children.

This victory proved hollow. Macdonald convinced British authorities to send a military expedition to Red River. Led by Colonel Garnet Wolseley, the army included in its ranks Ontario Orangemen who imposed a virtual reign of terror on the Métis. Riel fled to the United States, and other members of the provisional government went into hiding. Soon, white settlers poured into the province and received title for land, while the Métis were kept waiting for their grants. With the buffalo in Manitoba disappearing, no land grants in sight, and hostility from white immigrants, many Métis moved west to territory that is now part of Saskatchewan, where they could still hunt buffalo and establish communities under their own control.

THE INDIAN TREATIES

The Macdonald government hoped to avoid the Métis experience with the plains Natives. Between 1871 and 1877, seven treaties were concluded with Aboriginal peoples living east of the Rockies, whose estimated population was 34 000. Adams Archibald, the negotiator of Treaty One, outlined the intentions of the federal government: "Your Great Mother [Queen Victoria] wishes the good of all races under her sway. She wishes her red children to be happy and contented.... She would like them to adopt the habits of the whites, to till land and raise food, and store it up against a time of want."[1]

The Natives agreed to the treaties because they wanted guarantees for their future well-being which was threatened by the disappearance of the buffalo and the influx of settlers. The treaties established reserves where Natives could farm, and promised implements, seed, and training to launch them in their agricultural endeavours. Treaties also recognized traditional hunting and fishing rights.

The two sides interpreted treaty provisions differently. Indian commissioner Wemyss Simpson interpreted the Lower Fort Garry treaty to imply that implements and seed would be provided only when Natives had settled on reserves and built homes to demonstrate their readiness for an agricultural life. The distraught Lower Fort Garry Natives replied eloquently but futilely: "We cannot tear down trees and build huts with our teeth, we cannot break the prairie with our hands, nor reap the harvest when we have grown it with our knives."[2]

THE INDIAN ACT

In 1876, the federal government consolidated its policies with respect to Aboriginal peoples in the Indian Act. Its basic premise was that Natives remained incapable of integrating into "civilized" society and therefore needed supervision in their economic, political, and social activities.

The act replaced traditional political structures with band chiefs and councils chosen according to the legislation, and subjected all reserve activities to the supervision of white bureaucracies. In defining Indian status, the act made gender distinctions: the wives, widows, and children of registered men were accorded Indian status even if they had no Indian heritage; an Aboriginal woman who married a non-status man lost her status, as did her children. Later revisions of the act also denied status Indians the right to perform traditional religious practices or to drink alcohol.

The government's priority in the Northwest was European, not Aboriginal, settlement. In 1872, the Dominion Lands Act granted free homesteads of 160 acres to farmers who cleared 10 acres and built a home within three years of registering their intention to settle. In 1873, the North-West Mounted Police (NWMP) was established to maintain law and order in the Northwest and counter threats from American expansionists.

BRITISH COLUMBIA

Threats from the United States also stiffened Macdonald's resolve to negotiate the entry of British Columbia into Confederation. After the gold rush, both Vancouver Island and British Columbia were

Amor de Cosmos. In 1852, William Smith left his job in a Halifax grocery business for the gold fields of California, where he worked as a photographer and engaged in various speculative business ventures. He changed his name to Amor de Cosmos in 1854, claiming that the name "tells what I love most...order, beauty, the world, the universe." In 1858 he moved to Victoria, where he established a newspaper—the British Colonist—*and became involved in politics. A promoter of both responsible government and Confederation for his adopted province, he was premier of British Columbia from 1872 to 1874. He proved to be a poor politician and was defeated by the voters of Victoria in 1882 for advocating Canadian independence from Great Britain.*

National Archives of Canada/PA-025397

nearly bankrupt. The Colonial Office engineered their union in 1866, but, with combined debts of $1.3 million, the new colony of British Columbia was unable to initiate public projects. The jealousy between mainlanders and islanders further complicated the colony's politics. For two years New Westminster and Victoria fought to be the capital before Victoria prevailed.

By the 1870s, new economic activities had taken root on the West Coast, including coal mines in Nanaimo, sawmills along Alberni Canal and Burrard Inlet, a British naval base in Esquimalt, and small agricultural settlements scattered through the colony. While a few business people in Victoria called for British Columbia to join the United States, the proposal was denounced by the dominant British interests in the colony. The Canadian option was championed by Nova Scotia-born Amor de Cosmos, a Victoria-based newspaper editor whose adopted name reflected his flamboyant style.

Once the fate of the Northwest had been sealed, the Colonial Office encouraged British Columbia's entry into Confederation. The new lieutenant-governor, Andrew Musgrave, actively promoted the union. The colony's legislative council established terms for British Columbia's entry into Confederation: a wagon road connecting New Westminster to Fort Garry, with a railroad to follow in due course; the assumption by Canada of British Columbia's existing debt; and an annual grant of $100 000.

During negotiations held in June 1870 with council representatives, the Canadian delegation was led by George-Étienne Cartier. He accepted the British Columbian conditions and even agreed to complete the railway within 10 years of British Columbia joining Confederation. These generous terms raised eyebrows in Ottawa. British Columbia would have needed a non-Aboriginal population of 120 000 to justify its grant request. Instead, it had only about 10 500: 8576 Europeans, 1548 Chinese, and 462 African-origin residents. Despite these concerns, the Macdonald government stood by the agreement. British Columbia would give Canada a Pacific boundary and fulfil the Confederation promise of a dominion from sea to sea.

Elections in November 1870 gave every seat in the British Columbia legislature to supporters of Confederation. In June 1871, British Columbia became the sixth province of Canada. Few people in British Columbia—and certainly not the disfranchised Aboriginal peoples who made up 80 percent of the population—felt much attachment to Canada. The economic stimulus of the proposed railway and Canadian government grants made Confederation seem a lucrative economic arrangement that should not be rejected.

PRINCE EDWARD ISLAND

Similar economic reasons led Prince Edward Island into Confederation in 1873. When the Conservatives under James Pope took office in 1870, the island economy was stable, if not thriving. Its 94 021 people found export markets for the products of their farms and fisheries and, like other Maritimers, boasted a healthy shipbuilding industry. Only one thing was missing: railroads. An apostle of progress, Pope approved a costly line to link the island's communities. Subsequently faced with huge public debt, Pope argued that only by joining Canada and letting that country assume the island's debt could Islanders avoid financial disaster.

Once more the Americans were on the scene. General Benjamin Butler of Massachusetts came to the island in 1869 to negotiate a special trade deal, an apparent first step toward luring it into the American union. Although the American offers came to nothing, the Canadian government was spooked. Macdonald agreed not only to assume the railway debt and establish year-round communications between the island and the mainland, but also to buy out the remaining landlords so that tenants could become freeholders. With its interests thus addressed, Prince Edward Island became the seventh province of Canada in 1873.

NEWFOUNDLAND'S PERSPECTIVE

Unlike the other Atlantic colonies, Newfoundland faced neither an overwhelming debt nor intense British pressure to enter Confederation. The defence issue, which preoccupied leaders in the mainland colonies, inspired fears that the colony's young men would be conscripted to fight Canadian wars. Nevertheless, Conservative Premier Frederick Carter supported Confederation. In the months preceding the 1869 election, he persuaded the Assembly to pass draft terms for union, and negotiated an agreement with Canada.

Newfoundland voters were unpersuaded. Led by merchant Charles Fox Bennett, anti-Confederates won over two-thirds of the legislative seats. Several generations would pass before Newfoundlanders debated the issue of Confederation again. In the 1880s, railway mania swept Newfoundland with the usual accompanying public debt. Although Canada again put out feelers, local politicians refused to touch the Confederation issue.

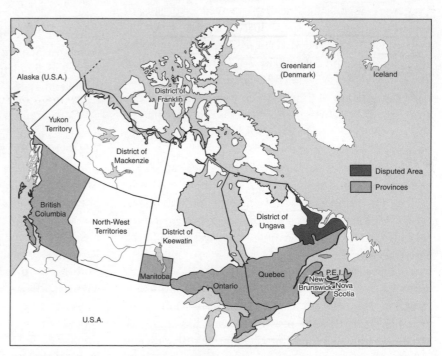

Map 15.2
Canada, 1882.

THE NORTH

In 1880, by an imperial order-in-council, the Arctic archipelago was added to Canadian jurisdiction as the District of Franklin. This move was precipitated by an American request in 1874 for mineral rights on Baffin Island. There was no thought of settling the region on the part of British or Canadian authorities. As one member of the Colonial Office remarked at the time, the main reason for turning the islands over to Canada was "to prevent the United States from claiming them, not from the likelihood of their being any value to Canada."[3]

THE PACIFIC SCANDAL

Macdonald's work to create a transcontinental nation did not win him widespread support in the 1872 election. Without the nine seats contributed by the new provinces of Manitoba and British Columbia, Macdonald would have had difficulty continuing to govern. His biggest threat came from Ontario where Alexander Mackenzie's Reformers—or Liberals, as they were increasingly called—revived criticisms of the Tories as corrupt spendthrifts and papist sympathizers. After the Red River uprising, sectarian issues intensified, and Ontario Liberals reminded Protestants that Macdonald had failed to bring the Métis murderers of Thomas Scott to justice. By contrast, opposition members from Quebec denounced Cartier for failing to settle Métis land claims or to win amnesty for Louis Riel.

Other issues surfaced during the campaign. Macdonald could not convince the United States to sign a new reciprocity agreement, a major item on the wish list of most primary producers. Nor, apparently, had his government determined who was to build the Pacific railway.

The desire to counter growing opposition support led Macdonald to indulge in activities that ultimately led to his downfall. In May 1871, the government introduced legislation to provide for building a railway to the Pacific. The bill offered extensive cash and land incentives to the successful bidder. Two companies sought the lucrative contract. One, headed by Ontario Senator David MacPherson, included leaders of the Toronto business community. The other, headed by Hugh Allan, president of Allan Steamship Lines, represented Montreal business interests and had backing from the Northern Pacific Railway in the United States. Attempts by Macdonald to have these two Canadian groups merge, and keep the Americans out, proved futile.

Cartier wished to see Montreal prevail over Toronto, but even he initially regarded Allan's demands as extreme. When Allan threatened to engineer his political defeat, a beleaguered and ailing Cartier capitulated. In return for Cartier's support in securing the railway contract, Allan contributed generously to the Conservative election effort. In February 1873, the Macdonald government named Allan as president of the Canadian Pacific Railway Company. Two months later, Lucius Huntington, a Liberal MP, charged that Allan had bought the charter with $360 000 in donations to the Conservative Party.

Macdonald reluctantly appointed a select committee to examine the charges. The Liberals apparently had a mole in the Conservative organization: incriminating letters and telegrams proved Cartier's corruption and left little doubt of Macdonald's. It was also revealed that behind Allan were American investors who would assume control of Canada's major railway company. Sensing that the government was doomed, many independents joined the Liberal opposition. On 5 November 1873, Macdonald resigned as prime minister.

THE LIBERALS AT THE HELM

Alexander Mackenzie formed the new government. A Highland Scot, stonemason, and Baptist, Mackenzie was also a teetotaller and workaholic. Mackenzie cobbled together a Liberal coalition consisting of Ontario Reformers, Quebec Rouges, moderate Liberals, and Maritimers of all political stripes disillusioned by Macdonald's government.

Hoping to use the Pacific Scandal to win majority support of his government, Mackenzie called an election for early 1874. He promised a new Pacific railway contract that would avoid large public expenditures for the benefit of private entrepreneurs. Emphasizing provincial rights and frugality, he presented a vision of the new dominion markedly at odds with Macdonald's "new nationality." Mackenzie won a majority of seats in every province except British Columbia.

Despite their strong mandate, the Liberals survived only one term in office. Their period in office coincided with a worldwide recession, which limited government revenues. When the United States rejected renewed efforts to negotiate a reciprocity treaty, the Liberals had no economic strategy other than retrenchment. It inspired little enthusiasm. British Columbia threatened secession if the federal government failed to follow Macdonald's railway timetable, and Canadians continued to move to the United States to find work.

The Liberal interlude nevertheless left its mark on the new nation. In addition to introducing electoral reforms that included simultaneous voting, the secret ballot, and trial of disputed elections by the courts, the Liberals tried to enlarge the powers of Canada within the British Empire. This was the special goal of Edward Blake, who served in several portfolios under Mackenzie's leadership. As minister of justice, Blake extended the nation's powers to create admiralty courts, exercise authority over shipping on the Great Lakes, and pardon criminals. He also established the Supreme Court of Canada in 1875 but failed in his attempts to make it, rather than the Judicial Committee of the Privy Council of Great Britain, the final court of appeal.

CANADA FIRST

Before joining Mackenzie's cabinet, Blake had associated himself briefly with the Canada First movement, dominated by Canadian nationalists based in Ontario. The Canada Firsters envisioned a more autonomous Anglo-Saxon, Protestant nation allied with Great Britain. While supporting policies that would give Canada greater political independence, they also hoped to inspire a national spirit that would triumph over the crass materialism that characterized the modern age.

The movement got underway following the assassination, in 1868, of D'Arcy McGee, a Conservative MP who played an influential role in promoting Confederation. When his death removed the most ar-

Alexander Mackenzie.

National Archives of Canada/C-020052

ticulate proponent of national idealism, a group of young men calling themselves Canada First decided to take action. The leading Canada Firsters included Ottawa civil servant Henry J. Morgan, Nova Scotia Coal Owners' Association lobbyist Robert Grant Haliburton, poet Charles Mair, militia officer and lawyer George Taylor Denison III, and lawyer W.A. Foster. Their mission was the promotion of "national sentiment" worthy of a great transcontinental nation.

Canada Firsters presented Canadians as robust Nordic races disciplined by their efforts to survive in a harsh environment. The place of French Canadians and First Nations in the new nation was problematic. Although Canada Firsters were willing in theory to include the "Norman French" among the Nordic elite, they failed in practice to demonstrate even this limited tolerance. Their bigoted attitudes toward French Canadians—and complete contempt for Aboriginal peoples—were fully exposed in their efforts to suppress the Red River Rebellion. Racist and ethnocentric, the Canada Firsters wanted white English

Canadian values to prevail in the new dominion. Their movement was too narrowly based to be successful and following the 1874 election both the movement and the party it sponsored quickly collapsed. The views they expressed nevertheless continued to thrive.

MACDONALD'S NATIONAL POLICY

It was widely conceded that the voters preferred Sir John A. drunk to Mackenzie sober, and the federal election of 1878 confirmed that verdict. The Pacific Scandal apparently forgiven, Macdonald's Conservatives won 142 of the 206 seats in the House of Commons. During the campaign, Macdonald advocated a development program that is often described as the National Policy. The centrepiece of the program was high tariffs to stimulate a strong manufacturing sector in the Canadian economy. In addition, Macdonald stressed rapid completion of the Pacific railway and the encouragement of population growth through immigration. These policies would form the framework of national development under both Conservative and Liberal administrations until the First World War.

Following the election, the Macdonald government quickly implemented its National Policy. In 1879, Finance Minister Tilley raised the tariff from 15 percent to levels ranging from 17.5 to 35 percent. Manufacturers welcomed a policy that they had long been promoting to fend off foreign competition. In 1880, the government approved a new Canadian Pacific Railway company. Headed by George Stephen, president of the Bank of Montreal, and Donald Smith, a major stakeholder in the Hudson's Bay Company, the company included American railway magnates Norman Kittson and James J. Hill. The CPR was from the outset a multinational enterprise with only about one-sixth of its stock held in Canada.

In both Canada and the United States, railway companies employed Chinese labourers to do some of the most dangerous and backbreaking work. They were responsible for the jobs of tunnelling and handling explosives, which helps to account for the death of 600 Chinese workers during the CPR construction process. In the words of the 1884 Royal Commission on Chinese Immigration, they were "living machines" working for the benefit of the capitalists who employed them and the fragile nation that was bound together by iron rails.

Notman Photographic Archives, McCord Museum of Canadian History, Montreal/2117

The Macdonald government offered the CPR syndicate generous support: $25 million in cash; 25 million acres of land (half of the land within 32 kilometres of the CPR's main line would be set aside until the company decided which parcels of land to claim); additional land for railway stations and road beds; 1100 kilometres of completed track built in the Mackenzie years; a 20-year monopoly on western rail traffic; exemption from tariffs on all materials required in railway construction; and a 20-year exemption for CPR properties from federal and provincial taxation and from taxation by municipalities not yet incorporated. More grants were required before the line was completed in 1885, and in 1888 the government guaranteed a $15-million bond issue in compensation for dropping the monopoly clause.

In the third area of the National Policy—immigration—the Macdonald government was less successful. Over 900 000 immigrants arrived in Canada in the 1880s, but over a million people left Canada during the decade. The exodus from the Maritimes and Quebec to the United States caused alarm in both regions. Ontarians were most likely to take up the challenge of western settlement, but the numbers were modest. The Prairie population was about 400 000 by 1901, not the millions that optimists had predicted 20 years earlier.

THE NORTHWEST

In the two decades following Confederation, the old Northwest was transformed, its society coming to resemble that of Eastern Canada in many ways. Outside of Manitoba, whose boundaries were extended in 1881, the region remained under federal government control. The Northwest Territories Act of 1875 gave power to an appointed council until such time as the population warranted government by elected officials. The act guaranteed denominational schools, and, by an amendment in 1877, French and English were made the official languages of the courts and council.

Plains Natives experienced little acknowledgment of their needs, not even the promised government help to become farmers. Before assistance arrived, Northwest Territories Lieutenant-Governor Edgar Dewdney reduced rations as a cost-cutting measure. This policy was implemented in the early 1880s just as the buffalo were disappearing from the Canadian prairies—the last Canadian hunt occurred in 1879. Between 1880 and 1885, an estimated 3000 Natives in the Northwest died from starvation.

In desperation, some Natives stole cattle from settlers, provoking conflict with the NWMP. As the situation worsened, Cree militants organized against the whites in the region, who symbolized the threat to the old plains way of life. Cree chiefs such as Big Bear and Poundmaker played key roles in Aboriginal resistance. Big Bear had refused to sign Treaty Six until starvation among his band forced his hand in 1882. Big Bear envisioned a confederation of the plains tribes that would force the Canadian government to provide Natives ironclad assurances of the right to hunt and live in their traditional territories.

In 1884, about 2000 Cree from several reserves gathered outside Battleford in an attempt to coordinate their resistance. When government policies failed to change, young militants called for armed protest. Meanwhile, there was growing discontent among the Métis living between the South and North Saskatchewan rivers. While the Métis had accepted the need for a transition to a largely agricultural existence, they wanted the same assistance that white settlers in the West received. Encouraged by the clergy, the Métis petitioned Ottawa for land, agricultural aid, schools, and a locally run police force.

When Ottawa ignored their petitions, the Métis decided in 1884 to invite Louis Riel to return to Canada from exile in the United States to lead his people. Initially, Riel attempted to pursue the peaceful route of pressuring the Macdonald government for concessions. This approach had the support of many white settlers in the region, who were growing impatient with their own treatment by Ottawa. Macdonald ignored Riel's petitions, with predictable results. On 18 March 1885, Riel proclaimed a provisional government and demanded that Ottawa grant the moderate demands outlined in a Bill of Rights. Riel still hoped for a peaceful settlement, but many Métis, including Riel's military adviser, Gabriel Dumont, felt that militant action was required.

Skirmishes between Métis and NWMP at Batoche and Duck Lake resulted in over 40 deaths and prompted the federal government to send a militia force under Major-General Frederick Middleton to the scene. Within two weeks, the first detachment of militia arrived on CPR trains. When word of the Métis rebellion reached Cree ears, the militants attacked the base at Frog Lake, killing a hated Indian agent and eight others. In another incident, two farming instructors regarded as hostile to Natives were murdered in the Battleford district. Riel withdrew his supporters to Batoche where they held out against the army for six weeks before surrendering. At least 35 Natives and 53 non-Natives lost their lives in the Northwest Rebellion. An all-white jury in Regina convicted Riel of treason and he was hanged in November 1885.

The First Nations paid dearly for their acts of resistance. Of 81 arrested, 44 were convicted. Of these, eight were hanged, three were sentenced to life imprisonment, and many others were incarcerated for shorter periods. Even Big Bear and Poundmaker, who had tried to prevent violence, were sentenced to three-year prison terms on charges of felony-treason. Military might and the legal system had broken armed

Following his capture in July 1885, Big Bear was incarcerated in Stoney Mountain penitentiary, north of Winnipeg. Like other prisoners, he had his hair cropped and was forced to do menial jobs. He was reported to have converted to Roman Catholicism while in prison. Released in 1887, he seemed broken in spirit and died within a year.

National Archives of Canada/C1873

resistance to white colonialism, but Aboriginal defiance continued. They secretly practised religious ceremonies that were banned under the Indian Act, and they protected each other against NWMP attempts to arrest them, often arbitrarily, for infractions of the white man's laws.

The Métis, too, faced dismal prospects. Instead of the unified nation that the rebels of '85 hoped to create, the Métis were dispersed across the Prairies in communities such as Green Lake, Saskatchewan, and Lac Ste Anne and Lac La Biche, Alberta. The Métis in Batoche finally won a land settlement in 1899–1900, receiving individual land grants rather than a reserve. Since farming required capital that the Métis lacked, many sold their lands. In 1896, the Roman Catholic Church, spurred by the missionary Albert Lacombe, established a reserve, St Paul des Métis, 100 kilometres northeast of Edmonton. Promises of livestock and equipment failed to materialize, and it soon became clear that neither the church nor the federal government planned to invest much money in the enterprise. For decades, the Métis remained a forgotten people, invisible even in the census until 1981 when, for the first time, "Métis" was recognized as an ethnic group.

RELIGION, LANGUAGE, AND POLITICS

Natives were not alone in questioning Macdonald's interpretation of Confederation. For francophones, Ottawa's handling of guarantees for French-language rights and denominational schools was disappointing. Both policies were resisted by provincial legislatures outside Quebec. Dominated by representatives of the English Protestant majority, the federal government also rejected pleas for legislation to protect francophone and Roman Catholic minorities throughout the country.

NEW BRUNSWICK SCHOOLS

The first contest over denominational schools occurred in New Brunswick. The New Brunswick Common Schools Act of 1871 authorized municipalities to tax all

Voices from the Past

The "Bill of Rights," 1885

The Métis demands in the "Bill of Rights" suggest that Riel's program was neither separatist nor racist, as Canadian opponents of Riel charged at the time. While the concerns of the Métis were uppermost in Riel's mind, the "Bill of Rights" included calls for better treatment of all peoples in the Northwest Territories. The following is a condensed version of the demands:

1. That the half-breeds of the Northwest Territories be given grants similar to those accorded to the half-breeds of Manitoba by the Act of 1870.

2. That patents be issued to all half-breeds and white settlers who have fairly earned the right of possession to their farms; that the timber regulations be made more liberal; and that the settler be treated as having rights in the country.

3. That the provinces of Alberta and Saskatchewan be forthwith organized with legislatures of their own, so that the people may be no longer subject to the despotism of Lieutenant-Governor Dewdney; and, in the proposed new provincial legislatures, that the Métis shall have a fair and reasonable share of representation.

4. That the offices of trust throughout these provinces be given to residents of the country, as far as practicable, and that we denounce the appointment of disreputable outsiders and repudiate their authority.

5. That this region be administered for the benefit of the actual settler, and not for the advantage of the alien speculator; and that all lawful customs and usages which obtain among the Métis be respected.

6. That better provision be made for the Indians, the parliamentary grant to be increased, and lands set apart as an endowment for the establishment of hospitals and schools for the use of whites, half-breeds, and Indians, at such places as the provincial legislatures may determine.

7. That the Land Department of the Dominion Government be administered as far as practicable from Winnipeg, so that settlers may not be compelled, as heretofore to go to Ottawa for the settlement of questions in dispute between them and land commissioners.[4]

ratepayers to support the public school system. The omission from the act of Roman Catholic schools, which had hitherto received public funding, though by convention rather than by law, was intentional.

Regarding the law as unfair, Roman Catholics in New Brunswick, who constituted one-third of the population, appealed to the courts. The legislation was declared valid, so they turned in vain to the federal government. While most Roman Catholics in New Brunswick vigorously opposed the school legislation, resistance was especially fierce among the province's Acadian population. They made up about half of provincial adherents to Roman Catholicism. Since only one Acadian child in six received any schooling, most Acadians balked at taxes to support any school, much less a school that excluded Catholic education.

Matters came to a head in the town of Caraquet. In January 1875, a group of angry Acadians broke up the meeting of Protestants who were setting aside parish elections on the grounds that most voters had been ineligible to cast ballots because they had not paid their school taxes. The Acadians had numbers on their side in Caraquet, where only 79 Protestants resided in a population of over 3000. When constables and volunteers tried to arrest the Acadians, a mêlée ensued in which one volunteer and one Acadian were shot. The trial of nine Acadians for murder became a cause célèbre and forced the government to compromise. It dismissed charges against the accused Acadians, and permitted religious orders to teach Roman Catholics in areas where numbers warranted.

THE ACADIAN RENAISSANCE

Confrontations over schools and language reflected the growing sense of political awareness among

The Caraquet Riot of 1875 resulted in two deaths and encouraged leaders in church and government to compromise on the issue of school policy in New Brunswick.

Courtesy Charles P. de Volpi Collection, Special Collections/Dalhousie University Libraries

Acadians. By the time of Confederation, an Acadian sense of identity was taking shape and their numbers, especially in New Brunswick, were growing rapidly. In 1880, the Société Saint-Jean-Baptiste invited all French-speaking communities in North America to a congress in Quebec. Acadians subsequently held their own congress at Collège Saint-Joseph in July 1881. Over 5000 people attended. In this and a subsequent congress in 1884 at Miscouche, Prince Edward Island, the Acadians chose a holiday, a flag, and a hymn to represent their sense of national purpose.

The emergence of a group identity and an expanding population base soon showed political results, with Macdonald appointing Pascal Poirier, a native of Shediac, as the first Acadian senator in 1885 and Acadian representation in the provincial legislature expanding in direct proportion to their growing numbers.

QUEBEC IN QUESTION

By the 1880s, religious and cultural concerns rivaled economic issues in determining party loyalties and shaping national policies. This was amply revealed in the aftermath of Riel's hanging in 1885. Because the Métis rebels were primarily French-speaking Roman Catholics, neither Orangemen nor Quebec nationalists took account of the regional and Aboriginal concerns behind the uprising. Instead, Orangemen regarded Riel as a French-speaking Roman Catholic determined to deprive the British Empire of the Northwest, while Quebec nationalists saw him as a hero whose undoing proved that French-Canadian rights were trampled outside Quebec. After Riel's execution, an outpouring of grief and rage, including a demonstration in Montreal attended by over 50 000 people, testified the extent of Québécois alienation.

Building on francophone discontent, Honoré Mercier led the Parti national, which included Quebec's Liberals along with Conservative dissidents, to a provincial election victory in 1886. Mercier's success demonstrated the erosion of the political alliance between Conservatives and the Roman Catholic Church that had prevailed in Quebec since the 1840s. By using the word national in the party name, Liberals also reminded the francophone majority in Quebec that they were a nation even if it was submerged in the larger nation-state of Canada.

ONTARIO FRANCOPHONES

French Canadians in Ontario, who numbered over 100 000 by the 1880s, became hostages to the cultural bigotry spreading across the country. Ontario's denominational schools were protected by the constitution, but French linguistic rights lacked similar guarantees. In the wake of the Northwest Rebellion, the Ontario government limited hours of instruction in languages other than English. Local school boards initially often ignored this regulation, but Protestant anglophones were determined to impose conformity.

The Jesuit Estates Act of 1888 galvanized the anti-Roman Catholic forces of Ontario into more concerted action. When the Jesuits returned to Quebec in the 1840s, they demanded compensation for properties confiscated by Britain following the conquest. The Quebec government invited Pope Leo XIII to arbitrate among the contending Roman Catholic claimants. Although the final settlement included funds for Protestant universities in Quebec, Protestant extremists in Ontario decried Vatican involvement in Canadian affairs. An Ontario-based group calling itself the Equal Rights Association launched a campaign to rid the province and the nation of papal influences. D'Alton McCarthy, one of the Conservative Party's most able lieutenants, urged the abolition of public funding for separate schools and called for the assimilation of French Canadians.

Wanting to curry favour with its overwhelmingly English and Protestant electorate, the Liberal government of Ontario removed all French books from the authorized list of textbooks in 1889. Local school boards began to enforce the province's restrictions against French instruction. In short order, the Ontario approach to education was taken up in Manitoba.

THE MANITOBA SCHOOLS QUESTION

The Manitoba Act of 1870 and the Northwest Territories Act of 1875 legislated official bilingualism on the Prairies, but demography favoured unilingualism. Although francophones were half the population of Manitoba in 1870, they represented only 11 000 of the 152 000 residents in 1891. The anti-French, anti-Catholic rhetoric of English Protestant settlers in the West and the ingrained image of the prairie soil as infertile, as well as the closer and stronger pull of New England, discouraged extensive Québécois migration to Canada's frontier.

In 1890, Thomas Greenway's Liberal government, influenced by Ontario developments, eliminated official bilingualism and the separate schools system guaranteed by the Manitoba Act. Following Manitoba's lead, the Northwest Territories in 1892 legislated an end to education in French after the third grade and removed French as an official language in legislative proceedings.

The Manitoba schools legislation quickly became a national issue. When the Judicial Committee of the Privy Council ruled that the federal government under the provisions of the British North America Act could pass remedial legislation to restore public funding for denominational schools, the Conservatives were torn between offering assistance to an aggrieved minority and defending education as an exclusively provincial matter.

Macdonald died in 1891, leaving the decision to his successors. In 1896 the federal Conservatives, under Charles Tupper, included remedial legislation in their election platform. Since they lost the election, the new prime minister, Wilfrid Laurier, had to negotiate a compromise acceptable to Liberals, who supported the principle of provincial rights. The Manitoba legislation was allowed to stand when the Manitoba government agreed to permit religious instruction and instruction in languages other than English where student numbers warranted such practices.

EMPIRE ONTARIO

Clearly, the defence of provincial interests had emerged as a major feature of the Canadian federal system. Macdonald made extensive use of the power of disallowance, which enabled the federal government to set aside provincial legislation, but the provinces challenged him in the courts. To Macdonald's dismay, the courts often sustained the provincial perspective.

Oliver Mowat, Liberal premier of Ontario from 1872 to 1896, emerged as the undisputed champion of provincial rights of his generation. Mowat insisted that Confederation was an agreement among provinces and that the provinces retained the jurisdiction they held prior to Confederation except for specific responsibilities that they granted to the federal government. From this "provincial compact" perspective, there was no new "political nationality" formed in 1867. Mowat believed that the federal government's frequent disallowances of provincial legislation amounted to unconstitutional interference in Ontario's sovereign areas of authority. When Macdonald attempted to restrict Ontario's boundaries by placing territories north and west of Lake Superior within the province of Manitoba, Mowat successfully challenged the decision in the courts. In 1889, Macdonald finally conceded the boundary that Ontario demanded.

THE PREMIERS' CONFERENCE, 1887

The Ontario boundary dispute was in full swing when Quebec Premier Mercier suggested a premiers' conference to discuss matters of common interest. Not surprisingly, Mowat was enthusiastic. Maritime premiers, experiencing difficulty managing on their federal subsidies and alarmed by the impact of federal economic policies on their economies, also favoured constitutional change. In May 1886, Liberal premier W.S. Fielding, angered by Ottawa's preoccupation with other areas of the country, introduced a resolution in the Nova Scotia legislature calling for repeal of the British North America Act and establishment of a Maritime union. In Manitoba, economic growth encouraged plans for railways to the United States, but these were banned by the CPR's monopoly clause. A frustrated John Norquay, Canada's first premier of Métis descent, therefore agreed to attend the conference despite being a Conservative.

In October 1887, five of Canada's seven premiers—the Conservative premiers of Prince Edward Island and British Columbia stayed home—met in Quebec City to demand changes in federal-provincial relations. The resolutions passed by the premiers included calls for a one-third increase in provincial subsidies; the handing of the power of disallowance from the federal to the British government; provincial selection of half of all senators; and provincial consent before local works could be placed under dominion control. Macdonald ignored the conference, accusing the four Liberal premiers of partisan mischief, but federal-provincial tensions continued.

THE NORTH ATLANTIC TRIANGLE

Canada had no Department of External Affairs until 1909. Nonetheless, Canada's leaders expected to be consulted by the British government on diplomatic initiatives that affected their nation's interests. In the discussions leading to the Treaty of Washington in 1871, and on several occasions thereafter, Britain included Canadian representatives on their negotiating teams, but Canadians always feared being sacrificed to good international relations by British negotiators.

Many of the problems between Canada and the United States revolved around fish. When the terms of the Treaty of Washington ended in the mid-1880s, Americans appeared uninterested in bargaining, with the result that Canada began enforcing measures to protect its fisheries. In 1886 and 1887, about 2000 vessels were boarded, and some were seized for violations. The Americans threatened to retaliate by cutting off all commercial relations with Canada.

In 1887, a British-American Joint High Commission was established to deal with the problem. Although Canada's delegate, Sir Charles Tupper, advocated a reciprocity agreement and at the very least Canadian access to the American market for fish, he ran into a brick wall of American resistance. There would be no reciprocity treaty and no access to the American market for fresh fish.

Canada fared better with regard to its sealing industry in the North Pacific. After buying Alaska from the Russians in 1867, the Americans claimed exclusive rights to the Bering Sea. The United States leased sealing rights off the Pribilof Islands in the Bering Sea to a company, which was enraged when British Columbia interests also began sealing in the region. The Americans and British charged each other with indiscriminate sealing that endangered the seal herd. The two sides agreed to an arbitration panel, which met in Paris in 1893, and decided largely in Britain's favour. The slaughter of the seals could continue, with all sides participating until a moratorium on sealing in the Bering Sea was imposed in 1911.

CANADA IN QUESTION

Notwithstanding the protectionist sentiment in the United States, the Liberals, under their new leader Edward Blake, still clung to their free trade agenda in the 1882 and 1887 elections. Macdonald, trumpeting the virtues of the National Policy, won both times. In June 1887, the Liberals chose Wilfrid Laurier as national leader. Within a decade, he reshaped the party into an election-winning machine, but he had to deal with the free trade issue first.

The idea of closer trade relations with the United States was popular with many Liberal voters. Among party radicals, there was even support for commercial

biography

Sir John Thompson

John Thompson (1845–1894) was born in Halifax, trained as a lawyer, and served briefly as Premier of Nova Scotia. In 1885, he joined Macdonald's cabinet as Minister of Justice. Raised a Methodist, Thompson had converted to Roman Catholicism as an adult which gave him a unique perspective on the religious and cultural wars that raged in the final decades of the nineteenth century. He was the logical successor to Macdonald but because of his religious affiliation was passed over in favour of John Abbott, who was a Protestant. Following Abbott's retirement in 1892, Thompson became Prime Minister but his tenure in the office was short-lived. He died in Windsor Castle, London, in December 1894 shortly after being sworn by Queen Victoria as a member of the Imperial Privy Council.

John Thompson's funeral cortège, Halifax, 3 January 1895.

Nova Scotia Archives and Records Management (Notman, N-1376)

union, a policy that would harmonize the tariff structures of the two North American nations as well as eliminate the border as a barrier to trade. Opposition to reciprocity rested both on economic and cultural arguments. For producers protected by high tariffs, free trade threatened competition that might well ruin them. There was also fear that overly close commercial ties with the United States would weaken Canadian identity and close economic and cultural ties with Great Britain.

Imperial sentiment was on the rise in the late nineteenth century. During the 1880s, many Canadian communities were celebrating the centenary of their Loyalist origins, while in Great Britain there was support for strengthening the bonds of empire. Although imperialists disagreed among themselves about what form closer imperial ties should take, most discussion centred on a common imperial tariff, colonial representation in an imperial parliament, and cooperation in imperial defence.

In the 1891 election, Macdonald's last, the prime minister offered no new remedies for his divided country. The Conservative slogan—"The Old Man, The Old Flag and the Old Policy"—said it all. The Liberals boldly declared their support for "unrestricted reciprocity." Such a position appealed to the radical wing of the party, but made many Canadians extremely nervous. It failed, however, to deter francophones in Quebec, who, for the first time since the Pacific Scandal, elected Liberals in a majority of their constituencies.

As Macdonald lay on his deathbed in June 1891, he must have wondered what manner of political entity he had helped to shape. Canadians remained at odds with each other and even the party he had worked so hard to build was in disarray. Following his death, it broke into squabbling factions and had four leaders—John Abbott, John Thompson, Mackenzie Bowell, and Charles Tupper—in five years. Little wonder that a majority of Canadians felt that it was time for a change.

CONCLUSION

Rounding out the borders of the Dominion of Canada proved to be the easy part of nation-building. Holding it together was more difficult. For many Canadians, the adjustment to new national policies as defined in the first three decades of Confederation brought only hardship and heartache. Aboriginal peoples experienced defeat and marginalization, while the outlying regions of West and East still wondered about their place in a Canadian firmament dominated by Ontario and Quebec. Throughout Canada religious and cultural differences focusing on school and language policy made some people feel that imperial federation, annexation, or provincial independence were happier alternatives to being yoked in a federation where every national policy was ringed with compromise and bitterness. Perhaps most disappointing of all, the rapid economic growth that Canada's leaders sought proved elusive.

NOTES

1. Alexander Morris, *The Treaties of Canada with the Indians of Manitoba and the North-West Territories* (Toronto: Belfords Clarke, 1880; reprinted Coles, 1971) 28.

2. Quoted in Manitoba Indian Brotherhood, *Treaty Days: Centennial Commemorations Historical Pageant* (Winnipeg: Manitoba Indian Brotherhood, 1971) 24.

3. Cited in Shelagh D. Grant, *Sovereignty or Security: Government Policy in the Canadian North, 1936–1950* (Vancouver: UBC Press, 1988) 5.

4. *Bill of Rights*, 13 April 1885, Provincial Archives of Alberta.

SELECTED READING

Biographies of major political leaders of this period include Donald Creighton, *Sir John A. Macdonald: The Old Chieftain* (Toronto: Macmillan, 1955); Dale C. Thomson, *Alexander Mackenzie: Clear Grit* (Toronto: Macmillan, 1960); Joseph Schull, *Edward Blake*, 2 vols. (Toronto: Macmillan, 1975/76); P.B. Waite, *The Man from Halifax: Sir John Thompson, Prime Minister* (Toronto: University of Toronto Press, 1985); Brian Young, *George-Étienne Cartier: Montreal Bourgeois* (Montreal: McGill-Queen's University Press, 1981); A.A. den Otter, *Civilizing the West: The Galts and the Development of Western Canada* (Edmonton: University of Alberta Press, 1982); J. Murray Beck, *Joseph Howe*, 2 vols. (Montreal: McGill-Queen's University Press, 1985/88); G.F.G. Stanley, *Louis Riel* (Toronto: McGraw-Hill Ryerson, 1963); and George Woodcock, *Amor de Cosmos: Journalist and Reformer* (Toronto: Oxford University Press, 1975).

Regional studies include Jean Barman, *The West Beyond the West: A History of British Columbia* (Toronto: University of Toronto Press, 1996); Margaret Ormsby, *British Columbia: A History* (Toronto: Macmillan, 1971); Cole Harris, *The Resettlement of British Columbia: Essays on Colonialism and Geographical Change* (Vancouver: UBC Press, 1997); Morris Zaslow, *The Opening of the Canadian North, 1870–1914* (Toronto: McClelland and Stewart, 1971); W.L. Morton, *Manitoba: A History* (Toronto: University of Toronto Press, 1957); Lewis H. Thomas, *The Struggle for Responsible Government in the North-West Territories, 1870–97* (Toronto: University of Toronto Press, 1978) Gerald Friesen, *The Canadian Prairies: A History* (Toronto: University of Toronto Press, 1987); John Herd Thompson, *Forging the Prairie West* (Toronto: Oxford University Press, 1998); John A. Dickinson and Brian Young, *A Short History of Quebec*, 2nd ed. (Toronto: Copp Clark Pitman, 1993); Paul-André Linteau, René Durocher, and Jean-Claude Robert, *Quebec: A History, 1867–1929* (Toronto: Lorimer, 1983); E.R. Forbes and D.A. Muise, eds., *The Atlantic Provinces in Confederation* (Toronto and Fredericton: University of Toronto Press and Acadiensis Press, 1993); Margaret R. Conrad and James K. Hiller, *Atlantic Canada: A Region in the Making* (Toronto: Oxford University Press, 2001); and William R. Morrison, *True North: The Yukon and Northwest Territories* (Toronto: Oxford University Press, 1998).

The Red River Rebellion is discussed in George Stanley, *The Birth of Western Canada: A History of the Riel Rebellions* (Toronto: University of Toronto Press, 1970); Gerhard J. Ens, *Homeland to Hinterland: The Changing Worlds of the Red River Métis in the Nineteenth Century* (Toronto: University of Toronto Press, 1996); D.N. Sprague, *Canada and the Métis, 1869–1885* (Waterloo: Wilfrid Laurier University Press, 1988); Thomas Flanagan, *Métis Lands and Manitoba* (Calgary: University of Calgary Press, 1991); and Frits Pannekoek, *A Snug Little Flock: The Social Origins of the Riel Resistance, 1869–70* (Winnipeg: Watson and Dwyer, 1991).

The causes and events of the 1885 rebellion are detailed in the Stanley works as well as Bob Beal and Rod MacLeod, *Prairie Fire: The Northwest Rebellion of 1885* (Edmonton: Hurtig, 1984) and Thomas Flanagan, *Riel and the Rebellion: 1885 Reconsidered* (Saskatoon: Western Producer Prairie Books, 1983). The military aspects of the rebellion are outlined in Desmond Morton, *The Last War Drum* (Toronto: Hakkert, 1972). On life for Native peoples in the West following the rebellions, see F.L. Barron and James B. Waldrom, eds., *1885 and After: Native Society in Transition* (Regina: Canadian Plains Research Centre, 1986). An important community study focusing on the Métis is Diane Payment, *Batoche, 1870–1910* (St Boniface: Les Éditions du Blé, 1983). The gender discourse of the rebellion's opponents is discussed in Sarah A. Carter, *Capturing Women: The Manipulation of Cultural Imagery in Canada's Prairie West* (Montreal: McGill-Queen's University Press, 1997).

One book establishes a valuable framework for analyzing the fate of the First Nations in Western Canada: Sarah Carter, *Aboriginal People and Colonizers of Western Canada to 1900* (Toronto: University of Toronto Press, 1999). Other important works on Aboriginal issues include Frank Tough, *"As Their Resources Fail:" Native People and the Economic History of Northern Manitoba, 1870–1930* (Vancouver: University of British Columbia Press, 1996); Katherine Pettipas, *Severing the Ties that Bind: Government Repression of Indigenous Religious Ceremonies on the Prairies* (Winnipeg: University of Manitoba Press, 1994); Sarah Carter, *Lost Harvests: Prairie Indian Reserve Farmers and Government Policy* (Montreal: McGill-Queen's University Press, 1990); R.E. Cail, *Land, Man and Law: The Disposal of Crown Lands in British Columbia, 1871–1913* (Vancouver: UBC Press, 1974); and Tina Loo, *Making Law, Order, and Authority in British Columbia, 1812–1871* (Toronto: University of Toronto Press, 1994).

On Canada's external relations see R.C. Brown, *Canada's National Policy, 1883–1900: A Study of American-Canadian Relations* (Princeton: Princeton University Press, 1964); J.L. Granatstein and Norman Hillmer, *For*

Better or For Worse: Canada and the United States to the 1990s (Toronto: Ryerson, 1991); and Edelgard E. Mahant and Graeme S. Mount, *An Introduction to Canadian-American Relations* (Toronto: Methuen, 1989). The Canada First Movement and aspects of early Canadian nationalism are discussed in Carl Berger, *The Sense of Power: Studies in the Ideas of Canadian Imperialism 1867–1914* (Toronto: University of Toronto Press, 1970). Works on the Loyalist tradition include Norman Knowles, *Inventing the Loyalists: The Loyalist Tradition and the Invention of Usable Pasts* (Toronto: University of Toronto Press, 1997) and Murray Barkley, "The Loyalist Tradition in New Brunswick," *Acadiensis* 4.2 (Spring 1975): 3–45.

General background on French-English and Protestant-Catholic conflict is provided in Robert Choquette, *Language and Religion: A History of English-French Conflict in Ontario* (Ottawa: University of Ottawa Press, 1975); Jean Daigle, ed., *Acadians of the Maritimes: Thematic Studies* (Moncton: Chaire d'études acadiennes, Université de Moncton, 1995); Sheila A. Andrew, *The Development of Elites in Acadian New Brunswick, 1861–1881* (Montreal and Kingston: McGill-Queen's University Press, 1996); Fernand Harvey and Gérard Beaulieu, eds., *Les relations entre le Québec et l'Acadie de la tradition à la modernité* (Québec: Éditions de l/IQRC/Éditions d'Acadie, 2000); Phyllis LeBlanc, "The Vatican and the Roman Catholic Church in Atlantic Canada: Policies Regarding Ethnicity and Language, 1878–1922," in *Papal Diplomacy in the Modern Age*, ed. Peter C. Kent and John F. Pollard (Westport: Praeger Press, 1994) 65–74; Robert Painchaud, "French-Canadian Historiography and Franco-Catholic Settlement in Western Canada, 1870–1915," *Canadian Historical Review* 59.4 (Dec. 1978): 447–66; Paul Crunican, *Priests and Politicians: Manitoba Schools and the Election of 1896* (Toronto: University of Toronto Press, 1974); Kenneth Munro, "Official Bilingualism in Alberta," *Prairie Forum* 12.1 (Spring 1987): 37–48; and Chad Gaffield, *Language, Schooling and Cultural Conflict: The Origins of the French-Language Controversy in Ontario* (Montreal: McGill-Queen's University Press, 1987).

 **WEBLINKS**

FATHERS OF CONFEDERATION
www.nlc-bnc.ca/confed/h18-2300-e.html

This site provides a collection of biographies for many of the people involved in the creation and building of Canada.

SIR JOHN A. MACDONALD
www.canadahistory.com/sirjohna.htm

This site offers photos of Macdonald and his family, as well as a comprehensive account of his life and career.

LOUIS RIEL
http://infoweb.magi.com/~shuttle/riel-index.html

The dichotomies of Riel's personality and character are explored at this site, in addition to his historical significance as a rebel leader. As well as biographical and political information, his contemporary and posthumous influences are examined thematically.

THE INDIAN ACT
www.ualberta.ca/~esimpson/claims/indianact.htm

A brief historical overview and links to a variety of sites, including the complete text of the Indian Act, can be found at this site.

ALEXANDER MACKENZIE
www.nlc-bnc.ca/primeministers/h4-3050-e.html

This site contains a list of quick facts, biographical and bibliographical information, anecdotes, and speeches relating to Alexander Mackenzie.

CANADIAN PACIFIC RAILWAY
www.cprheritage.com

The site of the CPR Archives includes an image gallery with a selection of photos and graphic art covering the history of Canada and the railway, including communities, railroad construction, trains, locomotives, ships, war, people, tourism, and settlement.

Entering the Twentieth Century

The more I advance in life... the more I thank Providence that my birth took place in the fair land of Canada. Canada has been modest in its history, although its history is heroic in many ways. But its history, in my estimation is only commencing. It is commencing in this century. The nineteenth century was the century of the United States. I think we can claim that it is Canada that shall fill the twentieth century.[1]

In retrospect, Wilfrid Laurier's comment during a speech to the Ottawa Canadian Club in 1904 proved over-optimistic. Nevertheless, the opening years of the twentieth century brought the economic growth that Canadian leaders had sought for their nation. Industries flourished, immigrants flocked to the West, and two more transcontinental railways were built. When the United States finally agreed to the long-sought-after Reciprocity Treaty in 1911, the Liberals were convinced that it would buy them another victory at the polls. They were wrong. The Conservatives under Robert Borden won the election and North American free trade would be rejected by a nation that was increasingly confident of its future.

LAURIER LIBERALISM

Wilfrid Laurier became Prime Minster of Canada in 1896 at the age of 55. Trained in law, he joined the Parti Rouge as a young man and edited a newspaper, Le Défricheur, in Quebec's Eastern Townships. Laurier initially opposed Confederation, but gradually became reconciled to the new political order. After serving a term in the Quebec legislature, he ran for a federal seat in 1874 and briefly served as Minister of Inland Revenue in the Mackenzie cabinet. Laurier's opposition to the ultramontanists endeared him to the majority of English Protestants, who admired his courage in standing up to conservative forces in Quebec. A stout defender of political liberalism and Canadian unity, Laurier was Edward Blake's choice as party leader and was chosen over the objections of a number of prominent Liberals.

Canadians voted for the Liberals in 1896 for a variety of reasons. Laurier's success in improving the party's organization was one of them. Another was the party's retreat in 1893 from its rigid free-trade philosophy, which was increasingly alienating voters in Ontario, where the tariff was credited with much of the province's recent economic growth. Laurier's talent for political management and his sensitivity to provincial aspirations no doubt helped as well. These qualities were evident in the formation of his first cab-

inet. In it he included powerful local chieftains—W.S. Fielding of Nova Scotia, Oliver Mowat of Ontario, and A.G. Blair of New Brunswick—and rising newcomers such as Clifford Sifton of Manitoba, who in 1897 became Minister of the Interior, responsible for development of the West.

Laurier's willingness to compromise was reflected in the tariff policy developed early in his adminstration. In 1897 his Finance Minister, W.S. Fielding, introduced the so-called British preference, which applied lower tariffs to any country admitting Canadian products on a preferential basis. Since Great Britain had a policy of global free trade, it was automatically granted tariff preference. This policy pleased those with imperialist leanings and did little to hurt

---

MORE TO THE STORY

Railroading Canada

William Mackenzie, born in 1849 in what would become Ontario, began his career as a subcontractor for the CPR and then made his fortune by investing in street railways and other utilities in Canada's burgeoning cities. In 1895, he teamed up with Donald Mann, another CPR subcontractor, to build a railway to Hudson Bay. This project failed to materialize, but the two men began buying short rail lines in Manitoba and soon had the basis for a second transcontinental railway. With bond guarantees and land grants from the Manitoba government, they marketed $14 million of securities for their Canadian Northern Railway in London and New York. Neither promoter put up any of his own money: one-third of the capital was guaranteed by governments at various levels, while Mackenzie's Toronto associate, George Cox, added the financial muscle of the Bank of Commerce.

The Grand Trunk Railway, whose conservative London-based directors saw their future survival dependent on tapping the booming West, tried to buy the Canadian Northern, but negotiations for a merger of the two companies failed. Under their new American general manager, Charles M. Hayes, the Grand Trunk embarked on a project to build its own new railway, incorporated as the National Transcontinental. Both companies would demand and get land grants, subsidies, and loan guarantees from the Laurier government. When Quebec and

the Maritimes laid on pressure, the federal government even agreed to build the Grand Trunk's Eastern Division from Moncton to Winnipeg and lease it to the company. Not to be outdone, Mackenzie and Mann knit together eastern lines to establish their claim to an Atlantic terminus.

Extravagance, greed, and patronage dogged the two ventures. When a royal commission was struck by the Borden government in 1911 to look into the skyrocketing costs of the Eastern Division, it was discovered that the project cost $70 million (out of $160 million) more than it should have. Nevertheless, the two companies pressed forward with construction, floating new security issues in London and demanding more subsidies and loan guarantees from Ottawa. Hayes was planning even grander schemes when he died in the sinking of the *Titanic* in 1912. Mackenzie and Mann continued to expand their railroad empire, but their days were numbered. European investors were beginning to have second thoughts about investing in Canadian railways, and the outbreak of the First World War closed European financial markets completely. Faced with bankruptcy, Mackenzie and Mann were forced to let their railway empire be amalgamated with other government-owned railways into the Canadian National Railway system, which was created in a series of mergers between 1917 and 1923.

Canadian manufacturers whose main competition came from the United States.

It was fortunate for the Liberals that they came to office just as international economic conditions were on the upswing and when most of the farmland on the American frontier had been taken up. Under the supervision of Clifford Sifton, immigration was vigorously pursued, and the results were spectacular. Nearly three million people came to Canada between 1896 and 1914, many of them settling in the four western provinces. In 1905, the Laurier government created two new provinces—Alberta and Saskatchewan—out of the Northwest Territories. It also created a continuing source of federal-provincial friction in deciding, as Macdonald had in the case of Manitoba, to keep public lands and natural resources under federal control.

Encouraged by what seemed to be unending growth, Laurier decided in 1903 to assist the eastern-based Grand Trunk and the western-based Canadian Northern railway companies to complete transcontinental lines. The vast sums of taxpayers' money invested in the projects meant that they, like the CPR, encouraged extravagance and political corruption. Unlike the CPR, the two new railways failed to

make a profit and continued to be a drain on the federal budget long after Laurier had departed the scene.

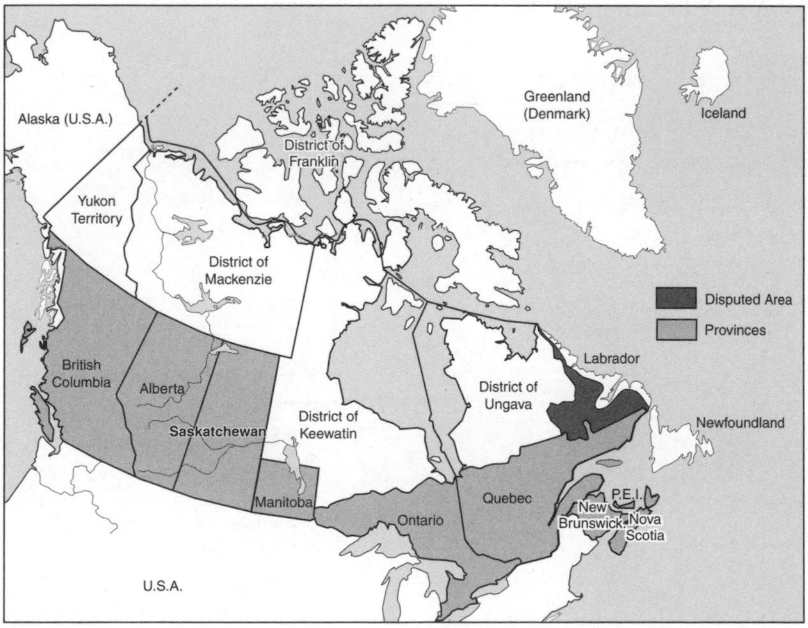

THE KLONDIKE GOLD RUSH

Coinciding with Laurier's success at the polls was the discovery of gold in the Klondike in 1896. The last great find in a series that began with California in 1849 and British Columbia in 1858, the Klondike gold rush began after California-born George Cormack, together with two Tagish brothers, Skookum Jim and Dawson Charlie, discovered gold nuggets on Rabbit Creek, which was renamed Bonanza. Within two years of the gold find on Bonanza Creek, the lure of instant wealth transformed Dawson from a tiny fur-trading post into Western Canada's second-largest city. The Klondike gold rush made a few instant millionaires, but most of the 40 000 people who made the difficult trek to Canada's new Eldorado returned home empty-handed.

At the height of the gold rush, Dawson City was a rough-and-ready place, with saloons and dance halls open 24 hours a day—though they closed on Sunday. Its reputation for lawlessness nevertheless was greatly exaggerated. Unlike Skagway, a roaring American frontier town ruled for a time by a gangster named Soapy Smith, Dawson was under the firm control of the Northwest Mounted Police, who were dispatched to the Yukon as soon as the news of the gold discovery reached Ottawa. Under Superintendent Sam Steele, the NWMP rigidly enforced the regulation banning firearms being carried in town, handed out stiff penalties to those who broke the law, and made sure that miners paid the royalty on gold.

A railway connected the Yukon with Skagway on the Pacific coast in 1900, but by that time the discovery of gold in Nome, Alaska, had shifted

Map 16.1
Canada, 1905.

Martha Munger Black. The Yukon gold rush drew many people into the Canadian North, including Martha Munger, who married George Black and in 1935 became the second woman to hold a seat in the House of Commons.

Yukon Archives. Martha Black fonds, #3258

the attention of gold-seekers elsewhere. Meanwhile, Canada's northern frontier settled down to a more mundane existence. Individual prospectors gave way to international corporations and the territorial government gradually became less authoritarian. Like other territorial governments, the Yukon was initially governed by a commissioner and appointed officials, backed by the NWMP.

A NATION ON THE MOVE

In the early years of Confederation, the slow rate of population growth was as great a concern as railways and tariffs for Canadian leaders. Despite the passage of the Dominion Lands Act in 1872, most immigrants to North America in the late nineteenth century preferred to settle in the

United States. So, too, it seemed, did many Canadians. Frontier lands and industrial jobs, as well as a better

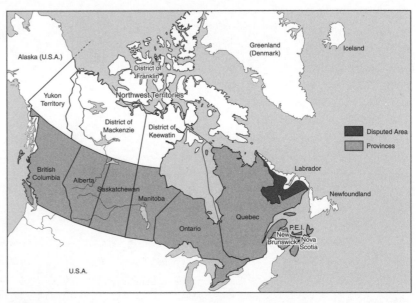

Map 16.2
Canada, 1912.

Voices from the Past

The Pioneering Experience

The Prairie pioneering experience offered singular hardship. One of the sons of Maria Aho, a founding settler of a Finnish community established in southwest Saskatchewan in 1888, recalled how difficult the early years were for his family:

My mother was so homesick, she never allowed us to dismantle her trunk insisting that she would not stay in this bush with no roads, nothing, just a small two-room hut with branches as a roof. The roof leaked. But every second year she had a new baby until there were twelve of us. She worked all the time, I never saw her sleep and still she kept insisting we act civilized. I was not allowed out to the nearest town till I could read and write. She taught us all that and she told us about Finland, her hometown Lapua. We dug a well by hand, but it kept drying up. Still we had a sauna every week and we were all scrubbed. Then we read the Bible and sang from the hymn book.... Mother never saw Finland again, she died at seventy-six, and I have never seen that country, but still if people ask me I tell them that I am a Finn.[3]

Belonging to the dominant Anglo-Canadian culture did not always make matters better. For example, Roy and Verna Benson, who settled in Munson, Alberta, were less than enthusiastic about their experience. Roy wrote in January 1911:

I suppose you are wondering what kind of country we have struck well there are a lot of people right here that are doing the same thing wondering. This past year has made a lot of them sit up and notice. Some have left the country, some couldn't.... I had a 10 a[cres] broke a year ago (cost me $50) last July. Last spring I let a fellow put in on shares and put

$20 into a fence—this fall I told him he could have it all but the fence.

In May of the same year, Verna offered her perspective:

I surely don't care anything about putting in another winter like last winter. I went to one of the neighbours New Years day and I wasn't away from home again until the last of April. There was two months last winter I never saw a woman and in fact the only persons I did see during that time was Roy and our bachelor neighbor. Then the men all wonder why the women don't like it here and the women all wonder what there is about the country that the men like so well.[4]

Verna's bachelor neighbour probably also suffered from loneliness. In her study of male labour in Prairie agriculture, Cecilia Danysk cites the case of Ebe Koeppen from Germany, who recorded in his diary that he had reached a "very sad point."[5] For Koeppen, life without a wife was "slow spiritual death." He admitted that he did not write home about such things because "the staggering dreariness of such existence is too difficult to make understandable." A popular prairie song, "The Alberta Homesteader," made light of this familiar lament of single men:

My clothes are all ragged, my language is rough,

My bread is case-hardened and solid and tough

My dishes are scattered all over the room

My floor gets afraid of the sight of a broom.

climate, attracted Canadians like a magnet, and there seemed to be nothing that the nation's leaders could do to stop the exodus.

Although many Canadians were sceptical, Minister of the Interior Clifford Sifton was prepared to welcome Eastern Europeans, assessing them as good prospects to survive the rigours of pioneering on the Canadian Prairies. "I think a stalwart peasant in a sheep-skin coat, born on the soil, whose forefathers have been farmers for ten generations, with a stout wife and a half-dozen children is good quality," Sifton declared.[2] Business people were similarly enthusiastic

about such recruits, seeing them as ideal candidates for the hard, low-wage labour needed in factories, resource industries, and homes.

Under Sifton's direction, the Department of the Interior, in cooperation with transportation companies and other private recruitment agencies, advertised extensively in Europe and the United States for immigrants to settle the Prairies and work in Canada's expanding industries. These efforts coincided with a number of global trends that combined to make immigration an attractive option for many people. In Europe, ethnic and religious tensions, persecution, industrial upheaval, and the collapse of peasant farming systems "pushed" many potential emigrants to seek a new life in Canada. An upswing in the international economy, vigorous recruitment campaigns, improved transportation by steam and rail, technological breakthroughs in farming, and the relatively high wages in Canada "pulled" people to what was increasingly perceived as a land of opportunity.

Frank Oliver, who was Sifton's successor as Minister of the Interior from 1905 to 1911, pursued a more restrictive immigration policy but it failed to stem the flow of people into the country before the First World War. From a low of 16 835 arrivals in 1896 to a high of 400 000 in 1913, immigrants came from Britain, Europe, the United States, and Asia. The majority of them came from the United States and Great Britain, but enough came from other nations of the world to alter the ethnic composition of Canada. By 1920, over 20 percent of Canadians traced their origins to countries other than Great Britain and France.

The three Prairie provinces, with 54 percent of the foreign-born, were entirely transformed by the newcomers. There, Canadian, British, and American settlers lived side by side with eastern and western Europeans, each of whom contributed about 20 percent to the population. On the Pacific Coast, the cultural mix varied again. Sixty percent of the 40 000 Chinese and virtually all of the 16 000 Japanese enumerated by the 1921 census were located in British Columbia, which otherwise was 60 percent British. Only the Maritime region, with its agricultural frontier taken up and its industrial base languishing,

failed to attract a significant number of immigrants outside of its coal-mining and steel-making communities.

Canadians harboured deep fears about immigration. For many English-speaking Canadians, the tide of foreigners threatened the dominance of British culture. Francophones were even more cautious. Since most immigrants came from English-speaking countries—and those who did not quickly assimilated to the Anglo-Canadian culture—French Canadians saw themselves disappearing in a sea of English-speaking North Americans. As a result of such views, the nation become a battleground for many cultures trying to establish their place in a rigid social pecking order.

SETTLERS AND SOJOURNERS

The federal government's early difficulties in attracting large numbers of farmers to the West created an interest in sponsoring block settlements for ethnic minorities. In the 1870s, about 7400 German-speaking Mennonites left their homes in western Russia to settle in Manitoba; two decades later, their descendants spread into the area that would become the province of Saskatchewan. Also in the 1870s, 2000 Icelanders settled in Gimli ("Paradise"), Manitoba, driven from their homeland by economic depression and volcanic eruptions.

In the 1880s, the first wave of Jewish immigrants, fleeing persecution in the Russian Empire, established farming settlements in what would become Saskatchewan. By the end of the century, Jews subjected to discriminatory policies in Poland, Austria-Hungary, and Germany also turned to Canada as a place of refuge, but they found that Canada was not without its own discriminatory practices. Jews were subject to quotas restricting their entrance to medical and law schools and covenants preventing them from buying homes in elite suburbs. The Prairies were home to about 25 000 Jews by 1921. Even more could be found in Quebec

Table 16.1
Canada's Population (in thousands), 1861–1921

Year	Natural Increase	Immigration	Emigration	Net Migration	Population
1861					3230
1861–71	650	186	376	–191	3689
1871–81	720	353	438	– 85	4325
1881–91	714	903	1108	–205	4833
1891–01	719	326	507	–181	5371
1901–11	1120	1782	1066	716	7207
1911–21	1349	1592	1360	233	8788

Source: David C. Corbett, *Canada's Immigration Policy: A Critique* (Toronto: University of Toronto Press, 1957) 121.

The Cardston Temple of the Church of Jesus Christ of Latter-Day Saints.

Glenbow Archives/ND27-12

and Ontario, each of which counted almost 50 000 Jews in their population in 1921.

In the 1880s the Mormons, adherents of the Church of Jesus Christ of Latter-Day Saints, began moving to Canada from their base in Utah. Using dry-land farming techniques developed in Utah, the Mormons brought into agricultural production areas of the Prairies that had hitherto supported only open-range ranching. The Mormon population in Alberta rose to 7000 by 1912. Like other religiously defined cultural groups, the Mormons often felt the prejudice of neighbours who condemned their religious beliefs, most notably their advocacy of polygamy. The Mormons gave up this practice soon after their arrival in Canada, but Canadians were slow to forget that this had once been a distinguishing feature of Mormon culture.

Under an agreement negotiated in 1898 with the help of Russian intellectual Leo Tolstoy and University of Toronto professor James Mavor, some 7400 Doukhobors settled on 400 000 acres of land near Yorkton, Saskatchewan. Mainly followers of visionary Peter Veregin, who required his flock to live communally, they soon became divided over the degree of loyalty the group should maintain to their leader's beliefs. The most fervent followers, called the Sons of Freedom, shocked Canadians by destroying their property and conducting nude demonstrations as visible evidence of their faith. In 1906, the government began forcing Doukhobors to follow the strict letter of the homestead law. About a third of the group abandoned their communalism and remained in Saskatchewan under their leader Peter Makaroff. In 1912, the rest joined Veregin in the creation of a new utopia in the interior of British Columbia.

During the First World War, the Hutterites, a German-speaking pacifist group with communal practices, negotiated entry into Canada. Most of them had spent one or two generations in South Dakota before moving northward. Settling in Manitoba and Alberta, they established communities that resisted all efforts at assimilation. Their distinctive communal arrangements included a children's nursery, women's spinning hall, and common dining room. When a community reached a population of between 100 and 200 people, another one was established, which remained as self-sufficient, remote, and autonomous as its predecessor.

Canada also became the homeland for people from the Hapsburg provinces of Galicia and Bukovyna.

Known today as Ukrainians, they were the largest of all European peasant cultures to come to Canada. Often poor, illiterate, and oppressed in their homeland, they were the prototype of Sifton's peasant in a sheepskin coat. As many as 150 000 Ukrainians had arrived by 1914, and another 70 000 came in the interwar years. The onion-shaped dome of their church architecture and the thatched-roofed homes built by the first generation of immigrants were the most distinctive symbols of a Ukrainian presence in Canada. Because of their numbers and varied political experiences, the Ukrainians were never a uniform cultural group. Nevertheless, in their insistence on maintaining their cultural distinctiveness, the Ukrainians were, more than any other single ethnic group, says historian Gerald Friesen, "responsible for the official adoption of today's bilingual-multicultural definition of Canadian society."[6]

The majority of newcomers came to stay, but another category of immigrant, called sojourners, planned to return to their homelands with some money in their pockets. A number of eastern Europeans, from the mountain villages where the borders of Greece, Bulgaria, Serbia, and Albania meet, fell into this category. Now known as Macedonians, they began migrating to Canada to find work in the first decade of the twentieth century. Overwhelmingly single or young married men, many of them found jobs in Toronto's factories, abattoirs, and construction sites, and lived in boarding houses located in ethnic enclaves such as Cabbagetown. When Balkan wars in 1912–13 divided their homeland, many Macedonian sojourners decided to stay in Canada, a decision confirmed by the difficulties of returning to Europe during the First World War.

Italians came both as settlers and sojourners, their numbers swelling in the first two decades of the twentieth century when over 120 000 Italians arrived in Canada. Like the Macedonians, most of the Italian immigrants were young single men. They were often recruited by Italian labour agents (*padrone*) based in Montreal and Toronto who sponsored contract labour for railway and mining companies. The majority of the Italians who chose to stay in Canada lived in Montreal and Toronto; others settled in communities across the nation. The low proportion of women among them— 10 834 out of a population of 45 411 in 1911— suggests one of the reasons why 10 years later only 66 769 people of Italian origin were reported living in Canada. Some men returned to their homeland once their work contracts expired; others moved to the United States.

The Chinese, who performed the most dangerous jobs in the construction of the CPR, were also expected to leave Canada once their contracts had expired. Because their families back in China depended upon the money they sent home, many of them stayed. Angry whites complained that they were unfair competition for jobs, and began to lobby for their deportation. Responding to pressure from British Columbia where most of the Chinese had settled, the federal government imposed a $50 head tax on Chinese immigrants in 1885. The tax was raised to $100 in 1901 and $500 in 1904, equivalent to a year's wages.

Galicians at immigration sheds in Quebec City.

National Archives of Canada/C4745

The result was a gender imbalance in the Chinese-Canadian population. Shunned by the broader society, the Chinese lived in segregated Chinatowns where support was available for the homeless, ill, and aged.

Like the Chinese, most Japanese immigrants to Canada (known as *Issei*) viewed themselves as sojourners who would return home after making some money. Many did so, but by 1910 a number of Japanese men in Canada had established themselves in farming, fishing, and trade in the Vancouver and Steveston areas of British Columbia. Soon they began to bring in Japanese women and establish families. Known as "picture brides" because husbands had only their pictures when they "proposed," the women were married by proxy in Japan, after negotiations between the couple's families. The economic success of the Japanese drew the ire of their racist neighbours, who wanted to keep British Columbia "white forever."

Whether immigrant or Canadian-born, Chinese and Japanese were denied the franchise in the western provinces, barred from access to the professions, subjected to discriminatory housing covenants, and segregated in public places. They were also threatened with physical violence. In 1907, whites marched through Japanese and Chinese sections of Vancouver, breaking windows and shouting racist slogans. While an isolated example, the incident indicated the depth of the hostility faced by Asian immigrants. The federal government responded to these racist sentiments by negotiating an agreement with Japan that restricted the number of Japanese allowed to enter the country to 400 annually.

While it was difficult for Canadians to impose restrictions on immigrants from India, which, like Canada, was a colony of the British Empire, the difficulty did not stop them from trying. The federal government passed an order-in-council in 1908 requiring East Indians to come to Canada by continuous passage from India. Since there was no direct steamship line between the two countries, the regulation virtually precluded immigration. In 1913, a group of 38 Sikhs contested the restriction and were admitted. This experience encouraged others to charter the *Komagata Maru*, a Japanese-owned freighter, to bring 376 Punjabis, mostly Sikhs, to Canada in 1914. Detained on board for two months in Vancouver harbour while their case was heard before the courts, the would-be immigrants were eventually ordered to leave. Due to such policies, only 1016 East Indians were enumerated in Canada in 1921, down from 2342 (2315 men and 27 women) 10 years earlier.

By the late nineteenth century, most whites had become adherents of racist beliefs that held blacks to be mentally and morally inferior. Thus the arrival on the Prairies of some 1300 African-American homesteaders from Oklahoma between 1910 and 1912 caused a major uproar. Because they were healthy American citizens and held property, immigration regulations could not be used to keep them out. Public petitions from all three Prairie provinces urged Ottawa to ban further admission of black immigrants. While the federal government resisted such a ban, agents were sent into the United States to discourage black immigrants, and border officials were rewarded for the rigorous application of immigration regulations against blacks trying to

Chinatowns such as this one in Victoria are among the legacies of racial segregation in Canada.

National Archives of Canada/C23415

enter the country—policies that, sadly, had the effect that was intended.

"NO ENGLISHMEN NEED APPLY"

Despite their talk about keeping the country British, Anglo-Canadians were not always welcoming of immigrants from their imperial homeland. Many Canadians found the superior attitude adopted by some British immigrants particularly hard to swallow. An even greater cause for concern, especially for employers, was the socialist perspective held by those who had been associated with labour politics in Great Britain. Because many of the British immigrants came from urban backgrounds, they often made disgruntled homesteaders. Dubbed "green Englishmen" by their neighbours, they drifted to Prairie towns to find work, where they were sometimes met with signs indicating that "No Englishmen need apply."

The demand for servants by Canada's growing middle class inspired immigration officials to recruit female domestics in Great Britain and elsewhere. Between 1904 and 1914, some 90 000 British women came to Canada to work in domestic service: 60 percent came from England, 29 percent from Scotland, and 10 percent from Ireland. British sources made up about three-quarters of the immigrants who came to work as domestic servants in this period. Others came from Scandinavia and Central and Eastern Europe. Domestic servants were believed to be especially desirable immigrants because they made the most likely marriage partners for the male farmers and labourers who were the majority of newcomers in the migration process.

While many British immigrants came as single men looking for work in Canadian towns and cities, in at least one instance it was British women who were actively sought as factory operatives. John Penman, the owner of Penman's woollen factories in Paris, Ontario, recruited 700 skilled hosiery workers from the East Midlands of England between 1907 and 1928. In addition, between the 1860s and the 1920s, over 80 000 poor and orphaned children from Great Britain were sent to Canada. Most of them were indentured to farm families as cheap labour. Known as

"Home Children" because they came from homes or orphanages, they seldom received the love and care reserved for "blood" children.

As many as one-third of the immigrants who came to Canada in this period arrived from the United States. Because most of them spoke English and came as individuals, they attracted less attention from nativistic Canadians. This was especially the case with the English-speaking Canadians living south of the border who took advantage of the incentives offered in the Canadian West to return to the land of their birth. Not only were they better able to adapt to institutions that were familiar to them, but they were also likely to have extended family members in Canada upon whom they could draw for assistance.

PROVINCIAL RIGHTS AND THE MANAGEMENT OF PROGRESS

While the prosperity that prevailed during Laurier's administration helped to cover up the cracks in Confederation, it did not stop the growing regional disparity that increasingly defined the country. Nor did it stop the provinces from demanding that Ottawa pursue their interests, whether or not they conflicted with national policies. For better or for worse, federal-provincial tensions had become an enduring feature of the new nation.

During Laurier's term of office, the West was a hotbed of political discontent. The high tariff that favoured eastern manufacturers and that forced farmers to pay higher prices for their agricultural machinery and supplies was the particular focus of their animus, but there were other grievances as well. After 1905, Manitoba became insistent that its northern boundary be pushed to the 60th parallel to give it a territorial base equal to Saskatchewan and Alberta. Westerners also wanted a railway to a Hudson Bay port to provide an alternative route to export markets. In British Columbia, the white majority were alarmed by the growing number of Asians arriving on their shores and insisted that Ottawa restrict Asian immigration.

In the Maritimes, regional resentment flourished as all three provinces fell behind the rest of the nation in economic and population growth. The expansion of industries related to coal and steel in the first decade of the twentieth century masked some of the deep structural problems facing the region's economy, but no one could deny that the Maritimes generally were losing power within Confederation. In 1867, the region had held over 20 percent of the seats in the House of Commons; by 1914, its representation had dropped to 13 percent. Declining representation made it difficult for the Maritime region to shape national policies to meet its needs.

Like Macdonald, Laurier built his success on support in Canada's two largest provinces. Yet Laurier could not count on Ontario to keep him in office. The province's seats split evenly between Conservatives and Liberals in 1896, but thereafter the Conservatives won a majority of Ontario's seats in federal elections. In 1905, James Whitney's Conservatives put an end to the 34-year reign of the Liberals in Ontario's provincial government. Holding more than a third of the seats in the House of Commons, Ontario wielded considerable influence in the corridors of power and caused Laurier as many problems as the other provinces put together. The strength of the province's industrial interests threatened the delicate balance between regional and national interests, while growing imperial sentiment within Ontario's overwhelmingly anglophone population continued to clash with nationalist sentiment in Quebec.

Laurier won large majorities in Quebec throughout his political career, but the nationalist movement remained an ongoing threat to his francophone support. Henri Bourassa, the grandson of Louis-Joseph Papineau—the patriote leader in the Rebellion of 1837–38—emerged as the leader of the nationalist cause. Although he was widely respected in his native province, Bourassa's vision of a bilingual and bicultural Canada put him at odds with some nationalists who felt that Quebec should pursue a destiny independent from the rest of Canada. Bourassa concentrated on influencing public opinion and existing parties rather than forming a new organization to promote his policies. Founded in 1910, his newspaper, *Le Devoir*, emerged as a major force in developing public opinion in Quebec.

COMPETING IMPERIALISMS

The growing rivalry between Germany and Great Britain for imperial and industrial ascendancy inevitably created problems in Canada. So, too, did the jingoistic attitude of the United States whose leaders continued to resist Canada's efforts to secure a free trade treaty or a generous settlement of the Alaska boundary. Laurier's genius for compromise was sorely tested as he attempted to steer a middle course in the conflicting demands generated by the two English-speaking empires that played such a major role in Canada's political and economic life.

When Britain declared war against Dutch settlers—called Boers—in South Africa in 1899, many anglophone Canadians felt it was their war too. Laurier faced enormous pressures to send a Canadian contingent to South Africa, not only from imperialist-minded English Canadians but also from the commander of the Canadian militia and the British Colonial Secretary. In sharp contrast, Bourassa and other French-Canadian nationalists in Laurier's party were determined that Canada not be involved in the conflict, which had nothing to do with Canada's interests. French Canadians identified with the Boers, who were fleeing the clutches of an aggressive world empire.

True to form, Laurier offered a compromise: Ottawa would equip and raise volunteers, but once in South Africa they would be paid by the British. On the grounds that the effort would cost Canada little financially, he refused to debate the issue in the Commons. More than 7000 Canadians eventually saw service in the so-called Boer War. Laurier's compromise pleased neither side: it lost him the support of Henri Bourassa, who resigned from the House of Commons in 1899 to protest the Liberal Party's policy on the war; at the same time, it did little to improve his image among the jingoistic imperialists.

Laurier's refusal to give more assistance to the British war effort encouraged a number of private initiatives. Donald Smith, a former Hudson's Bay Company fur trader and railway magnate who had been raised to the British peerage as Lord Strathcona, funded an entire contingent. In Montreal, Margaret Polson Murray launched a patriotic organization of

A one-time protégé of Wilfrid Laurier (right), Henri Bourassa (left) resigned from his seat in the House of Commons over Liberal policy on the South African War. He returned to Parliament as an independent in 1900 and soon emerged as the intellectual and moral leader of French-Canadian nationalism.

National Archives of Canada/A-119 (right) and C27360 (left)

women, the Imperial Order Daughters of the Empire, to support empire unity and assist in the war effort. The enormous interest that the war sparked on the home front also inspired the establishment of a Patriotic Fund, a Canadian branch of the Soldiers' Wives League, and a Canadian Memorial Association. This latter organization was dedicated to marking the graves of the 244 Canadian fatalities and to erecting monuments to the men who fought in South Africa.

The glamour of warfare quickly wore off for those fighting in South Africa. In the first few weeks of the war, the Boers inflicted humiliating defeats on British forces, and when the empire finally threw enough troops into the field to win formal engagements, the Boers refused to surrender. Instead, they resorted to guerrilla warfare, which prolonged the war for two years. Most of the Canadian casualties were a result of the diseases that ravaged the military camps.

Following the war, Laurier was determined to find a middle ground between subordination to imperial authorities and total independence, but the task proved difficult. Canada still needed British support in negotiating with the Americans, who, like the British, seemed to be entering another expansionary phase. In 1898, the Americans had trounced the Spanish in a nasty little war over Cuba and then went on to take Puerto Rico, Guam, and the Philippines from the humiliated Spaniards. Would they use the same tactics with Canada?

The disputed boundary between Alaska and the Yukon seemed to be the testing ground. With the discovery of gold in the Klondike, the width of the Alaska

In 1899, Minnie Affleck was one of four Canadian nurses who went with the First Contingent to South Africa. In 1901, the Canadian Army Nursing Service was established as part of the Army Medical Corps, making nurses the first women to officially serve in the Canadian army.

National Archives of Canada/C51799

Map 16.3
The Alaska boundary.

Panhandle suddenly became important for determining who owned the ports through which people and goods entered the fabled gold fields. Canada's dependence on Britain in foreign affairs was reflected in the makeup of an international judicial tribunal to decide the issue in 1903. The two Canadian delegates on the three-man British negotiating team found an uncertain ally in the British appointee, Lord Alverstone, who sided with the United States. In the minds of many Canadians, Alverstone's "betrayal" demonstrated that Anglo-American friendship was more important to Britain than were good relations with its senior dominion.

As a result of the meddling of British officers in Canada's affairs during the South African War, and the bad feelings lingering from the Alaska boundary decision, the Laurier government insisted in 1904 that the officer commanding the Canadian militia be appointed by Canada rather than by Britain. Canada theoretically also assumed greater responsibility for its own defence when Britain, in 1906, withdrew its troops from Halifax and Esquimalt, the last two British bases in Canada. In 1909 John A. Macdonald's former secretary, Joseph Pope was charged with the task of establishing a Department of External Affairs for Canada. Although Great Britain was still technically in control of Canada's external relations, the growing volume of paperwork surrounding trade, boundary disputes, and other matters pointed in the direction of better organization of—and more autonomy over—the nation's foreign affairs.

The major question facing Laurier as he entered his fourth mandate in 1908 was naval defence. Given the escalating Anglo-German naval rivalry, Canadians were pressed either to make a direct financial contribution to the British Admiralty or establish their own navy. Laurier once again took a compromise position. His Naval Service Bill, introduced in 1910, proposed a Canadian navy that, in times of war, could be placed under imperial control. United in their disdain for Laurier's "tinpot navy," the Conservatives were nevertheless deeply divided between an English-Canadian majority demanding a direct contribution to the British Admiralty, and a small band of French Canadians who opposed any money being spent on naval defence.

COMPETING NATIONALISMS

Like his predecessors, Laurier faced the problem of competing views on Canada's destiny and Canadian nationalism. Anglophones who identified with the imperialist goals of Great Britain demanded that Canadians establish closer relations with their mother country, while francophones, suspicious of imperialist aims, resisted these demands. Meanwhile, some Canadians, disappointed with slow growth of the Canadian economy, argued that Canada should join the United States. Canadian nationalism, it seems, had few defenders.

Ignoring the exploitative character of imperialism, many Canadians argued that British expansion was, at least potentially, a means of spreading the message of Christianity throughout the world. The Reverend G.M. Grant, principal of Queen's University, typified this brand of imperialism. Christian, imperial, and Canadian unity were all part of the same organic whole for people like Grant, who believed that by helping to bring the spiritual and cultural benefits of western civilization to "heathen" peoples, Canadians were contributing to global progress. George Parkin, the self-styled "wandering evangelist of empire," held similar views. As a leader in the Imperial Federation Movement, he left his position as principal of Upper Canada College in 1902 to become secretary of the scholarship trust established by Cecil Rhodes, an ardent imperialist and successful entrepreneur who made provision in his will for young men throughout the empire to study at Oxford with the help of Rhodes scholarships.

Support for imperialism among English Canadians was by no means unanimous. As the high degree of interest in closer economic links with the United States suggests, many English Canadians were comfortable with the view that Canada was a North American nation, free from the weight of tradition that plagued Europe. Goldwin Smith, a British-born academic who had settled in Toronto in 1871, argued that annexation to the United States was the best option for Canada. In his book *Canada and the Canadian Question* (1891), Smith maintained that annexation would consolidate North America's peoples into one progressive nation, enhance the global power of English-speaking peoples, and resolve, in one bold stroke, the nationalist issue in Quebec.

Goldwin Smith was not alone in seeing Canada's destiny firmly bound with that of the United States. Especially in the Maritimes and the West, there was strong support for commercial union with the United States among primary producers, though few went as far as calling for political annexation. Canadians who had moved to the United States to find work were also more receptive to closer relations between the two North American nations. In the Canadian Clubs that sprang up at the turn of the century in cities such as Boston, New York, and San Francisco, businessmen argued for closer Canada-United States relations, especially in matters of trade. Annexationism was always a latent force, ready to be called into service when economic circumstances looked bleak.

Few francophones in Canada found much in the national identity debate that appealed to them, though their leading spokesman, Henri Bourassa, shared Goldwin Smith's anti-imperialism. In 1901, Bourassa introduced a bill into the House of Commons making the Canadian Parliament the only authority that could declare war on behalf of Canada. Although the resolution was voted down, it put the nation's colonial relationship to Britain on the agenda of public debate. Bourassa also took the position that Canada should be an Anglo-French nation, with two cultures having equal rights throughout the country. Because English Canada was so unreceptive to the idea, Bourassa gradually retreated from his notion of a bilingual, bicultural Canada.

Bourassa increasingly became a spokesman for the nationalist forces that had been gaining momentum in Quebec since the Northwest Rebellion. He was a leading figure in La Ligue nationaliste canadienne, an organization established in 1903 that stood for Canadian autonomy within the British Empire, provincial rights, linguistic dualism, separate Roman Catholic schools, and the economic development of Canada by and for Canadians. Although the Ligue had only a few active members, its doctrines were widely disseminated through its newspaper, *Le Nationaliste*, and the speeches and writings of Bourassa and his coterie of young followers. The enthusiasm of young people for nationalist ideas was captured in L'Association catholique de la jeunesse canadienne-française, founded in 1904.

One of the most prominent leaders of the young nationalist movement was Lionel Groulx, a priest who taught at the Valleyfield Seminary. In his numerous publications, beginning with *Croisade d'adolescents*, Groulx proclaimed a mission for French Canadians, who, he argued, had been especially chosen by God to advance the cause of Roman Catholicism in North America. When he was appointed to teach history at Laval's Montreal campus in 1915, he had a platform from which to promote his providential view of French-Canadian history, an understanding of which he and other nationalistes felt was essential to the struggle for cultural survival.

In an age of competing imperialisms there were few voices arguing for either Quebec or Canadian independence. Nevertheless the idea of a separate Quebec was taken up by Jules-Paul Tardival, a Franco-American who moved to Quebec in 1868. He advanced his idea of an independent French Roman Catholic nation on the banks of the St Lawrence in his newspaper *La Vérité* as well as in a futuristic novel, *Pour La Patrie*, published in 1895. In English Canada, John S. Ewart, who served as legal counsel for the French-speaking minority of Manitoba, wrote a series of essays arguing for Canada to become constitutionally independent, but there was little popular support for achieving such a goal until the First World War spurred Canadians into re-evaluating their lingering colonial relationship with Great Britain.

NATIVE PEOPLES AND THE DOMINANT CULTURE

Despite their presence in all provinces and territories, Aboriginal peoples throughout industrializing Canada found themselves largely outside of the national debate. Victims of blinding racism, their voices went largely unheard. The combination of immigration and high death rates quickly reduced both the absolute and relative numbers of Aboriginal people, especially in Western Canada. For instance, in 1911 Native peoples constituted a mere 3 percent of the population of Alberta. Fifty years earlier, they had been the overwhelming majority in the territory. By the beginning of the twentieth century, with their total numbers in Canada dipping below 200 000, the very survival of Canada's First Nations seemed seriously in doubt.

Because white settlers tended to view Native peoples as a nuisance in the path of "progress," the major goal of federal policy became the removal of Aboriginal peoples from their lands without provoking a violent reaction. In 1908, Frank Oliver introduced a measure that would allow Aboriginal people to be removed from reserves near towns with more than 8 000 residents. Oliver won a further amendment to the Indian Act in 1911 that allowed portions of reserves to be expropriated by municipalities or companies for roads, railways, or other public purposes. Under this legislation, almost half of the Blackfoot reserve was sold for slightly over $1 million. The McKenna-McBride Commission, created in 1912 to resolve federal-provincial differences regarding Native land claims in the province, ignored Native claims and exchanged over 14 000 hectares of reserve land for larger but significantly less valuable holdings.

Those lucky enough to hold on to good lands in the face of predatory settlers often prospered. As early as the 1880s, the Cowichan and Fraser River Valley Natives raised livestock, cereals, and market produce. In Saskatchewan, Natives practised mixed farming, with the Assiniboine Reserve reporting in 1893, for example, the harvesting of good crops of wheat, barley, oats, potatoes, turnips, carrots, and onions. They also raised cattle and sheep. On many reserves, Natives made a reasonable living as carpenters, blacksmiths, and craftspeople; others owned trading schooners, hotels, inns, cafés, and small logging and sawmill operations.

Like many other Canadians facing the challenges of industrialization, Native peoples sought jobs in the industrial economy developing around them. With the rise of tourism, many Natives secured jobs as guides for recreational hunters and fishers. The Iroquois of Kahnawaké, near Montreal, took construction jobs in that city as well as in Ontario and the United States. Cree women and girls did laundry and cleaning for wages while men worked on railway construction. In the Maritimes, a few Mi'kmaq worked in the coal mines, on the railroads, and in the steel mills. On the West Coast, women and men from Native communities worked in the lumber mills, mines, canneries, and commercial fishery. Unfortunately, the position of Aboriginal peoples in the industrial economy was often marginal, and became even more so as economic growth became defined in terms of the immigrant population.

Remedies for injustice did not come easily. As litigants in a European-based judicial system, Natives faced major social, cultural, and economic obstacles. They gradually responded by using the tactics of their adversaries: cooperation among themselves, organized protest, and demands that white men's laws relating to property rights and personal freedom be applied equally to Native peoples.

Native industrial school students and their father, Saskatchewan, ca. 1900.

National Archives of Canada/C37113

The Grand Indian Council of Ontario and Quebec, founded in 1870 by Iroquois and Ojibwa, protested Ottawa's legislation designed to expropriate their land near towns and cities. Land claims in British Columbia were the subject of a Squamish delegation to King Edward VII in London in 1906 and of a petition from the Nisga to the Judicial Committee of the Privy Council in 1913. Pan-Indian revival movements such as the Council of Tribes were still more outspoken, stating bluntly that whites had demoralized and defrauded Native peoples, who should now fight back. The pressure from the Department of Indian Affairs, the indifference and outright hostility of most Canadians, and the military might of the majority doomed such protests.

As a last resort, Natives practised widespread defiance of measures taken to restrict their freedom. When a pass system was introduced on reserves in the Northwest Territories after the rebellion of 1885, this regulation proved largely unenforceable. Attempts to ban the sun dances of the Prairie Natives in the 1890s simply drove them underground: the dances were an essential component of communion with the spirit world and, like all dances among Native peoples, were an expression of group solidarity. In British Columbia, Natives similarly defied the 1885 government ban on potlatches, the elaborate gift-giving ceremonies widely practised in west coast cultures. The government regarded the time spent potlatching as a diversion from productive work and a deterrent to the development of capitalist values. For the Natives, it was a means both of redistributing wealth and conferring honours within the tribe.

Education policies proved particularly pernicious. The federal government delegated responsibility for Native education to the major churches, which had sent missionaries to reserves to convert their charges to Christianity. While the churches professed support for assimilation of Aboriginal peoples into white society, their school curricula suggested that Natives were only welcome in the lower ranks of the social hierarchy. Little time was devoted to academic subjects; instead, much of the day was divided between religious instruction and training in manual labour for boys and household work for girls. Although about two-thirds of the Native children enrolled in schools at the end of the century attended a day school on their reserve, the government policy favoured schools well away from reserves so that children would be divorced from their culture.

NORTHERN EXPOSURE

Canada's concept of the North was gradually changing in the years following Confederation. The provinces of Quebec, Ontario, Manitoba, Saskatchewan, and Alberta achieved their present configuration early in the twentieth century, and the general view developed that the "true North" was above the 60th parallel. In the late nineteenth century, the North still belonged to the Aboriginal peoples. Before the Yukon gold rush, over half of the white population living in northern climates could be found in Labrador.

As the fur stocks in the south dwindled, Aboriginal peoples in the North were increasingly drawn into the fur trade. This was particularly the case among the Dene who inhabited the Mackenzie River Valley. In the second half of the nineteenth century, free traders (many of them Métis), missionaries, and scientists (most of them associated with the Geological Survey and the Dominion Lands Branch of the Department of the Interior) increasingly encroached on the North. The Dene also became the target for salvation by two missionary organizations, the Oblate Missionaries of Mary Immaculate and the Anglican Church Missionary Society.

The potential wealth of the north, especially the oil-laden Athabasca tar sands and the iron-bearing rocks of Ungava, was gradually recognized by the federal government. In 1895 and 1897, orders-in-council affirmed the British cession of the Arctic to Canada, laid claim to all territory between 141 degrees west longitude and a vague line running west of Greenland, and created three new northern administrative districts—Mackenzie, Yukon, and Franklin. As early as 1891, the federal government declared its determination to negotiate treaties with the Dene but was slow to do so until the discovery of gold in the Klondike galvanized them into action. Treaties 8, 10, and 11 were signed with various Dene bands beginning in 1898.

Because Canada's claim to its Arctic sector was called into question by other nations, the federal government sponsored forays into the north by Captain Joseph Bernier between 1906 and 1911. Canada's pretensions notwithstanding, American explorer Robert Peary claimed the North Pole for the United States in 1909, but the Americans failed to follow up the claim. In 1913, Vilhjalmur Stefansson led an expedition under Canadian auspices to study the marine biology, oceanography, and Inuit people of the North. Soon after setting out, the primary government vessel, the *Karluk*, was crushed in the ice, and most of its crew, who set out on foot over the ice, were never heard of again. A few managed to reach Wrangel Island, 110 miles off the coast of Siberia. Rumours that they had claimed the island for Canada set in motion a protracted sovereignty debate with the Soviet Union in the 1920s.

Although the Inuit of the eastern Arctic remained largely outside European influences until the 1930s, the peoples of the central and western Arctic were not so fortunate. The uncontrolled slaughter of whales and walrus from the 1860s to the 1880s left starvation in its wake among a people already weakened by European diseases. As a result, the original Inuvialuit people disappeared from the region and were replaced by Alaskan Inuit.

THE 1911 ELECTION

As the 1911 election neared, the plight of Native peoples, most of whom were disenfranchised under the Indian Act, was not visible on the list of Laurier's concerns. Nationalist forces in Quebec, Western alienation, and charges of corruption were not new developments but they now threatened to undermine the Liberal administration.

A timely economic initiative by the Americans seemed to provide an issue to unite the country and defeat the prime minister's opponents. Under President William Howard Taft, the Americans proposed a comprehensive trade agreement that allowed the free entry of a wide range of natural products and set lower rates on a number of manufactured goods, including agricultural implements and machinery so necessary for Canadian farms. Here, it seemed, was the solution to agrarian grievances and a means of satisfying those who had long worked for closer trade relations between Canada and the United States.

At first glance, the phlegmatic Robert Laird Borden, federal Conservative leader since 1901, was not the man to challenge the charismatic Laurier. Yet this respectable Halifax lawyer had managed to rebuild a party shattered by the divisions of the 1890s. Like his predecessors, Borden was determined to pursue policies that would foster economic growth, but unlike Macdonald and Laurier, he was a progressive in his approach to policy. Borden emphasized morality, duty, and efficiency in government and struggled to eliminate some of the worst abuses of the old patronage-ridden system. In 1907, at a meeting in Halifax, the Conservatives unveiled a new platform that included endorsement of progressive policies such as free rural mail delivery, civil service reform, senate reform, provincial rights, public ownership of telegraphs and telephones, and federal aid to technical education. The Halifax platform failed to win many votes in 1908, but it remained the foundation for many of the policies promoted by the Conservatives in the 1911 campaign.

Conservative prospects were raised by the defection of two key interest groups from the Liberal fold. Enraged by the prospect of reciprocity, 18 prominent Toronto businessmen and financiers, along with the Canadian Manufacturers Association, deserted the party they had formerly supported so generously. Together with dissident Liberal MPs like Clifford Sifton, they denounced reciprocity as a threat to Canadian survival, a step toward absorption by the United States, and a threat to Canada's manufacturing interests.

Laurier's Quebec stronghold also crumbled as Bourassa's nationalists, damning the naval policy as a sell-out to English Canada, found common cause with Quebec francophone Conservatives. Borden promised to scrap Laurier's "tin-pot navy" and in its place make an "emergency" $35-million contribution to Great Britain's efforts to keep the imperial navy—on which Canada really depended—strong and efficient. This would buy time, Borden argued, for Canadians to reflect more deeply on their defence policy.

Reciprocity and the naval policy, the two issues that more than any other posed the question of Canada's future, combined with the usual appeal of patronage, local issues, and individual candidates to defeat the Liberals. Although the popular vote was close, the distribution of seats was decisive. The Liberals won only 13 of Ontario's 86 constituencies and altogether captured only 87 ridings; the Conservatives took 134 seats, including 27 in Quebec. Neither Laurier's liberalism nor his efforts to steer a middle course between differing visions of Canada proved sufficient to the problems of the day.

THE BORDEN ADMINISTRATION, 1911–1914

Having come to power in 1911 with the support of Quebec nationalists and the anti-free trade business community, Robert Borden faced the challenge of keeping the Conservative coalition together. To make matters worse, the economy began to sink into a recession in 1912. People across the country were thrown out of work, and the unemployed began drifting to cities, where they stretched municipal and charitable resources to the limit. Perhaps most frustrating for Borden was his inability to get some of his most innovative policies passed by Parliament. Although the Conservatives had a majority in the House of Commons, the Liberal-dominated Senate rejected or severely amended much of the government's legislation.

Borden's support in Quebec quickly evaporated after the election. The leader of the Quebec contingent of the cabinet, F.D. Monk, was uncomfortable in the anglophone milieu of Ottawa and held views on imperial policy that were diametrically opposed to those promoted by Borden's imperialist-minded colleagues. Quebec nationalists had formed an alliance with the Conservatives in 1911 because they opposed Laurier, but a common enemy was not enough to keep them together once the party came to power. A little over a year after taking office as Minister of Public Works, Monk resigned over the naval question. Like other Quebec nationalists, he was opposed to any policy that smacked of excessive subservience to the British.

Monk's defection from the cabinet did not make it easier to resolve the naval issue. When the Conservative Party's Naval Aid Bill was introduced into the House of Commons, it encountered such fierce opposition from the Liberals that the government invoked closure, a manoeuvre designed to limit debate. This was the first time that such a procedure had been used in Canada, and Laurier pointed to it as justification for instructing the Liberals in the Senate to defeat the bill. In making this decision, Laurier undoubtedly took into consideration the views of the nationalists in his native province, but he was probably also taking revenge for Borden's scrapping of his naval program.

Bills creating the Tariff Commission and providing subsidies to provincial highways also fell victim to the Senate's powers to veto and amend bills. In justifying their obstructionism, Liberal senators argued that the Borden administration was usurping powers that were not authorized by the BNA Act. Even the Grain Act of 1912, which created a Board of Grain Commissioners and gave the federal government the power to own and operate terminal grain elevators, had to be carefully administered so as not to invoke the wrath of the Liberal senators.

Not all programs foundered on the rock of Senate intransigence. In the West, Borden's popularity soared when he agreed to support the construction of a railroad to Hudson Bay. Farmers were pleased when many of the provisions of the aborted free trade agreement of 1911 were made available in the Underwood Tariff adopted by the United States in 1913. In 1912, Borden made good on his promise to Canada's most powerful provinces— Quebec, Ontario, and Manitoba—that he would grant them huge sections of federally administered territories on their northern borders. Many Canadians, including bankers and brokers, were relieved when the federal government stepped in to save the nation's two faltering railway companies from impending bankruptcy in 1914.

Borden appointed a commission headed by Sir George Murray, a British public servant with impeccable credentials, to investigate the federal civil service. In his report, Murray recommended a complete overhaul of a system that had become top-heavy, patronage-ridden, and inefficient. Borden's government took steps to introduce reforms, but the existing system was so inadequate that it was unable—and probably not all that eager—to preside over its own transformation.

Nothing was so disturbing in the long run as the economic recession that descended in 1912. While business and government leaders understood that a credit crunch and overexpansion had created the crisis, most people experienced it as bankruptcy, unemployment, and reduced purchasing power. The federal government responded in 1913 by appointing a commission on the cost of living and by urging the railways to maintain high levels of employment. In the larger cities, municipal governments established employment bureaus. These efforts proved inadequate. Many people were facing real misery and, with immigrants still pouring into the country, there was every possibility that social unrest would be more than local police forces could manage. In May 1914, 200 immigrants marched through the streets of downtown Winnipeg, waving shovels and

The Tories on tour in the West in 1911. Pictured is the lead car, with Borden seated behind the driver.

shouting "Work or bread." This incident was a harbinger of what could come if economic conditions failed to improve.

CONCLUSION

Borden's concerns over the economy and the Senate's obstructionism were quickly superseded with the outbreak of the First World War in the summer of 1914. Other concerns, some older than Confederation itself,

would remain to complicate wartime planning. Despite impressive economic growth and successful political compromises, Canada was still a fragile nation-state. Alternative destinies, including provincial independence, union with the United States, and imperial federation, continued to attract those who were disappointed in what Canada had to offer. The survival of the First Nations was seriously in doubt. When wartime stresses were added to the curious brew called Canada, the very survival of the nation would be called into question.

NOTES

1 "First Annual Banquet," January 18, 1904, *Addresses Delivered before the Canadian Club of Ottawa, 1903–1909* (1910), cited in *Colombo's Canadian Quotations*, ed. John Robert Colombo (Edmonton: Hurtig, 1974) 332.

2 Cited in J.W. Dafoe, *Clifford Sifton in Relation to His Times* (Toronto: Macmillan, 1931) 142.

3 Varpu Lindström-Best, *Defiant Sisters: A Social History of Finnish Immigrant Women in Canada* (Toronto: Multicultural History Society of Ontario, 1988) 27.

4 Cited in John W. Bennett and Seena B. Kohl, *Settling the Canadian-American West, 1890–1915: Pioneer Adaptation and Community Building* (Lincoln: University of Nebraska Press, 1995) 68.

5 Cecilia Danysk, *Hired Hands: Labour and the Development of Prairie Agriculture, 1880–1930* (Toronto: McClelland and Stewart, 1995) 71–72.

6 Gerald Friesen, *The Canadian Prairies: A History* (Toronto: University of Toronto Press, 1984) 265.

SELECTED READING

A good survey of the Laurier and Borden administrations can be found in R.C. Brown and Ramsay Cook, *Canada, 1896–1921: A Nation Transformed* (Toronto: McClelland and Stewart, 1974). Biographies of Laurier include Joseph Schull, *Laurier* (Toronto: Macmillan, 1965); Richard Clippendale, *Laurier: His Life and World* (Toronto: McGraw-Hill Ryerson, 1979) and Réal Bélanger, *Wilfrid Laurier: quand la politique devient passion* (Quebec: Presses de l'Université Laval, 1986). Borden's administration is discussed in R. Craig Brown, *Robert Laird Borden: A Biography*, 2 vols. (Toronto, Macmillan, 1980) and John English, *The Decline of Politics: The Conservatives and the Party System, 1901–1920* (Toronto: University of Toronto Press, 1977).

On the Yukon in this period, see William R. Morrison, *True North: The Yukon and Northwest Territories* (Toronto: Oxford University Press, 1998); William R. Morrison and Ken Coates, *Land of the Midnight Sun: A History of the Yukon* (Edmonton: Hurtig, 1988); and Charlene Porcild, *Gamblers and Dreamers: Women, Men and Community in the Klondike* (Vancouver: UBC Press, 1998).

On outmigration, see Yolande Lavoie, *L'émigration des Canadiens aux États-Unis avant 1930* (Montreal: Les Presses de l'Université de Montréal, 1972; Betsy Beatie, *Obligation and Opportunity: Single Maritime Women in Boston, 1870–1930* (Montreal: McGill-Queen's University Press, 2000); and Patricia A. Thornton, "The Problem of Outmigration from Atlantic Canada, 1871–1921: A New Look," *Acadiensis* 15.1 (Autumn 1985): 3–34.

On immigration and immigrants, the major surveys are Ninette Kelley and Michael Trebilcock, *The Making of the Canadian Mosaic: A History of Canadian Immigration Policy* (Toronto: University of Toronto Press, 1998); Jean Burnet with Howard Palmer, *"Coming Canadians": An Introduction to the History of Canada's Peoples* (Toronto: McClelland and Stewart, 1988); Dirk Hoerder, *Creating Societies: Immigrant Lives in Canada* (Montreal: McGill-Queen's University Press, 1999); Gerald Tulchinsky, ed., *Immigration in Canada: Historical Perspectives* (Toronto: Copp Clark Longman, 1994); and Franca Iacovetta et al., *A Nation of Immigrants: Women, Workers, and Communities in Canadian History, 1840s–1960s* (Toronto: University of

Toronto Press, 1998). Among other key works are Donald Avery, *Reluctant Host: Canada's Response to Immigrant Workers, 1896–1994* (Toronto: McClelland and Stewart, 1995); Howard Palmer, *Patterns of Prejudice* (Toronto: McClelland and Stewart, 1982); and Barbara Roberts, *Whence They Came: Deportation from Canada 1900–1935* (Ottawa: University of Ottawa Press, 1988). Much valuable information on immigration and settlement in this period is condensed in the pamphlets of the Canadian Historical Association's *Canada's Ethnic Groups* series. See also D.J. Hall, *Clifford Sifton*, 2 vols. (Vancouver: University of British Columbia Press, 1985). Also see Catherine Cavanaugh and Jeremy Mouat, eds., *Making Western Canada: Essays on European Colonizations and Settlement* (Toronto: Garamond Press, 1996) and Veronica Strong-Boag et al., eds., *Painting the Maple: Essays on Race, Gender, and the Construction of Canada* (Vancouver: University of British Columbia Press, 1998).

Publications dealing with specific groups and regions include Orest Martynowych, *The Ukrainian Bloc Settlement in East Central Alberta, 1890–1930: A History* (Edmonton: Alberta Culture, 1985); Lubomir Luciuk and Stella Hryniuk, eds., *Canada's Ukrainians: Negotiating an Identity* (Toronto: University of Toronto Press, 1991); George Woodcock and Ivan Avakumovic, *The Doukhobors* (Ottawa: Carleton Library, 1977); Lillian Petroff, *Sojourners and Settlers: The Macedonian Community in Toronto to 1940* (Toronto: University of Toronto Press, 1995); Bruno Ramirez, *The Italians of Montreal: From Sojourning to Settlement, 1900–1921* (Montreal: Éditions du Courant, 1980) and *On the Move: French-Canadian and Italian Migrants in the North Atlantic Economy, 1860–1914* (Toronto: McClelland and Stewart, 1990); John Zucchi, *Toronto Italians* (Montreal: McGill-Queen's University Press, 1988); Irving Abella, *A Coat of Many Colours: Two Centuries of Jewish Life in Canada* (Toronto: Lester and Orpen Dennys, 1990); Gerald Tulchinsky, *Taking Root: The Origins of the Canadian Jewish Community* (Toronto: Lester Publishing, 1992); Hans Lehmann, *The German Canadians 1750–1937: Immigration, Settlement and Culture* (St John's: Bassler Gerhard, 1986); Frank H. Epp, *Mennonites in Canada, 1786–1920: The History of a Separate People* (Toronto: Macmillan, 1974); Hugh Johnson, *The Voyage of the* Komagata Maru: *The Sikh Challenge to Canada's Colour Bar* (Delhi: Oxford University Press, 1979); Patricia E. Roy, *A White Man's Province: British Columbia Politicians and Chinese and Japanese Immigrants 1858–1914* (Vancouver: UBC Press, 1989); W. Peter Ward, *White Canada Forever: Popular Attitudes and Public Policy Toward Orientals in British Columbia*, 2nd ed. (Montreal: McGill-Queen's University

Press, 1990); and J. Brian Dawson with Patricia Dawson, *Moon Cakes in Gold Mountain: From China to the Canadian Plains* (Calgary: Detselig, 1991). On child immigrants, see Joy Parr, *Labouring Children: British Immigrant Apprentices to Canada, 1896–1924* (Montreal: McGill-Queen's University Press, 1980) and John Bullen, "Hidden Workers: Child Labour and the Family Economy in Late Nineteenth-Century Urban Ontario," *Labour/Le Travail* 18 (Fall 1986): 163-87.

The general context of Canadian-American relations in this period are provided in the books by Granatstein/Hillmer and Mahant/Mount cited in the previous chapter as well as C.C. Tansill, *Canadian-American Relations, 1875–1911* (Toronto: Ryerson, 1943). The Alaska Boundary Dispute is the focus of Norman Penlington, *The Alaska Boundary Dispute: A Critical Appraisal* (Toronto: McGraw-Hill Ryerson, 1972) and John Munro, *The Alaska Boundary Dispute* (Toronto: Copp Clark, 1970) and touched on by William R. Morrison, *The Mounted Police and Canadian Sovereignty in the North, 1894–1925* (Vancouver: University of British Columbia Press, 1985). On imperial relations, see Carl Berger, *The Sense of Power: Studies in the Ideas of Canadian Imperialism, 1867–1914* (Toronto: University of Toronto Press, 1970) and *Imperial Relations in the Age of Laurier*, ed. Carl Berger (Toronto: University of Toronto Press, 1969). The South African War is extensively covered in Carman Miller, *Painting the Map Red: Canada and the South African War, 1899–1902* (Montreal: McGill-Queen's University Press, 1993) and Robert Page, *Imperialism and Canada, 1895–1903* (Toronto: Holt, Rinehart and Winston, 1972). On the Department of External Affairs, see John Hilliker, *Canada's Department of External Affairs*, vol. 1, *The Early Years, 1909–1946* (Montreal: McGill-Queen's University Press, 1990).

The 1911 election is explored in Paul Stevens, ed., *The 1911 General Election: A Study in Canadian Politics* (Toronto: Copp Clark, 1970).

Clerical nationalism is explored in Susan Mann Trofimenkoff, *L'Action Française: French-Canadian Nationalism in the Twenties* (Toronto: University of Toronto Press, 1975); Joseph Levitt, *Henri Bourassa and the Golden Calf: The Social Program of the Nationalists of Quebec, 1900–1914* (Ottawa: University of Ottawa Press, 1969); Jean Hamelin and Nicole Gagnon, *Histoire du Catholicisme québécois*, Part 3, *Le XXe siècle* (Montreal: Boréal Express, 1984); and Arthur Silver, *The French Canadian Idea of Confederation, 1864–1900* (Toronto: University of Toronto Press, 1982).

On Native peoples in this period, J.R. Miller, *Shingwauk's Vision: A History of Native Residential Schools*

(Toronto: University of Toronto Press, 1996); Douglas Cole and Ira Chaikin, *An Iron Hand upon the People: The Law Against the Potlatch on the Northwest Coast* (Vancouver: Douglas and McIntyre, 1990); Rolf Knight, *Indians at Work: An Informal History of Native Indian Labour in British Columbia, 1858–1930* (Vancouver: New Star Books, 1978); Paul Tennant, *Aboriginal Peoples and Politics: The Indian Land Question in British Columbia, 1849–1989* (Vancouver: UBC Press, 1990); Katherine Pettipas, *Severing the Ties that Bind: Government Repression of Indigenous Religious Ceremonies on the Prairies* (Winnipeg: University of Manitoba Press, 1994); David C. Mandelbaum, *The Plains Cree: An Ethnographic, Historical and Comparative Study* (Regina: Canadian Plains Research Centre, 1978); Peter Schmalz, *The Ojibwa of Southern Ontario* (Toronto: University of Toronto Press, 1990); Ellice B. Gonzalez, *Changing Economic Roles for Micmac Men and Women: An Ethnohistorical Analysis* (Ottawa: National Museum, 1981); Ruth Holmes Whitehead, *The Old Man Told Us: Excerpts from Micmac History, 1500–1950* (Halifax: Nimbus, 1991); Keith J. Crowe, *A History of the Original Peoples of Northern Canada* (Montreal: McGill-Queen's University Press, 1991); and two books by Ken S. Coates, *Best Left as Indians: Native–White Relations in the Yukon Territory, 1840–1973* (Montreal: McGill-Queen's University Press, 1991) and *The Marshall Decision and Native Rights* (Montreal: McGill-Queen's University Press, 2000). Missionary work among Native peoples in the North is discussed in John Webster Grant, *Moon of Wintertime: Missionaries and the Indians of Canada in Encounter since 1534* (Toronto: University of Toronto Press, 1984) and Robert Choquette, *The Oblate Assault on Canada's Northwest* (Ottawa: University of Ottawa Press, 1995).

 WEBLINKS

WILFRID LAURIER
www.parcscanada.gc.ca/parks/quebec/laurier/en/index.html

The Sir Wilfrid Laurier National Historic Site includes detailed biographical information and photographs.

KLONDIKE GOLD RUSH
http://yukonalaska.com/klondike/index.html

The Klondike Weekly is an online magazine dedicated to celebrating the Klondike Gold Rush and the people who experienced it.

SOUTH AFRICAN WAR VIRTUAL LIBRARY
www.bowlerhat.com.au/sawvl

This site includes numerous links related to Canada's involvement in the Boer War, including photos and information on Canadian soldiers.

ROBERT BORDEN
www.nlc-bnc.ca/2/4/h4-3200-e.html

View a biography, several of Sir Robert Borden's speeches, and more at this National Library of Canada site.

The New Industrial Order, 1867–1914

In 1871 Edwige Allard, a carpenter's wife living in Montreal's St Jacques ward, kept a one-acre garden that provided much of the food for her household of nine: herself, her husband, their six children, and Edwige's father-in-law. According to the census taken in that year, she produced ten bushels of beans, ten bushels of potatoes, and four bushels of other root crops. Families in some Montreal neighbourhoods also kept cows, pigs, and chickens in their backyards. By the twentieth century, it was difficult for women in Canada's rapidly growing cities to contribute to the family economy through their farming activities. Only the wealthy could afford a home with enough land for a garden, while municipal by-laws made it illegal to keep animals in urban spaces. For housewives such as Madame Allard, options for contributing to the family economy were now limited to sharing her home with boarders, taking in laundry or sewing, doing piecework at home, or going out to work for wages.[1]

The new industrial order had a dramatic impact on the lives of all Canadians. The 1911 census showed that over 40 percent of Canadians lived in towns and cities, up from 20 percent in 1871. With their mechanized equipment, Canadian farms were more productive than ever before, but fewer people were making their living from agricultural pursuits. Urban-based industries employed people in increasing numbers and business cycles began to have more impact than the seasons in determining the rhythms of work.

ASSESSING THE NATIONAL POLICY

While not everyone had an easy ride on the rocky road to industrialization in Canada, the overall economic trends were in the direction of impressive growth. The total output of goods and services, known as the gross national product (GNP), multiplied several times between 1867 and 1921 and the population rose from 3.5 million to 8.5 million. By 1915, three rail lines stretched across the continent, linking cities, towns, and villages, many of which had not even existed in 1867. Wherever it went, the railway spurred economic growth and laid the foundations for a national economy dominated by the banks and businesses in Montreal and Toronto.

Three policies—a protective tariff, transcontinental railways, and sponsorship of immigration— emerged as the cornerstones of the federal government's national development strategy. By linking the provinces, the railways enabled tariff-protected goods to find national markets. Immigration ensured passengers for railways and markets for Canadian products. Together, these policies were designed to bring Canada into an age of sustained industrial growth. In retrospect the National Policy looks impressively integrated, but it actually developed in a piecemeal fashion and was challenged by regional, occupational, and individual agendas.

The importance of the National Policy in promoting industrial growth and economic expansion has long been debated. Detractors of the policy, then and now, charge that the tariff benefited producers at the expense of consumers and encouraged investors to establish firms destined for failure. By protecting domestic manufacturers from foreign competition, they argue, the National Policy encouraged the development of industries that could never compete in international markets. Regional critics maintain that the policy encouraged economic development in Central Canada to the detriment of the Maritimes and the West.

In contrast, supporters of the National Policy have argued that protection is necessary to allow infant industries to succeed against competition from established companies in other countries. Canada's model, after all, was the United States, where the importance of tariffs in promoting industrial development is generally conceded. Moreover, supporters point to statistics showing that, in the decade following the implementation of the National Policy tariff,

capital investment increased 114 percent, total wages paid by manufacturers rose by 68 percent, and the number of manufacturing establishments grew by 52 percent over the previous decade. They also argue that, because of the National Policy, Canada was in a better position to take advantage of improved economic conditions in the late 1890s.

While the role of tariffs in Canadian economic development remains controversial, there are several points of agreement. It is clear, for example, that under the protective cloak of the National Policy tariff, Canadian entrepreneurs moved to fill needs hitherto met by American imports. Southern Ontario, in particular, became the centre of specialized industries that served a national market. The agricultural implements industry is a good case in point. Using American patents as well as developing their own lines, the Ontario firms of Massey Manufacturing of Toronto and A. Harris and Son of Brantford had emerged as leaders in the industry before Confederation. The implementation of a 35 percent tariff on imported agricultural machinery in 1883 gave them a tremendous boost in the Canadian market. When in 1891 the two companies merged as Massey-Harris, capitalized at $5 million, they formed Canada's largest corporation, controlling over half the Canadian sales of agricultural machinery and accounting for 15 percent of the manufactures exported from Canada between 1890 and 1911.

There is also clear evidence that the National Policy laid the foundations for a branch-plant economy in Canada. Despite the success of such companies as Massey-Harris, many of the new companies, including Singer Sewing Machine, Gillette, Swift's, Coca-Cola, and Westinghouse, were American-owned. Their managers built factories in Canada to sell in a market that was protected from direct imports by high tariffs. In this period, the government welcomed foreign companies that sought to scale the tariff wall, and remained unconcerned about the nationality of company owners or the address to which profits were delivered.

The National Policy did little to shield Canada from dependence on foreign countries, primarily Great Britain and the United States, for capital and technology. Nor did it protect Canadians from international economic trends. Rising tariffs in the United States, fluctuating capital markets in Great Britain, and recessions in either country were immediately felt in Canada, and there was little Canadians could do economically or politically to alter that reality. International trends meant that economic growth remained sluggish from 1867 to 1896, then soared upward until 1912; the First World War sent it soaring again. Shorter business cycles resulting in slowdowns in 1873–79, 1893–96, and 1903–07, and 1913–14 were also felt in Canada.

It is impossible to determine whether another approach to economic development would have been more successful. No matter what they did, Canadians lived in a world dominated by the British Empire and were located on the border of the United States, an emerging industrial giant. When the Canadian economy was experiencing healthy growth, the American economy was often performing even better, encouraging people to move across the border to find work. In global terms, Canada's economic performance in this period was spectacular, but compared to the United States, the results seemed less impressive.

TRANSPORTATION AND COMMUNICATION

Railways played a major role in Canada's Industrial Revolution. By 1915, Canadians boasted over 55 000 kilometres of track capable of shuffling goods and people from the Atlantic to the Pacific and even into the Yukon. By reducing transportation costs, railways expanded the geographic range in which products could be marketed. There was, for example, little likelihood of a bushel of wheat selling at a profit in the London market before the completion of the Canadian Pacific Railway because the cost of transporting grain by cumbersome boat and overland trails made the product uncompetitive in international markets. With the introduction of lower freight rates on eastbound grain under the Crow's Nest Pass Agreement of 1897, and cutthroat competi-

tion resulting from the railway-building orgy of the early twentieth century, Prairie wheat farmers emerged as highly competitive players on international grain exchanges. The increased efficiency of rail communication was reflected in the inauguration of daily postal service across the nation in 1886, and rural postal delivery in 1908.

Ocean travel was also improving in safety and capacity. Reliable steamship service carried Prairie wheat, Ontario bacon, and Nova Scotia apples to British markets on time and usually in good condition. Under the auspices of the federal government, which had responsibility for navigational aids, Canada's coasts and inland waterways sprouted lighthouses, channel markers, and wharves. When the *Titanic* was sunk by an iceberg in 1912, it shocked Canadians, who had become less accustomed to marine disasters than their grandparents had been. Increased capacity and lower rates also encouraged the traffic in immigrants.

The major threat to the supremacy of steam-powered transportation was the internal combustion engine, used in both automobiles and aircraft. After the first manufacturing plant—a Ford branch plant—opened in Windsor, Ontario, in 1904, the auto industry thrived in Canada. By contrast, aircraft transportation was slow to get off the ground.

Intercolonial Railway works. Moncton's development as a manufacturing and distributing centre in the late nineteenth century had much to do with the fact that it became the eastern headquarters of the Intercolonial Railway.

Moncton Museum Collection

Aeronautical experiments by J.A.D. McCurdy and F.W. Baldwin under Alexander Graham Bell's Aerial Experiment Association in Cape Breton managed the first manned flight in the British Empire, with McCurdy in the cockpit, in 1909, but it had few practical results.

Developments in transportation were matched by equally revolutionary advances in communication. Before he experimented in aviation, Alexander Graham Bell had become a household name with his highly publicized telephone call between Brantford and Paris, Ontario, in 1876. Initially perceived as a novelty, the telephone quickly became a popular necessity for business and personal use. Yet another communication first occurred in 1901 when Guglielmo Marconi received a wireless signal from the other side of the Atlantic by hoisting an antenna on a kite on Signal Hill in St John's. Meanwhile, Canadian-born Reginald Fessenden was experimenting with wireless telegraph and voice transmissions, conducting the first broadcast of the human voice by radio from his laboratory in Massachusetts in 1906.

This conquest of time and space through developments in transportation and communication made traditional ways of telling time awkward. In 1867, clocks were set by astronomical calculations in each major locality. This meant, for example, that 12:00 noon was 15 minutes earlier in Halifax than in Moncton. The railway and telegraph demanded a more standardized approach, especially in a country as big as Canada. Appropriately, it was a Canadian, Sandford Fleming, who convinced those attending the International Prime Meridian Conference in 1884 in Washington to adopt a global system of telling time based on hourly variations from a standard mean, which is still in use today.

SECONDARY INDUSTRY

In the 50 years following Confederation, secondary industry went from strength to strength. The first phase of Canada's Industrial Revolution, which occurred roughly between 1850 and 1900, was characterized by a rapid expansion of consumer goods industries, such as textiles, clothing, footwear, and cigars. The second phase, beginning around 1900, was fuelled by a surge in capital goods industries, such as

MORE TO THE STORY

Measuring the Canadian Economy

Economists divide the economy into three sectors: primary or staple industries such as hunting, fishing, forestry, farming, and mining; secondary or manufacturing industries that add value through the processing of primary resources; and tertiary or service industries that facilitate the use and development of primary and secondary resources. The tertiary sector includes financial services, trade, transportation, utilities, and public administration as well as services ranging from street cleaning to teaching. Together, the output of goods and services is called the gross national product (GNP). In 1986, Statistics Canada adopted gross domestic product (GDP) to measure the nation's economic performance. The GDP is calculated in the same way as the GNP except that it excludes payments on foreign investment. Since the goods and services produced outside of the market economy, such as housework and voluntary labour, are not included in calculations of GNP, the na-

tional output is considerably greater than the official figures indicate. In 1996, Census Canada began collecting data on unpaid labour in and outside of the household, which accounts for much of the work performed by Canadians.

Table 17.1

Percentage Sectoral Distribution of the GNP, 1880–1920

Year	Primary	Secondary	Tertiary	Other
1880	43.5	22.7	22.4	11.4
1890	36.6	28.1	26.7	8.6
1900	36.5	25.0	29.4	9.1
1910	30.2	27.8	33.6	8.4
1920	26.6	29.7	35.3	8.4

Source: William L. Marr and Donald Paterson, *Canada: An Economic History* (Toronto: Gage, 1980) 22.

machinery and equipment, and new technologies that spurred development in mining, pulp and paper, and electrical and chemical industries. By 1921, nearly 30 percent of Canada's GNP was derived from manufacturing and construction (see Table 17.1), a proportion that remained virtually constant to the end of the twentieth century.

The emergence of a vigorous iron and steel industry at the turn of the century signalled Canada's arrival as an industrial nation. Located in convenient proximity to coal mines on Cape Breton Island and an abundant supply of iron ore shipped from Bell Island, Newfoundland, Sydney became home to two industrial giants: Nova Scotia Coal and Steel and Dominion Iron and Steel. After several false starts, the Hamilton Steel and Iron Company began pouring open-hearth steel in 1900 and established its dominance in the field following its reorganization as Stelco in 1910. By that time American visionary Francis Hector Clergue had capped his industrial empire at Sault Ste Marie with a massive steel and iron works. Between 1877 and 1900, Canadian iron production increased over sixfold and multiplied tenfold again by 1913.

biography

Max Aitken

Canada's most flamboyant financier was Max Aitken. The son of a Presbyterian minister, Aitken grew up in northern New Brunswick and turned to selling bonds and insurance when he failed the entrance examination to Dalhousie Law School. As the protégé of Halifax businessman John Stairs, Aitken became president of Stairs's new holding company, Royal Securities, in 1903. After speculating in utilities in the Caribbean and Latin America, Aitken moved to Montreal, used Montreal Trust to take over Royal Securities, and was a key figure in the merger movement of 1909–12.

His crowning achievement was putting together the Steel Company of Canada in 1910, a conglomerate that included the Montreal Rolling Mills, Hamilton Steel and Iron, Canada Screw, and Canada Bolt and Nut. Having made his fortune, Aitken moved to London where he had marketed much of his speculative stock, became a Member of Parliament, bought himself a title—Lord Beaverbrook—and continued to keep an eye on his Canadian interests. Among Beaverbrook's merger-making associates was a future Canadian prime minister, R.B. Bennett, whose millions were earned in part by collaborating with Aitken to merge grain elevators and hydro-electric stations on the Prairies.

Max Aitken.

National Archives of Canada/PA-006478

Canada's heavy industry expanded impressively during the first two decades of the twentieth century. In addition to the rails and rolling stock required for the railways, Canadian factories turned out binders and seed drills, bicycles and carriages, furniture, and appliances to satisfy the Canadian market. Stimulated by economic growth, construction materials such as lumber, bricks, glass, stone, and cement figured prominently in the secondary sector. The demand for factories, public buildings, homes, and tenements sustained a construction industry that accounted for over 5 percent of the GNP by 1921.

As manufacturing became more complex, intermediate goods required in the production process became a larger segment of secondary industry. Among the most successful intermediate goods industries were those producing the bolts, nails, nuts, screws, and similar products. Acids, alkalis, and heavy chemicals, essential ingredients in pulp and paper, iron and steel, oil refining, the electrical industry, and agriculture also experienced increased demand.

There was a clear geographical structure to the Canadian economy as it emerged under the National Policy. Neither the Maritimes nor the western provinces managed to emulate the manufacturing success of the central Canadian provinces, whose head start in the Industrial Revolution was evident even before Confederation. By 1901, Ontario accounted for fully half of the gross value of Canadian manufacturing and Quebec for nearly one-third. Once set, this pattern remained remarkably constant.

THE NEW FACE OF AGRICULTURE

Primary industries were also transformed in the industrial age. As agriculture evolved from a way of life to an industry, successful farms became larger and more highly mechanized, while subsistence farms on marginal lands were quickly abandoned. The decline in the relative importance of farming in this period reflects the fact that fewer farms were required to meet the Canadian and international demand for food.

Stimulated by local demand and the almost insatiable British market for staple foods, commercialized farming flourished in Ontario. With rail and steamship service offering more reliable transportation, cold storage facilities, and lower freight rates, huge quantities of Ontario's bacon, cheese, butter, and eggs found their way to British larders by the end of the nineteenth century. Ontario farmers also branched into industrial crops such as sugar beets, grapes, and tobacco and grew most of the fruit and vegetables that were canned in Canada prior to 1920.

Cattle raising in Quebec's Eastern Townships proved a highly profitable venture, and Quebec farmers exported butter and cheese to Great Britain. However, Ontario's farms remained more productive than those of Quebec, where families were larger, mechanization slower, and farm surpluses less abundant. The Maritimes, like Quebec, had a large number of marginal farms but, in fertile areas such as the St John River Valley, the Annapolis Valley, and Prince Edward Island, farmers took up commercial farming to take advantage of expanding urban markets at home and abroad. Potatoes were a successful

The longest steel cantilever bridge in the world, the Quebec City Bridge, opened in 1919, was designed to carry trains across the St Lawrence. It collapsed twice during construction, killing, in total, 84 workers, 37 of them Mohawk high steel workers from Kahnawaké.

Archives de la Ville de Québec: collection de documents iconographiques; photographie imprimée issue du volume intitulé The Quebec Bridge, Department of Railways and Annale; côte 21491

What a difference a century makes in the shoe industry.

McCord Museum of Canadian History, Montreal, M930.50.262 and M930.50.5.142

crop throughout the region, and in the Annapolis Valley of Nova Scotia, the production of apples, destined primarily for the British market, increased nearly tenfold between 1881 and 1911.

The Prairie wheat boom is the most spectacular agricultural success story of this period. Between 1901 and 1913, wheat production expanded from 56 million to 224 million bushels, grain exports increased by 600 percent, and wheat soared from 14 to 42 percent of total Canadian exports. A variety of factors came together to make the wheat boom possible: faster maturing strains of wheat, the chill steel plough (which could handle the prairie sod), gas-driven tractors, rising world prices, lower transportation costs, a steady supply of immigrant labour, and encouragement from public and private agencies. Together, these factors transformed the Prairies from a fur trade frontier to the breadbasket of the world, its wheat production second in volume only to that of the United States.

Although significant, wheat was by no means the only product of western agriculture. Dairy farming was important in Manitoba, as was mixed farming in the Park Belt of the Prairies and in British Columbia. Between 1885 and 1905, cattle ranching flourished in the Alberta foothills. Canada's "wild West" was developed by "gentlemen farmers" such as Senator Matthew Cochrane, a pioneer cattle breeder and successful shoe manufacturer from the Eastern Townships. With an embargo on American imports, generous terms for leasing land, and the completion of the CPR—all provided by the obliging Macdonald government in the 1880s—ranching fever gripped Alberta. Cattle ranching also flourished in the Okanagan Valley in the wake of the gold rush. Despite their initial success, ranchers in both Alberta and British Columbia were soon fighting a rearguard action against farmers who, armed with dryland farming techniques, insisted on breaking up the cattle range.

Scientific and technological innovation had an enormous impact on agricultural production. It has been estimated that the development of the fast-maturing Marquis wheat by Dominion Cerealist Charles E. Saunders added over $100 million to farm income between 1911 and 1918. While horse- and human-power continued to be the chief sources of energy on Canadian farms, engine power was introduced as early as 1877 when the first steam threshing machine was used in Woodbridge, Ontario. Steam threshers could process more in a day than the average farmer produced in a year and soon transformed the harvesting process. Gasoline engines and tractors became practical in the second decade of the twentieth century.

FISH, FOREST, AND FURS

The East Coast fisheries, like agriculture, adjusted unevenly to the new economic order. In the second half of the nineteenth century, the inshore fisheries came under increasing competition from deep-sea fleets, while canning and cold storage emerged as new ways of preserving fish, supplementing salting, drying, and pickling. Investment poured into canning factories designed to process lobster, herring, and sardines, and into cold storage facilities to handle fresh fish. While technology and transportation dictated that the fresh fish industry would become centralized in a few communities, the canned and salt fishery remained dispersed and uncoordinated. Because virtually every fishing port had a canning factory, the product varied widely in quality, and workers were relegated to seasonal employment. Quality control also plagued the saltfish industry, which was beginning to face stiff competition in its traditional Latin American and southern European markets.

On the West Coast, the salmon fishery developed quickly in the final decades of the nineteenth century, and by 1900 salmon had become the most profitable fishery in Canada, surpassing cod in the value of sales. Steveston, where a large number of canneries were built, became known as the sockeye capital of the world, exporting its canned salmon largely to a British market. In 1902, much of the industry was centralized under the British Columbia Packers Association. A company backed by eastern Canadian and American capital, it was based in New Jersey, a state whose liberal incorporation laws made it a popular base for companies avoiding anti-trust legislation. The new company consolidated and mechanized the packing process, increasing its profits by reducing the costs of both labour and fish supply. The Smith butchering machine, whose popular name, the "Iron Chink," reflected the racist attitudes toward Asian cannery workers, processed 60 to 75 fish a minute and encouraged the mechanizing of filleting, salting, and weighing. When the sanitary can and the double seamer were introduced in 1912, the automated assembly line became a reality.

British Columbia was also Canada's new timber frontier. By the 1880s, most of the white pine forests of Eastern Canada had been laid to waste. The demand for lumber for construction in rapidly growing North American cities was met by the majestic Douglas fir and cedar of the West Coast. Between 1871 and 1880, some 350 million board feet of timber were cut in British Columbia; in the second decade of the twentieth century, the figure had risen to a staggering 13.5 billion, and lumbering had emerged as one

of British Columbia's most lucrative industries. The forests of Eastern Canada continued to produce lumber, fine woods for furniture, pit props for mines, railway ties, shakes, shingles, and laths. They also came into their own in the production of pulp and paper, an industry that expanded rapidly at the end of the nineteenth century.

New technology and modern business practices also transformed the fur industry. By the first decade of the twentieth century, fur farming had begun to emerge as an alternative to hunting and trapping. Based primarily in Prince Edward Island, the raising of fox, mink, and other fur-bearing animals in captivity was made more practical by the introduction of woven wire enclosures in the late 1890s. Thereafter, the industry developed quickly, stimulated by improved breeding methods, the growing demand of the fashion industry, and the declining population of the world's wild fur-bearing animals. By 1910, Prince Edward Island breeders fetched as much as $15 000 a pair for their silver fox on the London market. Faced with this form of competition, the Hudson's Bay Company introduced bureaucratic management structures, used railways and steamships where possible, and pushed into new fur trade frontiers.

THE MINING INDUSTRY

Canada's mining industry grew dramatically in the years following Confederation. The new era of mining activity got off to a dramatic start when gold was discovered in the Klondike in 1896, but it had relatively less impact on the Canadian economy and business community than other mining ventures. Since the Industrial Revolution was built on resources of coal, iron, and other base metals, the discovery and exploitation of these resources drew most of the investment, if not the popular attention.

Coal mining in the Maritimes, Alberta, and British Columbia expanded in the late nineteenth century to supply Canadian trains, factories, and homes. By the beginning of the twentieth century, huge quantities of coal and iron were processed in Canada's steel plants. Surveys conducted for the CPR and the Canadian Geological Survey revealed the potential wealth locked in the Canadian Shield and the western mountain ranges. When the chemical and mechanical processes for separating complex ores were developed at the turn of the century, the nickel-copper deposits around Sudbury and zinc-lead-silver deposits in British Columbia became profitable fields for exploitation. Capital poured into Canada from all over the world to bring the vast storehouse of mineral wealth into production.

The discovery of copper-gold deposits at the base of Red Mountain in 1887 created an instant boom town at Rossland, British Columbia. By that time, an American promoter, F.A. Heinze, had built a smelter at Trail, which was connected to Rossland by a narrow-gauge railway. Following its decision to build a line through the Crow's Nest Pass, the CPR bought Heinze's interests and incorporated them in the Consolidated Mining and Smelting Company of Canada (Cominco) in 1906. As a CPR subsidiary, Cominco had access to extensive capital resources, which were used to develop hydro-electrical power in the region and to solve the metallurgical problem of separating ores. By 1910, British Columbia's mineral output was second in value only to Ontario's, much of it extracted from the fabulous Kootenay region.

Rich mineral resources were concentrated in "New Ontario," the area between Sudbury and Hudson Bay, which was granted in huge sections to Ontario by the federal government or the courts between 1874 and 1912. Following the discovery of copper sulphides in the Sudbury Basin in 1883, American promoter Samuel J. Ritchie established the Canadian Copper Company to develop Sudbury's deposits for refining by the Orford Copper Company in New Jersey. In 1888, a smelter was constructed at Copper Cliff to concentrate the nickel-copper matte prior to shipping.

In 1902, Canadian Copper and Orford merged to form the International Nickel Company, or INCO, of New Jersey. The increasing demand for nickel-steel armour plate in a rapidly militarizing Europe led Mond Nickel of Wales to establish a base in Sudbury, which emerged as the world's major supplier of nickel. At the same time, discoveries of gold, silver, and cobalt along the route of the Timiskaming and Northern Ontario Railway put the names of Cobalt, Timmins,

Kirkland Lake, and Porcupine on the map. The value of minerals produced in Ontario increased fourfold between 1900 and 1910 and nearly doubled again in the next decade, making Ontario Canada's leading province in the mining industry.

Quebec's rich mining frontier was slow to develop, but the extraordinary range of mineral resources inspired a variety of initiatives. At the end of the nineteenth century, foreign companies began working the asbestos deposits in the Eastern Townships. Although Quebec quickly became the world's leading producer of this rare mineral, most of the processing was done outside of Canada, and the fierce competition between mining companies resulted in overproduction, gluts, and slowdowns that made the industry highly unstable. The copper and gold deposits of the Abitibi region of Quebec, though identified, were not seriously exploited until the 1920s.

With nearly 80 percent of Canada's electrical generating capacity, Ontario and Quebec dominated the second industrial revolution based on mining, chemicals, and pulp and paper, which relied on abundant energy resources. Ontario's initiative in developing Niagara Falls gave the province a massive source of hydro-electric power. In Quebec, American capital developed the mighty Shawinigan Falls on the St Maurice River. Shawinigan soon attracted an aluminum smelter, pulp mill, and chemical factories. Unlike Ontario, which made hydro a government-run service in 1906, Quebec left the hydro industry to private enterprise, giving entrepreneurs free rein to charge lower rates to commercial customers if they chose to do so. Whether publicly or privately owned, the abundant supply of hydro-electric power served as a magnet to industry.

SERVING THE INDUSTRIAL ECONOMY

While the primary and secondary sectors provided much of the drama surrounding Canada's rise to industrial maturity, the service sector emerged as the major contributor to Canada's GNP by the end of the First World War. The Industrial Revolution in

Canada and elsewhere was carried forward by a growing army of clerks, cleaners, cab drivers, cooks, and secretaries as well as managers, bankers, lawyers, engineers, and civil servants. In 1921, as many people worked in service industries as in the primary sector, performing jobs, such as electrical repair, automobile sales, and switchboard operation, that could scarcely have been imagined in 1867.

Clerical work was one of the fastest-growing occupations in an industrializing Canada. While the general labour force grew by 10.4 percent between 1891 and 1901, the clerical sector rose 73.3 percent. The growth continued in the first decade of the twentieth century and reached an astounding 109.3 percent between 1911 and 1921. By the latter date, clerical workers represented nearly 7 percent of the labour force. Another change had also taken place in this 30-year period. In 1891, women comprised only 14.3 percent of those working in clerical positions; by 1921, 41.8 percent of clerical workers were women, and the trend toward feminization of clerical work continued throughout the twentieth century.

As transportation improved and nationwide markets emerged, retail operations grew and changed. The changes in retailing activity can be seen in the meteoric rise of the T. Eaton Company. In 1869, Timothy Eaton opened a dry-goods and clothing store on Yonge Street in Toronto. His method of selling, which included fixed prices, cash only, and money-back guarantees, proved so popular that he moved to larger premises, equipped with an elevator, in 1883. In 1884, Eaton reached across the country to grab business from local retailers when he issued his first mail-order catalogue. The expansion in sales allowed Eaton's to manufacture its own merchandise, thus bypassing wholesalers and suppliers. In 1893, Eaton's established the first of a number of overseas operations in London. Eaton's also opened a branch in Winnipeg in 1905, the first in a chain-store business that would expand dramatically in the 1920s. Robert Simpson, also of Toronto, paralleled the Eaton experience.

Until the First World War, men worked as bank tellers while women were assigned less visible roles as clerks, stenographers, and telegraphers.

City of Vancouver Archives CVA-17-57

MASS PRODUCTION AND MODERN MANAGEMENT

Market expansion led to reorganization of the structure of industry, encouraging small-scale, owner-operated businesses to evolve into bureaucratic, multipurpose, and multinational corporations. The limited liability corporation separated individual wealth from corporate wealth and made corporations independent legal entities. No longer tied to the fate of a single person or a few individuals, the corporation took on a life of its own. At the same time, ownership was divorced from management functions, which were increasingly carried out by salaried employees. No individual, no matter how energetic or gifted, could keep on top of the details of such rapidly expanding businesses. Nor was such control desirable. Chief executive officers needed their time to mobilize capital and plot long-range corporate strategy.

Control over day-to-day operations of large corporations was achieved through structural reorganization. At the turn of the century, management techniques became the focus of attention for business people trying to maximize the profits of their enterprises. Scientific management, a term coined by American Frederick W. Taylor, advocated that managers take responsibility for coordinating work processes and that employees be deprived of any initiative or authority in deciding how to do their work. On the shop floor this meant that the labour process was broken down into simple repetitive tasks and that employee output was closely monitored by supervisors.

At the management level, rigid hierarchies with clear lines of authority were developed and new accounting procedures implemented to control production and labour costs. When Henry Ford perfected the assembly line for his Model T in 1914, artisans who once performed the most skilled of manufacturing operations—the assembly of complex machinery—were forced to submit to the dictates of management and the machine.

SURVIVAL OF THE FITTEST

Driven by the Darwinian logic that held that only the fittest survived, corporate managers were forced to keep ahead of the competition or go to the wall. Not surprisingly, entrepreneurs were decidedly unenthusiastic about unrestrained competition. While giving lip-service to free enterprise, they secretly agreed to fix prices and agitated publicly for policies that would guarantee them a "living profit." Nationwide associations, such as the Dominion Wholesale Grocers Guild, Retail Merchants Association, Canadian Manufacturers Association, and Canadian Bankers Association, tried to regulate the activities of their members, but restrictions on "unfair" trading practices often failed to bring order to the marketplace because it took only one entrepreneur to break an agreement.

For most businesses, growing bigger meant becoming more efficient, reaping the benefits of economies of scale, and gaining an edge over competitors. If a company could become big enough, it might be possible to sweep all competition aside and establish a monopoly over the marketplace. Although "monopoly" was a bad word in industrializing Canada, anti-combine laws, first introduced in 1889, had little impact on corporate practices. A spate of mergers in the 1880s was followed by an even bigger merger movement in the early twentieth century. Between 1909 and 1912, some 275 Canadian firms were consolidated into 52 enterprises, capitalized at nearly half a billion dollars.

The merger movement brought to the fore some of Canada's major corporate giants. Vertically integrated companies were capable of handling all the functions of the industry, including supplying their own raw materials and shipping their products in company-owned boxcars. Their vast assets enabled them to mobilize capital on a scale hitherto unimaginable. Although such companies were technically not monopolies, their size gave them tremendous power in the reorganized marketplace. They could outbid and outlast their smaller competitors and make it difficult for new competitors to break into the industry. The fact that many of the companies established at the turn of the twentieth century are still household names in Canada—Imperial Oil, Bell Canada, General Electric, Stelco, and the Canada Cement Company—is visible testimony to their triumph over the "invisible forces" of the marketplace.

Consolidation was also the order of the day in banking. In 1871 Ottawa passed an act requiring banks to have assets of at least $500 000, resulting in the eventual dissolution of small banks. Between 1880 and 1920, while the number of branches rose from under 300 to 4676, the number of banks operating under dominion charter declined from 44 to 18. No longer simply vehicles for facilitating exchange, banks encouraged savings accounts by paying interest on deposited money, transferred funds from their many branches to profitable investment frontiers, and developed modern management structures. By 1920, four of the five Canadian banks that still tower over the business centres of most Canadian towns and cities—

Nova Scotia, Commerce, Montreal, and Royal—had established their position in the financial firmament.

HUMAN CAPITAL

By 1914, Canada had a charmed circle of multimillionaire businessmen who had made fortunes through mergers and investments. Their success was conspicuously displayed in palatial homes, knighthoods, and unprecedented power. On the other end of the social scale, life was not so rosy. In many occupations, 12-hour work days were common and compensation fell below a living wage.

Disease and injury were often the fate of industrial workers. Workers stricken by injury or disease were in the difficult position of having to prove employer negligence in order to sue for compensation. In the second decade of the twentieth century, Ontario, Nova Scotia, British Columbia, Alberta, and New Brunswick passed Workman's Compensation Acts, which conceded a limited right to industrial compensation. Still, many employees found no protection from the high levels of zinc, mercury, asbestos, dry-cleaning fluids,

dyes, and other chemicals that went unregulated. Coal miners and textile workers aged prematurely, their lungs so damaged by coal dust and fabric fibres that they coughed themselves to death.

Children in the workforce were particularly vulnerable. In Montreal, for example, young cigar makers who were unable to keep up with unrealistic demands, or who were unwilling to defer to the whims of supervisors, often had their wages docked and were subjected to physical discipline and confinement. Punishments were imposed to exact conformity, break a child's independence, and ensure regular work habits. In families where the child's income was critical to survival, parents often supported employers in their efforts to "train" young workers.

Women also faced discrimination in the workplace. In keeping with the gendered notions of work that prevailed in industrializing Canada, skill, while arguably an objective concept, was socially constructed. For example, printing, though it required little talent or training, was a well-paid "skilled" occupation that excluded women, while dressmaking, which required considerable skill, was a poorly paid "unskilled" line of work in which women were employed. As the structures of industrialization were gradually put in place, it became the ideal that a married man earned a "family wage" in the marketplace while his wife stayed home to do the housework and raise the children or, in middle-class families, to supervise servants who did this work.

Company owners kept unskilled male workers in line by threatening to replaced them with lower-paid women, children, and immigrants. Legislation was eventually passed limiting the age at which children could be hired and the types of work done by women, but employers' exploitation of immigrant men posed a major threat to workers attempting to bring fairer practices into the workplace. In response to demands of an increasingly organized labour

Garment workers in Quebec City.

Archives nationales du Québec à Québec/P535/N-79-12-43

movement, the Laurier government passed an Alien Labour Act (1897) designed to make it unlawful for "any person, company, partnership, or corporation, in any manner...to assist or solicit the importation of immigration of any alien or foreigner into Canada under contract or agreement...to perform labour or service of any kind in Canada." Despite its sweeping scope, the Alien Labour Act failed to prevent companies from importing contract labour and strikebreakers when they were determined to do so. The act was rarely enforced and applied only to the importation of labour from the United States.

Modern management techniques and hiring practices reduced the autonomy of many workers; so did the company-town phenomenon. Mining and textile-mill towns were frequently owned lock, stock, and barrel by companies. Homes, stores, schools, doctors, and even churches were firmly under corporate control. Cape Breton, Alberta, and British Columbia coal, Quebec asbestos, and Ontario gold, silver, and nickel were mined by workers who lived in company towns. While some factory owners took a paternal attitude toward their workers, most resorted to authoritarian control to keep their workers in line.

THE UNION MOVEMENT

At the time of Confederation, unionized labour was still too weak to exert much political pressure. The Trade Union Act of 1872 removed common-law prohibitions against unions as combinations in restraint of trade, but no laws forced employers to bargain collectively with their employees or prevented employers from dismissing employees who supported unionization.

Despite the obstacles, workers organized resistance. In 1871, Toronto printers struck all of the city's newspapers in an attempt to force the nine-hour day on the whole publishing industry. The publishers, led by Liberal Party notable George Brown, successfully prosecuted the strikers for seditious conspiracy, while 10 000 people paraded in support of the accused and their strike demands. Throughout 1872, the movement for the nine-hour day reverberated throughout industrial Canada, only to be quelled by the crushing recession of 1873. While the movement failed to

achieve its objective, it produced a degree of solidarity among workers that re-emerged once the recession lifted.

In the 1880s and 1890s, the strike became firmly established as labour's chief method of attempting to win improvements for workers. While there had been only 204 in the 1870s, there were 425 recorded strikes in the 1880s and 600 in the 1890s. A key player in the strike wave was the Noble and Holy Order of the Knights of Labor. The Knights originated in 1869 among Philadelphia garment cutters concerned about the loss of worker control in their industry, and spread quickly across the United States. By the early 1880s it had a foothold in Canada. Unlike craft unions, which organized workers according to their trade, the Knights were open to all workers regardless of skill and encouraged workers to support each other's struggles.

It was not only employers who recoiled at the class consciousness promoted by the Knights. Craft union leaders claimed that the exclusive right of workers to practise certain trades would be whittled away if the Knights succeeded in developing all-inclusive "industrial" unions. During the recession of the late 1880s, the craft unions began to force workers to choose between the Knights and separate craft unions. The Knights retained many locals, especially in Quebec, but their isolation increased as the Trades and Labour Congress (TLC), created in 1883, emerged as the major political voice of Canadian labour.

Dominated by craft-based unions, the TLC fought against industrial unions almost as hard as it did against employer intransigence. It also adopted the policy of its counterpart in the United States—the American Federation of Labor—of calling for higher wages and improved working conditions rather than for radical changes to the capitalist system. In 1902, at a meeting in Berlin, Ontario, the TLC formally affiliated with the American Federation of Labor. It then proceeded to expel industrial unions such as the Knights of Labor from its ranks and to consolidate its position as the dominant labour organization in the country. The TLC exiles established a rival organization, the National Trades and Labour Congress, in 1907. Although its numbers were small, it offered a national-ist alternative for Canada's working men and women.

LABOUR, CULTURE, AND REGION

During Canada's rise to industrial maturity, labour organizations were fragmented along regional and cultural lines. In Nova Scotia, the Provincial Workmen's Association (PWA), established in 1879, emerged as the most powerful voice of the province's working class. Militant in its early years, the PWA shut down all the province's mines on two occasions, and its fiercely independent locals waged over 70 strikes before 1900. When strike activity increased during the first decade of the twentieth century, Maritime coal miners turned to the even more radical American-based United Mine Workers (UMW) of America to help them in their struggles.

Miner militancy on the East Coast was matched in British Columbia, where a Mutual Protective Society was established in 1877 among workers at Dunsmuir, Diggle and Company. The society protested wage cuts and short-weighing of coal on company scales (the workers were paid by the ton) and closed down the Wellington mine on Vancouver Island. Robert Dunsmuir, the province's leading capitalist, convinced the government to use the militia to force the miners back to work, but a long history of miner organization and militancy in British Columbia had

begun. By 1905–06, the UMW had gained a foothold in the coal fields of southwestern British Columbia and Alberta.

In Quebec, francophone workers were encouraged to look for assistance from the Roman Catholic Church rather than from secular unions, which the church condemned as foreign-dominated and materialistic. Church-sponsored unions were initially conservative in their approach to labour rights, but priests assigned to the unions soon became sensitive to the plight of working people. In 1921, Catholic unions came together as the Confédération des travailleurs catholiques du Canada with an outlook similar to that of the TLC.

While many unionized workers held their own in the workplace, the position of common labourers remained precarious. The most vulnerable among male wage labourers were the navvies—men who worked in construction gangs that built the railways and other public works. Living in grim bunkhouses and eating stale bread, a navvy had experiences of the work world far removed from those of the proud craftsman. Such workers were ripe for the message of Industrial Workers of the World (IWW), an American-based organization, founded in 1905, that rejected both the parliamentary process and traditional unionism. The Wobblies, as they were called, focused on the strike as the most effective political weapon and urged their members to walk off the job collectively when a fellow worker was unjustly treated by an employer.

Women were largely excluded from labour organizations but this did not stop them from protesting labour practices in trades that they dominated. In 1900, female spoolers in Valleyfield's cotton industry walked off the job when apprentices were hired to perform their work. The women had limited bargaining power because textile workers could easily be replaced, but women in more skilled occupations also fared poorly in their confronta-

Bunkhouse men experienced some of the worst working and living conditions in industrializing Canada.

National Archives of Canada/PA-115432

tions with management. In 1907, over 400 Bell telephone operators in Toronto went on strike to protest a reduction in hourly rates for their highly skilled and physically taxing work. The strikers agreed to submit their grievances to a federal arbitration commission whose members were more concerned about the impact of dangerous working conditions on the maternal potential of the women, most of whom were between the ages of 17 and 22, than about the ability of the women to make a living wage.

Since most Asians and blacks were excluded from unions, they worked in manual jobs, many of them seasonal and part-time, which made it difficult for them to form their own unions. One exception was the occupation of railway porters. Although their hours were long and the pay low, working on the trains was almost a rite of passage for many African-Canadian men. In 1918, porters of the Canadian Northern Railway, then in the process of becoming part of the CNR system, organized Canada's first black union, the Order of Sleeping Car Porters. The Canadian Brotherhood of Railway Employees initially refused to accept the union but relented in 1919 to become the first craft union to abolish racial restrictions on membership.

Unions made their presence felt during Canada's rise to industrial maturity, but they had little success in restructuring capitalist development in the interests of labour or in expanding their membership. Only 5.6 percent of the labour force in Ontario and 8.4 in Quebec was organized by 1911. While some of the difficulties can be attributed to the conservative agenda promoted by the international unionism of the TLC, this was only partly the cause. Union leaders were often overtly racist and sexist, thereby alienating a significant proportion of their potential membership. Many employers, harking back to the paternalism that they felt characterized pre-industrial relations, tried to earn the loyalty of their skilled and

As this photo of the 1914 Street Railway Strike in Saint John suggests, peaceful demonstrations sometimes led to violence when police tried to disperse demonstrators.

Provincial Archives of New Brunswick Harold Wright Collection/P338-200

experienced employees by sponsoring company picnics, excursions to nearby tourist sites, and even company bands. When such inducements failed to work, employers used force, calling upon governments to send in police, militia, and troops to put down strikes and to coerce labour into compliance.

LABOUR AND THE STATE

Alarmed by the growing class conflict, governments at all levels tried to find a "middle way" that would reduce the worst excesses of the capitalist system while leaving its structure largely intact. The Macdonald government appointed the Royal Commission on the Relations of Labour and Capital in 1886 to investigate the cause of worker discontent. Its majority and minority reports submitted in 1889 provide a wealth of information on the shocking conditions in Canadian factories, but the commissioners' recommendations yielded few immediate reforms, other than the declaration in 1894 of a holiday—Labour Day—for Canada's working people.

In 1900, the federal Liberals established a Department of Labour and hired a university-trained

One Hundred and Two Muffled Voices 2

The Royal Commissioners studying the relations between labour and capital heard the testimony of nearly 1800 witnesses. Only 102 of those who testified were women. Although women made up over 20 percent of the paid labour force in 1891, nobody on the commission was very interested in hearing from them. As historian Susan Mann Trofimenkoff has revealed, it took a great deal of courage for working people generally and women in particular to speak before a formal body such as a royal commission. Saying something that offended employers might threaten a worker's job. Nearly half of the women testified anonymously; only 30 of the close to 1700 male witnesses did so.

The most dramatic testimony relating to women's work came from a woman identified as Georgina Loiselle. Beaten by her employer for her "impertinent" refusal to make a hundred extra cigars, she was still employed at the factory five years later when she gave her testimony. Her employer justified his behaviour to the commissioners on the grounds that "her mother had prayed me...to correct her in the best way I could." With three of Georgina's brothers also employed by the company, the factory's owner had assumed the role of disciplinarian to the fatherless Loiselle children. Georgina was 18 at the time of the beating, and no one, including Georgina herself, seemed particularly surprised by her employer's brutality.

When the commissioners submitted their report, they indicated much greater concern over the moral consequences of women working in unchaperoned settings and using common washrooms with men than they did about the poor salaries and working conditions that were uniformly the lot of wage-earning women in Victorian Canada.

labour relations expert, William Lyon Mackenzie King, to be its first deputy minister. In 1907, King helped to engineer the Industrial Disputes Investigation Act (Lemieux Act), which prohibited strikes and lockouts in public utilities and mines until the dispute had been investigated by a tripartite board of arbitration representing labour, capital, and government. By establishing a compulsory cooling-off period, the act deprived organized labour of its strongest weapon, the surprise strike, without any compensatory protection against retaliation by the employer, such as hiring strikebreakers. The TLC asked the Conservatives to repeal the act when they were elected to power in 1911, but Robert Borden let the legislation stand.

FAMILY AND WORK

The shift to an industrial economy had an enormous impact on the Canadian family. While self-sufficiency was rare even in pre-industrial British North America, a majority of family units produced a substantial proportion of the goods they consumed, relying only peripherally on the sale of their products and their labour in the marketplace. By the twentieth century, the market played a major role in the lives of virtually every Canadian. Urban dwellers, in particular, lacked the resources to produce most of their own food, clothing, or shelter, but even in the countryside, the true subsistence farm family was becoming rare and was, in most cases, desperately poor.

Families responded to the new market economy in a gendered way. In many farming families, women began in the mid-nineteenth century to increase their production for off-farm sales, becoming major producers in dairying, poultry raising, market gardening, and fruit growing. As these areas of farming expanded and wheat farming declined east of Ontario, men took over what had previously been considered women's work. Dairying was entirely transformed in the second half of the nineteenth century. Increasingly the pasturing, feeding, calving, and milking, once regarded as women's work, were appropriated by men. For many women, this shift in farm responsibilities was welcomed as a reduction of the heavy physical labour that characterized their daily lives, but it also reduced their power in the family and community context.

Farm children at work on the Prairies, ca. 1900.

Glenbow Archives/NA2157-1

Working-class children often entered the paid labour force at age 11 or 12—and even younger—and lived with their parents for perhaps another 15 years before marrying. In 1871, the census reported that 25 percent of boys and 10 percent of girls between the ages of 11 and 15 had occupations outside the home. Factory Acts passed in Ontario and Quebec in the mid-1880s, and later replicated in other provinces, prohibited employment of boys under 12 and girls under 14 in factories, but these laws were poorly enforced and frequently circumvented by families close to destitution.

Most working-class families were poor at some stage in their evolution. Generally, at the time of marriage, savings and two incomes allowed a couple to enjoy an acceptable, if modest, standard of living, but poverty was especially pronounced for large families consisting of children too young to work or to be left unsupervised while the mother entered the labour force. In such cases, the wife's marginal earnings from piecework, laundry, or boarders often meant the difference between a family's subsistence and destitution. Families headed by women—those who had never

married, were widowed, or whose husbands had deserted them—as well as families where the husband was too ill to work were in a particularly precarious position.

URBANIZATION

Industrialization was paralleled by an unprecedented movement of people from rural to urban areas of the country. In the boom years from 1901 to 1911, the populations of Montreal and Toronto increased by 49 and 58 percent, respectively. Even this growth paled in comparison with that of Winnipeg, Calgary, Edmonton, and Vancouver (see Table 17.2). Urbanization changed the way people thought about community and left rural areas scrambling to respond to the loss of population. Despite the problems surfacing in congested cities, they were exciting places to live, offering amenities and opportunities that rural folk were hard-pressed to emulate.

Cities in Western Canada grew out of nowhere to dominate their rural hinterlands. A sleepy village in 1871, Winnipeg would have remained a backwater except for the determination of local merchants to have the Pacific railway put its main line through town and construct its western yards and shops there as well. With the railway in place and Prairie agriculture under way, Winnipeg emerged as the third-largest city in Canada by 1911. Other Prairie cities, including Edmonton, Calgary, Saskatoon, and Regina, had begun to expand by the end of the century, but the railyards and Winnipeg's position as the main distribution point for the region gave it an advantage in attracting new industry. It became the home of the grain exchange whose speculators bid on the wheat crop, and developed a substantial manufacturing sector, including clothing, furniture, and food processing firms as well as metal shops dependent on the railway.

Table 17.2

Population of Selected Canadian Cities, 1871–1921
(ranked in order of size for 1921)

City	1871	1891	1901	1921
Montreal	115 000	219 616	328 172	618 506
Toronto	59 000	181 215	209 892	521 893
Winnipeg	241	25 639	42 340	179 087
Vancouver		13 709	29 432	163 220
Hamilton	26 880	48 959	52 634	114 151
Ottawa	24 141	44 154	59 928	107 843
Quebec	59 699	63 090	68 840	95 193
Calgary		3 867	4 392	63 305
London	18 000	31 977	37 976	60 959
Edmonton		700	4 176	58 846
Halifax	29 582	38 437	40 832	58 375
Saint John	28 805	39 179	40 711	47 166

Source: Alan Artibise, *Winnipeg: A Social History of Urban Growth* (Montreal: McGill-Queen's University Press, 1975) 132; George A. Noder, *Cities of Canada*, vol. 2, *Profiles of Fifteen Metropolitan Centres* (Toronto: MacMillan, 1976).

Jasper Avenue in Edmonton, 1890 (top) and 1910.

Provincial Archives of Alberta, E. Brown Collection/B4755 and National Archives of Canada/C7911

Like Winnipeg, Vancouver owed its growth to the CPR. To become the terminus of that company's transcontinental line, Vancouver provided subsidies and tax holidays to the company. Competing with Victoria, whose commission merchants continued for another 20 years to control trade with Britain and California, Vancouver's merchants sought to dominate the British Columbia economy. They convinced city council to provide a $300 000 subsidy to local promoters of a railway to the Upper Fraser Valley, spent $150 000 on a bridge across False Creek to connect the city with roads to the Fraser Valley, and gave subsidies to the initiators of a sugar refinery and a graving dock.

Wherever they were located, cities harboured the worst features of uncontrolled growth in this period. Noise, overcrowding, poor sewerage systems, and inadequate roads combined to make life unpleasant for most city dwellers. Yet, some urban dwellers lived in much better circumstances than others. The gap between rich and poor was evident in the segregated neighbourhoods of all major Canadian cities and in the stark contrast between the spectacular homes and office buildings of the wealthy and the substandard housing and dust-ridden factories of workers.

Montreal, Canada's largest city, manifested all the worst features of uncontrolled growth. By the end of the nineteenth century, most of its working class citizens lived in rundown tenements; its infant mortality rate was among the highest in the Western world; and the hierarchy of ethnic privilege was rigidly maintained.

In 1896 Herbert Ames, a businessman and social reformer, conducted a survey of living conditions in Montreal. Ames focused on two areas of the city, areas he labelled "the city below the hill" and "the city above the hill." Above the hill, Ames noted, there were "tall and handsome houses, stately churches and well-built schools," while below the hill "the tenement house replaces the single residence, and the factory with its

A one-room dwelling in Winnipeg, c. 1915.

Provincial Archives of Manitoba/N2438

smoking chimney is in evidence on every side." Beautiful parks and abundant greenery added to the charms of the homes in the upper city; below, "one paltry plot of ground, scarce an acre in extent, dignified by the title of Richmond Square, is the only spot where green grass can be seen free of charge." Above the hill, all the homes had modern plumbing and looked out on wide, well-paved, clean streets; below the hill, half the houses lacked running water and made use of pit-in-the-ground privies. Below the hill, population density was more than double the city average, and the residents suffered disproportionately from disease, crime, drunkenness, poverty, and early death.[3]

Later studies have confirmed the view that there were two cities in Montreal, with the rich and poor living completely different lives. As late as the 1920s, children of Montreal's wealthier families, the majority of them of English and Scottish Protestant backgrounds, had a much higher life expectancy than those who were born into poor families, many of them French and Irish Roman Catholics. The continuing high infant mortality rate in poor districts of Montreal can be traced in large part to contaminated milk and water. While affluent families could afford to purchase milk that was certified pure, 90 percent of the milk shipped to Montreal in freight cars was unfit for human consumption. The elite were also

more likely to be able to afford better food and to live in areas served by adequate water, sewerage mains, and municipal parks. When bad weather or epidemics rendered urban life especially unsafe or uncomfortable, they could escape to hideaways outside the city, like those in Ontario's Kawarthas or along Quebec's North Shore.

Toronto, Canada's second largest city, was only marginally better off than Montreal. Although falling land prices made home ownership possible for an increasing number of Toronto's working families, slum conditions prevailed in the back-lane cottages of St John's Ward and in areas close to railyards, factories, and packinghouses.

Despite the general recognition by the 1870s of the role of polluted water in carrying disease, many city governments were slow to install better water systems outside the wealthy neighbourhoods. Only in central Winnipeg where the commercial elite lived was the water supply adequate. In the working-class north end, water was delivered to homes but the sewage system emptied into the river with the result that deadly Red River fever (typhoid) was a continuing problem in the area. The combination of a poor water supply and wooden buildings could translate into uncontrolled fires that destroyed many homes. In 1877, a major fire left 15 000 people homeless in Saint John, and 15 years later the homes of 10 000 people were destroyed by fire in St John's.

Halifax, with its military base, was unique among Canadian cities. When the British withdrew their troops from Canada in 1871, they retained their garrison in Halifax, which served as Britain's naval and military base for the North Atlantic. Grog shops, brothels, and disreputable boarding houses thrived on Barrack Street just below the Citadel and helped to sustain the lifestyle of the repeat offenders committed to Rockhead Prison, a substantial octagonal building located in the north end of the city. After Barrack Street was closed to the military and its name changed to South Brunswick in the early 1870s, "soldiertown" drifted to adjacent areas and continued to be a major cause for concern among urban reformers.

CONCLUSION

By the turn of the century, few people could ignore the inequality that characterized the age of industry. In every Canadian town and city, hideous slums stood in sharp contrast to the elegant homes of the wealthy. The American investigative journalist Gustavus Myers claimed in 1914 that fewer than 50 men controlled $4 billion, or one-third of Canada's wealth. The conflict between labour and capital was a troubling feature of the industrial age, but it was by no means the only problem facing the new nation. As we shall see in the next chapter, immigration and urbanization were changing Canada's social fabric in ways totally unanticipated by the Fathers of Confederation.

A Historiographical Debate

The National Policy and Regional Development

It is a commonplace in Western and Atlantic Canada that the National Policy of the late nineteenth century was biased in favour of Central Canada. Some historians of these regions confirm popular perceptions and suggest that central Canadian industrialization occurred at the expense of the outlying regions as a result of deliberate public policy. There are also scholars, past and present, who argue that the National Policy had negligible impact on the economic fate of these two regions. Who is right?

S.A. Saunders argued in the 1930s that the economic problems of the Maritimes stemmed from decline in demand or price for the key staple exports. When British demand for timber and ships fell off in the 1880s, the region's economy began a decline from which it could not recover. The region's carrying trade meanwhile suffered a fatal blow from the competition of steam and steel ships.[4] This explanation, of course, does not address the issue of why the region's entrepreneurs did not adjust to changing economic times. According to T.W. Acheson, the failure of the Maritimes to generate a major metropolitan centre in the age of the National Policy contributed to the region's drift to outside control and industrial stagnation. "With its powerful mercantile interests," Acheson argues, "Halifax could have most easily adapted to this role, but its merchants preferred, like their Boston counterparts, to invest their large fortunes in banks and American railroad stocks than to venture them on building a new order."[5]

Economist Ken Norrie and historian Doug Owram, the authors of an economic history of Canada, are sceptical about the possibility of extensive industrialization of the Maritime region in the late nineteenth century. They are even more sceptical of attempts to pin the blame on the National Policy:

"To find the argument credible, one would need to believe that fairly small changes in transportation rates or in Dominion subsidies could have had enormous effects on industrial prospects. Simply putting the issue in that manner suggests the probable answer."[6]

Norrie and Owram also discount claims that the National Policy discriminated against Western Canada. T.D. Regehr, for example, states, "there has been deliberate and admitted freight-rate discrimination against the West."[7] Only constant battles by westerners resulted, over time, in partial amelioration of these rates, argues Regehr. In contrast, Norrie and Owram claim flatly, "rail freight rates in the development phase of the wheat economy were at least as low as they would have been under the next most likely alternative to the national policy."[8] Norrie rejects the view that federal tariff and freight rate policies hindered western industrialization:

> In some instances, Prairie industrialization being perhaps the best example, the problem lies in being small and isolated rather than with discriminatory treatment. The present economic structure of the region is adequately explained by standard location theory concepts. It is incorrect to suggest that the federal government or other institutions have industrialized the East at the expense of the West. It must be recognized rather that any significant decentralization of industry in Canada can only be achieved by committing real resources to that end and that this means a subsidy for persons residing in the recipient regions at the expense of other Canadians.[9]

Norrie's argument makes little allowance for the role that the state has played in the marketplace, demonstrating, in its purchasing policies, for example, a strong central Canadian bias. Nevertheless, he correctly points out a fallacy in the claims of many who focus on alleged discrimination against the regions: the assumption that the free market, left to its own workings, would have produced a more equitable distribution of industry in Canada. The tendency of capital left on its own to concentrate in a few areas with transportation and population advantages is a universal phenomenon of the capitalist system. In some countries, the state has intervened to force industries to locate in less favoured areas, but there is little evidence that in late-nineteenth-century Canada there were significant sections of popular opinion in any region who favoured more draconian intervention in the marketplace than that envisaged by John A. Macdonald and his business community supporters.

NOTES

1 Bettina Bradbury, "Pigs, Cows, and Boarders: Non-Wage Forms of Survival Among Montreal's Families, 1861–91," *Labour/Le Travail* 14 (Fall 1984) 46.

2 Susan Mann Trofimenkoff, "One Hundred and Two Muffled Voices: Canada's Industrial Women in the 1880s," *Atlantis* 3.1 (Fall 1977): 67–82.

3 Herbert Brown Ames, *The City Below the Hill* (1897; reprinted Toronto: University of Toronto Press, 1972) 103, 105, 48.

4 S.A. Saunders, *Economic History of the Maritime Provinces* (Ottawa: Royal Commission on Dominion-Provincial Relations, 1940).

5 T.W. Acheson, "The National Policy and the Industrialization of the Maritimes, 1880–1910," *Acadiensis* 1.2 (Spring 1972) 27–28.

6 Kenneth Norrie and Douglas Owram, *A History of the Canadian Economy* (Toronto: Harcourt Brace Jovanovich, 1991) 402.

7 T.D. Regehr, "Western Canada and the Burden of National Transportation Policies" in *Canada and the Burden of Unity*, ed. D.J. Bercuson (Toronto: Macmillan, 1977) 115.

8 Norrie and Owram, *History of the Canadian Economy*, 327.

9 Kenneth H. Norrie, "Some Comments on Prairie Economic Alienation," *Canadian Public Policy* 2.2 (Spring 1976) 222.

SELECTED READING

Major economic histories include Kenneth Norrie and Douglas Owram, *A History of the Canadian Economy* (Toronto: Harcourt Brace Jovanovich, 1991); Graham D. Taylor and Peter A. Baskerville, *A Concise History of Business in Canada* (Toronto: Oxford University Press, 1994); Michael Bliss, *Northern Enterprise: Five Centuries of Canadian Business* (Toronto: McClelland and Stewart, 1987) and *A Living Profit: Studies in the Social History of Canadian Business, 1883–1911* (Toronto: McClelland and Stewart, 1974); Tom Naylor, *The History of Canadian Business, 1867–1914*, 2 vols. (Toronto: Lorimer, 1975); Christopher Armstrong, *Blue Skies and Boiler Rooms: Buying and Selling Securities in Canada* (Toronto: University of Toronto Press, 1997); and David Monod, *Store Wars: Shopkeepers and the Culture of Mass Marketing, 1890–1939* (Toronto: University of Toronto Press, 1996). State-business relations are illuminated in H.V. Nelles and Christopher Armstrong, *Monopoly's Moment: The Organization and Regulation of Canadian Utilities, 1830–1930* (Toronto: University of Toronto Press, 1988). Biographies of early Canadian tycoons include Michael Bliss, *A Canadian Millionaire: The Life and Business Times of Sir Joseph Flavelle, Bart., 1858–1939* (Toronto: Macmillan, 1978); Gregory P. Marchildon, *Profits and Politics: Beaverbrook and the Gilded Age of Canadian Finance* (Toronto: University of Toronto Press, 1996); and Joy L. Stantik, *Timothy Eaton and the Rise of the Department Store* (Toronto: University of Toronto Press, 1990). A good history of one of the "big five" banks is found in Duncan McDowall, *Quick to the Frontier: Canada's Royal Bank* (Toronto: McClelland and Stewart, 1993).

Geographically focused studies include Morris Zaslow, *The Opening of the Canadian North, 1870–1914* (Toronto: McClelland and Stewart, 1971); Chester

Martin, *Dominion Lands Policy* (Toronto: Carleton Library, 1973); V.C. Fowke, *The National Policy and the Wheat Economy* (Toronto: University of Toronto Press, 1957); John Herd Thompson, *The Harvests of War: The Prairie West, 1914–1918* (Toronto: McClelland and Stewart, 1978); Ian M. Drummond, *Progress Without Planning: The Economic History of Ontario from Confederation to the Second World War* (Toronto: University of Toronto Press, 1987); H.V. Nelles, *The Politics of Development: Forests, Mines and Hydro-electric Power in Ontario, 1849–1941* (Toronto: Macmillan, 1974); Jean Hamelin and Yves Roby, *Histoire économique du Québec, 1851–1896* (Montreal: Fides, 1971); J.H. Dales, *Hydroelectricity and Economic Development: Quebec, 1898–1940* (Cambridge: Harvard University Press, 1957); William F. Ryan, *The Clergy and Economic Growth in Quebec, 1896–1914* (Quebec: Les Presses de l'Université Laval, 1966); Robert Armstrong, *Structure and Change: An Economic History of Quebec* (Toronto: Gage, 1984); Ronald Rudin, *Banking en français: The French Banks of Quebec, 1835–1935* (Toronto: University of Toronto Press, 1985); and the books by Gerard Bouchard, Peter Gossage and J.I. Little cited in Chapter 11.

Ontario's success compared to other regions is explored in John Isbister, "Agriculture, Balanced Growth and Social Change in Central Canada since 1850: An Interpretation," in *Perspectives on Canadian Economic History*, ed. Douglas McCalla (Toronto: Copp Clark Pitman, 1987) 58–80; Douglas McCalla, *Planting the Province: The Economic History of Upper Canada, 1784–1870* (Toronto: University of Toronto Press, 1993); and N.R.M. Seifried, *The Regional Structure of the Canadian Economy* (Toronto: Nelson, 1984). See René Hardy, *La Sidérurgie dans le monde rural* (Québec: Les Presses de l'Université Laval, 1995) for a discussion of the decline of Quebec's iron industry at the turn of the twentieth century. Prince Edward Island's adjustment to the industrial age is the subject of a fine study of Edward MacDonald, *"If You Are Strong-Hearted": Prince Edward Island in the Twentieth Century* (Charlottetown: Prince Edward Island Museum and Heritage Foundation, 2000).

On the post-Confederation fur trade, see Arthur J. Ray, *The Canadian Fur Trade in the Industrial Age* (Toronto: University of Toronto Press, 1990). On changes in the fishery see Peter S. Sinclair, *From Traps to Draggers: Domestic Commodity Production in Northwest Newfoundland* (St John's: ISER, Memorial University, 1985); Dianne Newell and Rosemary Ommer, eds., *Fishing Places, Fishing People: Traditions and Issues in Canadian Small-Scale Fisheries* (Toronto: University of Toronto Press, 1999). See also two books by Rosemary Ommer: *From Outpost to Outport: A Structural Analysis of the Jersey-Gaspé Fishery* (Montreal: McGill-Queen's University Press, 1991) and *Merchant Credit and Labour Struggles in Historical Perspective* (Fredericton: Acadiensis Press, 1990).

On the Aboriginal economy in the Industrial Age, see Bruce W. Hodgins and Jamie Benidickson, *The Temagami Experience* (Toronto: University of Toronto Press, 1989); Sarah Carter, *Lost Harvests: Prairie Indian Reserve Farmers and Government Policy* (Montreal: McGill-Queen's University Press, 1990); Kerry Abel, *Drum Song: Glimpses of Dene History* (Montreal: McGill-Queen's University Press, 1993); and Dianne Newell, *The Tangled Webs of History: Indians and the Law in Canada's Pacific Coast Fisheries* (Toronto: University of Toronto Press, 1994).

The tariff is discussed in Ben Forster, *A Conjunction of Interests: Business, Politics, and Tariffs, 1825–1879* (Toronto: University of Toronto Press, 1986) and J.H. Dales, *The Protective Tariff in Canada's Development* (Toronto: University of Toronto Press, 1966). Railway development is assessed in W. Kaye Lamb, *History of the Canadian Pacific Railway* (New York: Macmillan, 1977); G.R. Stevens, *History of the Canadian National Railways* (New York: Macmillan, 1973); T.D. Regehr, *The Canadian Northern Railway: Pioneer Road of the Northern Prairies, 1895–1918* (Toronto: Macmillan, 1976); John Eagle, *The Canadian Pacific Railway and the Development of Western Canada* (Montreal: McGill-Queen's University Press, 1989); and Ken Cruikshank, *Close Ties: Railways, Government, and the Board of Railway Commissioners, 1851–1933* (Montreal: McGill-Queen's University Press, 1991). Vernon Fowke's *National Policy and the Wheat Economy* (Toronto: University of Toronto Press, 1957) makes the Prairie case against the National Policy. An opposing view is presented in Kenneth H. Norrie, *The National Policy and the Prairie Region* (New Haven, CT: Yale University Press, 1971). Maritime assessments of national economic policies should begin with the much-reprinted essay by T.W. Acheson, "The National Policy and the Industrialization of the Maritimes, 1880–1910," *Acadiensis* 1 (Spring 1972): 3–28. See also S.A. Saunders, *Economic History of the Maritime Provinces* (Ottawa: Royal Commission on Dominion-Provincial Relations, 1940); and David G. Alexander, *Atlantic Canada and Confederation: Essays in Canadian Political Economy* (Toronto: University of Toronto Press, 1983). On the foreign ownership debate, see Glenn Williams, *Not for Export: Toward a Political Economy of Canada's Arrested*

Industrialization (Toronto: McClelland and Stewart, 1983); and Gordon Laxer, *Open for Business: The Roots of Foreign Ownership in Canada* (Toronto: Oxford University Press, 1989).

Surveys of the working-class experience and labour movement include Craig Heron, *The Canadian Labour Movement: A Brief History* (Toronto: James Lorimer, 1996); Bryan D. Palmer, *The Working Class Experience: Rethinking the History of Canadian Labour, 1800–1991* (Toronto: McClelland and Stewart, 1992); Desmond Morton, *Working People: An Illustrated History of the Canadian Labour Movement* (Toronto: Summerhill, 1990); Jean Hamelin, ed., *Les Travailleurs Québécois, 1851–1896* (Montreal: Presses de l'Université du Québec, 1973); Jacques Rouillard, *Histoire du Syndicalisme au Québec* (Montreal: Boréal Express, 1989); Terry Copp, *The Anatomy of Poverty: The Condition of the Working Class in Montreal, 1897–1929* (Toronto: McClelland and Stewart, 1974); Michael Piva, *The Conditions of the Working Class in Toronto, 1900–1921* (Ottawa: University of Ottawa Press, 1979); and Paul Craven, ed., *Labouring Lives: Work and Workers in Nineteenth-Century Ontario* (Toronto: University of Toronto Press, 1995).

Labour organization is discussed in Gregory S. Kealey and Bryan D. Palmer, *"Dreaming of What Might Be": The Knights of Labour in Ontario* (New York: Cambridge University Press, 1982); A. Ross McCormack, *Reformers, Rebels and Revolutionaries* (Toronto: University of Toronto Press, 1977); Martin Robin, *Radical Politics and Canadian Labour* (Kingston: Industrial Relations Centre, Queen's University, 1971); Donald Avery, *Dangerous Foreigners: European Immigrant Workers and Labour Radicalism in Canada* (Toronto: McClelland and Stewart, 1979); Linda Kealey, *Enlisting Women for the Cause: Women, Labour and the Left in Canada, 1890–1920* (Toronto: University of Toronto Press, 1998); and Ian McKay "'By Wisdom Wile or War': The Provincial Workmen's Association and the Struggle for Working-Class Independence in Nova Scotia," *Labour/Le Travail* (Fall 1986): 13–62. First-hand accounts of working conditions and attitudes are found in Greg Kealey, ed., *Canada Investigates Industrialism: The Royal Commission on the Relations of Labor and Capital, 1889* (Toronto: University of Toronto Press, 1973); Michael Cross, ed., *The Working Man in the Nineteenth Century* (Toronto: Oxford University Press, 1974); T. Phillips Thompson, *The Politics of Labour* (1887; reprinted Toronto: University of Toronto Press, 1975); and Edmund Bradwin, *The Bunkhouse Man* (Toronto: University of Toronto Press, 1972). Peter Baskerville and Eric Sager focus on the unemployed in *Unwilling Idlers: The Urban Unemployed and their Families in Late Victorian Canada* (Toronto: University of Toronto Press, 2000).

The impact of industrial capitalism on women and children's work is explored in Marjorie Cohen, *Women's Work, Markets and Economic Development in Nineteenth Century Ontario* (Toronto: University of Toronto Press, 1988); Joy Parr, *Labouring Children: British Immigrant Apprentices to Canada, 1869–1924* (Montreal: McGill-Queen's University Press, 1980), and *The Gender of Breadwinners: Women, Men and Change in Two Industrial Towns, 1880–1950* (Toronto: University of Toronto Press, 1990); Bettina Bradbury, *Working Families: Age, Gender, and Daily Survival in Industrializing Montreal* (Toronto: McClelland Stewart, 1993); Susan Mann Trofimenkoff, "One Hundred and Two Muffled Voices: Canada's Industrial Women in the 1880s," *Atlantis* 3.1 (Fall 1977): 67–82; Robert McIntosh, *Boys in the Pits: Child Labour in Coal Mines* (Montreal: McGill-Queen's University Press, 2000); John Bullen, "Hidden Workers: Child Labour and the Family Economy in Late Nineteenth-Century Urban Ontario," *Labour/Le Travail* (Fall 1986): 163–88; Janice Acton, Penny Goldsmith, and Bonnie Shepard, eds., *Women at Work: Ontario, 1850–1930* (Toronto: Women's Press, 1974); Franca Iacovetta and Mariana Valverde, eds., *Gender Conflicts: New Essays in Women's History* (Toronto: University of Toronto Press, 1992); Paula Bourne, ed., *Women's Paid and Unpaid Work: Historical and Contemporary Perspectives* (Toronto: New Hogtown, 1986); Graham Lowe, *Women in the Administrative Revolution: The Feminization of Clerical Work* (Toronto: University of Toronto Press, 1987); Elaine Bernard, *The Long Distance Feeling: A History of the Telecommunications Union* (Vancouver: New Star, 1982); Kathryn McPherson, *Bedside Matters: The Transformation of Canadian Nursing, 1900–1990* (Toronto: Oxford University Press, 1996); and Elizabeth Smyth et al., *Challenging Professions: Historical and Contemporary Perspectives on Women's Professional Work* (Toronto: University of Toronto Press, 1999).

Labour developments in specific industries and regions are the subject of many books and articles, including Bryan D. Palmer, *A Culture in Conflict: Skilled Workers and Industrial Capitalism in Hamilton, Ontario* (Montreal: McGill-Queen's University Press, 1979); Gregory S. Kealey, *Toronto Workers Respond to Industrialism, 1867–1892* (Toronto: University of Toronto Press, 1980); Craig Heron, *Working in Steel: The Early Years in Canada, 1883–1935* (Toronto: McClelland and Stewart, 1980); Robert A. J. McDonald, "Working-Class Vancouver,

1886-1914: Urbanism and Class in British Columbia," *B.C. Studies* (Spring/Summer 1986): 33–69; Ian McKay, *The Craft Transformed: An Essay on the Carpenters in Halifax, 1885–1985* (Halifax: Holdfast Press, 1985); Eric Sager, *Seafaring Labour: The Merchant Marine of Atlantic Canada, 1820–1914* (Montreal: McGill-Queen's University Press, 1989); Ian Radforth, *Bushworkers and Bosses: Logging in Northern Ontario, 1900–1980* (Toronto: University of Toronto Press, 1987); and Jeremy Mouat, *Roaring Days: Rossland's Mines in the History of British Columbia* (Vancouver: University of British Columbia Press, 1995).

On city life, see G. Stelter and A.F.J. Artibise, eds., *The Canadian City: Essays in Urban History* (Toronto: Copp Clark Pitman, 1984); A.F.J. Artibise, ed., *Town and City: Aspects of Western Canadian Urban Development* (Regina: University of Regina, 1981); and J.M.S. Careless, *The Rise of Cities: Canada Before 1914* (Ottawa: Canadian Historical Association, 1978). A series of illustrated urban histories published by James Lorimer is useful for studying the growth of the late-nineteenth-century city. Included are *Winnipeg* by Alan Artibise (1977); *Calgary* by Max Foran (1978); *Vancouver* by Patricia Roy (1980); *Toronto to 1918* by J.M.S. Careless (1984); *Hamilton* by John C. Weaver (1984), and *Ottawa* by John H. Taylor (1986). Also see Doug Baldwin and Thomas Spira, eds., *Gaslights,*

Epidemics and Vagabond Cows: Charlottetown in the Victorian Era (Charlottetown: Ragweed, 1988); John English and Kenneth McLaughlin, *Kitchener: An Illustrated History* (Waterloo, ON: Wilfrid Laurier University Press, 1983); Paul André Linteau, *Maisonneuve: Comment des promoteurs fabriquent une ville* (Montreal: Boréal Express, 1981); Robert A.J. McDonald, *Making Vancouver: Class, Status and Social Boundaries, 1863–1913* (Vancouver: University of British Columbia Press, 1996); Judith Fingard, *The Dark Side of Life in Victorian Halifax* (Porters Lake, NS: Pottersfield Press, 1989); and Judith Fingard, Janet Guildford, and David Sutherland, *Halifax: The First 250 Years* (Halifax: Formac, 1999). An examination of legal and police systems can be found in John C. Weaver, *Crimes, Constables and the Courts: Order and Transgression in a Canadian City, 1816–1970* (Montreal: McGill-Queen's University Press, 1995). A critical study of law-making can be found in Carolyn Strange and Tina Loo, *Making Good: Law and Moral Regulation in Canada, 1867–1939* (Toronto: University of Toronto Press, 1997), while policing generally is treated in Greg Marquis, *Policing Canada's Century* (Toronto: University of Toronto Press, 1993). Racism in law and culture is discussed in Constance Backhouse, *Colour Coded: A Legal History of Racism in Canada, 1900–1950* (Toronto: University of Toronto Press, and The Osgood Society, 1999).

WEBLINKS

THE NATIONAL POLICY
www.canadahistory.com/macdonald_moves_the_national_policy.htm

Read Sir John A. Macdonald's speech to the House of Commons on January 17, 1881, in which he discusses the National Policy.

CANADIAN NATIONAL RAILWAYS
http://collections.ic.gc.ca/cnphoto/cnphoto.html

The CNR Historic Photograph Collection provides visitors with an introduction to the significant role that railways have played in the development of Canadian society since the opening of Canada's first steam railway in 1836.

ALEXANDER GRAHAM BELL
http://history.acusd.edu/gen/recording/alexbell.html

This site contains photos and biographical information, a flow chart of Bell's invention processes, details of his early patents, notes and illustrated excerpts from his notebooks, and related links for further reading.

SANDFORD FLEMING
http://search.biography.com/print_record.pl?id=8593

A brief biography of Sir Sandford Fleming can be found at this site.

TIMOTHY EATON
http://collections.ic.gc.ca/heirloom_series/volume5/80-81.htm

This site offers photographs and a biography of the founder of the "department store" concept.

CHAPTER 18

Society and Culture in the Age of Industry, 1867–1914

Every large city on this continent has its fourfold problem of the slum, the saloons, the foreign colony and the districts of vice. The foreign colony may not properly be called a slum, but it represents a community that is about to become an important factor in our social life and will become a menace in our civilization unless it learns to assimilate the moral and religious ideals and the standards of citizenship.[1]

This comment, published in the *Missionary Outlook* in 1910, reflected views widely voiced in industrializing Canada. As immigration increased and industrial development transformed the economy, many Canadians mistook the symptoms for the causes of the poverty, conflict, and insecurity that threatened to undermine Canada's fragile unity. Reform became the watchword of the period, and few aspects of Canadian society escaped the impact of reform movements that swept across the nation. In cultural life, as well, there was a new energy and complexity. Everything from schools and universities to sports and fine arts adjusted to the challenges of the modern age, and in the process laid the foundations for many of the institutions and values that still define Canadian society.

THE AGE OF REFORM

The reform impulse in industrializing Canada took many forms. In the early years of Confederation, reformers commonly blamed the poor themselves for their plight, observing that the poor were often transient, drank too much, and failed to attend church. As time went on, more progressive approaches were adopted, most of which included some degree of state intervention to ensure compliance to reform goals. A few Canadians, often called "radicals," went further, demanding that the capitalist system be eliminated entirely, by peaceful means if possible, but if necessary by force.

LEGISLATING MORALITY

Alcohol was a favoured target of conservative reformers, who saw it as the cause of many of Canada's social problems. Over the course of the nineteenth century, the movement to encourage temperance in the use of alcohol had given way to a demand that the state impose laws to prohibit its manufacture, sale, and consumption. This transition from the personal to the political prompted a mass movement for reform. By the end of the nineteenth century, the Protestant churches, led by the Baptists, Methodists, and Presbyterians, and voluntary organizations such as the Sons of Temperance and the Woman's Christian Temperance Union had forged a formidable alliance.

Pressed by the mounting support for action, the federal government passed the Canada Temperance Act in 1878. Known as the Scott Act, it allowed municipalities to hold a plebiscite to determine whether liquor could be sold within their boundaries. Many areas of Canada voted "dry," and the consumption of alcohol actually declined, but it never totally stopped. What separated the "wets" from the "drys" was not the problem of alcohol abuse, which nearly everyone agreed was a cause for concern, but the means of addressing it. For many people, the demand for state intervention went too far. This was the position taken in Quebec, where the Roman Catholic Church resisted the growing power of the state and where people were less likely than Canadians in other provinces to exercise the local option to ban alcohol.

Prime Minister Laurier tried to avoid federal action by agreeing to a national referendum on the issue. Held in 1898, it yielded a predictable result: a majority for the drys in every province outside Quebec. The relatively small overall majority and a low voter turnout allowed Laurier to sidestep the issue that bitterly divided the country. For the time being, prohibition advocates had to be content with the existing system of local option, but their forces were not yet spent. They turned to their provincial governments to pass legislation prohibiting the liquor trade. They also demanded a wholesale reform of the political system, including giving women, who were believed to be more supportive of the temperance cause, the right to vote.

Most conservative reformers focused on the moral issues associated with social problems. Nowhere was this approach more diligently pursued than in Toronto, which earned the title "Toronto the Good" for its earnest efforts to legislate morality. In 1886, Toronto's reforming mayor, William Howland, established a Morality Department in the city police force. Anyone involved in prostitution, the illicit sale of liquor, gambling, or the mistreatment of children and animals was hauled into court by the new morality squad. Under the charge of vagrancy, young women innocently walking on the streets at night could be interrogated by the morality police.

Beer parlour, Boisetown, New Brunswick, 1912.

New Brunswick Provincial Archives/P145-61

Women and children were the special concern of moral reformers, who had difficulty accepting the freedom from parental and patriarchal control that city life encouraged. Taking the lead in the social purity movement, Torontonians created a flurry of institutions designed to focus on the plight of women and female children. A Children's Aid Society, two industrial schools for girls, a children's court, and a women's court were all established in the period between 1880 and 1910. Despite this energetic response, young women in Toronto continued to ply their trade as prostitutes, practise infanticide, and sink into destitution.

THE PROGRESSIVE IMPULSE

By the turn of the century, many people had come to the conclusion that reforming the individual would not produce a reformed society. Larger forces clearly were a cause of destitution and the power of the state would be necessary to achieve deep and lasting changes. Progressivism drew together an impressive coalition of professionals, journalists, church leaders, union organizers, and women's rights activists. Through their voluntary agencies and carefully documented studies, they promoted the view that hard work, judicious laws, scientific management, and reformed political structures would enable everyone to enjoy the benefits of the industrial system.

At the forefront of the progressive movement was an army of health professionals led by medical doctors and nurses. They argued that public health should be a priority of reform, and provided municipal officials and school boards with scientific evidence of the need for vaccinations, medical inspection, and better nutrition. Throughout the country, energies were marshalled to build new hospitals, establish clinics for young mothers and their babies, and teach schoolchildren that "Cleanliness is next to Godliness." Campaigns against smoking and spitting—both connected for those who pursued the popular pastime of chewing tobacco—encouraged habits that would lead to healthier Canadians.

Churches were also central to progressive reform efforts in many communities. By the turn of the century, the Methodists, Presbyterians, and Baptists, in particular, had adopted what is termed the "social gospel" approach to their work. While still concerned with spiritual salvation and social purity, they expanded their charitable activities to address the appalling conditions created by the industrial system. Canadian churches established missions, labour churches, and settlement houses in the inner city to minister to the spiritual and physical needs of the working class. One of the most prominent social gospellers was Methodist minister J.S. Woodsworth, who from 1907 to 1913 served as superintendent of Winnipeg's All People's Mission, which catered to the city's culturally diverse immigrant population.

The Protestant churches cooperated with union leaders, through the Lord's Day Alliance, to pressure the federal government to legislate Sunday observance. Passed in 1907, the Lord's Day Act banned paid employment, shopping, and commercial leisure activities on Sunday, a policy the churches argued not only conformed

Toronto Department of Health well-baby clinics instructed new mothers on how to care for their infants.

City of Toronto Archives/DPW32-234

to Canada's Christian beliefs but also gave working people a day of rest. Buoyed by this success, the Methodists and Presbyterians collaborated in the founding in 1907 of the Moral and Social Reform Council of Canada (its name was changed to the Social Service Council of Canada in 1913) to pursue an ambitious reform agenda.

The Methodist Church also took a lead in educating Canadians on issues of sexual hygiene. Since federal legislation passed in 1892 prohibited the promotion of birth control, the Church was eager to counsel self-control in sexual matters and distributed sex manuals targeted at various age levels for women and men. While criticized today as moralistic and wrong-headed, the manuals incorporated the thinking of the time in the field of "sexology" and moved some distance from the puritanical approach to sex characteristic of the Victorian age. Some progressives went even further and advocated a program of eugenics. Drawing on scientific findings relating to reproduction in the plant and animal world, eugenicists argued that society could be improved by preventing people with undesirable mental and physical traits from reproducing.

The desire for social control and scientific analysis led to same-sex relationships being labelled "homosexual" and deemed unnatural. While social purity advocates insisted on jail sentences for homosexuals, the medical profession began describing same-sex attraction as a form of insanity requiring confinement in a lunatic asylum rather than a prison. Practising homosexuals could face either fate in a society that subscribed to the view that sex should be confined to married couples. In Victoria, two men convicted of sodomy in 1891 were each sentenced to fifteen years in prison, a sentence later commuted to seven years. Sentences of a year or two were more common.

Progressives also took up the cause of environmental reform, arguing that Canada lagged behind other industrialized nations in attending to the problems of pollution and resource depletion. The example of the United States inspired the federal government to set aside Banff Hot Springs Reserve and Rocky Mountain Park for public use in 1885. Following the North American Conservation Conference called by President Theodore Roosevelt in 1909, the federal government established a Canadian Commission of Conservation (CCC). Under the energetic direction of Clifford Sifton, the CCC investigated everything from fur farming and migratory birds to power development and urban planning.

The "city beautiful" movement, with its notions of rational planning, handsome buildings, and public spaces, appealed to many progressives. Originating in Europe and the United States, the movement soon had Canadian converts, including Herbert Ames who, as we have seen, had catalogued Montreal's problems in his book *The City Below the Hill*. Urban reformers established their own voluntary associations, such as Montreal's City Improvement League, and enlisted the support of the Union of Canadian Municipalities. Urban planning experts argued that changing cities would also change the people who lived in them.

Progressive reformers were suspicious of private utilities in water, power, telephones, and transport, arguing for government control of such essential services. Municipal and provincial governments in the first decade of the twentieth century often responded to pressure from reformers to take over the utilities from private developers. Montreal's private utilities weathered the tide of consumer grievance, while Edmonton's streetcars, electricity, and telephones all became publicly owned. In Toronto, Bell survived as a private monopoly, but the Toronto Transit Commission assumed control of the street railways.

As progressives encountered resistance from municipal governments, they became critical of political processes. The ratepayers, critics argued, had become passive pawns in the hands of corrupt developers who could influence voting in the poorer wards. To curb the power of "special interests," cities were urged to establish boards of control, elected on a city-wide franchise. Because middle-class voters were more likely to vote than the working class, they could influence the results in a city-wide election, thereby putting an end to ward politics. Boards of control were adopted in Winnipeg (1906), Ottawa (1907), Montreal (1909), Hamilton (1910), and London (1914). Another way of wresting power from the masses was to delegate authority to "expert" city managers and appointed commissioners, policies adopted in Edmonton in 1904, Saint John in 1908, and a few years later in Regina, Saskatoon, and Prince Albert.

MORE TO THE STORY

The Grenfell Mission

In Newfoundland, the social gospel movement was represented in a dramatic way by the mission of Wilfred Grenfell. Born in England in 1865, Grenfell was a student at London Medical School when he was converted to active Christianity by American evangelist Dwight L. Moody. He subsequently joined the Royal National Mission to Deep Sea Fishermen. In 1892, he visited the coasts of Newfoundland and Labrador where he saw a great opportunity to combine medical and missionary work among people who rarely saw a doctor or a minister. The following year, he opened a hospital in Battle Creek, and by the end of the century had established his mission headquarters at St Anthony's on the northern tip of Newfoundland.

Backed by supporters in the United States, Canada, and Great Britain, Grenfell expanded his activities to include nursing stations, schools, cooperatives, and an orphanage. His well-publicized efforts to bring services to isolated areas—including a close brush with death on an ice floe in 1908—made him a popular hero and enabled him to earn more money for his mission through the lecture circuit. Following his marriage to a Chicago heiress in 1909, Grenfell spent less time in missionary work, which was carried on by dedicated men and women inspired by Grenfell's pioneering efforts.

THE RADICAL RESPONSE

By 1914, a growing number of Canadians were pursuing visions more radical than those championed by the progressives, whose main goal was to impose rational order on capitalism. Socialists were in the forefront of an international movement to abolish a system that they believed put property ahead of people and pitted labour against capital in an uneven struggle refereed by a state clearly biased in favour of the rich. Although socialists disagreed on the best means of achieving a society where each would receive according to his or her needs, their goal had wide appeal in early industrializing Canada.

The socialist movement that took root in Canada was a strange amalgam of Marxism, Christian socialism, and reformism. On one end of the spectrum, radicals such as the Industrial Workers of the World preached syndicalism, the view that labourers should join forces to overthrow the yoke of capitalism. These hardliners argued that a cataclysmic conflict between labour and capital was the only way the new order would be given birth. In contrast, the Christian Socialist League, whose leading spokesman was G. Weston Wrigley, maintained that Christ was the first socialist and advocated a more gradual and constitutional approach to a socialist utopia.

One of the earliest spokesmen for the gradual approach was T. Phillips Thompson, a journalist based in Toronto. Unlike most Anglo-Canadians, he sympathized with the francophone and Métis minorities and advocated the abolition of the monarchy. A free thinker, he was influenced by the work of American critic Henry George, whose book *Progress and Poverty*, published in 1879, caused a stir throughout Canada. George's message, that industrialism had unleashed an insupportable burden of poverty and distress, was not new, but his solution was a tax on the property of the rich. Dubbed the "single tax," it had the virtue of simplicity.

With the arrival of thousands of immigrants with a tradition of socialist politics, efforts to achieve unity in the cause of socialism were further complicated. No sooner had local socialist groups on the West Coast come together to produce the Socialist Party of Canada in 1904 than they were weakened by the defection of members who founded the more moderate Social Democratic Party (SDP) in 1907. With its language locals, the SDP appealed to Finnish, Ukrainian, and Russian communities on the Prairies, who felt excluded from the established political parties. The SDP also proved more open to women's issues, including the problems of unpaid domestic labour and prohibition, than the Socialist Party of Canada, whose leaders considered such issues as detracting from "scientific" socialist goals.

Many Canadian workers followed the example of labourers in Great Britain who were throwing their support behind the Independent Labour Party. While socialists preached the total abolition of capitalism, labourites focused on improving the lot of workers within the capitalist system. In addition to supporting public ownership of railways, banks, and utilities, Labour Party leaders urged state enforcement of safe working conditions and the introduction of social insurance programs such as unemployment and health insurance and old age pensions. In the first decade of the twentieth century, labour parties began to appear on the Canadian scene and scored a few successes. A.W. Puttee, a founder of the Winnipeg Labour Party, and Ralph Smith, TLC president, were elected to Parliament in 1900.

THE RURAL RESPONSE

While cities served as a focus for reform, people living in rural communities were far from passively resigned to the changes taking place around them. Western farmers began to question the power of eastern-based institutions such as railways, banks, and governments. In the eastern provinces, rural people were also disturbed by the growing power of urban-based institutions, and their concerns focused on the depopulation of rural areas, which had few of the amenities available to their city neighbours.

The transformation of rural life and the flight of large numbers of people to the city also troubled many urban dwellers. In Montreal, Henri Bourassa wrote frequently and eloquently about the danger to society of abandoning the values associated with rural life. So, too, did Andrew Macphail, a Montreal-based medical doctor who edited *University Magazine* between 1907 and 1920. Macphail looked back nostalgically upon his childhood in rural Prince Edward Island and lamented the rapid disappearance of what he saw as a superior way of life. For these men, rural living was as crucial to the moral and spiritual well-being of the nation as it was to physical survival and food production.

The flight of women from the farm was a particular concern of reformers. When markets became the focus of production, the balance of power in the family enterprise shifted in favour of men. Profits from farming, if there were any, were more likely to be invested in farm machinery than in appliances to relieve domestic drudgery. Discouraged by discriminatory homestead laws, unequal inheritance patterns, and the unending domestic toil that confronted them, young women began deserting the farm for jobs in the city. Industrial wages were lower for women than men, but at least in the cities women had access to an income that was often denied them on the farm.

Rural discontent blossomed into a full-blown movement that demanded major changes in Canada's political structures. In Central Canada and the Maritimes, the Grange Movement of the 1870s paralleled efforts by labour and capital to use collective action to achieve their goals. The Grange movement focused on educational activities and avoided direct political action, but another American import, the Patrons of Industry, led to the election of candidates to the Ontario and Manitoba legislatures as well as to the House of Commons in the 1890s. The Patrons were succeeded by the Ontario Farmers' Association, which in 1902 emerged as a critic of high transportation costs and the protective tariff. By 1907, it had joined with the Grange to form the United Farmers of Ontario. Led by E.C. Drury and J.J. Morrison, it was determined to make Ottawa listen to the concerns of the farming community.

Meanwhile, on the Prairies, agrarian discontent led to the creation of the Territorial Grain Growers' Association in 1901, which became the basis for provincial associations following the creation of the provinces of Saskatchewan and Alberta in 1905. The Manitoba Grain Growers' Association was founded in 1902. In 1908, the *Grain Growers' Guide*, a newspaper based in Winnipeg, was established as a mouthpiece for agrarian discontent. Francis Marion Beynon's column in the *Guide* gave women plenty to think about. Recognition of women's contribution to farm life led to the creation of women's auxiliaries to the prairie farm organizations and to support for female suffrage.

Rural areas of Newfoundland were also ripe for the message of social reform. Under the dynamic leadership of William Coaker, the Fishermen's Protective Union (FPU), founded in 1909, swept through the outports gaining support from the workers in the fishing and forest industries. The FPU demanded state intervention to ensure fair return to the people who caught and processed the fish, improvements in education and health care in the outports, and the implementation of an old-age pension program. In alliance with the Liberal Party, the FPU won eight seats in the Newfoundland legislature in 1913 and applied pressure on the government to legislate reforms.

One of the most significant challenges to capitalist industrial development came from the cooperative movement, which was particularly strong in rural Canada. Originating in Britain in the 1840s, cooperatives were organized on the principle of cooperation rather than competition and were owned by their members rather than by anonymous investors. Between 1860 and 1900, farmers in the Maritimes, Quebec, and Ontario developed over 1200 cooperative creameries and cheese factories. They also organized insurance companies to provide protection against crop failure and fires. In Quebec, Alphonse Desjardins used cooperative principles to establish a chain of credit unions, the caisses populaires. Grain farmers in the West, led by E.A. Partridge, organized the Grain Growers' Grain Company in 1906 to market directly to buyers in Europe.

The creation in 1909 of the Cooperative Union of Canada brought like-minded cooperators together for education and lobbying activities. In the same year, Ontario farmers and western grain growers established the Canadian Council of Agriculture. Tariff policy emerged as the organization's major grievance. Roundly condemned as a charge on society's producers for the benefits of manufacturers, tariffs were seen by the farmers as an instrument of oppression by a class of businessmen who were sucking the nation dry through their greed and corruption.

In June 1910, Prime Minister Laurier set out on a three-month tour of the west and was besieged by petitions from well-organized farmers. Later in the year, nearly 1000 farmers from all across the country descended on Parliament Hill demanding lower tariffs, better rail and grain elevator service, and legislation supporting cooperative enterprises. When the Laurier government negotiated a free trade treaty with the United States in the winter of 1911, it did so because a clear majority of rural Canadians demanded an end to high tariffs. The fact that the Liberals lost the election late that year only confirmed the belief held by farmers that industrial interests controlled the levers of power in the nation.

THE "WOMAN MOVEMENT"

Women's involvement in Canada's reform movements was fuelled by the enormous changes in their lives and by new ideas about the role of women in society. With the introduction of manufactured clothes, foodstuffs, and household products, and the tendency toward smaller families and educating children in public schools, much of what was considered women's work moved outside the home. At the same time, middle-class women were told that their place was in the home. To reinforce that injunction, women were denied access to higher education, the professions, boardrooms, and political office.

The doctrine of separate spheres led middle-class women to organize separately from men in a variety of voluntary organizations. In the 1870s, Women's Missionary Aid Societies sprouted in various Protestant churches. Designed to spread the gospel at home and abroad, missionary aid societies sponsored single women for overseas service in countries such as India and China and taught women valuable organizational skills. While consistent with women's long-standing role in charitable activities, missionary work provided a source of employment for women in the public sphere, often in areas such as medicine and administration largely denied to them at home.

Two of the earliest women's organizations, the Young Woman's Christian Association (YWCA) and the Woman's Christian Temperance Union (WCTU), took middle-class women another step down the road to public service. Founded in Great Britain as a counterpart to the YMCA, the Canadian YWCA was first established in Saint John in 1870. The "Y" provided both lodging and job training, largely in domestic service, for girls arriving in the "dangerous" urban environment. The WCTU, an American organization

A group of women in front of a YWCA boarding house at 689 Ontario Street, Toronto.

National Archives of Canada/PA-126710

that took root in Canada in 1874, focused women's energies in the cause of prohibition, but it soon took on other reform causes. Spreading quickly throughout the nation, the WCTU formed a Dominion Union in 1883, and by the 1890s claimed over 10 000 members.

While many of the voluntary organizations that appealed to women originated in Great Britain and the United States, Canada made its own contribution to the voluntary cause in the form of the Women's Institutes. The first Women's Institute was established in Stoney Creek, Ontario, in 1897 by Adelaide Hoodless, who had watched her youngest child die as a result of drinking impure milk. Her major causes included domestic science courses in the schools, pure milk legislation, and public health reforms. These goals were taken up with zeal by the Women's Institutes after the Ontario government began subsidizing their efforts in 1900. By the 1920s, the Women's Institutes had spread throughout Canada

and had taken root in rural areas of Great Britain and around the world.

In Quebec, francophone women found an outlet for their energies in religious orders that had responsibility for education, health care, and social services. Between 1837 and 1899, 34 new female religious communities were established in Quebec. By 1901, 6.1 percent of the province's single women over 20 years of age were nuns. Nuns took up many reform causes. For example, the Grey Nuns in Montreal organized day-care centres for working-class families in the early 1870s. By the turn of the century, lay women in Quebec began to resist the conservative injunctions of their clerical leaders. In 1907, Marie Lacoste-Gérin-Lajoie played a leading role in founding the Fédération nationale Saint-Jean-Baptiste, an organization that pushed for access to higher education for women, improvements in their legal status, and reform of working conditions.

The Hospital of the Sisters of Charity in Rimouski, 1890.

R.E. Mercier, Archives nationales du Québec à Québec/P600-6/438-1

The growth in Canadian women's activism was capped by the formation of a national federation of women's clubs in 1893. Known as the National Council of Women of Canada (NCWC), it was the brainchild of Lady Aberdeen, the wife of the governor general. An enthusiastic supporter of reform causes, Lady Aberdeen was a founder of the Aberdeen Association (1890), which distributed reading material to isolated settlers, and of the Victorian Order of Nurses (1897), an organization to provide nursing services in areas where trained medical help was not available. The NCWC began cautiously but soon encompassed a wide range of organizations and causes, including temperance, child welfare, and professional advancement for women. In 1910, the NCWC endorsed women's suffrage, the final step in recognizing women as having public power in their own right.

By the 1890s, an increasing number of reformers supported what was known at the time as "woman suffrage." People came to the cause in a variety of ways: from lengthy struggles to open universities, professions, and businesses on an equal basis to women; from groups condemning women's subordination under the law; and from reform movements that felt their goals might be advanced by the support of women. Two feminist perspectives were evident in the suffragists' arguments: Equal rights and maternal, or social, feminism. Equal rights advocates hoped to sweep away the unfair laws and attitudes that encouraged discrimination against women. Maternal feminists wanted laws to support women in their roles as wives and mothers. In both lines of thinking, women's suffrage became a key element in the struggle for reform.

The hardships of the suffrage campaign deterred the less courageous from expressing their opinions publicly.

British suffragist Emmeline Pankhurst (first row, fifth from left) stands beside Nellie McClung (left of Pankhurst) during Pankhurst's tour of North America, 1917.

British Columbia Archives HP-39849

women in their place. Not surprisingly, given their education and sense of purpose, many professional women became active in the suffrage movement. Dr Emily Howard Stowe, for example, took the lead in establishing Canada's first women's suffrage organization, the Toronto Literary Society, in 1876. By 1883, the group felt confident enough to change its name to the Toronto Women's Suffrage Association and to launch the Canadian Women's Suffrage Association. In western Canada novelist, Nellie McClung became the most prominent leader of the suffrage cause. Her sense of hu-

Misogyny and anti-feminism were widely expressed both verbally and in print by people determined to keep women in their place. mour and clever repartee enabled her to survive the many taunts that came her way.

Voices from the Past

Women in Action

To be an active member of the WCTU, women needed a strong will. *The Ottawa Daily Citizen* published this account of a WCTU action on 5 February 1890:

> A Band of evangelistic workers announced a few days ago by handbills distributed throughout Hull, that meetings would be held every Tuesday evening in that city in a hall on the corner of Duke and Queen Streets.... It seems that preparations were made by a gang of roughs, headed by an unlicensed saloon keeper, to give the new-comers a warm reception; in fact, the intention was more or less openly expressed to "clean them out." The band of evangelists was composed of Miss Bertha Wright, accompanied by a considerable number of young ladies.... On opening the doors of the Hall a crowd of about TWO HUNDRED MEN well primed with liquor rushed in and filled the place. For a time, their interruptions were confined to noises, etc., but on being remonstrated with they made an attack on the speaker and singers. For a time everything was in confusion, and there was reason to fear the worst, missiles being thrown and blows freely given, but not returned. The young women then joined hands and formed a circle around the speakers, and the roughs refrained from striking them but confined their efforts to separating the little band.... Finally the police managed to clear the hall and took the Ottawa people to the station, fighting off the crowd with their batons all the way. At this time some of the young women were badly hurt by the missiles that were thrown.[2]

Despite the "warm reception," Bertha Wright and her "little band" from the Ottawa Young Woman's Christian Temperance Union were back in Hull the following week, this time to take on an angry mob of 400 "roughs."

RELIGION AND REFORM

The changing economic and intellectual climate of the late nineteenth century had a profound impact on Canadian churches. Following the publication of Charles Darwin's works on evolution, the literal truth of church teachings was called sharply into question. Many church leaders responded to the Darwinian challenge by rejecting the theory of evolution as speculative nonsense. Others argued that Biblical stories were figuratively rather than literally true. Protestant "higher critics" borrowed critical methods from contemporary German and British scholars, treating the Bible like any other literary work, and interpreting its truths in mythical rather than literal terms. By the end of the nineteenth century, a widening gulf was developing between church leaders who accepted higher criticism and those who remained faithful to the literal teachings of the Bible.

The social problems accompanying industrialization sparked another dispute within Canadian churches. While many religious leaders continued to ascribe poverty to personal failings, others began to criticize the new economic order. By focusing on the physical and material condition of people on earth, social gospellers moved away from the evangelical preoccupation with individual spiritual development and life after death. This direction troubled many church members, who became concerned about the abandonment of what they believed to be the fundamental issues of Christianity.

The mainstream churches also faced competition from new religious organizations. The Salvation Army, which took root in Canada in the 1880s, was the most successful and enduring of the new evangelical churches, especially among the urban working class. At the turn of the century, a variety of millenarian groups, which believed in the imminent return of Christ, came and went, attracting followers who were

John Joseph Lynch, archbishop of the Roman Catholic Church in Toronto, who tried to stop his parishioners from attending free-thought meetings, is portrayed here as slaying the serpent of free thought with the sword of faith.

By J.W. Bengough. *Grip,* 22 May 1880

disillusioned with the apparent secularization of the established churches. These groups, in turn, often disillusioned their followers when the predicted Second Coming failed to occur. By the late nineteenth century, scepticism about the teachings of mainstream churches was evident in the spread of spiritualism and theosophy. Most shocking to the churches were the free-thought societies founded by intellectuals who equated Christianity with superstition and promoted atheism and agnosticism.

Although the Roman Catholic Church was not without its sceptics and social reformers, the clerical hierarchy was limited in how far it could deviate from the injunctions of papal pronouncements. The church banned books that it considered irreligious and forbade the faithful from joining secular organizations, such as the Knights of Labor, that it felt distracted people from their religious duties. Nowhere was clerical control more successful than in Quebec, where Roman Catholicism claimed the allegiance of 85 percent of the population.

A celebrated case of the church's confrontation with its critics occurred in 1869 when it refused to allow the burial of Joseph Guibord, an activist of the Institut canadien, in a Roman Catholic cemetery. Founded in Montreal in 1844, the Institut championed freedom of conscience and had a library that included publications placed on the church's Index of forbidden books. Clerical leaders in Quebec had the Institut condemned by Rome in 1868. Guibord explicitly refused to renounce his membership and, when he died in 1869, Bishop Bourget of Montreal denied him burial in consecrated ground. Guibord's widow took the case to court. In 1874, after a series of appeals, the Judicial Committee of the Privy Council ordered that Bourget's ruling be overturned. Because feelings ran so high over the issue, Guibord's body, which had rested in a Protestant cemetery for five years, had to be accompanied by an armed military escort when it was transferred to its final resting place. Even then, Bishop Bourget had the last word: he immediately deconsecrated the ground where Guibord's body lay.

By the end of the nineteenth century, the Roman Catholic Church became more receptive to reform ideals. Pope Leo XIII lifted an ineffectual ban on the Knights of Labor in 1887, and in his encyclical of 1891, *Rerum Novarum*, he condemned an uncontrolled market economy. The pope's position that "some opportune remedy must be found quickly for the misery and wretchedness pressing so unjustly on the majority of the working class" eventually spurred a Catholic social action movement. In Quebec, this was centred in the Montreal-based École sociale populaire, established in 1911, which trained Catholic activists to work in the community.

Although its influence remained the greatest in Quebec, the Roman Catholic Church expanded throughout Canada, building churches, hospitals, orphanages, and schools to serve its increasingly diverse membership. In the case of Polish immigrants, Catholicism was closely allied to Polish nationalism, a connection that in 1901 turned the congregation of the Winnipeg Holy Ghost parish against the German-speaking Oblate Fathers. At the same time that it was suppressing Native languages in its residential schools, the Catholic Church played an essential role in maintaining minority eastern European languages through its networks of parochial schools. By 1916, for instance, there were 11 Polish and Ukrainian Catholic schools in Manitoba.

SCHOOLING AND SOCIETY

During the second half of the nineteenth century, school attendance increased dramatically. It also varied according to region and culture. By 1891, it was estimated that only 6 percent of Ontario residents and 13 percent of Maritime Canadians were totally illiterate. In Quebec, where compulsory schooling was enacted only in 1943, 26 percent of the population was deemed unable either to read or write; in Newfoundland, the figure was 32 percent.

In all Canadian provinces except Quebec, the education system was under a state-directed Department of Education, which set minimum standards for schools. Quebec had two systems, one Catholic and one Protestant, each eligible for provincial subsidies. The Roman Catholic Church in Quebec opposed compulsory education, tuition-free schooling, and free textbooks. While the trade union movement in the province battled for free, compulsory schooling, the church had the support of the textile, tobacco, and shoe industries, which employed many older children. Poor working-class and farm families also tended to regard the labour and wages of their children as necessary for family survival.

Elsewhere in Canada, education was experiencing a rapid transformation. Faith in the value of education, fear of social breakdown, and conviction that new skills were required in the industrial labour market contributed to the growth of schools and changes in curriculum. Beginning in Ontario in 1871, the introduction of high schools offered parents who could afford it a chance to further educate their children. By 1905, with the exception of Quebec, all provinces had legislated free

By the end of the nineteenth century, multi-room schools such as the Lunenburg Academy, built in 1895, were emerging in towns and cities as monuments to the faith in education as a panacea for society's ills.

Lunenburg Academy Foundation

schooling and compulsory attendance for youngsters under the age of 12. Between 1891 and 1922, elementary and secondary enrolments in Canada more than doubled from 942 500 to 1 939 700. The number of teachers grew still faster, from 21 149 in 1890 to 54 691 in 1920. Teachers' qualifications improved steadily, and women increased their numerical predominance to over 82 percent of the profession in 1921.

Under pressure from parents, teachers, and administrators, schools became more humane and child-centred, as well as more practical and relevant. Kindergartens, with their goal to improve the family life of the poor and to nurture creativity and independence in the child, expanded slowly from their Ontario urban base. To respond to pressures that the curriculum be made more applicable to the world of work, courses in household science and manual training were introduced. Pressure also increased for the establishment of minimum standards of health and safety in the schools. Montreal's schools set the pace in

1906 with Canada's first regular and systematic medical inspection of pupils. As an integral part of the health-reform effort, formal instruction in physical education was introduced in many schools. For boys this often meant cadet training, an option that regularly pitted peace advocates against more militaristically inclined nationalists.

Schools served as a vehicle for assimilating new Canadians, especially on the Prairies. As the region filled up with people from diverse cultures, educational systems based on the cultural conditions of Eastern Canada faced serious challenges. The 1897 compromise in Manitoba over French and Catholic schools, for example, had permitted a limited number of Catholic teachers, Catholic instruction at the end of the day, and bilingual teaching in English and any other language spoken by at least 10 pupils in the school. What was not anticipated in 1897 was the flood of new Canadians who would take advantage of the right to bilingual schooling. Immigrant parents, who spoke a variety of languages, proved intensely interested in both preserving their culture and securing the best schooling possible for their children.

The English majority in the western provinces refused to accommodate linguistic pluralism in their schools. In the face of strong opposition from French-Canadian, Polish, Mennonite, and Ukrainian communities, the Manitoba government withdrew funding from all bilingual schools in 1916. Despite the compromise of 1905, Saskatchewan in 1918 abolished instruction in languages other than English beyond the first grade. The Roman Catholic clergy in Alberta had made separate schools, not language, its cause in 1905. The result was that, officially anyway, there were no bilingual schools to outlaw. Nor were there any in British Columbia.

In Ontario, Anglo-Canadians also resisted efforts of the growing francophone minority to secure education in its own language. The ultra-Protestant Orange Lodges and English-speaking Catholics worked together to push Ontario's Department of Education to enact Regulation 17 in 1912. Under this law, only schools with English-speaking teachers, where English instruction was begun upon admission, and where French was not used beyond the second year, could be eligible for government funding. Public protests were staged and legal challenges were launched, but the courts supported the Ontario government. By the end of the First World War, bitterness was such that Quebec nationalists compared Ontario to wartime Germany in its treatment of minorities.

UNIVERSITIES IN THE INDUSTRIAL AGE

While universities served a much smaller clientele than schools, they were important barometers of change in post-Confederation Canada. Most of Canada's 17 degree-granting institutions in 1867 managed on meagre endowments, tuition fees, and small government grants. Despite pressure from provincial governments in Nova Scotia and Ontario for consolidation, denominational colleges survived, and more were founded, including the Anglican-inspired University of Western Ontario in 1878, and McMaster Baptist University in 1887. In the western provinces, governments asserted control over universities from the beginning. Manitoba combined Saint Boniface (Catholic), St John's (Anglican), Manitoba College (Presbyterian), and Wesley College (Methodist) under the umbrella of the University of Manitoba in 1877. In each of the other western provinces, a single provincial university was established: the Universities of Alberta (1906), Saskatchewan (1907), and British Columbia (1908).

Most Canadian anglophone universities opened their doors to women in the 1880s and 1890s but female students remained a minority in the student body and were often discouraged from enrolling in science and professional programs. By 1921, women made up about 15 percent of the professoriate but they could be found primarily in the bottom ranks. People of colour and cultural minorities, such as Jews and blacks, were rarely welcomed as students or professors.

Despite their reputation for conservatism, universities were changing. Areas of study were expanding to include natural and social sciences; students were less preoccupied with piety than with social issues and participated in a wide range of extracurricular activities; and ornate buildings, housing laboratories, lecture theatres, and lounges proliferated on expanding, landscaped campuses. The growth of professional schools in universities reflected an increasing demand for career-related education.

In their efforts to restrict entry into their fields, professionals pressured the state to grant them self-regulation. Increasingly, a specific university degree became a condition for receiving a licence to practise a profession. Physicians, lawyers, and engineers succeeded in winning self-regulation in most jurisdictions by the end of the century and required university training as a condition of licensing. As well, in most provinces, specialized technical and agricultural colleges were established to bring academic rigour to practical pursuits. Like other professionals, university professors expanded their training and increasingly turned to research as the basis for their academic credentials. The PhD, a German innovation, was emerging as the most coveted degree in arts and sciences, though few Canadian universities yet offered it.

REINVENTING NATURE

Industrialization led Canadians to approach the natural environment in a different way. No longer a wilderness to be tamed or a rich storehouse of resources to be exploited, nature was increasingly seen as a respite from the competition and anxiety of modern society. In organizations such as the Alpine Club and Field-Naturalists' Club, urban adults were initiated into nature's mysteries, while foundations were established to fund summer vacations in rural areas for slum children. Even religion could not escape the call of nature. Among theologians it became fashionable to refer to nature as a medium whereby people could communicate with God, and poets such as Bliss Carman, Archibald Lampman, and Charles G.D. Roberts wrote eloquently about the kinship between people and nature. In many towns and cities, branches of the Society for the Prevention of Cruelty to Animals gave practical focus to the growing sympathy for the "lower orders."

With urban life increasingly redefining what it meant to be a man, boys became the particular focus of reformers who saw nature as the vehicle for inculcating survival skills and manly virtues. Ernest Thompson Seton, who achieved fame as a naturalist and animal-story writer, inspired a club movement dedicated to teaching boys the skills of tracking, camping, canoeing, and woodcraft. Hundreds of Woodcraft Clubs sprang up all over North America in the first decade of the twentieth century before they were superseded in Canada by the Boy Scout movement. Founded in Britain in 1908 by South African War veteran Robert Baden-Powell, the Boy Scout movement was based on the view that the frontier experience toughened boys up so that they would make better men—and better soldiers.

Baden-Powell launched the Girl Guides as a counterpart to Boy Scouts in 1909 and by January 1910 Canada had its first Guide group in St Catharines, Ontario. Even more popular among girls was the Canadian Girls in Training (CGIT), an organization established by the YWCA in cooperation with the major Protestant denominations in 1915. Dedicated to training young women between the ages of 12 and 17 in Christian leadership, the outdoor experience was prominent in CGIT activities.

Nature enthusiasts also became converts to conservation. Under the combined assault of environmentalists, governments in most provinces passed Game Acts, and people were encouraged to hunt with cameras rather than guns. In 1904, Jack Miner established his first bird sanctuary in Kingsville, Ontario, thereby launching a lifelong career devoted to the preservation of birds. The federal government followed up its initiative in Banff by creating more federally designated national parks, including Yoho (1886) and Jasper (1907), while the Ontario government established the first provincial park reserve, Algonquin, in 1893. Although Canadians continued to gobble up resources at an alarming rate, there was a growing sense that some control over their exploitation was necessary.

The idea of nature as a refuge from the city led those who could afford it to buy or rent summer cottages in attractive rural areas outside the city. With railways providing access to hitherto remote areas, people flocked to the Lake of the Woods, Georgian Bay, and the Muskoka regions of Ontario and the Lower Lakes region and Murray Bay in Quebec. In the Maritimes, St Andrew's-by-the-Sea, New Brunswick, Cavendish Beach, Prince Edward Island, and the Bras d'Or Lakes in Cape Breton became favourite haunts of the rich and famous from all over North America. For many well-heeled tourists hunting and fishing with a Native guide was the ultimate wilderness experience, taking them back to simpler times when survival in the great outdoors, rather than in some stifling office, was what life was all about.

THE GROWTH OF ORGANIZED SPORTS

As with tourism, sporting activities were shaped by the opportunities and values of the industrial age. Competitive games, the codification of rules regulating play, and commercialization paralleled trends in the marketplace and sparked debates about the purpose of games. The expansion of railway and road networks enabled teams to develop regular schedules of intercommunity, interregional, and even international play. By the 1890s, specialized sports pages had become common to most newspapers, an indication that such activities were becoming commercially viable. Electrically lit indoor facilities, such as ice rinks, tracks, and gymnasia, made conditions more predictable for those sports that could be played indoors.

The middle class clung tenaciously to the amateur ideal, with its prohibition of payment to participants and its gentlemanly codes of conduct. Amateurism became the defining feature of the Olympic Games when they were reinstated in 1896 and also prevailed in athletic programs established in schools, universities, and most social clubs before 1914. The Montreal Athletic Association (1881) was the first organization to serve as an umbrella for amateur sports enthusiasts and it became the driving force behind the Amateur Athletics Association of Canada, founded in 1884. In 1893, the governor general, Lord Stanley, donated a cup to the Canadian amateur hockey champions, and his successor, Earl Grey, provided a trophy for the football champions on the condition that the "cup must remain always under purely amateur conditions."

Canada ultimately followed the United States down the slippery slope toward the professionalization of sports. By the mid-1890s, a marked expansion in the number of ice rinks and teams effectively transformed ice hockey into a commercial success. The Montreal Wanderers, after winning the last amateur Stanley Cup in 1908, immediately turned professional, and professional hockey soon eclipsed its amateur rivals. Professional baseball emerged as the most popular spectator sport by the end of the nineteenth century, attracting a huge working-class audience throughout English and French Canada.

For many Canadians the rise of professionalism not only violated their much-cherished ideal of amateurism; it also opened the door to other undesirable, even "un-Canadian," practices. The issues were addressed by Toronto lawyer W.A. Frost in a letter to the editor of the *Varsity*, the University of Toronto's student newspaper. Frost claimed not to be opposed to baseball as a sport—it "may be as good as either cricket or football," he conceded—but worried about the people associated with the game, who were "of the very lowest and most repugnant character." According to Frost, baseball "has been degraded by Yankee professionalism until the name of baseball cannot fail to suggest a to-bacco-chewing, loud-voiced, twang-nosed bar-tender, with a large diamond pin and elaborately oiled hair."[3] Despite such views, professional sports continued to attract a wide following.

By the turn of the century, Canadians were increasingly participating in international sports events. Canada sent a team to the Olympics in 1900 but its only victory came to George Orton, who won the 1500 metre steeplechase as a member of the American team. Given the migration of so many Canadians to the United States in this period, and the lure of

professional salaries, it is not surprising that many Canadians earned their sporting reputations in events sponsored south of the border. Nat Butler, a native of Halifax, began his career in bicycle racing in Boston and broke all records at the Winter Velodrome in Paris in 1905. Although basketball was developed by a Canadian—James Naismith from Almonte, Ontario— it was pioneered at the YMCA International Training School in Springfield, Massachusetts, where Naismith was a student and later a teacher.

Sports were often closed to racial minorities because whites would not allow them to join their teams and clubs. In the Maritimes, blacks began forming their own baseball teams in the 1880s and by the 1890s were hosting an annual regional championship. Tom Longboat, a rare exception to the increasing exclusion of Native peoples from competitive athletics, came first in the 1907 Boston Marathon. Like whites, individuals from racial minorities were often found sporting opportunities in the United States. Gabriel Dumont, for example, toured in the United States as a crack marksman in Buffalo Bill's Wild West show in the 1880s, and two black boxers from Nova Scotia, George Dixon and Sam Langford, won acclaim at

The Royals Baseball Club of Saint John, New Brunswick, Intermediate Champions, 1921.

Public Archives of New Brunswick Harold Wright Collection/P338-2

home as well as in the United States for their successes in the ring.

Sporting activities were also beginning to open up for women. In the 1880s, bicycling joined tennis, curling, and skating as amusements for middle-class women and as a cause for worry among those who identified an increase in women's physical freedom and scandalously scant sporting attire with moral laxity and, worse still, feminist sympathies. The participation of women in school and university sports, such as basketball, field hockey, and ice hockey, helped to break down proscriptions against female participation in competitive play.

By 1914, the prevalence of school athletics and the multitude of programs run by groups such as the YWCA, YMCA, the CGIT, the Girl Guides, and the Boy Scouts had given sports an unprecedented place in the lives of most Canadians. The discovery by sports promoters that good money could be made presenting professional baseball, football, and hockey on a regular basis meant that Canadian sport was well on its way to becoming a major North American industry. And, for all the predominance of middle-class anglophones, a shared interest in sporting activity may well have helped to begin to knit together diverse groups of Canadians.

THE ARTS IN THE AGE OF INDUSTRY

In the half-century following Confederation, Canadians lamented their lack of a distinctive artistic and literary culture. The dominion's youth, colonial inheritance, and proximity to the United States were advanced as reasons why Canadian writers, painters, and sculptors rarely achieved international recognition. At the end of the nineteenth century, novelist and essayist Sara Jeannette Duncan commented:

> In our character as colonists we find the root of all our sins of omission in letters.... Our enforced political humility is the distinguishing characteristic of every phase of our national life. We are ignored, and we ignore ourselves. A nation's development is like a plant's, unattractive under ground. So long as Canada remains in political obscurity, content to thrive only at the roots, so long will the leaves and blossoms of art and literature be scanty and stunted products of our national energy.... A national literature can-

not be looked for as an outcome of anything less than a complete national existence.[4]

In Quebec, where the Roman Catholic Church remained powerful, most authors stuck to conservative narratives. Quebec was presented in this literature as a devout Catholic nation with a mission to spread the Catholic word throughout the world. With its idealization of country life, the peasant novel, a popular European genre, took firm root in Quebec. Its most enduring example is Louis Hémon's *Maria Chapdelaine* (1913), which dealt with the difficult choice for many French Canadians of moving either to New England to find work or to communities on Quebec's agricultural frontier. A few writers resisted clerical dictates. Influenced by French modernists like Baudelaire and Rimbaud, bohemian Montreal poets such as Émile Nelligan and members of the École littéraire de Montréal espoused a highly individualistic literature preoccupied with the meaning of life, death, and love. Such writers risked clerical censure and faced minuscule markets for their work.

As a major sponsor of painting, sculpture, and architecture in its great cathedrals, the Catholic church encouraged some of the most impressive religious art produced anywhere in the world. A combination of church and private commissions supported fine contributions in the art nouveau tradition by painters such as Ozias Leduc and sculptors such as Alfred Laliberté. In Montreal, Louis-Philippe Hébert's monuments to Jacques Cartier and Maisonneuve stand out as some of the best sculpture produced in Canada. Outside of the commissions sponsored by the church, Quebec painters of the late Victorian period focused on landscapes and romanticized portraits of people's lives. Before the First World War, Quebeckers in search of more liberated artistic expression moved to Paris.

English-Canadian writers also found that the centres of English-language publishing were located in London, and, increasingly, New York and Boston, where there was only a limited market for Canadian themes. Indeed, one of the reasons that Canadians remained within the romantic literary tradition after other countries had abandoned it was that the popular demand for stories about New France, Acadia, Aboriginal peoples, and rural life remained strong in foreign markets. Dramatic readings by Pauline

Union Station, Toronto, and Union Mine, Cumberland, British Columbia (inset). While cities were becoming architectural monuments to the Industrial Age, company towns on the resource frontier bore a remarkable similarity to one another in their undistinguished architecture and lack of amenities.

City of Toronto Archives/SC244-594 and British Columbia Archives/A-4531

Johnson, Canada's "Mohawk Princess," on stages in and outside Canada drew on her Native heritage to conjure up a distinctive northern nationality that was far removed from the experience of most of her listeners.

By the end of the nineteenth century, literary production began to increase in range and output, fuelled in part by the growing tendency of newspapers to run serialized novels. Women, who were increasingly able to make a living as writers or journalists, particularly excelled as novelists. In *Roland Graeme Knight*, Agnes Machar fused her reformist, feminist, religious, and patriotic concerns in her highly romantic portrayal of a Knight of Labor and the woman who loved him. Margaret Marshall Saunders, the daughter of a Nova Scotia Baptist minister, published *Beautiful Joe*, the story of an abused dog, in 1894. After winning first prize in an American Humane Society competition, *Beautiful Joe* became a best-seller, reputedly the first work by a Canadian author to sell a million copies. One of Canada's best-known writers was Lucy Maud

Montgomery, whose first published novel, *Anne of Green Gables*, became an instant international success when it appeared in 1908.

A new realistic tradition was reflected in the work of Sara Jeannette Duncan, a disciple of the American novelist Henry James and the first woman to be hired as a full-time journalist at the Toronto *Globe*. Her novel *The Imperialist* (1904) dissected small-town Ontario life and explored the need to balance British sentiment with the reality of North American living. Only one major popular writer, Stephen Leacock, in heavily ironic volumes like *Sunshine Sketches of a Little Town* (1912) and *Arcadian Adventures of the Idle Rich* (1914), questioned the values and virtues of North American liberal capitalism. Leading periodicals of the day such as *Saturday Night* (established 1887), *Busy Man's Magazine* (1896–1911), which became *Maclean's Magazine*, and *Canadian Magazine* (1893–1939) were somewhat more inclined to express liberal sentiments but they were often narrowly provincial in their focus.

biography

E. Pauline Johnson

In the period before the First World War, E. Pauline Johnson was one of only a handful of Canadian authors who achieved an international audience for their work. The youngest child of an English mother (Susanna Howells) and a Mohawk father (George Johnson), Pauline was born in 1861 and grew up in Chiefswood, an elegant home on the Grand River's Six Nation Reserve near Brantford, Ontario. Educated in both Native and Euro-Canadian cultures, she drew upon her mixed heritage to produce poetry and prose that addressed such issues as racism, feminism, and Canadian national identity.

Pauline began writing to support herself following the death of her father in 1884. In 1892, she launched a career as a performance artist, reading her poems to primarily white audiences in Canada, the United States, and Great Britain. Wearing Native costume for the first half of her program and a drawing-room gown for the second half, "the Mohawk Princess" thrilled audiences with dramatic recitations of such poems as "The Song My Paddle Sings," "A Cry From an Indian Wife," and "As Red Men Die." Her first book of poems, *The White Wampum*, appeared in 1895 and her second collection, *Canadian Born*, in 1903.

In 1906, while touring in England, she met Joseph Capilano [Su-á-pu-luck] and his delegation who were protesting to Edward VII about recent hunting and fishing restrictions on Natives in British Columbia. Johnson's friendship with "Chief Joe" reinforced her growing attraction to the West Coast and its Native history which was being ignored by new immigrants to the region. In 1909, ill with breast cancer, she retired to Vancouver, where editor Lionel Waterloo Makovski and journalist Isabel McLean es-

Pauline Johnson.

National Archives of Canada/PA-111473

tablished a committee that included representatives of the Canadian Women's Press Club and the local Women's Canadian Club to raise money for Johnson's care and also to help with the publication of her work. She produced *Legends of Vancouver* in 1911 and a collection, *Flint and Feather*, in 1912. Johnson died in 1913 and, as she requested, was buried in Stanley Park within sight of Siwash Rock.

Academic art tended to follow the international trends, though often at some distance. In 1868, a Society of Canadian Artists was established to promote formal Canadian artwork in a variety of exhibits. The Royal Academy of Arts and the National Gallery of Canada were created in 1880 at the urging of the governor general, the Marquis of Lorne. Before the end of the century, a number of art schools had been established in urban centres. Overwhelmingly, professional artists were men who, like William Brymner, Robert Harris, and George Reid, trained either in the academic style of the Paris Salon school or later, like

Edmund Morris and Curtis Williamson, found inspiration in the atmospheric Hague school. An exception to the habit of European training was Homer Watson, who, like the French-Canadian Ozias Leduc, was self-taught and visited Europe only later in life.

Artists regularly took up identifiably Canadian subjects, particularly landscapes of settled areas of the country. In 1907, the creation of the Canadian Art Club (CAC) encouraged showings by early Canadian impressionists. These painters, who focused their attention on light, colour, and mood in their work, were roundly criticized by traditionalists who felt that art, like photographs, should strive to represent objects as they were, not as imagined. By the time of its last exhibition in 1915, the CAC was being overtaken by men such as Lawren Harris and J.E.H. MacDonald, who along with Tom Thomson, Frank Carmichael, Frank Johnston, Arthur Lismer, Fred Varley, and A.Y. Jackson, began applying new approaches to art in their sketches of Algonquin Park. The war and the death of Thomson in 1917 postponed the public arrival of the painters who came to be known as the Group of Seven, but they were part of a significant prewar effort to find artistic expression for what was deemed uniquely Canadian.

On the West Coast, Emily Carr was beginning to develop her own powerful, post-impressionist style to convey the majesty of Native life and the coastal landscape. Lacking the sympathetic community available to her eastern male contemporaries, she was forced to support herself by running a boarding house. Both Carr and the Algonquin Group, like the great majority of earlier Canadian painters, tended to avoid the city and its problems. Their world, like that of many writers, most often symbolized an effort to come to terms with the natural rather than the human world of early twentieth-century Canada.

THE DRAMATIC ARTS

Canadians were enthusiastic spectators of a host of foreign and domestic touring theatre companies that crossed the country on the expanding railway networks. In 1897, Corliss Powers Walker, an impresario with a string of small theatres in North Dakota, settled in Winnipeg, which he used as a base for controlling bookings and theatre management throughout the West. His flagship theatre seated 2000 people and hosted productions, some of them direct from Broadway, six nights a week, fifty-two weeks a year. The seven touring companies of the Marks Brothers entertained in small towns across the dominion.

In the 1890s, the first home-grown professional French-language companies were founded, following on the phenomenal success of Parisian companies that toured Quebec. The British Canadian Theatrical Organization Society (1912) attempted to balance extensive American influence by organizing tours of British theatrical troupes. Although the Trans-Canada Theatre Society (1915) was Canadian-owned, it stayed in business by organizing tours of foreign companies. Britons and Americans gradually acquired controlling interests in Canadian theatres, effectively monopolizing the booking of entertainment by 1914.

The difficulties faced by Canadian talent did not escape notice. In 1907, Governor General Earl Grey created the Earl Grey Music and Dramatic Competition for the dramatic arts, but this venture collapsed in 1911 and had only a minimal influence. There was significant progress in amateur little theatre, notably with the creation in 1905 of the Toronto Arts and Letters Players and in 1913 of the Ottawa Drama League. With the opening of the Hart House Theatre at the University of Toronto in 1919, financed by the Massey family, many distinguished Canadian actors, directors, and playwrights had a forum for their talents.

Canadian audiences were also introduced to the international world of dance, though not without earning the disapproval of church leaders. Acclaimed dancers Lois Fuller and Anna Pavlova as well as Nijinsky and the Diaghilev Ballet Russe all made Canadian appearances. Many dance performances were aimed at more well-to-do audiences, but the crowds they drew included Canadians from many walks of life. Spectators also found much to entertain them in dance halls, burlesque theatres, and taverns, where hypnotists, magicians, circuses, and vaudeville drew audiences into a rich world of political satire, popular music, risqué dancing, and bawdy comedy.

These years also saw the appearance of the "movie," a popular entertainment that would soon

Top:
Artist unknown, Crooked Beak of the
Sky, *c. 1880.*

wood, paint, and bark;
29.0 x 20.3 cm
McMichael Canadian Art Collection, Purchase 1977; 1977.2.3

Left:
Clarence Gagnon (1881–1942), Twilight,
Baie St Paul, *c. 1920.*

oil on canvas;
49.9 x 65.0 cm
McMichael Canadian Art Collection, Gift of Mr Syd Hoare; 1975.61

Right:
J.E.H. MacDonald (1873–1932), Beaver
Dam and Birches, *1919*.

oil on panel;
21.5 x 26.4 cm
McMichael Canadian Art Collection, Gift of the Founders, Robert and Signe
McMichael; 1966.16.49

Below:
James Wilson Morrice (1865–1924), Ice
Bridge over the St Charles River, *1908*.

Montreal Museum of Fine Arts

outdraw all others. In 1896, 1200 citizens of Ottawa paid 10 cents each to watch a production of Thomas Edison's "Vitascope." Because of the obvious potential of the medium to attract viewers, the Department of the Interior experimented with film in their efforts to promote western settlement. By 1914, sporadic screenings were beginning to give way to regular shows offered in movie theatres that charged each enthusiastic customer a nickel: hence the name nickelodeon. With more comfortable theatres, better story lines, and higher prices, films were also appealing to the middle class, who had at first scorned the medium's reputed vulgarity.

CONCLUSION

When Canada went to war in 1914, there was still little consensus on what it meant to be a Canadian. There was no distinctive Canadian flag, and while the beaver and the maple leaf seemed to sum up what was distinctive about Canada, they were not adopted as official symbols of the country. Calixa Lavallée, a composer born in Quebec, penned the words to "O Canada" in 1880, but the song was not heard in English Canada until the turn of the century. Outside of Quebec, "The Maple Leaf Forever," with its triumphant imperialist lyrics, was much more popular. Growing cultural diversity and rapid economic development in the first decade of the twentieth century only compounded the natural tendency to emphasize differences. As participants in the new industrial order, however, Canadians shared more than they realized, including an expanding literacy, a rich popular culture, and a small but growing number of nationwide organizations. Whether these cultural trends were sufficient to hold the nation together under the impact of a world war would remain to be seen.

NOTES

1 Cited in Robert Harney, "Ethnicity and Neighbourhoods" in *Cities and Urbanization: Canadian Historical Perspectives*, ed. Gilbert A. Stelter (Toronto: Copp Clark Pitman, 1990) 228.

2 Cited in Sharon Anne Cook, *"Through Sunshine and Shadow": The Woman's Christian Temperance Union, Evangelicalism and Reform in Ontario, 1874–1930* (Montreal: McGill-Queen's University Press, 1995) 3.

3 Colin D. Howell, *Northern Sandlots: A Social History of Maritime Baseball* (Toronto: University of Toronto Press, 1995) 55.

4 Cited in Gerald Lynch and David Rampton, eds., *The Canadian Essay* (Toronto: Copp Clark Pitman, 1991) 12.

SELECTED READING

Social reform in this period is discussed in Mariana Valverde, *The Age of Light, Soap and Water: Moral Reform in English Canada, 1885–1925* (Toronto: McClelland and Stewart, 1991); Ramsay Cook, *The Regenerators: Social Criticism in Late Victorian English Canada* (Toronto: University of Toronto Press, 1985); Joseph Levitt, *Henri Bourassa and the Golden Calf: The Social Program of the Nationalists in Quebec, 1900–1914* (Ottawa: University of Ottawa Press, 1969); Richard Allen, *The Social Passion: Religion and Social Reform in Canada, 1914–1928* (Toronto: University of Toronto Press, 1990); Paul Rutherford, ed., *Saving the Canadian City: The First Phase, 1880–1920* (Toronto: University of Toronto Press, 1974); and Ronald Rompkey, *Grenfell of Labrador: A Biography* (Toronto: University of Toronto Press, 1991). For surveys of the working-class experience and labour movement see Chapter 17. Rural responses are discussed in Vernon C. Fowke, *The National Policy and the Wheat Economy* (Toronto: University of Toronto Press, 1957); David Laycock, *Populism and Democratic Thought in the Canadian Prairies, 1910–1945* (Toronto: University of Toronto Press, 1990); Ian Macpherson, *Each for All: A History of the Cooperative Movement in English Canada, 1900-1945* (Ottawa: Carleton University Press, 1979); Ronald Rudin, *In Whose Interest? Quebec's Caisses Populaires, 1900–1945* (Montreal: McGill-Queen's

University Press, 1990); Paul Sharp, *The Agrarian Revolt in Western Canada: A Survey Showing the American Parallels* (New York: Octagon Press, 1971); Jeffery Taylor, *Fashioning Farmers: Ideology, Agricultural Knowledge and the Manitoba Farm Movement, 1890–1925* (Regina: Canadian Plains Research Centre, 1994); Ian McDonald, *"To Each His Own": William Coaker and the Fisherman's Protective Union in Newfoundland Politics, 1908–1945* (St John's: ISER, Memorial University, 1987); and Terry Crowley, "Rural Labour," in Paul Craven, ed., *Labouring Lives: Work and Workers in Nineteenth-Century Ontario* (Toronto: University of Toronto Press, 1995) 13–104. See also John MacDougall, *Rural Life in Canada: Its Trend and Tasks* (1913; reprinted Toronto: University of Toronto Press, 1973); and Andrew Macphail, *The Master's Wife* (1939; reprinted Toronto: University of Toronto Press, 1977). Recent work in rural history is explored in R.W. Sandwell, ed., *Beyond City Limits: Rural History in British Columbia* (Vancouver: University of British Columbia Press, 1999) and Daniel Sampson, ed., *Contested Countryside: Rural Workers and Modern Society in Atlantic Canada, 1800–1950* (Fredericton: Acadiensis Press, 1994).

On women in this period see Marta Danylewycz, *Taking the Veil: An Alternative to Marriage, Motherhood and Spinsterhood in Quebec, 1840–1920* (Toronto: McClelland and Stewart, 1987); Ruth Compton Brouwer, *New Women for God: Canadian Presbyterian Women and India Missions, 1876–1914* (Toronto: University of Toronto Press, 1990); Rosemary R. Gagan, *A Sensitive Independence: Canadian Methodist Women Missionaries in Canada and the Orient* (Montreal: McGill-Queen's University Press, 1992); and Lynne Marks, *Revivals and Roller Rinks: Religion, Leisure, and Identity in Late-Nineteenth-Century Small-Town Ontario* (Toronto: University of Toronto Press, 1996); Denise Lemieux and Lucie Mercier, *Les femmes au tournant du siècle, 1880–1940: Ages de la vie, maternité et quotidien* (Quebec: Institut québécois de recherche sur la culture, 1989); Barbara K. Latham and Roberta J. Pazdro, eds., *Not Just Pin Money: Selected Essays in the History of Women's Work in British Columbia* (Victoria: Camosun College, 1984); Franca Iacovetta and Mariana Valverde, eds., *Gender Conflicts: New Essays in Women's History* (Toronto: University of Toronto Press, 1992); Linda Kealey, ed., *Pursuing Equality: Historical Perspectives on Women in Newfoundland and Labrador* (St John's: ISER, 1993); Carmelita McGrath, Barbara Neis, and Marilyn Porter, eds., *Their Lives and Times: Women in Newfoundland and Labrador, A Collage* (St John's: Killick Press, 1995); Margaret Conrad, Toni Laidlaw, and Donna Smyth, *No Place Like Home: Diaries and Letters of Nova Scotia Women, 1771–1939* (Halifax: Formac, 1988); Janet Guildford and Suzanne Morton, eds., *Separate Spheres: Women's Worlds in the Nineteenth-Century Maritimes* (Fredericton: Acadiensis Press, 1994); and Karen Dubinsky, *Improper Advances: Rape and Heterosexual Conflict in Ontario, 1880–1929* (Chicago: University of Chicago Press, 1993). Victorian medical notions about women are dissected in Wendy M. Mitchinson, *The Nature of Their Bodies: Women and Their Doctors in Victorian Canada* (Toronto: University of Toronto Press, 1991). Women and the law are the subject of Constance Backhouse, *Petticoats and Prejudice: Women and Law in Nineteenth-Century Canada* (Toronto: Women's Press, 1991).

Social histories dealing with changing notions of families and of sexuality include Carolyn Strange, *Toronto's Girl Problem: The Perils and Pleasures of the City, 1880–1930* (Toronto: University of Toronto Press, 1995); Angus McLaren and Arlene Tigar McLaren, *The Bedroom and the State: The Changing Practices and Politics of Contraception and Abortion in Canada, 1880–1980* (Toronto: McClelland and Stewart, 1986); Angus McLaren, *Our Own Master Race: Eugenics in Canada, 1885–1945* (Toronto: McClelland and Stewart, 1990); Gary Kinsman, *The Regulation of Desire: Sexuality in Canada* (Montreal: Black Rose Books, 1987); Sharon Dale Stone, *Lesbians in Canada* (Toronto: Between the Lines, 1990); Neil Sutherland, *Children in English-Canadian Society: Framing the Twentieth-Century Consensus* (Toronto: University of Toronto Press, 1976); Patricia Rooke and Rudy Schnell, *Discarding the Asylum: From Child Rescue to the Welfare State in English Canada, 1800–1950* (Lanham, MO: University Press of America, 1983); and James G. Snell, *In the Shadow of the Law: Divorce in Canada, 1900–1939* (Toronto: University of Toronto Press, 1991) and *The Citizen's Wage: The State and the Elderly in Canada, 1900–1951* (Toronto: University of Toronto Press, 1996). Motherhood is the focus of Katherine Arnup, *Education for Motherhood: Advice for Mothers in Twentieth-Century Canada* (Toronto: University of Toronto Press, 1994); Cynthia R. Comacchio, *"Nations Are Built of Babies": Saving Ontario's Mothers and Children, 1900–1940* (Montreal: McGill-Queen's University Press, 1994) and *The Infinite Bonds of Family: Domesticity in Canada, 1850–1940* (Toronto: University of Toronto Press, 1999). See also Pauline Greenhill and Diane Tye, eds., *Undisciplined Women:*

Tradition and Culture in Canada (Montreal and Kingston: McGill-Queen's University Press, 1997).

On reform and suffrage movements, see Janice Newton, *The Feminist Challenge to the Canadian Left, 1900–1918* (Montreal: McGill-Queen's University Press, 1995); Linda Kealey, ed., *A Not Unreasonable Claim: Women and Reform in Canada* (Toronto: Women's Press, 1979); Veronica Strong-Boag, *The Parliament of Women: The National Council of Women of Canada, 1893–1929* (Ottawa: National Museum of Civilization, 1976); Naomi Griffiths, *The Splendid Vision: Centennial History of the National Council of Women, 1893–1993* (Ottawa: Carleton University Press, 1993); Carol Lee Bacchi, *Liberation Deferred? The Ideas of the English-Canadian Suffragists, 1877–1918* (Toronto: University of Toronto Press, 1983); Catherine L. Cleverdon, *The Woman Suffrage Movement in Canada* (1950; reprinted Toronto: University of Toronto Press, 1972); and Margot I. Duley *Where Once Our Mothers Stood We Stand: Women's Suffrage in Newfoundland, 1890–1925* (Charlottetown: Gynergy Books, 1993). See also Nellie McClung, *In Times Like These* (1913; reprinted Toronto: University of Toronto Press, 1972).

On the intellectual history of late Victorian Canada, see the books by Gerald Friesen and A.B. McKillop cited in Chapter 13. See also Ramsay Cook, *The Regenerators*, cited earlier; Denis Monière, *Ideologies in Quebec: The Historical Development* (Toronto: University of Toronto Press, 1981); and Allen Mills, *Fool for Christ: The Political Thought of J.S. Woodsworth* (Toronto: University of Toronto Press, 1991). See also Suzanne Zeller, *Inventing Canada: Early Victorian Science and the Idea of a Transcontinental Nation* (Toronto: University of Toronto Press, 1987); Allan Smith, *Canada An American Nation? Essays on Continentalism, Identity and the Canadian Frame of Mind* (Montreal: McGill-Queen's University Press, 1994); and Carl Berger, *The Sense of Power: Studies in the Ideas of Canadian Imperialism 1867–1914* (Toronto: University of Toronto Press, 1970) and *Honour and the Search for Influence: A History of the Royal Society of Canada, 1882–1994* (Toronto: University of Toronto Press, 1996). On the writing of history in the late nineteenth century, see M. Brook Taylor, *Promoters, Patriots and Partisans: Historiography in Nineteenth-Century English Canada* (Toronto: University of Toronto Press, 1990); Carl Berger, *The Writing of Canadian History* (Toronto: University of Toronto Press, 1976); Serge Gagnon, *Quebec and Its Historians, 1840–1920* (Montreal: Harvest House, 1982) and Beverley Boutilier and Alison Prentice,

eds. *Creating Historical Memory: English-Canadian Women and the Work of History* (Vancouver: UBC Press, 1997).

On religion and culture, see the books by Michael Gauvreau, John Webster Grant, Jean Hamelin and William Westfall cited in Chapter 11. See also Neil Semple, *The Lord's Dominion: The History of Canadian Methodism* (Montreal: McGill-Queen's University Press, 1996); Harry A. Renfree, *Heritage and Horizon: The Baptist Story in Canada* (Mississauga, ON: Canadian Baptist Federation, 1988); Michael Gauvreau, *The Evangelical Century: College and Creed in English Canada from the Great Revival to the Great Depression* (Montreal: McGill-Queen's University Press, 1991) and George Rawlyk, ed., *The Canadian Protestant Experience* (Montreal: McGill-Queen's University Press, 1990). See also Terence Murphy, ed., *A Concise History of Christianity in Canada* (Toronto: Oxford University Press, 1996).

Schools are discussed in books by Paul Axelrod, Susan Houston, Alison Prentice, Roger Magnuson, and J. Donald Wilson cited in Chapter 13. See also Nancy Sheehan, David C. Jones, and Robert M. Stamp, eds., *Shaping the Schools of the Canadian West* (Calgary: Detselig, 1979). The best treatment of universities is Brian McKillop, *Matters of Mind: The University in Ontario, 1791–1951* (Toronto: University of Toronto Press, 1994). For a penetrating look at one institution see Sara Z. Burke, *Seeking the Highest Good: Social Service and Gender at the University of Toronto, 1887–1937* (Toronto: University of Toronto Press, 1996).

Nature, the environment, and conservation are the focus of Chad Gaffield and Pam Gaffield, eds., *Consuming Canada: Readings in Environmental History* (Toronto: Copp Clark, 1995); Patricia Jasen, *Wild Things: Nature, Culture, and Tourism in Ontario, 1790–1914* (Toronto: University of Toronto Press, 1995); Janet Foster, *Working for Wildlife: The Beginning of Preservation in Canada* (Toronto: University of Toronto Press, 1978); J.G. Nelson, ed., *Canadian Parks in Historical Perspective* (Montreal: Harvest House, 1970); James C. Taylor, *Negotiating the Past: The Making of Canada's National Historic Parks and Sites* (Montreal: McGill-Queen's University Press, 1990); Michel Girard, *L'Écologisme retrouvé: Essor et déclin de la Commission de la Conservation du Canada* (Ottawa: Les Presses de l'Université d'Ottawa, 1994); Carl Berger, *Science, God, and Nature in Victorian Canada* (Toronto: University of Toronto Press, 1983); and Robert H. MacDonald, *Sons of the Empire: The Frontier and the Boy Scout Movement, 1890–1918* (Toronto: University of Toronto Press, 1993). On culture, see Keith Walden, *Becoming Modern in Toronto: The Industrial Exhibition and the Shaping of Late Victorian Culture* (Toronto: University of Toronto Press, 1997).

On sports and recreation, see Alan Metcalfe, *Canada Learns to Play: The Emergence of Organized Sport, 1807–1914* (Toronto: McClelland and Stewart, 1987); Colin Howell; *Northern Sandlots: A Social History of Maritime Baseball* (Toronto: University of Toronto Press, 1995); and Bruce Kidd, *Contested Identities: The Struggle for Canadian Sport* (Toronto: University of Toronto Press, 1996). Architecture in this period is comprehensively surveyed in the second volume of Harold Kalman's *A History of Canadian Architecture* (Toronto: Oxford University Press, 1994); Janet Wright, *Crown Assets: The Architecture of the Department of Public Works, 1867–1967* (Toronto: University of Toronto Press, 1997); and Peter Ward, *A History of Domestic Space: Privacy and the Canadian Home* (Vancouver: University of British Columbia Press, 1999).

Literary history is discussed in Carl F. Klinck, ed., *Literary History of Canada* (Toronto: University of Toronto Press, 1976) and Dennis Duffy, *Gardens, Covenants, Exiles: Loyalism in the Literature of Upper Canada/Ontario* (Toronto: University of Toronto Press, 1982). See also Veronica Strong-Boag and Carole Gerson, *Pulling Her Own Canoe: The Times and Texts of E. Pauline Johnson* (Toronto: University of Toronto Press, 2000) for a stimulating discussion of cultural developments in this period as they relate to one of Canada's best-known poets. Paul Rutherford assesses the explosion in newspaper publication and newspaper readership in *A Victorian Authority: The Daily Press in Late Nineteenth-Century Canada* (Toronto: University of Toronto Press, 1982). See also Minko Sotiron, *From Politics to Profit: The Commercialization of Canadian Daily Newspapers,*

1890–1920 (Montreal: McGill-Queen's University Press, 1996). On artistic developments, see Carman Cumming, *Sketches from a Young Country: The Images of* Grip *Magazine* (Toronto: University of Toronto Press, 1997); Maria Tippett, *Making Culture: English-Canadian Institutions and the Arts Before the Massey Commission* (Toronto: University of Toronto Press, 1990); J. Russell Harper, *Painting in Canada: A History*, 2nd ed. (Toronto: University of Toronto Press, 1977); Dennis Reid, "*Our Own Country Canada*": *Being the Account of the National Aspirations of the Principal Landscape Artists in Montreal and Toronto, 1860–1890* (Ottawa: National Gallery, 1980); Guy Robert, *La peinture au Québec depuis ses origines* (Ste-Adèle, PQ: Iconia, 1978); and Laurent Mailhot and Pierre Nepveu, *La poésie québécoise des origines à nos jours* (Montreal: L'Hexagone, 1986). For an introduction to Canadian theatre history, see Don Rubin, ed., *Canadian Theatre History: Selected Readings* (Toronto: Copp Clark Ltd., 1996). Helmut Kallmann et al., eds., *The Encyclopedia of Music in Canada*, 2nd ed. (Toronto: University of Toronto Press, 1992) is an excellent resource for matters musical. Folklore is explored in Edith Fowke and Richard Johnston, *Folk Songs of Canada* (Waterloo, ON: Waterloo Music, 1954) and in several volumes by Edith Fowke: *Sally Go Round the Sun* (Toronto: McClelland and Stewart, 1969), *Folklore of Canada* (Toronto: McClelland and Stewart, 1976), and *Ring Around the Moon* (Toronto: McClelland and Stewart, 1977). For a study of one of Canada's foremost photographers, see Roger Hall, Gordon Dobbs, and Stanley Triggs, *The World of William Notman: The Nineteenth Century Through a Master Lens* (Toronto: McClelland and Stewart, 1993).

WEBLINKS

IMMIGRATION IN THE EARLY TWENTIETH CENTURY
www.cic.gc.ca/english/about/legacy/index.html

Forging Our Legacy, prepared by Citizenship and Immigration Canada, is a survey history that traces the evolution of Canadian citizenship and the role immigration played in the development of the country from the turn of the century until 1977. Chapters 2 and 3 cover the early twentieth century, including the policies of Clifford Sifton and Frank Oliver.

ADVERTISING FOR IMMIGRANTS
www.civilization.ca/hist/advertis/adindexe.html

This virtual exhibition, called *The Last Best West*, discusses the Canadian government's role in advertising free land to farmers and farm workers in Britain, the United States, and Europe. View colourful government pamphlet covers, newspaper advertisements for immigrants, and promotional photographs and notices.

CLIFFORD SIFTON
http://timelinks.merlin.mb.ca/reference/db0053.htm

This site contains a biography of Sifton, with dynamic links to related information.

FRANK OLIVER
http://timelinks.merlin.mb.ca/reference/db0076.htm

A biography of Oliver, with related links, can be found at this site.

WORKERS UNITE
www.civilization.ca/hist/labour/lab03e.html

This online exhibit traces the conditions of workers and the evolution of organized labour in Canada, from the early nineteenth century craft unions to the present day. Read about the Knights of Labour and the Industrial Workers of the World in the section called "Workers Unite".

WOMAN'S CHRISTIAN TEMPERANCE UNION
http://womenshistory.about.com/cs/temperance/

A timeline, through documents, of the Women's Christian Temperance Union is contained here, including a list of social reforms the WCTU has helped work for in its more than 125 year history.

NATIONAL COUCIL OF WOMEN
http://www.ncwc.ca

The National Council of Women of Canada (NCWC), founded in 1893, has sought to empower women and improve the quality of life for their families through education and advocacy. This site provides information about the Council's history, mission, and ongoing work.

WHO KILLED WILLIAM ROBINSON?
http://web.uvic.ca/history-robinson/

This site contains a collection of historical documents that relate to the death of William Robinson, a Black American who was murdered in Salt Spring Island in the British Colony of British Columbia in 1868.

PART V SUMMARY

LESS THAN A HALF-CENTURY OLD WHEN THE WAR WAS declared, Canada had changed dramatically in the years since Confederation. The federal government had successfully extended the nation's geographical boundaries and developed a national economic policy on which both Conservatives and Liberals seemed to agree. Despite persistent federal-provincial wrangling and cultural differences, Canada was fast developing its industrial potential and was attracting immigrants and capital investment. The optimism of the modern age was reflected in the creation of organizations to reform society in everything from drinking habits and city planning to the status of women and labour conditions. While Native peoples and other minorities faced crippling discrimination from the dominant culture, they were beginning to fight back, drawing strength from their own communities and the growing belief that everyone was entitled to benefit from the new industrial order. Two world wars, a major depression, and the onset of mass consumer culture over the next three decades would test the capacity of the developing nation to make this belief a reality.

PART VI

THE TRANSITIONAL YEARS, 1914–1945

The Great War, which raged from 1914 to 1918, wasted the lives of a generation of Canada's youth and was the catalyst for many changes, the most enduring of which was the enhanced role of the federal government in the lives of all Canadians. It also exposed the fault lines of class, culture, gender, and region that would bedevil Canada's postwar leaders. During the 1920s many Canadians embraced consumer culture, increasingly defining their success by the extent to which they could purchase the cars, radios, household appliances, and fashions that poured out of Canadian factories. While mass production seemed to promise a better life for all, many people were left behind in the rush for material well-being. The problem of poverty in the midst of plenty was starkly exposed during the Great Depression of the 1930s. Prompted by the sheer scale of human misery, many Canadians joined movements to create a welfare state or usher in a socialist transformation of the economic system. The widespread support for reform coupled with the federal government's success in mobilizing the nation's resources to fight the Second World War between 1939 and 1945 paved the way for dramatic changes in Canadian government and society following the war.

The Great War and Reconstruction, 1914–1921

timeline

1911–20	Robert Borden serves as prime minister
1914–18	First World War
1915	Battle of Ypres
1916	Battle of the Somme; female suffrage granted in Manitoba, Saskatchewan, and Alberta; Manitoba government abolishes bilingual schools; National Research Council created; Canadian Council of Agriculture produces Farmers' Platform
1917	Battle of Vimy Ridge; Military Service Act (Conscription) passed; Wartime Elections Act; Halifax Explosion; Union Government wins election
1917–23	Canadian National Railway created
1918	Battle of Amiens; League of Indians established; women win the vote federally and in Nova Scotia
1919	Farmer-Labour government elected in Ontario; Winnipeg General Strike and other general strikes across the country; New Brunswick women win the vote; Progressive Party formed; Canada signs Treaty of Versailles
1919–20	Borden sends Canadian troops to help quell Russian Revolution
1920–21	Arthur Meighen serves as prime minister

I am terrified. I hug the earth, digging my fingers into every crevice, every hole.

A blinding flash and an explosive howl a few feet in front of the trench. My bowels liquefy. Acrid smoke bites the throat, parches the mouth. I am beyond mere fright. I am frozen with an insane fear that keeps me cowering in the bottom of the trench. I lie flat on my belly waiting....[1]

Charles Yale Harrison, an American soldier in the Canadian Expeditionary Force (CEF), was far from alone in his reaction to a German shelling. Many soldiers found the senseless slaughter in Europe too much to bear. Others volunteered with enthusiasm and, in retrospect at least, remembered the war years as a time of comradeship and great purpose. Whatever the response to the Great War that raged in Europe between August 1914 and November 1918, it touched the lives of most Canadians. It also marked a major turning point in the political history of the nation and served as a catalyst for various trends gaining momentum in the industrial age.

PREPARING FOR WAR

The assassination of Austrian Archduke Franz Ferdinand and his wife in Sarajevo by a Serb national-ist in June 1914 seemed at first to Canadians a remote tragedy. What led to war was less the murder of a future head of state than the military alliances among European nations, which produced a domino effect when efforts were made to redress the outrage. Austria-Hungary declared war on Serbia, and its German ally declared its support. This led Russia, an ally of Serbia, to mobilize its army; France, an ally of Russia, followed. As Germany prepared to invade neutral Belgium en route to France, Great Britain aligned itself with France and Russia. Italy and Romania eventually joined the effort to stop the German alliance, as did the United States in April 1917, while the Ottoman Empire sided with Germany.

A member of the British Empire, Canada was automatically at war when Great Britain was, but Canadians made the decisions about the character of the nation's participation in the war. In the early days of the war there were few voices raised against Canada's active involvement in the conflict. Conservatives and Liberals in the House of Commons united to pass the War Measures Act early in August 1914. This act gave the federal government authority to do everything deemed "necessary for the security, defence, peace, order, and welfare of Canada." Under its provisions, Ottawa imposed tough censorship laws, intervened in the marketplace, stripped many people of their democratic rights, and overrode provincial claims to jurisdiction.

Canada entered the war with a standing army of just 3110 men and a navy consisting of two aging vessels. Since the end of the nineteenth century, most of Canada's modest defence expenditures had been channelled to the militia. Militia strength stood at over 74 000 in the summer of 1914, and these summer-camp soldiers provided Canada's first eager recruits. Volunteers were grouped in numbered battalions of about 1000 men. Battalions, in turn, were organized into regiments, brigades, and divisions for what became known as the Canadian Expeditionary Force (CEF).

Ignoring his department's plans for war mobilization, Minister of Militia Sam Hughes appealed for volunteers for a division of 25 000 men. He was swamped with replies. More by good luck than good management, 31 000 men, 8 000 horses, and sundry equipment, much of it useless, were loaded onto transports and dispatched to Europe on 3 October. Among those travelling with the First Division were 101 nurses under the direction of Matron Margaret MacDonald. In this war Canada's Nursing Sisters would be full-fledged members of the CEF.

Because no Canadian had sufficient military experience, a British officer, Major-General E.A.H. Alderson, took command. At Ypres, Belgium, in mid-April, they had their first real test when they experienced a chlorine gas attack. It soon became clear that the war would be a long one and that Britain needed all the help it could get from the empire. In the end, over 600 000 of the combatants mobilized for the Great War would be Canadians. Over 60 000 of them died and nearly 170 000 were wounded.

Inadequate facilities and bottlenecks in military supplies plagued Canada's early efforts. Sam Hughes was part of the problem. Patronage and corruption riddled the Militia Department's massive purchasing program, and confusion reigned in the command structure of the Canadian forces. Hughes defended the Canadian-made Ross rifles, even though the guns had a tendency to jam in the heat of battle. In 1916, they were replaced by the British-made Lee-Enfields.

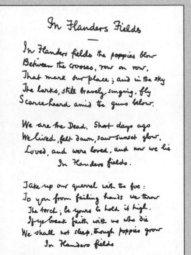

It was the battle of Ypres that inspired Lieutenant-Colonel John McCrae, a Canadian doctor, to write the poem "In Flanders Fields," a moving call to keep faith with the soldiers who had given up their lives.

Courtesy of Guelph Museums-McCrae House Collection

Hughes was finally dismissed from his portfolio in 1916. By that time, his administrative incompetence had brought an avalanche of criticism against the government's mishandling of the war effort.

Borden, meanwhile, had begun to bring efficiency to the war effort. A variety of committees, including the Imperial Munitions Board, War Purchasing Board, National Service Board, and Ministry of Overseas Military Sources, were established. They were staffed by people with administrative experience, mainly businessmen such as Joseph Flavelle, general manager of the William Davies Packing Company, who became chair of the Imperial Munitions Board (IMB). Flavelle spurred private firms to new levels of productivity, enticed American companies to locate in Canada, and, when all else failed, created government-run factories to produce everything from acetone to airplanes. By 1917, the IMB boasted 600 factories, 150 000 workers, and a turnover of $2 million a day.

THE WARTIME ECONOMY

Although the First World War did not effect major change in the direction of the Canadian economy, it sped Canadians faster down the road to industrial maturity. The value of Canadian exports quadrupled from 1914 to 1919. The percentage of Canadian manufactures sold overseas leaped from 7 percent in 1913 to 40 percent in 1917 and 1918. Grain acreage soared.

Government economic intervention increased markedly relative to peacetime. In addition to setting up agencies to ensure that the army was properly equipped, the government brought a wide range of supplies and services under its control. The Board of Grain Supervisors became the sole agent for Canadian wheat sales; the Fuel Controller decided the price and use of coal, wood, and gas; and the Food Board determined policy relating to the cost and distribution of food. To increase agricultural efficiency, the Food Board purchased 100 tractors from the Henry Ford Motor Company to distribute at cost to farmers.

Inevitably, there were complaints about government policy. The Food Board's "anti-loafing law," threatening punishment for any man or boy not gainfully employed, was unpopular, as were the "fuelless days" mandated by the Fuel Controller. The IMB's pattern of granting contracts sparked accusations from Western Canada that Flavelle was favouring central Canadian firms. Canadians were quick to observe that people like Flavelle prospered while servicemen's families were often forced to rely on charity.

By 1916, the Canadian economy was fully geared for war. The British-owned Vickers Company employed over 15 000 people in its shipyards near Montreal, while Davie Shipbuilding of Lauzon, Quebec, produced anti-submarine vessels and steel barges. Between 1914 and 1918, Canada's steel mills doubled their capacity to meet British demands for shells, supplying as much as a third of British artillery needs. Farm and factory production increased to meet the demand for food, clothing, and footwear.

Volunteers knitting socks.
City of Toronto Archives/SC244-873

Notwithstanding the enhanced role of government and industry, voluntary activities remained essential to the war effort. The 1200 branches of the Red Cross served as a virtual auxiliary of the Army Medical Corps. In many communities, the Women's Institute and the Imperial Order Daughters of the Empire collected money, knit socks, and packed parcels for the men overseas. A range of other organizations—the Great War Veterans' Association, the Next-of-Kin Association, the YM- and YWCA, Consumers' Leagues, Women's Patriotic Leagues, Vacant Lot Garden Clubs, and the Women's Volunteer Army Division—"did their bit." The federal government established a Canadian Patriotic Fund, an organization staffed largely by volunteers, whose role was to help the families of soldiers overseas. The volunteers in the Patriotic Fund helped dependants to apply for financial assistance—up to $50 a month by the end of the war—and also arranged services for a veteran who returned sick, wounded, insane, or addicted to alcohol.

The twin demand for workers and soldiers produced a labour shortage by 1916, causing the federal government to create the National Service Board to more efficiently mobilize the nation's resources. As men left their jobs for the front, women were recruited into transportation and metal trades. Over 30 000 women were hired in munitions factories and many more in positions temporarily opened to women because of the conditions created by the conflict. Women were paid less than the men they replaced, and they were fired from their "untraditional" jobs at the end of the hostilities.

As the economy moved into high gear, Canadians confronted inflation and a soaring cost of living. Wages, controlled by wartime regulation, failed to follow the upward spiral of prices and many people got caught in the financial squeeze. In the last two years of the war, strike activity and political unrest increased. In 1918, the government prohibited strikes and lockouts under its War Labour Policy, but labour shortages blunted the thrust of the legislation. Because there was no desperate reserve army of labour willing to take the jobs of striking workers, the workers had the upper hand. Union membership increased dramatically, and support for labour parties grew.

FINANCING THE WAR

Under the sweeping provisions of the War Measures Act, the federal government took a variety of financial initiatives that would have been unthinkable in peacetime. It suspended the gold standard, expanded the money supply, and engaged in deficit financing. Canadians also extended credit to Great Britain for the purchase of the necessities of war. In an effort to raise money domestically, the government sold Victory Bonds, War Savings Certificates, and, for children, War Savings Stamps. The Canadian economy proved capable of generating nearly $2 billion in loans, and at no time during the war did government expenditures exceed 10 percent of GNP. In 1917, the federal government began to nationalize half the country's railway capacity by taking control of the Grand Trunk Pacific and Canadian Northern and amalgamating them with other government-controlled railways to create the Canadian National Railway system. The government also used the wartime emergency to build a more effective civil service.

In response to farmer and labour demands that wealth as well as manpower be conscripted, Ottawa implemented a war profits tax in 1916. It was pegged at 25 percent on all profits greater than 7 percent of capital for corporations and 10 percent of capital for other businesses with a capitalization of $50 000 or more. In 1917, the federal government for the first time imposed personal income taxes. The tax was a mere 2 percent on annual incomes up to $6000, a substantial sum at the time; single people earning under $1500 and married men with family incomes under $3000 were exempted. Tax rates rose progressively to reach a maximum of 25 percent on income over $100 000. Although the "temporary" income and corporate taxes played a small role in financing the war effort, they outlived the crisis that sparked them. By 1939 they were generating nearly one-third of the federal government's revenues.

THE WAR IN EUROPE

Canadian men enlisted in the armed forces for a variety of reasons, patriotism, adventure, and unemployment among them. As Larry Nelson, a Toronto enlistee in 1914, recalled, "most of us were young and saw it as a wonderful opportunity to throw off the shackles of working in an office or a factory or on a farm or what-have-you."[2] Over 65 percent of the first wave of volunteers were recent British immigrants, and one-half of all enlistees in Canadian forces in the First World War were British-born.

The 6000 Canadians killed or injured in the April 1915 battle at Ypres were only the first in a long list of casualties. On 1 July 1916, the first day of the Allied offensive on the Somme, there were 21 000 British casualties, among them nearly 700 members of the Newfoundland Regiment, who fought at Beaumont Hamel. The Canadian Corps, now a full four divisions strong, had been brought in to sustain the failing offensive on the Somme and suffered over 24 000 casualties. But the worst was not over. With the Russian front crumbling, the Dardanelles taken by the Turks, and the Germans holding the line in Europe, there were fears that the Allies might lose the war. There were mutinies in the French army, and some Canadians were being shot for desertion as a warning to anyone else contemplating such a move.

In April 1917, the Canadian Corps took Vimy Ridge after a fiercely fought battle in which there were over 10 000 Canadian casualties. It proved to be a turning point for Canadians in the war. Until 1917, the soldiers of the CEF fought as "imperials" under Britain's Army Act. This did not always go over well with the troops or the folks at home. By the fall of 1916, Borden was determined to give Canadians more control over their own war effort. He created a Ministry of Overseas Military Forces under the control of Sir George Perley, the Canadian High Commissioner in London, and redefined the CEF as an overseas contingent of the Canadian militia. Many of the British officers were gradually replaced by Canadians and, after Vimy Ridge, the process accelerated until on 9 June 1917, Arthur Currie, the Canadian commander of the First Canadian Infantry Division, was made commander of the entire Canadian Corps.

Under the methodical Currie, Canadians developed a reputation for bravery and determination. In October 1917, the Canadians were summoned to Passchendaele, in Belgium, where the British Fifth Army had already lost 68 000 men. In October and November, the Canadian Corps broke through the German lines, but the price— 15 000 men—was high.

While the vast majority of Canadian military personnel were in the land forces, significant numbers also served at sea and in the air. The unexpected success of German submarines (known as U-boats) in sinking the merchant ships that carried North American war supplies to Britain and Europe brought a new dimension to naval warfare. As a result, nearly 10 000 Canadians served in the navy. Most of them operated Canadian-built anti-submarine craft on the East Coast, but over 1000 served with the British fleet in European waters. In the summer and fall of 1918, three German U-boats hunted off Nova Scotia

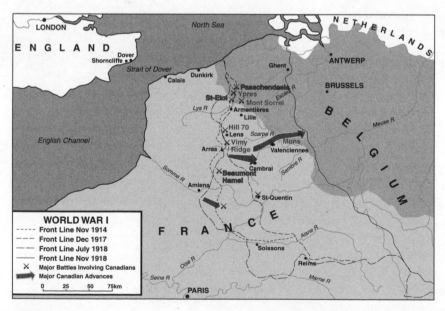

Map 19.1
The European Front, 1914–1918.

MORE TO THE STORY

The Realities of War

On the front, men lived in trenches that stretched from Switzerland to the English Channel. Their dugouts were pits of thick mud infested with fleas, lice, rats, and germs. Although soldiers devoured their rations of corned beef, biscuits, bread, and tea, it was not a healthy diet and left them constantly hungry and susceptible to diseases. If the enemy missed his mark, dysentery, pneumonia, and "trench fever" might be just as deadly. Chemical warfare was an entirely new and horrifying experience. To survive their first attack of chlorine gas at Ypres, men urinated in their handkerchiefs and held them to their noses. Rats nibbled the corpses of fallen comrades while those who were still alive dug new trenches and maintained existing ones, moved supplies, and tried not to think of their hunger and fear.

Fear was justified. Of the more than 600 000 Canadians who enlisted or were conscripted, about 60 000 died, and at least as many were so severely wounded, physically or mentally, that they were unable to resume a normal life. The mentally wounded, or "shell shocked" as they came to be known, returned to a society that was ill-prepared for such casualties. While a soldier whose wounds put him in a wheelchair received a government pension and the sympathy of other Canadians, there was little comfort for the emotionally disabled who remained unfit to resume their work and family life and who stared vacantly into space or sought comfort in the bottle.

Following the war, Canadians tried to find ways to come to terms with the sacrifice of so many men in the prime of their lives. Historian Jonathan Vance, in his book *Death So Noble*, shows that, as the memory of the war receded, the death and dismemberment of the ordinary soldier was idealized through monuments in town squares and reflections on the war that highlighted its role in fostering a national spirit that had been missing since Confederation. Such views conveniently glossed over the horror of war and the divisions it created among Canadians.[3]

Men remained in the trenches for a week or more at a time in all kinds of weather before they were relieved briefly to go to makeshift rest camps.

National Archives of Canada/PA-1326

and Newfoundland. The Canadian anti-submarine vessels, which escorted merchant ship convoys, helped keep losses of major vessels to only two. It was more difficult to protect the widely scattered fishing fleets, and over 30 schooners and trawlers were destroyed in Canadian and Newfoundland waters.

Canada authorized a tiny air unit early in the war, but airmen were encouraged to participate in British units. Over 20 000 Canadians served in the Royal Flying Corps (RFC), the Royal Naval Air Service, or, after 1 April 1918, the Royal Air Force. One of the most famous of Canada's fighting pilots was Lieutenant-Colonel W.A. "Billy" Bishop, who shot down 72 enemy planes. Unlike over 1500 other Canadians who pioneered in the use of the "aeroplane" in wartime, he lived to tell about it. The achievements of Canadian airmen such as Bishop, combined with the expertise Canadians gained in the

Jack Turner and Lee Allan from Prince Edward Island taking a break from battle in 1917. Lee reads the Island Patriot *while Jack holds* Jack Canuck, *a comic strip showing the heroics of soldier life.*

Courtesy of the Prince Edward Island Archives and Records Office/2767/107

British flying services and the tremendous growth of aircraft technology, helped to ensure national aviation development after the war, including the establishment of the Royal Canadian Air Force as a third armed service.

THE WAR AT HOME

The slaughter on the European front spread panic in the British War Office and led to the demand for more troops. Borden had pushed the approved strength of the CEF up to 500 000 in his New Year's message for 1916. But where would the soldiers come from? Lagging voluntary enlistments and high casualty rates at the front were already making it difficult to keep units up to strength.

In the early months of the war, it had looked as if voluntary enlistment would sustain the Canadian war effort. Overall, one in six Canadian men between the ages of 15 and 54, or nearly 233 000, had volunteered for the infantry by 1917. Canadians had also joined

other branches of the CEF, such as the artillery, engineer, medical, and army service corps, or had responded to appeals to join British forces, bringing the numbers almost up to the half-million demanded by Borden.

While most men of military age never volunteered, the proportion of recruits varied dramatically by region and culture. Only 13 000 were French-speaking, and men in Ontario and the West were more likely to sign up than those from the Maritimes and Quebec. The attachment of recent immigrants to their European homelands to some extent explains the lower recruitment rates in the longer-settled eastern provinces, but there were other reasons as well.

French Canadians were initially sympathetic to the Allied cause, but this feeling waned as the war progressed. During the first year of the war, French Canadians were dispersed among various units, creating language difficulties. The first and the last entirely French unit, the Royal 22nd Battalion, was established in October 1914. Anger at Ontario's 1912 legislation restricting French-language instruction in public schools also reinforced feelings of estrangement from a cause that was identified with Britain and English Canada. As wartime tensions mounted, provincial governments outside Quebec intensified their efforts to suppress French-language education in their jurisdictions, and English Canadians began accusing French Canadians of shirking their duty.

Borden tried to maintain volunteer strength by stepping up recruitment efforts, conducting a National Registration of all able-bodied men, and creating a Canadian Defence Force that would relieve soldiers stationed in Canada for European service. None of these measures worked. In May 1917, Borden announced his intention to impose conscription, or compulsory military service, on a war-weary nation. Opposition to his Military Service Act, which drafted single men between the ages of 20 and 35, was high, especially in Quebec and among farmers and labourers. Although Borden had postponed calling an election in wartime, he now changed his mind. An election would clear the air about the issue of conscription.

Before dissolving Parliament on 6 October, Borden approached Laurier to join him in a coalition to support an all-out war effort. The 78-year-old Liberal chief rejected conscription and therefore the coalition. Defying Laurier's decision, a rump of Liberals primarily from the West and Ontario joined with the Conservatives to create a Union government that campaigned on a platform of conscription, prohibition, and abolition of party patronage.

To ensure a victory for his unstable coalition, Borden also saw to it that the right people got the vote. A Military Voters' Act enfranchised every man and woman in the CEF, while the Wartime Elections Act gave the vote to mothers, wives, and sisters of soldiers—dead or alive—and took it away from citizens of enemy origin naturalized after 1902. The only compensation for those who were disenfranchised was an exemption from conscription. Even these draconian measures failed to convince Unionists that they would carry the day. Running scared during the election campaign, they promised sons of farmers an exemption from conscription, a promise that was later broken.

The results of the election held on 17 December surprised few people: the Union government won 153 seats, while the Liberals won 82. Sixty-two of Quebec's 65 seats went to Laurier, but the Liberals carried only 10 of 28 seats in the Maritimes, 8 of 82 in Ontario, and 2 of 57 in the West. The popular vote suggested greater division outside Quebec than the seat totals suggest. Civilian voters in the Maritimes gave a slight majority of their votes to anti-conscription candidates; even in Ontario, anti-

conscriptionists won almost 40 percent of the civilian vote.

Anti-conscriptionists constituted a substantial part of the electorate in English Canada, but they were the overwhelming majority in Quebec, where anti-conscription feeling continued to run high after the election. In 1918, the Quebec legislature even debated a secessionist resolution. When conscription tribunals began hearing applications for military exemptions, violence erupted in the province. The worst incident occurred in late March 1918 in Quebec City, where furious crowds attacked the military service registry and trashed English businesses. Ottawa sent in troops from Toronto who, when provoked, opened fire, killing four people and injuring many more.

Whether conscription served its military purpose has been much debated. Defaults and desertions were common, and tribunals were often sympathetic to local boys. Of the more than 400 000 men who registered under the legislation, only 24 000 went to France. Because of the difficulty of raising conscripts, the Fifth Division in Britain was dissolved and its soldiers distributed among the thinning ranks of other divisions. The war ended a year after conscription had been imposed, but its effects were felt for a long time,

Canadian nurses at a hospital in France vote in the 1917 election.
National Archives of Canada/PA-2279

not least in national politics, where the Liberal Party could claim that it had been Quebec's champion in a time of need.

ENEMIES WITHIN

The Wartime Elections Act revealed another source of tension for a nation at war: the people whose former homeland was in enemy territory. In 1914, there were about half a million people in Canada who had been born in, or traced their origins to, enemy countries. Many of the 100 000 enemy aliens—that is, people who still held citizenship in enemy countries—had arrived in the decade before the outbreak of war. Prewar apprehension about the number of immigrants pouring into Canada in the early years of the twentieth century turned into outright hostility under wartime pressures.

Enemy aliens in urban centres were forced to register with police authorities and were forbidden to carry arms. If unemployed, they were interned as prisoners of war in 26 camps scattered across the country, where they were required "to do and perform such work as may be...prescribed." Internment camps were initially established in northern Ontario and Quebec,

out of the way of nervous civilians. Between 1915 and 1917, some 900 men worked for six days a week at 25 cents a day, clearing land and building roads in various national parks. Others were contracted to private corporations to work as miners or farm labourers. Ultimately, over 8579 enemy aliens were interned, including over 3000 Canadian citizens.

Inevitably, tensions developed over disciplinary codes and labour demands imposed on prisoners. In the fall of 1917, the inmates at Kapuskasing refused an order to chop wood for the winter, resulting in an investigation of the conditions prevailing in the camp. The prisoners were eventually forced to comply, not only because authorities in Germany wrote a note approving of such tasks as chopping wood, but also because guards at the camp became more "vigilant" in their pursuit of those who violated the rules. In all the camps, a total of six prisoners were killed by gunshot and four wounded in the course of their internment. Over 100 others were confined to mental institutions and another 100 died in confinement, mostly of tuberculosis and pneumonia.

In some respects, harassment of people who traced their origins to enemy countries was even worse than official sanctions and internment. Universities fired German professors, judges threw cases brought by alien plaintiffs out of court, and angry mobs attacked businesses owned by Germans and Austro-Hungarians. Even people whose families were deeply rooted in Canada, such as the Germans of Lunenburg County, Nova Scotia, and Waterloo County, Ontario, felt the wrath of wartime prejudice. In an effort to demonstrate their patriotism, the citizens of Berlin, Ontario, changed the name of their city to Kitchener in 1916, while many people in Lunenburg County claimed their origins to be Dutch rather than German in the 1921 census.

Following the Bolshevik Revolution in the fall of 1917, radicals became the focus of attention in

Internees at their compound located in Castle Mountain in Banff, July 1915.

Glenbow Archives, Millican Collection/NA1870-6

Canada. The Union government issued an order-in-council making it an offence to print or possess any publication in an enemy language without a licence from the Secretary of State. "Foreign" organizations, including the Industrial Workers of the World, were banned as were meetings in which enemy languages were used. In British Columbia, tensions ran high when socialist labour leader "Ginger" Goodwin was shot by police constable Dan Campbell in 1918, ostensibly because Goodwin was evading the draft.

People who espoused pacifist views also found themselves subject to harassment. Francis Marion Beynon lost her job as a columnist for the *Grain Growers' Guide* because of her pacificist stance, and J.S. Woodsworth resigned from the Methodist Church in 1918 when it could no longer tolerate his pacifist and left-wing views. Groups such as the Mennonites and Hutterites, whose religious convictions included a rigorous pacifism, found themselves subject to both official and unofficial sanctions in a country that increasingly defined citizenship by the extent of one's military participation.

Acrimonious debates over the commitment to the war effort tore apart friendships, families, and organizations. Suffragist and novelist Nellie McClung recalled in 1945:

> The fall of 1914 blurs in my memory like a troubled dream. The war dominated everything. Some of my friends were pacifists and resented Canada's participation in the war of which we knew so little.... Chief among the Empire's defenders among the women was Miss Cora Hind. Her views were clear cut and definite. We were British and we must follow the tradition of our fathers. She would have gone herself if women were accepted. Miss Hind saw only one side of the question and there were times when I envied her, though I resented her denunciations of those who thought otherwise. The old crowd began to break up, and the good times were over.[4]

A WHITE MAN'S WAR

Prejudices based on gender and race, in large measure, determined who could participate in the fighting. Although women might keep the home fires burning and serve behind the lines as nurses, there was never any real thought given to allowing them to be combatants. Women, it was believed, were too weak and emotional to stand the rigours of battle and, in any event, it was men's role to protect them.

A few women, such as the Yukon's Martha Black, managed to get to Great Britain at their own expense. While they waited for word of their loved ones at the front, these women worked as volunteers in British hospitals and other service institutions. Most of the more than 3000 women who joined the Canadian Army Nursing Service went overseas. Forty-seven died on duty, and many received distinguished service awards, including Matron Ethel Ridley, who was invested a Commander of the Order of the British Empire for her work as principal matron in France.

For visible minorities, as for women, pervasive perceptions of their inferiority limited the roles they were allowed to play in wartime. Only Aboriginal peoples were specifically denied admission to the army from the outset, on the spurious grounds that "Germans might refuse to extend to them the privileges of civilized warfare." Not widely publicized, the directive was ignored by some militia officers. Throughout the war, officials repeatedly insisted that there was no "colour line," but when visible minorities offered their services, they were invariably turned down by militia officers. Fifty blacks from Sydney, Nova Scotia, who arrived at the recruitment office were advised: "This is not for you fellows, this is a white man's war."[5]

Many members of Canada's visible minorities believed that participation in the war would help them to improve the status of their people. So determined were they to be accepted that, in the face of rejection by recruitment offices, they formed their own segregated units and offered their services. On the West Coast, the Canadian Japanese Association enlisted 227 volunteers who drilled at their own expense. African Canadians were persistent in their demands that they be allowed to enlist for overseas service.

The crisis in recruitment helped to crack the wall of racial prejudice. In the fall of 1915, the directive against Native Canadians was lifted, and thereafter they were recruited for the 114th Battalion and accepted into other units. African Canadians faced a

Commanded by white officers, the No. 2 Construction Battalion included blacks from across Canada as well as 145 African Americans who crossed the border to participate in the war. The battalion was attached to the Canadian Forestry Corps, a labour unit whose job was to support the men fighting at the front.

Photo courtesy of the Black Cultural Centre for Nova Scotia

THE HALIFAX EXPLOSION

For all their problems at home and losses on the front, Canadians were relatively lucky as the belligerents went. Their territory was not invaded, and German submarines inflicted limited damage in Canadian waters. Only once were Canadians offered a taste of what it was like to have their world devastated by the horrors of war. Shortly after 9:00 am, on the morning of 6 December 1917, the French munitions ship *Mont Blanc*, laden with explosives, collided with the Belgian relief ship *Imo* in Halifax harbour, producing one of the largest explosions in human history up to that time. Over 1600 people were killed outright, another 9000 were injured—

more difficult battle, but they had champions in Conservative Party MPs from the Maritimes, including the prime minister. In April 1916, with Borden presiding, the Militia Council decided to form a black battalion—the No 2 Construction Battalion—headquartered in Nova Scotia. By the summer of 1916, Japanese men who had received basic training were admitted to 11 different battalions. Chinese men were also grudgingly accepted. When conscription was imposed, Natives and Asians were exempted because they were disenfranchised, and little effort was made to recruit black conscripts. In all, about 3500 Natives, over 1000 African Canadians, and several hundred Chinese and Japanese Canadians served in the Canadian forces.

Prejudice did not stop once they were in the army. Units composed of visible minorities were likely to be shunted into forestry and construction activities, and they were segregated whenever possible from whites. Nor did their service in the war change their status once they returned home. It had remained a white man's war to the end, and the service of visible minorities was largely forgotten in accounts of the war effort.

including 200 blinded by flying glass—and 20 000 were left without adequate shelter for the coming winter. Homes, factories, train stations, churches, and a great sweep of harbour facilities disappeared in the blast or the subsequent fires and tidal wave that engulfed the city. Makeshift mortuaries, hospitals, and shelters were set up in surviving churches, schools, and rinks, while people wandered aimlessly about the smoking rubble looking for lost loved ones.

As soon as word of the tragedy got out, help poured in from surrounding communities, from other provinces, from Ottawa, from Newfoundland, and eventually from around the world. The people of Massachusetts, where so many Maritime-born Canadians lived and worked, were particularly generous. Sir John Eaton, President of the T. Eaton Company, arrived in Halifax with his own train, food, sleeping car, staff, and medical unit. Some $30 million, over half of it from the federal government, was provided to help Halifax and its sister town Dartmouth, which had also suffered from the blast, to recover from the devastation.

Once people were sorted out and the debris cleared away, officials settled down to impose order on

The Acadia Sugar Refinery before and after the Halifax Explosion.

Nova Scotia Archives and Record Management, Notman Studio Collection, N-4264; Halifax Relief Commission Collection, 1976-166.78

the chaos caused by the blast. The progressive impulse was implicit in much of what was done. In January 1918, under the War Measures Act, the federal government established the Halifax Relief Commission to take charge of relief, medical care, and reconstruction. The commission decided to create a new community in the north end of the city, designed by urban planner Thomas Adams, who was in the employ of the Canadian Conservation Commission. To the marvel of visitors and residents alike, 10 parallel blocks containing 326 houses, shopping facilities, boulevards, and green spaces rose out of the ashes of the explosion in the north-end suburb of Richmond Hill. The homes were built of hydrostone, a type of cement block moulded under pressure, which was manufactured in a factory built especially for the purpose. Known thereafter as the Hydrostone district, the neighbourhood proved to be the only enduring monument to the garden city dreams of the Halifax Relief Commission. Other development projects fell victim to dwindling resources and flagging idealism.

CANADA ON THE WORLD STAGE

Borden's willingness to pursue an all-out war effort despite the opposition in Quebec owed much to his faith that Canada would emerge from the First World War with new international status. From the beginning, he pressed British authorities to give the dominion a voice in war planning, but his efforts bore little fruit before David Lloyd George became British prime minister in late 1916. Influenced by Max Aitken, Canada's London-based champion, and a leading figure in the political manoeuvring that made him prime minister, Lloyd George wanted help from the dominions in a war that was going badly. In 1917, he called an Imperial War Conference and created the Imperial War Cabinet—the British War Cabinet with dominion representation. These bodies gave Borden more information and the opportunity to express his views. Nonetheless, the British remained firmly in control of their empire's war effort.

The United States entered the war against Germany in 1917. In 1918, with Britain otherwise preoccupied, the Canadians turned to the Americans for help to defend the East Coast of Canada from German raids. Aid was supplied begrudgingly. It was for Borden another lesson in the importance of self-reliance.

The presence of fresh American troops provided a shot in the arm for war-weary allied forces. By August 1918, the tide had turned. The final Hundred Days leading to the armistice on 11 November 1918 began with the battle of Amiens, spearheaded by Canadian troops. The Canadian Corps played a major role in bringing Germany to its knees in the last days of the fighting, but the cost was great: over 30 000 casualties. At least the bloody war was over.

Canada was represented in the British Empire delegation to the Paris Peace Conference and separately signed the Versailles Treaty with Germany, the first time Canadians had signed a multilateral treaty. There would also be membership for Canada and other dominions in the new League of Nations, established to keep the peace, and the International Labour Organization, designed to maintain international labour standards. Despite these accomplishments, Canada had a long way to go before it would fully emerge as a nation in its own right.

DEMOBILIZATION AND RECONSTRUCTION

The task of bringing back over 300 000 combatants and reintegrating them into civil society was almost as difficult as fighting the war. In October 1917, the government formed a cabinet committee on reconstruction and a few months later created a new Department of Soldiers Civil Re-Establishment to oversee the problems of demobilization. Its minister, Senator James Lougheed, was charged with responsibility for the Board of Pension Commissioners, the Soldiers' Land Settlement Scheme, hospital treatment and vocational training for the returned men, and the re-employment of munitions workers. Under Lougheed, the new department began building hospitals, nursing homes, and sanatoria and helped to establish programs to retrain the disabled. In 1919, a new Department of Health took over many of the responsibilities formerly handled by the provinces and volunteers.

Health reform came too late to ward off yet another disaster associated with the war years. In the final months of the war a great influenza epidemic swept across the world. It killed at least 30 000 and perhaps as many as 50 000 Canadians—almost as many as died in the trenches—leaving citizens everywhere reeling with shock. Canadians and their government, already stretched to the limit by the war

effort, had few resources with which to fight this new enemy. Although the epidemic finally receded, it helped to contribute to a rising tide of discontent that swept the nation when the war ended.

What the cabinet did not predict, though it should have, was the rising tempers of soldiers when they were left hanging around Europe and Great Britain following the signing of the armistice. The lack of suitable transport and the inability of Canada's rail lines to carry more than 20 000 troops a month from the nation's only major ice-free winter ports—Halifax and Saint John—created an explosive situation. In March, discontent among Canadian soldiers stationed in Wales burst into violent protest when a black guard arrested a white soldier and placed him under a "coloured" escort. White soldiers attacked their black compatriots, and in the ensuing mêlée five people were killed and twenty-seven injured. More riots followed in May. Determined to rid themselves of the troublesome Canadians, the British managed to find extra shipping capacity, and most Canadians were home by July.

The Great War Veterans' Association (GWVA), founded in Winnipeg in 1917, emerged as the voice of the former members of the CEF. At the war's end, the organization was dominated by able-bodied men who demanded their rights and would brook no opposition from Conservative ministers. By 1925, the GWVA was amalgamated with a number of other smaller organizations into the Canadian Legion, which was more cautious and non-partisan in its approach.

The long-term costs of helping returned men and their families was immense. In 1920, more than 6500 men were still in hospital. Over 20 000 parents, wives, and children of dead soldiers qualified for pensions in 1925. As health problems surfaced, the number of people qualifying for disability pensions rose from nearly 28 000 in 1919 to 43 000 in 1933. In the interwar period, the total cost of these and other programs for veterans ranked second after the national debt in government expenditures, with accumulated costs of over $1 billion by 1935.

The costs of reconstruction helped to convince the government to demobilize its armed forces as quickly as possible. Only three warships, two submarines, and the Royal Naval College survived from the larger wartime military establishment. The infant airforce was reborn in 1920 but only because of assistance from Great Britain and the United States. As before 1914, the militia absorbed the bulk of the defence budget, but there would be no massive standing army in Canada as a testament to the nation's role in the Great War.

FEMALE SUFFRAGE

For many Canadians, the new era of liberal democracy offered potential for major reform. The Union government in 1918 followed up the Wartime Elections Act with legislation that gave the federal franchise to women on the same basis as men. During the war, the wall of opposition to female suffrage collapsed: in 1916, the three Prairie provinces adopted female suffrage, followed by Ontario and British Columbia in 1917, and Nova Scotia in 1918. Although New Brunswick extended the vote to women in 1919, they were not allowed to hold public office in that province until 1935. Prince Edward Island granted women the vote in 1922, and Newfoundland in 1925, but the latter based its legislation on British policy, which gave the vote to women over the age of 25—not, as for men, 21. By 1920, most of the property and income restrictions placed on voting rights had also been swept away. After 1922, only status Indians, Asians in British Columbia, women in Quebec, and conscientious objectors, including Mennonites and Hutterites, were denied the right to vote.

Women's suffrage advocates had the pleasure not only of seeing the franchise question largely resolved, they also saw the beginning of an era in which programs specifically designated "women's issues," such as prohibition, mother's allowances, and minimum-wage legislation, were addressed. Under the provisions of the War Measures Act, the federal government implemented full prohibition in 1918, and following the war all provinces except for Quebec and British Columbia maintained the policy, at least for a few years. Alberta, in 1917, was the first jurisdiction to pass a minimum-wage law for women, a policy adopted during the 1920s by all provinces except New Brunswick and Prince Edward Island.

For many women, the franchise served primarily as a means of pressing politicians to pass reform legislation. The National Council of Women developed a policy of adopting a Canadian Women's Platform to identify issues to be pursued through the established political parties. In 1920, the platform included demands for equal pay for equal work, the female minimum wage, and political equality of the sexes. Party organizations successfully resisted attempts to integrate women fully into their activities, much to the disappointment of some suffrage leaders who had hoped that the vote would transform Canadian political life.

LABOUR REVOLT

Suffragists were not alone in being disillusioned by the failure of the war to usher in a major transformation in society. Higher profits for a few were accompanied by low wages, repressive working conditions, and a spiralling cost of living for many. Desperate to mobilize resources for war, and with few close ties to labour, governments did little to rectify abuses. This failure set the groundwork for a level of class conflict unprecedented in Canadian history.

Domestic conflicts may have developed in response to specific Canadian conditions, but they did not develop in isolation. The Bolshevik Revolution in Russia and the rising tide of socialist and communist protest in Europe and the United States inspired many Canadians, just as it terrified Canadian politicians and capitalists. When Borden dispatched Canadian troops in 1918–19 as part of a combined Allied endeavour to put an end to the Russian Revolution, the labour movement was, not surprisingly, embittered.

Unhappy as it might be with the Union government, the labour movement was also deeply divided. Conservative eastern craft unionism took control of the Trades and Labour Congress at the 1918 convention, but the Western Labour Conference held shortly thereafter in Calgary broke with TLC policies of conciliation and restraint. Those attending the conference resolved to create a single industrial union, the One Big Union (OBU), to challenge conservative unionists, hostile employers, and unsympathetic governments. Before the fledgling OBU could hold its founding convention, its strike philosophy had an unanticipated dry run.

On 15 May 1919, the Winnipeg Trades and Labour Council called a general strike following the breakdown of negotiations between management and labour in the metal and building trades in the city. At stake were the principles of collective bargaining and better wages and working conditions. Although only 12 000 of Winnipeg's workers belonged to a union of any kind, about 30 000 workers joined the strike within hours of the call for action. They included telephone operators and department store clerks who had waged successful wartime strikes and hoped to consolidate their gains by working to strengthen the labour movement as a whole.

Winnipeg's strike sparked a series of general strikes of varying lengths across the country. Although these strikes were ostensibly held in support of the Winnipeg workers, local grievances came to the fore everywhere. Some Canadian leaders were convinced that they had a revolution on their hands. But internal divisions and lack of resources caused most of the strikes to come to an end within a month. The Winnipeg strike was the longest, stretching from 15 May to 26 June. While its leaders made every effort to keep it orderly, agreeing to have essential services such as milk delivery continue throughout the strike, it faced formidable obstacles. Opponents of the strike, drawn mainly from employer and professional groups in the city, organized a committee to crush the strike and discredit its leadership. Insisting that the strike was Bolshevik-inspired, the Citizens' Committee of One Thousand refused to let the issue of employees' right to collective bargaining become the sole focus of the debate.

With encouragement from the anti-strike forces, the federal government sent the Royal North-West Mounted Police to Winnipeg, allegedly to maintain order. On 21 June—a day that became known as Bloody Saturday—the Mounties attempted to disperse war veterans holding an illegal demonstration in support of the strike. The demonstrators refused to leave and the police fired a volley of shots into the crowd. By the end of the day, two men were dead and many other protesters were injured. Following the confrontation, strikers were arrested by the score. Among those jailed were two Winnipeg aldermen and a member of the Manitoba legislature. Recognizing the state's determination to crush the strike, those leaders who had not yet been imprisoned capitulated on 26 June. Winnipeg would remain a class-divided city for generations to come.

The federal government moved quickly to make radical protest difficult, if not impossible. Section 98 of the Criminal Code, passed in the House on 7 July, outlawed any organization whose professed purpose was to bring about "governmental, industrial or economic change" by force. Penalties for membership in such an organization included a maximum 20-year jail sentence. Even attending a meeting, advocating the principles, or distributing the literature of such an organization could result in charges under section 98.

EXPANDING POLITICAL HORIZONS

Like the differences that increasingly separated French and English Canada, a heightened awareness of class division was a long-term legacy of the First World War. Left-wing parties benefited from such divisions. In 1921, J.S. Woodsworth, who was imprisoned for his role as editor of the strike newspaper in the latter days of the Winnipeg General Strike, was elected to represent Winnipeg's working-class north end in Parliament as a member of the Independent Labour Party. Some veterans of the strike would join the Communist Party of Canada when it was formed clandestinely in 1921.

The Labour and Communist parties were not the only expression of political diversity that followed in the wake of the war. In 1916, the Canadian Council of Agriculture developed the Farmers' Platform, which included a call for free trade; graduated income, inheritance, and corporation taxes; nationalization of railway, telegraph, and express companies; and reform of the political process to eliminate the problems created by patronage, corruption, and centralized party discipline. Farmer candidates ran in the 1917 election on the Union ticket, but they were not converted to the Conservative cause. When exemption from con-

Voices from the Past

Bloody Saturday

Labour and capital viewed the events of 21 June 1919 in Winnipeg in entirely different ways. Following is the official strikers' view of the events of that afternoon as reported in *Strike Bulletin*, the newspaper published by the Strike Committee.

One is dead and a number injured, probably thirty or more, as a result of the forcible prevention of the "silent parade"

Demonstrations during the Winnipeg General Strike, June 1919.

Provincial Archives of Manitoba Winnipeg Strike 8 (N12299)

which had been planned by returned men to start at 2:30 o'clock last Saturday afternoon. Apparently the bloody business was carefully planned, for Mayor Gray issued a proclamation in the morning stating that "Any women taking part in a parade do so at their own risk." Nevertheless a vast crowd of men, women and children assembled to witness the "silent parade."

On Saturday, about 2:30 p.m., just the time when the parade was scheduled to start, some 50 mounted men swinging baseball bats rode down Main Street. Half were red-coated R.N.W.M.P., the others wore khaki. They quickened pace as they passed the Union Bank. The crowd opened, let them through and closed in behind them. They turned and charged through the crowd again, greeted by hisses and boos, and some stones. There were two riderless horses with the squad when it emerged and galloped up Main Street. The men in khaki disappeared at this juncture, but the red-coats reined their horses and reformed opposite the old post office.

Then, with revolvers drawn, they galloped down Main Street, turned, and charged right into the crowd on William Avenue, firing as they charged. One man, standing on the sidewalk, thought the mounties were firing blank cartridges until a spectator standing beside him dropped with a bullet through the head. We have no exact information about the total number of casualties, but these were not less than thirty. The crowd dispersed as quickly as possible when the shooting began.

scription for farmers' sons was cancelled in 1918, some 5000 farmers marched on Ottawa in protest. In the same year, the Farmers' Platform was fleshed out and rechristened the New National Policy. Soon, provincial farmers' parties and the National Progressive Party would challenge the old-line parties for the support of the nation's farmers.

In Newfoundland, as in Canada, politics lost their prewar simplicity. Labour shortages led to a spread of industrial unionism, with the Newfoundland Industrial Workers' Association organizing railway shops, longshoremen, street railway workers, and factory workers. In the outports, fishing families got bet-

ter prices for their fish but felt that the war effort was very much a St John's affair. When Fisherman's Protective Union leader William Coaker supported the government's efforts to form a coalition and impose military conscription, outport families felt betrayed. The collapse of the economy following the war resulted in a wave of bankruptcies and escalating unemployment, but the cash-strapped government had difficulty responding to the mounting crisis. In 1919, the National Government collapsed. It was replaced by a Liberal-Fishermen's Protective Union (FPU) alliance led by Richard Squires, but it, too, failed to find a solution to the postwar crisis. Demonstrations in St

John's underscored the social tensions that were unlikely to be resolved by any government.

CONCLUSION

Anyone surveying the Canadian scene in 1919 must have wondered if the nation could survive the challenges facing it. So much had changed since 1911, the last time that Canadians had voted in a peacetime election. Rather than bringing people together, the war had widened the gulf between Quebec and the rest of Canada and exposed deep regional and class divisions. A generation of young men had been lost in the trenches and even those who survived were often scarred for life. With the enfranchisement of women, the potential electorate had doubled. So, too, had the number of political parties. Canada's status as an independent nation had been further advanced by its involvement in the war, but decisions made in Great Britain and the United States still determined the nation's well-being. Would Canada, like many nation-states cobbled together in the nineteenth century, simply dissolve into chaos? Or would the sacrifices and conflicts generated by the Great War inspire Canadians to work harder to develop a sense of national purpose? Only time would tell.

A Historiographical Debate

Conscription

Why was conscription introduced? Was it a military necessity? Did its introduction signal Canada's desire to assert itself in international affairs or did it reflect subservience to Britain? Did its proponents carry the 1917 election by deliberately employing anti-French-Canadian messages? Historians of conscription have offered varied answers to these questions, and, perhaps not surprisingly, much of the division has been between francophone and anglophone historians.

According to one perspective, political pressure from English Canada forced the government's hand. Borden was "responding to the will of the English-speaking majority," write the authors of the authoritative history of Quebec in this period.[6] English-Canadian historians agree that there was pressure on the government for conscription, but they note that the government was aware that English Canadians were divided on the issue and feared that conscription might lose votes for a government already in difficulties.[7] Borden and his key ministers, they argue, imposed conscription because of British pressure for a greater Canadian commitment to the war effort. Moreover, Borden's own conviction that Canada should do more left the government few options when voluntary recruitment failed to meet the government's targets for fighting men.

From this viewpoint, conscription was a military necessity. Military historian A.M. Willms claims that, proportionate to its population, Canada before 1917 had contributed fewer military recruits than the other white-settler dominions. More recruits were necessary because of the heavy casualties of war.[8] French-Canadian historians have argued that this interpretation accepts the Allied view that a peace treaty was not negotiable. Robert Rumilly's biography of Henri Bourassa stresses the view that negotiations were possible if both sides gave up the idea that there had to be a clear victor.[9]

Rumilly and other French-Canadian historians have generally accepted Bourassa's view that no great principles were at stake in the war, but English-Canadian historians have rejected the view that Canada simply subordinated itself to British imperialism. Ramsay Cook, explaining the support for conscription by *Winnipeg Free Press* editor John W. Dafoe, suggests that many English Canadians who fought for greater Canadian autonomy from Britain believed the war was being fought over "cherished values" of democracy and not from motives of "sycophantic colonialism or aggressive imperialism."[10] The government's embrace of the view that this was a battle for "Canadian liberty and autonomy" is noted in a recent history of the First World War that emphasizes Borden's insistence on Canadian involvement both in war planning and in shaping the postwar world.[11]

How did the government win the election that allowed it to impose a measure it deemed necessary in this battle for "liberty"? Most historians agree that the Wartime Elections Act did not respect the liberty of all citizens, but there is less agreement about the extent to which the government resorted to ethnocentric appeals in its attempts to overcome anglophone divisions about the fairness of imposing conscription. Roger Graham, who wrote a biography on the influential cabinet minister and later prime minister Arthur Meighen, claims that the government attempted to avoid having the election contribute to national disunity.[12]

French-Canadian historians dismiss this claim, noting that the whole purpose of conscription was to assuage English-Canadian opinion that French Canadians were not doing their share.[13] Some anglophone historians also disagree with Graham's suggestion that the government took the high road in the election of 1917. Note J.L. Granatstein and J.M. Hitsman: "The Union Government campaign, founded on the Military Service Act and the War Time Elections Act, deliberately set out to create an English-Canadian nationalism, separate from and opposed to both French Canada and naturalized Canadians. No other conclusion can be drawn from this election campaign, one of the few in Canadian history deliberately conducted on racist grounds."[14]

NOTES

[1] Quoted in Desmond Morton and J.L. Granatstein, *Marching to Armageddon: Canadians and the Great War, 1914–1919* (Toronto: Lester and Orpen Dennys, 1989) 5–6.

[2] Robert Craig Brown and Ramsay Cook, *Canada: 1896–1921: A Nation Transformed* (Toronto: McClelland and Stewart, 1974) 230.

[3] See Jonathan Vance, *Death So Noble: Memory, Meaning, and the First World War* (Vancouver: UBC Press, 1997) for a fascinating discussion of the changing interpretations of the First World War after the event.

[4] Alison Prentice et al., *Canadian Women: A History* (Toronto: Harcourt, Brace Jovanovich, 1988) 207.

[5] Cited in James W. St G. Walker, "Race and Recruitment in World War I: Enlistment of Visible Minorities in the Canadian Expeditionary Force," *Canadian Historical Review* 70.1 (March 1989): 1–26.

[6] Paul-André Linteau, René Durocher, and Jean-Claude Robert, *Quebec: A History, 1867–1929* (Toronto: Lorimer, 1983) 524.

[7] See, for example, J.L. Granatstein and J.M. Hitsman, *Broken Promises: A History of Conscription in Canada* (Toronto: Oxford University Press, 1977) 67.

[8] A.M. Willms, "Conscription 1917: A Brief for the Defence," in *Conscription 1917*, ed. Ramsay Cook, Craig Brown, and Carl Berger (Toronto: University of Toronto Press, 1969) 1–14.

[9] Robert Rumilly, *Henri Bourassa: La Vie publique d'un grand canadien* (Montreal: Les Éditions Chantecler, 1953) 544.

[10] Ramsay Cook, "Dafoe, Laurier and the Formation of the Union Government," in *Conscription 1917*, 15–38.

[11] Morton and Granatstein, *Marching to Armageddon*, 145.

[12] Roger Graham, *Arthur Meighen*, vol. 1, *The Door of Opportunity* (Toronto: Clark, Irwin, 1960) 194–95.

[13] Linteau, Durocher, and Robert, *Quebec*, 524.

[14] Granatstein and Hitsman, *Broken Promises*, 78.

SELECTED READING

The military experience of the First World War is described in G.W.L. Nicholson, *Canadian Expeditionary Force, 1914–1919* (Ottawa: Queen's Printer, 1964) and *Canada's Nursing Sisters* (Toronto: S. Stevens, 1975); Desmond Morton and J.L. Granatstein, *Marching to Armageddon: Canadians and the Great War, 1914–1918* (Toronto: Lester and Orpen Dennys, 1989); Desmond Morton, *When Your Number's Up: The Canadian Soldier in the First World War* (Toronto: Random House, 1993); Michael L. Hadley and Roger Sarty, *Tin-Pots and Pirate Ships: Canadian Naval Forces and German Sea Raiders, 1880–1918* (Montreal: McGill-Queen's University Press, 1991); S.F. Wise, *Canadian Airmen and the First World War* (Toronto: University of Toronto Press, 1980); Stephen Harris, *Canadian Brass: The Making of a Professional Army, 1860–1939* (Toronto: University of Toronto Press, 1988); and Duff Crerar, *Padres in No Man's Country: Canadian Chaplains and the Great War* (Montreal: McGill-Queen's University Press, 1995). External affairs are the subject of Norman Hillmer and J.L. Granatstein, *Empire to Umpire: Canada and the World to the 1990s* (Toronto: Copp Clark Longman, 1994). For a ground-breaking discussion of changing views of the war, see Jonathan F. Vance, *Death So Noble: Meaning, Memory and the First World War* (Vancouver: University of British Columbia Press, 1997).

On the war at home, see the books by Brown, Brown and Cook, and English cited in Chapter 16, as well as Daphne Read, ed., *The Great War and Canadian Society: An Oral History* (Toronto: New Hogtown, 1978); Barbara M. Wilson, *Ontario and the First World War* (Toronto: University of Toronto Press, 1977); Frances Swyripa and John Thompson, eds., *Loyalties in Conflict: Ukrainians in Canada During the Great War* (Edmonton: University of Alberta Press, 1983); Jeffrey A. Keshen, *Propaganda and Censorship during Canada's Great War* (Edmonton: University of Alberta Press, 1996); and John Herd Thompson, *The Harvests of War: The Prairie West, 1914–1918* (Toronto: McClelland and Stewart, 1978). Thompson provides a useful summary of the treatment of ethnic minorities in both the First and Second World Wars in *Ethnic Minorities During the Two World Wars* (Ottawa: Canadian Historical Association, 1991). See Alison Prentice et al., *Canadian Women: A History*, 2nd ed. (Toronto: Harcourt Brace, 1996) on the experience of women during and after the war. See also Susan Mann, ed., *The War Diary of Clare Gass* (Montreal: McGill-Queen's University Press, 2000) for a nurse's

perspective on experiences behind the front lines in France.

Works dealing with conscription include J.L. Granatstein and J.M. Hitsman, *Broken Promises: A History of Conscription in Canada* (Toronto: Oxford University Press, 1977); Ramsay Cook, Craig Brown, and Carl Berger, eds., *Conscription 1917* (Toronto: University of Toronto Press, 1969); and Paul-André Linteau, René Durocher, and Jean-Claude Robert, *Quebec: A History, 1867–1929* (Toronto: Lorimer, 1983). The role of visible minorities is the subject of James W. St G. Walker, "Race and Recruitment in World War I: Enlistment of Visible Minorities in the Canadian Expeditionary Force," *Canadian Historical Review* 70.1 (March 1989): 1–26; Calvin W. Ruck, *The Black Battalion, 1916–20* (Halifax: Nimbus, 1987); and John G. Armstrong, "The Unwelcome Sacrifice: A Black Unit in the Canadian Expeditionary Force," in *Ethnic Armies*, ed. N.F. Dreiziger (Waterloo, ON: Wilfrid Laurier University Press, 1990) 178–97. Internment camps are discussed in Joseph A. Boudreau, "Interning Canada's 'Enemy Aliens,' 1914–1919," *Canada: An Historical Magazine* 2.1 (Sept. 1974): 15–27 and Bill Waiser, *Parks Prisoners: The Untold Story of Western Canada's National Parks, 1915–1946* (Saskatoon: Fifth House Limited, 1995). The Halifax Explosion is explored in Janet F. Kitz, *Shattered City: The Halifax Explosion and the Road to Recovery* (Halifax: Nimbus, 1989), and Alan Ruffman and Colin D. Howell, eds., *Ground Zero: A Reassessment of the 1917 Explosion in Halifax Harbour* (Halifax: Nimbus, 1994). Suzanne Morton discusses the Hydrostone development in *Ideal Surroundings: Domestic Life in a Working-Class Suburb* (Toronto: University of Toronto Press, 1995).

Problems relating to demobilization are discussed in Desmond Morton and Glenn Wright, *Winning the Second Battle: Canadian Veterans and the Return to Civilian Life, 1915–1930* (Toronto: University of Toronto Press, 1987). On pacifists, see Thomas Socknat, *Witness Against War: Pacifism in Canada, 1900–1945* (Toronto: University of Toronto Press, 1987). On the influenza epidemic, see Janice P. Dickin McGinnis, "The Impact of Epidemic Influenza, 1918–1919," *Canadian Historical Association Historical Papers* (1977): 121–40.

On worker radicalism during and after the war, see A. Ross McCormack, *Reformers, Rebels, and Revolutionaries* (Toronto: University of Toronto Press, 1977); David Bercuson, *Fools and Wise Men: The Rise and Fall of One Big Union* (Toronto: McGraw-Hill Ryerson, 1978); and

James Naylor, *The New Democracy: Challenging the Social Order in Industrial Ontario, 1914–1925* (Toronto: University of Toronto Press, 1991). On the 1919 strikes, see Harry Gutkin and Mildred Gutkin, *Profiles in Dissent: The Shaping of Radical Thought in the Canadian West* (Edmonton: NeWest, 1997); David Bercuson, *Confrontation at Winnipeg: Labour, Industrial Relations, and the General Strike* (Montreal: McGill-Queen's University Press, 1990); Alan Artibise, *Winnipeg: A Social History of Urban Growth, 1874–1914* (Montreal: McGill-Queen's University Press, 1975); Paul Philips, *No Power Greater* (Vancouver: BC Federation of Labour, 1967); and Gregory S. Kealey, "1919: The Canadian Labour Revolt," *Labour/Le Travail* 13 (Spring 1984): 11–44. Works on postwar repression include Larry Hannant, *The Infernal Machine: Investigating the Loyalty of Canada's Citizens* (Toronto: University of Toronto Press, 1995); Barbara Roberts, *Whence They Came: Deportation from Canada, 1900–1935* (Ottawa: University of Ottawa Press, 1988); and Donald Avery, *Dangerous Foreigners: European Immigrant Workers and Labour Radicalism in Canada* (Toronto: McClelland and Stewart, 1979).

 **WEBLINKS**

CANADA AND THE FIRST WORLD WAR
www.archives.ca/05/0518_e.html

This exhibition is designed to illustrate, through the National Archives of Canada's collections, the many roles that Canadian men and women played during the First World War, and the mark the war left on our society.

IN FLANDERS FIELDS
http://home.iae.nl/users/robr/poppies.html

This site describes the creation of the famous poem written by Canadian John McCrae after the battle at Ypres, and includes a transcript of the verses.

INTERNMENT OF UKRAINIANS IN CANADA, 1914–20
http://infoukes.com/history/internment/index.html

This site offers an extensive collection of articles and photos relating the internment of Ukrainian immigrants in Canada during World War I.

HALIFAX EXPLOSION
www.region.halifax.ns.ca/community/explode.html

The circumstances of the Halifax Explosion of 1917 are explored at this site, which includes links to several related virtual exhibits.

WINNIPEG GENERAL STRIKE
http://canadahistory.about.com/library/weekly/aa041500a.htm

A brief description of the Winnipeg General Strike and an extensive list of further online resources can be found on this site.

CHAPTER 20

Interwar Canada: Boom, Bust, and Reform

1920–24	Recession grips Canada
1921	Mackenzie King's Liberals form minority government; Progressive Party wins second-largest block of seats; United Farmers of Alberta form provincial government
1922	United Farmers of Manitoba form provincial government
1923	United Farmers of Ontario are defeated in provincial election
1925	Coal miners' strike in Cape Breton; Maritime Rights election in Nova Scotia
1926	Arthur Meighen forms three-day government; Mackenzie King wins federal election; Appointment of Duncan Commission
1927	Federal government introduces program for means-tested old-age pensions
1930–39	Great Depression
1930–35	R.B. Bennett serves as prime minister
1931	Statute of Westminster
1932	Imperial Economic Conference in Ottawa; establishment of federal relief camps
1934	British-appointed commission of government replaces parliamentary government in Newfoundland; Bank of Canada Act
1935	Mackenzie King forms majority government; Reconstruction Party founded; Bennett's New Deal; On-to-Ottawa Trek; election of Social Credit in Alberta; Canada–United States Trade Agreement.
1936	Election of Union Nationale government in Quebec
1937	UAW strike at General Motors in Ottawa

As the 1930s Depression descended, Ed Bates, a butcher in Glidden, Saskatchewan, faced with bankruptcy, moved his family and business to Vancouver. There, too, work was scarce and the Bates family was forced to seek relief. Denied welfare by the Vancouver authorities because of their recent arrival in that city, they attempted to get social assistance in Saskatoon, only to be told they must return to Glidden to apply for help. Too proud to return home to live on welfare, they rented a car and attempted suicide by carbon monoxide poisoning. Ed and his wife, Rose, survived, but their son Jack died, and they were charged with his murder. While the Bates's actions had caused Jack's death, local citizens blamed the politicians for the tragedy. A defence committee was formed, and a coroner's jury found Ed and Rose Bates not guilty in the death of their son.[1]

The Bates family tragedy occurred during the Great Depression, an economic catastrophe unprecedented in its intensity. As the human misery mounted, demands for ever-increasing numbers of people came to blame the political and economic system, rather than the individual, for widespread poverty. Demands for reform and even revolution led to the creation of new political parties and demands for social insurance and state regulation of industries so that ordinary people would never again be reduced to desperate measures because

they could not find work. This chapter explores the economic and political forces that shaped such changing social perspectives in the interwar period.

A CHANGING ECONOMIC LANDSCAPE

Where Canadians lived and what jobs they did changed dramatically during the 1920s. Particularly after the economy revived in 1924, Canadians found their lives reshaped by the acceleration of the second industrial revolution based on the internal combustion engine, resource development, electrical power, and new chemical processes. The long-term tendency away from primary industries continued and secondary industry held its own. Employment and investment growth was concentrated in the tertiary, or service sector, which accounted for over 50 percent of GNP in 1929.

Automobiles demonstrate how the economic sectors evolved. By the 1920s, a few Ontario cities had cornered the lion's share of the employment created in the manufacture of cars. Nevertheless, every city and most towns across Canada had car dealerships, gas stations, repair shops, auto insurance firms, and tire shops. Public demand for better roads led provincial governments to construct hard-surfaced highways along much-travelled routes. Taxes levied on gasoline and cars helped to finance the ribbons of asphalt that cost even more to build and maintain than railway lines. No longer tied to train routes, restaurants and cabins appeared along busy highways to cater to the motoring public. Tourism developed to new levels and required more service workers, many of them on a seasonal basis.

RIDING THE ECONOMIC ROLLER-COASTER

Canada, like most nations involved in the First World War, had trouble adjusting its economy to peacetime production. After the armistice, the Union government reduced state spending, slashing defence budgets and resisting pressures to enact social programs. Although veterans received some consideration, the government argued that market forces must make up for the slack resulting from the transition to peacetime conditions.

Apart from government indifference, the transition from a wartime to a peacetime economy was also hampered by a sharp contraction in export markets. The United States raised its tariff levels, which had a particularly detrimental effect on primary producers. In 1921, manufacturing, construction, and transportation industries stagnated, and the GNP dipped an ominous 20.1 percent. As the effects of the slump reverberated throughout the economy, company bankruptcies, unemployment, and migration to the United States rose in tandem.

Recovery only came in 1924, and from then until 1929 there was significant economic growth. The staples of wheat, pulp and paper, minerals, and hydroelectric power led the recovery. Automobiles and electrical appliances were the leading manufactured products. Foreign demand and foreign capital helped to spur the recovery. The long-established tendency toward North American economic integration accelerated. By 1924 American capital investment in Canada exceeded British investment. Trade with the United States was greater than with Britain, though

Clerical employment expanded in the postwar period as the service sector grew. As this photograph (ca. 1919) of the main office of the Great-West Life Assurance Company in Winnipeg illustrates, some of the new clerical employees were women. While office hierarchies reserved senior administrative posts and better salaries for men, an increasing number of women found employment as secretaries, stenographers, and file clerks.

Great-West Life Assurance Co. Archives

trade with the entire Empire still exceeded the American trade.

PRIMARY PRODUCTS

As markets for wheat in Britain and Europe rebounded, Prairie farmers expanded their acreage. Between 1925 and 1929, the Prairie provinces produced over 400 million bushels of wheat annually, and supplied 40 percent of the world's export market. Vancouver was a major beneficiary of the expanding grain economy. With the opening of the Panama Canal in 1914, which connected the Pacific and Atlantic Oceans for shipping, Vancouver became a major port for selling goods to Europe. From 1921 to 1928, Vancouver's annual shipments of grain leaped from 1 million to 100 million bushels. Meanwhile, Winnipeg's economy stagnated as the city lost its status as the warehouse for all the grain going to Europe.

Voices from the Past

Marketing Potatoes in Prince Edward Island

The frustration of Prince Edward Island farmers with complex marketing systems in the interwar years is revealed in the following tongue-in-cheek account, published in the *Charlottetown Patriot* in March 1928:

> Potatoes are seeds that are planted and grown in Prince Edward Island to keep the producer broke and the buyer crazy. The tuber varies in colour and weight, and the man who can guess the nearest to the size of the crop while it is growing is called the "Potato Man" by the public, a "Fool" by the farmer, and a "Poor Businessman" by his creditors.

> The price of potatoes is determined by the man who has to eat them, and goes up when you have sold and down when you have bought. A dealer working for a group of shippers was sent to Boston to watch the potato market, and after a few days' deliberation, he wired his employers to this effect: "Some think they will go up and some think they will go down. I do too. Whatever you do will be wrong. Act at once."[2]

Encouraged by orderly marketing procedures established during the war, western farmers in the 1920s experimented with a system of wheat pools. Producers agreed to sell their wheat to a common pool and share the returns, rather than gamble individually on the Winnipeg Grain Exchange. With high prices in the late 1920s, the system worked well, and just over half of the wheat crop was sold through co-ops in 1929. When markets became glutted and prices fell during the Great Depression, neither pools nor private companies could save farmers from ruin.

During the 1920s, pulp and newsprint began to rival King Wheat as Canada's principal export. Canadian output reached 2 985 000 tons in 1930, making Canada the world's largest producer of newsprint. The demand for pulp and paper breathed new life into the forestry industry of the Ottawa, St Maurice, Saguenay, Miramichi, and Humber rivers, and animated declining communities such as Liverpool, Nova Scotia, and Kapuskasing, Ontario. Price stability, however, proved elusive as the big American publishers proved more than a match for newsprint producers and their efforts to fix prices. Over half of the productive capacity was located in Quebec, which also surged ahead in electrical generating capacity. By the early 1930s, Quebec accounted for nearly 50 percent of Canada's electrical energy.

During the 1920s, Canada's mining frontier continued to attract investment. New developments included gold and copper mines in the Abitibi region of Quebec, and copper-zinc mines in Flin Flon, Manitoba. Sudbury's nickel mines enjoyed exploding demand while markets for British Columbia's silver, copper, lead, and zinc more than replaced slumping demand for its coal. Alberta's oil fields witnessed significant development but only 5 percent of Canadian energy consumption was supplied by Canadian wells.

SECONDARY INDUSTRY

In the manufacturing sector, consumer durables—automobiles, radios, household appliances, and furniture—were the big success story of the 1920s. Ontario, home to the largest number of consumers, was, not surprisingly, also home to most plants producing consumer durables.

Canada's independent automobile manufacturers were left in the dust by the Big Three American firms—Ford, General Motors, and Chrysler—that controlled two-thirds of the Canadian market. High tariffs on imported cars encouraged the American giants to establish branch plants to supply the Canadian market as well as the British Empire, in which Canada had a tariff advantage. By the 1920s, Canada's automobile industry was the second-largest in the world, and exported a third of its output. Between 1920 and 1930, car ownership jumped from one for every 22 Canadians to one for 8.5, and Oshawa, Windsor, and Walkerville, home to the major auto assembly plants, experienced spectacular growth. Like the automobile, household appliances fell in price during the 1920s, coming increasingly within reach of the middle-class consumer.

WINNERS AND LOSERS

The impressive growth in some sectors masked problems in other areas of the Canadian economy. Both farmers and fishers in the Atlantic provinces found exports blocked by tariffs, soft markets, and stiff competition. Primary producers were not alone in facing uncertainty in the 1920s. In many industries that defined the first phase of the Industrial Revolution, including railways, coal, and iron and steel, atrophy had set in. Canada's two national railways embarked on an orgy of spending on branch lines, steamships, and hotels. The debts piled up by this spending forced retrenchment that reduced demand for rails and rolling stock, causing the iron and steel industry to languish. Only the Hamilton-based companies Stelco and Dofasco, fattened by the demands of the automobile industry, survived the 1920s unscathed.

A few Canadians made fortunes by riding the waves of opportunity in the interwar years, but the economic transition brought only hardship to many. Historian Michiel Horn suggests that during the interwar period "it is likely that more than half of the Canadian people were never anything but poor."[3] In 1929, the average wage of $1200 per year was $230 below what social workers estimated a family required to live above poverty level. The "roaring twenties" did not even purr for many Canadians, but worse was yet to come.

ECONOMIC COLLAPSE

By late 1929, the problems experienced in a few industries and in some regions throughout the 1920s were becoming nation-wide. The crash of the New York stock market on 29 October 1929 signalled the beginning of the Great Depression. Merely a symbol of the underlying problems in the international economy, the crash reflected the shaky foundations upon which the prosperity from 1924 to 1929 had been based. The unprecedented productivity made possible by new technologies was unmatched by gains in consumer purchasing power. In most countries workers' incomes lagged far behind the availability of new goods. Economic growth was unsustainable without

It is easy to overestimate the distribution of new labour-saving devices for the home in the interwar period. Mary Tidd had neither running water nor electricity in her home in Ross River, in the Yukon. For her, wash day continued to involve a great deal of physical labour, particularly the constant hauling of water from the well and arduous scrubbing on a washboard.

Yukon Archives, Claude Tidd fonds, #8533

markets. Unable to have much of an impact on international trade, Canadian politicians were deeply divided about how to exercise the power they did have to promote prosperity and economic stability.

KING AND CANADA

The career of William Lyon Mackenzie King sheds some light on how political leaders tried to manage the contradictory demands placed upon them. When Laurier died early in 1919, the Liberal Party decided to hold a leadership convention in Ottawa to secure maximum publicity. Previously, both national parties had allowed a narrow party elite to choose the leader. In response to postwar labour and farmer radicalism, the Liberals adopted a platform that included promises of state-funded old-age pensions, unemployment insurance, and health care.

Liberal power-brokers viewed King as a logical candidate to convince Canadians of the party's reformist intentions while reassuring vested interests that they would not be unduly disrupted. King had

Mackenzie King governed the country from 1921 to 1930 and again from 1935 to 1948.

National Archives of Canada/C9062

served as Canada's first Minister of Labour in the final years of the Laurier regime. He then amassed a fortune as a consultant for American corporations attempting to dampen labour radicalism. Visionary yet cautious, King seemed to be just what was needed to put the Liberal Party back in Ottawa.

The Liberals won the 1921 federal election and King remained true to form. Once in power, he acted on social policy only when he was convinced that popular pressure gave him no other choice. Usually, he felt constrained in his liberal tendencies by the combined pressures of big corporations, conservative elements in his party, and provincial premiers determined to protect their constitutional jurisdictions. Nonetheless, by 1945, King's government had legislated a variety of reforms, including means-tested old-age pensions, national unemployment insurance, and family allowances.

King's caution in domestic policy was equalled on the international front. He believed firmly that both national unity and Liberal Party unity depended upon placating Quebec's anger over the imposition of conscription in 1917. Though he supported Canada's membership in the League of Nations and its ties with Britain, he emphasized Canada's North American character and its unwillingness to participate in European wars. He joined the leaders of Ireland and South Africa in pressing Britain for recognition of the white dominions as independent nations. An independent Canada might choose to join Britain if the latter went to war but it would not automatically be at war if Britain were at war.

THE CHANGING POLITICAL LANDSCAPE

The 1921 federal election set the stage for a new era in Canadian political life. Not only did new political parties win seats, but the result also produced the country's first minority government. The Conservative defeat came as no surprise. The Union government had begun to disintegrate shortly after the armistice, with its Liberal members either returning to their old political home or joining the new Progressive Party. While Arthur Meighen brought new leadership to the Conservative Party following Borden's retirement in

1920, he was unpopular. An arch-defender of high tariff policies, he also had to live down his involvement in imposing conscription in 1917 and in sending the Mounties against the Winnipeg strikers in 1919.

The Conservatives kept only 50 seats; the Liberals, 116. The Liberal sweep of Quebec's 65 ridings was expected, given the province's lingering hostility to conscription. The real surprise was the success of the Progressive Party, which came second to the Liberals with 64 seats. Calling for the public ownership of utilities and a speedy elimination of all tariffs, the Progressives apparently struck a responsive chord among rural residents in English Canada.

The result followed a provincial trend that began in Ontario in 1919 with the election of a minority government headed by the United Farmers in coalition with the Independent Labour Party. The following year, a Farmer-Labour coalition emerged as the opposition in Nova Scotia. In 1921, Alberta, and in 1922, Manitoba elected Farmers' governments. Yet, by 1929, the national Progressive Party was on life support and would be swept away entirely by the Depression. The Ontario Farmers enjoyed only one term of office, their Manitoba counterparts merged with the Liberals in 1932, and Alberta's Farmers were eviscerated by Social Credit in 1935. Why did this class-based political movement prove so ephemeral?

THE PROGRESSIVE PARTY

The Progressive Party arose as an attempt by the organized farm movement to unite farmers around a political program and elect members of Parliament who would speak for farmers' interests. Frustrated by their declining political power and business dominance in the Liberal and Conservative parties, many farmers found the idea of a new political party attractive.

Despite the widespread discontent in most farming communities, the Progressive Party faced real obstacles in becoming a truly national party. Its first leader, Thomas A. Crerar, had been a conscriptionist Liberal and a cabinet minister in Borden's Union government, which limited his appeal in rural Quebec. Like Canadians generally, the Progressives were divided on questions of economic restructuring. Opposition to tariffs held party supporters together,

but there were strong disagreements on the merits of public control of railways, utilities, and the marketing of grain.

At best, Progressives were a loose coalition of provincial organizations. On the conservative side, disenchanted imperialist Liberals, mostly from Ontario and Manitoba, focused on the party's reform agenda and rejected any notion of transforming the economic and political system. A more radical wing, based primarily in Alberta and led by Henry Wise Wood, rejected the party system altogether and claimed that elected representatives should be free to vote as their constituents wished rather than forced to support the party line. Wood felt that the party system subordinated local MPs to the urban central Canadian party leadership.

Although many Progressives were committed to more democratic, participatory politics, most party leaders simply wanted the Liberal Party to get rid of tariffs. First Crerar, and then his successor as Progressive leader, Robert Forke, accepted the wily King's invitations to join his party and cabinet when the radicals frustrated their attempts to create a traditional party machine. In an effort to lure moderate Progressives into the Liberal fold, King lowered tariffs on farm machinery and equipment and acceded to Prairie demands to complete a rail link to the port of Churchill. King also restored the Crow rate (the favourable freight rates on grain imposed on the CPR in 1897, and later applied to all railways), which had been suspended in wartime. In the late 1920s, he surrendered federal control over the natural resources of the Prairie provinces.

THE KING-BYNG AFFAIR

Prime Minister King's political manoeuvring also played a role in reducing the impact of the Progressive Party. In the 1925 election, the Liberals carried 101 seats, with the resurgent Conservatives taking 116, thanks to Maritime discontent and solid support from Ontario. King formed another minority government by wooing the low-tariff Progressives, who had been reduced to 24 seats, almost all in western Canada, and conceding a means-tested old-age pension for the support of the two Labour MPs.

The Progressives and Labour joined the Conservatives in defeating the government in June 1926 with a motion of censure regarding widespread corruption in the Customs Department. When King asked Governor General Byng to dissolve Parliament and call another election, Byng exercised his prerogative to ask Arthur Meighen to form a government. Meighen's ministry lasted less than three days, but it gave King the opportunity to shift the emphasis of the 1926 election away from the customs scandal.

During the campaign, King made political hay out of Byng's refusal to accept his advice to dissolve Parliament, making the questionable claim that the governor general had violated the principle of responsible government. In the end, the customs issue and the King-Byng disagreement may have cancelled each other out, allowing King to aim specific promises to both the West and the Maritimes, conceding only tariff-hungry Ontario to the Conservatives. Westerners seemed particularly prepared to abandon the Progressives to keep Arthur Meighen, viewed as the high priest of protection, out of office. On 14 September 1926, the Liberals won enough seats to give Mackenzie King his first of four majority governments.

POLITICAL WOMEN

For women, who had been recently enfranchised, the interwar period failed to yield significant political progress. Only nine women sat in provincial legislatures before 1940, none outside the western provinces, and only two won seats in the House of Commons. The reasons for this unimpressive showing are complex. Following the granting of suffrage, the women's movement lost its single focus, and women sorted themselves according to class, regional, and cultural interests. Professional women on the edge of the male-dominated public world continued to argue for equality of opportunity, especially in the context of blatantly discriminatory hiring practices, but they framed their arguments in the language of human, not women's, rights.

Their caution was understandable. In the interwar years, feminism and women's rights became equated with "man-hating" and the promotion of "sex wars" to

such an extent that virtually every woman in public life was quick to deny any association with feminist doctrines. A feminist agenda had to be disguised as an effort to strengthen the family, or the nation, to avoid immediate condemnation from the men who headed the country's political organizations.

The women's sections of the farm organizations demonstrated the strengths and weaknesses of 1920s feminism. Having won the battle for the vote, women's organizations used their political influence to convince governments to spend money to improve community services. Irene Parlby, president of the United Farm Women of Alberta (UFWA) from 1917 to 1921 and later the first female member of the Alberta cabinet, argued that rural homes could only be strong if their residents worked together to provide health, educational, and recreational facilities in their communities. Saskatchewan farm women, led by Irene McNaughton, spearheaded a movement to have municipalities hire salaried doctors and work together to create "union hospitals" that served a large agricultural district. Farm women's organizations also fought for better protection of women's property rights both within marriage and during divorce. The UFWA attempted to persuade the provincial government to establish family planning clinics, but it made little headway on "women's issues" with the largely male UFA cabinet.

One concession won by the women's movement in most provinces was modest mothers' allowances. Beginning in Manitoba in 1916, mothers' allowances had been instituted in all the western provinces and Ontario by 1920, and in Nova Scotia in 1930. This social program provided funds to women in desperate need, but its detailed regulations reflected a conservative gender ideology. There was close surveillance of recipients to ensure that they lived chaste lives and spent the allowances on necessities. Only widows and, in some provinces, wives of men unable to support their families for medical reasons were eligible. Never-married, single mothers need not apply.

While women achieved little electoral representation in the 1920s, they made some progress toward political equality. In 1929, five Alberta women were instrumental in convincing the Judicial Committee of the Privy Council that women were "persons" under the law. Without this recognition, women had been excluded from appointment to the Senate and other privileged bodies. The five women who took up the so-called Persons Case were Nellie McClung, suffrage activist, writer, and former Liberal MLA; Emily Murphy, writer and, in 1916, the first woman magistrate in the British Empire; Irene Parlby; former Alberta MLA Louise Mckinney; and Henrietta Muir Edwards, a founding member of the National Council of Women and the Victorian Order of Nurses. In 1930, Mackenzie King appointed Cairine Wilson, a mother of nine children and a prominent Liberal Party organizer, as the first woman senator in Canada.

Canada's first female MP, elected in 1921, was Agnes Macphail. A teacher from Grey County, Ontario, she sat as a Progressive and soon made her mark as a defender of farmers, workers, women, and prisoners. After her defeat in the federal election of 1940, she served as a socialist member in the Ontario legislature from 1943 to 1945 and 1948 to 1951, during which time she was responsible for the enactment of the first equal-pay legislation in Canada.

FIRST NATIONS IN THE AGE OF DEMOCRACY

In the 1920s Canada's Aboriginal peoples also began to organize more systematically to reform the political structures that kept them dependent on white authorities. They faced an uphill battle. Status Indians, except veterans, were still denied the franchise, and amendments to the Indian Act in 1920 gave the Department of Indian Affairs the explicit right to ban hereditary chiefdoms and regulate other forms of Native governance.

Interference with Native governance was a long-standing grievance among status Indians. Prior to the First World War, Chief Deskadeh, a Cayuga, had begun a movement to achieve independence for the Six Nations of Grand River, Ontario. Despite this campaign, in 1924, Indian Affairs imposed an elective council on the Six Nations and banned the hereditary council. Women, who had hitherto preserved their traditional veto in the selection of chiefs, had no vote on the elected council.

Another member of the Six Nations, Fred O. Loft, was the key organizer of the League of Indians of Canada. Established in December 1918, it included representatives from the three Prairie provinces, Ontario, and Quebec. Loft was a well-educated Mohawk who spent 40 years in the Ontario civil service, mostly as an accountant. Unlike the traditionalists of Grand River, he did not support independence from Canada or a total retreat from European ways. The League stressed the importance of improved educational opportunities on reserves and greater cooperation among Native people. Despite Loft's relative moderation, the Department of Indian Affairs considered the League to be subversive. Government harassment, police surveillance, and accusations of communism weakened the organization, which also suffered from internal divisions. By the time Loft died in 1934, the League was moribund. Nevertheless, the

Agnes Macphail.

National Archives of Canada/C21562

foundations for a pan-Canadian Native organization had been laid.

In the Northwest Territories, the discovery of oil at Norman Wells in 1920 led to greater outside interest in the region. The federal government quickly signed a treaty, number 11, with representatives of Natives in the region and established a council to support the Northwest Territories commissioner in his efforts to impose southern control. In the North, as elsewhere, Aboriginal people would eventually claim that treaty guarantees of Native rights to hunt, fish, and trap had been violated, that they failed to receive the reserve lands promised by the treaty, and that they had been misled at the time of the original negotiations.

The federal government was slow to take responsibility for the Inuit, whose contact with southern society was mediated largely through the Hudson's Bay Company. Not until 1939 did a federal court decision confirm that the welfare of the Inuit was a federal responsibility.

LABOUR POLITICS

During the 1920s, labour parties steered an uneasy course between socialism and reform. Several provincial labour parties espoused gradual nationalization of major industries and greater labour control of the workplace, but the struggle for immediate reforms for workers—minimum wages for women, improved workers' compensation, federal unemployment insurance—absorbed most of the time of elected Labour representatives. At the national level, the Labour Party elected few candidates during the 1920s, and only the popular J.S. Woodsworth was able to hold his seat for the entire decade.

Within the labour movement, craft union leaders had reasserted their supremacy and forestalled the advance of industrial unions. The increased conservatism of labour was partly a result of state repression following the Winnipeg General Strike, but it was also reinforced by the postwar recession. A marked contrast to this trend was the Communist Party of Canada (CPC). Organized furtively in a barn outside Guelph in 1921, the CPC included many of the nation's most committed labour radicals. Communist leadership in the coal fields, garment shops, hardrock mines, and among northern Ontario bushworkers brought a spirit of militancy to groups either ignored or poorly represented by established unions. Immigrant unskilled labour, particularly Ukrainians, Finns, and Jews, formed the backbone of Canada's Communist Party.

Communist doctrines appealed to Scottish immigrant J.B. McLachlan, whose uncompromising organizational work among the coal miners of Cape Breton brought him into conflict with both company bosses and the conservative American leadership of the United Mine Workers. Convicted in court of seditious libel, McLachlan spent a few months in prison before returning to Cape Breton in 1924 to edit the *Maritime Labour Herald*.

A protracted and bitter strike among Cape Breton coal miners in 1925 focused widespread attention on the troubled island. McLachlan described the company's efforts to starve the miners into submission in a letter to J.S. Woodsworth on 6 March 1925:

> Besco cut off all credit to all miners who are idle, that affected about 2500 families. Their jobs gone, their little bit of credit gone, left miners no alternative. The utmost gloom is settling over the mining towns and many of the men are talking the most desperate kind of talk…. The coal company is taking the horses and the pumps out of the mines and the local government is allowing this dismantling to take place without a word of protest.[4]

Before the strike ended, one miner had been killed by company police, and Cape Breton miners had become renowned throughout Canada and around the world for their resistance to capitalist exploitation.

THE MARITIME RIGHTS MOVEMENT

Labour unrest in Cape Breton was only one chapter in a large volume of woes facing people in the Maritime provinces. Manufacturing declined by 40 percent between 1917 and 1921, and the recession that gripped the national economy in the early 1920s never entirely lifted in the region. Nearly 150 000 people drifted to greener pastures to find work in the 1920s.

Meanwhile, Maritimers watched with dismay as national leaders ignored their problems—too busy, they bitterly concluded, catering to Central Canada and the West. Particularly galling was the policy of railway consolidation that merged the Intercolonial into the CNR and moved its head office to Toronto. Not only were jobs lost and freight rates dramatically increased, but also Saint John and Halifax were abandoned as major terminals of international trade.

The hope of redressing grievances seemed remote. As the population of the Maritimes declined relative to the rest of the nation, the political power of the region, including their representation in Parliament, plummeted. Convinced that their interests, already largely ignored, would be shunted aside completely, Maritimers of all classes and interests came together to fight for "Maritime rights." The Maritime Rights Movement was led by business and professional interests who hoped that by adopting a regional rather than a provincial approach they could force Ottawa to respond to their concerns. Within the movement, Maritimers demanded larger federal subsidies, national transportation policies that took the region's needs into account, and tariff policies that offered protection for the Maritime coal and steel industries.

The federal Liberal Party had won most of the Maritime constituencies in the 1921 election, but when King subsequently dismissed the concerns of his Maritime backbenchers, the region turned to the Conservative Party as a vehicle for its interests. Needing all the help he could get in the 1925 and 1926 elections, King promised action. He set up the Royal Commission on Maritime Claims in 1926, naming as its head British lawyer-industrialist Sir Andrew Rae Duncan. Recognizing that Maritime governments were forced to tax their citizens more than other

Lawren Harris (1885-1970), Miners' Houses, Glace Bay, *c. 1925. This grim representation of life in a mining town depicts the miners' lives and work as one. The pollution over the town and the rows of identical, stark-looking homes combine to make the miners' town look much like the underground of a coal mine, as well as a cemetery.*

oil on canvas; 107.3 x 127 cm; Art Gallery of Ontario, Toronto. Bequest of Charles S. Band Toronto, 1970

provincial governments to maintain a minimal level of services, Duncan called for a series of provincial subsidies based on need. He also recommended a revision of freight rates, assistance to the region's coal and steel industries, better ferry connections to Prince Edward Island, and improvements to port facilities at Halifax and Saint John to encourage international trade through the region.

While King appeared to embrace the Duncan Report, his government refused to implement fully its recommendations. The Maritime Freight Rates Act of 1927 helped the region's producers compete more effectively in central Canadian markets, but provincial subsidies based on need proved too hot a concept for the government to handle. So, too, was the plight of the region's fisheries, which became the subject for yet another commission of inquiry. Some assistance was provided to move Maritime coal to Quebec markets, but further aid to the coal and steel industries was deferred.

NEWFOUNDLAND'S DILEMMA

Newfoundland, like the Maritimes, saw little prosperity in the 1920s and sought political solutions to the dilemma of poverty in the midst of plenty. When Richard Anderson Squires became premier in November 1919, he headed a coalition government made up of members of the Liberal Reform Party allied with William Coaker's Fishermen's Protective Union. As minister responsible for the fisheries, Coaker set minimum market prices for cod and penalties for exporters who attempted to undersell. He also established a government-controlled fish-culling system, with trade agents hired in foreign markets. In 1921, the regulations were repealed because exporters simply ignored them. The fisheries failed to make the transition to an industrial economy, with results that would prove disastrous.

Although Newfoundland already carried a heavy debt load from earlier railway construction and the financing of the war effort, Premier Squires borrowed more money. He used it for projects designed to make Newfoundland a more attractive site for investors as well as to oil his party's patronage machine. One bright spot during the decade was the decision by the Judicial Committee of the Privy Council in 1927 in Newfoundland's favour in the long-standing border dispute between Labrador and Quebec.

POLITICS IN ONTARIO AND QUEBEC

The Farmer-Labour government of Ontario, formed after the 1919 election, lasted only one term. Unlucky to have their entire period in office marked by recession, this government alienated urban residents with its puritanical stances on liquor, gambling, and Sunday entertainments. George H. Ferguson's Conservatives roared back to power in 1923. Buoyed by a reviving economy, they succeeded in marginalizing the upstart class-based parties that had emerged so forcefully after the war. Ferguson invested public funds in a provincial highway system, promoting in particular roads linking the region's northern forestry and mining communities with southern Ontario. He established the Liquor Control Board of Ontario to replace prohibition with state regulation, and the Department of Public Welfare to increase the state's presence in the lives of the poor. A lifelong member of the Orange Order, Ferguson was able to repeal the contentious Regulation 17 and legislate a limited right to French-language education in elementary grades. While continuing Ontario's long-standing efforts to limit federal intervention in areas of provincial jurisdiction, he brought Ontario into the federal pension plan.

Quebec remained a Liberal fiefdom, with Louis-Alexandre Taschereau, premier from 1920 to 1936, emulating Ontario in building roads and encouraging foreign investors. Taschereau proposed educational and welfare reforms that drew on Ontario models as well but relented in the face of Church opposition to any weakening of its traditional monopoly in the areas of education and social services. A member of the board of directors of an array of large corporations, even as he served as premier, Taschereau had little sympathy with either clerical or labour critiques of the practices of the increasingly powerful companies in the province.

THE DIRTY THIRTIES

The panic that began with the Wall Street crash of October 1929 produced a virtual halt in new investments in the Western world that endured through most of the next decade. Once the global downward spiral started, it took on a life of its own. Prices dropped dramatically and then dropped again and again, as producers tried to convince someone to buy their products.

Canada was especially hard hit by the Depression. Its small and open economy was buoyed by exports of primary products, which the world now decided it no longer could afford. High American tariffs meant disaster for its major trading partner. Competition from Argentine and Australian wheat contributed to wheat prices dropping to their lowest in over a century. As the price of basic foods eroded, the market for fresh and salt fish collapsed. Automobile sales dropped to less than a quarter of their 1929 level, the contraction of the British Empire market compounding a shrinking domestic demand. By 1933, the value of Canada's exports was less than half of what it had been in 1929. Although export volumes resumed their earlier levels by the late 1930s, values remained below the 1929 figure (see Table 20.2 on page 391).

With companies collapsing, and those that survived firing workers, unemployment reached unprecedented levels. Although unemployment figures are elusive for this period, nearly 20 percent of the labour force was officially classified as unemployed in 1933, the worst year of the Depression. As had always been the case in Canada, seasonal unemployment added greatly to the poverty of working people. Hidden unemployment was rife in the 1930s as women were forced into unwanted retirement, and, in the case of married women, actually fired from their jobs, ostensibly to provide more work for men supporting families.

In cities, the unemployed were dependent upon social assistance, or "relief," from the municipal authorities. Rates varied across the country, but everywhere they were low, and dozens of regulations existed to restrict funds to recipients deemed morally worthy. Both the low rates of relief and the demeaning regulations provoked mass demonstrations and relief strikes across the country, which often met with success in convincing councils to treat the unemployed less parsimoniously. For example, in Saskatoon in 1932, a sitdown strike by 48 women and their children at city hall ended after two days when the council agreed to their demands to reduce the amount of money that

relief recipients had to pay back when they found work; to close the relief store where social assistance recipients were segregated as shoppers; and to limit the powers of bureaucrats regulating relief.

While the lives of all unemployed people were grim, gender and race determined how grim. Most cities made no provision for single unemployed women without dependents, or for never-married women with dependents. In November 1930, the Vancouver relief rolls included 4513 married men and 5244 single men. Only 155 women were on city relief, and they appear to have been mainly widows and deserted wives with dependants. Charity organizations were left to establish a women's hostel in the city. Reforms came gradually, mainly in response to a concerted campaign by the Women's Labour League and the Unemployed Women and Girls Club. At various times in 1933, the city provided milk to women with babies, relief for ill single women, medical care for pregnant women, clothing allowances for married

Table 20.1

Percentage Sectoral Distribution of the Gross National Product, 1920–1930

Year	Primary	Secondary	Tertiary	Other
1920	26.6	29.7	35.3	8.4
1930	15.9	26.1	52.3	5.7

Source: William L. Marr and Donald Paterson, *Canada: An Economic History* (Toronto: Gage, 1980) 22.

Destitute family in Saskatchewan, 1934.

Glenbow Archives/ND 3-6742

women and their children, and assistance to needy Japanese and Chinese families.

Asian and African Canadians were more likely to be denied relief than their European-origin counterparts among the unemployed. In British Columbia, the relief rates for Asian-origin recipients were set at half the rate for whites. In Calgary, only a spirited campaign by the Communist Party resulted in the city's destitute Chinese citizens becoming eligible for social assistance.

What added insult to injury for the poor, both employed and unemployed, were the great disparities in income that prevailed during the Depression. For example, Gray Miller, chief executive officer of Imperial Tobacco, earned $25 000 a year, at the same time that clerks in the company's United Cigar Stores earned as little as $1300 a year for a 54-hour week.

In the first four years of the Depression, per capita income dropped sharply throughout this nation. Saskatchewan, staggering under the double assault of the collapse of the wheat economy and massive crop failures, experienced the greatest descent in income. Drought plagued the southern Prairies for most of the decade and raised fears that the region might swirl away with the dust storms that characterized the hot, dry summers. Gophers, which flourished in this climate, provided food for many poor families. Saskatchewan's net farm income—that is, receipts minus costs of operation—was a negative figure from 1931 to 1933. Without federal relief, there would have been mass starvation or mass migration away from rural Western Canada during the Depression. Even with federal aid, approximately 250 000 people left the Prairies between 1931 and 1941.

MORE TO THE STORY

Environmental Catastrophe

The misery of the farmers of the southern Prairies during the Depression provides one of the enduring images of the decade. Southern Saskatchewan, southeastern Alberta, and southwestern Manitoba turned into a dust bowl where farmers' attempts to grow their cereal crops were mocked by drought, dust, and wind. "The Wind Our Enemy," by Anne Marriott, gave poetic voice to the farmers' disillusionment with nature's attack on their livelihood.

Prairie farmers liked to think of themselves as husbanders of the soil. Arguably, though, at the root of the farmers' problems was a futile attempt to dominate the natural environment rather than to respect its limitations. Dryland farmers ignored warnings from government experts about the dangers of one-crop farming, presuming that science and new technologies could conquer all obstacles. With wheat prices rising in the 1920s, farmers opted for short-term financial gains rather than for the longer-term security that might come from diversification of crops and animal husbandry.

A disastrous drought from 1917 to 1921, accompanied by an invasion of grasshoppers, was followed by frequent and devastating attacks of rust and smut. Sawflies, cutworms, and wireworms caused millions of dollars of damage annually to repeatedly sown cropland. In Saskatchewan alone, 57 percent of all homesteaders were forced to abandon their land between 1911 and 1931. By that time, there were few traces of the buffalo landscape that had characterized the region in the mid-nineteenth century. Natural predators had been eliminated or reduced to small populations, and the vegetation changed by cattle and horses overgrazing on fenced-in ranches.

The monoculture of wheat had transformed the environment and farmers' language testified to their view that this transformation represented "progress." As historian Barry Potyondi notes: "The everyday terminology of the farmers depreciated the value of the natural world and hinted at the artificiality of their intrusion: 'cultivated' crops and 'tame' grass replaced 'wild' hay; machinery replaced horsepower; 'correction' lines replaced ancient trails that followed natural contours. This was a collision of natural and human forces on a grand scale, legislated into being and mediated by science and technology." [5]

The Maritime provinces could ill afford to sink any lower, but they did. Dependent on primary industries and international trade, the Maritimes, like the Prairies, were devastated by the Depression. Even their major source of relief—outmigration—was closed as Maritimers who fell on hard times elsewhere returned home in the 1930s. The Depression highlighted the underdeveloped state of municipal and social services in the Maritime region as well as the utter inadequacy of the region's rapidly shrinking tax base.

Unable to find the money to participate in federal cost-sharing programs to help the destitute, the region's governments were responsible for some of the most mean-spirited relief policies in the nation. Unemployed miners in Cape Breton received less than a dollar a week to feed their families, and in New Brunswick, officials prosecuted relief recipients who produced a child out of wedlock. Without the aid of relatives, neighbours, and charitable organizations, many of the region's dependent citizens would have succumbed to starvation. As it was, an untold number of people on relief died because hospital services were denied them until they were too far gone to be cured.

NEWFOUNDLAND ON THE ROCKS

In Newfoundland, the impact of loss of external markets, so devastating for Canada's resource-extracting regions, was even more dramatic. The colony's long-standing efforts to preserve its relative political independence collapsed with its economy. With 98 percent of its exports coming from the fish, forestry, and mineral sectors, Newfoundland could neither repay its debts nor provide social assistance to destitute citizens. In August 1932, a demonstration of unemployed workers in St John's deteriorated into a riot that gutted the legislature and forced Premier Squires to call an election. The United Newfoundland Party, led by Frederick Alderdice, won an overwhelming victory, but it had no solutions to the financial crisis. In desperation, the government turned to Britain for help.

Britain established a commission of inquiry into the colony's future. Headed by Lord Amulree, the commission recommended the suspension of Newfoundland democracy and the handing over of power to a British-appointed commission of government headed by a governor. While humiliated, the members of the House of Assembly felt they had no choice but to acquiesce. The commission of government, which came into operation in February 1934, brought an injection of British funds to pay off interest on debts, and began programs to encourage cooperatives and a cottage hospital system in the outports.

HANGING ON BY THE FINGERNAILS

The Canadian economy managed to weather the crisis somewhat better than Newfoundland, but there were some tense moments. To pay its bills the federal gov-

Table 20.2
The Canadian Economy, 1926–1939

	1926	1929	1933	1937	1939
GNP*	5152	6134	3510	5257	5636
Exports*	1261	1152	529	997	925
Farm income*	609	392	66	280	362
Gross fixed capital formation*	808	1344	319	809	746
Automobile sales (thousands)	159	205	45	149	126
Common stock prices (1935–39=100)	200.6	203.4	97.3	122.4	86.1
Unemployment (thousands)	108	116	826	411	529
Unemployment (percent of labour force)	3.0	2.8	19.3	9.1	11.4
Cost of living index (1935–39=100)	121.7	121.6	94.3	101.2	101.5
Wage rates (1939=100)	46.1	48.5	41.6	47.3	48.9
Corporation profits ($millions pre-tax)	325	396	73	280	362

*millions, current dollars

Source: Michael Bliss, *Northern Enterprise: Five Centuries of Canadian Business* (Toronto: McClelland and Stewart, 1987) 418–19. Reprinted by permission of Michael Bliss.

These men formed the Royal Commission that recommended in 1933 that Newfoundland be governed by a Commission of Government of Newfoundland rather than self-governed. They are, left to right, Charles A. Magrath, P.A. Clutterbuck of the Dominions Office (secretary of the Royal Commission), Lord Amulree, and Sir William Stavert.

The Provincial Archives of Newfoundland and Labrador (PANL) B-16-36

As British war production increased, the demand for gold, nickel, zinc, copper, and other minerals strengthened the mining industry in northern Ontario, producing growth and a degree of prosperity in Sudbury and Timmins, among other centres. Toronto was the financial capital for this mining expansion, and in the late 1930s, for the first time, the Ontario capital surpassed Montreal as the major source of financial capital in the nation.

TRADE UNIONS AND HARD TIMES

Not everyone was content to try to deal individually with Depression-imposed hardships. Huge demonstrations of the unemployed and violent strikes by workers trying to limit wage cuts rocked many communities in the 1930s. Under the leadership of the Communist Party, the Workers Unity League (WUL), dedicated to the creation of militant industrial unions, was founded in 1929 and soon took root among miners, loggers, and garment workers.

ernment resorted to wartime precedents of borrowing from the public. A National Service Loan of $150 million— oversubscribed by $72 million—helped to pull Canada through the crisis. Ottawa also came to the rescue of the provincial governments, most of which were deeply in debt.

Some industries recovered relatively quickly from Depression conditions after 1934. While most entrepreneurs were slow to gamble on new investment, the automobile industry rebounded quickly. Radio stations, cinemas, and oil and gas companies showed steady growth. When the price of gold was artificially raised from $20 to $35 during the Depression, mining companies had little difficulty attracting investors. Ontario and British Columbia were the main beneficiaries of the gold-mining boom, but many provinces— and the territories—experienced their own gold rushes in the 1930s. Discoveries of the mineral pitchblende near Great Bear Lake made Eldorado Gold Mines one of the success stories of the Depression. The source of radium used in the treatment of cancer, pitchblende also contains uranium, initially considered a useless by-product of the mining process.

In the United States, meanwhile, workers began to join a brash new federation of industrial unions, the Congress of Industrial Organizations (CIO), which soon also had branches in Canada. Many of the early CIO organizers in Canada were activists in the WUL, which folded its tent in accordance with orders from the international organization of Communist unions for radicals to work inside the mainstream union movement. The CIO, gaining an early stronghold in Sydney's steel plant, played a role in convincing Nova Scotia's Liberal premier, Angus L. Macdonald, to pass in 1937 Canada's first provincial law establishing rules for state recognition of a union in a particular firm or industry, and forcing employers to engage in collective bargaining with certified unions.

Mitch Hepburn, Ontario's Liberal premier from 1934 to 1943, was less open to accommodation. When the CIO-inspired United Auto Workers (UAW) called a strike in 1937 against General Motors in Oshawa, the union brought 4000 workers onto the streets, Hepburn organized a special police force which quickly became dubbed "Hepburn's hussars." Afraid that things would get out of hand, General Motors instructed its Canadian managers to negotiate an agreement with the UAW.

In 1939, on orders from the American Federation of Labor, CIO affiliates were expelled from the crafts-dominated Trades and Labour Congress. Undeterred, they joined a group of Canadian-controlled unions to form the Canadian Congress of Labour (CCL). The unions were biding their time. Only the high rate of unemployment gave employers and the state the power to prevent willing workers from unionizing. When and if the economy turned around, the unions would be ready to assert themselves.

In Quebec, the Confederation des travailleurs catholiques du Canada, formed in the 1920s, continued to be a strong force within the trade union movement. Associating strikes with socialism, church leaders believed that international unions were promoting an adversarial model that pitted class against class. In practice, the Catholic unions and many of the priests associated with their operations soon came to the view that workers needed the weapon of the strike to deal with those intransigent employers who could not otherwise be persuaded to treat their workers fairly.

In Newfoundland, as in Canada, the Depression provided a spur to union organization. The Newfoundland Lumbermen's Association was formed in 1935 by 12 000 loggers to fight for a just piece rate for the wood that they cut. Railway clerks unionized, and when both their employer and the commission of government refused to recognize the union, they took their case to Britain, which granted recognition of their rights as workers.

Western Canadian workers continued to prove receptive to radical labour leadership during the Depression. The WUL spearheaded strikes among New Westminster sawmill workers, Vancouver Island loggers, and fishers on the Skeena and Nass Rivers. But repression limited labour's gains in the region. The RCMP were used to suppress strikes such as the Estevan coal miners' strike in 1931, during which three miners were killed. Such repression highlighted the apparent league of the state with employers against workers.

THE BENNETT YEARS, 1930–1935

Slow to grasp the seriousness of the situation as Canada faced its first Depression winter, Mackenzie King lost his temper during a parliamentary debate and said that he would not help out any Tory provincial government with so much as "a five-cent piece." The "five-cent piece speech" became the theme of Conservative candidates stumping the country in the July 1930 campaign, and, under their new leader Richard Bedford Bennett, the Conservatives won a resounding victory, carrying 137 seats to 91 for the Liberals, 12 for the Progressives, and 3 for Labour. King was luckier than he realized at the time. With the nation sinking under the weight of the Depression, it was the Conservatives who would become associated with hard times, and the Liberals who would be waiting in the wings to pick up the pieces in 1935.

Born in 1870 in Albert County, New Brunswick, R.B. Bennett was a Tory's Tory. He was proud of his alleged Loyalist roots, his Methodist values, and his rise to prominence from humble origins. He made his fortune in Calgary as a lawyer for powerful clients such as the CPR and through wise investments. In 1911, he won the Calgary seat in the House of Commons, and in 1927 he was the first Conservative leader to be chosen by a national convention.

Eager to make good on his election promise to address the problems created by the Depression, Bennett called a special session of Parliament soon after taking power. The government introduced the Unemployment Relief Act to provide $20 million—an unprecedented sum—to help people get back to work and also embarked on a program of tariff increases designed to protect languishing Canadian industries from foreign competition. It was not enough. Bread lines lengthened, prices continued to plummet, and municipal and charitable organizations collapsed under the weight of the demands placed upon them. At a loss as to how to stem the crisis, Bennett resorted to desperate measures and soon found his party embattled from without and divided from within.

PROTEST FROM THE LEFT

In 1932, the Bennett government established relief camps under military control to house the single, unemployed men who had been travelling from city to city in search of work. From the government's perspective, these unfortunate people were a potentially explosive group who should be segregated from society until the economy improved. The transients were to be denied welfare unless they agreed to live in the camps, where they would labour on public works for their board and receive an allowance of 20 cents a day. As Irene Baird's powerful novel *Waste Heritage* (1939) vividly illustrated, Communist organizers had little difficulty convincing these desperate young men to organize to demand "work and wages" and the closing of the camps.

Communism had attracted little support during the 1920s, but it thrived in the appalling conditions of Depression Canada. Bennett moved quickly to suppress dissent. In 1931, the Communist Party was declared illegal and seven of its members—including its leader, Tim Buck—were imprisoned. The party was legalized in 1936, only to be banned in Quebec in 1937. The use of state violence to protect the established order was not new in Canada, but the intensity of the repression, which included jail sentences, beatings, and, for those who were not Canadian citizens, deportation, reached a new level in the hysteria fostered by the Depression.

While there were several tragic instances in the 1930s of strikers being killed by the police, the clash between the authorities and the victims of the Depression that gained the most national attention occurred in Regina in 1935. Relief camp workers, fed up with their lot, were enthusiastic recruits to the Relief Camp Workers Union (RCWU) organized by the Workers Unity League. In April 1935, the RCWU led nearly half of the 7000 relief camp inmates in British Columbia on a strike for work and wages. Early in June, 1200 of the strikers boarded freight trains heading east. Picking up support along the way, they planned to converge on Ottawa and put their demands directly to the prime minister.

The On-to-Ottawa Trek, as it became known, quickly attracted the nation's attention. Bennett responded by calling on the RCMP to stop the demonstrators in Regina. One constable was killed and hundreds of strikers and constables were injured in the mêlée that ensued as the strikers resisted RCMP orders to disperse. The next year, Mackenzie King abolished the relief camps, which by that time had provided temporary homes and education in radical politics to about 170 000 Canadians.

THIRD PARTIES

With as much as one-third of the nation facing destitution by 1932, many Canadians looked to new political parties to find a solution to their problems. The Co-operative Commonwealth Federation, Social Credit, and the Union nationale were all born in the Dirty Thirties, each with its own formula for preventing capitalist boom-bust economic cycles.

THE CCF

The Co-operative Commonwealth Federation (CCF), established in 1932, enjoyed modest success in the 1930s. Altough it formed no governments during the Depression decade, the CCF ultimately proved influential. Forerunner of the New Democratic Party, the CCF provided the first dem-

Communists and socialists led marches of unemployed men and women demanding better treatment of those unable to find work and more efforts on the part of the state to create work. In 1935, the United Married Men's Association marched in Calgary, carrying a banner that read, "We stand behind 12 000 on relief."

Glenbow Archives/NA 2800-12

ocratic socialist government in North America when Tommy Douglas was elected premier of Saskatchewan in 1944.

The CCF was a democratic socialist party formed as the result of a decision by the small contingent of Labour and Progressive MPs to capitalize on grassroots pressure to unite the disparate left-wing labour and farm organizations in the country. It inherited the often contradictory traditions of labourism, socialism, social gospelism, and farm radicalism. Early election results demonstrated that, outside of industrial Cape Breton, the CCF had taken root mainly in the West. By 1939, it formed the opposition in British Columbia, Saskatchewan, and Manitoba, and was poised for greater success in the future.

Led by J.S. Woodsworth, a Winnipeg Labour MP, the CCF rejected both capitalism and the revolutionary rhetoric of the Communists. The CCF's manifesto, adopted at the party's Regina convention in 1933, proclaimed the possibility of a parliamentary road to socialism, and recommended state planning as the best route to social justice.

SOCIAL CREDIT

Not all western Canadians who rejected the mainstream political parties turned toward socialism for a solution to economic ills. When popular Alberta radio evangelist William "Bible Bill" Aberhart began in 1932 to inject "social credit" into his weekly radio broadcasts, he found a receptive audience. Aberhart adapted doctrines espoused by a British engineer and fanatic anti-Semite, Major C.H. Douglas, to Alberta conditions and built on traditional provincial suspicion towards central Canadian financial institutions. Claiming that the Depression had been caused by the failure of the banks to print enough money so that consumer spending could match industrial production, Aberhart offered a blueprint for getting monetary policy back on track. To many free enterprisers, disillusioned by the severity of the Depression, Aberhart's nostrums proved appealing. If only the banks could be forced to supply consumers with money, they believed, prosperity could be restored.

Social credit meant that governments would replace financial institutions as the vehicle for deciding how much money should be in circulation and in whose hands. It claimed to offer a scientific formula to determine the shortfall in purchasing power, advocating that the government simply credit all citizens equally with a share of this shortfall to keep the economy healthy.

Aberhart turned the social credit study clubs spawned by his radio appeals into a political movement that won 56 of 63 seats in the provincial election of 1935. Once in power, he failed to deliver on his promises to issue social dividends or to control prices, and he only attempted to regulate banks and currency when a revolt by backbenchers in the party forced him to stop procrastinating. Legislation to this end was disallowed by the federal government and ultimately by the courts, which upheld federal jurisdiction over banking and currency. Aberhart was thus able to blame the federal government for his failure to implement his election promises and could maintain provincial support for his party with his strong stand against Ottawa.

UNION NATIONALE

In Quebec, the reform movement resulted less from popular pressure than from clerical responses to the 1931 papal encyclical *Quadragesimo Anno*, which supported state intervention to achieve social justice. The Jesuit-sponsored École sociale populaire, an organization that propagated church teachings, assembled representatives of lay Catholic organizations, including unions, caisses populaires, and professional groups, to produce a document on desirable social reforms in line with the pope's thinking. In 1933, they published *Le Programme de restauration sociale*, a program of non-socialist reforms including government regulation of monopolies, improved working conditions in industry, a system of farm credits, and a variety of social insurance measures.

The business-oriented Liberal regime of Louis-Alexandre Taschereau proved resistant to reform. In frustration, more progressive Liberals, led by Paul Gouin, formed a breakaway party, the Action libérale nationale. Maurice Duplessis, a Trois-Rivières lawyer who led the province's moribund Conservative Party, sensed a political opportunity and formed an electoral alliance with the renegade Liberals. In 1935, the rechristened Union nationale contested the provincial election, with *Le Programme de restauration sociale* as its platform and with its two component parties maintaining organizational autonomy.

Disillusionment with the long-governing Liberals produced a close result: 48 Liberal and 42 Union nationale seats. Shortly after the election, the Union nationale was able to capitalize on evidence of government corruption and nepotism to force Taschereau's resignation. The hastily formed new government, forced to call an election in 1936, was badly mauled by the Union nationale, which made corruption rather than reform the theme of its campaign.

Duplessis out-manoeuvred Gouin to take full control of the Union nationale, submerging its two founding parties into a new organization under his personal control and becoming the new political chief of the province.

In power, the Union nationale delivered only on its promises to help farmers with cheap loans and programs to settle the unemployed in remote (and generally infertile) areas of the province. Employers, not labour, received a sympathetic ear from the government, and the reform program was abandoned. In 1937, Duplessis demonstrated how far he would go in repressing dissent when he passed the Padlock Act. Designed to suppress communism, the act was fre-

Maurice Duplessis and Mitchell Hepburn, the two central Canadian premiers, worked together for several years, resisting federal social programs and economic regulation. While both men were economic conservatives, their motives for opposing the federal government differed in important respects. Hepburn wanted to avoid a redistribution of wealth away from the country's richest province, while Duplessis was leery of any proposals that might threaten the French-speaking, Catholic character of Quebec.

National Archives of Canada/C19518

quently invoked to intimidate any labour organization that the government considered undesirable.

BENNETT'S NEW DEAL

Not immune to the mounting pressures for action, Bennett's first instinct was to turn to the traditional Tory nostrum: the tariff. He promised to create jobs by raising tariffs as a means of forcing Canada's trading partners to sue for mercy. Britain was the first country to respond to Bennett's initiative, agreeing to preferential treatment for Canadian agricultural and forest products at the Imperial Economic Conference held in Ottawa in 1932. The agreement did little to help Canada's floundering manufacturing sector or the devastated wheat economy, but it was welcome news to apple growers in Nova Scotia, lumbermen in British Columbia, and Ontario's beef and dairy farmers. In 1935, the United States began its retreat from high tariffs when it signed a comprehensive trade treaty with Canada, the first since 1854.

There was also pressure to manipulate the money supply as a means of stimulating the economy. Bennett resisted most of the "soft money" proposals that circulated during the decade but did provide relief to hard-pressed farmers through the Farmers' Creditors Arrangement Act. As banking practices became increasingly restrictive, there was widespread agreement that Canada needed a central bank, like the Bank of England or the Federal Reserve Bank in the United States, to convince the public that someone was in control. In 1934, the Bank of Canada Act made provision for a central bank. Its major function, in the words of the preamble to the act, was "to regulate credit and currency in the best interests of the economic life of the nation."

The bank's first governor, Graham Towers, was recruited from the Royal Bank. Towers pursued a policy of modest growth in the money supply in order to cut interest rates and stimulate the economy. Bankers' commitment to "sound money" was too strong for him to undertake bolder efforts to make credit available to most Canadians. Although the economy was flat as a pancake, conservative economists and bankers worried that an increase in the money supply would result in an unacceptable level of inflation.

Responding to pressing problems relating to wheat exports, municipal funding, and housing, Ottawa pumped money into the economy through programs established under the Prairie Farm Rehabilitation Act, the Municipal Improvement Assistance Act, and the Dominion Housing Act. The federal government also passed the Natural Products Marketing Act, providing a legal framework for marketing boards, and created the Canadian Wheat Board to manage the sale of Canada's most troubled staple. Given the magnitude of the crisis, it no longer seemed wrong to fix prices and regulate output in the farming sector.

Nor was the notion of a government-sponsored social security system so steadfastly resisted. In 1935, R.B. Bennett, facing an election, introduced legislation to regulate hours of work, minimum wages, and working conditions, and to provide unemployment insurance. Many voters were unimpressed. What good were social insurance programs to the jobless who were ineligible to make a claim? And would this legislation be upheld in the courts? Most of Bennett's New Deal pronounced on matters that the BNA Act placed under provincial control.

THE 1935 ELECTION

Whatever his motives, Bennett received few benefits from his conversion to social security. He not only lost the 1935 election, but also watched his party split into warring factions. One revolt was led by Trade and Commerce Minister H.H. Stevens in response to public outrage against the apparent callousness of big corporations in the face of widespread human misery.

In 1934, Stevens headed a parliamentary committee established by the government to investigate the gap between what producers were receiving and what consumers were required to pay for necessities of life. Testimony in the committee hearings revealed damning evidence that big meat-packing companies, such as Canada Packers, made huge profits while farmers who raised the cattle and hogs had been paid "ruinous" prices. Similarly, seamstresses who did piecework for big department stores were paid a few pennies for dresses that sold for $1.59 at Eaton's or Simpson's.

When Bennett resisted taking the captains of industry to task for their exploitative policies, Stevens resigned and established the Reconstruction Party. While the party of "the little man" won only one seat—its leader won his Vancouver riding—it split the Conservative vote in constituencies from Nova Scotia to British Columbia. King, also resisting pressure to adopt new policies for new times, campaigned under the slogan "King or chaos," and won the largest majority of his political career.

As had been predicted, much of Bennett's New Deal was declared unconstitutional, and even marketing boards were deemed by the courts to be a matter for provincial rather than national legislation. King resisted appeals for dramatic action. In typical King fashion, he had the situation studied, appointing a National Employment Commission to investigate and recommend policy on unemployment and relief, and a Royal Commission on Dominion-Provincial Relations as a means of resolving the constitutional impasse. Only time would tell if Ottawa could introduce legislation to expand its role in the social and economic lives of Canadians.

CANADA AND THE WORLD

Mackenzie King's efforts, along with leaders of other white dominions, had led to informal British recognition of virtual sovereignty for the dominions. By the Statute of Westminster, passed by the British Parliament in 1931, Canada and the other dominions were given full legal freedom to exercise their independence in domestic and foreign affairs. While Canadian autonomy was not complete—amendments to the BNA Act still had to be approved by the British Parliament, and the Judicial Committee of the Privy Council remained the final court of appeal—the Statute of Westminster paved the way to complete independence for Canada in foreign affairs.

Canada proved cautious in its approach to world events, unwilling to do much to defend either sovereignty or democracy for other nations. It was hardly alone. The ambivalence of League of Nations members ensured an ineffectual response to the aggressive behaviour of Japan, Germany, and Italy in the 1930s. When Walter Riddell, Canada's representative at the League, called for stronger measures against Italy after its invasion of Ethiopia in 1935, he was told by Ottawa to change his position: Canada had no interest in the fate of Ethiopia.

Canada was equally unwilling to provide aid to the Spanish republic when its armed forces, led by General Franco, who was supported by German and Italian arms, overthrew the country's elected government during a bloody three-year civil war (1936–39). Some 1200 Canadians fought as volunteers for the republic, but their government regarded them with suspicion and the Roman Catholic hierarchy in Quebec was openly sympathetic to Franco and the fascists. Canada made no official protest when Hitler annexed Austria or invaded and dismembered Czechoslovakia. Even after Germany invaded Poland and imposed a murderous regime, Mackenzie King suggested to the British government that he try to mediate between the Allies and Nazi Germany.

CONCLUSION

Canadians emerged from the Depression with few political illusions. Although Canada had become a player in its own right on the international stage, the game of global politics was a dangerous one that threatened to engulf Canadians in another world war. Nor did Canada's new international status do anything to inspire a new national identity. Canadians were divided as never before along class, regional, and cultural lines, and many had abandoned the old two-party system to support new political parties that promised to address these interests. If there was cause for hope, it was that all parties professed to seek a solution to the problem of poverty in the midst of plenty and to make Canada a better place for all Canadians.

Populism, Right and Left

The Co-operative Commonwealth Federation and Social Credit are sometimes seen as polar opposites, but not all scholars view them in this manner. Some point to the similarity in origin of these movements: both had urban roots but found a mass audience among Prairie farmers; both claimed a national platform but focused on regional and provincial strategies for political change; neither had an important base outside Western Canada in the 1930s. Both parties were populist—that is, they claimed to be people's movements against the interests of the entrenched political and economic elites who dominated the country.

The CCF's populism was directed against all big capitalists, while Social Credit's populist attack targeted only financial institutions. The CCF may therefore be described as a "left-wing populist" movement because it identified farmers' interests with workers' interests against the interests of big business. Social Credit may be described as "right-wing populist" because it was suspicious of unions and suggested that workers and farmers had interests in common with capitalists other than bankers.

But were these two parties very different in practice? Some scholars say yes.[6] When the CCF assumed office in Saskatchewan in 1944, it nationalized auto insurance and the distribution of natural gas and established a provincial inter-city bus company. By contrast, the Alberta government denounced all state ventures in the economy. The CCF pioneered universal free hospital and medical care insurance in Saskatchewan; the Social Credit regime in Alberta insisted that medical care schemes must be voluntary and must in-

volve some direct payment for services by subscribers to prevent abuse of the program. The CCF passed labour legislation that favoured union organization in Saskatchewan, while Social Credit produced a labour code that made unionization difficult. Welfare recipients were subjected to mean-spirited treatment in Alberta, but received some sympathy in Saskatchewan.

Despite these contrasts, many scholars believe that the gap in performance between the CCF in Saskatchewan and Social Credit in Alberta has been exaggerated.[7] They claim that the farm programs of the two governments were similar and that, whatever philosophical differences existed between them, both governments spent lavishly on health, education, and roads. The provincial takeovers in Saskatchewan are held to have had a negligible impact on overall private ownership and direction of the provincial economy.

The claims of the two sides are difficult to adjudicate, in part, because the Alberta government, awash in oil revenues by the 1950s, had a vastly superior financial base compared to its Saskatchewan counterpart. It could afford to spend extravagantly, all the while deploring the tendencies of governments generally to spend more than they earned. Nonetheless, left-wing critics of Alberta Social Credit suggest that the poor in Alberta were largely passed over in the orgy of public spending. Their point of comparison is usually Saskatchewan, which they allege had more humanitarian social policies. Left-wing critics of the Saskatchewan CCF suggest that, in office, the party attempted to appease elite interests at the ultimate expense of the poor.

NOTES

1 James Struthers, *No Fault of Their Own: Unemployment and the Canadian Welfare State, 1914–1941* (Toronto: University of Toronto Press, 1983) 83–84.

2 Charlottetown Patriot, 26 March 1928, cited in Ruth A. Freeman and Jennifer Callaghan, "A History of Potato Marketing in Prince Edward Island, 1920–1987" (prepared for the Royal Commission on the Potato Industry, April 1987).

3 Michiel Horn, ed., *The Dirty Thirties: Canadians in the Great Depression* (Toronto: Copp Clark Pitman, 1972) 14.

4 David Frank, *J. B. McLachlan: A Biography* (Toronto: James Lorimer, 1999) 373.

5 Barry Potyondi, "Loss and Substitution: The Ecology of Production in Southwestern Saskatchewan, 1860–1930," *Journal of the Canadian Historical Association*, n.s. 5 (1994) 235.

6 The view that there are sharp differences between Social Credit's performance in Alberta and the CCF performance in Saskatchewan is defended in Alvin Finkel, *The Social Credit Phenomenon in Alberta* (Toronto: University of Toronto Press, 1989), 202–13, and Walter D. Young, *Democracy and Discontent: Progressivism, Socialism and Social Credit in the Canadian West* (Toronto: McGraw-Hill Ryerson, 1978). On the general distinction between left and right variants of populism, see John Richards, "Populism: A Qualified Defence," *Studies in Political Economy* 5 (Spring 1981): 5–27.

7 The best case for the convergence in the behaviour of the two parties in office is made in John F. Conway, "To Seek a Goodly Heritage: The Prairie Populist Responses to the National Policy" (PhD diss., Simon Fraser University, 1978). Peter R. Sinclair argues that the Saskatchewan CCF had lost its early radicalism before winning office. See "The Saskatchewan CCF: Ascent to Power and the Decline of Socialism," *Canadian Historical Review* 54.4 (Dec. 1973): 419–33. An opposite view is found in Lewis H. Thomas, "The CCF Victory in Saskatchewan, 1944," *Saskatchewan History* 28.2 (Spring 1975): 52–64.

SELECTED READING

On the economy in the 1920s, see Tom Traves, *The State and Enterprise: Canadian Manufacturers and the Federal Government, 1917–1931* (Toronto: University of Toronto Press, 1979); Ian Macpherson, *Each for All: A History of the Cooperative Movement in English Canada, 1900–1945* (Ottawa: Carleton University Press, 1979); and Trevor J. Dick, "Canadian Newsprint, 1913–1930: National Policies and the North American Economy," in *Perspectives on Canadian Economic History*, ed. Douglas McCalla (Toronto: Copp Clark Pitman, 1987).

On the political history of the interwar period, general works include John Thompson and Alan Seager, *Canada, 1922-1939: Decades of Discord* (Toronto: McClelland and Stewart, 1985); Ian Drummond, Robert Bothwell, and John English, *Canada, 1900–1945* (Toronto: University of Toronto Press, 1987); Douglas Owram, *The Government Generation: Canadian Intellectuals and the State, 1900–1945* (Toronto: University of Toronto Press, 1986); Robert A. Wardhaugh, *Mackenzie King and the Prairie West* (Toronto: University of Toronto Press, 2000); J.W. Pickersgill, ed., *The Mackenzie King Record*, vols. 1–3 (Toronto: University of Toronto Press, 1960-70); and Larry A. Glassford, *Reaction and Reform: The Politics of the Conservative Party Under R.B. Bennett, 1927–1938* (Toronto: University of Toronto Press, 1992).

On Western protest, see David Laycock, *Populism and Democratic Thought in the Canadian Prairies, 1910–1945* (Toronto: University of Toronto Press, 1990); W.L. Morton, *The Progressive Party in Canada* (Toronto: University of Toronto Press, 1989); Kenneth McNaught, *A Prophet in Politics: A Biography of J.S. Woodsworth* (Toronto: University of Toronto Press, 1959); Allen Mills, *Fool for Christ: The Political Thought of J.S. Woodsworth* (Toronto: University of Toronto Press, 1991); Bob Hesketh, *Major Douglas and Alberta Social Credit* (Toronto: University of Toronto Press, 1997); Alvin Finkel, *The Social Credit Phenomenon in Alberta* (Toronto: University of Toronto Press, 1989); L.H. Thomas, ed., *The Making of a Socialist: The Recollections of T.C. Douglas* (Edmonton: University of Alberta Press, 1982); and Seymour Martin Lipset, *Agrarian Socialism: The Co-operative Commonwealth Federation in Saskatchewan* (Berkeley: University of California Press, 1971).

On Quebec political developments, see Paul-André Linteau, René Durocher, Jean-Claude Robert, and François Rocard, *Quebec since 1930* (Toronto: Lorimer, 1991); Andrée Lévesque, *Virage à gauche interdit: les communistes, les socialistes, et leurs ennemis au Québec* (Montreal: Boréal Express, 1984); Conrad Black, *Duplessis* (Toronto: McClelland and Stewart, 1979); Bernard L. Vigod, *Quebec Before Duplessis: The Political Career of Louis-Alexandre Taschereau* (Montreal: McGill-Queen's University Press, 1986); and Herbert F. Quinn, *The Union Nationale* (Toronto: University of Toronto Press, 1979). Ontario politics are the subject of Kerry Badgley, *Ringing in the Common Love of Good: The United Farmers of Ontario, 1914–26* (Montreal: McGill-Queen's University Press, 2000); Peter Oliver, *G. Howard Ferguson, Ontario Tory* (Toronto: University of Toronto Press, 1977); and James Naylor, *The New Democracy: Challenging the Social Order in Industrial Ontario, 1914–1925* (Toronto: University of Toronto Press, 1991).

On political developments in the Atlantic region, important works include Ernest R. Forbes, *Maritime Rights: The Maritime Rights Movement, 1919–1927* (Montreal: McGill-Queen's University Press, 1979); E. R. Forbes and D.A. Muise, eds., *The Atlantic Provinces in Confederation* (Toronto: University of Toronto Press, 1993); David Frank, ed., *Industrialization and Underdevelopment in the Maritimes, 1880–1930* (Montreal: McGill-Queen's University Press, 1979); Robert J. Brym and R. James Sacouman, eds., *Underdevelopment and Social Movements in Atlantic Canada* (Toronto: New Hogtown, 1979); and Gary Burrill and Ian McKay, eds., *People, Resources and Power: Critical Perspectives on Underdevelopment and Primary Industries in the Atlantic Region* (Fredericton: Acadiensis Press, 1987).

The Canadian economy during the Depression is discussed in A.E. Safarian, *The Canadian Economy in the Great Depression* (Ottawa: Carleton University Press, 1970); Ian M. Drummond, *British Economic Policy and the Empire, 1919–1939* (London: Allen and Unwin, 1972); Ian M. Drummond and Norman Hillmer, *Negotiating Freer Trade* (Waterloo, ON: Wilfrid Laurier University Press, 1989); Gillian Creese, "The Politics of Dependence: Women, Work and Unemployment in the Vancouver Labour Movement before World War II," in *British Columbia Reconsidered: Essays on Women*, ed. Gillian Creese and Veronica Strong-Boag (Vancouver: Press Gang, 1992) 364–90; and E. R. Forbes, "Cutting the Pie into Smaller Pieces: Matching Grants and Relief in the Maritime Provinces during the 1930s," in *Challenging the Regional Stereotype: Essays on the Twentieth-Century*

Maritimes (Fredericton: Acadiensis Press, 1989). The background to the environmental debacle that produced "dust bowl" conditions on the southern Prairies is traced in Barry Potyondi, *In Palliser's Triangle: Living in the Grasslands 1850–1930* (Saskatoon: Purich Publishing, 1995).

On the relief camps, see Laurel Sefton MacDowell, "Relief Camp Workers in Ontario During the Great Depression of the 1930s," *Canadian Historical Review* 76.2 (June 1995): 205–28, and Ronald Liversedge, *Recollections of the On-to-Ottawa Trek* (Ottawa: Carleton University Press, 1973). Works on the labour movement include Ian Radforth, *Bushworkers and Bosses* (Toronto: University of Toronto Press, 1987); Craig Heron, *Working in Steel* (Toronto: McClelland and Stewart, 1988); Joan Sangster, *Earning Respect: The Lives of Working Women in Small-Town Ontario, 1920–1960* (Toronto: University of Toronto Press, 1995); David Frank, *J. B. McLachlan: A Biography* (Toronto: James Lorimer, 1999); Bryan D. Palmer, *Working-Class Experience: Rethinking the History of Canadian Labour, 1800–1991* (Toronto: McClelland and Stewart, 1992); Michael Earle, ed., *Workers and the State in Twentieth-Century Nova Scotia* (Fredericton: Acadiensis Press, 1989); and Margaret Hobbs and Joan Sangster, eds., *The Woman Worker, 1926–1929* (St John's: Canadian Committee on Labour History, 1999).

On Canadian communists, see Ian Angus, *Canadian Bolsheviks* (Montreal: Vanguard, 1981) and William Beeching and Phyllis Clarke, eds., *Yours in the Struggle: The Reminiscences of Tim Buck* (Toronto: NC Press, 1977). On the national CCF, see Walter Young, *Anatomy of a Party: The National CCF, 1932–61* (Toronto: University of Toronto Press, 1969); Norman Penner, *From Protest to Power: Social Democracy in Canada 1900–Present* (Toronto: Lorimer, 1992); and William Brennan, ed., *Building the Co-operative Commonwealth: Essays on the Social Democratic Tradition in Canada* (Regina: Canadian Plains Research Centre, 1984). On women in the CCF and the Communist Party, a critical account is Joan Sangster, *Dreams of Equality: Women on the Canadian Left, 1920–1950* (Toronto: McClelland and Stewart, 1989). A biography of a major woman founder of the CCF is Terry Crowley, *Agnes Macphail and the Politics of Equality* (Toronto: Lorimer, 1990). On intellectuals and the left, see Michiel Horn, *The League for Social Reconstruction* (Toronto: University of Toronto Press, 1980).

On women's political activities and lives more generally, key works include Veronica Strong-Boag, *The New Day Recalled: Lives of Girls and Women in English Canada, 1919–1939* (Toronto: Copp Clark Pitman, 1988); Andrée

Lévesque, *Making and Breaking the Rules: Women in Quebec, 1919–1939* (Toronto: McClelland and Stewart, 1994); and Catherine A. Cavanaugh, "Irene Marryat Parlby: An 'Imperial Daughter' in the Canadian West, 1896–1934," in *Telling Tales: Essays in Western Women's History*, ed. Catherine A. Cavanaugh and Randi R. Warne (Vancouver: UBC Press, 2000).

On social welfare developments, see Nancy Christie, *Engendering the State: Family, Work and Welfare in Canada* (Toronto: University of Toronto Press, 2000); James Struthers, *The Limits of Affluence: Welfare in Ontario, 1920–1970* (Toronto: University of Toronto Press, 1994) and *No Fault of Their Own: Unemployment and the Canadian Welfare State, 1914–1941* (Toronto: University of Toronto Press, 1983); Gerard William Boychuk, *Patchworks of Purpose: The Development of Provincial Social Assistance Regimes in Canada* (Montreal: McGill-Queen's University Press, 1998); Raymond B. Blake and Jeff Keshen, eds., *Social Welfare Policy in Canada: Historical Readings* (Toronto: Copp Clark, 1995); James G. Snell, *The Citizen's Wage: The State and the Elderly in Canada, 1900–1951* (Toronto: University of Toronto Press, 1995); Cynthia R. Comacchio, *"Nations Are Built of Babies": Saving Ontario's Mothers and Children, 1900–1940* (Montreal: McGill-Queen's University Press, 1993); and Alvin Finkel, *Business and Social Reform in the Thirties* (Toronto: Lorimer, 1979).

On foreign policy developments, see Norman Hillmer and J.L. Granatstein, *Empire to Umpire: Canada and the World to the 1990s* (Toronto: Copp Clark, 1994) and B.J.C. McKercher and Lawrence Aronson, eds., *The North Atlantic Triangle in a Changing World: Anglo-American-Canadian Relations, 1902–1956* (Toronto: University of Toronto Press, 1996).

 **WEBLINKS**

WILLIAM LYON MACKENZIE KING
www.mackenzieking.com

This site aims to be a primary online source of information and resources pertaining to Canada's tenth Prime Minister.

ARTHUR MEIGHEN
http://trulycanadian.freeservers.com./Ameighen.htm

This site includes brief biographical information, with a link to a more detailed exploration of Meighens' life and career.

THE GREAT DEPRESSION
www.escape.com/~paulg53/politics/great_depression.shtml

This article considers the main causes of the Great Depression and its political, economic, and social effects.

R.B. BENNETT
www.nlc-bnc.ca/primeministers/h4-3275-e.html

A profile of R.B. Bennett, as well as an account of his speeches, is offered on this site.

REGINA MANIFESTO
www.arts.uwaterloo.ca/ECON/needhdata/Regina_Manifesto.html

Read the text of the Regina Manifesto, adopted at the first national convention of the Co-operative Commonwealth Federation in 1933.

ON TO OTTAWA TREK
www.workingtv.com/oto/otohome.html

View historical photographs and read about the On to Ottawa Trek at this site.

THE "PERSONS" CASE
www.famous5.org

This site is dedicated to the five women (Henrietta Muir Edwards, Nellie McClung, Louise McKinney, Emily Murphy, and Irene Parlby) who petitioned the Canadian to have women declared "persons" under Section 24 of the British North America Act so that they could serve in the Senate of Canada.

CHAPTER 21

Mass Consumer Society and the Search for Identity, 1919–1939

During the Christmas season one Depression year, an Eaton's saleswoman witnessed throngs of little girls admiring Shirley Temple dolls. Priced at between nine and sixteen dollars, dolls cost a month's income for a family on welfare.

> Some used to come at opening time and just stand there looking at those pink-cheeked, golden-haired lovely Shirley Temples. Little faces, they needed food. You could see a lot who needed a pint of milk a day a thousand times more than they needed a Shirley doll. They'd stare for hours. We tried to shush them away, but it didn't do any good…. One [clerk] had a crying fit over just that, those hundreds of poor kids who would never own a Shirley Temple in a hundred years. They were lucky if they had breakfast that morning, or soup and bread that night.[1]

This moving account of would-be juvenile consumers speaks volumes about Canada in the interwar years. By creating desire through advertising, corporate capitalism touched most people, including children. The commercial media, dominated by radio, movies, magazines, and newspapers, focused on the good life and encouraged people to indulge the whims of the moment. Defying the sexual and social taboos of the prewar period, many women wore shorter skirts and displayed a devil-may-care attitude. Men returning from the trenches in Europe ignored the petty conventions that characterized polite society in the prewar years.

Nonetheless, prohibition, poverty, and a domestic ideal in which gender roles were rigidly prescribed also marked the interwar years. The clash of old and new values created tensions and sparked debates about many issues, including how families should raise children and what it meant to be a man or woman in the modern age.

POPULATION

In 1941, Canada's population was over 11 500 000. Immigration peaked during the late 1920s but dried up during the Depression (see Table 21.1). In the interwar years, Canada still gave preferential treatment to immigrants from Great Britain and the United States. The federal government bowed to pressure from railway companies, manufacturers, and farmers—all facing labour shortages—and opened the doors to wider European immigration after the postwar recession began to ease. Southern Ontario, largely an Anglo-Celtic preserve before 1920, joined the West in becoming home to tens of thousands of southern and eastern European immigrants.

Table 21.1

Canada's Population (in thousands), 1911–1941

Year	Natural increase	Immigration	Emigration	Net Migration	Population
1911–21	1349	1592	1360	233	8 788
1921–31	1486	1198	1095	103	10 377
1931–41	1242	149	262	–112	11 507

Source: David C. Corbett, *Canada's Immigration Policy: A Critique* (Toronto: University of Toronto Press, 1957) 121.

Some of Canada's new immigrants fled religious persecution at home. Between 1922 and 1930, over 20 000 Mennonites arrived from the Soviet Union. Most settled on Prairie farms, reliving the harsh lives of earlier generations of settlers. Ukrainian-Canadian politics of the interwar period was strongly influenced by the debate about the future of the Ukraine. While radicals supported the Soviet Union, conservative Ukrainians wanted an independent, non-communist Ukraine.

Racism continued to dog many new Canadians. In 1923, federal legislation excluded Chinese nationals from immigrating to Canada. This policy prevented men working in Canada from bringing their families from China, and unemployment, especially during the Depression, meant there was no money to send home to the family. Many accepted Vancouver City Council's offer of a free one-way ticket to China, on condition that they never return. The Japanese invasion of China in 1937 cut communications be-

CPR card for Mennonite immigrants.

Courtesy of Barbara Tessman

tween China and Canada, leaving Chinese Canadians without knowledge of the fate of their loved ones back home.

The Japanese in Canada were also caught up in the web of international developments. Since most were second-generation Canadians, or *Nisei*, they spoke English and shared the liberal democratic outlook of other Canadians. Nevertheless, they continued to face discrimination in educational and job opportunities and were subject to growing hostility as Japan began its military assault in Asia. An articulate minority of Nisei formed associations to discuss their mutual problems and founded English-language newspapers such as *The New Canadian*. Their elders, by contrast, clung to the language and traditions of their Japanese homeland.

CANADA'S NATIVE PEOPLES

In the interwar years, the living conditions of most Natives continued to deteriorate. Courts, dominated by whites, rejected Native efforts to establish land claims. A 1928 decision in the case of *Rex v Sylliboy* found that eighteenth-century treaties in the Maritimes had no validity because the Mi'kmaq had allegedly not been competent to sign. Prairie provinces, having just received jurisdiction over their natural resources, tended to ignore treaties with the federal government that granted hunting and fishing rights in traditional Native territories.

In the North, Southern trappers similarly ignored Native hunting rights, and overtrapping led to resource depletion. The Inuit, drawn into the whaling industry off Herschel Island in the western Arctic, suffered massive epidemics. The population began to rise only in the 1930s as the Inuit began to develop immunities to European diseases. Ultimately, a new northern society emerged which was characterized by "limited growth, federal government neglect, dependence on a small number of mines, a vibrant fur trade and a bicultural society."[2]

The Métis, who lacked even treaties, lived under appalling conditions. A provincial commission in Alberta heard shocking medical evidence suggesting

These Métis trappers at their winter camp in the foothills of the Rockies cked out a bare living for their efforts.

Glenbow Archives, Brady Collection/PA-2218-985

that the Métis faced extinction. As much as 90 percent of the Métis population was infected with tuberculosis. The province responded in 1939 by establishing six Métis colonies where schools and health care were provided, but the colonies lacked an economic base. In Saskatchewan and Manitoba, the Métis were almost completely ignored by their provincial governments.

SEXUALITY AND RESPECTABILITY

As Canadians moved to cities, and movies and radio vied with churches and schools for the minds of the masses, fears spread of a moral breakdown in society. Church leaders, in particular, regarded modern culture as hedonistic, violent, and profane. Traditionalists countered modernism by reaffirming long-standing moral conventions that sex was only acceptable if it was heterosexual, infrequent, and confined to married couples. They also railed against drinking, smoking, swearing, and gambling.

Heterosexual men who violated this moral code faced few penalties, but women risked their reputations if they became sexually available "flappers." A pregnant unwed woman lost all claims to "respectability," and if she could afford it, concealed her condition. Both public and private institutions were prepared to exploit her for their own ends. In Chester, Nova Scotia, the Ideal Maternity Home charged hefty fees both for unwed pregnant women who stayed in the home and for would-be parents who adopted the babies. Many of the babies born in the home died. Their bodies were packed in empty butter boxes and hastily buried behind the home.

In Montreal and Quebec City, unwed mothers could give birth at homes run by the Sisters of Misericorde in return for labour in the homes. Poverty forced most of them to leave their children to be adopted. Over a third of the children died in the home during their first year, mostly from preventable diseases. So deep was the social disapproval that haunted "illegitimate" children that a nun wrote to the grandfather of one of the children in 1934: "Dear Sir: We regret to say that the baby born to E.C. is dead. Thank God for this great favour."[3]

In the interwar period, birth-control information became more readily available and the birth rate continued its steady decline. Defying the 1892 law that forbade provision of birth-control information, advocacy groups and a few birth-control clinics, beginning in Hamilton in 1932, informed people how to avoid unwanted pregnancies.

In 1937, birth-control advocates won an important legal victory in Ottawa. Dorothea Palmer, a field worker for the Parents' Information Bureau, was found not guilty of violating the law because her provision of birth-control information to working-class people in Ottawa was done for the public good. Resolute resistance of Quebec and the Roman Catholic Church prevented the federal government from making birth-control devices legal.

A darker side of the birth-control movement was the idea that the human race would be improved by sterilizing people deemed physically and mentally inferior to some defined standard. Nazi Germany's grim implementation of this policy eventually discredited eugenics, but in the interwar years it had the support of many Canadians.

Women who were victims of sexual assaults were often wary of using the courts to have their assailants punished. Any suggestion of sexual impropriety in her life could turn the trial against the victim rather than the rapist. Women who laid complaints against rapists risked disbelief and ostracism within their communities.

THE BURDEN OF RESPECTABILITY

Apart from condemning as immoral women who transgressed the sexual conventions, respectability required that a married woman be seen as a good mother, frugal consumer, tidy housekeeper, and devoted wife. Similarly, men wanted the image of good providers who turned over enough wages to their wives for the family to live decently. Depression poverty caused many men to become hopelessly depressed, to commit suicide, or desert their families as it became impossible to fulfil their breadwinning roles.

Even during the Roaring Twenties, meeting the ideal of respectability eluded many people. A letter written by a Mrs Richards to her landlord, the Halifax Relief Commission, in 1926, illustrates efforts to cling to an image of respectability in the face of extreme poverty. Asking for time to make up back rent, she argued that her husband's limited income made it "pretty hard to be respectable a[nd] to keep up under the conditions we are living." This family of six had one bed, where the father and three children slept while the mother and baby slept on a mattress with a broken spring. There was too little money for food and fuel, but Mrs Richards wrote that she would go to prison before going on the streets. Her father-in-law had offered to help in exchange for sex. "I'm an Englishwoman and I'd not touch one cent of money belonging to that man," wrote Mrs Richards.[4]

Those without pretensions to respectability found ways to get by that often involved the complicity of their social betters as clients. An ambitious young man might make moonshine, run gambling dens, or pimp for prostitutes. For women, almost the only alternative to destitution was prostitution.

Divorce remained uncommon in interwar Canada. The 1931 census indicated that fewer than 8000 Canadians were legally divorced. Most desertions of homes involved men leaving their wives. While some women left abusive husbands, sometimes taking the children with them, most accepted the economic logic that fleeing simply plunged the family into permanent poverty. The judicial system continued to be unsympathetic to most women's accusations of batterings and deaf to claims from children about abuse by relatives.

MOTHERHOOD IN THE MODERN AGE

Mothers in the interwar years became the particular focus of a campaign to reform and homogenize child-rearing practices. Mass-circulation magazines and government-sponsored child welfare departments dispensed "scientific" advice on how to be a better mother. "Old-fashioned" methods and "maternal instinct" came under harsh criticism. While reformers worked to reduce infant mortality through better hygiene, dietary practices, and prenatal care, there was a tendency to medicalize motherhood. In 1926, only 17.6 percent of births took place in hospitals, a figure that rose steadily to 94.6 percent in 1960.

Experts increasingly intruded in the nursery, with middle-class families leading the way in embracing new methods of bringing up baby. Funded by private sources, two nursery schools, one in Montreal, one in Toronto, were established to study children. The University of Toronto Institute of Child Study became world-famous under Dr. William Blatz for its pioneering work on child development.

Views about raising children departed dramatically from the prewar period. Reflecting new notions of behavioural science pioneered by American psychologists, families were encouraged to teach their children good habits from an early age by establishing fixed schedules for every activity. At its height, the trend toward regimentation included toilet training at the age of two weeks. "If the time and place are always the same and the mother shows her approval of the first successes," one 1943 pamphlet opined, "the baby will soon learn what is expected of him."[5]

HOUSING CANADIANS

By international standards of the period, Canadians were relatively well housed. Toronto in 1921 had the highest rate of home ownership of the 20 largest North American cities. During the Second World War, a government-sponsored report provided a detailed picture of the shelter available to Canadians that highlighted deficiencies. The report concluded that 10 percent of existing dwellings should be demolished while another 25 percent required major repairs. There was overcrowding in one dwelling in five.

Ethnicity influenced housing options. Land titles often had restrictions that kept non-whites, Jews, and eastern Europeans out of new developments. French Canadians and eastern European immigrants were far more likely than Anglo-Canadians to be living in overcrowded conditions. Visible minorities fared worst, being easy targets for prejudiced realtors. Natives on reserves lived in unheated shacks. Families in the Chinese business quarters east of Dewdney Street in Vancouver lived shabbily, and single Chinese males lived in crowded, poorly lit, poorly ventilated boarding houses. This was hardly surprising since British Columbia gave Chinese men an accommodation voucher worth a third of white men's vouchers.

Child-care experts opined that regimentation was best for both mother and baby. Such advice was reflected in attempts to "toilet train" infants almost immediately after birth.

National Archives of Canada/PA-803178

Tenants being evicted in Montreal during the Depression.

National Archives of Canada/C30811

In the early 1920s, both workers and the middle class lived in the heart of the cities, though the middle class had larger lots and better access to sewer and water services. Many workers escaped the pollution, noise, and squalor of the neighbourhoods where they could afford to rent by building homes on the urban fringes. But by the mid-1920s, middle-class families, now in possession of cars, viewed the previously unattractive urban fringes as ideal places to raise families. Urban planners and developers alike pressed city councils to implement regulations requiring that suburban homes meet certain building standards and be subject to municipal taxes. These measures often forced the original low-income suburbanites to return to the city centres. Following the planners' models, the new suburbs were residential oases separated from commercial and industrial life and characterized by curved streets, large parks, and generous-sized lots.

By international standards of the period, Canadians were relatively well housed. They enjoyed better sanitary standards than Europeans and less overcrowding. In 1921, Toronto could boast the highest rate of home ownership of the 20 largest cities in North America. Such statistics nevertheless hid vast differences in the living arrangements of Canada's increasingly industrialized population; poor renters were least likely to be paying fair prices in relation to their incomes.

Wherever they lived, Canadians of the interwar period were influenced by the new domestic ideal propagated in the media. This ideal suggested that the home, rather than institutions such as the church and community hall, should be the major centre for entertainment. Radios, gramophones, and fine furnishings were necessary accoutrements for the ideal home. As "labour-saving devices" such as electric stoves, vacuum cleaners, and washing machines began to replace servants, wives increasingly did all their own housework, often in isolation from other women. Men were expected to spend less time at public places and more time with their families. Some Canadians paid outrageous rents to secure an accommodation that could help them approximate the goals of the new cult of domesticity.

WOMEN, WORK, AND THE FAMILY

Work, including waged work, meant different things to men and women. Gendered attitudes to work were reinforced by the different socialization that girls and boys received. As historian Joy Parr notes:

> Through waged work, boys learned manliness; they mastered disciplines and discriminations, ways of appraising their work and one another, which they would practice through their adult lives; varied though these ways of being manly were, they shared one trait: they were lessons males alone might learn. Girls did not learn womanliness through their paid employment. Their experience of waged work was important in their growing into womanhood because it became them to remain under the protection of male kin while they waited for their life's work, in marriage and outside the market, to begin. [6]

Many rural women dreamed of escaping to the city and many of them sought waged labour there. As their diaries and letters attest, they went to movies, dances, and shops with friends whom they had met at work and in boarding houses. However, their work lives were rarely glamorous. Most were underpaid store clerks, office workers, and domestics. Immigrant women whose first language was not English were clustered in the lowest-wage occupations, such as home sewing by the piece, cleaning, and laundering.

Women's work was central in establishing a sense of community in new single-industry towns such as Powell River, BC, and Gagnon, Quebec. While the men toiled in the town's main industry, their wives established community facilities. A woman who arrived in Flin Flon, Manitoba, in 1926 when the town was still a bush camp, later recalled: "Women organized the community centre, the schools, the hospital…. Women looked after the home and that's what makes this town great. It's a family town."[7]

Female single parents faced dismal prospects. Rose and Edith Biscun were nine and six when their widowed Russian mother placed them in the Winnipeg Jewish Orphanage in 1931. Until 1936, she worked all week in a *shmata* factory, seeing them only occasionally. Children in single-parent families enjoyed few opportunities, as their labour was needed for financial support. In 1931 Halifax, 25 percent of 15- to 19-year-olds were in school, versus 12 percent for children of widows.

RURAL LIFE

As late as 1921, a majority of Canadians lived in communities of less than 20 000 people, and even in 1941, over 44 percent of Canadians were rural residents. During the Depression, three of every ten Canadians lived on a farm. Most farmers depended on the sale of their produce to buy farm implements and consumer goods. When hard times descended, they could survive by subsistence farming, an option unavailable to most city-dwellers. This was particularly true for farmers in the fertile belt of southern Ontario, Quebec, and the Maritimes. Many farmers' sons and daughters returned to farms during the 1930s to wait out the Depression.

More than ever before, rural Canadians were connected to metropolitan centres. By the late 1920s, 40 percent of Alberta farmers owned an automobile and used it to shop in the larger towns and cities. Town merchants lost business and often closed shop, leaving the small towns to languish, a trend that would continue throughout the twentieth century.

In the interwar period, the farm population of Ontario and Quebec declined, but it remained stable in the Maritimes and increased on the Prairies. More farms were created in northern Saskatchewan and Alberta as well as in the foothills of the Rocky Mountains. These provided an alternative to unproductive areas on the southern Prairies, the driest of which were abandoned

after homesteaders had made heartbreaking efforts to turn deserts into productive farmlands.

During the 1930s, provincial governments settled landless families without income on infertile lands where it was hoped that they could eke out a subsistence. The "back-to-the-land" movement of the 1930s suggested the strength of agrarian ideology in Canada, which held that it remained possible in an industrial age for families to live off the land without help from the state. The bleakness of life in the new farming areas disillusioned those who had been resettled, and many families relocated to cities and towns when the Second World War offered them employment.

THE COMMUNICATIONS REVOLUTION

In the interwar period, the isolation of even the remotest rural region was shattered by new developments in communication. Radio made its first appearance in Canada in 1920. Three years later, three Canadian households in four owned a radio. Most of the early Canadian radio stations were owned by electric retailers or newspapers. Advertising provided revenues to owners while selling products and dreams to a largely uncritical and unsuspecting audience.

American stations and programs dominated the early Canadian radio scene. Fears that unregulated radio would contribute to the Americanization of Canadian culture sparked the formation of the Canadian Radio League. The League, taking its inspiration from the state-owned British Broadcasting Corporation, declared that, in broadcasting, it was "the state or the United States."

In 1928, Mackenzie King created a royal commission to advise on the future control, organization, and financing of broadcasting. Sir John Aird, president of the Bank of Commerce, chaired the commission, which recommended the creation of a public broadcasting company to own and operate all radio stations and to build seven stations across the country. In 1932, Prime Minister R.B. Bennett established the Canadian Radio Broadcasting Commission, which in 1936 was reorganized as the Canadian Broadcasting Corporation. The CBC was to supervise the operations of the private stations and use its own stations to foster a "national spirit." Limited funding left the CBC largely unable to

MORE TO THE STORY

The Dionne Quintuplets

The five girls born to a poor rural francophone couple on 28 May 1934 in Corbeil, Ontario, illustrate the impact of show business on Canadian society. They also reveal the increasing power of the state and medical experts in the lives of Canadian families. From the moment they were born, Annette, Emilie, Yvonne, Cecile, and Marie Dionne were famous. The media immediately focused on what was indeed a remarkable event—the birth and survival of quintuplets. Almost as quickly, the state removed the infants from the care of their parents, who were already raising five older children. Two months after their birth, the Ontario government placed the girls under the control of a local board of guardians and moved the babies to a specially equipped hospital where their upbringing was overseen by Dr Allan Roy Dafoe, who had helped to deliver them. Only after a long battle were the girls restored to their outraged parents.

It was little wonder that everyone wanted custody of the quints. The girls were a major economic asset: they had endorsements of over $1 million, were the subjects of Hollywood films, and became a major tourist attraction—three million curiosity seekers flocked to view them from behind a one-way screen. The girls never recovered from their first traumatic years and felt little bond with their parents or older siblings after their return to the family home.

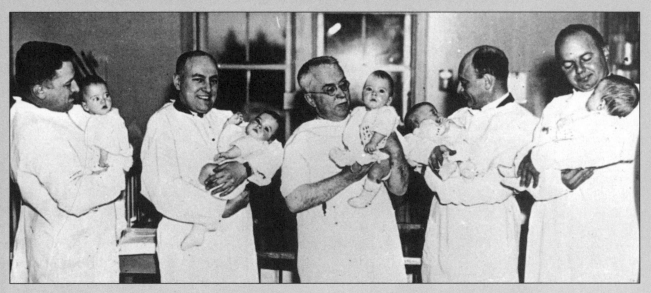

Ontario cabinet minister David Croll (left) poses with Dr A.R. Dafoe (centre) and "the Quints."

Archives of Ontario S801

create programs that would lure audiences away from the American-dominated private stations. Apart from airing American shows, these stations focused on recorded music from New York's Tin Pan Alley and Nashville's Grand Ole Opry.

Canadians also watched American movies. After the First World War, movies had become a favourite pastime for Canadians of all social classes. The average Canadian went to 12 movies a year in 1936, and children in cities watched far more. Most of the movies were made in Hollywood. Marginalization of the Canadian film industry was apparent by the early 1920s as major American studios came to dominate the distribution as well as production of films. By 1930, Famous Players distributed about 90 percent of all feature pictures shown in Canada.

Movies defined the material desires of mass consumer society. The silver screen shaped individual fantasies, established trends in clothing and hairstyles, and encouraged new patterns of leisure and recreation. Canadian politicians recognized that film was a powerful medium. In 1939, the National Film Board was created with a mandate to interpret Canada to Canadians and to the larger world. Quickly swept up in producing wartime propaganda, the NFB thrived under its first commissioner, John Grierson, a British film producer.

Magazines also helped to establish standards of taste and behaviour. In 1925, American magazines outsold their Canadian counterparts in the country by eight to one. Tariff protection in the Bennett years reduced the gap to three to two, but by the end of the Depression, as trade agreements removed tariff protection for made-in-Canada magazines, American magazines regained their former market share.

Interwar governments had little interest in legislating greater Canadian content in the popular media. They focused instead on censoring materials deemed unsuitable, especially in movies. Quebec's censorship board was hardly alone as it snipped not only sexual scenes but also depictions of burglaries, gambling, divorce, suicide, or unpatriotic behaviour. A prime reason for much of this censoriousness was that the new mass culture was supposedly corrupting the younger generation. If radio, movies, and dance halls took up all the time of young people, it was argued, they would soon reject the moral values and religious convictions of their elders.

THE CHRISTIAN CHURCH IN A SECULAR AGE

The Protestant churches, concerned about the worldly focus of modern society, often tried to turn back the tide of modernism. In 1925 the Methodist, Presbyterian, and Congregationalist churches merged into the United Church of Canada in an effort to support the cause of ecumenism and to increase their influence. United Church leaders were motivated by lofty notions of the Christian mission in Canada, but many Presbyterians, particularly in Ontario and the

Maritimes, were more concerned with preserving Scots and Scots-Irish cultural traditions than in pursuing the exalted goals of their ministers. A large minority of Presbyterians rejected the union and maintained the Presbyterian Church as a separate entity.

The founders of the United Church hoped to influence legislators in such areas as temperance, censorship, Sunday observance, and gambling. The prohibition issue illustrates their limited success. The federal government had yielded to distiller pressure after the war to abandon national prohibition, leaving the fate of "demon rum" to the provinces. Soon the prohibition front began to crumble, beginning with a vote by British Columbians in 1920 to create a government monopoly on hard liquor sales, with beer to be sold in grocery stores. By the end of the 1920s, only Prince Edward Island clung to prohibition.

The conservatism of Canadian churches was evident in attitudes to women. Although the majority of active church members were women, they were not welcome in the pulpit. The United Church ordained Canada's first female minister, Lydia Gruchy, in the 1930s, but few women were encouraged to follow in her footsteps. Of course, for some Canadians, the

The campaigns of Protestant churches for prohibition and, later, stringent regulation of liquor sales created a great deal of work for police forces. Here, two Saskatchewan Mounties proudly demonstrate a still that they seized in the 1930s.

Saskatchewan Archives Board/R-A7536

mainline Protestant churches remained too liberal and lacking in fervour. The Pentecostals and the Jehovah's Witnesses were among religious sects that grew in the interwar period that focused almost exclusively on the individual's relationship with God.

The Roman Catholic Church was, if anything, more conservative than the major Protestant denominations, on most issues of individual behaviour. While the Protestant churches cautiously endorsed mechanical contraceptives to limit family size in the 1930s, the Roman Catholic Church would only endorse the use of the unreliable rhythm method. It was also implacably against divorce and all efforts to foster equality for women.

In the Maritimes, the Roman Catholic Church sponsored the Antigonish Movement, a unique combination of cooperatives and adult education to help producers to escape exploitation by middlemen. The movement was led by Father Moses Coady, the founding director of the Extension Department of St Francis Xavier University in Antigonish, Nova Scotia.

Beginning in 1928, cooperatives were established in many communities dependent on farming, fishing, coal mining, and steel production. The movement was particularly successful among Acadians, who responded enthusiastically to Coady's message of community cooperation.

EDUCATION

By the 1920s, parents who could afford to delay their children's entry into the workforce generally encouraged them to complete as many years of secondary schooling as possible. The Ontario government endorsed this goal by extending the school-leaving age to 16 in 1921, a move that other provinces gradually copied. As the value of academic skills was increasingly recognized, high school matriculation became a prerequisite for many jobs. Public schools reinforced gender stereotypes in the workforce, streaming boys who were not academically-minded into trades programs while girls received commercial or domestic training. In keeping within the gender stereotype, elementary education remained primarily in the hands of poorly-paid single women while men predominated among the higher-paid high school teachers.

Quebec francophones, indeed francophones generally, did not share in the trend toward increased schooling. As late as 1926, only 6 percent of Quebec francophones attended school beyond the elementary level. The Catholic Church in the province still resisted pressure to force children to remain in school, its leaders arguing that higher education was needed only for future priests, teachers, church administrators, and other professionals. Since

In July 1939, 105 French-Canadian couples, having received formal instruction in the Church's doctrines regarding married life, were wed en masse in Delormier baseball stadium in Montreal.

Conrad Poirier/Archives Nationales du Québec/P48, S1, P371.1

the labour of older children often kept families out of poverty, many Quebeckers were pleased that schooling was not compulsory. By the early 1940s, reformist elements within the church joined with trade unions and liberal women's organizations in recognizing the need for a better-educated citizenry. In 1943, the Liberal government of Adelard Godbout passed legislation making education compulsory for children from ages 6 to 15.

Outside Quebec, only New Brunswick did not restrict French-language education. Poor educational opportunities and an association of French with poverty caused many francophones outside Quebec to assimilate to the anglophone culture. In 1931, the percentage of Ontarians whose first language was French but who later became primarily English speakers was reported as 22.1 percent. Acadians in the Maritimes were also finding it difficult to resist assimilation in the age of mass consumer culture, which was overwhelmingly delivered in the English language.

Enthusiasm for schooling extended only slowly to the post-secondary sector. With university education generally still confined to an elite minority, provincial governments were reluctant to increase spending on universities. Between 1929 and 1940, Canadian university enrolments increased from 23 418 to 37 225. Women's participation jumped from 16 to 24 percent of all enrolments, but their increase was concentrated in areas stereotyped as women's professions: nursing, household science, library science, and physical and occupational therapy. Women were rarely hired as professors outside the departments offering training in "women's professions."

In the interwar years women seeking educational challenges or career training became an important part of the audience for adult education programs. Several universities established extension programs aimed first at rural areas and eventually at the non-university population of the cities.

Nor was adult education restricted to universities. At the turn of the century, Frontier College had been founded by Alfred Fitzpatrick, a Nova-Scotia-born Presbyterian minister, to provide basic education to workers, particularly immigrants. In the interwar years university students flocked to work sites on the indus-trial frontier to teach people with little other hope of receiving formal education. Trade unions and political parties of the left ran schools in an attempt to counter the information dispensed by the media, which the left viewed as tools of the capitalist class.

LITERATURE AND ART

A better-educated public provided an increasing market for the arts, despite the overweening influence of American popular culture. The creation of the Canadian Authors' Association in 1921 testified to a new sense of national identity among Canadian writers. With 800 members and a French-Canadian branch, it sponsored an annual book week and encouraged sales of the works of Canadian authors.

In Quebec novels written by francophones remained preoccupied with the idealization of the land, but a few writers, led by Ringuet, stressed that the traditional Quebec was disappearing and could not be restored. Social realism marked much of the literature of English Canada. From Irene Baird's *Waste Heritage*, chronicling class strife in British Columbia during the Depression to Sinclair Ross's *As For Me and My House*, with its bleak narrative of Prairie sexual repression and hypocrisy, the writing of this period reflected the critical perspectives that had emerged from the First World War. Hugh MacLennan's 1941 novel *Barometer Rising*, which focused on the Halifax explosion of 1917, was widely acclaimed for its insights into the Canadian colonial mentality.

In the interwar years, many Canadian painters were in revolt against conventional subject matter and styles. Emily Carr's work was enriched by Native art forms and themes. In New Brunswick, Miller Brittain was a leading member of a group of artists who abandoned idyllic landscape art to portray the harsher side of Maritime life. Perhaps the most influential art of the period was the work produced by the Group of Seven. Although originally based in Toronto, members of the group worked across the country. More popular than the new experimental art, their work contributed to a nature-based Canadian nationalism. Over the years, A.Y. Jackson and Arthur Lismer re-

Emily Carr (1871–1945), A Haida Village, c. 1929.

oil on canvas;
82.7 x 60.7 cm
McMichael Canadian Art Collection; Gift of Dr and Mrs Max Stern, Dominion Gallery, Montreal; 1974.18.1

MUSIC AND THEATRE IN THE INTERWAR YEARS

When film and radio reduced the audience for the popular prewar vaudeville shows, many music halls became cinemas. Movies posed a threat to touring theatre troupes, but community theatre groups flourished. In 1933, the first Canadian Drama Festival was held in which community theatre groups competed for prizes in acting, directing, design, and production after a series of regional run-offs. This annual event stimulated amateur theatre across Canada.

Radio and records increased the audience for live bands, and a variety of nightclubs sprang up in Canadian cities. Guy Lombardo and his Royal Canadians and Wilf Carter (who had morphed into Montana Slim) were among the Canadian acts beamed into Canadian homes on American airwaves. In Quebec, Marie Travers, known as La Bolduc, became the province's first successful recording artist. Her songs focused on the realities of daily life. Although the Church regarded her lyrics as naughty, francophone Quebeckers lined up to buy her records. The classical music tradition was strengthened by the creation of schools of music at the University of Toronto, McGill, and Laval. New symphony orchestras in Toronto, Montreal, and Vancouver gave professional classical musicians an outlet for their talents.

mained especially faithful to the Group of Seven's original work, while Lawren Harris's art became more abstract, and Fred Varley, through Emily Carr, discovered Native art.

THE INVENTION OF TRADITION

As Canadians contemplated the rapid changes that had occurred since Confederation, they often viewed the past through a romantic haze, inventing traditions, and imagining golden ages. The National Museum of Canada, created by an Act of Parliament in 1927, and the Historic Sites and Monuments Board, established in 1919, symbolized this new interest in the past. Upon the advice of the board, the government designated national historic sites. Most of the sites recognized by the board in the interwar period—for example, Port Royal and Queenston Heights—related to military and political developments in the nation's past.

With a long recorded history of European settlement, Maritimers and Quebeckers eagerly embraced historical approaches to identity creation. The pre-Confederation pioneers were increasingly depicted as happy folk, living in farming and fishing communities untouched by the materialism of the industrial age. Researchers sought descendants of the folk still living in the "traditional" way, claiming to find in these people the essence of regional identities.

The "cult of the folk" sold well to consumers of culture and tourism in the modern age. In Nova Scotia, many of the symbols of provincial identity—Peggy's Cove, the *Bluenose*, and the Scottish bagpiper—emerged in the interwar years. Historian Ian McKay underlines the contradictions embodied in the cult of the folk: in upholding their premodern, quaint, therapeutic otherness, he argues, it was simultaneously drawing the folk into the commercial and political webs of modern society.[8]

In Quebec, clerical-nationalists continued to cultivate their particular vision of the folk: pious, rural, and sedentary. Henri Bourassa's pan-Canadian cleri-

Frank Carmichael (1890–1945), Northern Tundra, *1931.*

oil on canvas;
76.4 x 91.6 cm
McMichael Canadian Art Collection, Gift of Col R.S. McLaughlin; 1968.7.14

cal-nationalist vision for francophones gave way in the aftermath of conscription and discriminatory language legislation in anglophone provinces to a focus on Quebec alone as the homeland of francophone Catholic culture. Abbe Lionel Groulx emerged as the new leader of clerical-nationalism, founding a newspaper, *L'Action Française*, and inspiring a new youth group, Association Catholique de la Jeunesse. Groulx firmly fixed his gaze on a romanticized past, insisting that only the preservation of the French language and the strictest adherence to the dictates of the Church hierarchy could protect Quebec from being absorbed into the North American secular, materialist culture that was seducing French Canadians.

Despite clerical efforts to defend rural life, Quebec was becoming more urban. Progressive nationalists, ignoring Groulx, embraced the more liberal teachings of their church, and formed the École Sociale Populaire to study and propagate ways in which Catholicism and the new social order could be reconciled.

SPORTS IN THE MODERN AGE

In the interwar years, interest in professional sporting events increased among all social classes. Hockey's claim to be the national sport was cemented, as indoor stadiums, artificial ice, and the expansion of the National Hockey League to American cities gave the game new prominence. The Montreal Forum opened in 1924, followed by Maple Leaf Gardens in 1931. After the Ottawa Senators folded in 1934, the only Canadian teams in the NHL were the Montreal Canadiens and the Toronto Maple Leafs. Still, all four American teams in the league had a majority of Canadian-born players.

Baseball remained a popular participant sport, as did softball, the latter regarded as an acceptable sport for women. There was also a semi-professional baseball league in Quebec, and both Montreal and Toronto had teams in the International League, headquartered in the United States.

Although the sports world was still largely a male preserve, Canadian women fared well in international competitions. Fanny Rosenfeld stands out among women athletes of the period, having won the silver medal in the 100-metre dash at the 1928 Amsterdam Olympics. She had also been lead runner for the gold-medal relay team and was Canada's leading woman broad jumper and discus thrower. In basketball, the Edmonton Grads pursued a remarkable career through the interwar period. When they disbanded in 1941, they left a record that has yet to be equalled, winning 93 percent of their games and 49 out of a possible 51 domestic titles.

SERVICE ORGANIZATIONS

Spurred by increased urbanization and a shorter work week, voluntary organizations proliferated in the interwar years. Churches, fraternal associations, and the militia continued to provide men with opportunities to bond on the basis of religious, ethnic, or patriotic inclinations. Community-service organizations such as the Rotary Club, Kiwanis, Gyros, and the Elks, which had no ethnic or religious affiliation, raised funds for local facilities such as libraries, swimming pools, community halls, and parks, participated in parades to boost community spirit, and supported community groups such as the Boy Scouts.

Women remained active in both mixed-sex and women's church groups and secular voluntary organizations. In 1919 women who had university degrees founded the Canadian Federation of University Women and involved themselves in both social reform and charitable activities. In 1930, the Canadian Federation of Business and Professional Women's Clubs was organized to convince business leaders that better training and fairer treatment for women were ultimately in the interests of business. In Ontario and Nova Scotia, black women established clubs that organized cultural programs, studied African-Canadian history, and worked for better local race relations.

One of Canada's outstanding sports stories was supplied by a female basketball team, the Edmonton Grads, students and alumnae of that city's Commercial High School. Beginning in 1915 and continuing for 25 years, the Grads put together an unrivalled record of wins over domestic and international opponents.

Provincial Archives of Alberta/A-11.428

CONCLUSION

Interwar Canada was a society in transition. Older ways rubbed uneasily against the new mass culture and its commercially oriented values. Self-styled experts on raising children, urban planners promoting suburban living, and birth-control advocates challenged conventional perspectives, while churches led the defence of traditional values. Attracted by American movies, records, magazines, and radio programs, Canadians struggled to establish their own national culture, but it was an uphill battle. The threat of American cultural dominance was balanced by identities that were regional, local, and political. In the 1930s, hard times exposed class and gender differences that had been easier to minimize in the better economic times of the 1920s. With the outbreak of the Second World War in September 1939, Canada's fragile unity would again be tested.

A Historiographical Debate

The Farming Community

The farming community of the interwar years was anything but unified. While some farmers identified with the working class, others viewed themselves as middle-class business people. Historians also take opposing sides on the issue. In the classic work *The National Policy and the Wheat Economy* by economist Vernon Fowke, Prairie farmers are presented as a uniform group oppressed by national tariff and railway policies.[9] C.B. Macpherson's study of the Social Credit movement in Alberta, *Democracy in Alberta*, presents a similar though less sympathetic view of the farmers of that province. Macpherson portrays farmers as "independent commodity producers," who were, in fact, dependent upon market forces over which they exercised little control. Still, as individuals who owned modest farmsteads and employed few labourers, their self-image prevented identification with the cause of working people.[10]

Other historians present a more diversified farming community and question the notion of "independent commodity producers." David McGinnis indicates that off-farm labour was required by most farmers in the interwar period to make ends meet; they might view themselves as independent commodity producers, but this perspective was largely an illusion.[11]

Jeffery Taylor argues that false views of farmers' true position were not accidental but largely the creation of agricultural colleges and other institutions in Canadian society that shaped the view that farmers held of themselves.[12] The Manitoba Agricultural College, for example, rejected the older language of agrarianism in which farmers joined workers as a producing class exploited by greedy monopolists. Instead, its professors encouraged farmers to see themselves as scientific managers of a producing property who could, if they behaved intelligently, make market forces work to their advantage.

John Herd Thompson notes that many farmers employed labourers on a seasonal basis and that they often proved to be very harsh employers.[13] In a study that focuses on farm labourers, Cecilia Danysk details the increasing stratification of the farm community in the interwar period. As the costs of farming soared, only the farmers who developed large holdings could survive. The lifestyles of these farmers were quite different from those of farmers on small homesteads or from farm labourers. While farm labourers could once have looked to eventually owning a farm, the number of permanent farm labourers was on the rise in the interwar period because the cost of getting into farming had become prohibitive.[14]

NOTES

1 Cited in Veronica Strong-Boag, *The New Day Recalled: Lives of Girls and Women in English Canada, 1919–1939* (Toronto: Copp Clark Pitman, 1988) 13.

2 Kenneth Coates, *Canada's Colonies: A History of the Yukon and Northwest Territories* (Toronto: Lorimer, 1985) 100.

3 Andrée Lévesque, "Deviants Anonymous: Single Mothers at the Hôpital de la Misericorde in Montreal, 1929–1939,"*Historical Papers/Communications Historiques* (1984) 178.

4 Suzanne Morton, *Ideal Surroundings: Domestic Life in a Working-Class Suburb in the 1920s* (Toronto: University of Toronto Press, 1995) 41–42.

5 Cited in Katherine Arnup, *Education for Motherhood: Advice for Mothers in Twentieth-Century Canada* (Toronto: University of Toronto Press, 1994) 92.

6 Joy Parr, *The Gender of Breadwinners: Women, Men, and Change in Two Industrial Towns 1880–1960* (Toronto: University of Toronto Press, 1990) 186.

7 Cited in Meg Luxton, *More than a Labour of Love: Three Generations of Women's Work in the Home* (Toronto: Women's Press, 1980) 29.

8 Ian McKay, "Helen Creighton and the Politics of Antimodernism," in *Myth and Milieu: Atlantic Language and Culture, 1918–1939*, ed. Gwendolyn Davies (Fredericton: Acadiensis Press, 1993) 16.

9 Vernon C. Fowke, *The National Policy and the Wheat Economy* (Toronto: University of Toronto Press, 1957).

10 C.B. Macpherson, *Democracy in Alberta: Social Credit and the Party System* (Toronto: University of Toronto Press, 1962).

11 David McGinnis, "Farm Labour in Transition: Occupational Structure and Economic Dependency in Alberta, 1921–1951," in *The Settlement of the West*, ed. Howard Palmer (Calgary: University of Calgary Press, 1977): 174–86.

12 Jeffery Taylor, *Fashioning Farmers: Ideology, Agriculture Knowledge and the Manitoba Farm Movement, 1890–1925* (Regina: Canadian Plains Research Centre, 1994).

13 John Herd Thompson, "Bringing in the Sheaves: The Harvest Excursionists, 1890–1929," *Canadian Historical Review* 59.4 (Dec. 1978): 467-89.

14 Cecilia Danysk, *Hired Hands: Labour and the Development of Prairie Agriculture, 1880–1930* (Toronto: McClelland and Stewart, 1995).

SELECTED READING

On immigrant experiences, see Dirk Hoerder, *Immigrant Lives in Canada* (Montreal: McGill-Queen's University Press, 1999) and Donald H. Avery, *Reluctant Host: Canada's Response to Immigrant Workers, 1896–1994* (Toronto: Viking, 1994). On Native peoples generally, the texts by Miller, Ray, and Dickason are useful. A particularly compelling provincial history is Mary-Ellen Kelm, *Colonizing Bodies: Aboriginal Healing in British Columbia, 1900–1950* (Vancouver: UBC Press, 1998).

For a longer-term context on interwar family life, see Cynthia Comacchio, *The Infinite Bonds of Family: Domesticity in Canada, 1850–1940* (Toronto: University of Toronto Press, 1999). The interwar period for women has a rich literature that includes Veronica Strong-Boag, *The New Day Recalled: Lives of Girls and Women in English Canada, 1919–1939* (Toronto: Copp Clark Pitman, 1988); Andrée Lévesque, *Making and Breaking the Rules: Women in Quebec, 1919–1939* (Toronto: McClelland and Stewart, 1994); Denyse Baillargeon, *Making Do: Women, Family and Home in Montreal During the Great Depression* (Waterloo, ON: Wilfrid Laurier University Press, 1999); Joan Sangster, *Regulating Girls and Women: Sexuality, Family, and the Law in Ontario, 1920–1960* (Toronto: Oxford University Press, 2001) and *Earning Respect: The Lives of Working Women in Small-Town Ontario, 1920–1960* (Toronto: University of Toronto Press, 1995); Suzanne Morton, *Ideal Surroundings: Domestic Life in a Working-Class Suburb in the 1920s* (Toronto: University of Toronto Press, 1995); Frances Swyripa, *Wedded to the Cause: Ukrainian Canadian Women and Ethnic Identity, 1891–1991* (Toronto: University of Toronto Press, 1993); Ruth A. Frager, *Sweatshop Strife: Class, Ethnicity, and Gender in the Jewish Labour Movement of Toronto, 1900–1939* (Toronto: University of Toronto Press, 1992); Karen Dubinsky, *Improper Advances: Rape and Heterosexual Conflict in Ontario, 1889–1929* (Chicago: University of

Chicago Press, 1993); Margaret Little, *"No Car, No Radio, No Liquor Permit": The Moral Regulation of Single Mothers in Ontario, 1920–1997* (Toronto: Oxford University Press, 1998); and Cynthia R. Comacchio, *"Nations Are Built of Babies": Saving Ontario's Mothers and Children 1900–1940* (Montreal: McGill-Queen's University Press, 1993).

Varying experiences of men and women in the work force and home are discussed in Mary Kinnear, *In Subordination: Professional Women, 1870–1970* (Montreal: McGill-Queen's University Press, 1995); Joy Parr, *The Gender of Breadwinners: Women, Men, and Change in Two Industrial Towns, 1880–1950* (Toronto: University of Toronto Press, 1990); and Thomas Dunk, *It's a Working Man's Town: Male Working-Class Culture in Northwestern Ontario* (Montreal: McGill-Queen's University Press, 1991). On housing, see Peter Ward, *A History of Domestic Space: Privacy and the Canadian Home* (Vancouver: UBC Press, 1999); Michael Doucet and John Weaver, *Housing the North American City* (Montreal: McGill-Queen's University Press, 1991); Richard Harris, *Unplanned Suburbs: Toronto's American Tragedy 1900 to 1950* (Baltimore: John Hopkins University Press, 1996); and Jill Wade, *Houses for All: The Struggle for Social Housing in Vancouver, 1919–1950* (Vancouver: UBC Press, 1994).

On social developments in the Atlantic provinces, see the chapters on the 1920s and 1930s in E.R. Forbes and D.A. Muise, eds., *The Atlantic Provinces in Confederation* (Toronto and Fredericton: University of Toronto and Acadiensis Press, 1993); Edward MacDonald, *If You're Stronghearted: Prince Edward Island in the Twentieth Century* (Charlottetown: Museum and Heritage Foundation, 2000); and Ian McKay, *The Quest of the Folk: Antimodernism and Cultural Selection in Twentieth-Century Nova Scotia* (Montreal: McGill-Queen's University Press, 1994). On British Columbia, see Patricia E. Roy, *A History of British Columbia: Selected Readings* (Toronto: Copp Clark Pitman, 1989) and R.W. Sandwell, ed., *Beyond City Limits: Rural History in British Columbia* (Vancouver: University of British Columbia Press, 1999). On the Prairies, social histories of the period include Cecilia Danysk, *Hired Hands: Labour and the Development of Prairie Agriculture, 1880–1930* (Toronto: McClelland and Stewart, 1995); Jeffery Taylor, *Fashioning Farmers: Ideology, Agricultural Knowledge and the Manitoba Farm Movement, 1890-1925* (Regina: Canadian Plains Research Centre, 1994); and Kenneth M. Sylvester, *The Limits of Rural Capitalism: Family, Culture, and Markets in Montcalm, Manitoba, 1870–1940* (Toronto: University of Toronto Press, 2000). Quebec's social and cultural evolution is detailed in Paul-André Linteau, René Durocher, and Jean-Claude Robert, *Quebec Since 1930* (Toronto: Lorimer, 1983) and Susan Mann Trofimenkoff, *Action Française: French-Canadian Nationalism in Quebec in the 1920s* (Toronto: University of Toronto Press, 1975). The Canadian North is analyzed in Kenneth Coates, *Canada's Colonies: A History of the Yukon and Northwest Territories* (Toronto: Lorimer, 1985); William R. Morrison, *True North: The Yukon and the Northwest Territories* (Toronto: Oxford University Press, 1998); and Morris Zaslow, *The Northward Expansion of Canada, 1914–1967* (Toronto: McClelland and Stewart, 1988).

On the media, see Mary Vipond, *The Mass Media in Canada* (Toronto: Lorimer, 1989) and *Listening In: The First Decade of Canadian Broadcasting* (Montreal: McGill-Queen's University Press, 1992). On the Dionne quintuplets, see the articles in *Journal of Canadian Studies* 29.4 (Winter 1995). Rival views of the survival of the social gospel in this period are found in David B. Marshall, *Secularizing the Faith: Canadian Protestant Clergy and the Crisis of Belief, 1850–1940* (Toronto: University of Toronto Press, 1992) and Nancy Christie and Michael Gauvreau, *A Full-Orbed Christianity. The Protestant Churches and Social Welfare in Canada, 1900–1940* (Montreal: McGill-Queen's University Press, 1996). Robert A. Campbell, *Sit Down and Drink: Regulating Vancouver's Beer Parlours 1925-1954* (Toronto: University of Toronto Press, 2000), and Angus McLaren and Arlene Tigar McLaren, *The Bedroom and the State: The Changing Practices and Politics of Contraception and Abortion in Canada, 1890-1980*, 2nd ed. (Toronto: Oxford University Press, 1997) treat issues that caused endless difficulties for churches.

On higher education, see Paul Axelrod, *Making a Middle Class: Student Life in English Canada during the Thirties* (Montreal: McGill-Queen's University Press, 1990). On art history, consult Ann Davis, *The Logic of Ecstasy: Canadian Mystical Painting, 1920–1940* (Toronto: University of Toronto Press, 1992). On sports, see Bruce Kidd, *The Struggle for Canadian Sport* (Toronto: University of Toronto Press, 1996) and Colin Howell, *Blood, Sweat, and Cheers: Sport and the Making of Modern Canada* (Toronto: University of Toronto Press, 2001).

 **WEBLINKS**

REX V SYLIBOY
http://library.usask.ca/native/cnlc/vol04/430.html

Read the full text of the 1928 decision that found eighteenth century treaties with the Mi'kmaq in the Maritimes to be invalid.

DIONNE QUINTUPLETS
www.city.north-bay.on.ca/quints/digitize/dqdpe.htm

This site contains digitized historical information about the Dionne Quintuplets, including a timeline, digital collections, and information about the museums and libraries owning original artifacts.

THE DISCOVERY OF INSULIN
http://web.idirect.com/~discover/

The mission of this site is to preserve and promote the history behind one of the most important medical discoveries of our time—the discovery of insulin. Brief biographies of the scientists, a scrapbook of old newspaper clippings, pictures, and a voice recording, and several interesting links are featured.

IMPORTANT MOMENTS IN THE HISTORY OF CANADIAN VISUAL CULTURE, 1919–1945
www.arts.ouc.bc.ca/finearts/1918_45.html

This site includes a detailed timeline describing significant exhibitions, important architectural achievements, and the founding of various art clubs, schools, and societies in Canada.

THE CANADIAN BROADCASTING CORPORATION
http://cbc.radio-canada.ca/htmen/4_1.htm

View major milestones of the CBC's history at this site.

THE NATIONAL FILM BOARD OF CANADA
www.nfb.ca/E/index.html

Read about the creation and early years of the National Film Board.

CHAPTER 22

Canada's World War, 1939–1945

On 16 July 1945, scientists and other observers gathered in bunkers near Los Alamos, New Mexico, one of the locations where work had been carried out on the top-secret Manhattan project, to view the first explosion of an atomic bomb. Overwhelmed by the bomb's frightening power, Dr J. Robert Oppenheimer, who headed the project's team of international scientists, recalled the words from the sacred Hindu text, the *Bhagavad Gita*: "I am become death, Destroyer of Worlds."

Rich in uranium, a necessary ingredient of atomic energy, Canada played a major role in the Manhattan project. Early in the Second World War, a team of British, European, and Canadian scientists under the umbrella of the National Research Council had begun working on aspects of the atomic energy puzzle in laboratories based in Montreal. The Canadian government made uranium resources available for American atomic research, and a Combined Policy Committee consisting of three Americans, two British, and one Canadian—Minister of Munitions and Supply C.D. Howe—was established to oversee the project. In September 1945, Canada's first nuclear facility was operating at Chalk River, but Oppenheimer's team in the United States had already made history. Two of their bombs had been dropped on Japan in August 1945.

CANADA'S WAR

Canadians had hoped that the Great War would be the war to end all wars, but it was not to be. Under Nazi leader Adolf Hitler, who came to power in 1933, Germany adopted a fascist program to reconstitute its "homeland," which included destroying other nations and cultures. In 1938, Germany annexed Austria and then gobbled up Czechoslovakia. Italy's fascist leader, Benito Mussolini, taking his cue from Hitler, annexed Albania in the spring of 1938. In August Hitler signed a non-aggression pact with the Soviet Union under Joseph Stalin, freeing the way for the depredation of their mutual neighbour, Poland. The Japanese, who had long been running roughshod over China, saw an opportunity to further extend their influence in the Pacific. On 3 September, two days after Hitler had invaded Poland, Great Britain and France decided to stop his mad grasp for power. The Second World War had begun.

Canada joined the war against the Nazis on 10 September. Even more than the First World War, this war was an easy one for most Canadians to see as a struggle between good and evil. It was also a difficult war to avoid. With submarines, fast surface warships, and long-range aircraft capable of rapidly spanning great distances, all nations were becoming vulnerable. Indeed, the Japanese bombing of Pearl Harbor in Hawaii on 7 December 1941 jarred the United States out of its isolationist stance and into the war.

As in 1914, the Canadian government invoked the War Measures Act to ensure that it had all the powers it needed to fight an all-out war. Also, as in 1914, the cabinet was initially slow to mobilize the nation's military and economic might. This earned King harsh criticism from Premier Hepburn of Ontario, among others, but it helped to reassure Quebeckers that Great Britain would not dictate Canada's wartime policy. Early in 1939 King had promised that his government would not impose conscription for overseas service in the event of war. It was a pledge that he would repeat in two elections held in the early months of the conflict.

After war was declared, Premier Maurice Duplessis called a snap election and made Canada's wartime involvement the major campaign issue. Quebec's federal ministers threatened to resign if Duplessis won. Fearing that without its Quebec contingent, the cabinet might renege on King's anti-conscription promise, Quebeckers elected the provincial Liberal Party, led by Adélard Godbout. Hepburn's stinging criticisms of Ottawa's war effort prompted King to call a national election for March 1940. Defending voluntary enlistment, the Liberals won convincingly, taking over 51 percent of the popular vote and 184 of 245 seats.

King was shrewd or just plain lucky to have gone to the polls when he did. In April 1940, Hitler's forces struck down Denmark and Norway and then conducted a *blitzkrieg*, literally a lightning war, through the Netherlands, Belgium, and France. The surrender of France early in June and the evacuation of the British Expeditionary Force from Dunkirk raised fears that Great Britain might also be defeated. Canada was forced to consider a much larger contribution to the war effort than King had originally envisaged. The government promptly enacted the National Resources Mobilization Act (NRMA), which provided for the conscription of soldiers for home defence and state control of economic resources.

As the war dragged on, pressures from army commanders, cabinet ministers, opposition members, and many Canadians caused King to re-evaluate his position on conscription. He called a national plebiscite on 27 April 1942, which asked Canadians whether the

The provincial wing of the Bloc populaire was led by André Laurendeau, a young journalist shown here speaking in Montreal before the 1944 election.

Centre de recherche Lionel Groulx/P2-B302

government should be released from its pledge not to impose conscription for overseas service. While 64 percent of Canadians voted "yes," at least 85 percent of Quebec francophones demanded that King honour his original promise. The threat of conscription sparked the formation of the Bloc populaire canadien, a new nationalist political party in Quebec, and returned the ardently anti-conscriptionist Union nationale to power in a 1944 provincial election.

King made every effort to avoid conscription, including firing pro-conscription Defence Minister J.C. Ralston. In November 1944, Ralston was replaced by General A.G.L. McNaughton, King's choice in 1939 to command the army overseas. When McNaughton failed to secure the necessary voluntary enlistments, the government passed an order-in-council in late November 1944 allowing the armed forces to dispatch 16 000 NRMA men to overseas duty. This decision was not always well received. In Terrace, British Columbia, NRMA men seized an anti-tank gun to defend themselves against officers who were trying to send them overseas; in London, Ontario, 600 men of the Oxford Rifles went absent without leave; and in Drummond, Quebec, 2000 civilians attacked RCMP and military police sent to hunt down deserters. These events went undisclosed in the media, whose war reporting was subject to censorship. Eventually, only 13 000 NRMA men were sent overseas. As in the First World War, conscription added to feelings of betrayal among French Canadians without doing much to help the war effort.

French-Canadian enlistment in the Second World War was significantly higher than in the First World War. Nineteen percent of the volunteers for overseas service were French Canadians, compared to 12 percent in the earlier war. Overall Canadian participation in the war was impressive: nearly 1.1 million men and women joined the forces, including 100 000 in the NRMA, from a population estimated at 11.5 million in 1941. Most served in the army, although about 250 000 joined the Royal Canadian Air Force, and nearly 100 000 joined the Royal Canadian Navy. Over 42 000 died in service, including over 17 000 members of the RCAF. Another 54 000 were wounded or injured.[1] The Canadian losses paled in comparison to the overall tally. The total dead and wounded in the Second World War reached a staggering 55 million. Many were civilians, killed by bombs, invading armies, or concentration camp personnel. The USSR alone lost 20 million people; and the Nazis slaughtered 6 million Jews.

Although only men participated in combat, 50 000 women served in the Canadian armed forces. Women began volunteering their services as soon as war was declared. The military establishment accepted them because of manpower shortages, creating separate female auxiliaries in each armed services branch. In 1941, the Canadian Women's Army Corps (CWAC), and the Women's Division of the RCAF were established, and the Women's Royal Canadian Naval Service (WRENS) the following year.

Women's divisions were kept separate and subordinate to men's. Initially slotted into jobs as nurses, clerks, secretaries, drivers, stretcher bearers, and cooks, women gradually took on less traditional roles

A member of the WRENS operating direction-finding equipment in New Brunswick, 1945.

National Archives of Canada/PA-142540

such as mechanics, truck drivers, technicians, and spies. If their usefulness was unquestioned, their morality was. Rumours spread about their lax morals, especially in the CWAC, where, allegedly, women had a high incidence of "illegitimate" children and venereal disease. Men were encouraged to vent their sexual energies; women, clearly, were not. Nor did women receive the same pay and benefits as men, even when they performed the same job. When the war ended, all three women's services were abandoned.

DESCENT INTO WAR

With control of French air bases, Hitler's Luftwaffe conducted a destructive blitz on London and other British cities beginning in the summer of 1940. At the same time the Nazis launched a devastating but inde-

cisive U-boat campaign against Allied shipping in the Atlantic. Turning his army on the Soviet Union in June 1941, Hitler forced that country into the Allies' embrace. Meanwhile, Japan destroyed the Far East fleets of both the United States and Britain, defeated the British and Australians in Malaya and Singapore, and captured the American army in the Philippines.

It is in this context that two incidents in the war, one in Hong Kong and the other in British Columbia, must be understood. In December 1941, two battalions of Canadian troops, totalling nearly 2000 men, participated in a questionable effort to defend Hong Kong, a British colony, against the Japanese. Almost 1300 Canadians died and another 1700 were taken prisoner. Mistreatment in prison camps in Hong Kong and as forced labour in Japanese mines killed nearly 300 before the end of the war. At the time and later, there was much criticism of political and military

Japanese-Canadian internees packing to leave for camps in the interior of British Columbia.

Tak Toyota/National Archives of Canada/C-046350

leaders for allowing Canadians to get involved in such a hopeless campaign.

In February 1942, President Franklin Roosevelt announced that, by reason of military necessity, persons of Japanese ancestry were to be removed from the Pacific Coast of the United States. A few days later, the Canadian government also decided to remove nearly 22 000 people of Japanese ancestry—nearly three-quarters of whom had been born in Canada or were naturalized Canadians—from coastal British Columbia. Their homes, businesses, and personal property were auctioned to the highest bidder in 1943. About 700 men who had expressed support for Japan or had protested vigorously against Ottawa's repressive policies were interned in a prisoner-of-war camp in Angler, Ontario. Women, children, the old, and the sick were moved to abandoned mining towns in the British Columbia interior. Able-bodied men were sent to work in road camps in the province. Families who wished to remain together were shipped to sugar beet farms in Alberta and Manitoba. Among the children removed from their homes in 1942 were David Suzuki, the future scientist, and Joy Kogawa, whose 1981 novel *Obasan* dealt with her family's internment.

Beginning in May 1945, all Japanese Canadians were forced to choose between deportation to war-devastated Japan or relocation east of the Rockies. Nearly 4000 people were shipped to Japan between May and December 1946. Other than suspicions about a few individuals, Ottawa had no evidence of disloyalty of Japanese Canadians and no one was ever charged with treason. Yet Mackenzie King's government suspended the civil liberties of the entire Japanese-Canadian population until 1949. Wartime hysteria coupled with the long-standing racist attitudes of British Columbians toward Japanese Canadians made a more humane policy unlikely. Only in the 1980s did the Canadian government officially acknowledge its mistreatment of Japanese Canadians during the war and provide compensation to survivors.

THE WAR ON LAND

In Europe, the Allies had difficulty bringing the Axis powers to heel. Although the German army was stalled in its drive to Moscow, Allied efforts to create a front in France ended in dismal failure. An ill-conceived landing on French beaches at Dieppe in August 1942 left 907 Canadians dead and almost 2000 prisoners. In November 1942, good news finally came. At El Alamein, the British Eighth Army broke through the German and Italian lines, forcing General Erwin Rommel's Afrika Korps into retreat. In December, the Soviets soundly defeated the enormous Nazi forces outside the gates of Stalingrad. The war had reached a turning point.

By 1943, the Canadian Army Overseas had expanded to a full field army, the 1st Canadian Army, with two corps, three infantry, and two armoured (tank) divisions, and an array of additional formations and support units. Most of the army stood guard in Britain until the liberation of Western Europe began in the summer of 1943 with the Allied invasion of Sicily and then mainland Italy. The 1st Canadian Infantry Division took part in these operations, which became increasingly difficult as the Allies pushed up the boot of Italy against fortified lines the Germans had established in the mountainous terrain. During December 1943, in appalling conditions amid winter rains, the 1st Division suffered 2300 casualties fighting for the town of Ortona, on the Adriatic coast. In early 1944, Canadians played a key role in breaking through the strongly defended approaches to Rome.

Meanwhile, there had been a massive build-up of forces in Britain for the invasion of France at Normandy, on 6 June 1944. Among the initial assault force was the 3rd Canadian Infantry Division. Over 100 Royal Canadian Navy warships helped to clear mines, keep enemy warships and submarines at bay, land troops, and provide gunfire support to the soldiers struggling ashore. The huge air armada that forced back the Luftwaffe and saturated the German defences with bombs included many squadrons of the Royal Canadian Air Force. During the following weeks, the 1st Canadian Army, under the command of Lieutenant-General H.D.G. Crerar, crossed to France. The push inland from the beaches was a slow-moving, brutal campaign, with the Germans concentrating their strongest armoured forces in the British–Canadian sector. By the last week in August, two German armies had been destroyed, but the

Canadians paid heavily, with 5000 dead and over 13 000 wounded.

After the defeat of the main German forces in Normandy, the 1st Canadian Army moved up the coast of the English Channel, clearing strongholds. The culmination of these operations was a bitter five-week battle in October and early November that opened the Belgian port of Antwerp. The port was essential to keeping supplies moving to the Allied armies in northwest Europe, but was opened at the price of over 6000 Canadian casualties.

THE WAR AT SEA

The significant role that the Royal Canadian Navy played in the Normandy assault was only a small part of that service's work. By 1944, it provided most of the escort forces for the north Atlantic convoys that sustained Britain and the invasion force. The RCN also helped to protect British waters against the German U-boat force, joined in offensive strikes at German naval bases in Norway, and contributed escort ships to convoys that supplied the Russian forces through the Arctic port of Murmansk.

When the war began, there were only six destroyers, a few small minesweepers, and about 3500 personnel in the RCN. The fall of France forced the government to accelerate and expand programs to build corvettes and other anti-submarine vessels. The entry of the United States into the war brought U-boats streaming into Canadian and American coastal waters in January 1942. Because the Americans were short of anti-submarine vessels, the RCN maintained its Newfoundland force. Although the RCN was generally effective in protecting Canadian waters, it had less success in the Gulf of St Lawrence, where deep waters provided advantage to the U-boats. Two small warships and 19 merchant ships were sunk in the gulf and in the lower reaches of the St Lawrence River. Among them was the

Map 22.1
The European Front, 1944–45—
Italian Campaign and Northwest Europe Campaign.

Sydney–Port-aux-Basques ferry, which went down in October 1942 with the loss of 237 lives. In all, 12 000 Canadians in the Merchant Marine perished when their ships were sunk.

Measures to improve the RCN's escort organization gradually came into effect. The British turned over additional destroyers to the Canadians to reinforce the corvettes. In April 1943, Rear-Admiral L.W. Murray, RCN, at Halifax, became commander-in-chief of the Canadian Northwest Atlantic theatre, the only Canadian to command an Allied theatre of war. Soon thereafter, the Allies allocated to the RCAF bombers that could effectively provide support to convoys across the whole breadth of the Atlantic. The benchmarks of their success were the thousands of ships and tens of millions of tonnes of cargo that safely reached port under Canadian protection.

THE WAR IN THE AIR

Soon after war was declared, Canada agreed to play host to the British Commonwealth Air Training Plan (BCATP), which trained allied pilots and aircrews for the war effort. Canada had ample space beyond the range of enemy aircraft and was close to vital American aircraft industries. At its height, the BCATP employed over 100 000 ground crew at 231 sites across the country. The program trained almost half the total aircrews supplied by Great Britain and the Commonwealth for the war effort.

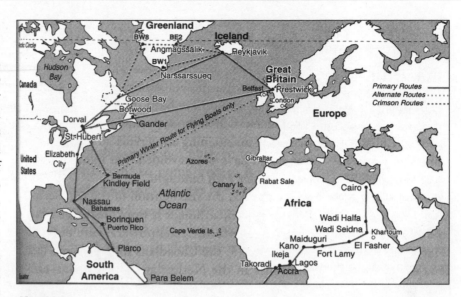

Map 22.2
Principal Routes Flown by Ferry Command, 1940–1945.

Another successful joint venture was Ferry Command, which delivered planes built in North America to Britain. Based in Montreal, Ferry Command flew nearly 10 000 aircraft from enlarged or newly created air bases such as Gander and Goose Bay to Great Britain. Over 500 people lost their lives in Ferry Command, but it was, in the words of historian Carl A. Christie, "one of the most spectacular achievements of the war."[2]

Far more controversial was the Allied bomber offensive against Germany. From its bases in northeastern England, the Royal Air Force's Bomber Command targeted German cities in an effort to disrupt industrial production and reduce German morale. Because the attacks were often on city centres or residential districts rather than industrial areas, critics claim that the campaign was neither efficient nor effective and that it was immoral to boot. Allied bombing, it seems, spurred the Nazis to greater productivity, just as the bombing of London in 1940 made the British determined to carry on. Only in the final months of 1944 did German production of war materiel begin a rapid decline. Allied bombing forced the Germans to employ over half a million workers in repairing the bomb damage and almost a million men to operate the flak defences around their cities, personnel that could otherwise have been used in factories or on the battlefield.

The bombing offensive was pressed in spite of the high casualty rates among the bomber crews themselves. In 1942, only one airman in three survived a 30-mission tour of duty. By 1944, the success rate had improved due to better training and new aircraft, but critics argued that the money and manpower committed to Bomber Command could have been better spent elsewhere—for example, on the understaffed and poorly equipped convoy service or in maintaining army ranks so that conscription could have been avoided. But fighting wars is always easier in hindsight.

THE BUSINESS OF WAR

The experience of the Great War had demonstrated the need for tighter controls on a wartime economy. The system of planning, rationing, taxation, and wage and price controls imposed by the federal government early in the Second World War prevented the devastating inflation that had seriously disrupted the economy in the earlier conflict. Following a decade of increasing intervention in the economy, the government was better equipped in 1939 to coordinate a major war effort. Economic policy was

MORE TO THE STORY

War Artists

During the First World War, Lord Beaverbrook had commissioned artists to record Canada's war effort. It was the first large official commission for Canadian artists. The well-established, such as Maurice Cullen, and promising unknowns, such as David Milne, were hired for the task. So, too, were four men who would later become associated with the Group of Seven: A.Y. Jackson, Frederick Varley, Arthur Lismer, and Franz Johnston.

In 1943, the war art program was reactivated, and artists were commissioned into the three divisions of the armed services. For the first time, female artists were included to document women's contribution: Molly Lamb eventually received a lieutenant's commission in the CWAC; Pegi Nicol MacLeod painted many aspects of the women's forces; and Paraskeva Clark and Alma Duncan recorded women's work in the war industries. Artists captured on canvas some of the worst horrors of the war. Charles Goldhamer painted RCAF flyers at a plastic surgery hospital in England; Aba Bayefsky and Alex Colville had the difficult job of documenting the Belsen concentration camp. Confronted with a larger-than-life situation, Canadian war artists produced some of their finest, if most disturbing, work during the war.

Alex Colville, Tragic Landscape, *1945.*

Canadian War Museum

centralized and orchestrated to achieve desired ends. From April 1940, the Department of Munitions and Supply, under its energetic minister C. D. Howe, was given sweeping powers. With the help of members of Canada's business community who were seconded to Ottawa, Howe expanded existing industries, created new ones, and focused the total resources of the country on the successful prosecution of the war.

The federal government's role in the war economy was pervasive. Its 28 Crown corporations produced everything from synthetic rubber to airplanes. In 1943, Ottawa made the Canadian Wheat Board the exclusive international sales agent for the nation's precious wheat crop. Under the auspices of the Wartime Prices and Trade Board, an army of controllers, regulators, and troubleshooters fanned out across the country allocating output, rationing consumer purchases, and cutting through red tape. The federal civil service more than doubled, from 46 000 in 1939 to 116 000 in 1945. Ottawa would never return to its prewar size and sleepy pace.

In the First World War, federal spending represented 10–15 percent of the GNP. By 1944, Ottawa's expenditures accounted for nearly 40 percent of GNP. Extensive taxation of both corporate and personal incomes, the sale of Victory Bonds, and the careful regulation of the money supply through the Bank of Canada enabled Canadians to finance their war without massive foreign borrowing.

Despite the impressive record, Canada's wartime economy encountered problems. Britain imposed exchange controls, including restrictions on the convertibility of sterling into dollars. As Britain's wartime purchases in Canada escalated and Canada came to depend on the United States for war supplies, Canadians faced the prospect of having a huge surplus of sterling and a crippling deficit in American currency. Ottawa responded with stringent exchange controls, monitored by a Foreign Exchange Control Board. Imports were permitted only under licence. By 1940, there were restrictions on travel to the United States and an embargo on importation of many commodities from countries outside the sterling bloc. Still, the Canadian trade deficit with the United States mounted alarmingly.

Canada could do little to solve the problem. During the interwar years, Canadian and American industry had become so integrated that virtually everything Canada produced included American components. Parts for Canadian automobile factories, coal for Stelco's furnaces, and machinery for mining companies all came from the United States. The problem was eventually solved when the United States entered the war in 1941. By that time, North America already functioned as a unit in defence production, and the problem for Canada became too much, rather than too little, American exchange.

The Second World War tended to reinforce Canadian economic geography. Wartime production was initially expanded in existing industries, and virtually all plants built and operated by the government were located in the industrial heartland of the country. There were some notable exceptions. Winnipeg became a centre for munitions and communications industries. Adjacent to Alberta's oil and natural gas reserves, Calgary was the obvious site for nitrogen and high-octane fuel production. Vancouver sprouted a Boeing aircraft factory and a modern shipbuilding industry. New military bases quickened the economic pace in communities from Summerside to Esquimalt, while such projects as Ferry Command brought development to the northern territories and Newfoundland. Nevertheless, the bias in favour of central Canada was blatant in decisions relating to shipbuilding and repair. The ice-free ports of Halifax and Saint John were treated as secondary to Montreal, which was ice-bound during the winter and whose narrow access was infested with German U-boats. The failure to develop repair facilities in the Maritime provinces both consolidated regional disparity and impeded the effectiveness of the Canadian navy.

Traditional attitudes toward labour were challenged during the war. By 1941, the labour pool had dried up, and a shortage of workers loomed. In 1942, the government began a campaign to recruit women into the paid labour force. Before the war, only 21 percent of women between the ages of 15 and 65 worked outside the home, and of these, less than 13 percent were married. At first only unmarried women were recruited, but by 1943 even married women with children were strongly encouraged to do their patriotic duty. In Quebec and Ontario, a government-sponsored day-care system offered support for a handful of mothers. The number of women in the workforce increased from 638 000 in 1939 to over a million by 1944, some 255 000 of whom were engaged in what were defined as war in-

Day care was a problem for mothers who took jobs in the paid labour force. This Mi'kmaq woman brought her child with her to the Pictou shipyards in 1943.

National Archives of Canada/PA-116154

dustries. When the war ended, the prewar sex-typing of jobs resumed.

CONTROLLING THE ENEMY WITHIN

As in the First World War, the Canadian government took measures against enemy aliens and others perceived as potential troublemakers. The Defence of Canada Regulations included sweeping powers to curb freedom of expression and arrest anyone who might threaten public safety or recruitment efforts. Besides the Japanese Canadians, several other groups also experienced the heavy hand of government control.

Among the first targets were members of political organizations associated with enemy nations. The RCMP, in charge of public security, arrested 358 known supporters of Nazi organizations and sent them to camps at Petawawa and Kananaskis. Another sweep after the fall of France and the entrance of Italy into the war netted over 850 more. Canada's official Nazi party was banned and its leaders were interned.

On 4 July 1940, the government passed an order-in-council declaring the Jehovah's Witnesses illegal. The order made 7000 Canadian Jehovah's Witnesses subject to surveillance and arrest, while their meeting halls and property were handed over to the Custodian of Enemy Property. The treatment of the Jehovah's Witnesses, like the evacuation of the Japanese, indicates how prewar prejudices are acted upon in wartime contexts. Because the Witnesses criticized the Roman Catholic Church, Cardinal Villeneuve loathed them and appealed to Justice Minister Ernest Lapointe to curb their activities. Lapointe, eager to maintain the Catholic hierarchy's support for the war effort, promptly had the ban issued and enforced. It lasted until 1943.

Even refugees were treated with suspicion. Canada accepted only about 3500 refugees from enemy countries between 1939 and 1945. Quebec's opposition to Jewish immigration contributed to Ottawa's minimal compliance with Britain's request to admit German and Austrian refugees, many of them Jews. Jewish refugees were initially put in prison camps with German prisoners of war. Although they were eventually housed separately, many remained under guard in rough internment camps. Not even reports, widespread by 1943, of Nazi extermination camps changed official or public sentiment.

The treatment of refugees became a major concern of the Canadian National Council on Refugees (CNCR), whose president was Senator Cairine Wilson. Under pressure from the CNCR, the government passed an order-in-council in December 1943 releasing enemy alien refugees from internment and granting them one-year permits to stay in Canada. The CNCR tried to find work for these unfortunate people, many of whom eventually made major contributions to their adopted country as scientists, university professors, and artists.

Anti-war dissidents also came under surveillance. Since the Communist Party spoke out against the war, the party was outlawed in June 1940, and 133 of its leaders were arrested. Most Communist internees were released after Hitler invaded the Soviet Union in 1941. Apart from political dissidents, an estimated 12 000 Canadians, mainly Quakers, Mennonites, and Brethren in Christ, declared themselves conscientious objectors. Many were required to work in rural camps or factories, on pain of being interned in labour camps.

No internees were deported after the war. Although the Canadian government planned to deport the Japanese evacuees, the legality of the policy was soon called into question. By the time the courts handed down their decision, Canadians and much of the world were beginning to adopt a new attitude toward cultural minorities and refugee populations. The increasingly popular concept of human rights was reflected in the human rights codes banning discrimination in hiring and accommodation passed by the governments of Ontario and Saskatchewan in 1945.

THE WELFARE STATE

Almost as soon as the war started, Canadians began to worry about the nation's postwar agenda. Government planning of the economy during wartime had resulted in a higher standard of living for ordinary people. Why, they asked, could governments not continue such a role in peacetime?

biography

Tommy Douglas

Born in Scotland in 1904, Tommy Douglas immigrated with his family to Winnipeg in 1919, where he witnessed the General Strike. After serving as a printer's apprentice, he decided, in 1924, to enter the Baptist ministry. He attended Brandon College for six years where he was exposed to social gospel teachings. Following his ordination in 1930, he moved to Weyburn, Saskatchewan, where he witnessed first-hand the suffering of farmers during the Depression. He soon became deeply involved in politics, establishing a local association of the Independent Labour Party in 1931 and attending the founding convention of the CCF.

In 1935, he was elected to the House of Commons and soon developed a reputation as a skillful and witty debater. He resigned his seat to lead the CCF to victory in Saskatchewan in 1944 and remained premier of the province until he resigned in 1961 to become leader of the federal New Democratic Party. Under his leadership, Saskatchewan earned a reputation for innovative and efficient government. Indeed, Douglas pioneered many of the social welfare programs that would eventually be implemented in other provinces of Canada.

Tommy Douglas.
National Archives of Canada/C-036220

The two major parties appeared at first to ignore such concerns, but they would soon change their tunes. In early 1942, Arthur Meighen, recently re-elected as the federal Conservative leader, sought a parliamentary seat in a by-election in the supposedly safe Conservative riding of York South. King, who feared Meighen's pro-conscription campaign, decided not to run a Liberal candidate, leaving the CCF to challenge Meighen. Throughout the by-election, Meighen talked of the need to impose conscription; the previously unknown CCF candidate, Joseph Noseworthy, spoke of the need to plan employment and insurance programs for the postwar era. The majority of constituents liked his message. Meighen's defeat and subsequent resignation as Conservative leader had repercussions throughout the political system.

Reform-minded Conservatives argued that the country could not be allowed to fall to the socialists. In 1942, the Conservatives chose John Bracken, the Liberal-Progressive premier of Manitoba, as national leader. The convention delegates also adopted a platform that went beyond Bennett's New Deal to embrace universal pensions, medical insurance, equality for women, and union rights. At Bracken's insistence, the party changed its name to "Progressive Conservative" in the hope of shedding its reactionary image.

Despite attempts to steal its thunder, the CCF advance continued. In 1943, the party captured 34 of the 89 seats in the Ontario legislature and became the official opposition. Provincial Conservative leader George Drew was obliged to promise a comprehensive social security program in an attempt to blunt the

CCF advance. Meanwhile, in Saskatchewan, the CCF under the leadership of the dynamic Tommy Douglas won the 1944 provincial election. Douglas capitalized on the popular policies of the CCF and the widespread disenchantment among Saskatchewan farmers with Ottawa's price controls on grain. The shift in public opinion toward the left was not unique to Canada. In Great Britain, voters elected a Labour government in 1945 to preside over postwar reconstruction. A report published in Britain in 1942 by Sir William Beveridge, a distinguished social planner, argued for a government-sponsored social security system from the cradle to the grave.

Ever vigilant of trends that might undermine his power, King decided the time had come to implement major reforms. The government had introduced a national unemployment insurance program in 1940, but it was a cautious initiative. An insurance plan rather than a welfare scheme, the program required earners and employers to make contributions to a fund from which employees could draw if they were laid off work. As it was initially designed, unemployment insurance covered only a small proportion of the labour force, and even that unequally. Some exemptions, such as farm labourers, were testimony to the influence of special interest groups. Other exemptions reflected patriarchal notions of women's place in the economy. Married women were excluded from coverage as were domestic workers. Benefits were tied to wages and weeks of continuous work, provisions that discriminated against low-wage and part-time workers.

Many Canadians felt that Ottawa's plans to stabilize the economy should go beyond insurance policies for a small proportion of the labour force. Their perspective was supported in a report prepared for government by a committee but generally known by the name of its principal author, Leonard Marsh. A McGill economist, Marsh brought his CCF sensibilities and the insights of the Beveridge Report to the problems of reconstruction. The Marsh Report argued that full employment should be a major goal of the postwar industrial state; to that end, the government and the whole society should play a role in ensuring that people found work, remained healthy, and were properly fed, housed, and educated. Although the cost of programs such as universal old-age pensions and family allowances was high, Marsh argued that such spending constituted "investments in morale and health, in greater family stability,... in human productive efficiency."

Conservative critics were appalled by such thinking. Charlotte Whitton, one of Canada's leading social workers, claimed that Marsh's schemes would make Canadians dependent on the state, destroy initiative, and encourage the feeble-minded to procreate. King's finance minister, J.L. Ilsley, wondered where the government would get the money to implement such programs. Proponents of the new social programs responded that maintaining the high taxes of the war period would be the key to financing peacetime social schemes.

Provincial cooperation would be necessary because the courts had ruled that provinces had jurisdiction over social policy. To proceed with national unemployment insurance, the federal government had been obliged to secure an amendment to the BNA Act. The King government had established a Royal Commission on Dominion-Provincial Relations in 1937 to explore ways of reforming the constitution to permit the federal government to intervene directly in the field of social welfare. When the proposals of the royal commission were unveiled in 1940, they were strongly opposed by the premiers of Ontario, Alberta, and British Columbia, who refused to concede their taxation powers so that the federal government could establish a national policy to create full employment and social services.

Most Canadians were unconcerned about constitutional niceties. They wanted reform. At a meeting of the National Liberal Federation in September 1943, the party followed the CCF and the Progressive Conservatives in adopting a platform supporting social security. King moved quickly to establish three new departments—Reconstruction, National Health and Welfare, and Veterans Affairs—to preside over the government's postwar planning. His administration introduced family allowance legislation, by which mothers of children under 16 received a monthly stipend. The first cheques, amounting to between five and eight dollars per child, were sent out in 1945.

In the last two years of the war, the government focused on policies that would help cushion the shock of returning to peace. It passed a National Housing Act to generate construction, established an Industrial Development Board to help companies retool for peacetime production, created a Veterans' Charter to provide benefits for those who served in the war, and developed policies to help primary producers survive the transition to peacetime markets. In all, the government appropriated $3.12 billion for reconstruction, an incredible sum even today. These policies went some distance in helping the Liberals to ward off the CCF threat and to win the 1945 election.

LABOUR AND THE STATE

Another reason for the Liberal government's success in fending off socialism was its change of heart on trade union rights. King's initial wartime response to labour alienated the unions. The Industrial Disputes Investigation Act was vastly extended under the War Measures Act to allow the government to use conciliation to avoid strikes. If managers fired workers attempting to form unions, the government looked the other way.

Under wartime conditions, workers were no longer forced to submit silently to the dictates of government and hostile managers. Recognizing that labour shortages prevented employers from firing them for union activities, workers joined industrial and craft unions in droves. They used strikes and work slowdowns to combat companies that refused to accept the unions formed by the democratic votes of their workers. In 1943, there were over 400 strikes involving more than 200 000 workers.

Eager to keep war industries functioning smoothly and his political popularity high, King felt compelled to act. In February 1944, Order-in-Council PC 1003 ushered in a new era of labour policy in Canada. The order guaranteed workers the right to organize and to bargain collectively, established procedures for the certification and compulsory recognition of trade unions, defined unfair labour

practices, and created an administrative apparatus to enforce the order.

The move to accommodate labour and a massive anti-socialist campaign by business interests reduced support for left-wing parties. In 1945, the Ontario Conservatives decisively won a provincial election that reduced the CCF to third place in the legislature. On 11 June, the CCF won only 28 of 245 seats in the federal election, with 15 percent of the popular vote. Although they received a reduced parliamentary majority, the Liberals were given a mandate to govern the country in peacetime. King had proven his ability to stay in the middle of the political road, no matter what direction that road took.

THE NEW WORLD ORDER

King also walked down a new road in international affairs. During the Second World War, Canada moved closer to the Americans, economically, politically, and militarily. The distinguished political economist Harold Innis would later claim that Canada moved

When British prime minister Winston Churchill (right) and American president Franklin Roosevelt (left) met in Quebec City in 1943, Mackenzie King (centre) was on hand for a photo opportunity.

National Archives of Canada/C-31186

from "colony to nation to colony" in its efforts to maintain good relations with the superpower next door. In other words Canada had achieved independence from Britain only to lose it to the United States.

As Hitler's armies erased national borders with ease, King had recognized Canada's dependence on the United States for its defence. President Roosevelt, in turn, feared that Canada's combatant role made the whole North American continent vulnerable to the fascist dictators. In August 1940, Roosevelt invited King to meet him at Ogdensburg, New York. Their meeting established a Permanent Joint Board on Defence to prepare for mutual assistance in defence of North America.

The United States also considered Canadian interests in framing its wartime economic policies. In 1941, the American Congress empowered the president to order the manufacture of defence materiel for friendly governments, whether for sale, loan, or lease. In March 1941, a Lend-Lease arrangement was concluded between the United States and Britain. Initially, Lend-Lease, which made available $7 billion for the purchase of equipment and supplies in the United States, excluded Canada. This "oversight" was rectified at another meeting between Roosevelt and King at Hyde Park, New York, in April 1941. The Americans would increase purchases in Canada and would charge many of the components bought by Canada in the United States to the British account, thereby easing the balance of payment difficulties.

King told Parliament that the Hyde Park declaration "involves nothing less than a common plan for the economic defence of the western hemisphere," and "the enduring foundation of a new world order."[3] Valuable wartime arrangements as they were, Ogdensburg and Hyde Park symbolized an intimate Canadian-American relationship that was becoming a dominant fact of life for Canada in peacetime as well.

Once the United States officially entered the war, Canada figured less prominently in American calculations. Roosevelt resisted Canadian efforts to have a military mission in Washington to learn more about American military strategy. The United States also protested loudly when Canada quietly supported the successful efforts of Charles de Gaulle's Free French forces to seize St Pierre and Miquelon from the Vichy government. King suspected that Vichy—the pro-German government in that part of France unoccupied by the Nazis—was using the islands as a base from which to report to the Germans on Allied convoy movements.

Canadians developed what became known as the "functional principle" in wartime planning. When Canadian interests were at stake, they would insist on having a voice in determining international policy. So, for example, Canadians won a seat on the Allied Combined Food Board, which allocated food resources for the war effort, but had less success in gaining influence in organizations established to manage international relations in peacetime.

As the war dragged on, the American presence loomed ever larger. Roosevelt had arranged for American bases in Newfoundland, which Canada had agreed to protect for the duration of the war. When the Japanese occupied the Aleutian Islands in the summer of 1942, the United States, with Canada's permission, built an overland route through Canada to Alaska. The Alaska Highway was a marvel of American efficiency. Between March and October 1942, 11 000 engineers and workers carved a highway from Alaska, a total of over 2000 kilometres, at a cost of nearly $150 million. To ensure oil supplies, the Americans built the Canol pipeline from Whitehorse in the Yukon to Norman Wells in the Northwest Territories. The Americans also developed northern staging routes of rough airstrips to transport bombers and fighter planes to Europe and the USSR. By 1943, 33 000 Americans worked in the Canadian North.

Concerned to establish sovereignty over Canada's North, the government offered to pay the Americans in full for all permanent military installations that they built in Canada. Canada ultimately paid $123.5 million for 28 airfields, 56 weather stations, and other facilities. In 1943, the Canadian government upgraded its diplomatic presence in Washington, and the Canadian legation took on embassy status.

Cooperation more than conflict also characterized Canadian-American relations after the war. In the spring of 1945, meetings were held in San Francisco to establish the United Nations, an organization designed to replace war with negotiation as a vehicle for settling international disputes. Although Canadian diplomats had their own ideas about the economic structures that should govern the postwar world, they went along with American plans for the International Monetary Fund and the World Bank.

The prospects for a peaceful postwar world were grim. When the war in Europe ended, the leaders of the Soviet Union, Great Britain, and the United States met in Potsdam, Germany, in July 1945 to discuss how to manage the peace process. The conference revealed the growing tension between the Soviet Union and the West, tension that ultimately led to the partition of Germany and to the Cold War that was to characterize international relations for decades to come.

DEMOBILIZATION AND POSTWAR RECONSTRUCTION

Early in 1945, the Canadians in Italy joined their comrades in the Netherlands for the final campaign. Overrun from all sides, Hitler committed suicide and the Germans surrendered on 5 May. The war in the Pacific came to an abrupt halt following the dropping of atomic bombs on Hiroshima and Nagasaki on 6 and 9 August. On 14 August, the Japanese surrendered.

The Canadian government was determined to avoid the mistakes that created unrest following the Great War. Planning for postwar reconstruction began early in the war. In January 1940, the government created the General Advisory Committee on Demobilization and Reconstruction under Great War veteran H.F. McDonald. A new Department of Veterans Affairs was established in 1944 to help soldiers make a successful transition to civilian life. The Veterans' Charter of 1944 offered veterans more generous benefits than those available in 1919, including gratuities totalling $752.3 million to help them get reestablished in civilian life.

In 1942, the government passed an act requiring companies to rehire veterans in their former jobs under conditions "not less favourable" than if they had never enlisted. Nearly 200 000 veterans benefited from this injunction. About 150 000 veterans had their entry into the labour market postponed for several years by the provision that helped them to attend uni-

versity or college. Others took up land offered by the Veterans' Land Act and settled into farming.

While it was crucial to plan for the end of the war, victory in Europe brought the predictable problem of getting the forces home. Repatriation went faster than expected, but there were too few ships for too many soldiers. The worst disorder took place in Aldershot, in England, in July 1945, when Canadian forces erupted in a two-night riot. By the end of 1945, only half of the nearly 350 000 Canadians in Europe were home. A division of 25 000 troops and 11 air force squadrons was committed to the occupation of Germany. When few Canadians volunteered for this tour of duty, Canada informed the Allied Command that it would pull its forces out of Germany by the spring of 1946.

Most ships arriving from Europe docked at Halifax. The city did its best, under difficult circumstances, to welcome "the boys" home, but not before VE day (victory in Europe) celebrations blew the city apart. As news of the German surrender spread, Haligonians closed their offices, stores, and restaurants, while throngs of service people and civilians celebrated in downtown streets. Seamen were free to come and go, but there was nothing for them to do. Liquor stores were looted, a tram trashed, and chaos reigned in the streets of Halifax. Neither the naval patrols nor the city police were strong enough to keep the peace, and Rear-Admiral Murray was at a loss as to how to restore order among his men. The two-day riot caused $5 million worth of damage and left civilians and military authorities pointing fingers at each other for causing the fracas. In the inquiry following the riot, 41 soldiers, 34 sailors, and 19 airmen were among the 211 indicted for offences. Murray was relieved of his command because of the affair, and the navy took most of the blame for the damage.

Among those returning on the big ships from Europe were 44 886 war brides (and a few war husbands) and their children, numbering nearly 22 000. The vast majority of war brides were British, although Canadian soldiers also married Dutch, Belgian, French, Danish, Italian, and German women. Once in Canada, the war brides faced a difficult adjustment to new families, new communities, and a new country. Some, such as Betty Oliphant, divorced their husbands but ended up staying in Canada anyway. Oliphant became the founder of the National Ballet School.

As in the First World War, the re-establishment of family life was difficult for many veterans. The number of marriages and births increased after the war but so, too, did divorces. For many veterans, it was impossible to pick up the threads of civilian life. Some women resented being pushed out of civilian jobs and being encouraged to stay at home. Others responded enthusiastically to state and business propaganda to establish homes in the suburbs and raise their children in one of the world's luckiest democracies.

Much of the responsibility for establishing Canada's postwar economy on a peacetime footing fell on the shoulders of C.D. Howe, who was appointed Minister for Reconstruction in 1944. Howe reduced rationing, converted war industries to peacetime purposes, and re-established Canada's export sales. Canada's merchant marine was scrapped, and most Crown corporations were closed down or sold. To meet 15 years of pent-up civilian demand, companies were given tax breaks to get their factories producing consumer goods.

The loss of overseas markets was in part compensated for by sales made possible under the Marshall Plan. When it looked as if communism might sweep war-torn European countries, the United States agreed in 1947 to a generous aid program, named after American Secretary of State George C. Marshall who proposed it, to help them restore their capitalist economies. Funds were initially tied to purchases in the United States but soon Canada was included and sold a billion dollars' worth of its products overseas by 1950. Instead of the postwar slump predicted by many economists, Canada experienced growth, its GNP rising from $11.8 billion in 1945 to $18.4 billion in 1950.

Canada was not spared the wave of strikes that followed the First World War. In 1945 and 1946, proportionately more time was lost in strike activity than in 1919. A major strike was conducted at the Ford Motor plant in Windsor in 1945, and a national steel strike shut down plants in Sault Ste Marie, Hamilton, and Sydney in 1946. The results of arbitration at Ford and the willingness of federal and provincial governments to enshrine the principles of PC 1003 in postwar legislation helped to prevent the stand-off between labour and capital that occurred after the Great War.

CONCLUSION

Canada was vastly changed by the Second World War. With a stronger federal state and the beginnings of a social welfare system, the nation was in a position to avoid the misery experienced during the Depression. The booming economy seemed to hold its own in a peacetime context. In comparison to the devastated cities and countrysides of Europe and Asia, Canada was an untouched utopia and the destination of choice for many European refugees. Canadians were also assuming a new place among the nations of the world. Although not a major power like Great Britain or the United States, Canada began to embrace the term "middle power," a small nation no more, and one with an expanding role to play in international affairs. It was also a country in the process of creating its own identity independent from the British Commonwealth. In 1946, Secretary of State Paul Martin introduced a bill, passed the next year, to establish a distinct Canadian citizenship, since up to that point Canadians still carried British passports. Clearly issues of Canadian identity were on the agenda as Canada entered the atomic age.

Origins of the Welfare State

Social scientists generally agree on the various factors contributing to the evolution of the welfare state in Canada, but the relative weight of these factors is in dispute. In identifying the groups pressing for the creation of federal social insurance programs, scholars list the following: the unemployed; business groups; municipalities and provinces; liberal churches; and elements within the state bureaucracy. They also note the support of key politicians. Is there evidence to suggest that one group more than another left its mark on the kind of welfare state that emerged in Canada? The contours of the debate can be understood by looking at how scholars explain the emergence of an unemployment insurance program in 1940.

Alvin Finkel has suggested that pressure from big business was largely responsible for producing an unemployment insurance program.[4] According to Finkel, business people felt that unemployment insurance would help prevent public finances from being besieged by unplanned expenditures when unemployment rose. Business leaders wanted the scale of payments to be modest so that people would be encouraged to find work. They also wanted the cost to be borne by working people themselves rather than by companies or the government. To a considerable degree their views prevailed in the program that was introduced in 1940.

James Struthers argues that this scenario is too one-sided, suggesting that popular pressures, both from the unemployed and from liberal-minded citizens, generally played a role in securing unemployment insurance.[5] Some argue that the business community, though divided, was largely opposed to unemployment insurance. According to sociologist Carl Cuneo, unemployment insurance was an example of the state implementing reforms to save capitalism from itself. By providing a social safety net for workers, the state helped to prevent widespread social unrest that might lead to revolution and the total destruction of the market economy.[6]

Still others stress the role of specific politicians. R.B. Bennett's need to appear reform-minded before the 1935 election is often mentioned.[7] Since Bennett had promised unemployment insurance as early as 1931, it is not surprising that it emerged as an item in his "New Deal" package of reforms in 1935. J.L. Granatstein attributes Mackenzie King's reintroduction of unemployment insurance in 1940 to his desire to plan for expected postwar unemployment.[8] Struthers also sees the war as the major catalyst for the welfare state. "When King finally pushed for speedy passage of the Unemployment Insurance Act, it was out of his own fear of post-war unrest," Struthers argues. "No one expected that veterans or unemployed war workers would queue up meekly in front of local relief offices. In the final analysis it was war and not the depression which destroyed the poor-law heritage."[9]

Most scholars concede that the state bureaucracy shaped the character of Canada's unemployment insurance program. While admitting that a variety of forces caused politicians to accept the need for some form of social insurance, political scientist Leslie Pal suggests that a state-centred, rather than society-centred, perspective explains the character of the program itself. In its formative years, he argues, unemployment insurance became grounded in administrative logic when it came to determining contributions, benefits, duration, and coverage. Whereas employee groups tended to view unemployment insurance in terms of rights, and employers saw it in terms of costs and the effect on the labour supply, officials were preoccupied with administrative feasibility, actuarial soundness, and strict insurance principles. This led to a similarity of views between employers and officials, particularly on the abuse question, but this similarity was coincidental in that the official view was arrived at independently. It was not the result of "pressure."[10]

When examined from the perspective of gender, there is also a remarkable coincidence of views between the state bureaucrats, businessmen, and union leaders on the treatment of female workers under the unemployment insurance program.[11] Indeed, as Ruth Pierson has pointed out, neither progressives nor conservatives, labour nor management, organized to defend the right of married women workers to receive fair compensation when they lost jobs.

NOTES

1 Enlistment and casualty figures vary widely. The figures cited in this chapter are taken from Desmond Morton and J.L. Granatstein, *Victory 1945: Canadians from War to Peace* (Toronto: HarperCollins, 1995) 19.

2 Carl A. Christie, *Ocean Bridge: The History of RAF Ferry Command* (Toronto: University of Toronto Press, 1995) 3.

3 J.L. Granatstein and Norman Hillmer, *For Better or for Worse: Canada and the United States to the 1990s* (Toronto: Copp Clark Pitman, 1991) 147.

4 Alvin Finkel, *Business and Social Reform in the Thirties* (Toronto: Lorimer, 1979).

5 James Struthers, *No Fault of Their Own: Unemployment and the Canadian Welfare State, 1914–1941* (Toronto: University of Toronto Press, 1981).

6 Carl J. Cuneo, "State, Class and Reserve Labour: The Case of the 1941 Canadian Unemployment Insurance Act," *Canadian Review of Sociology and Anthropology* 16 (May 1979): 147–70.

7 See, for example, Larry A. Glassford, *Reaction and Reform: The Politics of the Conservative Party under R.B. Bennett, 1927–1938* (Toronto: University of Toronto Press, 1992).

8 J.L. Granatstein, *Canada's War: The Politics of the Mackenzie King Government, 1939–1945* (Toronto: Oxford University Press, 1975).

9 Struthers, No Fault of Their Own, 213.

10 Leslie Pal, *State, Class and Bureaucracy: Canadian Unemployment Insurance and Public Policy* (Montreal: McGill-Queen's University Press, 1975) 109.

11 Ruth Roach Pierson, "Gender and the Unemployment Insurance Debate in Canada, 1934–1940," *Labour/Le Travail* 25 (Spring 1990): 77–103.

SELECTED READING

On Canada's wartime experience, see Norman Hillmer, Robert Bothwell, Roger Sarty, and Claude Beauregard, eds., *A Country of Limitations: Canada and the World in 1939* (Ottawa: Canadian Committee for the History of the Second World War, 1996); J.L. Granatstein and Desmond Morton, *A Nation Forged in Fire: Canadians in the Second World War* (Toronto: Lester and Orpen Dennys, 1989); J.L. Granatstein and Peter Neary, eds., *The Good Fight: Canadians and World War II* (Toronto: Copp Clark, 1995); W.A.B. Douglas, ed., *The RCN in Retrospect, 1910–1968* (Vancouver: UBC Press, 1982), and *The Creation of a National Airforce* (Toronto: University of Toronto Press, 1968); Brereton Greenhous et al., *The Crucible of War, 1939–1945* (Toronto: University of Toronto Press, 1994); Marc Milner, *North Atlantic Run: The Royal Canadian Navy and the Battle for the Convoys* (Toronto: University of Toronto Press, 1982); Roger Sarty, *The Maritime Defence of Canada* (Toronto: Canadian Institute for Strategic Studies, 1997); C.P. Stacey, *Arms, Men and Governments: The War Policies of Canada, 1939–1945* (Ottawa: Queen's Printer, 1970); G.W.L. Nicholson, *The Canadians in Italy, 1943–1945* (Ottawa: Queen's Printer, 1957); Terry Copp and Bill McAndrew, *Battle Exhaustion: Soldiers and Psychiatrists in the Canadian Army, 1939–1945* (Montreal: McGill-Queen's University Press, 1990); Daniel Dancocks, *The D-Day Dodgers: The Canadians in Italy, 1943–1945* (Toronto: McClelland and Stewart, 1992); J.L Granatstein, *The Generals: The Canadian Army's Senior Commanders in the Second World War* (Don Mills, ON: Stoddart, 1993); Carl A. Christie, *Ocean Bridge: The History of RAF Ferry Command* (Toronto: University of Toronto Press, 1995); and Donald Avery, *The Science of War: Scientists and Allied Military Technology During the Second World War* (Toronto: University of Toronto Press, 1998). On women's participation at home and abroad, see Ruth Roach Pierson, *"They're Still Women After All": The Second World War and Canadian Womanhood* (Toronto: McClelland and Stewart, 1986).

On political developments at home during the war, see J.W. Pickersgill and D.F. Foster, *The Mackenzie King Record*, vols. 1 and 2 (Toronto: University of Toronto Press, 1960, 1968); Reg Whitaker, *The Government Party* (Toronto: University of Toronto Press, 1977); Douglas Owram, *The Government Generation: Canadian Intellectuals and the State, 1900–1945* (Toronto: University of Toronto Press, 1986); J.L. Granatstein, *Canada's War: The Politics of the Mackenzie King*

Government, 1939–1945 (Toronto: Oxford University Press, 1974); Robert Bothwell and William Kilbourn, *C.D. Howe* (Toronto: McClelland and Stewart, 1979); Lita-Rose Betcherman, *Ernest Lapointe, Mackenzie King's Great Quebec Lieutenant* (University of Toronto Press, 2001); Leonard Marsh, *Report on Social Security for Canada, 1943* (Toronto: University of Toronto Press, 1945); Gary Evans, *John Grierson and the National Film Board, 1939–1945* (Toronto: University of Toronto Press, 1984); and E.R. Forbes, "Consolidating Disparity: The Maritimes and the Industrialization of Canada during the Second World War," *Acadiensis* 15.2 (Spring 1986). For a discussion of labour policy during the war, see Bryan Palmer, *Canadian Working-Class History: Character of Class Struggle* (Toronto: McClelland and Stewart, 1986); Irving Abella, *Nationalism, Communism and Canadian Labour* (Toronto: University of Toronto Press, 1973); and Laurel Sefton MacDowell, "The Formation of the Canadian Industrial Relations System during World War II," *Labour/Le Travailleur* 3 (1978).

The treatment of minorities is the subject of Norman Hillmer, Bohdan Kordan, and Lubomyr Luciuk, eds., *On Guard for Thee: War, Ethnicity, and the Canadian State, 1939–1945* (Ottawa; Canadian Committee for the History of the Second World War, 1988); Irving Abella and Harold Troper, *None Is Too Many* (Toronto: Lester and Orpen Dennys, 1982); Daniel Dancocks, *In Enemy Hands: Canada's Prisoners of War, 1939–1945* (Edmonton: Hurtig, 1983); Marjorie Wrong, *The Dragon and the Maple Leaf: Chinese Canadians in World War II* (Toronto: Dundurn Press, 1994); and Tom Socknat, *Witness Against War: Pacificism in Canada, 1900–1945* (Toronto: University of Toronto Press, 1987).

Security and intelligence are the subject of John Bryden, *Best-Kept Secret: Canadian Secret Intelligence in the Second World War* (Toronto: Lester, 1993); Gregory S. Kealey and Reg Whitaker, eds., *RCMP Security Bulletins: The War Series*, 2 vols. (St John's: Canadian Committee on Labour History 1989, 1993); and Larry Hannant, *The Infernal Machine: Investigating the Loyalties of Canada's Citizens* (Toronto: University of Toronto Press, 1995).

On Newfoundland, see Peter Neary, *Newfoundland and the North Atlantic World, 1929–1949* (Montreal: McGill-Queen's University Press, 1988), and the useful synthesis by James K. Hiller, "Newfoundland Confronts Canada, 1867–1949," in *The Atlantic Provinces in Confederation*, ed. E.R. Forbes and D.A. Muise (Toronto: University of Toronto Press, 1993).

On the Japanese evacuation, see Ken Adachi, *The Enemy that Never Was* (Toronto: McClelland and Stewart, 1976); Ann Gomer Sunahara, *The Politics of Racism* (Toronto: Lorimer, 1981); W. Peter Ward, *White Canada Forever: Popular Attitudes and Public Policy toward Orientals in British Columbia* (Montreal: McGill-Queen's University Press, 1978); and Pat Roy et al., *Mutual Hostages: Canadians and Japanese During the Second World War* (Toronto: University of Toronto Press, 1989).

On foreign policy during the war, see James Eayrs, *In Defence of Canada*, vol. 2: *Appeasement and Rearmament* (Toronto: University of Toronto Press, 1965); Stanley Dziuban, *Military Relations Between Canada and the United States, 1939–1945* (Washington: Office of the Chief of Military History, Dept. of the Army, 1959); and J.L. Granatstein and Norman Hillmer, *For Better or For Worse: Canada and the United States to the 1990s* (Toronto: Copp Clark Pitman, 1991) and *Empire to Umpire: Canada and the World to the 1990s* (Toronto: Copp Clark Longman, 1994).

War's end is described in Desmond Morton and J.L. Granatstein, *Victory 1945: Canadians from War to Peace* (Toronto: HarperCollins, 1995). On the Halifax riots of 1945, see Graham Metson, *An East Coast Port: Halifax at War, 1939–1945* (Scarborough, ON: McGraw-Hill Ryerson, 1981); and Stanley Redman, *Open Gangway: The (Real) Story of the Halifax Navy Riot* (Hantsport, NS: Lancelot Press, 1981). The experience of the war brides is described in Joyce Hibbert, *The War Brides* (Toronto: Peter Martin Associates, 1978).

Farley Mowat has produced two evocative memoirs of his wartime experience: *The Regiment* (Toronto: McClelland and Stewart, 1973) and *And No Birds Sang* (Toronto: McClelland and Stewart, 1979). See also Barry Broadfoot, *The Veterans' Years* (Toronto: Douglas and McIntyre, 1985); Murray Peden, *A Thousand Shall Fall* (Stittsville, ON: Canada's Wings, 1979); and E.L.M. Burns, *General Mud* (Toronto: Clarke Irwin, 1970). Heather Robertson offers a fine sampling of Canada's war art in *A Terrible Beauty: The Art of Canada at War* (Toronto: Lorimer, 1977).

 **WEBLINKS**

CANADA AND WORLD WAR II
http://canadaonline.about.com/cs/canadaww2/index.htm

This site includes an extensive list of links to Canadian history resources on the Second World War, including Canadian units, secret agents, battles, Books of Remembrance, and the home front.

JAPANESE CANADIAN INTERNMENT
www.lib.washington.edu/subject/Canada/internment/intro.html

This site briefly describes the internment of Japanese Canadians during World War II and includes an extensive bibliography.

TOMMY DOUGLAS
www.weyburnreview.com/tommydouglas/welcome.html

A brief biography, photos, and essays describing Douglas' accomplishments are presented here.

INTERNATIONAL RELATIONS
www.canschool.org/relation/history/5world-e.asp

This site describes the history of Canadian international relations, from pre-confederation through the Trudeau years. The challenges of post-war reconstruction after 1945 are discussed in a global context.

VETERANS AFFAIRS CANADA
www.vac-acc.gc.ca

This site provides information on programs and services for veterans, Canadian Forces members, qualified civilians and their families, and all Canadians who desire to learn more about the sacrifices that helped to build Canada.

PART VI SUMMARY

CANADIANS BORN BY THE TURN OF THE TWENTIETH century had experienced the First World War, a revolution in communications and values, the Great Depression, and the Second World War. In 1945, they lived with the realization that atomic energy could destroy all life on the planet. Would the new technology be harnessed for war or peace? Canadians were well positioned to prosper if peace prevailed, but would postwar adjustment bring another recession? As in the past, Canada's fate rested more on international than domestic developments, but Canadians were finally in a position to make their presence felt in the new world order that emerged in the second half of the twentieth century.

PART VII

REINVENTING CANADA, 1945–1975

In the 30 years following the Second World War, Canada emerged as one of the world's great industrial nations, with all the benefits and problems associated with its new status. Wealth continued to be unequally distributed, but the state assumed increasing responsibility for ensuring the basic welfare of all Canadians. No longer tied to Great Britain's apron strings, Canadians developed a stronger sense of their own identity. The arts flourished, buoyed by the new prosperity and government grants. As the centennial of Confederation approached, many Canadians felt that they had much to celebrate, and Ottawa hosted a birthday party worthy of a great nation. Yet the country's survival remained at risk, threatened by regional fissures, a sovereignty movement in Quebec, and the overwhelming impact of the United States on Canadian economic, political, and cultural life. The Cold War, which periodically threatened to become hot, helped to impress the American view of the world on the consciousness of Canadians, who were increasingly called upon to define their place in a North American context.

CHAPTER 23

Redefining Liberalism: The Canadian State, 1945–1975

Letters exchanged between a prominent Canadian businessman and a socialist, feminist Member of Parliament in 1972 demonstrated the poles of political debate in postwar Canada. Taking exception to a speech in Parliament by Grace MacInnis, New Democrat MP for Vancouver-Kingsway, Eric Harrington, president of Canada Vickers Ltd., wrote, in part:

> Could you please tell me what on earth "day centers" of which you claim we need 130 000 and "family planning centers" of which you claim we need 700 have to do with "equal rights for women?"
>
> Surely family planning and day-care centres for children are purely a family responsibility and a personal matter and don't have a damn thing to do with equal rights.
>
> Please all of you, stay out of our family affairs and our bedrooms, leave our children alone and do some planning that might help the economy, the unemployment situation and a hundred other more important problems on which to date you have been ineffectual.

MacInnis replied pointedly:

> The fact that you can believe that family planning and day-care centres for children are purely a family responsibility and a personal matter, indicates very clearly that you enjoy an income standard where you and those who surround you are well able to handle such matters from your own resources. Such, I regret to have to tell you, is not the case for a very large percentage of the Canadian people.[1]

With the war over and memories of the Depression still alive, Canadians developed a much greater sense of entitlement than they had felt in earlier periods. A decent income, good medical care, pensions, child-care, a minimum standard of housing: none of these were seen as rights of citizenship before the war; rather they were goals that individuals could set for themselves and work individually to attain. Scarred by the economic devastation of the 1930s and impressed by their government's ability to plan for war, Canadians increasingly argued that planning for peacetime purposes could prevent another depression and improve the quality of living for everyone.

THE POSTWAR LIBERAL CONSENSUS

In the period from 1945 to 1975, Canadians embraced what is often described as a "postwar liberal consensus." Liberalism once meant freedom from state intervention: it endorsed such principles as freedom of trade, freedom of speech, and freedom of worship. The new liberalism, while confirming support for such goals, also emphasized freedom from want. State intervention, rather than being the enemy of liberalism, became its essence, provided that the state limited its intervention to the economic sphere. As the Harrington-MacInnis exchange demonstrates, there was much debate about the limits of that sphere.

The term "welfare state" is often used to describe government programs designed to give cradle-to-grave security to citizens. It includes the broad set of programs by which the state ensured a guaranteed minimum income and social opportunities for all citizens as a matter of right. Minimum wages and programs for employment creation, farm subsidies, and public education were included in the definition; so, too, were universal programs, such as medical insurance, and narrower programs, such as social assistance and old-age pensions, that targeted certain groups.

Opponents of state intervention for the purpose of redistributing wealth put a different spin on the welfare state. Although they rarely attacked spending on education or pensions, they derided social assistance and unemployment insurance as programs that robbed people of initiative and cost too much money. These arguments tended to fall on deaf ears in times of prosperity, but they were never completely put to rest. When economic clouds appeared on the horizon in the 1970s, those advocating less ambitious welfare state policies began to gain more influence in policy circles.

FEDERAL PARTIES AND LEADERS

In the 1945 federal election, both Liberals and Conservatives embraced the welfare state. Tariffs and relations with Britain, the hot-button issues of prewar elections, became largely irrelevant in an age of international trade agreements and Britain's loss of super-power status. The result was that, for a generation, little differentiated the two major political parties. Both supported the basic premise of the Cold War, namely that the world was polarized between supporters of "evil" communism, led by the Soviet Union, and democratic capitalism, led by the United States. This caused both parties to support closer continental ties in foreign and defence policy. Both favoured the cautious addition of social programs to appease public demands for social security. Neither condoned a degree of state intervention that might alarm private investors. Personalities and regional interests, rather than overarching ideologies, determined the public image of the main parties.

The Liberal victory in the 1945 election demonstrated that most Canadians trusted Mackenzie King's programs to prevent a postwar depression. King, however, remained a fiscal conservative, unwilling to sponsor a great deal of social experimentation. In 1948, King stepped down as prime minister and was succeeded by Louis St Laurent. King had recruited St Laurent, a successful lawyer with a string of corporate directorships, to his cabinet in 1941. Pleased with their relative postwar prosperity, Canadians gave the avuncular "Uncle Louis" resounding election victories in 1949 and 1953.

Support for the Liberals eroded in 1956 when the government invoked closure on debate in the House of Commons over its controversial bill to support a private gas pipeline. Tiring of Liberal arrogance after 22 years in power, Canadians shifted their allegiance to the Conservatives. John Diefenbaker formed a minority Conservative government in 1957 and then went on to win the biggest electoral majority held by any government to date—208 out of 265 seats—in 1958.

Diefenbaker was a Saskatchewan lawyer with a burning ambition to succeed in politics. As a Member of Parliament since 1940, he had become one of the leading figures in his party but was twice rejected in national party leadership contests. Sixty-one when he became party leader in 1956, Diefenbaker was a powerful orator. His calls for a larger old-age pension, huge expenditures to open up Canada's North, and subsidies to the economically challenged Atlantic provinces demonstrated that the postwar Conservative need not be a fiscal conservative. Diefenbaker's pursuit of closer trade and foreign policy ties between Canada and Britain suggested that old-style Tory imperialism might not be dead, but in practice he could not divert trade to Britain or remake that country into an independent player on the international scene.

Lester Pearson became Liberal leader shortly before the 1958 election that so humbled his party. A long-time bureaucrat in the Department of External Affairs, Pearson was deputy minister when his old boss, St Laurent, became prime minister and asked him to become Minister of External Affairs. In 1957 Pearson won the Nobel Peace Prize for his role in defusing the Suez Crisis in 1956.

Pearson formed minority governments in 1963 and 1965, dependent on socialist support. The Pearson period represented the heyday of social reform in twentieth-century Canada, with medicare capping a series of new programs designed to provide Canadians with a social safety net. By the time he left office, Pearson could boast that he had taken the reins of power in a country whose social programs paralleled American policy and in five short years had left the Americans in the dust.

Pierre Trudeau, elected Liberal leader and then prime minister in 1968, had the image of a reformer. The son of a Montreal millionaire, Trudeau was an intellectual and world traveller who entered politics in the 1965 federal election. Associated with progressive causes in his home province, Trudeau maintained this image in the federal arena. As justice minister from 1965 to 1968, he was responsible for legislation that decriminalized homosexual relations, liberalized divorce laws, and made abortion legal under some circumstances.

Trudeau captured the public imagination with his promise to create a "just society." Cosmopolitan and debonair by Canadian political standards, he projected an image of a vigorous, trendy, forward-looking leader. The spellbound media lapped it up, and Trudeaumania was born. In 16 years of government, Trudeau consolidated existing social and regulatory programs and proved responsive to new social forces within Canadian society. Nevertheless, the wave of reform that characterized the Pearson years ebbed as the economy slowed down in the early 1970s.

John F. Kennedy, Governor General Georges Vanier, John Diefenbaker, Jacqueline Kennedy, and Olive Diefenbaker, Ottawa, 1961.

National Archives of Canada/PA-154665

THIRD PARTIES IN POSTWAR CANADA

Between 1945 and 1975, third parties remained important in the nation's politics.

1960s, he called without success for a realignment of Canada's political parties to unite the Conservatives and Social Credit behind a truly conservative program. Social Credit had faded as a force in federal politics in English Canada by the 1960s, but the Créditistes, the Quebec wing of the party, carried 26 of 74 federal seats in that province in the 1962 election. The charismatic leadership of Réal Caouette, resentment against the power of the big banks over people's lives, and Diefenbaker's perceived indifference to francophones helped the Créditistes to make their breakthrough.

PROVINCIAL POLITICS

Social Credit's power base was essentially provincial. Its Alberta bastion was finally assaulted when Peter Lougheed's Conservatives upset 36 years of continuous rule in 1971. In 1952, Social Credit, led by the charismatic W.A.C. Bennett, began a 20-year reign in British Columbia. In the postwar period, Social Credit, while maintaining its obsession with the power of financiers, was largely a right-wing party even more hostile to socialists than to bankers.

The West also provided provincial strongholds for democratic socialism. In Saskatchewan the CCF-NDP governed from 1944 to 1964 and pioneered state hospital insurance and medicare. NDP governments elected in Manitoba in 1969, Saskatchewan in 1971, and British Columbia in 1972 were responsible for a degree of social experimentation well exceeding that of other provinces.

In Quebec provincial politics, Duplessis's Union nationale provided a conservative administration until the death of *le chef* in 1959. Quebec voters elected the Liberals in 1960 and 1962, a party that proved both reformist and nationalist. But the pace of reforms left

Pierre Elliott Trudeau.

National Archives of Canada/C-25000

CCF support declined after the 1945 election and the party joined forces with organized labour in 1961 to create the New Democratic Party (NDP). In an attempt to shake off paranoid Cold War allegations that linked the party with communism, the CCF largely abandoned its commitment to public ownership. Instead, it accepted private enterprise as long as it was regulated by a strong state that implemented extensive social programs and progressive taxation to redistribute wealth. Despite its third-party status, the CCF-NDP had a significant impact on policy since the two main parties feared losing votes to the socialists if they avoided new social programs.

On the political right, Ernest Manning, the Social Credit premier of Alberta from 1944 to 1968, denounced the federal Progressive Conservative Party's embrace of the liberal postwar consensus. In the

many behind, and the Union nationale was returned to office one last time in 1966. Thereafter, Quebec politics polarized between the federalist Liberals and the sovereignist Parti québécois.

Politics in the Atlantic provinces mirrored national politics: indistinguishable reform-minded Liberal and Conservative parties differentiated in the public mind by the personalities of their leaders. With the lowest standard of living in the country and a shrinking proportion of House of Commons seats, Atlantic Canadians felt the need to be allied to a national party that could throw some policy and patronage crumbs their way. Meanwhile, the region's political leaders began cooperating across party lines to pressure Ottawa for special regional subsidies and development projects that would jumpstart their economies. Although their tactics brought some concessions, the region continued to lag behind the rest of the nation.

Ontario politics seemed the most predictable, with the Conservatives in power without interruption from 1943 to 1985, usually with a comfortable majority of legislative seats. The ruling Conservatives were sometimes called "Red Tories" because of their willingness to spend lavishly on education and health. The well-funded, efficiently-run party, commonly known as the "Big Blue Machine," was a force to be reckoned with throughout the postwar decades, not only in Ontario, but also in Ottawa where it exercised enormous influence on the direction of national policy.

NEWFOUNDLAND ENTERS CONFEDERATION

Newfoundland's entry into Confederation illustrates the impact of both the welfare state and the Cold War on postwar developments. While Canada's social programs enticed many Newfoundlanders, the demands of the Cold War made Canada especially eager to accept the new province. Newfoundland sat astride the sea lanes of the North Atlantic, and therefore played an important role in Cold War strategy.

For Newfoundlanders, the first order of postwar business was to replace the British-dominated commission. In June 1946 Newfoundlanders elected delegates to a National Convention to recommend future forms of government. While some people, especially in the outports, favoured Confederation with Canada, others, including many leaders of the Roman Catholic Church, wanted Newfoundland to regain the status of a self-governing dominion. A few wanted to retain commission government.

Through radio broadcasts of the convention, Joseph Smallwood emerged as the principal proponent of joining Canada. Journalist, trade unionist, and farmer, the colourful Smallwood promised that Confederation would banish economic uncertainty forever, thanks to the social safety net provided by family allowances, unemployment insurance, and old-age pensions.

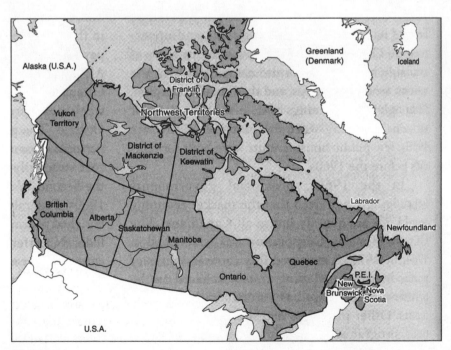

Map 23.1
Canada, 1949.

Symbols of Independence

In the period after 1945, Canada moved quickly to break many ties that smacked of colonial subordination. The Canadian Citizenship Act of 1947 enabled immigrants, for the first time, to become citizens of Canada, as opposed to "British subjects." In 1949, Canada's Supreme Court became indeed supreme in legal matters, as appeals to the Judicial Committee of the Privy Council in Great Britain were abolished. In 1952, Vincent Massey became the first governor general to be named by the government of Canada rather than by the British government. He was also the first native-born Canadian to hold the post.

The flag debate of 1964 showed that some Canadians, particularly former Prime Minister John Diefenbaker, were unhappy with the severing of symbolic ties with Great Britain. The Pearson government proposed a distinctive Canadian flag with the maple leaf as the symbol of the nation. Diefenbaker's unsuccessful counter-proposal was a new flag that incorporated the Union Jack and the fleur-de-lys as a way of paying tribute to Canada's "two founding peoples." Such a proposal ignored not only Native peoples, but also the increasing numbers of Canadians whose origins were neither British nor French.

Anti-confederates, by contrast, suggested that closer economic ties to the United States would make a self-governing Newfoundland prosperous.

The Convention majority opposed including the Confederation option on the referendum ballot, but the British, who favoured Newfoundland joining Canada, ignored its wishes. It took two referenda to get a majority vote for one of the options for Newfoundland governance. A mere 52.4 percent voted in favour of Confederation with Canada. On 31 March 1949, Newfoundland and Labrador became the 10th province of Canada, rounding out the nation from the Atlantic to the Pacific.

POLITICS AND REPRESENTATION

The federal Parliament and provincial legislatures remained largely the privileged arena of wealthy white males of British and, in the case of Quebec, French extraction. The upper levels of the civil service were staffed with men from the same backgrounds. As the period progressed, there were slight gains for other groups. Grace MacInnis was the only woman in Parliament from 1968 to 1972, but five women were elected in 1972 and eight in 1974. Ellen Fairclough became Canada's first female cabinet minister when she was appointed Secretary of State by Diefenbaker

in 1957, and Judy LaMarsh held major portfolios in the Pearson administration.

Not all politicians came from French or English backgrounds. Diefenbaker was partly of German-Canadian extraction, as was Ed Schreyer, who became Manitoba's first NDP premier in 1969. Herb Gray was appointed by Pierre Trudeau to cabinet, becoming the first Jew to hold such a position; Dave Barrett, the first NDP premier of British Columbia, was also of Jewish descent. Visible-minority Canadians fared less well, although Dave Barrett's cabinet included one Native and his caucus included two African Canadians. One of these was Rosemary Brown, who won 37 percent of the ballots for the NDP federal leadership in 1974 in a contest with Ed Broadbent.

SHAPING THE WELFARE STATE

The postwar welfare state had an inauspicious start. After the 1945 election, Mackenzie King called the Dominion-Provincial Conference on Reconstruction and tabled a comprehensive national program to care for the old, the sick, and the unemployed. To fund these costly endeavours, Ottawa suggested it would require exclusive rights to income and corporate taxes and to succession duties. The provinces, led by Ontario and Quebec, argued that they could not sur-

Ellen Fairclough with the Great Seal of the Secretary of State.

Copyright © City of Ottawa Archives/Ottawa Journal Collection/CA-19893

render all major taxes and still fulfil their responsibilities. After nine months of meetings, King announced that the talks had collapsed. The pace of social reform would be slower than the parties had promised in 1945.

Instead of a comprehensive program of welfare measures, the government implemented reforms piecemeal. In 1951, a system of state-funded universal old-age pensions was introduced. The next step was hospital care. In 1957, a hospital insurance program with costs shared by the provincial and federal governments was implemented. A full-fledged system of state-funded medicare was the next item on the agenda but it proved to be a harder sell. Many physicians argued that doctor-controlled and voluntary private insurance schemes were preferable to a state program forcing all doctors and patients to enroll. National public opinion disagreed. In 1944 and again

in 1949, 80 percent of Canadians endorsed a federal health plan to cover complete medical and hospital care for a monthly flat rate.

Prosperity allowed more people to consult doctors and to access hospital services, but prosperity was uneven. The regional distribution of medical personnel paralleled regional patterns of wealth. Although Canadians collectively had one doctor to serve every 938 people in 1959, Ontario, British Columbia, and Alberta residents were even better served. Newfoundland had only one doctor for every 2190 residents. The lack of local medical services caused the Newfoundland Federation of Labour to mock the posters that Ontario public health organizations sent to schools:

> "Brush your teeth three times a day and see your dentist twice a year" say posters in the school. The dentist is 150 miles away.

> "Fight cancer with a checkup and a cheque." The checkup means a trip by coastal boat to a doctor with no training or equipment to diagnose cancer.

> "Prize your eyes" says the CNIB. But on the coast of Labrador or at the head of Bay d'Espoir, there has never been an eye specialist, not even in transit.[2]

Diefenbaker established a Royal Commission on Health Services in 1961. Its report in 1964 called for a universal medicare scheme embracing hospital, physician, dental, and prescription costs. The Liberals promised medicare in the 1965 election and, on their return to office, announced the first stage of a national health insurance program. While to some extent a response to the royal commission, the government's action also owed much to the province of Saskatchewan, which had introduced medicare in 1962. The province had persisted with its legislation, despite a strike by its doctors.

The federal medicare plan added physician care and the services of some non-physician specialists to the earlier federal-provincial hospital insurance scheme. Ottawa would share costs with the provinces if provincial programs adhered to four principles: universality of coverage, coverage of most medical treatment, portability of benefits, and provincial administration. By 1970, all provinces had established programs embodying the four federal principles.

biography

Elsie Gregory MacGill

One of the strong voices within the Royal Commission on the Status of Women for a welfare state more attuned to women's needs was Elsie Gregory MacGill (1905-1980). MacGill was the daughter of British Columbia's first woman judge, Helen Gregory MacGill, a lifelong campaigner for women's rights. Refusing to be held back by a bout of childhood polio, Elsie MacGill embarked on a brilliant career as an aircraft designer. After becoming University of Toronto's first woman graduate in engineering, she earned a masters degree in aeronautical engineering at MIT in 1929, a North American first for a woman. From 1938 to 1943, MacGill was chief aeronautical engineer, at the Fort William plant of Canadian Car and Foundry. In this position, she designed Hawker Hurricane planes, the prize of the Allies' Second World War fighter aircraft. Responsible for the production of over 2000 planes, she headed a staff of 4500 at the peak point of Hawker fabrication.

After the war, Elsie MacGill set up her own consulting practice, continuing to design aircraft for most of her life. She became an activist in women's groups, serving for a time as president of the Canadian Federation of Business and Professional Women's Clubs. She fought for paid maternity leave, liberalized abortion laws, and publicly-supported daycare. Appointed as one of the members of the Royal Commission on the Status of Women, Elsie MacGill, as one of Canada's best known feminists and scientists, was regarded by many as almost a co-chair to the official Commission chair, broadcaster Florence Bird.

Elsie Gregory MacGill.

National Archives of Canada/PA-148380

Apart from universal medicare, there were other significant Pearson-era reforms, beginning with the introduction of the Canada Pension Plan (CPP), an earnings-related pension, in 1965. Low-interest loans for postsecondary students made their appearance in 1966. The Canada Assistance Plan (CAP) of the same year built upon the 1956 cost-sharing agreement on welfare and assured all Canadians of the right to receive social assistance. CAP established national guidelines that provinces had to incorporate in their welfare programs to receive federal assistance.

There is no doubt that CAP improved the lives of poor Canadians. Marion Dewar, executive director of the Canadian Council on Children and Youth and former mayor of Ottawa, recalled in 1990:

When I was nursing with the Victorian Order of Nurses in the early 1960s, it was a very different society from the one we live in today. We gave bedbaths to elderly people living in cold rooms, or living with relatives who refused to feed them. I particularly recall one woman who had suffered a stroke. She had lost her ability to speak. I went in once a month to see her at first. Each visit she clutched my uniform and pointed to her mouth. I realized she was hungry. I started going in two or three times a week. I would bring her soup and feed her. When government assistance became available, she went to live in a nursing home....

In those days welfare was granted to those persons whom local politicians decided to give it to. If you were a young person out of work, very often having run away from an abusive home, you could be refused welfare. If you were a juvenile, you could be sent to one of the "reform schools," in some of which, we are hearing today, the young people were abused.[3]

CANADA'S WELFARE STATE IN PERSPECTIVE

How did Canadian efforts in the social policy arena compare with other countries? Critics of big government stress the rapid increase in Canadian social expenditures. According to the Organization for Economic Co-operation and Development (OECD), the cost rose from 12.1 to 21.7 percent of gross domestic product from 1960 to 1981. These figures were modest relative to other OECD countries. West Germany had the OECD's largest per capita social expenditures in 1960, and yet it continued to post the greatest productivity gains of any OECD country. Sweden, Italy, Austria, and the Netherlands, all successful in global trade, also exceeded Canada in growth and volume of social expenditures.

The Canadian welfare state generally treated women less fairly than men. CPP pensions, which were calculated on the basis of individual earnings, penalized women on two fronts: first, women workers earned on average far less than men; second, many women withdrew completely from the labour force to raise their children. Unemployment insurance policy was also discriminatory. Men could leave jobs for any reason and, if they had worked the required number of weeks, collect unemployment insurance, provided they demonstrated that they were making reasonable efforts to find new work. Women who left or lost jobs during or after pregnancy were deemed automatically

ineligible to collect unemployment insurance. Women's organizations and the labour movement successfully campaigned to have this exclusion lifted.

The 1970 Report of the Royal Commission on the Status of Women argued that a major barrier to women's economic equality was the lack of affordable daycare. The commission concluded: "Parents require supplementary help, and society may legitimately be called upon to contribute to community services for its younger generation. The equality of women means little without such a programme, which should include ... day-care centres."[4]

Studies by women's groups and social agencies pointed to the inadequacies of existing private arrangements for childcare. Forced by economic desperation to work, yet unable to find affordable and reliable childcare centres, women sometimes left very young children with abusive, neglectful, or alcoholic caregivers. Researchers documented many cases of children warehoused in quarters infested with parasites, in facilities without toys or play areas, and in spaces so cramped that closets became sleep areas. A disturbing number of children, including pre-schoolers, spent much of the day alone. Daycare advocates maintained that it was time to stop arguing about

Table 23.1

Social Expenditures by Country (percentage of gross domestic product)

Country	1960	1981
Belgium	17.0	38.0
Netherlands	16.3	36.1
Sweden	14.5	33.5
Germany	20.5	31.5
Italy	16.5	29.1
Denmark	10.2	29.0
Austria	17.9	27.9
Ireland	11.7	27.1
Norway	11.7	27.1
United Kingdom	13.9	24.9
France	13.4	23.8
Canada	12.1	21.7
United States	10.9	21.0
New Zealand	13.0	19.6
Australia	10.2	18.6
Japan	8.0	17.5

Source: *OECD Bulletin*, no. 146 (Jan. 1984). Reprinted in Andrew Armitage, *Social Welfare in Canada: Ideas, Realities and Future Paths*, 2nd ed. (Toronto: McClelland and Stewart, 1988) 22.

whether it was desirable that mothers work, recognize that many were working, and insist that the state assist them to find quality, affordable day care.

In some countries, such as Sweden and France, state programs of free daycare for all children had contributed to dramatic reductions in the rates of poverty for single mothers and fairer distribution of income between men and women. Canada did not join these nations. Both the federal and provincial governments proved unwilling to fund universal, public daycare, though some provincial governments, notably the NDP administration in British Columbia from 1972 to 1975, gave subsidies to the neediest families.

Discussions about the cost of state-sponsored social programs tended to assume that the poor were the main recipients, but this was misleading. In 1954, a government body, the Canada Mortgage and Housing Corporation (CMHC), hoping to encourage more private initiative, agreed to guarantee mortgages from private financial companies. To reduce the potential for default, CMHC limited its loan guarantees to middle- and upper-income Canadians. Although some state-subsidized senior citizens' housing was in evidence by the late 1950s, few public housing units were built for families before the 1960s.

In the 1960s, provincial governments begrudgingly admitted that the market economy would not adequately house all Canadians. The Ontario Housing Corporation was established in 1964; by 1972, it managed 50 000 units of public housing. Other provinces had similar, if less ambitious, programs. Most of the public-housing developments built in the 1960s and 1970s were notable for overcrowding, cheapness of construction, and lack of green space.

THE PROVINCES AND THE NEW LIBERALISM

The provinces extended their social welfare policies in areas other than public housing. In addition to providing funds for new schools, universities, hospitals, and highways, provinces established vocational programs to train young people in the skills demanded in the new economy.

To allow poorer provinces to provide education, health, and social services comparable to those in the wealthier provinces, generous equalization payments were built into the tax system which came into effect in 1957. All provinces received per capita grants from Ottawa based on the average revenues of the two wealthiest provinces, British Columbia and Ontario. The percentage of federal corporate and personal income taxes that was rebated to provinces rose gradually from a mere 5 percent in 1945 to 24 percent by the early 1960s. Federal cost-sharing programs and grants enriched provincial coffers but created the threat of federal interference. Alberta's Social Credit government, for example, objected to federal financial penalties against the province for charging hospital user fees. At the same time, the Atlantic provinces, with their lagging economies, had no choice but to become dependent on federal largesse. In 1958, the federal government established subsidies in the form of Atlantic Provinces Adjustment Grants in recognition of the region's difficult position.

Transfer payments were not the only federal schemes to help have-not provinces. Ottawa also implemented targeted development programs. For example, in the early 1960s, the government passed the Agriculture Rehabilitation and Development Act, which poured money into rural areas to improve efficiency in the development of local resources and to create alternative employment in depressed regions. Prince Edward Island became the focus in 1969 of a 15-year Comprehensive Development Plan that promised an investment of $725 million to help restructure farming and fishing activities, improve infrastructure, and diversify the economy, most notably in the area of tourism.

Both the federal and provincial governments attempted to lure industries into depressed provinces as well as to the poorer regions of wealthy provinces. Unwilling to have the state itself take an entrepreneurial role, governments searched for private investors who, with the help of public funds, would agree to establish new industries. The major recipients of regional assistance grants were corporations. In the 1960s and 1970s, garment firms that set up low-wage sweatshops in rural areas of Manitoba, for instance, received a dizzying array of federal, provincial, and municipal subsidies. These included grants to introduce new technologies, "forgivable loans" from the federal government, federal wage subsidies, tax concessions, government-paid training for employees, subsidized hydro-electricity rates, and reduced tariffs on fabrics. Programs by have-not provinces to lure corporate investment were equally wasteful, encouraging, it appeared, a take-the-money-and-run attitude on the part of investors.

Regional assistance incentives generally failed in their stated objectives: they served to maintain rather than change the relative distribution of wealth in the country. The Atlantic region, Manitoba, and Saskatchewan became dependent for much of their income on federal transfer payments. Fully half of the Atlantic region's income was derived from federal transfer payments by 1975. The failure of regional development programs encouraged Atlantic Canadians to fight to at least hold on to what they already had. When DOSCO abandoned its steel mill in Sydney and coal mines at Glace Bay, popular pressures forced the province to operate the mill and the federal and provincial governments to work together to keep the mines open.

Public money was also wasted in central Canada as the federal government lavished funds on an unneeded second international airport for Montreal, and on high-technology firms in the Ottawa region. Quebec seemed the most successful in using provincial subsidies to attract new industries. The investment arm of the Quebec Pension Plan offered competing incentives to companies thinking of building new plants or moving existing ones. Wealthier provinces had the luxury of focusing on indirect subsidies. Ontario stepped up existing infrastructure programs, while British Columbia and Alberta used low provincial taxes to encourage diversification.

Secondary industry nonetheless continued to concentrate mainly in central Canada. Alberta, in the midseventies, made a highly-publicized, though initially largely unsuccessful, effort to use its energy wealth to challenge this pattern. In 1975, Conservative premier Peter Lougheed created the Heritage Trust Fund, into which a portion of oil royalties was committed to provide moneys to stimulate new economic activity. Saskatchewan's NDP government followed a different tack, buying shares for the state in private companies in order to encourage economic development. It was responsible for establishing a steel-manufacturing firm in Regina, but the province's limited resources relative to the Heritage Trust Fund restricted many achievements of these kinds.

The energy-producing provinces responded bitterly when the federal government attempted to increase its revenues from oil and gas developments in the wake of the huge increases in oil prices undertaken by the Oil and Petroleum Exporting Countries (OPEC) in 1973. Resource policy was added to a roster of western grievances against the federal government, including monetary policy, the promotion of bilingualism, the introduction of the metric system, and indifference to the plight of farmers. Ironically, while Lougheed and the other premiers of Western Canada and the Atlantic region accused the federal government of following policies that negated provincial development strategies in favour of central Canadian economic development, the province most alienated from Ottawa was in Central Canada: Quebec.

MODERNIZATION AND NATIONALISM IN QUEBEC

The new liberalism almost guaranteed a collision between Ottawa and Quebec City. With Ottawa insisting that the federal government play a large role in all areas of social and economic development, Quebec's resistance to federal involvement in provincial jurisdictions heightened. In the 1950s Duplessis spurned over $200 million in federal moneys earmarked for Quebec universities. Determination to resist federal encroachments increased during the Quiet Revolution ushered in by the election of Jean Lesage's Liberals in 1960. Following the Second World War, francophones in Quebec, particularly in the cities, embraced the secular values of the rest of North America and developed new ideas about the role of the state in their society. Nationalists in the province expected their provincial government to follow policies that both reflected a new liberal consensus and ensured the preservation of the national identity of Quebec's majority.

The Lesage administration's main thrust was economic development under francophone control. This meant a significant expansion of the role of the state. René Lévesque, a member of Lesage's cabinet, lead the campaign to nationalize private hydro companies. Hydro-Québec became a model for nationalist goals of economic development, including the hiring of francophone managers and engineers. The establishment of the Quebec Pension Plan, as noted earlier, provided Quebec with an investment fund to encourage economic diversification.

Quebec's determination to run its own social programs soon led to confrontation with Ottawa. The Pearson government's solution was to allow a province to opt out of a federal program, retaining its share of funding as long as it established a similar provincial program with the moneys. In practice, only Quebec availed itself of this option, and Trudeau removed the opting-out option for future programs.

As the Quiet Revolution worked its way through the fabric of Quebec society, a growing number of Quebeckers became sovereignists—supporters of a sovereign Quebec nation-state. Resistance by the Trudeau government and most English-Canadians to the de facto special status that Quebec had begun to develop in the Pearson period strengthened the hand of sovereignists. In 1968, René Lévesque cobbled together an alliance of pro-sovereignty forces to create the Parti québécois (PQ). By the mid-1970s, the PQ platform was sovereignty-association—the creation of a separate Quebec state with the maintenance of close economic links with Ottawa.

THE MOVE TO OFFICIAL BILINGUALISM

The federal government did not remain idle as Quebec drifted from Confederation. In 1963, the Pearson government established a Royal Commission on Bilingualism and Biculturalism under co-chairs André Laurendeau and Davidson Dunton. The commission revealed that the rate of assimilation of French Canadians outside Quebec and northern New Brunswick was so alarming as to support Quebec nationalist claims that Confederation had failed to protect French culture. Pierre Trudeau, who distrusted Quebec nationalism, was determined to make francophones feel "chez nous" throughout the country.

In 1969, Parliament passed the Official Languages Act, which placed French on an equal footing with English throughout the federal government. The bill created an official languages commissioner responsible for ensuring that federal departments served the public equally well in both languages. A significant percentage of new hirings required functional bilingualism. The federal government also tried to expand the use of French nationally by providing funds for French-language schools, French immersion programs for anglophones, and organizations for francophones outside Quebec. The success of these programs in strengthening either the French community or national unity was debatable. Francophones outside Quebec complained that economic realities in most of the country still forced them to become proficient in English to get well-paying jobs.

Acadians experienced their own quiet revolution. Their numbers grew in the postwar period, though the rate of assimilation to anglophone culture was high. As in Quebec, education was identified as a key to maintaining cultural identity. Acadians pushed for more French-language instruction and for institutions of higher learning to prepare their children for the new opportunities of the service economy.

In New Brunswick, sheer numbers made these goals viable. Confrontations with Moncton's anglophone mayor, student sit-ins at the Université de Moncton, and a well-attended Day of Concern over unemployment in January 1972 brought attention to Acadian demands for programs that would protect their culture and improve their economic condition. New Brunswick became Canada's only officially bilingual province, its status declared in 1969 and confirmed in the Constitution of 1982.

Opposition to official bilingualism ran deep in English Canada, though polls suggested majority support. Canadians whose backgrounds were neither French nor English wondered where they fit into the Canadian mosaic. The Trudeau government established a Secretary of State for Multiculturalism in 1971 to stem criticism from ethnic minorities, but by

Protest in Ottawa following proclamation of the War Measures Act, October 1970.

National Archives of Canada/PA-126347

that time acts of terrorism in Quebec were calling Canada's peaceable image sharply into question.

THE OCTOBER CRISIS

On 5 October 1970, James Cross, the British trade commissioner in Montreal, was kidnapped by members of the Front de libération du Québec (FLQ). Five days later, Pierre Laporte, the Quebec Minister of Labour and Immigration, was abducted by another FLQ cell. Although consisting of only a few dozen members, the FLQ had been associated with over 200 bombings between 1963 and 1970.

In return for release of the hostages, the kidnappers demanded, among other things, the freeing of FLQ members who were imprisoned or detained and the broadcasting of the group's manifesto. On 16 October, the federal government, for the first time in peacetime, proclaimed the War Measures Act, under which it banned the FLQ, suspended civil rights, and imposed martial law on the nation. The act played little role in the apprehension of the revolutionaries and the release of the trade commissioner in early December. It may well have precipitated the murder of Laporte, whose body was found in the trunk of an abandoned car on 17 October. The use of the act to detain over 450 people, most of whom were charged with no offences, became another example for Quebec nationalists of the injustice imposed by an English-dominated Parliament.

THE "SPECIAL STATUS" DEBATE

Although Quebec's Liberal premier Robert Bourassa worked closely with Trudeau to destroy the small revolutionary separatist movement, the two disagreed about how to react to the surging Parti québécois. Trudeau rejected requests from Quebec for special status as the homeland of a French-Canadian nation. Wishing to appease nationalist sentiment, Bourassa followed his predecessors in calling for Quebec City to have absolute control in many areas increasingly dominated by Ottawa, particularly social programs, communications, and immigration.

At a federal-provincial conference in Victoria in 1971, Trudeau offered Bourassa a veto for Quebec over constitutional change in return for the premier's support for patriation of the Canadian constitution from Britain. Bourassa spurned the prime minister, warning that Quebec would not support patriation until it was given extra powers.

Bourassa's language legislation also appalled the prime minister. In 1974, the Quebec legislature passed Bill 22, making French the only official language in Quebec and promoting its use in the workplace. All children were to be educated in French unless their parents were Canadian-born anglophones. Immigrant children wishing to enrol in English-language schools would have to pass a language test. Unilingual English signs were banned. Quebec anglophones criticized the bill for infringing on civil liberties. For nationalist francophones, the legislation did not go far enough in restricting the use of English.

Given the city's unique demography, Montreal was one of the centres of resistance to Bill 22. While over four-fifths of Quebeckers had French as their first language, on Montreal Island the ethnic French constituted little more than 60 percent of the total population in 1971. Allophones, Quebeckers of neither French nor English ancestry, constituted 23 percent of Montrealers, and joined the 16 percent of the city's population of British descent in opposing restrictions on the language of education.

INTERNATIONAL RELATIONS AND THE NEW LIBERALISM

If the new liberalism was reflected in federal social welfare programs and the Quiet Revolution in Quebec, it was also evident in international affairs. The image that Canada cultivated was that of a peacekeeper and benevolent donor of foreign aid. Like its American counterpart, the Canadian government subscribed to the view that poverty in the so-called Third World was the result of "underdevelopment" rather than the effects of colonialism and a vastly uneven distribution of wealth. Foreign aid, liberals argued, would allow the governments of poor countries to build the infrastructure, including transportation systems and schools, necessary to encourage industrial development and agricultural improvement.

In 1950, Canada was a signatory of the Colombo Plan, meant to provide assistance to former British colonies in Asia as they gained their independence. Over the next two decades, aid was extended to Commonwealth nations in other parts of the world, to francophone Africa, and, in 1970, to Latin America. The Canadian International Development Agency (CIDA) was established in 1968 to coordinate the nation's foreign aid efforts. Critics of the foreign aid program lamented its lack of generosity and its heavy reliance on "tied aid": countries received funds on condition that they spent specified amounts of their grants to acquire Canadian goods or services.

Canada was perhaps more successful in its role as international peacekeeper. In 1956, Canadian diplomacy was responsible for finding a solution to the Suez Crisis when British and French troops attacked Egypt following its nationalization of the Suez Canal. Canada was a member of the United Nations Emergency Force that kept the peace between Egypt

and Israel from 1956 until 1967, when Egyptian President Gamal Abdel Nasser expelled the UN forces. Among other hot spots where Canadian peacekeepers served were the Congo (now Zaire), Yemen, and Cyprus.

THE COLD WAR

Overarching Canada's foreign policy deliberations after 1945 was the Cold War, in which capitalist democracies vied globally with the communist states for resources, trade, and political allies. Their fierce ideological battles created a simplified view of the political and economic options available to nations on either side of the capitalist-communist divide.

After the war, the Soviet Union insisted upon friendly regimes in Eastern Europe as a protection against Germany, which had devastated their country during two world wars. The western countries, particularly the United States, rejected such concerns, insisting that the Soviet Union's neighbours had the right to military and economic independence. The Soviets responded by tightening the screws on Eastern Europe and imposing Communist-dominated regimes. Each side then declared that the other was bent on world domination. But both sides tried to avoid a direct confrontation—a "hot war"—instead limiting themselves to virulent rhetoric and to support for either pro-Soviet or pro-western forces in localized conflicts.

Canada tended to take the American lead. The Permanent Joint Board on Defence, established during the Second World War, remained in operation to coordinate the defence policies of the two nations. In 1949, Canada became a founding member of the North Atlantic Treaty Organization (NATO), a military pact that included the United States and Britain as well as continental western European nations. Both organizations were designed to contain the Soviet threat.

THE KOREAN WAR

In 1950, Canada agreed to contribute troops to the United Nations forces sent to hold the line against

MORE TO THE STORY

The Gouzenko Affair

In September 1945, Igor Gouzenko, a cipher clerk in the Soviet Embassy, revealed to the Canadian government that a Soviet spy ring had been in operation in Canada throughout the war. Gouzenko's story created a sensation in the country when it became public news in February 1946. By then Western-Soviet relations had deteriorated, and many Canadians were prepared to view their wartime ally as a bogeyman.

The information leaked to the Soviets was not particularly significant. Still, the government was concerned with the potential for real secrets to arrive in the hands of the "enemy," particularly information from Canadian laboratories that had been involved in the research leading to the invention of the nuclear bomb.

Hence the hysteria that surrounded the biggest "spycatch" based on the Gouzenko papers. Scientist Raymond Boyer and Canada's only Communist MP, Fred Rose, were found guilty of conspiracy for having passed scientific information to the Soviets in 1943. Boyer had been involved in improving a chemical explosive, and wanted to share the discovery with Canada's Soviet allies. The Canadian government denied him permission. Boyer gave the information to Rose, who passed it to Soviet embassy officials. Ironically, a year later the government passed on the same information, unaware that the Soviets already knew.

Rose and Boyer's defence that they were aiding the anti-Nazi cause counted for nothing in the atmosphere of the Cold War. As civil libertarians protested, the Canadian state seemed to want to crucify these men, not for having consorted with an enemy but for lacking the foresight to realize that Canada's wartime friend would become its postwar enemy. Rose was jailed and ejected from his parliamentary seat.

The government established a commission to investigate the Gouzenko files. The commission was allowed to detain individuals without laying charges. Only half of the 22 individuals fingered by the commission were found guilty of criminal offences, generally of lesser charges than the commission had made.

In the aftermath of the Gouzenko affair, a chill fell over political activity on the part of Canadian scientists. State authorities branded the pacifist Canadian Association of Scientific Workers as communist, causing most of its members to quit and the organization to collapse.

Igor Gouzenko, masked to protect himself from Soviet spies.

National Archives of Canada/PA-129625. Reprinted by permission of *The Montreal Gazette*

---

communism in Korea. Korea had been divided after the war into two zones, North Korea, under Soviet supervision, and South Korea, under American control. Cold War antagonism stalled the amalgamation planned for the two Koreas by the UN. When troops from North Korea invaded South Korea in June 1950, the United States manoeuvred the UN into sending a peacekeeping force into the region. Canada worked behind the scenes to restrain its aggressive ally but with little success.

In total, about 25 000 Canadians participated in the hostilities, and 300 lost their lives. Again, however, war proved a boon to the Canadian economy. The federal government poured money into defence production and the United States invested in Canadian resources to replace those rapidly being depleted by its expanding Cold War economy. By contrast, the two Koreas, both controlled by ruthless dictators, experienced economic devastation and the loss of millions of lives.

THE NUCLEAR ISSUE

Canada and the United States also poured billions of dollars into an elaborate defence program designed to protect North America from a Soviet air attack. Between 1949 and 1957, three radar defence systems—the Pine Tree, Mid-Canada, and Distant Early Warning (DEW) lines—were built. The DEW Line stretched from Alaska to Baffin Island, and cooperation on this project helped pave the way for the North Atlantic Air Defence Treaty (NORAD) agreement of 1958, which produced a unified air command for North America.

America's exclusive possession of nuclear weapons from 1945 to 1949, followed by a decade of clear nuclear superiority over the Soviet Union, encouraged political leaders in the United States to enunciate a policy of "deterrence": the Americans threatened to use "nukes" against communist states if they intervened in other countries' affairs. In 1954, NATO members, hoping to avoid the expense of large conventional armed forces, adopted nuclear deterrence as the mainstay of their defence strategy. In December 1957, in line with NATO policy, Canada agreed to play a role in surveillance of possible military strike plans by the communists. In 1959 and 1960, Canada ordered a variety of aircraft and missiles meant to help serve this objective. In 1958, Canada received a reward for its close cooperation with American defence policies: the Defence Production Sharing Agreement, which guaranteed that Canadians would benefit from the industrial potential of military production for the Cold War.

SUPPORTING DEMOCRACY?

Close ties to the Americans sometimes compromised Canada's vaunted peacekeeping role. This was the case in policy relating to Vietnam, which, like Korea, became a Cold War hot spot. In 1954, French colonizers of Vietnam had been forced to recognize communist control over the northern half of Vietnam and to cede South Vietnam to anti-communist Vietnamese landlords and businessmen. Negotiations in Geneva that year produced an accord calling for reunification of North and South Vietnam after elections to be held in 1956. An International Control Commission (ICC) with Canada, Poland, and India as its members was established to monitor implementation of provisions of the Geneva accord.

Fearing that the communists would win, the United States refused to call a nation-wide election. Instead, the Americans supported a permanent division of the two Vietnams, and appeared to approve of the South Vietnamese government's reign of terror, including the murder of suspected communist sympathizers and the uprooting of peasant villages. As an ICC member, Canada seemed to see only North Vietnamese violations while Poland saw only South Vietnamese violations. A report in 1962 prepared by Canada and co-signed by India, desperate for American goodwill because of border wars with China, was regularly brandished by American officials during their undeclared war in Indochina (1965–75) to demonstrate North Vietnamese atrocities.

Canada made one effort to counsel reason to the Americans during the Vietnam War. In April 1965, Prime Minister Pearson, addressing students at Temple University in Philadelphia, cautiously advocated that the American government temporarily cease bombing North Vietnam in an effort to seek diplomatic solutions in Indochina. Meeting Pearson afterwards, American president Lyndon Johnson grabbed him by the shirt collar and shouted, "You pissed on my rug!" Pearson never issued another indictment of American policy in Indochina, admitting candidly to journalists in 1967 that open criticism of American foreign policy could lead to American economic retaliation that might be disastrous for Canada.

Such thinking likely led to Ottawa's silence as repressive military dictatorships, supported by the Americans, overthrew a string of democratic governments that struck the United States as too leftist or too nationalist. It would, however, be misleading to overstate the extent to which Canadian foreign-policy makers cowered in fears of American economic retaliation. The shared views of the elites of the two countries led Canada's political leaders to support the main lines of American foreign policy. Canada's leaders were supporters of international capitalism and wanted to see the defeat of communism at any cost.

As critics of Canadian silence regarding the Vietnam War suggested, Canada benefited economically from the war. Thanks to the Defence Production Sharing Agreement, Canadian weapons producers were able to bid as equals with American arms manufacturers in supplying US military contracts. The close trade and investment links between the two countries assured that the war-induced boom in the American economy would translate into economic buoyancy for Canada as well.

VOICES OF DISSENT

Many Canadians were concerned by the apparent contradictions that resulted from Canada's special relationship with the United States. Even at the height of the Cold War in the 1950s, campaigns for nuclear disarmament, human rights, and a more balanced assessment of various communist regimes were waged. In 1960, women from across Canada formed the Voice of Women to promote disarmament and peace. Dissenting voices soon grew louder, stimulated by the student rebellions that swept North America and Western Europe.

The voice of dissent was fuelled in the 1960s by one of Canada's most purposeful immigrant groups: Americans evading the draft, military deserters, and others opposed to the Vietnam War. Estimates of the numbers of American war resisters who emigrated to Canada range as high as 100 000. Most of them were young and well-educated. They settled all over the country but were concentrated in Montreal, Toronto and Vancouver, where the peace movement was most vocal.

THE RESPONSE FROM OTTAWA

In the early 1960s, there were indications that Canada might chart an independent course on defence rather than continue to offer unquestioning support to the Americans. Howard Green, named Secretary of State for External Affairs by Diefenbaker in 1959, supported nuclear disarmament. Green influenced Diefenbaker to reconsider Canada's agreement to acquire nuclear warheads as part of its commitment to NATO and NORAD defence strategies.

His cabinet divided, Diefenbaker vacillated on defence issues and caused consternation in Washington. Relations between the two countries reached a new low when Diefenbaker resisted demands from President John F. Kennedy to put Canada's NORAD forces on alert during an American-Soviet showdown over Cuba in October 1962. The Cuban missile crisis occurred because the Americans had tried to overthrow a Communist regime in Cuba, the product of a revolution led by Fidel Castro, who took power in 1959. Castro had responded by accepting Soviet missiles to defend his besieged country, but Kennedy demanded that the missiles be removed. Although the two super-powers settled the matter peacefully, Diefenbaker's lack of cooperation infuriated the Americans.

In the months preceding the 1963 federal election, statements from the American State Department and from a retiring American NATO leader drew attention to Diefenbaker's about-face on defence policy. The Americans revealed that Diefenbaker's earlier agreement to purchase weapon systems associated with NORAD and NATO commitments necessitated acquisition of nuclear warheads, notwithstanding public statements by Diefenbaker to the contrary. Diefenbaker decried American interference in a Canadian election and finally decided to reject nuclear weapons for Canada. His unpopular government went down to defeat by Pearson's Liberals, who acquired the nuclear warheads in order to improve Canadian-American relations.

When Pierre Trudeau came to power, he initiated a reassessment of Canada's NATO and NORAD commitments but the results were mixed. Plans were announced to gradually cut Canada's NATO troops in Europe by half, but its NORAD commitment remained unchanged. The obsolescence of the nuclear weapons Canada acquired allowed Trudeau to return Canada to its non-nuclear status. Trudeau also tried to move away from the Americans in some areas of foreign policy. In 1970, two years before the Americans took the same step, he recognized the People's Republic of China.

CONCLUSION

The postwar liberal consensus in Canada embraced several contradictory threads. While postwar prosperity was to be guaranteed by extensive state regulation of the economy and new programs of social spending, it was sustained by American military expenditures resulting from the Cold War. Similarly, although Canada was striving to be an independent nation with an influence in world councils, it often felt the need to subordinate its foreign policy and defence policy to American policies. In domestic policy, the desire to create national programs conflicted with regional demands for greater local control, and Quebec's wish to be regarded as a nation unto itself within or without the Canadian Confederation. As we will see in the following chapter, the contradictions also had an impact on the Canadian economy.

A Historiographical Debate

The Development of Quebec Nationalism

What have been the causes of growing sentiment for sovereignty in Quebec since the 1960s? Political scientist Kenneth McRoberts offers one of several theories rooted in economics to explain this phenomenon. The Quiet Revolution, he argues, raised francophone hopes that they would take over the levers of economic power in the province and experience a measurable increase in their standard of living. When this failed to occur, the upwardly mobile professional middle classes were particularly offended. They provided the impetus for the Parti québécois as well as movements that preceded its founding.[5] A somewhat more radical view is provided by sociologist Marcel Rioux, who argues that Quebec francophones identified with the movements for decolonization in the Third World and wished to end their own colonial status. According to Rioux, the Quebec francophones were an ethnic group relegated to working-class status and therefore gradually began to develop the view of themselves as an ethnic class that must break free not only from the Canadian Confederation, but also from the capitalist ethos that pervaded anglophone North America.[6]

Several authors have challenged the view that the educated middle class, and indeed francophones generally, failed to benefit from the reforms of the Quiet Revolution. Historian Ramsay Cook, comparing incomes of male workers in Montreal, notes that the spread of average earnings between francophones and anglophones fell from 51 percent in 1961 to 32 percent in 1970 and 15 percent in 1977.[7] Economists Francois Vaillancourt and Pierre Saint-Laurent demonstrate that increased public employment for francophones has accounted for much of the decline in the income gap between the two linguistic groups.[8]

Political scientist Mary Beth Montcalm argues that it is the very economic success of the francophone middle classes that has impelled them toward the creation of their own nation. Comparing Quebec separatism with similar breakaway nationalist movements in Belgium, France, Spain, and Britain, she argues that the rise of middle-class groups with distinct ethnic identities has been a common catalyst for modern separatist movements. It is not economic anxiety but rather the wish of such groups to establish an ethnic state in their own image that motivates such movements. Thus Montcalm sees cultural goals rather than economic ones as the primary motivation of the Quebec sovereignty movement.[9]

Political scientist André Bernard goes further, suggesting that the struggle to preserve the French language united secessionists, regardless of social class:

> The French language…is a fundamental characteristic of the French-Canadian nation, but it is also more than that. It is the symbol of identity for French Canadians as a group, the rallying force among them, their pride and their wealth. It has an appeal which compares to no other group characteristic. In the last analysis, it is what French Canadians fight for. In this light, the idea of a unilingual French-speaking people in the territory populated and dominated by French Canadians is more a reflection of ideology than a formula prompted by narrow economic interests.[10]

NOTES

1 National Archives of Canada, MG 32, C 12, *Grace MacInnis Papers*, vol. 19, File "Women, Status of, 1972," J. Eric Harrington, president, Canada Vickers Ltd., to MacInnis, 9 May 1972; MacInnis to Harrington, 18 May 1972.

2 Canada, *Royal Commission on Health Services*, brief presented by the Newfoundland Federation of Labour, Oct. 1961.

3 Quoted in *Canadian Council on Social Development*, "Canada's Social Programs Are in Trouble" (Ottawa: CCSD, 1990) 5.

4 *Report of the Royal Commission on the Status of Women in Canada* (Ottawa: Information Canada, 1970) 261.

5 Kenneth McRoberts, *Quebec: Social Change and Political Crisis*, 3rd ed. (Toronto: McClelland and Stewart, 1988) 173–208.

6 Marcel Rioux, *Quebec in Question* (Toronto: Lorimer, 1971).

7 Ramsay Cook, "Canada's New Quiet Revolutionaries," in *Canada, Quebec, and the Uses of Nationalism* (Toronto: McClelland and Stewart, 1986): 87–104.

8 François Vaillancourt and Pierre Saint-Laurent, "Les determinants de l'evolution de revenu entre Canadien anglais et Canadien francais, " *Journal of Canadian Studies* 15.4 (Winter 1980-81): 69–74.

9 Mary Beth Montcalm, "Quebec Nationalism in a Comparative Perspective," in *Quebec: State and Society in Crisis*, ed. Alain Gagnon (Toronto: Methuen, 1984): 45–58.

10 André Bernard, *What Does Quebec Want?* (Toronto: Lorimer, 1978) 45.

SELECTED READING

Key works that deal broadly with postwar national political developments include Ian Drummond, Robert Bothwell, and John English, *Canada Since 1945: Power, Politics and Provincialism*, rev. ed. (Toronto: University of Toronto Press, 1989); Alvin Finkel, *Our Lives: Canada After 1945* (Toronto: James Lorimer, 1997); J.L. Granatstein, *Canada, 1957–1967: The Years of Uncertainty and Innovation* (Toronto: McClelland and Stewart, 1986); Reginald Whitaker, *The Government Party: Organizing and Financing the Liberal Party of Canada, 1930–1958* (Toronto: University of Toronto Press, 1977); Norman Penner, *From Protest to Power: Social Democracy in Canada 1900–Present* (Toronto: Lorimer, 1992); John English, *The Life of Lester Pearson*, vol. 2, *Worldly Years* (New York: Alfred A. Knopf, 1992); Stephen Clarkson and Christina McCall, *Trudeau and Our Times* (Toronto: McClelland and Stewart, 1990); and Denis Smith, *Rogue Tory: The Life and Legend of John G. Diefenbaker* (Toronto: McFarlane Walter & Ross, 1995).

Provincial political histories dealing with this period include Roger Graham, *Old Man Ontario: Leslie Miscampbell Frost* (Toronto: University of Toronto Press, 1990); Allan Kerr McDougall, *John P. Robarts: His Life and Government* (Toronto: University of Toronto Press, 1986); Nelson Wiseman, *Social Democracy in Manitoba: A History of the CCF-NDP* (Winnipeg: University of Manitoba Press, 1983); Raymond B. Blake, *Canadian at Last: Canada Integrates Newfoundland as a Province* (Toronto: University of Toronto Press, 1994); James Hiller and Peter Neary, eds., *Twentieth Century Newfoundland: Explorations* (St John's: Breakwater, 1994); David Mitchell, *W.A.C. Bennett and the Rise of*

British Columbia (Vancouver: Douglas and McIntyre, 1983); Alvin Finkel, *The Social Credit Phenomenon in Alberta* (Toronto: University of Toronto Press, 1989); Verner Smitheram et al., *The Garden Transformed: Prince Edward Island, 1945–1980* (Charlottetown: Ragweed, 1982); Margaret Conrad, "The Atlantic Revolution of the 1950s," in *Beyond Anger and Longing: Community and Development in Atlantic Canada*, ed. Berkeley Fleming (Fredericton: Acadiensis Press, 1988): 55–96; Thomas H. McLeod and Ian McLeod, *Tommy Douglas: The Road to Jerusalem* (Edmonton: Hurtig, 1987); and Della Stanley, *Louis Robichaud: A Decade of Power* (Halifax: Nimbus, 1984).

Studies of postwar Quebec include Paul-André Lintcau, René Durocher, and Jean-Claude Robert, *Quebec Since 1930* (Toronto: Lorimer, 1991); Kenneth McRoberts, *Quebec: Social Change and Political Crisis*, 3rd ed.(Toronto: McClelland and Stewart, 1988), René Lévesque, *Memoirs* (Toronto: McClelland and Stewart, 1986); Alain Gagnon, *Quebec: State and Society in Crisis* (Toronto: Methuen, 1984); Dale C. Thomson, *Jean Lesage and the Quiet Revolution* (Toronto: Macmillan, 1984); William Coleman, *The Independence Movement in Quebec, 1945–1980* (Toronto: University of Toronto Press, 1984); and Michael Behiels, *Prelude to Quebec's Quiet Revolution: Liberalism Versus Neo-Conservatism, 1945–1960* (Montreal: McGill-Queen's University Press, 1985).

On the views of Quebec's most noted federalist, see Pierre Trudeau, *Federalism and the French Canadians* (Toronto: Macmillan, 1977), *Against the Current: Selected Writings 1939–1996* (Toronto: McClelland and Stewart, 1996), and *Towards a Just Society: The Trudeau Years* (Markham, ON: Viking, 1990). Among useful works on francophones outside Quebec are Richard Wilbur, *The Rise of French New Brunswick* (Halifax: Formac, 1989); la Fédération des francophones hors Québec, *The Heirs of Lord Durham: A Manifesto of a Vanishing People* (Toronto: Gage, 1978); Sally Ross and Alphonse Deveau, *The Acadians of Nova Scotia: Past and Present* (Halifax: Nimbus, 1992); and Georges Arsenault, *The Island Acadians, 1720–1980* (Charlottetown: Ragweed Press, 1989).

Federal-provincial relations are discussed in David Milne, *Tug of War: Ottawa and the Provinces Under Trudeau and Mulroney* (Toronto: Lorimer, 1986) and Keith Banting, *The Welfare State and Canadian Federalism*, rev. ed. (Montreal: McGill-Queen's

University Press, 1987). Among useful works on the evolution of the welfare state more generally, see Dennis Guest, *The Emergence of Social Security in Canada*, rev. ed. (Vancouver: UBC Press, 1997); John C. Bacher, *Keeping to the Marketplace: The Evolution of Canadian Housing Policy* (Montreal: McGill-Queen's University Press, 1993); James Struthers, *The Limits of Affluence: Welfare in Ontario, 1920–1970* (Toronto: University of Toronto Press, 1994); James Snell, *The Citizen's Wage: The State and the Elderly in Canada, 1900–1951* (Toronto: University of Toronto Press, 1996); and Raymond B. Blake and Jeff Keshen, eds., *Social Welfare Policy in Canada: Historical Readings* (Toronto: Copp Clark, 1995). On medicare and the Canada Pension Plan, the most recent work is P.E. Bryden, *Planners and Politicians: Liberal Politics and Social Policy, 1957–1968* (Montreal: McGill-Queen's University Press, 1998). An excellent work on the welfare state in Quebec is Dominique Marshall, *Aux origines sociales de l'État-providence. familles québécoises, obligations scolaires et allocations familiales 1940–1955* (Montreal: Les Presses de l'Université de Montréal, 1998). On provincial welfare regimes more generally, a comprehensive overview is found in Gerald William Boychuk, *Patchworks of Purpose: The Development of Provincial Social Assistance Regimes in Canada* (Montreal: McGill-Queen's University Press, 1998). On daycare, see Alvin Finkel, "'Even the Little Children Cooperated': Family Strategies, Childcare Discourse, and Social Welfare Debates, 1945-1975," *Labour/Le Travail* 36 (Fall 1995): 91–118.

Canada's aims and roles throughout the Cold War are discussed in the Hillmer and Granatstein texts mentioned in earlier chapters, as well as Denis Smith, *Politics of Fear: Canada and the Cold War, 1941–1948* (Toronto: University of Toronto Press, 1988); James Eayrs, *In Defence of Canada*, vols. 4 and 5 (Toronto: University of Toronto Press, 1980, 1983); and Ernie Regehr and Simon Rosenblum, eds., *Canada and the Nuclear Arms Race* (Toronto: Lorimer, 1983). On Canada in Korea, see Ted Barris, *Deadlock in Korea: Canadians at War, 1950–1953* (Toronto: Macmillan, 1999). Canada's role in Vietnam is discussed in Victor Levant, *Quiet Complicity: Canadian Involvement in the Vietnam War* (Toronto: Between the Lines, 1986) and Douglas Ross, *In the Interests of Peace: Canada and Vietnam, 1945–1973* (Toronto: University of Toronto Press, 1985).

 **WEBLINKS**

JOHN DIEFENBAKER
www.nlc-bnc.ca/primeminister/h4-3325-e.html

This site contains a biography, a list of quick facts, anecdotes, links for further reading, photographs, and speeches pertaining to Canada's thirteenth Prime Minister.

LESTER B. PEARSON
www.nlc-bnc.ca/history/4/h4-3350-e.html

This site includes a biography and highlights of Pearson's career, as well as some useful links.

PIERRE ELLIOTT TRUDEAU
http://collections.ic.gc.ca/canspeak/english/pet

Biographical information and a transcript of Trudeau's Statement on the Introduction of the Official Languages Bill of October 17, 1968 are presented on this site.

CANADA AND THE COLD WAR
www.kn.pacbell.com/wired/fil/pages/listcanadama2.html

This site includes an extensive list of online resources dealing with Canadian involvement in and perspectives on the Cold War.

THE KOREAN WAR
www.vac-acc.gc.ca/general

Read about Canada's involvement in the Korean War at the website of Veterans Affairs Canada.

Growth at All Costs: The Economy, 1945–1975

In 1964, Cominco began operating a lead-zinc mine in the Northwest Territories, creating the instant community of Pine Point. About $100 million of federal money was invested in the project, which included developing the townsite and building highways, hydro-electricity plants, and a railway to haul minerals to markets. By 1975, about 1800 people, mainly white southerners, lived at Pine Point. Their high wages and modern homes were evidence of the good lives that many Canadians attained in the postwar period.

Forty miles west of this new town created by business and government was the long-established Native community of Fort Resolution. Speaking to a federal inquiry established in 1974 to determine whether energy pipelines should be built across the Mackenzie Valley, Mike Beaulieu of Fort Resolution provided a different view of the economic benefits of the mine than Cominco's.

> We, the Dene people, do a lot of hunting and trapping and fishing. Our hunting has decreased a lot due to the construction of the highway, the building of the mine, and the increase of the people from the South.... Our traditional grounds are slowly being overtaken by these [mine] employees. There is virtually no benefit to be spoken of from the mine.[1]

The impact of the Pine Point mine on the environment and on Native peoples provides an example of the other side of the equation of the unprecedented economic growth that characterized the period from 1945 to 1975. Dramatic improvements in overall living standards were accompanied by environmental degradation, uneven distribution of the new wealth, and destruction of many communities. This chapter traces the economic history of the period when the American dream of unlimited prosperity became a realistic goal for many Canadians, but an unattainable—even undesirable—illusion for others.

THE WELFARE AND WARFARE ECONOMY

In 1945, the federal government proposed to prevent a postwar depression by expanding the money supply and incurring government deficits in times of unemployment. According to Reconstruction Minister C.D. Howe's White Paper on postwar reconstruction, the government would redeem those deficits by cutting spending when the economy boomed. The private sector would continue to operate companies, price goods, and make investment decisions. Even this moderate Keynesianism shocked economic conservatives. Traditional economic theory held that large government debts would produce uncontrollable inflation. In

1945, the federal debt alone was 1.5 times the nation's gross national product.

Ottawa ignored prewar nostrums about the sinfulness of debt and government intervention in the economy. While moving quickly to jettison wartime price controls and to privatize Crown corporations, the federal government expanded the money supply to finance the debt and increased spending on social programs and later on defence. If growth in output and productivity are the measures of success, the government's strategy worked well.

Immediately after the war, when production slowed, exports contracted, and inflation soared, the federal government stoked the economy with tax incentives to industry and programs targeted at veterans, the private-housing market, and municipalities. Soon, consumer demand picked up the slack. War plants were quickly converted from producing troop carriers, uniforms, bombs, and barracks to making cars, clothes, appliances, and housing materials.

Since Canada's economic prosperity depended on exports, trade liberalization became a cornerstone of Canadian postwar foreign policy. In November 1947, Canada signed the General Agreement on Tariffs and Trade (GATT), aimed at reducing trade barriers. Ironically, shortly afterwards, Finance Minister Douglas Abbott announced a series of restrictive trade measures. Another exchange crisis precipitated by postwar spending on American products had forced the government to reimpose import controls. By 1949, controls were lifted again, foreign investment resumed, and exports rose.

The cyclical upswing was reinforced by massive military spending, sparked by the escalating Cold War. Between 1949 and 1953, defence expenditures rose from 16 to 45 percent of the federal budget, and a new ministry was created to orchestrate the business of war. C.D. Howe became the Minister of Defence Production, and in this guise he continued to play godfather to the business community. With over $1 billion spent annually on defence in the 1950s, every aspect of the Canadian economy was shaped by military considerations. As late as 1960, when defence had slipped back to a quarter of federal budgetary expenditures, military purchases accounted for 89 percent of the shipments in the aircraft industry, 41 percent in electronics, and 21

percent in shipbuilding. Research and development in both Canada and the United States was increasingly related to defence priorities. Strategic stockpiling by the American military led to large-scale purchases of Canadian primary products, particularly minerals. In the United States, the term "military-industrial complex" was coined to describe this new era of defence-induced growth. It was equally applicable to Canada.

Contrary to the philosophy espoused in C. D. Howe's White Paper in 1945, federal planners failed to tailor their policies to cyclical swings. Ottawa ran budget surpluses from 1949 to 1956, but they were not sufficiently large to offset private investment or the ambitious spending by provincial and municipal governments. In the heady atmosphere of postwar prosperity, politicians and the public believed that both welfare and warfare could be accommodated. Their treasuries fattened by higher taxes, governments at all levels spent money at an unprecedented rate, investing in infrastructure (roads and electrical power facilities) and building up social capital (schools and hospitals).

In cooperation with provinces and private industry, the federal government supported several megaprojects, including the Trans-Canada Highway, the Trans-Canada Pipeline, and Beechwood Power. Most impressive as an engineering and construction feat was the St Lawrence Seaway, a jointly-funded project with the Americans, built between 1954 and 1959. Its purpose was to enlarge the canals and develop the power potential along the inland waterway. Nearly 3800 kilometres from Anticosti Island to Lake Superior, the seaway cost the Canadian government over $1 billion.

Owing to the booming economy, the unemployment rate for 1956 was only 3.2 percent, the lowest rate for the rest of the century. Wages increased faster than prices throughout the postwar decade while consumption increased by 5.1 percent a year. The government's debt as a proportion of gross national product halved from 1946 to 1956 because a wealthier population was paying enough taxes to cover both increased spending and debt reduction.

Much of the postwar productivity was stimulated by technological innovation leading to new product lines. While many new products such as synthetic fibres, plastics, and pesticides had been stimulated by

American Fast Food and the Service Industry

The fast-food industry was one example of an American-dominated service industry that made its entry into Canada in the postwar period. Franchise operations, such as Colonel Sanders' Kentucky Fried Chicken, Burger King, and, after 1968, McDonald's, defined the eating-out experience for teenagers and for two-income families who sought occasional relief from having to prepare a meal.

Sociologist Ester Reiter worked at a Toronto Burger King in the early 1980s and interviewed fellow employees as part of a thesis project. Each Burger King is operated by a franchisee who pays Burger King's Miami headquarters a large fee for the right to operate a firm with the Burger King name and every outlet is required by Miami to follow unswervingly the procedures laid out in the Manual of Operating Data. "Burger King University" in Miami trains managers so that they know how to implement these procedures uniformly. Headquarters is linked by computer to each franchise and monitors performance daily. For employees this means a rigid work schedule in which the time allowed to take an order, prepare a specific item, or to get the food to the customer is measured in seconds.

Reiter's fellow minimum-wage workers were teenagers, often working part-time, and immigrant women for whom better jobs were unavailable. Few liked the work, which paid minimum wage, and many felt like robots, waiting for their breaks in the "crew room" for a chance to listen to rock music and talk about plans for the weekend. On the job, "hamburgers are cooked as they pass through the broiler on a conveyor belt at a rate of 835 patties per hour. Furnished with a pair of tongs, the worker picks up the burgers as they drop off the conveyor belt, puts each on a toasted bun, and places the hamburgers and buns in a steamer. The jobs may be hot and boring, but they can be learned in a manner of minutes."[2]

wartime needs, others, including televisions, the self-propelled combine harvester, and the snowmobile, had been developed prior to the war but became commercially viable only in the improved postwar economic climate. Developments in the chemical industry revolutionized agriculture and sparked massive forest-spraying programs. The pharmaceutical industry could hardly keep up with the demand for new products, including such miracle drugs as penicillin, polio vaccines, and the birth-control pill.

Stimulated by government spending and strong export markets, multinational economic empires bloomed in Canada, including the Macmillan-Bloedel forestry complex headquartered in British Columbia, Ontario's investment giant, Argus Corporation, and K.C. Irving's New Brunswick-based conglomerate. Times had never seemed so good but in 1957, the economic bubble burst. The American economy went into recession, and the Canadian economy, so closely integrated with that of its southern neighbour, followed suit. By 1958, the rate of unemployment was twice its 1956 level.

Table 24.1
Canada's Economic Growth, 1945–1976

Year	GNP*	GNP in 1971 dollars*	GNP per capita in 1971 dollars*
1945	11 863	29 071	2400.81
1951	21 640	35 450	2530.52
1956	32 058	47 599	2959.95
1961	39 646	54 741	3001.48
1966	61 828	74 844	3739.40
1971	94 450	94 450	4379.17
1976	191 031	119 249	5195.02

*millions of dollars

Source: Adapted from F.H. Leacy, ed., *Historical Statistics of Canada*, 2nd ed. (Ottawa: Statistics Canada, 1983), Catalogue 11-516, tables A1, F 13, and F 15.

PRIMARY INDUSTRIES

In the postwar period, marketing boards revolutionized farming in Canada by establishing quotas, setting prices, and defining market boundaries. A larger percentage of farm products was destined for canning and, increasingly, freezing. Farms became larger and could increasingly be viewed as full-fledged business enterprises, part of a delicately balanced network of production, processing, and marketing required to feed an increasingly urbanized North American society.

The crops in demand in the marketplace changed. During the war, federal subsidies encouraged Prairie farmers to diversify their output to oats, barley, and flax. The price of wheat remained low on international markets throughout the 1950s, discouraging further expansion of the wheat economy. A similar transformation occurred in the Annapolis Valley where farmers were paid to uproot their apple orchards and concentrate on other fruits as well as vegetables, poultry, and dairy products for a domestic rather than a British market.

The transformation of the east coast fishing industry in the postwar decade paralleled that of agriculture. As European markets for saltfish disappeared, sales of fresh and frozen fish were increasingly geared to an oversupplied North American market. At the same time, technology revolutionized productivity in the fisheries. By the 1960s there were 1400 trawlers engaged in the Grand Banks fishery, netting an unprecedented 2.6 million metric tonnes of fish. Interest in ocean resources led the United Nations to institute the Law of the Sea Conference. The third Law of the Sea conference in 1977 gave nations the right to control ocean activities within 200 miles of their shores, opening a new resource frontier of great potential—if it were managed well.

Impressive growth also occurred in mining and hydro-electric power generation, benefiting from the booming North American domestic and military economies. Companies developed copper deposits at Murdochville on the Gaspé Peninsula, lead-zinc-copper ores in the Dalhousie-Bathurst region of New Brunswick, and potash in Saskatchewan. In 1949 the Iron Ore Company was formed to bring the vast deposits on the Ungava–Labrador border into production.

Canada's energy resources seemed to know no bounds. On 3 February 1947, Imperial Oil's Leduc No. 1 well struck oil, and energy discoveries in Alberta soon became regular fare. From 1945 to 1960, Alberta's annual production of crude petroleum increased sixteenfold while natural gas production increased tenfold. Saskatchewan also made promising finds of energy resources. By 1952, pipelines in which Imperial Oil was a major shareholder funnelled oil from Alberta either to Vancouver or through Wisconsin to Sarnia, Ontario.

Oil well at Leduc, Alberta, 1947.

Imperial Oil Archives

In 1956, the Canadian government entered an agreement with an American company, Trans-Canada PipeLines, to build a gas pipeline from Alberta to Montreal. In addition to providing a generous loan to the company, Ottawa agreed to create a Crown corporation to build the uneconomical section of the pipeline through northern Ontario. The United States absorbed about half of the Canadian output of oil and gas, but cheap imports of crude oil from the Middle East kept the industry lean until the early 1970s.

Other provinces did what they could to keep pace with the burgeoning economies of Ontario and Alberta. Newfoundland premier Joey Smallwood convinced overseas capitalists to develop the mighty Churchill Falls in Labrador, while New Brunswick premier Hugh John Flemming wrung $30 million out of the federal government to help complete his Beechwood Power complex on the St John River. Nova Scotia developed coal-generated thermal power plants. In the early 1950s, Alcan built a huge generating station at Kemano, British Columbia, to supply its $450-million aluminum smelter at Kitimat. Saskatchewan's premier, Tommy Douglas, with generous subsidies from Ottawa, planned an ambitious power-generating project on the South Saskatchewan River.

THE POSTINDUSTRIAL ECONOMY

The increasing importance of communications in determining the pace of economic change in the second half of the twentieth century led analysts to coin the term Information Age to describe the new phenomenon. While industrial and service industries remained significant players in the economy, communications technology, represented by computers and satellites, contributed to quantum leaps in productivity. With the development of satellite and space communications in the late 1950s and 1960s, signals could be transmitted around the world in a split second. Computers were linked to telecommunications systems in the early 1970s, permitting vast quantities of information to be sent over telecommunications networks.

Canada was among the first nations to experiment with the communication technologies that defined the Information Age. In 1958, Canada's television network was the longest in the world. Canada also established cable-television systems ahead of most countries. When *Alouette 1* was launched on 29 September 1962, Canada became the third nation in space after the Soviet Union and the United States. With its *Anik* (the Inuit word for "brother") series launched in the 1970s, Canada led the world in the use of satellites for commercial communications. It was the first nation to establish a digital data network for computer users.

Virtually every human activity has been altered in some way by computer technology. Computer technology helped to send people to the moon, revolutionized the office, and automated manufacturing processes. The initial research on computers was conducted in Britain and the United States. During the Second World War, British scientists used primitive computers to crack German codes. Canada's first entry into the computer age was UTEC, developed by scientists at the University of Toronto between 1947 and 1951. A massive structure that filled a whole room, UTEC experienced more down time than computing time. In 1952, the University of Toronto purchased a British-made computer.

The invention of the transistor in 1949 transformed the whole field of electronics. The replacement of vacuum tubes with solid-state transistors—ultimately made of chips of silicon sand—allowed computers to become smaller, more reliable, and less expensive to build and operate. Integrated circuitry, developed in 1958, led to further miniaturization. By 1977, Apple, a microcomputer company based in California, was selling desktop computers to the technology-fixated consumer.

Once the commercial potential of the computer was realized, IBM and other big multinational corporations soon dominated the field. A Canadian-based corporation, Northern Electric (later renamed Northern Telecom), eventually carved a niche for itself by producing telephone equipment and switching devices for a global telecommunications market. Nevertheless, Canada's trade deficit in electronic goods reached $850 million in 1973 and rose quickly in the years that followed.

While their labour force participation continued to expand, women, such as these typists at the Dominion Bureau of Statistics, worked in traditional, poorly paid occupations.

C. Lund/National Archives of Canada/PA-133212

THE END OF THE ECONOMIC MIRACLE

By the early 1970s, there were dark clouds on the horizon. The American government had failed to raise taxes to offset expenses associated with the unpopular Vietnam War. Allowing the economy to overheat, it then attempted vainly to reduce inflation by cutting spending and tightening credit. American unemployment increased, and the government responded with trade restrictions, which had repercussions for Canadian trade and therefore Canadian rates of employment and inflation.

Then the OPEC oil price shocks late in 1973 seemed to knock the stuffing out of western economies, which had relied throughout the postwar boom on cheap energy. In 1974, though unemployment was a manageable 5.3 percent, inflation stood at 14.5 percent. A year later inflation was down to 9.9 percent, but unemployment had reached a postwar high of 6.9 percent. The combination of high unemployment and high inflation was labelled "stagflation," a short form for stagnation plus inflation.

A political debate ensued about how to combat this unsettling phenomenon. In the August 1974 federal election, Conservative leader Robert Stanfield called for wage and price controls. Prime Minister Trudeau won re-election after vigorously opposing this prescription. In October 1975, Trudeau reversed himself, announcing a three-year program of controls. Trudeau's economic policies to deal with stagflation proved contradictory. Government spending increased substantially in accordance with Keynesian prescriptions for a stagnating economy but, beginning in 1975, the money supply was severely restricted.

The business community, concerned about profit margins, began to abandon the postwar consensus on economic policy. Low rates of unemployment and generous unemployment insurance benefits, they complained, were forcing employers to pay wage in-

In the Postindustrial Age, seven of ten employed Canadians provided services rather than producing goods. A striking feature of Canada's service economy was the growth of government spending and jobs. Public spending increased from 5 percent of GNP in 1867 to 30 percent by 1960 and 48.2 percent in 1985. Nearly half of government expenditure was on goods and services; the rest involved transfer payments, which moved private income from one group of citizens to another. The federal share of GNP rose only marginally after 1960, but the provinces' share doubled as their responsibilities grew rapidly.

The trend toward urban concentration, typical of the Industrial Age, was consolidated by the service economy. Only in the 1970s did this trend ease as people moved from congested city cores and monotonous suburbs to rural "exurbia." To improve their tax bases, many city councils expanded their boundaries into exurbia, becoming vast, sprawling administrative units. In 1971, three out of four Canadians were classified as urban dwellers.

creases that hurt profits. Tight money policies, they stressed, were necessary to slow down the Canadian economy in the short run to stop inflation and create long-term stability.

THE COSTS OF GROWTH

Following the Second World War, government policy and economic activity was focused on bringing every Canadian into the modern age. Subsistence survival by farming, fishing, and hunting was deemed unworthy, and rural life, unless fully commercialized, experienced a rapid decline. As a result, many communities became ghost towns.

Farming communities lost population as the agriculture industry was restructured. While the new corporate giants in the food industry prospered, farmers often did not. In Saskatchewan, where a majority of the population still farmed in 1941 and earned most of their income from harvesting grains, the farm population fell over the next 30 years from 514 677 to 233 792. Those who remained had larger, more diversified farms, but federal farm subsidies and income from off-farm jobs provided most of their livelihood. Except in British Columbia, similar patterns prevailed across the country. Prince Edward Island witnessed the most change as costs of production for its major farm products, particularly potatoes, increased well out of proportion to rising prices to consumers. Between 1951 and 1981 the size of farms increased while the number of farms dropped from 10 137 to 3154. Over one Canadian in four lived on a farm at the end of the Second World War. Thirty years later, fewer than 1 in 15 farmed.

In the fisheries the story was the same. The magnificent trawlers sealed the fate of inshore fishers. By the 1950s, the real choice for most fishers was between becoming a labourer on a corporate trawler or changing occupations. Cooperative fishing organizations founded before the war lost control of processing and marketing structures as the fishery on both coasts became part of the continental corporate universe. Most fishers earned a wage rather than being self-employed. In 1956, the remaining poverty-prone self-employed fishers became eligible for unemployment insurance.

Most Canadians moved voluntarily from their rural communities to urban centres where they had better access to jobs and services, but there were exceptions. In Newfoundland, families in outport communities had to be enticed by government grants to move to anticipated "growth centres." Inuit in the Arctic were also reluctant to be relocated from their traditional communities to "northern suburbs,"[3] where they were expected to live under government surveillance. In both cases, the move failed to live up to its promise. The housing and sanitary conditions in communities created by the state for the Inuit were appalling. Outport Newfoundlanders found few jobs in the communities where they were encouraged to relocate.

The transformation from subsistence to consumer society was evident in every corner of the nation. In the North the Inuit were incorporated into the North American economy through their painting and sculpture, which had become popular in the art market in southern climes. With factories turning out textiles and clothing at unprecedented rates, women no longer engaged in domestic production. A vacationing antique dealer in the late 1950s bought 1200 spinning wheels in rural areas of Cape Breton. In fashionable

Figure 24.1
Farm Populations in Canada, 1941–1971 (Millions)

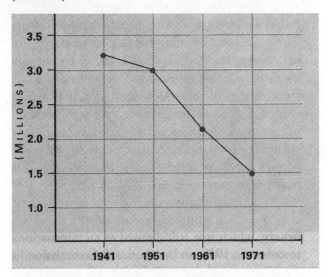

Source: Adapted from F.H. Leacy, ed., *Historical Statistics of Canada*, 2nd ed. (Ottawa: Statistics Canada, 1983), Catalogue 11-516, Series M1-M11.

middle-class homes, such items now became collectors' items, a happy reminder of the past when people had to work hard for a living.

WORKING CONDITIONS

Industrial workers benefited more from the economic growth of the post-1945 period than farmers and fishers. In some industries, working conditions improved noticeably. Ontario's lumber industry, finding it difficult to retain workers in an economy with low unemployment, replaced logging camps—once notorious for their crowded, cold, and poorly maintained bunkhouses—with suburban-like accommodations. In other industries, however, employers reckoned that highly paid workers would put up with unsafe or unhealthy conditions. In the mining industry, for example, innovations such as scooptrams meant back injuries and respiratory problems for nickel miners.

Machines that improved productivity posed problems both for worker safety and eventually the preservation of jobs. By the 1970s, the net impact of technology on employment prospects appeared to be negative. Microprocessors, first introduced in 1971, displaced blue-collar workers by controlling systems that automatically cut boards, stitched seams, and assembled parts. Women-dominated white-collar jobs, such as file clerk and keypunch operator, were among the first to be automated. Many workers who lost their jobs proved ill-equipped to take up other available jobs, thus becoming victims of "structural unemployment."

GROWTH AND THE ENVIRONMENT

Of all the costs of economic growth, the impact on the biosphere that supports life is of greatest importance in the long term. The long-term consequences of industrial pollutants received little attention in the postwar boom, but the age of innocence came to an abrupt end in 1962 when American scientist Rachel Carson published *Silent Spring*. Carson provided stunning revelations about the dangers posed by the "tide of chemicals born of the Industrial Age." Rivers and oceans, the air and soil, animal and human species, she argued, were being rapidly destroyed. She singled out the "Rivers of Death" created in New Brunswick and other forested areas of Canada where aerial pesticide-spraying programs begun in the 1950s were more effective in killing fish than their intended target, the spruce budworm.

Soon, scientists discovered that polychlorinated biphenyls (PCBs), a family of highly toxic chemicals used in electrical equipment, continued to poison the food chain after their use had been discontinued. No one knew how to dispose of the hazardous waste from nuclear power plants. Even the emissions released into the atmosphere by tall smokestacks came back to earth hundreds of kilometres away as acid rain and snow, which ravaged lakes and forests.

Workers in fluorspar mine, St Lawrence, Newfoundland.
National Archives of Canada/PA-130784

Perhaps the Canadians who suffered most from the "growth at all costs" philosophy were the Aboriginal peoples. Although they fought in the courts to stop megaprojects that would harm the ecology of their hunting and fishing territories, their concerns were largely brushed aside by the larger society. Hydro-electric projects, mines, pulp and paper mills, and new transportation systems displaced Native peoples or jeopardized their traditional ways of life. For example, effluent from the Reed paper mill made it unsafe for Natives to fish in the English–Wabigoon River system near Kenora. Not only was their major food supply affected, but also the tourism that had made the reserves outside Kenora relatively prosperous and which depended on good local fishing dried up. Moreover, mill operators rarely hired Native labour. Thus, for Native peoples in the area, chronic unemployment accompanied environmental degradation.

As the environmental movement gained momentum, public and private institutions began to alter their behaviour. The Soviet Union, Britain, and the United States signed an agreement to ban atmospheric testing of nuclear weapons in 1963. A United Nations Conference on the Human Environment met in Stockholm in 1972 to discuss the decaying state of the planet. Chaired by a Canadian, Maurice Strong, the conference produced a declaration of environmental rights and established a program to fund and coordinate investigations into environmental problems. Environmental legislation came slowly because of its potential impact on growth. Economic growth had been the liberal answer to the socialist call for a more egalitarian distribution of wealth. How could the standard of living of the lowest people on the economic scale be improved if the economy remained static?

ECONOMIC DISPARITY

In postindustrial Canada, age, class, ethnicity, gender, and geography remained important factors in determining how one fared in the quest for economic well-being. In 1965, John Porter published *The Vertical Mosaic*, an impressive analysis of stratification in Canadian society. Porter showed that an economic elite of less than 1000 men—mostly of British and Protestant background, and graduates of private schools—dominated the Canadian economy. Even in Quebec, anglophone elites controlled the economic structures.

Women figured prominently in the ranks of Canada's economically disadvantaged despite increasing participation in the work force. As services moved from the domestic economy into the market economy, women often moved with them but their wages failed to match those of men. Paid domestic work declined under the impact of household appliances, but teaching, nursing, secretarial, clerical, and cleaning jobs expanded and remained dominated by women. Overall, women's labour force participation in Canada increased from 23.4 percent in 1953 to 48.9 percent in 1979, while the male participation rate fell from 82.9 percent to 78.4 percent. Despite their increasing participation in the labour force, in 1971 women with full-time jobs made on average less than 60 percent of men with full-time jobs. Women were also far more likely to be employed in part-time work.

Visible minorities, especially First Nations, Métis, Inuit, and African Canadians, remained at the bottom of the economic scale throughout the nation. Immigrants, many of them illegally in the country, also suffered exploitation by factory owners and farmers. In Montreal, immigrants from the Caribbean, Latin America, India, Pakistan, Greece, Portugal, and Italy worked 12-hour days for subsistence wages. According to one journalist writing in 1974, they "man the clanging textile and clothing factories which line St. Lawrence and Park….clean toilets in glittering highrises, wash dishes in grimy restaurant kitchens, pull switches and operate machinery in fuming plastics and chemical factories, abattoirs, machine shops."[4] It was estimated in the late 1970s that 100 000 illegal immigrants worked in Canada, generally in sweatshops in Montreal and Toronto. Intimidated by the threat of discovery and deportation, they often had to accept work at less than the legislated minimum wage.

Far from industrial sites, farmworkers also often laboured under conditions and rates of pay that few Canadians were aware existed in their prosperous society. Excluded from minimum-wage protection, im-

Native dwellings contrast sharply with houses in Fort George, Quebec, 1973.

John Flanders/National Archives of Canada/PA-130854

migrant orchard workers in British Columbia and Ontario and Native sugar-beet pickers in Manitoba worked long hours for negligible pay and slept in miserable accommodations provided by the employers. Many farmworkers were illegal immigrants; still others were contract workers for the growing season and were required to return home to Latin America or the Caribbean once the growing season was over. Canada apparently wanted their labour power, but did not want them as citizens.

Despite economic growth and the advent of the welfare state, the overall distribution of wealth in Canada remained remarkably static. The Economic Council of Canada, an advisory group to the government on economic planning, calculated in 1961 that 27 percent of Canadians received incomes low enough to qualify them as poor. Eight years later, the federal government, using the same measures, announced that poverty had been cut in half thanks to economic growth and the increase in the number of two-income families. The poverty rate would rise again in the slow-growth seventies.

Whether the national economy was booming or in recession, certain provinces and regions of provinces lagged well behind the national average. Southern Ontario generally prospered far more than the rest of the country, while northern Ontario suffered high rates of unemployment and poverty, particularly in Native areas. Even within southern Ontario, there were large pockets of poverty in the southeast. Montreal had a vibrant mixed economy, but northern Quebec and the Gaspé experienced grinding poverty even during economic upswings. In wealthy Alberta and British Columbia, northern residents had little to show for the resource boom that created high average incomes in their provinces.

The Atlantic region, Saskatchewan, and Manitoba constituted the country's have-not provinces. Dependent on equalization grants to provide reasonable levels of service to their citizens, they remained unable to provide the economic diversification that would create more jobs. The bias of federal fiscal and monetary policies toward the more populous and wealthy regions compounded the problem. How, for instance, could the bank rate be set to meet the needs of the lagging Atlantic region when the central Canadian economy was facing inflationary pressure?

TAXATION AND THE DISTRIBUTION OF WEALTH

An assessment of the taxation system helps to explain why there was little redistribution of the nation's wealth. Before the war, most working Canadians earned less than the minimum income required before personal income tax had to be paid. After the war, most workers became income taxpayers. Corporations and the wealthy also paid taxes. But taxes on profits were ameliorated by generous capital cost (depreciation) allowances and, for many firms, by a variety of loopholes. Dividend holders by 1953 received a 20 percent tax credit in recognition of dividends forgone because of corporate tax assessments.

The Diefenbaker government established a Royal Commission on Taxation in 1962, headed by Kenneth Carter, a leading chartered accountant. According to the commissioners: "The present system does not afford fair treatment for all Canadians. People in essentially similar circumstances do not bear the same taxes. People in essentially different circumstances do not bear appropriately different tax burdens."5 Commission studies revealed that the poorest Canadians paid proportionately more taxes than well-off citizens. Carter recommended that indirect taxation be substantially reduced and that the base for personal and corporate income tax be broadened by removing most loopholes. The poor would be compensated through the tax system by the institution of a "negative income tax"—that is, a payment from the government to individuals whose incomes were too low to support a decent standard of living.

Industry's negative reaction caused the Pearson government to delay its response to the Carter recommendations, tabled in 1966. In the early 1970s, the Trudeau government made a half-hearted attempt at tax reform, taxing most capital gains at half the rate of other income and increasing income exemptions so as to remove the poorest citizens from the tax rolls. But negative income taxes were rejected, and most of the exemptions of rich individuals and corporations remained on the books. Indeed, the federal government abandoned estate taxes in 1972, leaving the provinces to decide how to tax the wealth of individuals who had died. The provinces abolished the tax. The overwhelming influence of the corporate elite in Canadian political and economic decision-making limited the impact of Carter's recommendations.

THE TRADE UNION MOVEMENT

The trade union movement was the most vocal opponent of the liberal consensus in the postwar period.

Although legislation recognized the right of workers to organize, the Industrial Relations Disputes Act of 1948, which applied to federal workers, and its provincial equivalents, also attempted to co-opt union leaders into the planning mechanisms of corporations and governments. Under the new labour laws, workers found their rights to negotiate limited to wages and narrowly defined working conditions. Unions were expected to enforce contracts and to keep their members in line. Decisions to reduce the size of the workforce, to speed up production, or to use hazardous materials in the workplace were rarely covered by contracts. Even when management appeared to violate a contract, workers were not allowed to strike. Instead, drawn-out grievance procedures had to be followed to seek redress.

Despite such restraints, workers were not prepared to return to prewar conditions. Long-time United Electrical Workers staffer and Communist activist Bill Walsh recalled: "We had just won the war, freed the world from fascism and to advance to a new social order and good times for all…There was a whole new spirit in the world. Returning soldiers were not looking for jobs but they weren't going to sit around waiting for handouts. They talked with new authority. They had been through hell and they weren't going to accept the world they had left behind—including the depression wages still being paid at Westinghouse and the other big companies."6

When better wages and working conditions could not be won at the bargaining table, unionists resorted to the strike weapon. Wartime wage freezes created pent-up demands for increases at war's end. In 1946 and 1947, about 240 000 workers struck for a total of almost seven million workdays. Automobile, steel, rubber, textile, packing, electrical manufacturing, forestry, and mining companies all felt the sting of such action. Average wages rose from 69.4 cents per hour in 1945 to 91.3 cents per hour in 1948.

Women, who were generally not unionized, did not share in the wage gains. In 1948, the Retail, Wholesale, and Department Store Union (RWDSU), supported by the Canadian Congress of Labour, initiated a three-year drive, headed by Eileen Talman, to organize Toronto's Eaton's store. The company pulled out all the stops to oppose the union, linking unions with communism, raising wages just before the vote on unionizing took place, and warning part-time workers that unionism would cost them their jobs. When only 40 percent of the workers supported affiliation with the RWDSU, the CCL leadership, almost exclusively male, concluded that women were too passive to unionize and ceased its attempts to organize sectors dominated by female labour.

Such stereotypical views were being exploded in Quebec, where women endured a bitter and ultimately successful strike at Dupuis Frères department store in 1952 to win better pay and working conditions. Members of the increasingly secular Confédération des travailleurs catholiques du Canada, these women were a harbinger of things to come in postwar Quebec, where the provincial government often came to the armed defence of strike-bound employers. In 1949, workers in the town of Asbestos, unwilling to delay a strike until a government-appointed board of arbitration reported on their grievances, struck so that

the company would not have time to stockpile asbestos before the inevitable walkout. During the five-month strike, the workers faced a large contingent of provincial police who protected replacement workers hired by the company. Many strikers were arrested or beaten in clashes with the police.

The brutal state response to the strike galvanized considerable resistance to the Union nationale. Liberal-nationalist intellectuals, including future prime minister Trudeau, were increasingly united on the need to defeat Duplessis and to protect workers' interests. Even within the church, there were dissenters against Duplessis's heavy-handed tactics. Rank-and-file clergy who supported the Asbestos strikers briefly had a champion in Archbishop Charbonneau of Montreal, but his ecclesiastical superiors transferred him out of the province.

It was not only in Quebec that striking workers were confronted by police. In November 1945, the Ontario government sent provincial police and rein-

Voices from the Past

Factory Women on Strike

The predominantly young female labour force of Lanark Manufacturing Company, a firm making wire harnesses for the automobile companies, went on strike in August 1964. On strike for six months, their militancy countered popular stereotypes of women as passive workers. Here are some of their reflections about why they struck, what they faced during the strike, and what they gained by striking. Worker Rosemary Cousineau described factory conditions as:

> just total exhaustion and stress. Sometimes you'd come home and the tightness in your back felt like you were all in knots…You had to work so hard and so fast. If you made a mistake, the verbal abuse you'd get…Predominantly young women were put on the rotary because, as one worker described it, 'you had to hurry up. That's why we had more energy than the older girls, because we were young.'

One young woman recounted the struggles on the picket line.

> It broke our hearts when we saw people still going in…and they did everything they could to stop the scabs from work-

ing. The police used to protect the scabs going in and out…So we'd fight back—even with the police. We'd do anything to get back at 'em. They're supposed to be protection for the public, right? They're not supposed to be biased. But they sure were…It was all one-sided…I was in court every week for something or other.

Striker Yvette Ward, sizing up the results of the strike years later, concluded:

> A lot of times I sit and think about it. Lanark, to me, was a landmark in the history of labour because these kids weren't afraid. They went ahead and did it, even though they knew they might lose their jobs forever…
>
> I can't help but remember the unity and the courage and the knowledge that all of the girls from that time had—and the few men that were working there. We were bound together so tight. These girls were working for peanuts, and didn't have much to fight for, but they did. They fought for six months steady without a stop and never gave up for one minute…It was the experience of a lifetime.[7]

forcements from the RCMP into the gates of the Ford plant at Windsor to end a five-week-old strike. The strikers responded by blockading the plant with cars. The federal government appointed Justice Ivan Rand to mediate the conflict. The major issue was the closed shop, or compulsory union membership for employees. Rand successfully proposed a formula for union membership: in a bargaining unit where a majority voted to join a union, employers must collect union dues from all members of the unit, but individuals could formally apply to have their dues sent to a designated charity rather than the union. A less happy ending greeted the loggers of Newfoundland who struck in 1959, only to have Premier Joseph Smallwood use the RCMP to enforce his decision to decertify the International Woodworkers' Association as the bargaining agent of the loggers.

Opposition by employers to unions meant that the rate of unionization of private sector workers stalled after the 1950s. By contrast, public sector workers increasingly joined unions. Because women were heavily concentrated in the lower echelons of the public service, four-fifths of Canada's new unionists from 1966 to 1976 were women. Women in the "caring" professions, such as nursing, social work, and teaching, also questioned the stereotype that "women's work" was mainly community service rather than remunerative professional labour. Strikes of teachers, social workers, and civil servants, unheard-of before the 1970s, began to become commonplace by the end of the decade.

An increase in militancy was especially noticeable in Quebec. In 1960, there were 38 strikes in the province; in 1975, there were 362. The province's Catholic unions formally ended their affiliation with the church in 1960, organizing the Confédération des syndicats nationaux (CSN). The CSN played a major role in the Common Front formed by Quebec public sector unions in 1972, conducting general strikes to improve the position of the lowest-paid public sector workers, most of whom were women. The Common Front provoked much opposition. The Bourassa government invoked legislation to end the labour disruption, jailing the heads of Quebec's three largest labour federations when they encouraged their members to defy back-to-work orders.

CONTINENTAL ECONOMIC INTEGRATION

Economic integration characterized Canadian-American relations in the postwar period. As the Americans became concerned that they were running out of the raw materials required to fuel their military and civilian economy, they began to invest heavily in Canadian minerals, oil, and lumber. The need for uranium for atomic bombs and nuclear reactors allowed Canadian uranium companies to sell their product at fabulous prices to the United States Atomic Energy Commission. With Canada supplying a third of the world's military and civilian requirements for uranium in the 1950s, Uranium City, Saskatchewan, and Elliot Lake, Ontario, were added to the pantheon of boom towns on Canada's resource frontier.

In 1952, Atomic Energy of Canada was created as a Crown corporation to develop peaceful uses of atomic energy. It sold Candu reactors at home and internationally. Ontario was the first province to enter an agreement with AECL to build nuclear power stations, and the first demonstration plant at Rolphston came into operation in 1962.

Defence production, particularly after the Defence Production Sharing Agreement of 1958, further encouraged continental economic integration.

Table 24.2

Percentage of Foreign Control of Selected Canadian Industries, 1939–1973

Industry	1939	1948	1958	1968	1973
Manufacturing	38(32)*	43(39)	57(44)	58(46)	59(44)
Petroleum and natural gas**	–	–	73(67)	75(61)	76(59)
Mining and smelting	42(38)	40(37)	60(51)	68(58)	56(45)
Railways	3(3)	3(3)	2(2)	2(2)	2(2)
Other utilities	26(26)	24(24)	5(4)	5(4)	7(4)
Total†	21(19)	25(22)	32(26)	36(28)	35(26)

*Numbers in brackets indicate percentage controlled by American residents
**Petroleum and natural gas combined with mining and smelting to 1948
†Total includes merchandising, not shown separately

Sources: F.H. Leacy, ed., *Historical Statistics of Canada*, 2nd ed. (Ottawa: Statistics Canada, 1983), Series G, 291-302; John Fayerweather, *Foreign Investment in Canada: Prospects for National Policy* (Toronto: Oxford University Press, 1974) 7.

Fuelled by the Vietnam war, armaments production accounted for an estimated 125 000 Canadian jobs in the late 1960s. Shells, military aircraft, and radio relay sets poured out of Canadian factories while metal mining companies received record orders for minerals required in defence production.

The structure of trade as it emerged in the postwar period had one enduring characteristic. Exports, which made up a quarter of GNP, consisted largely of unprocessed and semi-processed products. By contrast, Canada's imports were mainly manufactured goods. While the Americans imported only 10 percent of the manufactured goods they consumed, Canadians imported 36 percent. There was a small decline in the percentage of Canada's imports from the United States

from 1946 to 1975. In 1946, when the war-wrecked economies of most countries provided little for Canada to import, 75.3 percent of all Canadian imports were from the United States; in 1975, the figure was 68.1 percent. By contrast, Canada's dependence on the American market for its exports grew considerably from 38.9 percent in 1946 to 64.7 percent in 1975.

THE GORDON REPORT

Canadians were ambivalent about this transformation in their economic relations. In 1955, the Canadian government appointed chartered accountant Walter Gordon to chair a Royal Commission on Canada's

Voices from the Past

Views of Foreign Ownership

In the 1950s and 1960s, Canada's political and business leaders expressed conflicting views regarding the benefits of foreign ownership of Canadian industries. The following excerpts provide a hint of the flavour of the debate.

> With an enormous area still of almost virgin country to be opened, Canadians need and welcome foreign investments and with their own healthy stake in the national development they have no fears of any domination.
>
> —G.K. Shiels, president of the Canadian Manufacturers Association, in the *Financial Post*, 1953

> The free and unhampered flow of foreign investment into Canada has brought so many benefits to this country that it certainly is entitled to a fair and unbiased hearing from the Canadian people.
>
> …If one allows for Canadian investment abroad and the use of foreign resources as a percentage of net capital formation, it turns out that not more than 6 per cent of Canadian investment in the postwar world depended on foreign resources.
>
> …Canada's economy has been growing at such a rapid rate that the role of foreign investment in relation to our productive capacity has diminished and will continue to do so.
>
> —C.D. Howe, Minister of Trade and Commerce, in the House of Commons, 1956

> No other country in the world with something like our relative state of development has ever had such a degree of foreign domination, or even one half or one quarter the degree of foreign domination. Canada is being pushed down the road that leads to loss of any effective power to be masters in our own household and ultimate absorption in and by another.
>
> —James Coyne, president of the Bank of Canada, to the Canadian Chamber of Commerce, 1960

> During the two-and-one-half years I held that office [minister of finance], the influence that financial and business interests in the United States had on Canadian policy was continually brought home to me. On occasion, this influence was reinforced by representations from the State Department and the American Administration as a whole. It was pressed by those who direct American businesses in Canada, by their professional advisors, by Canadian financiers whose interests were identified directly or indirectly with American investment in Canada, by influential members of the Canadian civil service, by some representatives of the university community, and by some sections of the press. [9]
>
> —Walter Gordon, *A Choice for Canada*, 1966

Economic Prospects. The commission report, submitted in 1958, expressed concerns that American branch plants in Canada hired few Canadian managers, did little exporting, and devoted little attention to research and development. The high level of foreign investment in Canada contributed to Canada's growing balance of payments problem as capital flowed out of the country in the form of interest and dividends. The commissioners suggested that foreign corporations be required to employ more Canadians in senior management positions, and sell an "appreciable interest" in their equity stocks to Canadians.

Not all Canadians agreed with Gordon's concerns. Economist Harry Johnson spoke for many conservatives in arguing that economic nationalism was "a narrow and garbage cluttered cul-de-sac."[8] He wanted all restrictions on foreign trade and investment removed. Despite interest in free trade in some quarters, the only tangible result was the Auto Pact of 1965. The pact, which created an integrated continental market for automobiles and automobile parts, included quotas for Canadian production, making it more an example of "managed trade" than unfettered free trade.

The Diefenbaker government introduced tax incentives for Canadian-based industries, and incurred the wrath of the United States by trading with communist countries such as Cuba and the Soviet Union. The Pearson government at first appeared to be willing to go even further. Pearson named Walter Gordon Minister of Finance. Gordon's first budget included a 30-percent "take-over tax" on the sale of publicly held Canadian companies to foreigners. He withdrew the provision because of pressures from an angry business community and the American government.

Over the next two years, Gordon introduced legislation to protect Canadian financial companies from foreign control, and took steps to reduce American dominance of the Canadian media. He was fighting an uphill battle. By the time that he resigned as finance minister in late 1965, his cabinet influence had waned. Nevertheless, Pearson agreed with Gordon's proposal to establish a Task Force on the Structure of Canadian Industry to examine whether it really mattered who owned industry in Canada. Gordon's choice for its head was a respected economist, Mel Watkins of the University of Toronto.

THE WATKINS REPORT

The Watkins Report, appearing in 1968, proved more damning of American economic impact on Canada than even the Gordon report 11 years earlier. He challenged the myth that Canada remained short of capital and needed foreign investment. If Canadians who invested abroad had kept their money at home, he argued, they would have reduced the need for foreign capital by half. The task force painted a picture of an inefficient branch-plant manufacturing economy geared to serving the Canadian market alone, leaving international markets to American-based plants.

Released at a time of growing nationalism in Canada and misgivings about the United States, it led to some actions on the part of the Trudeau government. The Canada Development Corporation (CDC) was created in 1971 to encourage Canadian ownership and management in vital sectors of the economy. In 1974, the Foreign Investment Review Agency (FIRA) was established to screen proposals for foreign takeovers of existing Canadian businesses. In late 1973, the federal government created Petro-Canada, a Crown corporation with a broad mandate to develop a Canadian presence in the petroleum industry.

The American oil giants responded with considerable hostility to Canada's nationalistic economic initiatives, which seemed to be part of a larger policy to frustrate the goals of the abitious multinational corporations. American oil companies operating in Alaska claimed the right to have their supertankers travel across the Arctic passage to transport their product to eastern American markets. In 1969 and 1970, the American tanker *Manhattan* carried several cargoes across the Arctic. Canada responded with the Arctic Waters Pollution Prevention Act, meant to protect the fragile northern environment and assert Canadian sovereignty in the North.

Such confrontations with the Americans help explain why President Richard Nixon, introducing import controls on manufactures in 1971, failed to exempt Canada as American governments had in the past. The Trudeau government's response was to seek what became known as the "Third Option" in Canadian foreign policy. Option one, maintaining Canada's existing relationship with the United States, seemed impossible. Option two, closer integration with the Americans, seemed undesirable. Option three, reduction of Canada's vulnerability to American actions by expanding global political and economic links, seemed the obvious choice. Diplomatic efforts to expand Canada's trade with other nations bore some fruit, but Canada remained overwhelmingly dependent on the American economy for its imports and exports.

CONTINENTALISM AND THE PROVINCES

Federal efforts to control American investment in Canada often met a hostile response from the provinces. Since the provinces had constitutional jurisdiction over resources and could earn much-needed income from their development, they increasingly resisted the use of the federal power over trade and taxation to shape patterns of resource exploitation. Alberta governments opposed any "discriminatory" treatment of foreign capital, to which they attributed their energy boom.

Provincial pressures broke down the long-standing federal resolve to prevent large-scale hydro-electricity exports as a means of insuring Canadian self-sufficiency in electricity. British Columbia was able to exploit the American Northwest's greed for more power, and to persuade the Pearson government in 1964 to sign the Columbia River Treaty and Protocol, which committed Canada to sell power to the western American states. Soon Manitoba was signing deals with the Americans to deliver power from the province's North. In the 1970s the Quebec government began its ambitious James Bay project to meet not only provincial power needs but also considerable demand from the state of New York. Both Manitoba's and Quebec's hydro plans were achieved at the expense of Native communities that were flooded by the huge dams that were the centerpiece of ambitious hydroelectricity schemes.

CONCLUSION

Canada's economic sovereignty, like its political sovereignty, was compromised by the country's growing economic integration with the United States. Steps were taken in the early 1970s to achieve greater independence, but they were tempered by a fear of risking Canada's postwar prosperity. Measured by purchasing power, most Canadians had never been so well off but millions remained on the outside of the new consumer society, looking in. Trudeau came to office promising a just society but by the mid-1970s concerns about the environment, added to stagflation, cautioned that Canadians would be forging their national policy in a much different atmosphere in the closing decades of the twentieth century.

A Historiographical Debate

Causes and Solutions for Stagflation

Why did the so-called Keynesian policies that promoted over a quarter of a century of unprecedented economic prosperity prove inadequate in the early 1970s to prevent stagflation? Some scholars argue that changes in the labour market made rising unemployment inevitable and that government efforts to stem the growth in unemployment simply caused inflation to balloon, without significantly affecting unemployment rates. Others argue that governments did not do enough to control both unemployment and inflation.

In their text on the Canadian economy, Kenneth Norrie and Douglas Owram argue that higher unemployment resulted from a combination of factors. Technological change reduced industry's labour requirements just as more women and younger workers were entering the labour market. Workers were able to quit their jobs and take advantage of generous unemployment insurance benefits. Governments, Norrie and Owram argue, vainly tried to counter these factors by expanding the money supply and increasing state expenditures, hoping these policies would create economic growth and produce more jobs. Such policies proved counterproductive because they increased the rate of inflation and made employers hesitant to borrow money. It had become necessary for public policy to aim deliberately at increasing the rate of unemployment in order to improve the operations of the market economy.[10] This monetarist analysis advocated restricting the money supply, which would force governments to spend less. If governments did not increase either money supply or spending to create jobs, employers would have an incentive to keep wages down, and fear of unemployment would force workers to accept this new state of affairs.

Some post-Keynesian economists have argued that the monetarist solution to stagflation meant a return to the economic thinking that preceded the Great Depression. Taken to its logical extreme, it would recreate the conditions that produced the economic catastrophe of the 1930s. These economists reject the view that a higher rate of unemployment was a natural outgrowth of changes in the structure of the economy and that expansionary economic policies necessarily led to unacceptable levels of inflation. Economist Pierre Fortin, studying the economies of industrialized countries from 1960 to 1985, disputed the assertion that low rates of inflation were necessary for increases in economic productivity. He found that some countries with low inflation had weaker economic growth than countries with relatively high Inflation.[11]

Economist Harold Chorney observed that Keynes had always been sceptical that low unemployment and low inflation could be achieved without substantial state economic intervention. In the postwar period, the fear of returning to Depression conditions had caused employers and unions to make compromises that made such intervention less necessary. With the postwar compromise in tatters by the early 1970s, it was up to governments to take a clearer stand on how wealth was to be distributed. According to Chorney, post-Keynesians advocated either wage and price controls or a tax-based system that penalized those deemed to be causing inflation as an alternative to the monetarism espoused by the anti-Keynesians.[12]

NOTES

[1] Mr Justice Thomas R. Berger, *Northern Frontier, Northern Homeland: The Report of the Mackenzie Valley Pipeline Inquiry* (Ottawa: Minister of Supply and Services Canada, 1977), 1: 123.

[2] Ester Reiter, "Life in a Fast-Food Factory" in *On the Job: Confronting the Labour Process in Canada*, ed. Craig Heron and Robert Storey (Montreal: McGill-Queen's University Press), 317–18.

[3] Frank James Tester and Peter Kulchyski, *Tammarniit (Mistakes): Inuit Relocation in the Eastern Arctic, 1939–1963* (Vancouver: UBC Press, 1994) 7.

[4] Sheila Arnopolous, "Immigrants and Women: Sweatshops of the 1970s" in *The Canadian Worker in the Twentieth Century*, ed. Irving Abella and David Millar (Toronto: Oxford University Press, 1978) 204.

[5] Canada, *Report of the Royal Commission on Taxation, vol. 1, Introduction, Acknowledgements and Minority Reports* (Ottawa: Queen's Printer, 1966) 1.

[6] Cy Gonick, *A Very Red Life: The Story of Bill Walsh* (St John's: Canadian Committee on Labour History, 2001) 171.

[7] Ester Reiter, "First Class Workers Don't Want Second-Class Wages: The Lanark Strike in Dunnville," in *A Diversity of Women: Ontario, 1945–1980*, ed. Joy Parr (Toronto: University of Toronto Press, 1995) 179, 186, 194.

[8] Harry Johnson, *The Canadian Quandary* (Ottawa: Carleton University Press, 1963) 11-12.

[9] Quoted in Philip Resnick, *The Land of Cain: Class and Nationalism in English Canada 1945–1975* (Vancouver: New Star Books, 1977) 79, 102, 114, 115.

[10] Kenneth Norrie and Douglas Owram, *A History of the Canadian Economy* (Toronto: Harcourt Brace Jovanovich, 1991) 602.

[11] Linda McQuaig, *Shooting the Hippo: Death by Deficit and Other Canadian Myths* (Toronto: Viking, 1995) 138.

[12] Harold Chorney, "The Economic and Political Consequences of Canadian Monetarism" (paper presented to the British Association of Canadian Studies Annual Meeting, 1991).

SELECTED READING

Works covering postwar economic developments include Lawrence Robert Aronsen, *American National Security and Economic Relations with Canada, 1945–1954* (Westport, CT: Greenwood, 1997); Kenneth Norrie and Douglas Owram, *A History of the Canadian Economy* (Toronto: Harcourt Brace Jovanovich, 1991); Harold Chorney, *The Deficit and Debt Management: An Alternative to Monetarism* (Ottawa: Canadian Centre for Policy Alternatives, 1989); David A. Wolfe, "The Rise and Demise of the Keynesian Era in Canada: Economic Policy, 1930–1982," in *Modern Canada 1930–1980s*, ed. Michael S. Cross and Gregory S. Kealey (Toronto: McClelland and Stewart, 1984); and Robert M. Campbell, *Grand Illusions: The Politics of the Keynesian Experience in Canada, 1945–1975* (Peterborough, ON: Broadview Press, 1987). On taxation debates, see Canada, *Report of the Royal Commission on Taxation* (Ottawa: Queen's Printer, 1966); John N. McDougall, *The Politics and Economics of Eric Kierans: A Man for all Canadians* (Montreal: McGill-Queen's University Press, 1993), chap. 6; and J. Harvey Perry, *A Fiscal History of Canada: The Postwar Years* (Toronto: Canadian Tax Foundation, 1989).

Growing concern for the environment and uncontrolled technological innovation is discussed in Chad Gaffield and Pam Gaffield, eds., *Consuming Canada: Readings in Environmental History* (Toronto: Copp Clark, 1995); Rachel Carson, *Silent Spring* (Boston: Houghton Mifflin, 1962); Donella J. Meadows, Dennis L. Meadows, Jorgen Randers, and William W. Behrens III, *Limits to Growth: A Report for the Club of Rome's Project on the Predicament of Mankind*, 2nd ed. (New York: Universe, 1974); and E.F. Schumacher, *Small Is Beautiful: The Study of Economics as if People Mattered* (New York: Harper and Row, 1975). Donald Savoie discusses the economic implications of regionalism in *Regional Economic Development: Canada's Search for Solutions* (Toronto: University of Toronto Press, 1986). Thomas Berger's report for the Mackenzie Valley Pipeline Inquiry, *Northern Frontier, Northern Homeland*, rev. ed. (Vancouver: Douglas and McIntyre, 1988) offers a classic statement on Native dilemmas over the development ethic, as does Mel Watkins, ed., *Dene Nation: The Colony Within* (Toronto: University of Toronto Press, 1977). On the impact of hydro-electric projects on Native communities and the environment more generally, see James Waldram, *As Long as the Rivers Run: Hydroelectric Development and Native Communities in Western Canada* (Winnipeg: University of Manitoba Press, 1988), and Sean McCutcheon, *Electric Rivers: The Story of the James Bay Project* (Montreal: Black Rose Books, 1991). On Natives and the economy, see also Dianne Newell, *Tangled Webs of History: Indians and the Law in Canada's Pacific Coast Fisheries* (Toronto: University of Toronto Press, 1993).

Works with extensive coverage of regional economic developments include Gerald Friesen, *The Canadian Prairies: A History*, rev. ed. (Toronto: University of Toronto Press, 1987); Rennie Warburton and Donald Coburn, eds., *Workers, Capital and the State of British Columbia* (Vancouver: UBC Press, 1987); Patricia Marchak, *Green Gold: The Forest Industry in British Columbia* (Vancouver: UBC Press, 1983); Miriam Wright, *A Fishery for Modern Times: The State and the Industrialization of the Newfoundland Fishery, 1934–1968* (Toronto: Oxford University Press, 2001); Edward MacDonald, *"If You Are Strong-Hearted": Prince Edward Island in the Twentieth Century* (Charlottetown: Prince Edward Island Museum and Heritage Foundation, 2000); Verner Smitheram, David Milne, and Satadal Dasgupta, eds., *The Garden Transformed: Prince Edward Island, 1945–1980* (Charlottetown: Ragweed Press, 1982); Gary Burrill and Ian McKay, eds., *People, Resources and Power in Atlantic Canada: Critical Perspectives on Underdevelopment and Primary Industries in the Atlantic Region* (Fredericton: Acadiensis Press, 1987).

On the impact of the Cold War on Canadian-American economic relations, see Melissa Clark Jones, *A Staple State: Canadian Industrial Resources in the Cold War* (Toronto: University of Toronto Press, 1987); and J. L. Granatstein and Robert Cuff, *American Dollars and Canadian Prosperity* (Toronto: Samuel-Stevens, 1978). On Canadian-American economic relations more generally from 1945 to 1975, useful sources include Mel Watkins et al., *Foreign Ownership and the Structure of Canadian Industry: Report of the Task Force on the Structure of Canadian Industry* (Ottawa: Ministry of Supply and Services, 1968); Kari Levitt, *Silent Surrender: The Multinational Corporation in Canada* (Toronto: Gage, 1971); H.G. Johnson, *The Canadian Quandary* (Ottawa: Carleton University Press, 1977); and Walter Gordon, *Gentle Patriot: A Political Biography of Walter Gordon* (Edmonton: Hurtig, 1973).

Among excellent accounts on postwar trade union developments are Irving M. Abella, *Nationalism, Communism, and Canadian Labour: The CIO, the Communist Party, and the Canadian Congress of Labour, 1935–1956* (Toronto: University of Toronto Press, 1973);

Judy Fudge and Eric Tucker, *Labour Before the Law: The Regulation of Workers' Collective Action in Canada, 1900–1948* (Toronto: Oxford University Press, 2001); Cy Gonick, *A Very Red Life: The Story of Bill Walsh* (St John's: Canadian Committee on Labour History, 2001); Sam Gindin, *The Canadian Auto Workers: The Birth and Transformation of a Union* (Toronto: Lorimer, 1995); Pamela Sugiman, *Labour's Dilemma: The Gender Politics of Auto Workers in Canada, 1937–1979* (Toronto: University of Toronto Press, 1994); and Doug Smith, *Cold Warrior: C.S. Jackson and the United Electrical Workers* (St John's: Canadian Committee on Labour History, 1997).

 **WEBLINKS**

PROJECTS, CAMPAIGNS, AND BOYCOTTS OF THE CANADIAN LABOUR CONGRESS
www.clc-ctc.ca/campaigns/workers/index.html

This site provides links to campaigns in support of workers' rights, in Canada and internationally.

BURGER KING CORPORATION
www.burgerking.com/CompanyInfo/onlinepressroom/ bkfactsheet/histfacts.html

This site offers a list of quick facts about Burger King's evolution from the 18-cent hamburger to the Whopper, now sold at more than 11,000 locations worldwide.

JAMES BAY HYDROELECTRIC PROJECT
www.pearson-college.uwc.ca/pearson/ensy/mega/kinwa/ kinwa.htm

The environmental, socioeconomic, and political impacts of the James Bay Hydroelectric Project are discussed at this site. The controversial nature of this energy creation plan, begun in 1972, is explored through both native and non-native perspectives.

JOHN MAYNARD KEYNES AND RIVAL ECONOMIC THEORIES
http://bized.ac.uk/virtual/economy/library/economists/ classical.htm

A glossary of economic terms, profiles of noted economists, examinations of key economic theories, case studies, and economic policy tools can be found at this comprehensive site.

CHAPTER 25

Community and Nation, 1945–1975

I n 1962, the Governor General's Award for Canadian literature was given to Jacques Ferron, a physician, committed socialist, and indépendantiste, for his *Tales from the Uncertain Country*. In 1963, Ferron founded the Rhinoceros Party, whose candidates in the 1968 federal election all took the name of Lucien Rivard, a convicted drug dealer whose escape from prison in 1965 was alleged to have been abetted by bribery of federal Justice Department officials.

Like the Rhinoceros Party, the stories in *Tales from the Uncertain Country* used humour to raise serious issues. In "Back to Kentucky," for example, a Kentucky druggist serving in the American armed forces in Belgium during the Second World War marries a French-speaking Belgian woman though neither can speak the other's language. The two search for a place to live where they can each speak their own language. "We nearly opted for Lowell in New England. Human geography evolves fast in America. Our books were already out of date: Lowell, too late. We arrived in time in Montreal."[1] In Montreal, too, they discover that the French language is threatened in the anglophone sea of North America and that the struggle for identity is fraught with contradictions.

The Québécois were not alone in attempting to define a new identity for themselves in the postwar period. Like Ferron's linguistically-challenged couple, most Canadians were eager to find a zone of comfort between the conservative values of the past and the mass consumer culture sweeping North America.

POPULATION

Due to the combination of a postwar baby boom and extensive immigration, Canada's population grew from about 12 million in 1945 to 23 million in 1975. Women had limited their pregnancies during the Depression and the war, but the relative security of the postwar period encouraged couples to marry young and have more children. At the peak of the baby boom in 1959, the fertility rate of women in their childbearing years was about 50 percent greater than in 1941.

From 1946 to 1962, almost 1.8 million immigrants came to Canada. Only 4 percent came from Asia and Africa because government policy for most of this period ensured that immigrants were primarily Europeans. By the 1960s, it became clear that Western Europe, back on its feet after postwar rebuilding, would no longer produce the steady stream of immigrants required to support Canada's expanding economy. Immigration regulations were changed to open the door to skilled people, as well as domestic servants, both in short supply, from regions other than Europe and the United States. Revisions of the Immigration Act in 1962 and 1967 reduced the colour bias that once kept Canada's gates largely closed to non-whites. People from the Caribbean and Asia in particular took advantage of Canada's changing immigration policy.

As Table 25.1 suggests, immigration accounted for a dramatically larger proportion of the population increase in the early 1970s than in the late 1950s when immigration levels were almost the same. This is explained by the huge decline in the birth rate from 28.3

newborns per 1000 population in 1959 to 15.7 in 1976. Better nutrition, preventive medicine, and the use of antibiotics increased both infant survival and life expectancy more generally. Children born in 1976 could expect to live 13 years longer than children born in 1931. By the 1970s, life expectancy had reached 70 years for men and 77 for women, though the poor and, most strikingly, Aboriginal Canadians, died, on average, much younger.

CHANGING SOCIAL VALUES

For the majority of Canadians, education levels and income increased, and so too did material expectations. The nuclear family, consisting of a husband, a wife, and several children, remained the ideal for most Canadians, but with each census, it accounted for a noticeably smaller proportion of households. In 1969 divorce laws were liberalized, allowing more unhappy marriages to be dissolved and increasing the number of single-parent households. The effectiveness of "the Pill," which was widely prescribed in the 1960s, allowed women the option of delaying childbirth or of not having children at all. Reflecting somewhat greater tolerance of homosexuality, same-sex couples "came out" in unprecedented numbers. Common-law marriages, once associated with the poorer classes, became popular across the economic spectrum, particularly among young adults. Divorce and remarriage substantially increased the number of "blended" families, which might include a couple's biological children

Table 25.1
A Growing Population, 1941–1976*

Period	Population increase	Births	Population increase due to births (%)	Net immigration	Population increase due to immigration (%)	Population at the end of period
1941–51	2141**	1972	92.1	169	7.9	13 648
1951–56	2072	1473	71.1	594	28.9	16 081
1956–61	2157	1675	77.7	482	22.3	18 238
1961–66	1777	1518	85.4	259	14.6	20 015
1966–71	1553	1090	70.2	463	29.8	21 568
1971–76	1425	934	65.5	491	34.5	22 993

*All population figures in these tables are in thousands.
**Excludes Newfoundland

Source: Adapted from the Statistics Canada publication *Canada Year Book* (1994) Catalogue 11-402, page 113.

Figure 25.1
Total Fertility Rates,* 1946–1976**

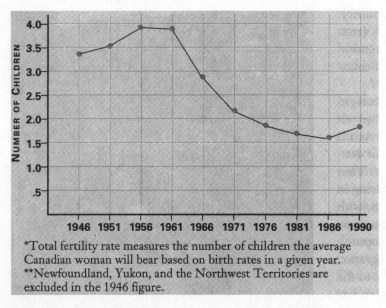

*Total fertility rate measures the number of children the average Canadian woman will bear based on birth rates in a given year.
**Newfoundland, Yukon, and the Northwest Territories are excluded in the 1946 figure.

Source: Created from and published in the Statistics Canada publications *Historical Statistics of Canada*, 2nd ed., (Ottawa: Statistics Canada, 1983), Catalogue 11-402, Series B1-14; and *Canada Year Book*, Catalogue 11-402, various years.

as well as each partner's offspring from earlier marriages.

The baby boomers, children of a prosperous and media-dominated age, fostered an ever-changing youth culture characterized at first by rock music and blue jeans and later by premarital sex, mind-altering drugs, unisex clothing and hairstyles, and political protest. The changes were most evident among middle-class teenagers enrolled in expanding liberal arts programs at universities, but they had their impact throughout the postwar generation. Even at the conservative University of Alberta, where only 1 percent of students in residence had used drugs in 1965, fully a quarter in 1971 had experimented with illegal drugs, usually marijuana.

Surveys among Canadian young people showed that by the mid-1960s, a majority of university students were sexually active; a decade later the same was true for high school students. The widespread availability of contraceptives meant that fear of pregnancy became a less important reason for unmarried people to avoid sex. But many young women, while

pleased that the compulsory heterosexual monogamy of the past was no longer their only sexual option, believed that changing values relating to sex were "scripted by men for men's benefit."[2] They often felt compelled by peer pressure to have sex with their boyfriends and were too often subject to physical force when they were reluctant to consent.

EDUCATION

Most young people in the postwar years experienced more schooling than their parents. In an increasingly urbanized society, the illiterate, self-educated, and those lacking formal training found fewer employment prospects. In the 1950s, a high school diploma was essential for all but the least skilled, lowest paying jobs. By the 1970s, employers expected university degrees or college diplomas for many junior positions.

University degrees, once limited to a numerically negligible, if extremely influential, elite, became more common, with one in ten Canadians aged 25 to 44 in 1976 holding at least one university degree. The gender balance in higher education also began to change, though gender still governed what programs students pursued. Fields such as engineering, law, and medicine remained male bastions, while schools of social work and nursing had a largely female clientele.

Responding to public pressure, governments made huge outlays on education between 1945 and 1975. Throughout rural areas, the one-room schoolhouses where poorly paid, inadequately trained young women taught eight grades gave way to modern, centrally located facilities. By the 1970s, most public school boards across the country required that new teachers hold at least a university degree in education. Powerful teachers' associations had won professional wages for teachers, sometimes using strikes or the threat of strikes to achieve their demands. Generally, schools became more humane, as corporal punishment and rote learning gave way to child-centred education and attempts to encourage critical thinking.

MORE TO THE STORY

Who Is Fit to Have a Baby?

Despite the high birth rate from 1945 to 1960, society and the state continued to frown upon women who had children out of wedlock. In Quebec, thousands of "illegitimate" Catholic children were placed in homes for the feeble-minded, regardless of their actual intelligence, to hide them from society. At least until the late 1950s, single mothers in Canada were denied mothers' allowances, thus virtually ensuring that they had to give their children up for adoption.

Single mothers were not the only Canadians deemed unworthy to have children. People labelled mentally unfit were also discouraged from reproducing. According to popular psychology of the period, the offspring of such people would grow up to become criminals. The province of Alberta has a particularly shameful history of enforcing such eugenicist policies. From 1929 to 1972, the provincial Eugenics Board ordered the sterilization of 2822 "mentally defective" people. The board interpreted this category broadly: it included, among others, some adult sexual offenders, young women whom the board determined to be promiscuous or potentially promiscuous, and school-age children whose parents could not cope with them and whose intelligence appeared to be less than average. The children were placed in the Provincial Training School for Mental Defectives in Red Deer.

Most of the men and boys ordered sterilized by the board were vasectomized, but some sexual offenders were castrated. Girls in the school were routinely sterilized at puberty. Among them was Leilani Muir, an inmate of the school from 1955 to 1965. An abused child at home, Muir suffered developmental delays and scored poorly on an IQ test. School officials had her Fallopian tubes tied during an unnecessary appendectomy. Muir left the school when she was 21. At the age of 45, after her mother finally informed her of the sterilization, she sued the provincial government. In 1996, the Court of Queen's Bench awarded Muir $750 000 in compensation. Two years later the province agreed to substantial financial compensation for other living victims of the eugenics policy.

The enthusiasm for more schooling gradually extended to the postsecondary sector. Between 1944 and 1947, university enrolment doubled as a result of federal grants to veterans wishing to pursue university educations. Federal grants to universities, recommended by the Massey Commission in 1951 and quickly implemented by Ottawa, supplemented provincial grants to these institutions. In the 1960s, new universities including York in Toronto, Simon Fraser in Burnaby, and the University of Regina were opened. Some affiliated colleges, such as United College in Winnipeg and Brandon College, became full-fledged universities. Church-affiliated universities, particularly important in postsecondary education in the Maritimes, became more secular in their governing structures in order to become eligible for government grants.

EDUCATION IN QUEBEC

Educational changes were most dramatic in Quebec. In 1960, 11 percent of anglophones in the province aged 20 to 24 attended universities, but only 2.9 percent of francophones in that age group did. Not only was the number of graduates from Catholic secondary schools poor relative to the Protestant system, but the Catholic curriculum was antiquated. For boys, education still focused on classical thought; for girls, the system taught above all else "preparation for family life, the beauty of the home, its virtues, and its unique position in society."[3]

Dissatisfaction with the conservative, clerically run educational institutions of Quebec revealed itself in the phenomenal success of *Les Insolences du Frère Untel* (*The Impertinences of Brother Anonymous*), which was published in 1960. Written by Brother Jean-Paul Desbiens, it was a stinging indictment of Quebec education by someone within the ranks of the Roman Catholic Church. The Lesage government appointed a commission to make recommendations for improvement in Quebec education. Although the commissioners decided that schools should remain organized along religious lines, they recommended that the state play a larger role in administration and curriculum development.

In 1964, for the first time since 1875, the provincial government established a Ministry of Education. New curricula were introduced to bring Quebec schools in line with education systems in the rest of North America. The ministry set up a network of secular junior colleges, or CEGEPs, to provide post-secondary vocational and academic training. Between 1960 and 1970, enrolment in Quebec's secondary schools rose 101 percent, college enrolments rose 82 percent, and university enrolments rose 169 percent.

CITIES AND SUBURBS

Demands for more and better housing were common in a generation that had weathered the Great Depression by sharing living space and deferring the purchase of goods. Aided by government-guaranteed mortgages, veterans' housing grants, and consumer credit, people flocked to homes in the suburbs. The media, especially in their advertisements, portrayed the suburbs as a world of quiet, privacy, modern appliances, and fine furnishings.

The new suburbs increased the costs of urban administration. In addition to utility lines and sewers, new roads were needed for the cars and public transport that became indispensable to suburban life. More schools, police, and firefighters were also required. In the prosperous 1950s, the municipalities raised the funds for such developments from property tax increases and grants from provincial governments.

In most cases, new suburbs initially lacked shopping areas, community centres, theatres, taverns, sport complexes, and other recreational areas. Many suburbanites either sought privacy or had it thrust upon them in anonymous settings that brought the term "community" sharply into question. Television replaced community events. Supermarkets, department stores, and malls eventually substituted for neighbourhood shops where customers and merchants all knew each other.

Stay-at-home moms experienced this new privatization most directly, sometimes with devastating psychological consequences. Often well-educated, suburban women suffered from what American feminist Betty Friedan, in her groundbreaking book *The Feminine Mystique* (1963), called "the problem that has no name." Some sought refuge in paid work despite social proscriptions, others in voluntary activities in community leagues and church auxiliaries that attempted to create community feelings within the suburbs. A surprisingly large number developed various nervous disorders for which a male-dominated medical profession prescribed tranquilizers that often created long-term addiction and left the underlying problems unresolved.

HOUSING STANDARDS

While middle-class ideals defined the suburban lifestyle, many postwar neighbourhoods on the urban fringe were shantytowns. Tarpaper shacks in Villes Jacques Cartier on Montreal Island, unserviced homes in Bridgeview on the British Columbia lower mainland, and shacks without water or sewer facilities, garbage collection, or street lighting outside St John's demonstrated that many suburbs had greater problems than middle-class angst.

Opportunities to find decent housing varied dramatically among regions. Atlantic Canadians, Natives, Northerners, and Gaspésiens, for example, were far less likely to live as well as people in southern Ontario. While less than one in ten new homes built in Ontario in the early 1960s lacked either a furnace or a flush toilet, over four in ten built in Atlantic Canada during that period lacked one or both of these amenities.

By the 1970s, the core areas of many cities had become rundown. Slumlords refused to maintain their properties and city governments controlled by suburban councillors funnelled municipal funds away from the downtown areas. Tenants formed organizations to demand stricter implementation of municipal housing standards and more funding for public housing. The authorities, by contrast, often supported programs for "redevelopment," which often meant simply levelling existing homes and replacing them with fancier houses that only the well-off could afford.

Where the basic architectural structures were sound, as in Cabbagetown in downtown Toronto, slumlords renovated homes to meet the tastes of affluent Torontonians who preferred to live close to their offices and the city's night life. In other cities, poor districts were transformed into chic shopping areas, such as Osborne Village in Winnipeg. Increasingly, the poor were forced to live further from the urban core.

THE IMMIGRANT EXPERIENCE

If the postwar suburbs often appeared colourless, the established areas of cities were often reinvigorated by the huge influx of immigrants. The majority of the postwar immigrants settled in cities, and by the 1970s the initial destination of over half of all immigrants to Canada was Greater Toronto, Montreal Island, and Greater Vancouver. The colourful, multilingual store-fronts, the smells of a variety of cuisines, and the pref-erence for streets and cafés over privatized living transformed these cities into cosmopolitan metropoles.

Male immigrants in the early postwar period were usually blue-collar workers who received modest pay. Their wives often had little choice but to seek work, even if they had young children. Maria Rossi's experi-ence was not atypical. In November 1956, she and her daughter arrived in Toronto. Her husband had emi-grated one year earlier from their peasant farm in southern Italy. The family rented a basement flat in the home of another Italian émigré family. Four days after her arrival, she began work as a steam press operator at a local laundry. For the next 20 years she worked continuously in a variety of low-paying jobs including sewing, cooking, and cashiering.

Poverty initially left many immigrants with little money or time for joining and participating in ethnic organizations. However, within a generation most im-migrant groups had spawned dozens of organizations, from community centres to businessmen's clubs and from sports teams to charities. Political organizations also abounded in ethnic communities. Ukrainian-Canadian politics still pitted pro-Soviet communists and supporters of an independent Ukraine, but with 80 000 mostly nationalist immigrants arriving after the war, the nationalists, who enjoyed financial support from the Canadian government, became the main voice of the Ukrainian community.

Zionism, the movement to create a Jewish home-land in Israel, became a uniting cause for Canadian Jews in the aftermath of the Nazi Holocaust. Led by the Canadian Jewish Congress, Jews in Canada stepped up their campaigns for legal sanctions against open manifestations of anti-Semitism and other forms of racism.

Immigrant efforts to preserve their home lan-guages and cultural practices led to the federal decision in 1971 to appoint a Secretary of State for Multiculturalism and to fund ethnic organizations and festivals. Provinces with large ethnic minorities also introduced heritage-language instruction in the schools. Such developments muted, though they did not eliminate, racism and bigotry in Canadian society.

ASIAN-CANADIAN COMMUNITIES

When Hing Chang, an exceptional student, decided to attend business college in Vancouver in the late 1940s, her high school principal admitted that college train-ing, a ticket to success for white Canadians, would not help Hing find a job. His top Chinese-Canadian graduates, he admitted, had faced unrelenting discrim-ination in their job searches.

Before the 1970s, Chinese Canadians had good reason to feel embattled in Canadian society. Their communities were close to downtown and viewed with contempt by urban redevelopers. Two-thirds of Toronto's Chinatown was bulldozed in the 1960s to build a new city hall. In Vancouver, city by-laws eroded the distinct character of Chinatown. As author Denise Chong, daughter of Hing Chang, recalled:

> Vancouver's city council enacted bylaws to sanitize the squalor and ordered commerce off the sidewalk—gone were the squawking chickens in cages, the barbecued pork and duck that once hung for the customer's perusal. The gambling dens that used to be my grandmother's liveli-hood and entertainment had also disappeared; the last one had been padlocked long ago by city police.[4]

After Canadian recognition of the communist govern-ment in Mainland China, new Chinese immigrants began to arrive in Canada, reinvigorating the Chinese-Canadian community and eventually giving it enough clout to resist the redevelopers.

Immigration from India and Pakistan increased dra-matically following the reform of immigration laws in the 1960s. Although their numbers included much-in-

Events such as the Chinese dragon parade celebrate the cultural diversity of Canadian society.

Vancouver Public Library/79795-A

demand doctors, engineers, and teachers, those without university degrees were often ghettoized in low-wage, supposedly unskilled factory jobs. South Asian women workers were confined, in many factories, to the lowest-paying and most difficult tasks on the worst shifts. South Asians also provided much of the farm labour force in British Columbia, picking pesticide-sprayed crops without protective clothing or masks, and living in converted barns without running water or electricity.

AFRICAN CANADIANS

Canada's restrictive immigration laws permitted entry to only handfuls of blacks in the 1950s, about half of whom were Caribbean domestics needed to fill a shortage of maids for wealthy homes. In Nova Scotia,

home to 30 percent of Canada's mostly long-established black population in 1961, blacks fought for their rights through the Nova Scotia Association for the Advancement of Coloured People (NSAACP), founded in 1945. In 1946, the NSAACP raised money to help Viola Desmond fight segregation in movie theatres. Desmond, a Halifax beautician, was arrested in a New Glasgow theatre for sitting downstairs rather than in the balcony to which blacks were usually restricted. Sentenced to 30 days in jail or a $20 fine, she paid the money but appealed the decision. The case was thrown out on a technicality, but the incident resulted in so much negative publicity that such discriminatory laws were soon abandoned.

Elsewhere, discrimination on the basis of race was also common and was even upheld by the courts. In 1949, the Appeal Court of Ontario ruled that there was nothing illegal about a clause in property deeds that barred Jews and blacks from buying property in Beach O'Pines near Sarnia. In Dresden, Ontario, where blacks made up 17 percent of the town's 2000 people in 1950, restaurants, poolrooms, and barber and beauty shops refused patronage from non-whites.

Encouraged by the Black Power Movement in the United States, African Canadians in the 1960s became more assertive in their struggle against discrimination. A new generation of black leaders, many of them recent immigrants from the West Indies and Africa, refused to accept discrimination in employment and housing. Numbers contributed to a greater community confidence. Between 1971 and 1981, over 140 000 West Indian immigrants came to Canada, with two-thirds settling in Ontario. Their concentration in southern Ontario allowed them to establish a rich institutional culture, including social clubs, newspapers, the annual Toronto International Festival (formerly Caribana), and anti-racist organizations.

The plight of blacks in Nova Scotia received international attention when the city of Halifax decided to demolish Africville. Home to Halifax's black population since the middle of the nineteenth century, Africville had been shamefully neglected by the city authorities, who had provided no public utilities and had located the municipal dump nearby. In 1961, city council decided to remove the 400 citizens of Africville to make way for an industrial development

Africville in the 1960s.

Nova Scotia Archives and Records Management, Bob Brooks Collection, Neg. Sleeve No. 6

a special joint committee of the House and Senate reviewed the Indian Act. Its report defended assimilatory goals, but called for limited reforms. In 1951, ineffectual bans on the potlatch and sun dance were lifted. Elected band councils could make decisions in areas that traditionally concerned municipal governments. The provinces began gradually to enfranchise Natives, and status Indians finally received the vote federally in 1960.

By this time, Native peoples were becoming increasingly militant in their pursuit of fairer treatment. A catalyst for action by treaty Indians was the unveiling of the Trudeau government's White Paper on Indian policy in June 1969. Ottawa planned to relinquish Native lands while at the same time removing Indians' special status, giving the provinces responsibilities for services to Native people. The Native response was overwhelmingly negative. The National Indian Brotherhood (NIB), which was formed in 1968 to speak for treaty Indians, led the resistance, claiming that they wanted self-government and not the assimilation implied in becoming ordinary citizens of the provinces. Surprised at the vehemence of Native reaction, the government withdrew the White Paper but offered no framework for negotiating Native demands for self-government.

During the 1970s, pressures from the NIB—renamed the Assembly of First Nations in 1982—led the government to gradually give Native peoples the responsibility for their own education. Although the residential education system was phased out in the 1960s and 1970s, its scars remain. In 1990, the head of the Manitoba Association of Chiefs, Phil Fontaine, made a public issue of claims that had frequently been heard privately: Native children in residential schools had been victims of violence, including sexual abuse, at the hands of members of religious orders as well as lay

on the site. Residents' protests were ignored, the city believing that financial compensation was sufficient for bulldozing a community into history.

In the wake of the demolition of Africville, the Black United Front (BUF) was founded in 1968 to intensify the struggle for change. In an effort to defuse what appeared to be a growing militancy among blacks in Canada—a student protest against racism at Sir George Williams University (now Concordia) ended in the destruction of the university's computer system—the federal government offered to fund BUF and other black organizations. Beginning in the late 1960s, provincial human rights legislation, backed up by human rights commissions with powers to investigate and prosecute cases of clear discrimination on the basis of race, sex, or religion, demonstrated a greater desire on the part of authorities to reduce systemic racism in Canada. But visible minorities, including Canada's Aboriginals, continued to struggle against social exclusion.

NATIVE PEOPLES FIND A VOICE

Canada's First Peoples probably felt the sting of intolerance even more than immigrant groups. In 1946–48,

MORE TO THE STORY

Recovering Community

In the early 1970s, almost every resident of Alkali Lake, a Shuswap community of 400 people in the British Columbia interior, was an alcoholic. Phyllis Chelsea and her husband, Andy, were typical. He had been in hospital on several occasions for kidney trouble after binge drinking, and Phyllis had required medical care twice after Andy had beaten her while in a drunken stupor. One evening, after again drinking heavily, Phyllis stopped to pick up her children at their grandmother's house. There she was confronted by her eldest daughter, then only seven, who refused to go home, accusing her parents of being violent drunks. Phyllis was shocked and resolved to stop drinking immediately. Andy was initially unwilling to follow her example until, one day, he was deeply struck by the many bruised, hungry faces among local children on the way to school, a reflection of the effects of alcohol on families in the community.

The Chelseas began to spread their anti-alcohol message zealously on the reserve. They persuaded the band council to make treatment for alcoholism a condition for receiving financial help. They and their converts looked after the children of reserve residents who had enrolled in Native treatment programs. As people sobered up, it soon became clear that alcohol was a symptom, not the primary cause, of the degradation of many Native people. The extent of sexual abuse that had occurred at the Catholic-run St John's Mission residential school near Williams Lake became public. Sexual abuse had, in turn, become common in the households of Alkali alcoholics. Healing circles became crucial in allowing people to overcome the shame that had caused generations of local residents to seek comfort in drunkenness. By the early 1980s, Phyllis Chelsea could point proudly to a community in which 95 percent of the adults were sober. The children attended a new school built by the band and where elders "came to share prayers, pipe ceremonies, and songs in Shuswap," thus renewing the traditional culture that had all but died out in the wake of poverty, abuse, and despair.[5]

teachers. Native people who left the reserves for towns and cities were rarely assimilated into the larger society. Undereducated and faced with discrimination, many succumbed to lives in urban ghettos marked by poor housing, poverty, and drunkenness.

The marginalization of Native adults often resulted in family problems in which children were innocent victims. Although many families struggled to provide caring environments for their offspring, their children often grew up in abusive situations. On remote reserves, glue-sniffing and other forms of dependency on mind-numbing drugs became common among Native children, with a high number of drug-related deaths. Native groups increasingly demanded that traditional cultural practices, once suppressed by governments and churches, be restored so that Native children could grow up with positive images of their culture.

Not all Native peoples had the option of living on reserves. Despite having signed Treaty 11 in 1921, the Mackenzie Valley First Nations had no reserves. Other Yukon Indians and the Inuit had never signed treaties with the federal government. Such a situation made northern Native peoples particularly vulnerable to the burgeoning development in the postwar North and resulted in opposition to energy pipelines proposed in the 1970s. Mackenzie Valley Indians and some Métis declared the existence of a Dene nation seeking independence within the framework of Canadian Confederation.

In 1974, the Trudeau government appointed Justice Thomas Berger to study the impact of a pipeline in the Mackenzie Valley on local residents and the environment. Berger proved sympathetic to the Dene and Inuit who stressed the extent to which they still subsisted on local resources. Although the government accepted Berger's call for a halt to pipeline developments for a decade, it was slow in pursuing comprehensive land-claims settlements for the North.

THE WOMEN'S MOVEMENT

Natives were not alone in questioning their position in postwar Canadian society. Women of all backgrounds increasingly challenged sexual stereotypes and double standards. Inspired by the feisty women's liberation movement in the United States, some Canadian women joined feminist organizations to fight for full equality. An increasing number of women, whether professing to be feminists or not, joined the paid labour force.

Although they participated more than ever in paid work, women found that their employment options were limited. Their pay was deflated by notions that women's wages were "pin money," unlike the wages of a male "breadwinner," and by the fact that society had come to depend so heavily on women's unpaid and underpaid work. While employers and families required women's paid work, social institutions adapted slowly. There were virtually no arrangements for childcare outside the home and both single and married women returned from work to find the housework waiting. The "double day" of housework and paid work often left women even less leisure time than their mothers had enjoyed, although their wages sometimes allowed them to purchase labour-saving devices, prepared foods, and off-the-rack clothing.

Individual reactions to the obstacles facing women slowly coalesced into political action. In Quebec in 1966, Thérèse Casgrain, a leading figure in the peace group Voice of Women, helped to found the Fédération des femmes du Québec (FFQ), an umbrella group of women's organizations, to fight for women's rights. In English Canada, women's groups, galvanized by leaders such as Laura Sabia, president of the Canadian Federation of University Women, and *Chatelaine* magazine editor Doris Anderson, pressured Ottawa for action. Feminist pressures, supported by outspoken cabinet minister Judy LaMarsh, led

Berger Commission hearings in the Northwest Territories.

Northern News Services Ltd.

Pearson to create the Royal Commission on the Status of Women in 1967, which reported in 1970. The National Action Committee on the Status of Women (NAC), an umbrella organization for the many women's groups springing up across the country, was created in 1972. It lobbied governments to ensure that the commission's recommendations—which included calls for reform in education, employment, immigration, criminal and family law, and childcare—would not simply gather dust.

A CULTURE OF PROTEST

The women's movement emerged in the context of increasing dissent within Canadian society in the 1960s. Expanded university campuses spawned movements for greater democratization of society beginning with the university itself. In the 1960s, the "New Left," a loose grouping that embraced a socialist vision of society but rejected the authoritarianism and puritanism of traditional Marxism as well as the gradualism of social democracy, was transplanted from the United States to Canada. Environmental movements and the gay rights movements, while their major successes occurred after 1975, were well established by the early 1970s.

Homosexuality lost its criminality in 1969, but it did not lose its stigma. In the postwar period, under the influence of psychology, the view that sex with someone of the same gender was conscious criminal behaviour gave way to the view that homosexuality was a pathology that psychotherapy could cure. As long as gays and lesbians were regarded as mentally deranged, they remained the target of discrimination in employment and housing. Fledgling gay rights organizations pressed for an end to such discrimination, and for recognition of sexual orientation as largely biologically determined.

They had their work cut out for them. As late as 1963, the RCMP persuaded the Diefenbaker government, still convinced that homosexuality and communism were perversions and therefore related, to allow it to use a "fruit machine" to root out homosexual applicants for civil service jobs. Only the apparent unreliability of the machine in measuring erotic responses resulted in this fruity idea's demise.

Nor did the new culture of social protest in the late 1960s guarantee acceptance of gay and lesbian relationships. Within the women's movement, for example, conservative feminists were often uncomfortable with lesbians, who often provided sharp criticism of the assumptions built into feminist processes and policies. Until homosexuality was legalized in 1969, lesbians were rarely public about their sexual orientation and focused on social support rather than political lobbying. Increasingly, lesbians came out of the closet and attacked "compulsory heterosexuality," the pervasive social and cultural images that extolled heterosexual relations as the only acceptable sexual option. In company with gay men, they called for an end to discrimination in such areas as adoption and spousal benefits.

THE POOR ORGANIZE

The new culture of protest among the young middle class in the 1960s encouraged a revival of lobbying organizations among working people and the poor. By the 1970s, hundreds of groups representing tenants, welfare rights advocates, single mothers, the unemployed, and other categories of the poor and powerless were organized. Demonstrations at provincial legislatures, city halls, and sometimes the homes of slumlords brought increased media attention to those who lived destitute lives within a prosperous society.

Thousands attended a conference of poor people's organizations in Ottawa in 1971 that led to the creation of a national poverty organization to fight for a guaranteed annual income and other legislation that would benefit the country's poorest citizens. In Quebec, where both nationalist sentiment and social grievances spurred tens of thousands to join community groups, there was a close alliance between grass-roots movements and the powerful trade unions. "Social animators," often university-educated facilitators paid by the unions, mobilized citizens and provided a link between the protests of radical baby boomers, organized workers, and the poor.

RELIGION IN A SECULAR AGE

The era of mass society and rampant consumerism posed unique challenges to churches. Believers were increasingly unlikely to attend church services, and they told pollsters that they, not their ministers, made the moral decisions that shaped their lives.

While some people were abandoning organized religion, claiming their church was not addressing social issues, fundamentalist Protestant denominations, with an otherworldly orientation, were gaining memberships. In the 1950s and early 1960s, the mainstream Protestant denominations tried to strike a balance in their views, supporting social programs such as medicare while staking out more conservative ground on other issues, opposing homosexuality, abortion, divorce, and jobs for married women.

Ironically, while they opposed greater social opportunities for women, the Protestant churches offered them opportunities to demonstrate leadership skills in social and charitable activities as well as in missionary roles. The United Church, the largest Protestant church, reported 401 757 members in its Women's Auxiliary and Women's Missionary Society in 1955.

By the 1970s, the mainstream Protestant churches, influenced by the growing women's movement within the churches, began to change their views on gender roles. While progress, particularly in the ordination of women, occurred slowly—the Anglican Church agreed to ordain women in 1976—the churches joined with other social groups in calling for state-subsidized quality daycare and for greater economic equality between the sexes.

At the same time, the Roman Catholic Church was undergoing its own soul-searching, in response to liberal trends in Rome. Radicals preached "the preferential option of the poor" and were likely to support the ordination of women and the relaxing of celibacy requirements. Conservatives held sway on these issues, but many Catholics followed their own instincts on moral issues. Despite the church's condemnation of effective contraception, the birth rate among Catholics paralleled the rate for non-Catholics. Quebec, though nominally overwhelmingly Catholic, had the country's lowest birth rate by the 1970s. Pollsters found that most Catholics, like most Canadians generally, supported a woman's right to abortion, despite the official position of their church.

Fewer Catholics were going to church at all. In Montreal, church attendance dropped by half in the 1960s. The church had difficulty recruiting enough priests and nuns to minister to their congregations. Convents, the mainstay of the religious work force, were deserted as jobs in teaching, nursing, and social work opened up for women in the paid labour force.

AMERICANIZATION OF CANADIAN CULTURE

Many regarded the increasing secularism of Canadian society as one of many reflections of the American cultural impact on the country. Concerns about the overwhelming American influence on Canadian culture, particularly in Anglophone Canada, led to the creation in 1949 of a royal commission to study national developments in the arts, letters, and sciences. Headed by Vincent Massey—scion of the farm-implements giant Massey-Harris and, in 1952, Canada's first native-born governor general—the royal commission recommended government programs to strengthen Canadian cultural production.

Among the commission's recommendations were CBC control over private radio and television stations. CBC-TV, which began broadcasting in 1952, was to focus on Canadian-produced arts programming. Other recommended policies included federal grants for universities and increased funding to national cultural agencies such as the National Film Board and National Museum. The commission's most ambitious recommendation was for an agency to finance cultural production in such areas as music, drama, and ballet. In 1957, the federal government established the Canada Council with a mandate based on the Massey Commission's recommendations.

The Canada Council strengthened the Canadian presence in literature, music, and art. But popular culture seemed firmly within the American grip, causing scholars to question whether Canada's survival as a nation clearly distinct from the United States was likely. Harold Innis, Canada's most celebrated political economist, argued in several works in the early postwar period that media empires in the United States were shaping the thinking of people the world over. Democratic discussion and national differences both seemed to be casualties of technologies that permitted a limited number of individuals who controlled access to information to influence global perspectives.

In 1965, George Grant wrote *Lament for a Nation*, in which he explored the career of John Diefenbaker as a metaphor for Canada's efforts to develop outside of the shadow of the Americans. While defending Diefenbaker's genuine desire to uphold Canadian sovereignty, Grant argued that the Conservative prime minister had been waylaid less by American intervention in Canadian politics than by his own social values, which were fundamentally the same as the dominant American values. He accepted the supremacy of the market over the state, and of individual acquisitiveness over collective goals. Canadians generally, lamented Grant, shared Diefenbaker's contradictions. They had embraced American social values, all the time protesting that they wished to be a sovereign people. Driven by their materialistic pursuits, Canadians had integrated their economy and their foreign policy with that of the Americans and consumed what the American entertainment industry served them.

Even universities appeared to be part of the problem. In the 1960s, they had coped with exploding enrolments by hiring a significant number of foreign, mainly American, academics, many of whom ignored Canadian topics in their teaching and research. Only in the 1970s did the federal government establish programs to encourage Canadian Studies and pass legislation to give preference to qualified Canadians in university hirings.

An example of the American influence on Canadian thinking was Canada's copycat response to American suppression of dissenters and "subversive" ideas during the Cold War. Following the Second World War, American legislators, led by Senator Joseph R. McCarthy of Wisconsin, attempted to remove Communists and critics of American foreign policy and capitalist insititutions from public life. Canadian governments responded accordingly, though "witch hunts" were comparatively milder in Canada than in the United States.

Anti-communism became a key ingredient in immigration policy in the early postwar years. While ex-Nazis were gradually welcomed into the country, communists and ex-communists were unwelcome even as visitors. Radicals were rooted out of the civil service, trade union leadership, and teaching positions. Within Canadian society generally, a reticence descended on fundamental criticism of American or Canadian foreign policy and economic institutions. Ironically, this changed only in the 1960s when the American civil rights and anti-war movements created a North America-wide questioning of fundamental social values.

CULTURE AND QUEBEC SOVEREIGNTY

The society-wide questioning of existing structures and social values unleashed by the Quiet Revolution resulted in a flowering of Quebec culture. By the 1960s, political commitment, particularly support for sovereignty, marked much of the celebrated literature in Quebec, including novels by Hubert Aquin and Jacques Godbout and the autobiography of convincted FLQ bomber Pierre Vallieres. The plays of Michel Tremblay, the province's most successful playwright, focused on the ways that domination by both the English and the church had dampened people's ability to communicate their thoughts to others or to demonstrate social solidarity. Tremblay portrayed francophone women as the main victims of a social disintegration resulting from the long suppression of independent thought in Quebec.

By the 1970s Quebec's airwaves, once saturated with pop music from France, were dominated by home-grown talents such as Robert Charlebois, Monique Leyrac, and Pauline Julien. Gilles Vigneault became the major songwriter of the sovereignist movement, with his "Mon pays" and "Gens du pays" becoming anthems of the independence forces.

State subsidies, both provincial and federal, were crucial to the creation of many of the new cultural groups and products in postwar Quebec. In no area was state funding more crucial than in film. The National Film Board was the pivotal player in film financing before the late 1970s, when the Parti québécois government established a provincial film board. Quebec francophones wanted to see movies in their own language and about places and events familiar to them, and locally produced movies drew large audiences. An early success was Claude Jutra's *Mon Oncle Antoine* (1971), which also drew good crowds for its English-language version. More controversial was Michel Brault's *Les Ordres* (1974), which won prizes at the prestigious Cannes Film Festival but was denounced by the federal and provincial governments as an inaccurate portrayal of the arrests and detentions during the October Crisis in 1970. Denys Arcand, eventually to become Quebec's major filmmaker in the twentieth century, also had begun his film-making career in the early 1970s.

Television in Quebec, as elsewhere in North America, became the most important medium for cultural production and political awareness. During the Duplessis years, Radio-Canada, the federally-funded francophone wing of the CBC, provided one of the few media sources of criticism of Duplessis, the Quebec-based newspapers and radio stations fearing retaliation if they criticized the autocratic premier. Radio-Canada produced a number of celebrities, one of whom was René Lévesque, the future premier. By the late 1960s, Quebec federalists accused Radio-Canada journalists of using the network to broadcast sovereignist propaganda. Both Radio-Canada and Radio-Québec, the Quebec broadcasting service established by the provincial government in 1968, provided Quebec entertainers with important outlets for their creative talents.

Quebec anglophones made significant contributions to Quebec and Canadian culture. Hugh McLennan, Nova Scotia-born but resident in Montreal, examined Canadian social values, including conflicts between francophone and anglophone approaches to life, in his novels. In the 1950s, Dorothy Livesay, F.R. Scott, A.M. Klein, and Louis Dudek were key figures in Montreal-centred social realist poetry. Mordecai Richler became the best-known of the Jewish novelists of Montreal, gaining an international reputation with novels which provided vivid portrayals of the Jewish experience in the city. Another product of Montreal's Jewish community, Leonard Cohen, achieved national fame as a poet and novelist and then international recognition as a composer of poetic popular-music lyrics.

CULTURAL PRODUCTION OUTSIDE OF QUEBEC

In the 1960s many artists outside Quebec also struggled to define regional and ethnic identities, and the rate of cultural production in many areas of the arts was impressive. By the 1950s, writers from a number of regions—including Thomas Raddall and Ernest Buckler from the Maritimes, Ontario's Morley Callaghan and Hugh Garner, and the West's W.O. Mitchell, Sheila Watson, and Adele Wiseman—were gaining a national audience. By the 1960s, several Canadian writers began to develop an impressive international following, including Marie-Claire Blais, Robertson Davies, Timothy Findlay, Margaret Laurence, Antonine Maillet, Alice Munro, and Mordecai Richler.

Few Native authors of fiction developed a national reputation before 1975, but several non-fiction works were influential. Harold Cardinal's *The Unjust Society* (1969) and George Manuel's *The Fourth World* (1974) placed before a broad public the perspectives of

Natives clamouring for dramatic legislative changes in Canadian-Native relations. Native autobiographical works also attracted attention. In her 1973 best-selling autobiography, *Halfbreed*, Maria Campbell describes the dire poverty of her childhood in northern Saskatchewan. While Métis traditions partly compensated for grim living conditions and racial discrimination, the death of Campbell's mother in 1952 put an end to this source of solace. Only 12 years old, Maria struggled to hold together her large family. She drifted across Western Canada, becoming a prostitute and drug addict in Vancouver and later doing low-paid "women's work"—cooking, waitressing, hairstyling. In the late 1960s, she became a militant Native activist in Alberta.

From its founding in 1957, the Canada Council played a major role in supporting theatre and film production in Canada. The town of Stratford, Ontario, demonstrated the potential for theatre in the country when local people launched the Stratford Festival in July 1953. Hiring the country's top actors and creating a blend of Shakespeare and other classics, Stratford became a tourist attraction. Professional theatres opened in most urban centres, initially concentrating, like Stratford, on the classics. By the 1970s, many Canadian playwrights were having their works staged at major theatres, which began to include Canadian fare among the classics and Broadway imports.

English-Canadian films were generally less successful than the country's theatrical productions. In the 1970s, the federal government began to provide tax concessions to financial backers of Canadian films. This resulted in a quantitative leap in the number of films produced in the country, and a few films reached high levels of excellence but few Canadians saw them. As in the interwar years, American distributors owned the theatres that remained dominated by Hollywood productions.

Before the 1970s, Canadian radio stations mainly played American recording artists. A few Canadians—the Crew Cuts, the Diamonds, and Paul Anka in the 1950s, and the Guess Who in the 1960s—achieved success in both Canada and the United States. For the most part, however, record sales in Canada simply meant an export of Canadian funds to American record companies and artists. In 1970, the Canadian

biography

Margaret Atwood

Margaret Atwood was the best-selling Canadian author of the twentieth century. Born in Ottawa in 1939, Atwood's childhood was divided between Toronto, where her father taught biology at the University of Toronto, and northern Ontario, where he conducted research. After completing a Bachelor's degree in English at the University of Toronto, Atwood studied in the United States, earning a Masters at Harvard. Her publishing career began with *The Circle Game*, her first book of poetry, in 1966. It won the Governor General's Award for poetry, but poets in Canada cannot earn a living from their publications and Atwood earned her keep by lecturing at the University of British Columbia, Sir George Williams University, the University of Alberta, and York University from 1964 to 1972. Her first novel, *The Edible Woman*, appeared in 1969 followed by *Surfacing* in 1972. That year, Atwood also published her first book of Canadian literary criticism, *Survival: A Thematic Guide to Canadian Literature*.

A prolific writer, Atwood became a public figure in Canada, defending causes that both her fictional and non-fictional writings raised. An ardent nationalist, feminist, and defender of civil liberties, her voice was raised against the Toronto police raids on gay bath houses in 1981, and against the Canada-United States Free Trade Agreement in 1988.

Atwood's international reputation took off with the publication of *The Handmaid's Tale* in 1986, an eerie futuristic account of American society in which the subordination of women to men was total. As Atwood told interviewers, she simply pasted together historical accounts of the treatment of women to create the dystopia of *The Handmaid's Tale*. The book won the Governor General's Award for fiction in 1986 and Atwood's first of four nominations for Britain's prestigious Booker Prize, a prize she finally won for *The Blind Assassin* in 2000.

Margaret Atwood.

Peter Bregg/CP Photo Archive

Atwood's work covers a variety of themes and locales. But Canadian history is central to much of it. From her poetry collection *The Journals of Susanna Moodie: Poems* (1970) to her novel *Alias Grace* (1996), the latter dealing with the complexities surrounding a nineteenth-century Ontario murderer, Atwood has demonstrated an abiding interest in uncovering the past of her country and particularly its women.

Radio-television Commission (CRTC), established by the federal government in 1968 to regulate Canadian broadcasting, introduced regulations requiring radio stations to ensure that no fewer than 30 percent of the recordings they played were of Canadian origin. Within a year, artists such as Anne Murray, Neil Young, Gordon Lightfoot, and Joni Mitchell were common fare on the radio, and their Canadian success spilled across the border.

There was a growing audience for dance in Canada in the postwar period. Canadian dance companies such as Les Grands Ballets Canadiens and the Danny Grossman Dance Company came into their own, and dancers such as Karen Kain and Frank Augustyn of the National Ballet and Evelyn Hart of the Royal Winnipeg Ballet won prestigious international competitions. With grants from the Secretary of State for Multiculturalism, cultural groups began to revive dance traditions that had been pushed aside in the rush to fleeting popular dance styles such as the twist, the monkey, and the mashed potatoes.

In art, as in theatre and literature, regional, ethnic, and gender sensibilities struggled to emerge. Native artistic expression finally received some recognition. On the West Coast, Bill Reid earned an international reputation for his revival of traditional Haida carving. In the 1950s, Norval Morrisseau, an Ojibwa from Sand Point reserve in Ontario, began to create paintings that incorporated the pictography of rock paintings and Ojibwa spiritual themes. Largely due to the promotional energy of Toronto artist James Houston, what is now known as Inuit art was introduced to southern buyers. Beginning in the late 1940s, he encouraged Inuit to develop cooperatives as a vehicle for marketing their prints and ivory and soapstone carvings.

Artists increasingly turned to the land and its people for their inspiration. Northwest Coast Native art and the British Columbia landscape influenced the work of Vancouver surrealist painter Jack Shadbolt. On the Prairies, William Kurelek's work re-

flected his attempts to deal with a difficult childhood as a Ukrainian Canadian growing up in rural Alberta and Manitoba. Ontario film-maker and artist Joyce Wieland produced provocative works that reflected her nationalist and feminist values. Several artists from London, Ontario, among whom Greg Curnoe was best-known, created a regional art celebrating local identity and the Canadian struggle to be free of American control. With the east coast environment as his context, Alex Colville inspired a generation of artists, including Christopher Pratt, Mary Pratt, and Tom Forrestall, to produce works that collectively became known as Atlantic realism.

HERITAGE CONSERVATION

Heritage conservation became an important means by which national, regional, and ethnic identities could

Frank Augustyn and Karen Kain dance in the National Ballet's production of "The Sleeping Beauty."

Andrew Oxenburg/National Ballet of Canada

be preserved. Outside of the work of the Historic Sites and Monuments Board and the National Museum, little attention had been paid before 1960 to preserving historic buildings and artifacts. An explosion of conservation and historical reconstruction activities accompanied the centennial celebrations in 1967 and continued thereafter.

Such activities involved all levels of government and were carried out for a variety of reasons. Sometimes the goal was job creation, as in the federally sponsored reconstruction of Louisbourg as a tourist attraction in Cape Breton in the early 1960s. Provincial projects such as the Acadian Historic Village in Caraquet, New Brunswick, and the Ukrainian Village outside Edmonton represented a recognition by government of the voting power of ethnic groups. At other times, projects involved attempts to invigorate decaying areas of cities, as in the conversion of dilapidated buildings on the Halifax waterfront and in Winnipeg's warehouse district into fancy shops. The sites at King's Landing in New Brunswick and Upper Canada Village in Ontario were assembled from buildings threatened with demolition when hydro-electric dams flooded the land on which they had been originally built. In some cases, such as the remains of a Viking settlement at l'Anse-aux-Meadows in Newfoundland and the well-preserved buildings in old Quebec City, historic sites received international recognition. Museums, like historic sites, mushroomed after 1960, most focusing on some aspect of the history of Canada.

Preservation of historic sites, as many commentators pointed out, was not quite the same thing as preservation of history. While the object of much enthusiasm and capital investment, the history of preserved places and buildings was often presented in a romantic and simplified way to tourists. The thousands of visitors who parked their vehicles for a day at pretty-as-a-picture Peggy's Cove, near Halifax, learned little of the difficult lives of the fishermen and their various battles with fish buyers or banks. For all its meticulous detail in reproducing the exteriors and interiors of buildings, the Ukrainian Village gave little hint of the political divisions that were important to pioneer life for the early generations of Ukrainian immigrants to western Canada.

PROFESSIONAL SPORTS

Postwar prosperity resulted in a larger potential audience of paying customers for professional sporting events. Hockey remained the national passion, and fans were often quite demonstrative in their feelings for their teams. In March 1955, after the legendary Maurice "Rocket" Richard of the Montreal Canadiens was suspended for the balance of the season as a penalty for brawling, fans at the Forum pelted National Hockey League president Clarence Campbell with food. They then took to the streets, breaking windows and looting stores in what many saw as a demonstration of Quebec nationalism. Canada's victory in the first Soviet-Canadian hockey series in 1972 was a cause of nation-wide celebration. National pride was on the line when a series was arranged between the Soviets and the best Canadian players in the NHL. Paul Henderson's famous series-ending goal has come to be seen as one of the classic moments in Canadian sports history.

Though racial integration in North American sport advanced in the postwar period, the National Hockey League remained virtually lily-white until the late 1980s. Before 1986, only one black player, Willie O'Ree, had been allowed to play in NHL major-league games. A Fredericton-born left-winger and speed demon, O'Ree was asked to play in two Boston Bruins games in 1958. Three years later, he played most of the Bruins' regular season games, but despite a strong performance, was traded several times after the season and relegated back to the minors for the remaining 14 years of his hockey career.

While professional sports teams were almost exclusively male, both female and male Canadian athletes won international honours in individualized sports. Two women received particular media attention in the early postwar period. Barbara Ann Scott won the 1948 Olympic figure-skating title and then skated professionally in ice shows. Marilyn Bell was hailed for her swimming achievements beginning in 1954 with her 52-kilometre swim across Lake Ontario when she was only 16 years old. She later went on to become the youngest swimmer to cross the English Channel and the Strait of Juan de Fuca.

As in other nations, sports became increasingly identified in Canada with the "national identity." In 1961, the Fitness and Amateur Sports Act was passed, which made federal funds available for sports activity. Amateur sports became more bureaucratized, presided over by paid administrators rather than enthusiastic volunteers.

CONCLUSION

Canadian society in the postwar decades was both a reflection of and reaction to American developments. While everything from suburbs to popular entertainments seemed to embody the American spirit, there were tenacious efforts to create distinctly Canadian or regional institutions. In the case of Quebec, the sovereignty movement gave a particular poignancy to such efforts. Canadians success in this period were often due to the efforts of governments, both through subsidies and regulations to protect the Canadian market for home-grown talents. As Canadians began seeing themselves reflected in cultural productions they developed a sense of their own identity. This did not mean that national differences were erased. Cultural production reflected the growing diversity of Canadian society as the twentieth century drew to a close.

NOTES

1 Jacques Ferron, *Tales from the Uncertain Country* (Toronto: Anansi, 1972) 100.

2 Myrna Kostash, "Dissing Feminist Sexuality," *Canadian Forum* (Sept. 1996) 16.

3 Kenneth McRoberts and Dale Posgate, *Quebec: Social Change and Political Crisis*, 2nd ed. (Toronto: McClelland and Stewart, 1980) 53.

4 Denise Chong, *The Concubine's Children: Portrait of a Family Divided* (Toronto: Viking, 1994) 228.

5 Dan Smith, *The Seventh Fire: The Struggle for Aboriginal Government* (Toronto: Key Porter, 1993) 57.

SELECTED READING

On baby boomers, see Douglas Owram, *Born at the Right Time: A History of the Baby Boom in Canada* (Toronto: University of Toronto Press, 1996). On postwar education, see Paul Axelrod, *Scholars and Dollars: Politics, Economics, and Universities of Ontario, 1945–1980* (Toronto: University of Toronto Press, 1982) and Henry Milner, *The Long Road to Reform: Restructuring Public Education in Quebec* (Montreal: McGill-Queen's University Press, 1986). Canadian suburbanization is addressed in Stanley R. Barrett, *Paradise: Class, Commuters, and Ethnicity in Rural Ontario* (Toronto: University of Toronto Press, 1994), and Veronica Strong-Boag, "Home Dreams: Women and the Suburban Experiment in Canada, 1945–60," *Canadian Historical Review* 72.4 (Dec. 1991): 471–504.

Immigration policies are analyzed in Ninette Kelley and Michael Trebilcock, *The Making of the Mosaic: A History of Canadian Immigration Policy* (Toronto: University of Toronto Press, 1998); Donald H. Avery, *Reluctant Host: Canada's Response to Immigrant Workers, 1896–1994* (Toronto: McClelland and Stewart, 1995); Reginald Whitaker, *Double Standard: The Secret History of Canadian Immigration* (Toronto: Lester and Orpen Dennys, 1987); and Freda Hawkins, *Canada and Immigration: Public Policy and Public Concern* (Toronto: Institute of Public Adminstration of Canada, 1972). Among excellent works on immigrant and ethnic experiences are Franca Iacovetta, *Such Hardworking People: Italian Immigrants in Postwar Toronto* (Montreal: McGill-Queen's University Press, 1992); Frances Swyripa, *Wedded to the Cause: Ukrainian Canadian Women and Ethnic Identity, 1891–1991* (Toronto: University of Toronto Press, 1993); Jean Burnet, ed., *Looking into My Sister's Eyes: An Exploration in Women's History* (Toronto: Multicultural History Society of Ontario, 1986); Bridglal Pachai, *Beneath the Clouds of the Promised Land: The Survival of Nova Scotia Blacks*, vol. 2, *1800–1989* (Halifax: Black Education Association, 1990); and E. Wickberg, ed., *From China to Canada: A History of the Chinese Communities in Canada* (Toronto: McClelland and Stewart, 1982). On the Canadian Jewish Congress and the struggle for religious tolerance, see Janine Stingel, *Social Discredit: Anti-Semitism, Social Credit and the Jewish Response* (Montreal: McGill-Queen's University Press, 2000).

The lives of Canada's Native peoples are explored in Kenneth Coates, *Canada's Colonies: A History of the Yukon and Northwest Territories* (Toronto: Lorimer, 1985); Boyce Richardson, *Strangers Devour the Land*, 2nd ed. (Vancouver: Douglas and McIntyre, 1991); Sally Weaver, *Making Canadian Indian Policy:The Hidden Agenda, 1968–1970* (Toronto: University of Toronto Press, 1980); and J.R. Miller, *Shingwauk's Vision: A History of Native Residential Schools* (Toronto: University of Toronto Press, 1996).

On the postwar ideal of families and of sexuality, see Mona Lee Gleason, *Normalizing the Ideal: Psychology, Schooling, and the Family in Postwar Canada* (Toronto: University of Toronto Press, 1999) and Mary Louise Adams, *The Trouble With Normal: Postwar Youth and the Making of Heterosexuality* (Toronto: University of Toronto Press, 1997). On the women's movement in Canada, see Constance Backhouse and David Flaherty, eds., *Challenging Times: The Women's Movement in Canada and the United States* (Montreal: McGill-Queen's University Press, 1992); and Jeri Dawn Wine and Janice L. Ristock, eds., *Women and Social Change: Feminist Activism in Canada* (Toronto: Lorimer, 1991). On African-Canadian women, see Peggy Bristow, et.al., *"We're Rooted Here and They Can't Pull Us Up": Essays in African Canadian Women's History* (Toronto: University of Toronto Press, 1994). On the changing position of women in Canada, important works include Angus McLaren and Arlene Tigar McLaren, *The Bedroom and the State: The Changing Practices and Politics of Contraception and Abortion in Canada* (Toronto: McClelland and Stewart, 1997); Pat Armstrong and Hugh Armstrong, *The Double Ghetto: Canadian Women and Their Segregated Work*, 3rd ed. (Toronto: McClelland and Stewart, 1994); and Mary Kinnear, *A Female Economy: Women's Work in a Prairie Province 1870–1970* (Montreal: McGill-Queen's University Press, 1999).

The state campaign against homosexuals is discussed in Daniel J. Robinson and David Kemmel, "The Queer Career of Homosexual Vetting in Cold War Canada," *Canadian Historical Review* 75.3 (Sept. 1994): 319–45, and Gary Kinsman, "'Character Weaknesses' and 'Fruit Machines': Towards an Analysis of the Anti-Homosexual Security Campaign in the Canadian Civil Service," *Labour/Le Travail* 35 (Spring 1995): 133-61 as well as his *Regulation of Desire*, 2nd ed. (Montreal: Black Rose, 1996). On lesbians, see Sharon Dale Stone, *Lesbians in Canada* (Toronto: Between the Lines, 1990); Becki Ross, "Down at the Whorehouse? Reflections on Christian Community Service and Female Sex Deviance at Toronto's Street Haven, 1965-1969," *Atlantis* 23.1 (Fall 1998): 48-59; and Line Chamberland, "Remembering Lesbian Bars: Montreal, 1955-1975," in Veronica Strong- Boag and Anita Clair Feldman, eds., *Rethinking Canada: The Promise of Women's History*, 3rd ed. (Toronto: Oxford University Press, 1997) 402–23.

Religion in postwar Canada is discussed in Tony Clarke, *Behind the Mitre: The Moral Leadership Crisis in the Canadian Catholic Church* (Toronto: HarperCollins, 1995); Gregory Baum, *Compassion and Solidarity* (Toronto: CBC Enterprises, 1987); John Webster Grant, *The Church in the Canadian Era* (Toronto: Welch Publishing, 1988); Pierre Berton, *The Comfortable Pew: A Critical Look at Christianity and the Religious Establishment in the New Age* (Toronto: McClelland and Stewart, 1965); and Reginald Bibby, *Fragmented Gods: The Poverty and Potential of Religion in Canada* (Toronto: Irwin,1987).

On cultural identities in Canada, see William Dodge, ed., *Boundaries of Identity* (Toronto: Lester, 1992) and Neil Bissoondath, *Selling Illusions: The Cult of Multiculturalism in Canada* (Toronto: Penguin, 1994). On Quebec cultural developments, see Renate Usmiani, *Michel Tremblay* (Vancouver: Douglas and McIntyre, 1982); Gabrielle Roy, *Letters to Bernadette* (Toronto: Lester and Orpen Dennys, 1990); and Guy Bouthilier and Jean Meynaud, *Le choc des langues au Québec* (Montreal: Presses de l'Université du Québec, 1972). On Canadian literature generally, see Margaret Atwood, *Survival* (Toronto: Anansi, 1972) and Northrop Frye, *The Bush Garden: Essays on the Canadian Imagination* (Toronto: Anansi, 1971). On authors writing in English, see Judith S. Grant, *Robertson Davies: Man of Myth* (Toronto: Penguin, 1994); Janice Williamson, *Sounding Differences: Conversations with Seventeen Canadian Writers* (Toronto: University of Toronto Press, 1993); Ed Jewinski, *Michael Ondaatje: Express Yourself Beautifully* (Toronto: ECW Press, 1994); and Beverly Rasporich, *Dance of the Sexes: Art and Gender in the Fiction of Alice Munro* (Edmonton: University of Alberta Press, 1990). On Native cultural assertion, see the texts by Arthur Ray, Olive Dickason, and J.R. Miller referred to in earlier chapters as well as G. Gottfriedson and R. Schneider, *In Honour of Our*

Grandmothers: Visions of Cultural Survival (Penticton, BC: Theytus Books, 1994).

Histories of Canadian film include Michael Dorland, *So Close to the States: The Emergence of Canadian Feature Film Policy* (Toronto: University of Toronto Press, 1998); Gary Evans, *In the National Interest: A Chronicle of the National Film Board of Canada from 1949 to 1989* (Toronto: University of Toronto Press, 1991); and R. Bruce Elder, *Image and Identity: Reflections on Canadian Film and Culture* (Waterloo, ON: Wilfrid Laurier University Press, 1989).

Key works on Canadian art include *Visual Arts in Canada: Painting, Drawing, and Sculpture* (Ottawa: Canadian Heritage, 1993); Dennis Reid, *A Concise History of Canadian Painting* (Toronto: Oxford University Press, 1988); and Elizabeth McLuhan and Tom Hill, *Norval Morrisseau and the Emergence of the Image Makers* (Toronto: Methuen, 1984).

On the media in Canada, see Paul Rutherford, *When Television Was Young: Primetime Canada, 1952–1967* (Toronto: University of Toronto Press, 1990); Mary Vipond, *The Mass Media in Canada* (Toronto: Lorimer, 1989); Frank Peers, *The Public Eye: Television and the Politics of Canadian Broadcasting, 1952–1968* (Toronto:

University of Toronto Press, 1979); and Gerry Friesen, *Citizens and Nation: An Essay on History, Communication, and Canada* (Toronto: University of Toronto, 2000).

On heritage preservation, see C.J. Taylor, *Negotiating the Past: The Making of Canada's National Historic Parks and Sites* (Montreal: McGill-Queen's University Press, 1990); *Prairie Forum* 15.2 (Fall 1990), special issue on heritage conservation; and Ian McKay, *The Quest of the Folk: Antimodernism and Cultural Selection in Twentieth-Century Nova Scotia* (Montreal: McGill-Queen's University Press, 1994).

On sports in Canada, see Colin Howell, *Blood, Sweat, and Cheers: Sport and the Making of Modern Canada* (Toronto: University of Toronto Press, 2001); Bruce Kidd, *The Struggle for Canadian Sport* (Toronto: University of Toronto Press, 1996); Richard S. Gruneau and David Whitson, *Hockey Night in Canada: Sport, Identities and Cultural Politics* (Toronto: Garamond, 1993); Ann Hall, *Sports in Canadian Society* (Toronto: McClelland and Stewart, 1991); and Donald Macintosh, *Sports and Politics in Canada: Federal Government Involvement Since 1961* (Montreal: McGill-Queen's University Press, 1987).

WEBLINKS

CANADIAN BLACK HERITAGE IN THE THIRD MILLENNIUM
http://fcis.oise.utoronto.ca/~gpieters/blklinks.html

This online resource allows students to research Black history from a Canadian perspective.

CANADA'S HISTORIC SOUL: PIER 21
http://pier21.ns.ca/

This site for a major historic point of entry to Canada includes downloadable education kits.

ASSEMBLY OF FIRST NATIONS/ASSEMBLÉE DES PREMIÈRES NATIONS
www.afn.ca

This comprehensive bilingual site provides links to a vast range of information on First Nations people.

AFRICVILLE
www.hartford-hwp.com/archives/44/170.html

An exercise in "urban removal" in Canada, the social significance of Africville, as well as the history of black settlers in Nova Scotia, is examined at this site.

MACKENZIE VALLEY PIPELINE INQUIRY
www.yukoncollege.yk.ca/~agraham/nost202/berger1.htm

This excerpt from Thomas R. Berger's *Northern Frontier, Northern Homeland* outlines the environmental, social, and economic consequences—to the northern territories and their people—of the proposed Mackenzie Valley energy corridor.

PART VII SUMMARY

POSTWAR PROSPERITY SPAWNED THREE DECADES OF unprecedented social reform and cultural development in Canada. Until the 1960s, Cold War hysteria limited public debate on many issues and fostered a climate of conformism characterized by a rigid gender stratification and all-embracing consumerism. Under the surface, regional and class antagonisms persisted. The 1960s ushered in a new spirit of public debate. Protest groups, often dominated by "baby boomers," challenged gender roles, the distribution of wealth and power in Canada, the impoverishment of Native peoples, racism, and homophobia. While resistance to American domination of Canada's economy and culture peaked in English Canada, in francophone Quebec a sovereignty movement was equally resistant to anglophone-Canadian domination. The political and corporate elite alternately tried to co-opt such concerns and to resist demands for change, the latter reaction becoming more prominent as economic growth began to decline in the early 1970s.

POST-MODERN CANADA

If the first three decades after the Second World War were years of hope for most Canadians, the quarter-century that followed gave Canadians cause for anxiety. Economic growth stalled, the liberal consensus cracked, and international relations were thrown into disarray by terrorist attacks on the World Trade Center in New York on 11 September 2001. In this period, Canadian governments adopted a neo-conservative agenda that focused on eliminating deficits and consolidating an even closer relationship with the United States. The new era of economic globalization, it was argued, made concern for economic competitiveness more important than efforts to improve the lives of disadvantaged members of society or concerns about Canadian sovereignty. In 1982, the Canadian constitution was finally patriated and a Charter of Rights and Freedoms offered some hope for groups struggling for social justice, but they faced an uphill battle. Meanwhile, nationalist forces in Quebec continued to call into question the legitimacy of a nation-state called Canada, and both the Atlantic and Western provinces voiced angry reservations about a federal government so clearly dominated by Ontario and Quebec. As the twenty-first century dawned, Canadians lived in one of the richest nations in the world, but its future seemed as uncertain as it had in the past.

CHAPTER 26

Canada in the Global Village, 1976–2002

On 25 November 1997, the Asia-Pacific Economic Cooperation (APEC) summit, a meeting of political and corporate leaders of Pacific Rim countries, took place at the University of British Columbia's Museum of Anthropology. While the leaders talked trade and investment, protesters, mainly students, demonstrated against the presence at the summit of Indonesia's tyrannical President Suharto. RCMP officers pepper-sprayed protesters, and evidence suggested that the Prime Minister's Office had directed much of the security strategy for the Vancouver conference. Bruce Arthur, a student commenting on the pepper-spraying and Prime Minister Jean Chrétien's reaction in Parliament to questions about the event, wrote:

> It's such an innocuous name for such a brutally painful thing, really. When asked about it Jean Chrétien said, "For me, I put pepper on my plate." I saw those people writhing, face on fire, eyes shut so tight that the tears could barely roll out, screaming. Screaming so hard I thought they'd break apart. I put pepper on my plate, he said, and the media laughed like Chrétien was Johnny Carson.[1]

The APEC confrontation said volumes about the Canadian government's priorities in the late twentieth century. Increasingly political leaders evinced a single-minded determination to export goods or services to a much-enlarged global marketplace.

They simply shrugged when confronted with the human rights records of countries such as China or Sudan, where economic opportunities beckoned. At home, too, from many people's perspective, Canada had become a more callous country, less willing than in the three postwar decades to use the power of the state to prevent the weak from being crushed by the power of capital.

GLOBALIZATION

The new world order had been developing for several decades. By the 1970s, the rising economic power of Japan led giant corporations in the West to believe that their postwar compromise with labour and governments was no longer workable. Japanese radios, televisions, stereo equipment, appliances, computers, and cars were putting North American factories out of business. A close business-government alliance had promoted Japan's industrial cause, and the "Four Tigers" of Asia—Hong Kong, South Korea, Taiwan, and Singapore—benefited from similar strategies to make important strides in industrial development.

Their well-being threatened by new competitors, the energy crisis, and the environmental movement, corporations began moving their production facilities overseas. Developing countries, desperate for capital investment, offered these "transnational" corporations cheap labour, lower taxes, and fewer corporate and environmental regulations to eat into profits. Soon corporate managers could also extract favourable conditions from governments of Western nations eager to prevent jobs from being exported. Corporate taxes were cut, trade union protection reduced, environmental regulations relaxed, and social programs pared back.

In the face of these developments, ecologists' hopes that the world community would recognize that the future of the biosphere depended on collective action to avert alarming trends received a setback. Environmental disasters at Three Mile Island (1979), Bhopal (1984), and Chernobyl (1986) underscored the difficulty of controlling technology. The destruction of the ozone layer by chlorofluorocarbons (CFCs) and the rapid disappearance of tropical rain forests caused further deterioration of the atmosphere. With both the greenhouse effect and nuclear winter threatening the future of the planet, the limits of technology and the people who planned it were plain for all to see. The collapse of the east coast cod stocks in 1992 emphasized, as environmentalists had been warning for decades, that there was a limit to growth. For the time being, the power of transnational corporations and the unwillingness of governments collectively to challenge this power limited what could be achieved to protect the environment.

Instead, governments focused on maintaining their nation's share of world trade. Regional trading blocs established policies to expand trade among their own members. The European Economic Community, created by six Western European nations in 1958, expanded to include almost all of Western Europe in what became known as the European Union (EU). A Free Trade Agreement (FTA) between Canada and the United States went into effect early in 1989. Three years later, the North American Free Trade Agreement (NAFTA) brought Mexico into the North

American trading bloc, and plans were soon underway to include all South American nations by 2005 as well.

The corporate agenda of "restructuring" for a leaner and meaner global economy had become evident even before these events. When a recession descended in late 1981, the corporate response was to automate production processes, reduce the number of workers, and offer a more flexible response to changing market conditions so that only the fittest survived. A wave of mergers and takeovers followed, which further concentrated economic power. By 1986, thirty-two families and nine giant conglomerates controlled over one-third of Canada's non-financial assets.

NEO-LIBERALISM

In the new climate of corporate concentration and "downsizing," government intervention—deficit financing, tax incentives, and the expansion of the money supply—was condemned as a dead weight on the economy. The solution was to encourage efficient production to improve the supply of goods and services rather than to stimulate demand through government spending. If governments simply reduced taxes, controlled inflation, and let the private sector adjust to changing economic conditions, the global economy would right itself soon enough. Above all, argued the so-called monetarists who championed this theory, economic discipline should be maintained by resisting temptations to expand the money supply.

Both the terms "neo-liberalism" and "neo-conservatism" were used to describe this perspective, the former because such views harkened back to classical liberal economic theory and the latter because parties that called themselves conservative were the major, though not the only, proponents of this theory. Supply-side economics inspired the policies of conservative governments in Britain under Margaret Thatcher (1979–90), in the United States under Ronald Reagan (1981–88), and in Canada under Brian Mulroney (1984–93). Although their economies were experiencing the worst dislocation since the 1930s, these leaders reduced social spending, privatized government activities, cut back the civil service, and exercised tighter control over the money supply. Keynesians objected that such policies had been pursued during the Great Depression, with disastrous results, but reminders of this kind, voiced by Canadian-born economist John Kenneth Galbraith, were increasingly ignored by political leaders.

Since governments felt compelled to cut corporate taxes, and generally resisted significant increases to the individual tax rate, imbalances between revenues and expenditures produced annual deficits. Over time, large debt loads accumulated that had to be financed through loans from financiers. As a result, an increased portion of state expenditure went simply to repaying debts, further limiting funds available for social programs.

Opponents of neo-liberalism charged that high unemployment, resulting from the credit squeeze that tight money produced, was not simply an unfortunate consequence of the battle against inflation: it was the goal of the exercise. Such accusations gained steam from statements made by officials such as Bank of Canada governor John Crow (1987–94), who publicly opined that allowing the rate of unemployment to fall below 8 percent would produce a new round of inflation. Ironically, while neo-liberals claimed that the welfare state and Keynesian economics had mollycoddled individuals, discouraging them from taking the jobs on offer, they promoted a monetary and fiscal regime that reduced demand for workers.

FEDERAL MANOEUVRES

The Liberal Party had been the chief political beneficiary of postwar prosperity. Given credit by Canadians for implementing welfare state policies, it governed the country for 32 of the 39 years from 1945 to 1984. It was weak in Western Canada, where competition between the right-wing Progressive Conservatives and the left-wing New Democrats squeezed out the party that was seen less as centrist than as central Canadian.

By contrast, the party was strong in Quebec, if only because the Conservatives and New Democrats were viewed as anglophone parties.

By the late 1970s, the Progressive Conservatives were beginning to tap the resentment among middle-class Canadians against increasing taxes and increasing state intervention. The Liberals lost the federal election of 1979 to the Progressive Conservatives led by Joe Clark. Once in office, the willingness of Clark's minority government to allow energy price increases met little favour outside the energy-producing provinces of Western Canada. The government's first budget met Commons defeat, forcing a second election in less than a year. In 1980, Trudeau's Liberals remained the safest bet for many Canadians.

By 1984, Trudeau was gone, and the new Liberal leader, John Turner, had a different legacy with which to contend. After almost three years of a

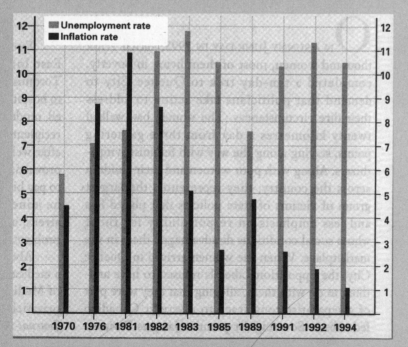

Figure 26.1
Unemployment and Inflation Rates in Canada, 1970–1994

Source: Richard Layard, Stephen Nickel, and Richard Jackman, *The Unemployment Crisis* (Oxford: Oxford University Press, 1994) 134, 138; Statistics Canada

bruising recession and increasing government deficits, Canadians were ready for a change. Brian Mulroney, the new Progressive Conservative leader, promised Canadians that he would restore employment and reduce deficits without touching Canada's social programs, which he labelled a "sacred trust." Cynically recognizing that most Canadians had not yet been won over to the hard-hearted politics of Thatcher and Reagan, he promised Canadians gain without pain. He even took advantage of a televised forum on women's issues to announce that his party would implement a national daycare program if he won the election.

THE FREE TRADE AGREEMENT

In 1984, Mulroney claimed that he opposed free trade between Canada and the United States. This old idea had been revived by the Royal Commission on Canada's Economic Union and Development Prospects. Appointed by Trudeau in 1982 when the country was mired in recession, the commission was chaired by Donald Macdonald, a former Liberal finance minister. Its report, released in September 1985, argued that Canada had to maintain a flexible economy, capable of adjusting to global economic change and new technologies. With over one-third of Canada's GNP derived from foreign trade, and over three-quarters of Canada's exports sold to the United States, Canadians would experience an inescapable crisis if the flow of goods across the Canada–United States border was disrupted. The time had come, the commissioners claimed, to shake up the industries that remained sheltered behind the old National Policy and to lay the foundations for a New Age economy that would serve Canadians in the twenty-first century.

Ignoring his pre-election statements, Mulroney followed the commission recommendation and initiated trade negotiation with the Americans. In taking this step, his government had powerful backing from Canada's major industry lobby groups. The details of the free trade agreement were negotiated in the fall of 1987. According to its provisions, tariffs on primary and manufactured goods would be eliminated over a 10-year period and free trade in services would gradually be implemented. Most non-tariff barriers to trade,

such as quotas and content regulations, were also slated for elimination. Following a year of heated debate, Mulroney called an election on 25 November 1988 that focused almost exclusively on the free-trade debate.

Leaders of the NDP, labour unions, feminists, some church groups, and several nationalist coalitions opposed free trade in principle, while the Liberal Party, which waffled about the concept, rejected certain features of the actual proposal. Opponents of the free trade agreement maintained that it would allow multinational corporations to consolidate their North American operations in locations with better climates and lower wage levels than those prevailing in Canada. Jobs would be lost in the goods-producing sectors, and the wages of those remaining in the labour force would be substantially reduced. Moreover, Canada's cultural industries would be threatened, and Canadians would be forced to "harmonize" their welfare, environmental, and regional development policies with the goals of the larger economic partner. Under such pressure, Canada as a nation would surely fall apart.

In her autobiography, Pat Carney, who was Trade Minister in the Mulroney government, maintains that she's proud of the role she played in helping to eliminate the economic border between Canada and the United States.

Glenn Baglo/The *Vancouver Sun*

Brian Mulroney maintained that Canada would remain a sovereign nation once the agreement was in effect. Although the government could no longer levy tariffs to protect industries, he claimed that the opening of the American market to more Canadian-produced goods and services would, overall, benefit workers in the manufacturing and service sectors. Moreover, the agreement merely furthered the work of the GATT, which, after 1947, had effectively removed tariffs on 80 percent of all goods produced in Canada.

If the 1988 election is taken as a referendum on the issue of free trade, its opponents won, since the Liberals and New Democrats together received over 52 percent of the total votes cast. Supporters of the agreement, the Conservatives and the fledgling Reform Party, won about 46 percent of the vote. The Liberals and New Democrats had formed no alliance in the campaign, and the large plurality of Conservative voters returned a second Mulroney majority government. On 24 December 1988, the legisla-

tion authorizing the free trade agreement between Canada and the United States passed in the House of Commons by a vote of 141–111, and the agreement went into effect on 1 January 1989.

THE FREE TRADE ERA

The ink was barely dry on the Free Trade Agreement when firms, beginning with Gillette, announced that they were closing all or part of their Canadian operations and centralizing their manufacturing in the United States. In every case, they insisted that their plans to vacate Canada were unrelated to the agreement and had been in place prior to its enactment. Supporters of free trade minimized the importance of the exodus, arguing that Canadians should turn the companies that remained into world-class firms with markets around the globe.

By 1990, Canada was in the grip of a deep recession. Although it affected all Western nations, the recession was more severe in Canada than in most other countries, lasting for three years and being followed by a "jobless recovery." Mel Hurtig, a long-time champion of Canadian nationalism, charged in his book *The Betrayal of Canada* (1992) that, in its first two years, the free trade agreement was responsible for the loss of 264 000 manufacturing jobs as branch plants closed and new operations were located in Mexico and elsewhere. Supporters of the agreement accused the nationalists of blaming free trade for job losses that were the result purely of the recession. Even without the FTA, Canadians would have been victims of the restructuring and downsizing policies that were part of global economic strategy, they argued.

While free traders argued that nothing could stop this irresistible force toward global marketplace decisions regulating everything, their opponents took another perspective. An equally global movement developed that called into question the type of globalization being imposed on nation-states. Its leaders argued that globalization led by transnational corporations constituted a new and particularly vicious form of imperialism that was impoverishing the peoples of most countries and creating a race for the bottom in such areas as environmental standards and

Mel Hurtig was one of the leading opponents of the Free Trade Agreement in 1988. In the years that followed, he documented the Agreement's negative impact on the Canadian economy and attempted in vain to lead a political struggle to force the Canadian government to tear up the agreement.

Courtesy of Mel Hurtig

MORE TO THE STORY

Massey-Harris: A Tale of Canadian Capitalism

As we have seen in earlier chapters, the agricultural machinery company founded in 1847 by Daniel Massey went from strength to strength in the late nineteenth and early twentieth centuries. The company moved from Newcastle to Toronto in 1855 and, in 1891, merged with its chief competitor to become Massey-Harris, the largest company of its kind in the British Empire. By the first decade of the twentieth century, it had captured a huge share of the rapidly expanding Prairie market for farm machinery and had established branch operations in the United States. When the company ran into difficulties following the Second World War, it was reorganized under the direction of its holding company, Argus Corporation, and continued to prosper. As Massey- Ferguson, it developed a global market and reached annual sales of over $1 billion in the 1960s.

In the difficult economic climate of the late 1970s, Massey's fortunes again began to slip. Conrad Black, the ambitious young head of Argus, became chair of the troubled company in 1978, but the bottom fell out of the farm machinery market in 1980, and Argus wrote off its Massey-Ferguson shares as worthless. In an effort to save the capital and jobs that Massey represented, banks, governments, and shareholders poured $1.2 billion into the failing firm between 1978 and 1984. By 1987, when Massey-Ferguson changed its name to Varity Corp (after the Varity Plough Company, which had been acquired in 1892), it was a third of its former size, but nonetheless ranked as the forty-ninth largest firm in Canada with sales and operating revenue of $1.8 billion. Following the signing of the Free Trade Agreement, it moved its head office to the United States.

working conditions. This view seemed confirmed by the creation in 1995 of the World Trade Organization (WTO), whose sole purpose appeared to be to break down the barriers to international trade. When the WTO met in Seattle in 1999, well-orchestrated protests publicized opposition to the brand of globalization that the WTO promoted.

Huge demonstrations and street theatre greeted international trade and finance organizations in the years following the Seattle confrontation. In April 2001, it was Quebec City's turn to play host to both the globalizers and their opponents. The Summit of the Americas brought together national leaders to plot the Free Trade of the Americas, a gradual extension of free trade throughout the hemisphere to be completed by 2005. Social justice, environmentalist, and labour groups, together with students, created a carnival-like atmosphere in the city as they counterposed a hemispheric agenda of cooperation among governments and social groups to the Summit's celebration of transnational capitalism. A four-kilometre steel fence around the Old City, erected by the federal government to separate heads of state from protesters, symbolized the gulf between free marketers and social justice advocates.

THE JOBLESS RECOVERY

Although moderate economic growth had succeeded the recession, one-tenth of the Canadian labour force remained unemployed in 1995. Both governments and profitable businesses were reducing their workforces. Business cutbacks were justified on the grounds that trade liberalization forced companies to be more competitive. That meant mergers, factory shutdowns, and the introduction of technology, particularly computerization, all of which reduced the economy's demand for labour. Because they were determined to cut taxes, governments were forced to follow the business model based on downsizing.

Between 1990 and 1998, the real after-tax income of Canadian families fell 7 percent. While most households still had a comfortable income, a growing number of Canadians were living under the poverty line. Rates of poverty had dropped gradually during the era of prosperity, but they climbed during the recessions of the early 1980s and 1990s. In 1993, 4.9 million Canadians were classified as poor, including over one in five Canadian children. Sixty percent of poor children lived in homes headed by single mothers, whose ability to find work had been undermined first by the recession and then by the jobless recovery.

Women's labour force participation nonetheless continued to rise. By 1994, women made up 45 percent of the workforce, an increase of 8 percent from 1976. Although women increasingly unionized and fought successfully for better wages, there was still a considerable degree of inequality in income. In 1994, women's incomes overall were only 58 percent of men's. Apart from gender, colour was a factor in labour-force earnings. Members of visible minorities earned 30 percent less than other Canadians in the labour force in 1998, with African-Canadian males and all Aboriginals encountering the greatest income disparities.

INFLATION VERSUS UNEMPLOYMENT

Federal economic policies, both under the Progressive Conservatives and their Liberal successors, elected in 1993, continued to emphasize the battle against inflation and government debt rather than the battle against unemployment. At the same time, high unemployment drained the federal treasury, as unemployment insurance and social assistance costs mounted, and it deprived that treasury of the income taxes that resulted from more people working. Unemployment insurance, rather than unemployment, then became a target of government policy. It was made much harder to get and in 1997–98, only a third of the unemployed received unemployment insurance compared to 80 percent in 1990–91.

Young people were disproportionately the victims of the new unemployment. In an economy that was producing few new jobs, experienced workers were favoured over newcomers, making it difficult for the young to get a start in the labour market. "McJobs" in the service industry appeared to be the fate of large numbers of people in their twenties, even if they had excellent qualifications for professional employment. While some young people beat the odds and either found good jobs in the profession for which they had trained or created their own fortune through an entrepreneurial venture, it was clear that opportunities were limited. The term "Generation X" entered the language to denote a generation who, some pessimists suggested, could only live well if they remained in their parents' homes throughout their adult lives.

Even as the economy gathered steam in the late 1990s and deficits began to fall, governments argued that there was no money for job creation programs. Instead, as surpluses replaced deficits at the federal level and in most provinces, the mantra of the upper middle class became tax reduction. Business-financed think-tanks, supported by a compliant media, made it appear that wealthy Canadians were being whacked by the taxman and were lining up for their green cards to enter the United States. In fact, wealth in Canada was being redistributed in favour of the rich. In 1973, the wealthiest 10 percent of families had 6.77 times the income of the poorest 10 percent after the impact of taxes and social transfers was factored in. The comparable figure in 1998 was 7.24. Both federally and provincially, tax cuts in 1999 and 2000 were targeted disproportionately in favour of the well-heeled.

Summit of the Americas, 2001.

Tom Hanson/CP Picture Archive

A HIGH-TECH ECONOMY

In the late 1990s, Candians were experiencing a robust export trade, mainly the result of a booming American economy and its demand for Canada's resources. Increases in resource prices were only part of the story. Canada's high-technology sectors, especially transportation and communications, were winning large contracts abroad. Bombardier of Valcourt, Quebec, was a prime example. Before the 1970s, this firm had both Canadian and international markets for its recreational equipment. By the 1990s, Bombardier had established itself firmly as an international player in the aerospace, defence, and mass transit sectors. With production facilities in 19 countries, Bombardier seemed the picture postcard for those arguing that Canada was a net beneficiary of globalization. Meanwhile, various federal and Quebec industry grant programs quietly aided this allegedly private-enterprise success story.

With the World Wide Web (WWW) and cellular phones providing expanding global markets, Canada's fibre-optics firms, particularly Nortel, also performed well in the late 1990s. The WWW was launched in December 1990 as a project in a physics laboratory in Geneva, Switzerland. Soon governments, including Canada's, were talking about an "information highway" that would connect all citizens, and corporations were using "the Net" to lure new customers for everything from books to stocks. Overnight "dot-com" millionaires and billionaires sprouted. In 2000, Jozef Strauss, chief executive officer of JDS Uniphase, earned at least $300 million, and John Roth, the chief executive officer of Nortel, earned $150 million in stock options. Like most media-hyped developments in the Information Age, the dot-com revolution offered its enthusiasts a bumpy ride. In 2001, most of the news from companies like Nortel and JDS Uniphase involved huge layoffs and steeply declining share prices. Being so closely tied to their southern neighbour, Canadians shared the economic slowdown that descended on the United States in the fall of 2000.

CANADIAN FOREIGN POLICY AND THE AMERICANS

That downturn was compounded by the shocking developments on 11 September 2001. Suicide bombers hijacked airplanes and turned them into gigantic bombs that they used to destroy the twin towers of the World Trade Center in New York and to inflict damage on the Pentagon. The terrorists were members of an extremist Islamic sect operating clandestinely in a variety of countries and more openly in a few states in the Moslem world. Their goal was to retaliate for perceived injustices against Islam on the part of the United States and Western countries more generally. In response to this outrageous act of terrorism, the United States under President George W. Bush created a coalition of nations to fight a "war on terrorism."

The consequences of these events for the world and for Canada were enormous both in the short and long term. In the short term, the western economies entered into a deep recession as the airline industry and tourism lost much of their business, and anxious investors and consumers kept their money out of circulation. The longer-term consequences, while still unfolding, seemed to include a narrowing in the areas in which individual nations would be permitted to follow different policies from the Americans. Concerns about security caused Canada to integrate its policies on immigration and security with American policies, as well as to beef up military forces that had been depleted during years of budget cuts. Canada was also expected to fight alongside the Americans in whatever battles the "war on terrorism" might bring, and to mute any criticisms that it might have had about American foreign policy.

The events of 11 September 2001 brought a return to the gloomiest days of the Cold War, when countries were expected to choose either the American or the Soviet camp, rather than to search for middle ground. Both Diefenbaker and Trudeau had attempted to break from Cold War subservience of Canada to the United States, but with little effect. Trudeau denounced the American invasion of Grenada in 1983 and called for international efforts to improve the global imbalance in wealth between the North and South. The Americans responded coolly to such efforts. Diefenbaker had been openly scorned for his refusal to follow the dictates of the Kennedy regime during the Cuban Missile Crisis.

By contrast, under Mulroney, Canada and the United States moved even closer on foreign policy issues. As the Cold War thawed in the late 1980s, neither country seemed to have a clear vision of what diplomatic issues were likely to preoccupy the "new world order." Iraq's invasion of Kuwait, an American ally, in August 1990 marked the first major post-Cold War incident. Canada supported a tough United Nations embargo against Iraq and appeared ready to endorse American plans for an invasion of Iraq should it refuse to withdraw from Kuwait. Iraq proved intransigent, and the United States led massive strikes against the country. The Gulf War was enormously popular in the United States, but less so in Canada, particularly in Quebec where a majority opposed Canadian participation. Nonetheless, Mulroney lent his full support to President George Bush, extending him a hero's welcome when he visited Ottawa after the war.

The morality of Canadian external policies appeared particularly suspect in the area of arms sales, including sales to both Iraq and Iran as the two countries waged a territorial war in the 1980s. In 1985, Canada sold $1.9 billion in military commodities, an increase of nearly sixfold since 1970. Almost 90 percent of these arms were sold to the Americans. The federal government continued to subsidize defence industries, even though studies suggested that the expenditures would create more jobs in other areas of the economy.

Canada's role in peacekeeping remained the aspect of foreign policy that made Canadians proudest. The nation's long record of service in Cyprus and the Middle East drew praise from many quarters in the world. That record was supplemented by Canada's peacekeeping efforts in the chaotic and dangerous atmosphere of a Yugoslavia that flew apart in the early 1990s, leaving a variety of competing ethnic-based groups to vie for territory in a series of bloody civil wars. The image of Canadian peacekeeping was tarnished by racist and murderous behaviour on the part of some of its peacekeepers in Somalia. In any given year, Canada spent far less on peacekeeping than it received in receipts from foreigners for its weapons.

The Chrétien government's public pronouncements defended the need for citizens of all countries to have basic human rights such as free speech and the right of assembly, but Ottawa's actions on the trade front belied this rhetoric. In 1994, Chrétien and nine of the ten provincial premiers (Jacques Parizeau, premier of Quebec, stayed home) conducted a trade mission to the People's Republic of China. Largely willing to ignore Chinese human rights abuses, "Team Canada" came home with $1 billion in contracts. A similar leaders' visit in 2001 showcased the Canadian government's unwillingness to apply more than token pressure on China's government to respect human rights. The government also rejected calls to suspend defence orders for such countries as Turkey, Vietnam, and Thailand because of their questionable human rights records, and was slow to respond to concerns over the use of child labour by some of its Asian trading partners.

CONCLUSION

With the rediscovery of the market as the arbiter of social and economic justice in the late twentieth century, Canada's economic policies based on protectionism and social welfare seemed old-fashioned. The United States appeared to be Canada's best bet in a world dominated by trading blocs and the embrace of the Free Trade Agreement ushered in a new phase of Canadian national life. As the two countries became ever closer intertwined, it was inevitable that the terrorist attack on the United States in 2001 would appear to Canadians as virtually an attack on themselves and their values as well. For better or for worse, Canada had tied its destiny to that of the United States, though the relative size and power of the two countries meant that Canada would accept subordinate status rather than an equal-partner relationship in its dealings with its southern neighbour.

NOTES

[1] Quoted in W. Wesley Pue, ed., *Pepper In Our Eyes: The APEC Affair* (Vancouver: UBC Press, 2000) 1.

SELECTED READING

International economic and environmental developments are assessed in Robert Gilpin, *The Challenge of Global Capitalism: The World Economy in the 21st Century* (Princeton: Princeton University Press, 2000); M. Patricia Marchak, *The Integrated Circus: The New Right and the Restructuring of Global Markets* (Montreal: McGill-Queen's University Press, 1991); and Susan George, *A Fate Worse Than Debt* (New York: Grove Press, 1988).

On the Canadian economy after 1975, directly opposed views are found in Harold Chorney, John Hotson, and Mario Seccarecia, *The Deficit Made Me Do It* (Ottawa: Canadian Centre for Policy Alternatives, 1992) and Linda McQuaig, *Shooting the Hippo: Death by Deficit and Other Canadian Myths* (Toronto: Viking, 1995), on the one hand, and David Laidler and William Robson, *The Great Canadian Disinflation: the Economics and Politics of Monetary Policy in Canada, 1988–1993* (Toronto: C.D. Howe Institute, 1993); and Kenneth Norrie and Douglas Owram, *A History of the Canadian Economy* (Toronto: Harcourt Brace Jovanovich, 1991), on the other. Focusing on the threats to the welfare state are Gary Teeple, *Globalization and the Decline of Social Reform: Into the Twenty-First Century* (Toronto: Garamond, 2000) as well as such feminist readings of the changing socio-economic environment as *Rethinking Restructuring: Gender and Change in Canada*, ed. Isabella Bakker (Toronto: University of Toronto Press, 1996); *Women and the Canadian Welfare State: Challenges and Change*, eds. Patricia M. Evans and Gerda R. Werkele (Toronto: Oxford University Press, 1997); and Sylvia B. Bashevkin, *Women on the Defensive: Living Through Conservative Times* (Chicago: University of Chicago Press, 1998). An attempt to place recent Canadian economic developments within the country's larger economic and intellectual history is Harold Chorney and Philip Hansen, *Toward a Humanist Political Economy* (Montreal: Black Rose, 1992). Maureen Baker, *Canadian Family Policies: Cross National Comparisons* (Toronto: University of Toronto Press) places changes in Canadian social policy in international perspective.

On Canadian-American economic relations before the Free Trade Agreement, useful works include Stephen Clarkson, *Canada and the Reagan Challenge*, 2nd ed. (Toronto: Lorimer, 1985) and G. Bruce Doern and Glen Toner, *The Politics of Energy* (Toronto: Nelson, 1985). The argument for free trade is put forward in the three-volume *Report of the Royal Commission on Economic Union and Development Prospects for Canada* (Macdonald Report) of 1985. Views from the opposite side are found in James Laxer, *Leap of Faith: Free Trade and the Future of Canada* (Edmonton: Hurtig, 1986) and Marjorie Griffin Cohen, *Free Trade and the Future of Women's Work: Manufacturing and Service Industries* (Toronto: Garamond, 1987). On the impact of the Canadian-American Free Trade Agreement, see Duncan Cameron, Daniel Drache, and Mel Watkins, eds., *Canada Under Free Trade* (Toronto: Lorimer, 1993); Mel Hurtig, *The Betrayal of Canada*, rev. ed. (Toronto: Stoddart, 1992); and Maude Barlow and Bruce Campbell, *Take Back the Nation* (Toronto: Key Porter, 1991). Works on NAFTA include Mario F. Bognanno and Kathryn J. Ready, eds., *The North American Free Trade Agreement: Labor, Industry and Government Perspectives* (Westport, CT: Praeger, 1993); Ricardo Grinspan and Maxwell A. Cameron, eds., *The Political Economy of North American Free Trade* (New York: St Martin's Press, 1993); and *Women Working the NAFTA Food Chain: Women, Food and Globalization*, ed. Deborah Brandt (Toronto: Sumach, 2000). Opposing perspectives by Canadians are represented by Ian Robinson, *North American Trade as if Democracy Mattered: What's Wrong with NAFTA and What Are the Alternatives?* (Ottawa: Canadian Centre for Policy Alternatives, 1993) and Stelios Loizides and Gilles Rheaume, *The North American Free Trade Agreement: Implications for Canada* (Ottawa: Conference Board of Canada, 1993).

On Canadian foreign policy, see Norman Hillmer and J.L. Granatstein, *Empire to Umpire: Canada and the World to the 1990s* (Toronto: Copp Clark Pitman, 1994), and Ernie Regehr and Simon Rosenblum, eds., *Canada and the Nuclear Arms Race* (Toronto: Lorimer, 1983).

 **WEBLINKS**

THE EGOYAN NUCLEUS
http://members.cruzio.com/~akreyche/atom.html

    This site is dedicated to the career of Atom Egoyan, Canadian independent film director and writer.

NATIONAL HOCKEY LEAGUE
www.nhl.com/

    News, schedules, scores, statistics, players, teams, and the history of the NHL can all be found on this official site.

CANADIAN FOOTBALL LEAGUE
www.cfl.ca/

    This official CFL site includes league history, player biographies, news, schedules, scores, statistics, and links to team sites.

THE MEECH LAKE ACCORD
http://members.tripod.com/pc9899/cc/meechlake.html

    This site provides an overview of the Meech Lake Accord.

The Politics of Uncertainty, 1976–2002

O n 30 October 1995, Quebec voters marked ballots "oui" or "non" in answer to the following question:

Do you agree that Quebec should become sovereign, after having made a formal offer to Canada for a new economic and political partnership, within the scope of the bill respecting the future of Quebec and of the agreement signed on June 12, 1995?

The result of the voting was a virtual dead heat. With 2 362 355 votes for "non" and 2 308 504 for "oui," the margin of victory was razor thin. Canada was clearly at a crossroads that would determine whether it had any future as a country.

In the last quarter of the twentieth century, Canadian politics became increasingly fractious and complex. Economic uncertainty and state responses to it meant that governments were less generous in programs to address the needs of less favoured groups, whether defined in terms of region, ethnicity, class, or sex. When the federal government decided to drastically cut funding to the provinces in the 1990s, the howls of protest indicated widespread disagreements about how Canadian federalism should work. Quebec's increasing demands for independence represented just one of many strands in the debate about who owed what to whom within the Canadian federation.

QUEBEC SOVEREIGNTY

The success of the Parti québécois (PQ) in the 1976 provincial election in Quebec ushered in a new era in Canadian political life. Apart from high unemployment, the major impetus for sovereignty in Quebec came from the flowering of cultural nationalism. No longer protected from assimilation into North American values by an omnipresent Catholic Church and a high birth rate, francophone Québécois attempted to create a distinct secular identity for themselves. For the more nationalist among them, it became intolerable that the province lacked the trappings of nationhood: a seat in the United Nations, ambassadors abroad, a central bank. They claimed that the federal government's efforts to exercise control over social programs and civil rights were intended to erode the ability of the people of Quebec to determine their own future.

The rest of the country was sceptical about such claims. Quebec received more than its per capita share of transfer grants and of federal government contracts. Once virtually closed to French speakers, especially at senior levels, Ottawa's bureaucracy came to reflect the linguistic balance in the nation. Sovereignists argued that the poverty that federal programs were trying to compensate was itself the product of a long history of colonialism. Only by seizing their destiny in their own hands could the Québécois become a prosperous, entrepreneurial people, no longer dependent on outsiders who were trying to assimilate them.

In 1980, the PQ sponsored a referendum on sovereignty-association. Nearly 60 percent of Quebeckers, including half of all francophones and most anglophones and allophones, voted "non" to a question that asked for authorization for the Quebec government to negotiate political sovereignty with economic association.

Claude Ryan and René Lévesque.

National Archives of Canada/PA-117480

PATRIATING THE CONSTITUTION

Once the referendum was over, Trudeau announced that the federal government was determined to patriate the constitution. With or without provincial approval, Ottawa planned to ask the British government to place the constitution in Canadian hands. The patriated constitution would include a Charter of Rights and Freedoms and a new amending formula.

Most provinces resisted Trudeau's initiative, seeing it as a bid to weaken provincial rights. Only Ontario and New Brunswick, which had few grievances with Ottawa at the time, supported the plan. René Lévesque had the support of seven other premiers in opposing Trudeau. The eight provinces challenged the procedure in the courts. The Supreme Court ruled in September 1981 that "substantial consent," but not unanimity, of the provinces was needed for patriation. With the British prime minister, Margaret Thatcher, unwavering in her declaration that Britain would accept a request by the federal government for patriation, the premiers began to fear that constitutional reform would be achieved without the provinces winning any concessions.

On 5 November 1981, nine premiers came to terms with Trudeau, leaving Lévesque to claim betrayal. Lévesque argued that the actions of anglophone premiers demonstrated that Quebec would never receive justice in the federal system.

THE CHARTER OF RIGHTS AND FREEDOMS

The premiers' deal with Trudeau created the Constitution Act, 1982, which consisted of the renamed British North America Act, an amending formula, and the Charter of Rights and Freedoms. The amending formula allowed the federal government to change the constitution with the approval of the federal Parliament plus two-thirds of the provinces representing a combined population of at least 50 percent of all Canadians. Unanimous consent of all provinces as well as both houses of Parliament would continue to be required for amendments affecting representation in the House of Commons, Senate, and Supreme Court and for changes affecting the use of the French and English languages.

Furthermore, a province that believed that its legislative or proprietary rights were compromised by an amendment could declare that amendment null and void within its boundaries. A province would also have the right to opt out with full financial compensation from a program established by amendment that affected educational or cultural matters. As a concession to Atlantic Canada as well as to Saskatchewan and Manitoba, section 36 of the constitution committed Canadian governments to the principle of equalization to "ensure that provincial governments have sufficient revenue to provide reasonably comparable levels of public services at reasonably comparable levels of taxation."

The Charter guaranteed Canadians freedom of speech, association, conscience, and religion and prohibited discrimination on the basis of colour, sex, or creed. There were also restrictions on Canadians' constitutional freedoms. Legislatures could place "reasonable limits" on citizens' enjoyment of their rights. Provinces could also override constitutional rights by specifically exempting pieces of legislation from the Charter's reach. This clause, dubbed the "notwithstanding clause" because it allowed legislatures to assert that a law would apply notwithstanding Charter

provisions, was used by Quebec to exempt all of its legislation from the Charter.

Section 28 declared that Charter rights "are guaranteed equally to male and female persons." This section owed its existence to concerted pressure from women's groups, as the proposed Charter had originally said nothing about gender equality. Effective feminist lobbying also succeeded in exempting section 28 from the override provisions of the Charter.

Native lobbies also campaigned to enshrine rights in the constitution. Their attempts to win the right to self-determination failed, but the Charter did guarantee that nothing in the document would affect existing treaty rights or prejudice later land settlements. A constitutional conference on Native rights was to be called within one year of the proclamation of the constitution.

For women, the new constitution would prove a disappointment in practice. Early Charter decisions regarding gender rights suggested that the courts, dominated by men, were blind to the differences in social power between the sexes. In 1989, a study prepared for the Canadian Advisory Council on the Status of Women reported that "women are initiating few cases, and men are using the Charter to strike back at women's hard-won protection and benefits."[1]

Aboriginal peoples were no more successful. Three first ministers' conferences yielded nothing on attempts to win an amendment guaranteeing Native self-government. The three westernmost provinces were unwilling to surrender any control over resources, and Quebec boycotted all constitution-related conferences. At the third conference in 1987, British Columbia, Alberta, and Saskatchewan, all with Conservative or Social Credit governments, claimed that Native demands were imprecise. They feared that their provinces' rights to control resources would be compromised by a self-government amendment. After 1982, the focus of constitutional talks shifted solely to the rights of provinces, especially Quebec, and away from Native rights.

THE MEECH LAKE ACCORD

In the 1984 federal election, Brian Mulroney had swept Quebec and was determined to cement his party's new-found respect in the province. Robert Bourassa, returned to power as Quebec premier the following year, was equally determined to win constitutional concessions that could blunt the sovereignist thrust. He presented five requirements for Quebec's signature on the constitution. The first was a clause recognizing Quebec as a distinct society. The second was a Quebec veto for constitutional amendments. The remaining three would give all provinces a greater role in immigration, allow them to remain outside any new cost-sharing programs without financial penalty, and have the federal government choose Supreme Court judges from lists of nominees provided by premiers.

A first ministers' conference held at Meech Lake, near Ottawa, in April 1987 tentatively approved a package that met Quebec's demands. To win support from premiers who balked at Quebec having a veto over constitutional change, Mulroney granted all provinces a veto. The first ministers gave themselves three years to get the Accord passed by all legislatures and the federal Parliament. To close off public debate, Mulroney announced that not one word of the document could be changed.

To Mulroney's chagrin, opposition to the Meech Lake Accord quickly took shape. Most sovereignists and some federalists in Quebec rejected the agreement, although polls showed that the majority of Quebeckers favoured it. How the courts would interpret the distinct society clause was hypothetical, but Quebec's Meech opponents, both federalist and sovereignist, rejected a clause that abandoned such an important question to the judiciary. Apart from the distinct society clause, the two aspects of the accord that drew the most fire were cost-sharing provisions and the unanimity required for constitutional amendments. Supporters of particular amendments believed that the unanimity clause would permanently dash hopes of reform.

Outside Quebec, a large majority of Canadians opposed the accord. Women's groups, trade unions, and anti-poverty groups rejected the provision that allowed provinces to exempt themselves from new federal shared-cost programs to set up their own programs. Groups working for new national policies, particularly in childcare, suspected that provincial op-

position would block the establishment of new programs. Aboriginals charged that their interests had been sacrificed on the altar of provincial rights.

Much of the Meech Lake debate might have become academic had three elections between 1987 and 1989 not changed the provincial arithmetic. Newly elected Liberals Frank McKenna in New Brunswick and Clyde Wells in Newfoundland and Conservative Gary Filmon in Manitoba all sought changes in the accord. Just weeks before the ratification deadline, Mulroney reassembled the premiers and used the threat of Quebec separation to try to force consensus. To that end, he offered a statement accompanying the accord that granted a degree of Senate reform and acknowledged the views of several constitutional lawyers regarding the scope of the distinct society clause. The New Brunswick and Manitoba governments were won over. Clyde Wells, who opposed Meech because it weakened the federal government and failed to recog-

Clyde Wells and Brian Mulroney.
Ron Poling/CP Picture Archive

Elijah Harper.
Office of Elijah Harper

months, polls suggested that a majority of Québécois were prepared to vote in favour of sovereignty. A group of nationalist MPs from Quebec, mainly Conservatives, responded by forming the Bloc québécois, a federal party supporting Quebec independence. The party was headed by Lucien Bouchard, a renegade Conservative cabinet minister.

THE CHARLOTTETOWN ACCORD

Brian Mulroney tried to reconcile Quebec and other Canadians by convening a marathon session of the premiers and some Native leaders. This produced the Charlottetown Accord of 28 August 1992. The accord included concessions to each of the players in the room. Quebec was to receive much of what it had been promised during the Meech Lake discussions, but it did not gain important new powers.

To achieve agreement on special status for Quebec, Bourassa had to concede equal provincial representation in the Senate. Bourassa agreed to accept this approach to Senate reform but only after its proponents agreed to whittle down Senate powers. The other provinces agreed to guarantee Quebec that its representation in the House of Commons would not fall below 25 percent, its approximate percentage of the population of the country in 1992. The premiers recognized Native rights to self-government, but the perimeters were to be determined in subsequent negotiations. Several provinces, including Quebec, decided to test support for the constitutional proposals in binding referenda. To make the process more uniform, the Mulroney government decided to hold a national referendum on the Charlottetown Accord.

The referendum campaign focused on a variety of issues. In Quebec, nationalists urged the defeat of the Charlottetown Accord on the grounds that it failed to recognize Quebec's need for control over such jurisdictions as communications and banking. The Reform

nize the concept of the equality of the provinces, resolved to have a free vote on the revised accord in the Newfoundland legislature.

Meanwhile, Elijah Harper, the lone Native member in the Manitoba legislature, used procedural methods to prevent the accord's passage before the deadline. The accord's unpopularity dissuaded Manitoba's political leaders from changing procedures to force a vote on time, and Harper's last stand for Native peoples seemed a fitting way to let the accord die. When it became clear that Manitoba could not pass the accord in time, Clyde Wells called off the Newfoundland vote.

Bourassa and Quebec francophones generally reacted angrily to the defeat of the accord: for several

Cartoonist's view of Brian Mulroney turning his attention from the constitution to the economy.

Reprinted with permission from *The Globe and Mail*

Party argued, by contrast, that Quebec had been given too much power. Issues regarding what the Accord did or did not offer women, Natives, and other groups also divided Canadians.

Ultimately, the "Yes" forces could not withstand the many-pronged "No" campaign. Some Canadians felt left out of the constitutional process; many more did not like certain features of the accord and resented being told that they had to accept the deal as a package. Weary of continued constitutional impasse, disillusioned by political dishonesty and scandal, and uneasy because of the long recession that showed no sign of lifting, many Canadians simply wanted to send their politicians a message. On 26 October 1992, three have-not provinces—Newfoundland, Prince Edward Island, and New Brunswick—supported the accord in the hope that constitutional bickering could be put to an end. Ontario voters were split virtually down the middle.

In the remaining six provinces, the accord suffered a clear defeat.

Popular disillusionment with the constitutional process and politics in general was directed primarily at Prime Minister Mulroney. When he announced early in 1993 his intention to resign as prime minister, there was widespread rejoicing. Voters virtually obliterated his party in the federal election that year. Only two Conservatives were elected across the country, and the new party leader, Kim Campbell, Canada's first woman prime minister, was soundly defeated in her own Vancouver riding. The Liberal Party under Jean Chrétien returned to power with a comfortable majority.

QUEBEC AFTER CHARLOTTETOWN

The Bloc québécois won 49 percent of the Quebec vote in the federal election, enough to give the party

54 of Quebec's 75 seats and to make it the official opposition in Parliament. In the provincial election in 1994, the Parti québecois, led by Jacques Parizeau, won an impressive majority of seats though, thanks to a solid non-francophone vote for the Liberals, earned few votes more than the main opposition party. About 10 percent of the francophone vote went to a new party, the Action démocratique du Québec, led by the former president of the Liberal youth wing, Mario Dumont, who called for continuing negotiations for greater Quebec independence within the Canadian federation.

During the 1994 election, Parizeau promised a referendum on sovereignty during the PQ's mandate. Federalists charged that the question that the sovereignists chose for the referendum, quoted at the beginning of this chapter, was a trick to get Québécois to think they could have their cake and eat it too. Voters were confused. Polls suggested that a third of the voters planning to vote "Yes" believed that a sovereign Quebec would continue to have representatives in the Canadian Parliament and that its citizens would keep Canadian citizenship and social benefits. The "No" side pointed out that the government of Canada, contrary to what the sovereignists said, could not negotiate sovereignty-association with Quebec. Quebec would have to negotiate with the other nine provinces, all of which had already indicated that they would refuse to negotiate.

In the early stages of the referendum, such arguments seemed to sway a comfortable majority of the people of Quebec, but the campaign momentum took a swing in the other direction when Lucien Bouchard became its unofficial leader. Bouchard was popular in Quebec; for some, he became an almost saintly figure when he survived an attack of a rare and usually deadly disease in 1994. Publicly less strident than Parizeau, he seemed better able to convince the Québécois that Canada was bluffing when it claimed that it would not negotiate with Quebec.

Prime Minister Chrétien's decision not to offer Quebec any changes, constitutional or otherwise, should its citizens vote no, alienated some wavering voters. Only in the last week of the campaign, with polls suggesting the sovereignty forces were taking the lead, did Chrétien actively step into the campaign. On nationwide television, he made an emotional plea to Quebec not to throw away the benefits of Confederation, promising recognition of the province as a distinct society as well as decentralization of power in Canada.

Referendum night was a nail-biter for both sides. Premier Parizeau responded gracelessly to defeat, telling supporters, "It's true we have been defeated, but basically by what? By money and the ethnic vote." While the "ethnic" vote was solidly against leaving Canada, about 40 percent of francophones also voted to reject the vague offer represented in the referendum question. Within months after the referendum defeat, Parizeau had resigned the premiership, and Bouchard had moved from Ottawa to Quebec City to become the province's premier.

Language tensions heightened in the wake of the referendum. Although most of the population opposed any changes to the province's existing language legislation, well-organized sovereignist groups demanded that the province further restrict the use of English. Quebec's anglophones and allophones were also in a more combative mood. Earlier, their leaders had cautioned that militancy on their part might alienate federalist-leaning francophones. New leaders arose who suggested that federalists must demand the right to linguistic pluralism and militantly oppose separatism to ensure that soft nationalists understood that sovereignty would be costly. A militant "partition" movement gained considerable support for its demand that should Quebec separate, federalist regions of the province such as the West Island of Montreal, the Hull region, and northern Quebec be allowed to hold a referendum on remaining in Canada.

Meanwhile, former sovereignist Guy Bertrand sought, via the Supreme Court, to establish the illegality of any attempt by Quebec to declare independence unilaterally. Both federalists and sovereignists claimed to find vindication in the Court's ruling in August 1998 that while the Quebec National Assembly could not unilaterally declare independence, the federal government would have little option but to negotiate the issue with the province if a large majority of the population voted to separate.

Two years later, the federal government passed the Clarity Bill, which insisted that no referendum was valid unless its wording was clear and unambiguous. While the Bouchard government denounced the federal intervention in Quebec political life implied by the bill, few people in the province seemed much interested in the debate. When Bouchard resigned as Quebec premier early in 2001, he admitted that the sovereignty movement, which he still supported, was losing momentum. Nonetheless, in the aftermath of the second referendum, Canada's future seemed less assured than ever.

ONTARIO'S UNINTERRUPTED PROSPERITY

Quebec separatism was not the only cause of Canadian uncertainty. In every region of the country, economic slowdown had produced social and political instability. Even Ontario, the most prosperous of Canadian provinces throughout the twentieth century, was engulfed by the economic crisis. Manufacturing jobs disappeared, particularly during the recessions of 1982–85 and 1990–93. In 1985, the Conservative dynasty that had held power in Ontario since 1943 came crashing down as it came slowly around to the business view that the state must make deep cuts in social services. The Liberals formed a minority government with NDP support and then won a big majority in 1987. By then, the Ontario economy was booming again and the Liberals, led by David Peterson, eliminated extra-billing by physicians and extended full funding to separate schools up to grade 13. As quickly as it appeared, the Liberal bubble burst. A party fund-raising scandal weakened the Liberals, and, in 1990, voters replaced Peterson with the New Democrats headed by Bob Rae.

The New Democrats proved unable to adopt a consistent policy. In their first budget in 1991, they defied the neo-conservative logic that had gripped most governments in Canada, producing a stimulative budget with a $10 billion deficit. The business community and the media condemned this return to Keynesianism. Over the next two years, the NDP largely recanted its first budget and cut social spend-

ing. Rae also alienated much of the union movement when he imposed an across-the-board wage cut of 5 percent on all public sector workers in provincial or municipal institutions earning over $30 000 a year.

In 1995, Ontario voters were in a mood to punish Bob Rae, who had had the misfortune to govern during five years of economic stagnation. Mike Harris's Conservatives received 45 percent of the vote, running on a campaign of cutting the civil service, slashing social assistance, privatizing government services, and cancelling employment equity programs. In office, the Harris government cut taxes for the middle and upper classes while slashing health, education, and welfare expenditures to pay for the tax cut. The government cut programs to aid battered women, the disabled, and the mentally ill, closed dozens of hospitals throughout the province, and weakened environmental regulation. It initiated extensive reform at the municipal level, attempting to offload welfare expenditure on to the municipalities and initiating plans to create a "mega-city" in Metro Toronto.

All of these policies provoked vocal resistance. Labour and community groups organized "Days of Action," but Harris dismissed them as "special interest groups" and stayed true to his neo-conservative agenda. By the 1999 provincial election, the Ontario economy was booming and Harris was talking about reinvesting in the province, particularly in health and education. He was re-elected but with a decline in the popular vote and seats.

THE NEW WEST

Throughout the 1970s, energy policy created tensions in Ottawa's relations with the West. In 1980, the National Energy Program (NEP) brought matters to a head. Introduced by Trudeau, the main features of the NEP were a low "made-in-Canada" price for oil, larger federal revenue from energy production, and greater Canadian ownership of the energy industry.

The energy-producing provinces wanted Canadians to pay international prices for energy, claiming that the made-in-Canada price simply deprived them of revenues and made it uneconomical to extract higher-cost heavy oil in northern Alberta. This debate pitted Alberta, British Columbia, and

Saskatchewan and the oil-producing "wannabes"—Newfoundland and Nova Scotia—against energy-poor provinces and the federal government, at least while oil prices were high. Although the NEP was modified sufficiently to effect a truce between Trudeau and Alberta premier Peter Lougheed in 1981, it would be blamed by many westerners for an economic downturn, beginning in 1982, in which many people lost their homes and their savings.

The NEP was not the only source of western alienation. Grain farmers were angry at the decision of the Trudeau government in the early 1980s to phase out the historic Crow rates, which had kept the cost of grain shipment competitive with American farmers' transportation costs. Another common complaint was that the lion's share of federal contracts were awarded to Quebec. Western outrage greeted the announcement that Bombardier had received a large contract for maintenance of Canada's CF-18 military aircraft despite the fact that Winnipeg's Bristol Aerospace had submitted a lower and technically superior bid.

Such events joined to a resurgence of right-wing sentiments helped to produce the Reform Party in 1987. Led by Preston Manning, son of Alberta's long-time Social Credit premier Ernest Manning, the Reformers declared that the West did not want out of Confederation: rather it wanted in, and it wished to reconstruct that Confederation to better reflect the regions. They wanted the federal deficit slashed, even if it meant sacrificing subsidy programs to farmers and abandoning universality in social programs.

By the 1993 federal election, the Reformers were wooing Ontario voters, appearing more like a Canadian version of the Republican Party in the United States than a regional protest party. They appealed to many traditional Conservative voters who believed that the Mulroney Tories had been too awash in patronage and shady dealings. In Alberta and British Columbia, the Reformers swept all before them, becoming, for the moment, the major federal party in the two westernmost provinces.

BRITISH COLUMBIA

From 1975 to 1991, the divide between right and left remained fairly rigid in British Columbia. The New Democrats narrowly but repeatedly lost to Social Credit in what was essentially a two-party province. The Socreds under William Bennett demonstrated the shift away from the postwar consensus after the 1983 provincial election, when they implemented a program of massive cuts in education and social spending. In response, civil servants, and state employees such as teachers, nurses, and social workers, joined with client groups to form Operation Solidarity. For a week they shut down most state operations in the province to protest the cuts.

Social Credit became a spent force after Bennett's successor, William Vander Zalm, a charismatic millionaire, resigned over allegations of conflict of interest in his sale of the family firm. Vander Zalm was replaced by Rita Johnson, Canada's first woman premier. In the election that followed, the New Democrats won a large majority without increasing their traditional vote. Much of the Social Credit vote had gone to the Liberals, who formed the official opposition. Despite great hopes for a new era in politics, Mike Harcourt, the New Democrat premier, resigned in late 1995 over yet another scandal.

The Harcourt government had faced difficulties trying to balance the demands of environmentalists and unionized forest workers, both traditional NDP supporters in the province. Clear-cutting at Clayoquot Sound on Vancouver Island became a defining issue for the organized environmental movement not only in British Columbia but across the country. The NDP's solid record of achievement in social programs and the environment won them a narrow re-election in 1996 under their new leader, Glen Clark. But stagnating resource exports in the late 1990s fuelled voter discontent. When scandal forced Clark out of the premier's office in 1999, NDP stock in the province fell to a new low. His elected replacement, Ussal Dosanjh, who took office in February 2000, was Canada's first Indo-Canadian premier. Dosanjh and the NDP were crushed by Gordon Campbell's Liberals in a provincial election in 2001.

THE PRAIRIE PROVINCES

In Alberta, the Conservatives remained in office continuously after 1971, but they underwent an ideological sea change as prosperity oozed away in the 1980s and 1990s. Attempts by Premier Don Getty (1986–1992) to use government subsidies to industry to promote economic diversification failed spectacularly. By the government's own figures, an estimated $1.5 billion was lost as firms went bankrupt without repaying their loans and the government sold their assets for a pittance. Getty's successor, Ralph Klein, promised a new approach. Klein slashed the costs of government, with social programs taking most of the punishment. Nurses, schoolteachers, welfare recipients, and the elderly suffered the most. Within the province, the most controversial move was closing down a large number of intensive care units in hospitals and encouraging private medical entrepreneurs to make up for deficiencies in a slimmed-down public health system. As provincial energy revenues soared in the late 1990s, the "Klein Revolution" gave way to generous spending on health and education once again. But true to their new right-wing ideology, the Conservatives also passed legislation that permitted a degree of privatization of both hospitals and universities.

Saskatchewan replaced the NDP administration of Allan Blakeney in 1982 with a free-enterprise Conservative government under Grant Devine. The Tories privatized some Crown corporations and copied Alberta's attempt to lure businesses with subsidies and loans, with much the same dismal results. Floundering in a sea of corruption, the Conservatives lost the 1991 election to the NDP led by Roy Romanow, but much of its populist zeal was gone. By 2001, when Romanow retired, the NDP had lost its legislative majority, mainly because of rural disaffection, and governed in coalition with the Liberals.

Manitoba's political parties were perhaps more sharply divided than Saskatchewan's. A neo-conservative Progressive Conservative administration from 1977 to 1981 was succeeded by a high-spending NDP government under Howard Pawley. Tax increases necessary to maintain public expenditures eventually led to a tax revolt that deposed Pawley's government. The Conservatives under Gary Filmon, first elected in 1988, followed neo-conservative policies, but in 1999, provincial voters, angry with health-care cuts, put the NDP, this time under Gary Doer, back in office.

ATLANTIC CANADA

In the Atlantic provinces, regional economic development programs had failed to produce sustained prosperity and people continued to leave the region to find work. Federal fisheries policies changed little despite the declaration of the 200-mile limit in 1977. Weak federal efforts to prevent foreign overfishing caused the fisheries boom of the 1970s to quickly turn into a bust. By the early 1980s, processing companies were in trouble, and two corporate giants swallowed up their competitors. As fish stocks began to collapse in the late 1980s, quotas were cut, fish plants shut down, and many fishing communities faced extinction.

In July 1992, the federal government announced that there would be a two-year moratorium on northern cod fishing. This meant unemployment for 19 000 Newfoundland fishers and plant workers. Even before the moratorium expired, it was clear that the Atlantic cod fishery was over for at least a generation.

In the late 1970s, the large Hibernia oil field was discovered off Newfoundland. Brian Peckford, Newfoundland's Conservative premier, insisted that the province have equal control with Ottawa over offshore developments. Trudeau disagreed, and the Supreme Court in 1984 upheld federal control over the offshore. The election of the Mulroney Conservatives resulted in a victory for Peckford, as Ottawa conceded Newfoundland's claims for co-management of offshore oil developments. While stimulating economic growth, Hibernia provided few jobs after the construction phase ended.

Expectations in Newfoundland and Nova Scotia that they might follow Alberta's lead to become energy-rich provinces proved slow to materialize. Instead, the four Atlantic provinces joined the rest of the country in trying to attract manufacturing and service companies with offers of low wages and few government regulations.

Governments in Atlantic Canada resorted to desperate measures to accommodate corporate interests in the region. Responding to company pressures, Nova Scotia passed legislation that made it impossible for unions to organize one of Michelin's three sites in the province. By contrast, the government seemed deaf to complaints from miners at the Westray coal mine in Pictou County about rock slides, cave-ins, and dangerous levels of methane gas. When an explosion destroyed the mine in 1993, eight months into its operation, 26 men were left dead below the earth.

Discontent with the sluggish economy of the region led to a degree of political instability. In New Brunswick, voters unhappy with flamboyant Conservative premier Richard Hatfield gave every seat in the province to Frank McKenna's Liberals in 1987. There was a general swing to the Liberals in the region. One of the Liberal premiers was Catherine Callbeck in Prince Edward Island, who made history in 1993 as the first woman to be elected to a provincial premiership.

The differences between the two major parties in the region remained, for the most part, differences of personalities, and by 2000, the pendulum had swung back to the Tories except in Newfoundland. Both parties, having embraced the welfare state in the postwar era, began to proclaim the need for more entrepreneurship and for cuts to state expenditures in an effort to attract global corporations with the promise of low taxes. Although the region's need for federal subsidies to provide a minimal standard of health, education, and social assistance was unchanged, demands by Atlantic premiers for a more generous equalization formula and a larger share of royalties from offshore oil fell on deaf ears.

FEDERAL CUTBACKS

Public funds had helped throughout the postwar period to place a floor on poverty and to guarantee citizens of all social classes improved access to quality education and health services. In the post-prosperity era, governments became less willing to provide these funds. Attempts by the federal government to limit growth in grants to the provinces had begun under Trudeau in 1977 when block funding replaced equal federal-provincial sharing of medicare and postsecondary education costs. The new arrangement was called "established programs financing" and gave the provinces a percentage of federal income and corporate taxes plus a cash grant. Beginning in 1982, the Trudeau government set limits below the rate of infla-tion to increases in federal spending on postsecondary education for 1982 and 1983.

In 1986, the Mulroney government announced that federal cash grants for medicare and postsecondary education would be reduced by 2 percent annually. Four years later it sped up withdrawal from established programs financing so that by 2004 the federal government's cash transfer for medical and educational spending would disappear. Campaigning in 1993, the Liberals promised to stop the cuts to the provinces, but once they were in office, they announced they would actually speed up the Conservative timetable for getting rid of established programs financing. The Liberals also cancelled one of the pillars of the Pearson social reforms: the Canada Assistance Plan. Under the plan, there had been some federal control over provinces to ensure that legitimate social welfare recipients were not denied aid.

The neo-conservative focus on the deficit made cutbacks appear to be an almost technical matter and across-the-board cuts were presented as fair to the entire population. In fact, the cutbacks affected women as a group more than men. Women were more likely to be in the jobs gutted or privatized by the government, they were more likely to be recipients of social assistance, and they figured large among the groups targeted when the employment insurance program was "reformed" in 1995. Women, especially single women with children, also dominated the lines at food banks. Food banks started modestly in the early 1980s in some urban centres. By 1992, 150 000 people were served each month by the Daily Bread Food Bank in Toronto alone, and an estimated 2 million Canadians relied on food banks at some point that year.

THE TRADE UNION MOVEMENT

Canada's trade union movement was under attack in the age of neo-conservatism, but it fared much better than its American counterpart. In the United States, southern and western states passed "right to work" legislation that banned the closed shop. As northern firms moved south to take advantage of cheap labour and poor environmental standards, workers in the northeast often abandoned their unions to preserve their jobs, albeit at a high cost in wages and working conditions. By the mid-1990s, only about 15 percent of American workers were unionized, about half the rate 20 years earlier.

In Canada, by contrast, the fall-off was less steep. From a peak of 37.2 percent of the non-agricultural labour force in 1984, the rate of unionization in Canada had fallen to 32.5 percent in 1998. Nevertheless, in the era of free trade, Canadians were not immune to trends south of the border. As many Canadians were learning in the age of globalization, local governments had little ability to protect citizens against the often take-it-or-leave-it demands of mobile multinational corporations.

The trend toward a greater feminization of the labour movement, apparent since the 1960s, continued after 1975, though mainly in the public sector. The huge retail and service sectors proved determined to resist attempts by their largely female workforce to organize. When Manitoba's Labour Relations Board imposed a first contract on a recalcitrant Eaton's in Brandon, the store responded by firing half of its workers and demanding concessions from the union for the workers who remained.

Some of the success of Canada's unions in the last quarter of the twentieth century may have resulted from Canadian sections of many American industrial unions breaking away to form national unions. The Canadian Auto Workers, for example, formed after a rupture between the Canadian wing of the United Auto Workers and the union's American headquarters. With only 120 000 members in 1984, CAW doubled in size over the next 17 years, partly through mergers with smaller unions in other sectors and partly by organizing unorganized workers.

NATIVE STRUGGLES

Aboriginal social activism increased after 1975, sometimes involving violent conflicts with authorities over land claims. Native militancy occurred in a context of continued desperate conditions on and off reserves. The low life expectancy relative to the rest of the population, high rates of suicide, high unemployment, and poor living conditions testified to the slow rate of change Natives experienced in Canadian society. Incarceration rates tell a startling tale. In Saskatchewan, for example, where 11.4 percent of the population is Native, they made up fully 72 percent of the inmate population.

Many Northern Natives, in the wake of the Berger Commission, eventually reached settlements with the federal government. In 1984, the Inuit of the Mackenzie Delta and in 1988 the Yukon First Nations received land settlements. In November 1992, the Inuit of the eastern Arctic made a land deal and also voted for the eastern Arctic to become a separately administered territory called Nunavut (meaning "the people's land" in the Inuktitut language). In March 1999, Nunavut officially became a territory and elected its own assembly. Nunavut's population in 2000 was 27 700, of whom about 80 percent were Inuit.

Outside the territories the process of land claims seemed virtually stalled. In an effort to make Canadian authorities take notice, First Nations resorted to direct action. An early confrontation occurred in 1974 when Natives occupied Anicinable Park in Kenora, claiming that the park, like much of Kenora, belonged to the Aboriginal peoples. In the years that followed, the Lubicon Cree in northern Alberta, the Temagami in Ontario, and the Cree of northern Quebec, among other groups, engaged in struggles to prevent resource extraction on their territory that they had not authorized and to receive recognition of their land claims. Nova Scotia Mi'kmaq pursued their hunting and fishing rights against an unsympathetic provincial government and used an investigation into the wrongful conviction of a young Mi'kmaq, Donald Marshall, to expose the racism they faced on a daily basis. In Manitoba, the Public Inquiry into the Administration of Justice and Aboriginal People was sparked by two tragic deaths: the conspiracy of silence that followed the murder of Helen Betty Osborne in The Pas in 1971 and the shooting of an unarmed Native leader, John Joseph Harper, in Winnipeg in 1988.

The most sensational conflict occurred in the summer of 1990 between the Quebec Provincial Police and Mohawk Warriors at a reserve near Oka, Quebec. The Warriors were resolved to stop the town of Oka from developing a golf course on lands the Mohawk regarded as sacred. As the standoff escalated,

MORE TO THE STORY

British Columbia Natives and the Struggle for Self-Determination

The history of British Columbia's dealings with its first peoples was perhaps the most shameful in the country. After British Columbia entered Confederation, the non-Aboriginal minority who deprived the First Nations of voting rights insisted to the federal government that treaties could not be signed with Natives in that province. For a century, Native lands were seized for industrialization and urban expansion without negotiating with the landowners. Gradually things began to change. In 1985, the Supreme Court of Canada awarded the small Musqueam band $10 million in compensation for Indian Affairs duping them into granting an unfair golf course lease on their land. Increasingly, many Native people, rather than hoping for monetary compensation after their resources were depleted and their traditional lifestyle was destroyed, began to actively resist developers, even if it meant breaking Canadian law. In the late 1980s, in various parts of the province, Natives clashed with loggers whose activities despoiled traditional Native lands.

In 1990, the province finally agreed to negotiate land issues. A year later, however, Judge Allen McEachern of the British Columbia Supreme Court issued a verdict in the Delgamuukw case that suggested British Columbia's first people did not hold Aboriginal rights to the land. That ruling was invalidated in 1997 when the Supreme Court, hearing an appeal of this case involving the Gitskan-Wet'suwet'en Nation, rejected McEachern's logic. Not only did the first peoples have Aboriginal rights, but those rights went beyond hunting and fishing rights to broader rights to be involved in determining what activities occurred on their traditional lands.

The Supreme Court decision placed some pressure on British Columbia's NDP government to negotiate agreements with Native nations if only to counter the economic uncertainty that business representatives claimed the court's words created for them. Perhaps fittingly the first successful negotiations between the government and a First Nation was with the Nisga'a of the Nash Valley. The Nisga'a had fought their dispos-

session by non-Aboriginals for over 100 years. Mainly relying on the courts and petitions to governments, they had persisted in their claims of ownership of their traditional lands even as the government of Canada, at British Columbia's request, kept handing away their lands to forestry and mineral companies.

It was Frank Calder, a Nisga'a leader, whose Supreme Court appeal of a court decision that denied that Aboriginal title had ever existed in British Columbia had started the ball rolling for comprehensive land claims in Canada. While the Supreme Court, in a 1973 decision, split on the issue of whether Aboriginal title had been extinguished, a majority agreed that it had existed before colonization began. This led Pierre Trudeau to accept the notion that comprehensive land claims had to be negotiated with First Nations that had never signed treaties.

In 1998, the governments of British Columbia and the Nisga'a people reached agreement on a treaty, which was subsequently ratified by a referendum of the Nisga'a and a vote of both the British Columbia Legislature and the Parliament of Canada. Finally this was ratified by a Senate vote on April 13, 2000 and became the law of the land.

The opposition parties in British Columbia made exaggerated claims about the treaty and played upon non-Aboriginal fears of being displaced by the original owners. Arguably, as many Nisga'a opponents of the treaty claimed, it was the Nisga'a that gave away most in the negotiations. They received 1930 square kilometres as a territory in which they would exercise law-making authority in such areas as land use, cultural practices, and employment policies. The various benefits and monetary grants that accompanied the treaty were worth $487.1 million. But, in the process, they had to give up all claims to 80 percent of their traditional territory and accept the Canadian Criminal Code and the Canadian Charter of Rights and Freedoms rather than exercise complete sovereignty within their lands.

Ronald Cross, also known as Lasagna, was a prominent Native figure in the Oka crisis. For his part in his people's resistance at Oka, Cross received a five-year sentence for criminal assault.

Tom Hanson/CP Picture Archive

Native and non-Native fishers in St Mary's Bay, Nova Scotia, subsequently worked out an agreement to jointly manage the lobster fishery, but at Burnt Church, New Brunswick, Natives faced resistance from both non-Native fishers and the Department of Fisheries and Oceans in their efforts to lay enough traps to make a modest living for their fishers.

Native women's rights in Canada also seemed unclear. Under the Indian Act, a woman who married someone other than a treaty Indian lost her treaty status, as did her children, even though Native men could marry non-Native women without any loss of status. In the early 1970s, Native women organized to end such discriminatory treatment. Supported by non-Native women's groups, they persuaded the federal government to remove the offending section from the act in 1985.

Although the 76 000 women and children who were potentially eligible to be reinstated as status Indians had won a legal victory, they were not always welcomed back into reserve communities. Native women often charged that white imperialism had eroded women's traditional influence in Native communities. They organized support groups and healing centres and demanded that elected band councils implement programs to counsel men who had abused women and to protect their potential victims.

THE WOMEN'S MOVEMENT

The women's movement continued to play an important role in Canadian society, focusing attention on a variety of issues. Liberalization of divorce laws and the flight of men from family obligations increased the number of self-supporting women. By the 1980s, one marriage in three ended in divorce. The number of single-parent families correspondingly jumped, rising from 477 525 to 714 005 from 1971 to 1981 alone, with 85 percent of such families headed by women. In 1998, Statistics Canada reported that 59.5 percent of children raised only by mothers were growing up poor.

If the women's movement could point to only modest successes in its campaigns against poverty, it

a police officer was killed and the Canadian military was called to intervene. While denouncing the Warriors as terrorists, the federal government was forced to buy the disputed land to make it available to the Mohawk.

Other confrontations followed, including a still-unresolved dispute regarding the rights of Mi'kmaq to engage in commercial fishing. A Supreme Court ruling in 1999 upheld several eighteenth-century treaties that recognized Native fishing and hunting rights.

Voices from the Past

Women on the March

I was alarmed by most of the lists of top 10 Canadians this year because they were almost all men. I think Quebec Federation of Women's President Francoise David should have made the list. She took a good idea, a woman's march on poverty, and took it to the global level. Hundreds of thousands of women in almost 200 countries marched against poverty and violence.

In many countries, women mobilized for the first time. In Canada, we saw the largest women's marches in Canadian history in Montreal and Ottawa when more than 30,000 women marched in each city. The media in English Canada virtually ignored the whole thing. But then, I forgot feminism is dead and nothing good ever happens in Quebec.[2]

Broadcaster and long-time feminist activist Judy Rebick's tongue-in-cheek comment on the huge women's marches of October 2000 demonstrated some of the flavour of Canadian politics at the turn of a new century. There was widespread opposition to policies that contributed to immiseration of the poor, the majority of whom were women and children. But media indifference often greeted such opposition. The growing divide between Quebec and the rest of Canada made it particularly noticeable that a global organization of women's solidarity that received much attention in Quebec was treated as barely newsworthy in the rest of the country.

The Fédération des Femmes du Québec were no strangers to anti-poverty demonstrations. They had organized a women's march on Quebec City in June 1995 that forced Premier Jacques Parizeau to announce a few policy changes of benefit to women. About 4000 women, most of them living in poverty, completed a 10-day trek to Quebec City to demand that politicians take direct action to address their dire circumstances. The women had walked twenty kilometers a day from three gathering points, staying along the way with feminist sympathizers. Along with poor women and their children across the country, they represented the largest group of victims of state policies that placed less and less emphasis on responsibility for those whose social conditions disadvantaged them in the marketplace.

When the women arrived in Quebec City, the opposition Liberals refused to have anything to do with them, alleging that they were part of a separatist conspiracy to discredit Canadian federalism. Sovereignist premier Jacques Parizeau told the women that their demand for a program of social infrastructure spending could only be met when Quebec was independent from Canada. He then announced an increase in Quebec's minimum wage from $6 to $6.45 an hour, 20 percent of the increase that the marchers had demanded. Many of the protesters were understandably disappointed that their efforts to draw attention to the plight of the poor were being manipulated by politicians with their own agendas.

Women's March Against Poverty, Ottawa, 1996. Standing to the right of the banner is then-NAC president Sunera Thobani.

Canadian Women's Movement Archives/Morisset Library/University of Ottawa

had more success in its demands for a woman's right to choose to terminate a pregnancy. After the relaxation of the abortion law in 1969, access to abortion was uneven across the country, leading the Supreme Court to rule in 1988 that the law, which required an abortion to be approved by a three-doctor panel, violated the guarantees in the Charter of Rights and Freedoms of equal rights for all Canadians. After the court decision, Parliament grappled unsuccessfully with this divisive issue, leaving Canada with no law restricting rights to an abortion.

Violence against women was an important focus of the women's movement and became a more urgent concern following the Montreal massacre. On 6 December 1989, a deranged young man fatally shot 14 female engineering students at the École Polytechnique in Montreal while shouting his hatred of feminists. In the wake of this tragedy, women's groups continued to press for battered women's shelters, rape crisis centres, counseling for abusers and their victims, and increased court charges and convictions for rapists, batterers, and harassers. Government action proved slow in coming, and what few programs were available were often among the first victims of fiscal restraint in the debt-conscious 1990s.

THE ENVIRONMENTAL MOVEMENT

Apart from the women's movement, the most visible popular movement against the status quo in late twentieth-century Canada was the environmental movement. Greenpeace was particularly astute at focusing public attention and creating controversy. In 1970, a small group of American and Canadian activists created Greenpeace to protest nuclear testing at Amchitka, in the Aleutian Islands. Publicity generated by the fledgling organization prompted the Americans to abandon the tests. Soon, Greenpeace was conducting dramatic non-violent protests on a range of issues. Its successes included the abandoning of the Newfoundland seal hunt and reforms to the whaling industry.

By the turn of the twentieth century, the environmental movement in Canada consisted of hundreds of local movements organized to deal with environmental issues generally or with a specific environmental problem. A key focus for many groups was the reduction in greenhouse gases that were contributing to global warming. In 1997, the Canadian government had signed the Kyoto Accord, an international agreement on greenhouse gas emissions. But, despite Canadian promises to cut emissions substantially, there was an increase in emissions over the next four years.

GAY RIGHTS

Gays and lesbians continued to struggle for acceptance in Canadian society and for legal protection from discrimination. Although fundamentalist preachers and masculinist culture with its strict gender definitions promoted homophobia, there were several legislative victories. In 1977, sexual preference was removed as a criterion for immigration. The Parti québécois added sexual orientation to Quebec's human rights code, and most other provinces eventually followed. Activists won court battles that gave same-sex partners benefits similar to heterosexual spouses. After legal challenges, the Canadian Army agreed in 1992 to end long-standing policies against homosexuals.

There were setbacks as well. Ontario's NDP government failed to win enough votes from its own caucus to implement a bill in 1994 that would have removed discrimination in such areas as adoption rights. The federal government balked at efforts to allow gays to become legally married. While gays won the right to be ordained ministers in the United Church, the Roman Catholic Church joined evangelical Protestants in continuing to denounce homosexuality, along with abortion and divorce, as threats to the traditional family. Governments balked at requests to make gay and lesbian marriages legal, arguing spuriously that the purpose of marriage was procreation. The issue arrived at the Supreme Court in 2001.

Intolerance against homosexuality sometimes manifested itself in violence. Homophobic thugs beat up and in some cases killed gay men. In the 1980s, Toronto's gay newspaper, *The Body Politic*, was slapped with obscenity charges, while police raids on gay bars and bathhouses indicated a continuing willingness to harass gays in the name of public morality.

AIDS awareness campaign poster.

Canadian AIDS Society

The spread of AIDS—Acquired Immune Deficiency Syndrome—provided a daunting challenge to the gay community, whose male members initially formed the majority of its victims. AIDS organizers developed support systems for persons infected with AIDS and educational campaigns to halt the spread of the disease. They also pressured governments to spend more money on medical research to fight AIDS.

Gay and lesbian activists of the 1990s, unlike their counterparts a generation earlier who struggled just to make homosexuality legal, proudly celebrated homo- sexual culture. Gay Pride Days became annual events in many cities, with the Gay Pride parade in Toronto attracting more than 100 000 participants and spectators. No longer confined to the closet, gays and lesbians published newspapers and magazines, founded bookstores, established theatre compa- nies, and made films and wrote books dealing with gay lifestyles and concerns.

THE FEDERAL ELECTIONS OF 1997 AND 2000

In June 1997 and October 2000, Canadians re-elected Jean Chrétien's Liberals to federal office. In both elec- tions, the Liberals, though winning around 40 percent of the national vote, formed majority governments, by a small margin in 1997 but comfortably in 2000. These elections confirmed the regional split that had been so evident in the 1993 election, with the West giving a majority of its seats to the Reform Party and its successor, the Canadian Alliance, and a majority of Quebec seats going to the Bloc québécois. Ontario gave the Liberals 101 of 103 seats in 1993 and 100 of 103 in 1997. The Liberals strength- ened their majority in 2000 by injecting more cash into economic development and social programs, producing a suffi- cient revival in Liberal support in the Atlantic region and Quebec to make up for the party's mediocre performance in the West.

Shortly before the 2000 election, the Reform party had made an effort to unite forces to the right of the Liberal party by creating the Canadian Alliance. Stockwell Day, a former lay Pentecostal school admin- istrator who became Alberta's Provincial Treasurer, was elected party leader. Well financed by Bay Street, Day attempted to convince Canadians to adopt his national agenda of huge tax cuts, especially for the wealthy, and an end to regional development programs.

The Liberals moved to stop the new party in its tracks by offering both tax cuts and modest increases in social spending, including an increase in transfers to provinces for health spending. While the Alliance, more so than Reform, attempted to fudge its policies on social issues such as gay rights and the right to abortion, Day's well-established, religious-based social conservatism hurt his party's chances of winning the support of moderate voters. Many of them opted for Joe Clark's emaciated national Progressive Conservative party (see Tables 27.1 and 27.2). After the election, the Canadian Alliance seemed to tear itself apart with internecine battles, mainly over the party leadership.

Table 27.1
2000 Federal Election Results

Party	Popular Vote %	Seats
Liberal	40.82	172
Canadian Alliance	25.46	66
Bloc Québécois	10.72	38
Progressive Conservative	12.21	12
New Democratic Party	8.51	13
Green Party	.81	0
Marijuana Party	.521	0
Canadian Action Party	.21	0
Marxist-Leninist Party of Canada	.101	0
Communist Party of Canada	.071	0
Independent/No affiliation	.442	0

Source: Elections Canada

CONCLUSION

In the past quarter-century the postwar liberal consensus became unstuck. A slowdown in economic growth, growing regional discontent, and a new pessimism about the efficacy of governments to solve economic problems created a profusion of mainly regionally-based political parties with no consensus among themselves about what policies a national government should follow. Meanwhile, extra-parliamentary groups, often with little patience for the political games and stale formulae that seemed to emanate from the House of Commons and provincial legislatures, became more organized than ever before. While the state, corporate, and media elites branded organized women, Natives, workers, and anyone else outside the privileged elites as "special interest groups," politicians tried to placate these groups with limited responses to demands from below.

Table 27.2
2000 Federal Election Results by Region

Party	West	Ontario	Quebec	Atlantic	North
Liberal	14	100	36	19	3
Alliance	64	2	0	0	0
Bloc Québécois	0	0	38	0	0
Progressive Conservative	2	0	1	9	0
NDP	8	1	0	4	0

Source: Elections Canada

A Historiographical Debate

If Quebec Leaves

Increasingly, social scientists—if not governments—have been prepared to speculate on the political and economic impact of Quebec sovereignty on both Quebec and the remaining Canadian provinces. Historian David J. Bercuson and political scientist Barry Cooper have marshalled arguments as to why the rest of Canada would be better off without Quebec. They argue that Quebec nationalism is incompatible with the liberal-democratic values that they believe are central to English-Canadian politics. Quebec nationalists, they maintain, place the rights of

French Canadians above both majority and individual rights. Bercuson and Cooper suggest that majority rule ought to be—and, without Quebec, would be—the essential principle of governance in Canada.[3]

Some authors point to liberal democracies that accommodate minority communities without losing their liberal character. Political scientist Alain Gagnon cites the examples of Switzerland and Belgium, where regional governments "have the right and the obligation to protect their respective linguistic community against any infringements." Gagnon labels this "a charter of rights and freedoms whose application varies according to specific regions."[4]

Bercuson and Cooper reject such regionalism, and they suggest that a Quebec-free Canada could avoid decentralization by giving each province equal representation in the Senate. Other scholars are sceptical that such a proposal would be acceptable to Ontario. They predict that, if Quebec left Confederation, Canada would begin to fall apart. Economist Tim O'Neill observes that Ontario's dominance in population and economic activity could lead other provinces to "forge separate regional and interregional alliances with other provinces and possibly with contiguous areas of the United States."[5]

Federal bilingual policy is a sore point for many scholars. Bercuson and Cooper scoff at those who claim that "what makes us great is official bilingualism and French on our cereal boxes."[6] While few other anglophone scholars share this rejection of legislated bilingualism, many Quebec nationalists do. They argue that Quebec's government should operate only in French, while governments outside Quebec should offer services in French only in heavily francophone areas. Sociologist Hubert Guindon, a sovereignist who supports unilingualism for Quebec, maintains that "the official bilingualism adopted by the Canadian state was politically irrelevant."[7]

Bercuson and Cooper argue that Canada without Quebec would be more prosperous than today's Canada. Adopting the neo-conservative view that the federal government's spending has been out of control for several decades, they suggest that Quebec pressures have played a key role in preventing the government from trimming its programs. Although they provide no figures to corroborate this view, they conclude, "By ending the wasteful transaction costs of official bilingualism and especially the ongoing transfer of wealth from Canada to Quebec, the citizens of Canada would undoubtedly be more wealthy, not less."[8]

Quebec economists of a nationalist bent have rejected the view that Quebec is a net gainer from tax transfers in Canada. Georges Mathew has produced "a balance sheet of federalism for Quebec," which claims that Quebec had a marginally favourable balance from 1973 to 1986 but afterwards was a net loser.[9] Pierre Fortin also argues that Confederation continues to have a negative economic impact on Quebec. He claims that the federal debt, failed federal development policies, and monetary instability as well as duplication in powers between the federal and provincial governments have hurt Quebec's economy.[10] Indeed, such policies hurt every province's economy, and Fortin suggests that radical decentralization might be of benefit to the whole country. If emotional attachments to Canada make residents of other provinces reluctant to support decentralization, then Quebec must either receive special status or become sovereign.

Scholars in have-not provinces, especially Atlantic Canada, have been less sanguine about the economic prospects of their provinces should Quebec leave. Tim O'Neill notes that "neither extensive decentralization nor separation will have a positive impact on Atlantic Canada" because the region depends more on federal transfers than other areas.[11] O'Neill also observes that notions that either Quebec or the rest of Canada will benefit economically from a break-up take as a given that the break-up will be amicable and cause little short-term economic disruption. Yet there has already been an indication that the two sides would have difficulty determining how to divide up the national debt.

Political scientist Peter Russell suggests that the aftermath of Quebec sovereignty might well depend on how it is achieved. If it comes through a unilateral declaration of independence rather than through a long process of negotiations, "the climate of uncertainty and tension generated by such a move will reduce international confidence and put severe strain on the Canadian economy."[12] Opponents of independence, particularly anglophones and First Nations, "might insist on federal protection of their rights against a Quebec government operating outside Canadian law. Civil disobedience and violence cannot be ruled out."

While such views strike many as alarmist, some Quebec nationalist intellectuals readily concede that the sovereignty-association formula is probably impossible. There is no guarantee that the rest of Canada would negotiate a common market with a seceding province. Hubert Guindon, reflecting on the debate in the 1980 Quebec referendum, observes: "The common myth shared by both those opposed to sovereignty association and those in favour was that should the 'oui' forces have won decisively, it would have led automatically to the creation of a sovereign state with association with Canada.... Such naïveté, in a sense, honours us. But it augurs poorly for the kind of sophistication that will be required to inch our way toward sovereignty."[13]

NOTES

1 Gwen Brodsky and Shelagh Day, *Canadian Charter Equality Rights for Women: One Step Forward or Two Steps Back?* (Ottawa: Canadian Advisory Council on the Status of Women, 1989) 3.

2 CBC News, *Viewpoint*, Judy Rebick column, 3 Jan. 2001.

3 David J. Bercuson and Barry Cooper, *Deconfederation: Canada Without Quebec* (Toronto: Key Porter, 1991) 15–16.

4 Alain Gagnon, "Other Federal and Nonfederal Countries: Lessons for Canada," in *Options for a New Canada*, ed. Ronald L. Watts and Douglas M. Brown (Toronto: University of Toronto Press, 1991) 232.

5 Tim O'Neill, "Restructured Federalism and Its Impacts on Atlantic Canada," in *The Constitutional Future of the Prairie and Atlantic Regions of Canada*, ed. James N. McRorie and Martha L. Macdonald, (Regina: Canadian Plains Research Center, 1992) 63.

6 Bercuson and Cooper, *Deconfederation*, 134–35.

7 Hubert Guindon, *Quebec Society: Tradition, Modernity, and Nationhood* (Toronto: University of Toronto Press, 1988) 143.

8 Bercuson and Cooper, *Deconfederation*, 140–41.

9 Georges Mathews, *Quiet Resolution: Quebec's Challenges to Canada* (Toronto: Summerhill Press, 1990) 139–40.

10 Pierre Fortin, "How Economics Is Shaping the Constitutional Debate in Quebec," in *Confederation in Crisis*, ed. Robert Young (Toronto: Lorimer, 1991) 3–44.

11 O'Neill, "Restructured Federalism," 63.

12 Peter H. Russell, "Towards a New Constitutional Process," in *Options for a New Canada*, 148.

13 Guindon, *Quebec Society*, 166–67.

SELECTED READING

On Quebec since 1975, see Paul-André Linteau et al., *Quebec Since 1930: A History* (Toronto: Lorimer, 1991); Kenneth McRoberts, *Quebec: Social Change and Political Crisis*, 3rd ed. (Toronto: McClelland and Stewart, 1988); René Lévesque, *Memoirs* (Toronto: McClelland and Stewart, 1986); Pierre Godin, *René Lévesque: un enfant du siècle* (Montreal: Boréal, 1994); and Robert Chodos and Eric Hamovitch, *Quebec and the American Dream* (Toronto: Between the Lines, 1994). Ontario developments are discussed in Thomas L. Walkom, *Rae Days* (Toronto: Key Porter, 1994); Patrick Monahan, *Storming the Pink Palace: The NDP in Power, a Cautionary Tale* (Toronto: Lester, 1995); and Daniel Drache, ed., *Getting on Track: Social Democratic Strategies for Ontario* (Montreal: McGill-Queen's University Press, 1992).

On Western Canada, see Gerald Friesen, *The Canadian Prairies*, rev. ed. (Toronto: University of Toronto Press, 1987); Trevor Harrison and Gordon Laxer, eds., *The Trojan Horse: Alberta and the Future of Canada* (Montreal: Black Rose, 1995); James M. Pitsula and Ken Rasmussen, *Privatizing a Province: The New Right in Saskatchewan* (Vancouver: New Star, 1990); Patricia Marchak, *Green Gold: The Forest Industry in British Columbia* (Vancouver: UBC Press, 1983); Rennie Warburton and Donald Coburn, eds., *Workers, Capital, and the State of British Columbia: Selected Papers* (Vancouver: UBC Press, 1987); and Jim Silver and Jeremy Hull, eds., *The Political Economy of Manitoba* (Regina: Canadian Plains Research Centre, 1990). On the Reform Party, see Trevor Harrison, *Of Passionate Intensity: Right-Wing Populism and the Reform Party of Canada* (Toronto: University of Toronto Press, 1995).

On the Atlantic provinces, see E.R. Forbes, "The Atlantic Provinces, Free Trade, and the Constitution," in *Challenging the Regional Stereotype* (Fredericton: Acadiensis Press, 1989): 200-16; Gary Burrill and Ian McKay, eds., *People, Resources, and Power in Atlantic Canada: Critical Perspectives on Underdevelopment and Primary Industries in the Atlantic Region* (Fredericton: Acadiensis, 1987); Wallace Clement, *The Struggle to Organize: Resistance in Canada's Fisheries* (Toronto: McClelland and Stewart, 1986); and Shaun Cornish, *The Westray Tragedy: A Miner's Story* (Toronto: Fernwood, 1994).

Useful works on the constitutional debates include David Milne, *The New Canadian Constitution* (Toronto: Lorimer, 1982); Keith Banting and Richard Simeon, eds., *And No One Cheered: Federalism, Democracy and the Constitution Act* (Scarborough, ON: Nelson, 1983); Michael D. Behiels, ed., *The Meech Lake Primer: Conflicting Views of the 1987 Constitutional Accord* (Ottawa: University of Ottawa Press, 1989); C.E.S. Franks, *The Myths and Symbols of the Constitutional Debate in Canada* (Kingston: Institute of Intergovernmental Relations, 1993); and Deborah Coyne, *Roll of the Dice: Working with Clyde Wells During the Meech Lake Negotiations* (Toronto: Lorimer, 1992).

On the trade union movement, see Bryan D. Palmer, *Working-Class Experience: Rethinking the History of Canadian Labour, 1800–1991* (Toronto: McClelland and Stewart, 1992) and Leo Panitch, *The Assault on Trade Union Freedoms: From Wage Controls to Social Contract*, rev. ed. (Toronto: Garamond, 1994). The lives of Canada's Native peoples are explored in the texts mentioned in earlier chapters as well as Geoffrey York, *The Dispossessed: Life and Death in Native Canada* (Boston: Little Brown, 1992) and Pauline Comeau and Aldo Santin, *The First Canadians: A Profile of Native People Today* (Toronto: Lorimer, 1990).

On Native peoples, apart from the readings in Chapter 25, see John L. Steckley and Bryan D. Cummins, *Full Circle: Canada's First Nations* (Toronto: Prentice Hall, 2001); Peter Kulchyski, ed., *Unjust Relations: Aboriginal Rights in Canadian Courts* (Toronto: Oxford University Press, 1994); Patricia Monture-Angus, *Thunder in My Soul: A Mohawk Woman Speaks* (Toronto: Fernwood, 1995); Geoffrey York, *The Dispossesed: Life and Death in Native Canada* (London: Vintage, 1990); James S. Frideres and Rene R. Gadacz, *Aboriginal Peoples in Canada: Contemporary Conflicts*, 6th ed. (Toronto: Prentice Hall, 2001); and Ken Coates, *The Marshall Decision and Native Rights* (Montreal and Kingston: McGill-Queen's University Press, 2000).

On the Women's movement see the references in Chapter 25 as well as Ruth Roach Pierson, et.al., *Canadian Women's Issues*, 2 vols. (Toronto: James Lorimer 1994/95).

On the environmental movement, see Mary Richardson, Joan Sherman, and Michael Gismondi, *Winning Back the Words: Confronting Experts in an Environmental Public Hearing* (Toronto: Garamond, 1993); George N. Hood, *Against the Flow: Rafferty-Almeda and the Politics of the Environment* (Saskatoon: Fifth House, 1994); and John Dyson with Joseph Fitchett, *Sink the Rainbow! An Enquiry into the "Greenpeace Affair"* (London: Victor Gollancz, 1986).

On gay liberation and AIDS organizing, see Gary Kinsman, *The Regulation of Desire: Homo and Hetero Sexualities* (Montreal: Black Rose, 1996) and David M. Rayside and Evert A. Lindquist, "AIDS Activism and the State in Canada," *Studies in Political Economy* 39 (Autumn 192): 37–76.

 **WEBLINKS**

NORTH AMERICAN FREE TRADE AGREEMENT
www.dfait-maeci.gc.ca/nafta-alena/menu-e.asp

The Department of Foreign Affairs and International Trade site contains links to the Agreement itself, frequently asked questions, related publications and Web sites, and disputed settlements under NAFTA.

THE RIGHT HONOURABLE MARTIN BRIAN MULRONEY
www.nlc-bnc.ca/primeministers/h4-3450-e.html

This site contains biographical information, selected speeches, photos, and related links.

PARTI QUEBECOIS
http://partiquebecois.org/nouvelles_derniereheure.phtml

This is the official site of the Parti Quebecois, offering a history of the party as well as current news, leadership, and membership information.

GREENPEACE CANADA
www.greenpeace.ca

The history of Greenpeace, its campaigns, and news releases are presented at this site.

BEHIND THE BARRICADES: OKA
www.geocities.com/av_team2001/oka.html

Details of the 1990 Oka crisis are presented here, through text, photos, and sound clips. A chronology of events and mediography of sources is also available.

ATLANTIC FISHERIES
www.hssfc.ca/english/policyandadvocacy/ breakfastonthehill/breakfast-fishers.cfm

Rosemary E. Ommer explores the sustainability of communities of fish and fishers in Canada in this presentation. An environmental history of Canada's east coast fishing regions and their social, economic, and cultural implications are examined.

Community and Culture, 1976–2002

Kids are expensive. If it were just my wife and I, she wouldn't have to work. But at one point when there was five in here…Your kids want everything now. You can't just buy them 'adventure' running shoes. They want Adidas or Reeboks. That's the killer…My parents didn't have much. To me, what I wanted and what I got were two different things. I just saw a kid walk by with a $150 starter coat. My son's got one too [laughs] and I'm thinking when does it end? I think I would have been satisfied growing up, to have a decent coat, never mind a starter coat with a Montreal Canadiens logo. Sure, I'd like my kids to have better than what I had or at least better than what my parents could give me, but then we put a gun to our head by doing this…When does it stop?[1]

These comments by "Dom," a Niagara Falls man in his early forties in 1995, reflected the conflicting values of many Canadians as the twentieth century closed. While most adult Canadians worked outside the home, some people looked nostalgically upon earlier times when supposedly a single income had supported a family. Participating in the rampant materialism of society, many Canadians nonetheless also viewed consumerism as more a curse than a blessing. In this chapter we look broadly at the social and cultural developments in Canada as one millennium ended and another began, providing some context for the hopes and worries of people like Dom.

POPULATION

Canada's population increased from 23 450 000 in the census of 1976 to a Statistics Canada estimate of 30 007 094 in 2001 (see Table 28.1). Natural increase accounted for 60 percent of the population growth with immigration accounting for the rest. While recent immigrants, as a group, had once been relatively poor compared to other Canadians, in the 1980s the average immigrant in the labour force earned more than Canadian-born workers. The averages masked the poverty of some immigrant groups, but they demonstrate the extent to which the immigrants, often having superior job credentials to the Canadian-born, succeeded in their new country. Among the poorer groups were refugees from Indochina and Latin America fleeing persecution and ethnic discrimination in their war-torn countries.

The countries of origin of immigrants to Canada had changed significantly because of the gradual elimination of racist restrictions on non-Europeans entering the country. While only 4 percent of new immigrants from 1945 to 1962 were from outside Europe or the United States, that figure had reached 75 percent in 1998–99. Asia was the major continent supplying new residents for Canada, accounting for 125 903 of the 205 469 immigrants to Canada in that fiscal year.

While Canada remained a country in which an overwhelming majority had European origins only, that profile was rapidly changing. In the 1996 census, almost 4 million of Canada's 28 528 125 people were members of visible minorities. Just short of 800 000 Canadians were reported to be Aboriginal, including status and non-status "Indians" as well as Métis. The Chinese-Canadian population had reached 860 000 while South Asians accounted for 670 590 Canadians and there were 574 000 African-origin Canadians. Arabs, Filipinos, Southeast Asians, and Latin Americans each contributed about 200 000 members of the Canadian mosaic.

Visible minorities, largely dominated by recent arrivals, flocked to the major population centres where jobs were easier to find. The result was that Ontario accounted for over half of all visible-minority Canadians, with British Columbia, a magnet for many Asians, proving the second most attractive province for non-Europeans. The four western provinces continued to be the home of almost two-thirds of Aboriginal peoples, while the Atlantic provinces, still continuing to leak population to the rest of the country, offered too few opportunities to attract more than a slim minority of new Canadians. While visible minorities, other than Natives, comprised 11.2 percent of all Canadians in 1996, in Toronto their share of the total population was 32 percent, and in Vancouver 31 percent.

It was not only visible-minority immigrants who flocked to a few cities and a few provinces in Canada. From 1961 to 1996, fully 90 percent of immigrants located in Ontario, British Columbia, and Quebec. In the latter year, the foreign-born made up 17.4 percent of the population of Canada, but again the big three cities were home to most of them: 42 percent in Toronto, 17 percent in Vancouver, and 12 percent in Montreal. By 2000, the number of Chinese-speaking homes in provinces other than Quebec was just shy of the number of French-speaking homes.

The federal government had reduced immigration levels to below 100 000 a year in response to the recession of 1982, but they were allowed to rise once the economy rallied. During the recession of the early 1990s, smaller cuts in immigration were made as it became clear that Canadians were having too few children to maintain the population through natural increase alone. Because of more effective contraception and changing social values, Canadian fertility rates had fallen by 1976 below the 2.1 children per woman required to maintain current populations and remained below that level into the new millennium.

Infant mortality rates continued to fall, and in 1997, only 5.5 per 1000 children failed to reach their first birthday. Life expectancy for a girl born in 1998 had reached 82 years, while boys could expect on average to live for 76 years, in both cases six years longer than their counterparts born in 1971.

The trend to urbanization and suburbanization continued apace, with farmlands being gobbled up by voracious metropolitan developers. In 1996, the largest 25 metropolitan census areas accounted for three of every five Canadians, with the four largest

Table 28.1
Growth of Canada's Population, 1971–1996

Period	Census Population at End of Period	Total Population Growth	Births	Deaths	Immigrants	Emigrants
1971–76	23 450	1882	1755	824	1053	358
1976–81	24 820	1371	1820	843	771	278
1981–86	26 101	1280	1872	885	677	278
1986–91	28 031	1930	1933	946	1199	213
1991–96	29 672	1641	1936	1024	1137	229

All numbers above are in thousands.

Source: Adapted from the Statistics Canada Website http://cansima.statcan.ca/cgi-win/CNSMCGI.EXE, Table 051-001

metropolitan areas alone—Toronto, Montreal, Vancouver, and Ottawa-Hull—containing over a third of the country's population.

EDUCATION

Formal education became more important than ever as a means to finding satisfying and high-paying work in the last quarter of the twentieth century. As secure blue-collar jobs with good union wages began to evaporate, the doors to young people with limited education shut tight. In 1995, 20 percent of both high-school drop-outs and high-school graduates looking for work were unable to find even part-time positions, and many of those able to find employment worked for the legal minimum wage.

Studies of the career paths of the "baby boomers" demonstrated that by the 1990s, almost half of university graduates who were in the labour force had reached high-level management or professional positions. Their earnings easily outstripped those of their high-school classmates without postsecondary education, while the income of community college graduates sat between those of university and high-school graduates. University education proved particularly important to immigrant youngsters as a means of improving their economic situation relative to their parents, though social class continued to be the major determinant of which young people would go on to postsecondary education.

While education became more important, it also became less affordable. Government cutbacks in grants to postsecondary institutions resulted in higher tuition fees. In the 1960s, tuition had paid about a fifth of the cost of a university education in most provinces. By 2000, it paid about half. The consequence, of course, was that students had to dig deeper to pay for their education. Part-time jobs helped but they were hard to find in the high-unemployment 1990s. More and more students lived at home throughout their education years, or relied on student loans.

Tales of recent graduates who had accumulated debts of as much as $50 000 but could only find modest jobs abounded in the 1990s. However, studies suggested that in 2000, university graduates of the early 1990s were out-earning people of their age who had not attended university. Still, the high cost of postsecondary education acted as a deterrent to many youth. Stagnating university and college enrolments told the story. Full-time university enrolment, having reached 575 713 in 1994–95, had climbed only another 5000 by 1998–99, while part-time enrolments plummeted by almost 40 000 to 246 000. Community college enrolments increased slightly—from 380 000 full-timers to almost 404 000 in the same period, with part-time enrolments steady at around 91 000.

By the 1996 census, women outnumbered men among university graduates, but this did not mean that they were bound, as a group, toward better financial futures than men. In 2000, as in 1980, proportionately more women, in spite of generally superior academic performances, were tracked into sex-segregated occupations that paid lower salaries. Eighty percent of engineering graduates and two-thirds of the graduates in the physical sciences in 1996 were men, while women made up two-thirds of the graduates in Arts programs. In a few high-paying areas such as law and medicine, significant advances had been made in gender parity.

If education in Canada was seen increasingly as a vehicle for providing highly-trained workers for industry, it had yet another purpose as well for Quebec governments: maintaining French language and culture. Shortly after its election in 1976, the Parti québécois government passed Bill 101, which, among other things, permitted only Quebec-born anglophones to educate their children in English. The Supreme Court later extended that right to all Canadian-born anglophones who lived in the province. Under this law, all immigrants, regardless of linguistic background, were obliged to send their children to French-language schools.

Some allophones initially resisted the French-Canadian majority's imposition of French as the only language of instruction. From their point of view, they had moved to Canada, or indeed just to North America, and they did not see why they had to embrace the cultural aspirations of French Canadians. Immigrants often found that Canada's claims to support multiculturalism seemed to be contradicted by prejudices favouring linguistic and cultural conformity on the part of the two largest linguistic groups.

IMMIGRANT EXPERIENCES

Asian immigrants had quite varied experiences in Canada. In the 1980s and 1990s, for example, wealthy Hong Kong residents, skittish about the impending return of their city to the Chinese government in 1997 after a century of British control, were actively courted by the Canadian government because of the capital and expertise they promised to inject into the country.

By contrast, South Asian farm labourers and South Asian women factory workers continued to work in exploitative conditions. Vietnamese and other Indochinese immigrants, often "boat people" fleeing either political repression or economic hardship, began arriving in Canada in the late 1970s. While many prospered in their new home, the rate of unemployment among Canadians of Vietnamese descent in the early 1990s was double the Canadian average.

Three new Canadians take their citizenship oath.

Aaron Harris/CP Picture Archive

Violent youth gangs in the Vietnamese community reflected the presence of an underclass for whom racism made the future appear quite bleak. Middle-class Vietnamese resented the media spotlight on the gangs and the limited attention paid both to those who were succeeding despite the odds and to the conditions that caused some youth to turn to gangs.

In this period, African Canadians continued to experience a great deal of racism in employment and housing, and they also regarded themselves as victims of police racism. A series of shootings of unarmed blacks in Montreal and Toronto led to accusations that many police officers were racists who stereotyped all blacks as criminals. Neo-Nazi skinheads—largely unemployed white male youths—attacked non-whites of Asian and African origin and desecrated Jewish cemeteries. Intolerance had its violent side, even in Canada.

State and unofficial discrimination against an ethnic minority also surfaced in Canada in the wake of 11 September 2001. Since the perpetrators of the crime had been mostly Muslims who were religious fundamentalists, state vigilance against potential terrorists often seemed to consist of more rigorous security checks of people of Arabic origins than other Canadians. Some Canadians of Arab descent lost their jobs, allegedly because they were security risks, without being informed as to how the government had come to this conclusion. Public hysteria over the American events led to tragic reports of Arab and other Muslim children being stoned on their way to school, to desecration of mosques, and to threats and intimidation of Arabs and those who looked like they might be Arabs. Religious institutions were often key to creating greater acceptance of a diversity of peoples in Canada, but some actually promoted intolerance.

THE CHURCHES

Evangelical Protestant churches enjoyed the greatest relative growth in membership in the last quarter of the twentieth century. Still, the numbers of Canadians who indicated affiliation with the mainline denominations easily dwarfed the congregations of the Pentecostal Churches, Adventists, Churches of Christ, and other groups that tended to identify with the New Right because of its opposition to changing

Table 28.2

Religious Affiliations of Canadians
(in percentages)

Religious Organization	1911	1951	1991
Roman Catholic	39.4	44.7	45.7
United Church	–	20.5	11.5
Anglican	14.5	14.7	8.1
Presbyterian	15.6	5.6	2.4
Lutheran	3.2	3.2	2.4
Baptist	5.3	3.2	2.5
Pentecostal	–	.7	1.4
Other Protestant*	17.3	2.5	7.9
Eastern Orthodox	1.2	1.2	1.5
Jewish	1.0	1.5	1.2
No religion	.4	.4	12.4
Other	2.0	1.4	2.8**

*Includes Methodists and Congregationalists for 1911; Adventists, Churches of Christ, Disciples, and Salvation Army for 1951 and 1991, along with smaller groups.
**Includes Muslims, 1 percent; Hindus, 0.6 percent; and Buddhists, 0.7 percent.

Source: Adapted from the Statistics Canada publication *Canada Year Book*, 1994, Catalogue 11-402, page 123

gender roles and notions of personal moral choice (see Table 28.2).

The churches continued to face the dilemma of the extent to which they should become involved in secular issues, and which ones. During the 1980s recession, the Canadian Conference of Catholic Bishops' Social Affairs Commission issued a manifesto entitled *Ethical Reflections on the Economic Crisis.* The bishops set forth the ethical priorities that they wanted governments to follow: "The needs of the poor have priority over the wants of the rich; the rights of workers are more important than the accumulation of machines or the maximization of profit; the participation of the marginalized takes precedence over an order that excludes them."[2] With unemployment in double digits, the bishops called on the government to focus on policies that would create jobs rather than continuing to emphasize the battle against inflation, as the business community urged.

The leaders of the Anglican and United Churches praised the Catholic bishops for their stand, but within all three churches, there were voices against economic radicalism as well. Much of the hierarchy identified with the business leaders, whose corporate sponsorship was essential to the churches' charitable work. In

1988, the limits of the churches' social justice movement were demonstrated by the decision of the Roman Catholic and Anglican churches to take no position on the Canadian-American Free Trade Agreement and the mildness of the United Church's public opposition to the deal.

While the percentage of Canadians who identified themselves as Catholics rose 1 percent from 1951 to 1991, Protestant denominations accounted for 15 percent fewer Canadians in 1991 than 40 years earlier. Much of the decline was accounted for by the increase in Canadians who followed no religion. Even among professed Christians, there were many people who were attracted to New Age religions, spiritual movements with an affinity to Asian and ancient New World religions.

For traditional Catholics and Protestants, Canada's evolution as a multicultural country began to pose new issues. Was Canada really a "Christian" country? As new Canadians of non-Christian faiths protested that public schools were requiring their children to participate in Christian ceremonies, many school boards agreed to take the religion out of Christmas and to end such practices as prayers and Bible readings in the school. The growing number of atheists and agnostics similarly applied pressures upon schools and other public institutions to end religious observances.

CULTURAL DEVELOPMENTS

Trends from the 1960s and early 1970s in Canadian cultural development continued: Canadian literature blossomed, a respectable recording industry developed, and almost no one paid money to watch Canadian films except the rare one that achieved American acclaim. In this period, it became clear that culture, like resource development and manufacturing, was an industry, contributing as much to the GDP as farming or textile production.

Governments at both federal and provincial levels paid close attention to the policies regulating cultural industries, offering incentives for Hollywood moguls to make their films in Canada, sponsoring overseas junkets for artists and writers to promote their products, and supporting cultural workers through such programs as the Public Lending Right Commission to compensate writers for the availability of their books catalogued in Canadian libraries.

FILM IN A VISUAL AGE

In this period, film maker Denys Arcand emerged as one of Canada's success stories. *Le Déclin de l'empire americain* (1986) was a huge international success and his *Jésus de Montréal* won the Jury prize at the Cannes Film Festival in 1989. He also directed an English-language film in 1993, *Love and Human Remains*, an adaptation of a play by an acclaimed homosexual playwright, Edmonton's Brad Fraser. While Arcand and a few others continued to draw large audiences in the 1990s, Quebec filmmakers complained that reduced government subsidies and chain ownership of cinemas made it difficult to make French-Canadian films or find an audience for them. Increasingly, filmmakers had to be content with having their movies screened on television, where they often found large audiences, rather than in movie houses.

The situation for filmmakers in English Canada was even worse. While a few feature films such as Cynthia Scott's *The Company of Strangers*, Anne Wheeler's *Bye Bye Blues*, and several films by Atom Egoyan received distribution in theatres, on the whole cinema in Canada continued to be dominated by American products. In this period National Film Board documentaries continued to receive acclaim. A feminist film unit within the NFB, Studio D, was particularly successful, producing *If You Love This Planet*, an Academy Award-winning anti-nuclear documentary; *Not a Love Story*, an anti-pornography film; and *Forbidden Love*, an examination of lesbian relationships.

English-Canadian television faced new challenges in an era of government cuts and competition from the "200-channel universe" that allowed Canadians to use satellites to beam endless numbers of American programs into their homes. There were exceptions. Canadians warmed to their political and social humorists, and shows such as *This Hour Has 22 Minutes* and *Royal Canadian Air Farce* drew audiences in the millions. Despite the success of the American television station CNN in dominating international newscasts, Canadians continued to watch news programs produced within the country.

CBC's new Newsworld channel in particular quickly developed a loyal following. CBC's *People's History of Canada* series, aired in 2000 and 2001 to celebrate the millennium, was popular with most viewers. Nevertheless, Canadians increasingly had difficulty distinguishing between the sitcoms, dramas, and game shows produced at home and those beamed in from American channels, and gave more of their time to the latter than the former.

The French language assured Quebec's television producers of a bigger audience. In the 1980s and 1990s, hundreds of thousands of francophones watched Pierre Gauvreau's *Le Temps d'une paix* (Peacetime), a dramatization of life in Quebec from 1918 to 1930, and *Cormoran*, which highlighted political and class struggles in Rimouski during the Great Depression. Fernand Dansereau's *Le Parc des Braves* focused on the Second World War while his *Shehawek* was set in the period of Montreal's founding. Beginning in 1997, Jacques Lacoursière's *Épopée en Amerique*, a series chronicling the history of Quebec, drew large television audiences. Among TV series focusing on modern Quebec, several by the feminist author, broadcaster, and former PQ cabinet minister Lise Payette have been particularly successful. Her *Marilyn*, which began a long TV run in 1991, had as its protagonist a charwoman whose experiences put her in contact with people from all walks of life in Quebec.

By the 1980s, Canadian educators were beginning to recognize that students brought up in the age of television and the computer responded well to visual media and increasingly used film and video to stimulate student interest. The National Film Board had long been the mainstay of such approaches but private corporations were also beginning to develop educational film. The growing alienation of Quebec prompted the Bronfman family in 1986 to channel some of their corporate profits into the CRB Foundation, designed to foster a better knowledge of Canadian history and culture. Despite the skepticism of critics, the Foundation's well-crafted Heritage Minutes, aired widely on television and in movie theatres in both English and French, proved a great success. In 1998, the Foundation became involved in the founding of Historica, whose mandate was to promote Canadian history in Canadian schools.

LITERARY ACHIEVEMENTS

The popularity of Canadian literature in the postwar period continued to grow late in the twentieth century, and international audiences became more and more interested in Canadians' work as well. Margaret Atwood, Michael Ondaatje, Carol Shields, Rohinton Mistry, Anne Michaels and others won major international book awards, and a host of writers such as Wayne Johnston, Alice Munro, M. G. Vassanji, Anne-Marie MacDonald, Alistair Macleod, Bonnie Burnard, Mordechai Richler and Guy Vanderhaeghe also topped Canadian and international best-seller lists.

The multicultural character of Canada's contribution to world literature was striking. Mistry and Vassanji are Indian expatriates, while Ondaatje was born in Sri Lanka. Other key contributors were Trinidad-born Neil Bissoondath and poet and literary social critic Himani Bannerji. Nova Scotia's black community has produced two fine poets in Maxine Tynes and George Elliot Clarke, while Toronto poet Dionne Brand explored the issues of sexism, racism, imperialism, and homophobia in her work.

Native authors were also beginning to be noticed by the broader society. Thomas King's portraits of Native life in works such as *Medicine River* (1990) and Tomson Highway's plays, including the critically acclaimed *Dry Lips Oughta Move to Kapuskasing* (1989), represented just a few of the Native attempts to bring their stories to Canadians as a whole. The Mi'kmaq found a voice in the poetry of Rita Joe.

RECORDING ARTISTS

Sales of "Canadian content" recordings had increased from $53.6 million in 1990–91 to $127.2 million by 1995–96. By the latter date, 14.5 percent of sales in Canada, against 10.5 percent five years earlier, were of records whose artists, writers, or producers were Canadian citizens. In part, this was simply because Canada produced a number of international superstars in the 1990s, many of them women. Céline Dion,

Alanis Morrissette, Shania Twain, Sarah MacLachlan, and Diana Krall were the world's best-selling female artists in pop, country, folk, and jazz. Among male artists, Bryan Adams, Barenaked Ladies, and The Tragically Hip were Canada's best-known exports.

Popular music was one of the few occupations that a talented few could use to transform their economic prospects. Céline Dion, for example, was the 14th child of a working-class Quebec family and had become Quebec's leading francophone pop star. In the 1980s, while a teenager, she rose to stardom in Quebec and established an equally solid reputation in France. At the time she spoke barely a word of English, but in the 1990s she learned it well enough to become the world's best-selling female artist. Another rags-to-riches story is the career of Shania Twain, who had grown up in poverty in Timmins, Ontario, with her mother and Métis stepfather. When her parents died in a car crash, the teenage Twain raised her younger brothers and sisters with money she earned as a local singer. By 2000, she was country music's all-time best-

Sarah MacLachlan.
Courtesy of Nettwerk Management

selling female artist. Folk-pop singer Sarah MacLachlan was responsible for Lilith Fair, a female musicians' summer festival that for several years drew large numbers in the United States and Canada.

While some of these artists might have found success without the Canadian-content regulations, the rules encouraged more diversity in the types of music aired by radio stations and broadcast on the video channels that appeared in the 1980s. Political tunes such as Bruce Cockburn's "Rocket Launcher" and Parachute Club's "Rise Up," which may not have been played in Canada in the period before the "Can Con" rule, proved to be big sellers. Rita MacNeil's "Working Man"—featuring Men of the Deeps, a coal miners' choir from Cape Breton, singing with MacNeil—made every country music station playlist in Canada and also became a chart-topper in Great Britain. Apart from MacNeil, who hailed from Big Pond, Cape Breton, many other Atlantic artists, including Ashley MacIsaac, Natalie MacMaster, Great Big Sea, the Barra MacNeils, Figgy Duff, and the Rankin Family, performed folk music with Celtic roots.

Edith Butler's compositions, inspired by folk traditions, became popular hits in Canada and France, while Prince Edward Island's Angèle Arsenault, after becoming known for both her folk songs with historical messages and her pop tunes, won acclaim for her revival of the songs of La Bolduc, Quebec's popular diva. Stompin' Tom Connors, who grew up in Skinners Pond, Prince Edward Island, appealed to both folk and country audiences with his working-class perspective on Canadian themes. Ontario-born Stan Rogers also drew a large following with ballads that chronicled the difficulties facing working people in the post-modern age. In Western Canada, artists such as Connie Kaldor, James Keelaghan, Spirit of the West, and Tom Russell drew on regional themes and often spoke to the lives of the disadvantaged.

In the 1990s, some Native artists gained recognition. Kashtin, two Innu performers from northern Quebec who sang in their Native language, produced a hybrid of Native music and rock and roll, and played to large audiences of both francophones and anglophones in the south. Susan Aglukark, although singing mainly in English, paid tribute to her Inuit heritage and dealt with social problems of the North. Native dance troupes performing traditional dances in ceremonial costumes performed before their own people and increasingly before white audiences as well, attempting to reproduce the dances as they had been performed by their ancestors rather than refashioning them for commercial broadcasters.

MEDIA CONCENTRATION

The mass media, which has so great an impact on Canadian social values, has come to be controlled by fewer and fewer corporations and individuals. In 1980, the Royal Commission on Newspapers reported that three chains controlled 90 percent of French-language newspapers and that another three conglomerates controlled over two-thirds of English-language newspapers in Canada. Since that time, the problem of concentration of ownership has only worsened. The Southam chain dominated most large anglophone urban markets outside the Atlantic provinces, though it faced well-established competitors in Toronto. Once owned by the Southam family, the chain was controlled by magnate Conrad Black from 1996 to 2000, when it was bought by I.H. Asper, a Winnipeg entrepreneur and former Manitoba Liberal leader who had already built a television empire.

Such media concentration, which also occurred in other Western democracies, raised questions about the degree to which the media could be counted on to provide a range of points of view. While alternative sources of information were available through small magazines, newsletters, and chat lines on the new Internet, the need to lure corporate advertisers made it difficult for groups such as trade unions to establish their own newspapers or television stations.

Entry was easier in the book-publishing industry, but a smaller number of corporations made most of the money, and increasingly Canadian firms were absorbed by mega-corporations. Ryerson Press was taken over by the American firm McGraw-Hill in 1970; Copp Clark, Canada's oldest publisher, was bought first by the British firm Pitman in the 1950s and then by the conglomerate Pearson in 1995. In the 1980s, while Canadian-owned firms were responsible for most of the new textbooks that appeared in Canada, they garnered less than a third of the revenues from book sales.

PROFESSIONAL SPORTS

Hockey continued to be the major spectator sport in Canada. When the World Hockey Association faced bankruptcy in 1979, all of the WHA teams but Ottawa joined the NHL, and the transfer of the NHL's Atlanta franchise to Calgary increased the number of Canadian teams to seven. The Edmonton Oilers won five Stanley Cups from 1984 to 1990, and Oiler Wayne Gretzky became almost synonymous with the game. To the chagrin of most Edmontonians, Gretzky was sold to the Los Angeles Kings in 1988 by Oiler owner Peter Pocklington for $18 million. It was a reminder that hockey, like most professional sports, had become big business and that a franchise belonged to owners rather than a particular city. By the mid-1990s, the cost of signing star players had forced both Quebec City and Winnipeg to concede that they could not draw the home audiences needed to sustain a professional hockey team, and their teams headed south of the border.

Football fans proved reluctant to pay the high ticket prices necessitated by the 1990s to pay lucrative players' contracts. Though the ownership of Ontario teams was private, the Western teams were owned and operated by non-profit community organizations. An attempt to increase interest in the Canadian Football League by expansion of franchises to the United States in the mid-1990s flopped. American football fans proved uninterested in the Canadian version of the game. By 1996, the CFL was once again made up of only Canadian teams.

Professional baseball in Canada was represented by American major league teams based in the two largest cities. The Montreal Expos had difficulties filling the stadium; baseball was never as popular as hockey among the city's francophones. The Toronto Blue Jays attracted large crowds in their hometown, even though no member of the team was a Torontonian or even a Canadian. After spending almost $50 million on player salaries, the Blue Jays won the World Series in 1992 and 1993.

While professional sports teams were almost exclusively male, both female and male athletes won international honours in individual sports, bringing home medals in a variety of events at Olympic, Commonwealth, and Pan-American Games as well as world championships in individual sports. Competitive figure skating in particular drew spectators in large numbers.

SPORTS AND SOCIETY

For many Canadians, the country's most inspiring athlete had never attempted to win any competition. In April 1980, Terry Fox, a 21-year-old Vancouver student, who had lost a leg to bone cancer, began a run across Canada to raise funds for cancer research. After five months of running almost 40 kilometres per day on his "Marathon of Hope," Fox was forced to give up his run at Thunder Bay when doctors found that the cancer had spread to his lungs. He died in June 1981, but the Terry Fox Run, an annual fund-raising event for cancer research, became one of the major participatory sports events in Canada. British Columbia wheelchair athlete Rick Hansen, inspired in part by Fox's achievement, dramatized the oft-ignored capabilities of people with disabilities by circling the globe in his wheelchair.

For Terry Fox, running was a means to a noble end but running was also big business. As in many other sports, the desire to win often led athletes and coaches to cheat. A steroids scandal rocked Canada after sprinter Ben Johnson was stripped of a gold medal at the Seoul Olympics in 1988. In the media circus and official inquiry that followed, Canadians learned that many athletes used performance-enhancing steroids. Questions of amateurism that had plagued earlier international competition seemed rather quaint as sports took on a big-business atmosphere where millions of dollars in endorsements could await Olympic gold medallists. Canada's reputation in running rebounded with Donovan Bailey's convincing 100-metre win in the 1996 Olympics.

While many young Canadians dreamed of becoming sports celebrities, studies suggested their chances were best if they were Anglo-Canadian males with professional or white-collar parents. The costs in-

Terry Fox during his Marathon of Hope.

CP Picture Archive

year-old Justine Blainey from participating on a leading boys' hockey team. Several courtrooms and thousands of dollars later, Justine got her wish in 1987, but the OHA continued to grumble that the bodychecking and slapshots of the boys' league made the inclusion of girls inappropriate.

While sports for youngsters was supposed to be about fun, it sometimes became a nightmare. In 1997, Sheldon Kennedy, a former member of the Swift Current Broncos, a junior team, who had made it to the NHL, revealed that in the late 1980s the Bronco coach had persistently sexually abused him. It soon became clear that Kennedy was not his only victim and that coaches for other teams had sexually abused players as well. The hockey scandal followed revelations about sexual abuse of both boys and girls in other sports, alarming parents and sports authorities at a time when more and more children were becoming involved in organized sporting activities.

Canadians in the postwar period spent a great deal of money and time as sports spectators, both at children's and professional games, but attending sports activities and participating in them were two different stories. In the early 1970s, it was estimated that 90 percent of adults did not do the minimum amount of exercise recommended for protection against heart disease and stroke. While Canadians were living longer, poor nutrition habits, lack of exercise, and smoking were ending many lives prematurely and causing many other Canadians, who survived cancer surgery, heart attacks, or strokes, to live restricted lives.

Increasingly the federal government, aided by campaigns of nutritionists, physical education specialists, and physicians, encouraged Canadians to rethink their lifestyles. Urged on by a federal body called Participaction, which placed clever ads on radio and television, previously indolent Canadians took up jogging, enrolled in aerobics classes, swam, or at least took the occasional long walk. The physical fitness craze meant new business for leisure industry operators from ski hills to fitness clubs.

Anti-smoking campaigns also had an impact. By the 1990s, the intrepid smoker stood out in the snow or rain during a coffee break at most workplaces, public buildings, and halls of education. Airlines banned

volved in training athletes who could compete in national and international events excluded most working-class children. Girls faced particular challenges as sexual segregation continued to make sports a largely male preserve. Attempts by girls and women to share the same opportunities as boys were mightily resisted. In 1985, the Ontario Hockey Association barred 13-

smoking altogether, and intercity buses, once thick with smoke, became havens for the non-smoker as well. In most cities, restaurants were divided by law into smoking and non-smoking sections, and some city councils legislated smoking out of all establishments where food was served. The percentage of adults who smoked halved between the 1960s and the 1990s, but today young people seem to be beginning to smoke at rates similar to those that had prevailed when their parents' generation was young.

The diets of many Canadians have changed and are now more likely to meet Nutrition Canada's requirement for "balanced" eating. Consumption of red meat, one of the items that physicians linked to cardiovascular problems, fell, and the cattle industry changed breeding habits to develop leaner meats. The focus on diet, however, had its seamy side. Social images, especially for young women, created the view that the ideal body was fat-free, an unhealthy suggestion that led to a rise in anorexia and bulimia, with their risks of death by starvation in a prosperous society.

More commonly, unhealthy diets that ignored nutritionists' guides for getting all the necessary vitamins and minerals were pedalled by diet gurus out to make a buck at the expense of women and sometimes men who were misled by the pervasive images that "fat is not where it's at." Social class was a big factor in people's response to the new ideas of healthy living. Surveys suggested that the working class and the poor had less time and money to devote to "participaction" and that, in any case, they often regarded the new opposition to smoking, drinking, and relaxation as an attack on the few pleasures in their lives.

CONCLUSION

The anxiety and conflict that characterized formal political and economic developments over the past three decades stood in sharp contrast to the effervescence that marked Canadian community and cultural life. In this period, Canada had become a more multicultural and pluralist society and the creativity of its diverse peoples seemed to know few boundaries. The dominance of American culture remained an issue that preoccupied many Canadian critics but ordinary people seemed comfortable with the fact that Canada was a North American nation with access to the markets of the world's richest nation for their films, books and recordings. As the twenty-first century dawned, living next door to the United States promised to continue to provide the creative tension that has long been a stimulus to Canadian cultural production.

NOTES

1   Paul Anisef, Paul Axelrod, Etta Balchman-Anisef, Carl James, and Anton Turritin, *Opportunity and Uncertainty: Life Course Expectations of the Class of '73* (Toronto: University of Toronto Press, 2000) 239–40.

2   Tony Clarke, *Behind the Mitre: The Moral Leadership Crisis in the Canadian Catholic Church* (Toronto: HarperCollins, 1995).

SELECTED READING

On immigration and cultural developments, see the Selected Reading in Chapter 25. In addition, see Paul Anisef et al., *Opportunity and Uncertainty: Life Course Expectations of the Class of '73* (Toronto: University of Toronto Press, 2000) and Ted Madger, *Canada's Hollywood: The Canadian State and Feature Films* (Toronto: University of Toronto Press, 1993). For a provocative reflection on Canadian culture as reflected in film, see Geoff Pevere, "Ghostbusting: 100 Years of Canadian Cinema, or Why My Canada Includes the Terminator," *Take One* (Summer 1996): 6–13.

WEBLINKS

NUNAVUT
www.nunavut.com/home.html

This site describes Canada's newest territory, including its government, business, land and wildlife, education, culture, health, and tourism.

THE STANLEY CUP
www.nhl.com/hockeyu/history/cup/cup.html?clk=001

This site contains the history of the Stanley Cup, which started with a dinner of the Ottawa Amateur Athletic Association on March 18, 1892.

EDMONTON OILERS
www.edmontonoilers.com

The official website of the Edmonton Oilers hockey club includes news, statistics, ticket information, an on-line store, and video and audio links.

TERRY FOX
www.terryfoxrun.org/terry/introduction.htm

A biography of Terry Fox, the history of his Marathon of Hope, and information about the Terry Fox Foundation, Run, and cancer research are offered at this site.

PART VIII SUMMARY

IN THE LAST QUARTER-CENTURY, THE FREE TRADE agreements with the United States and Mexico were the pivotal events for Canadians. They defined new limits on Canadian sovereignty and challenged Canadians to find ways of preserving national identity in a world where national economic barriers were steadily eroding. As governments capitulated to the neo-liberal economic policies of the United States and Great Britain, efforts to strengthen national institutions were less pronounced than efforts to strengthen regional economic power. Nearly half of the people of Quebec seemed to want out of the federation altogether, and discontent with national policies remained high in the Western and Atlantic provinces. At the same time, many Canadians resisted both the neo-liberal tide and the American vortex, and both social movements and Canadian cultural production remained as vigorous in 2001 as they had been 25 years earlier.

CONCLUSION TO THE TEXT

WHERE THEN HAD THE NATIONAL JOURNEY TAKEN Canadians in the years from pre-contact times to a new millennium in 2000? In many respects the issues confronting Canadians in the early 2000s were much the same as those of centuries past: relations between French and English, regional disparities, the status of Native peoples and minorities, the roles and rights of women and men, the relations between workers and capitalists. Although none of these were new, much had changed over time. Canada had been transformed from a largely rural set of colonies closely allied first with France and then with Great Britain to a largely urban nation dominated by the United States with which it shared what largely amounted to a common market. Its governments had gone from being primarily the financiers of railways and promoters of trade to being the organizers of vast social welfare programs, the desirable size of which was, however, in some dispute. The churches, which once had been able in large measure to direct the lives of most, played a far more modest role in a secular country.

In the context of such changes, the form in which class, gender, racial, regional, and ethnic issues played out, changed dramatically as well. Canadians in 1763 or 1867 might have been largely content to accept hierarchical social relationships, but their struggles over the years had created very different Canadians by the 2000s, with far more demands for democratization of social institutions and for inclusion in decision-making within society. Although no one could predict how long the nation-state known as Canada would exist and particularly whether Quebec would remain part of it for the long haul, it was clear that Canadians had achieved a great deal collectively since 1867. Many Canadians hoped that the new millennium would become the occasion for new achievements that would produce a more just and civil society and strengthen Canada's sense of purpose to remain an independent nation despite the pressures for integration with the United States, a global superpower with a determination to recreate the world in its own image.

INDEX

Page numbers in italics indicate an illustration. Page numbers followed by an "m" indicate the presence of a map; those followed by a "w" indicate a Web site.

ADDITIONAL PHOTO CREDITS